8th edition

Ernest J. McCormick

Purdue University

Daniel R. Ilgen

Michigan State University

INDUSTRIAL AND ORGANIZATIONAL PSYCHOLOGY

Prentice-Hall, Inc., Englewood Cliffs, New Jersey 07632

Library of Congress Cataloging in Publication Data

McCormick, Ernest James.
   Industrial and organizational psychology.

   Rev. ed. of: Industrial psychology. 7th ed. c1980.
   Bibliography: p.
   Includes index.
   1. Psychology, Industrial.   I. McCormick, Ernest James.
Industrial psychology.   II. Ilgen, Daniel R.   III. Title.
HF5548.8.M383   1985   158.7   84–11718
ISBN 0-13-463092-0

Editorial/production supervision and
   interior design: *Edith Riker*
Cover design: *Whitman Studio, Inc.*
Manufacturing buyer: *Barbara Kittle*
Cover photograph: *Stan Wakefield*

TO EMILY AND BARBARA

Previously published as *Industrial Psychology*

© 1985, 1980, 1974, 1965, 1958, 1952, 1947, 1942
by Prentice-Hall, Inc., Englewood Cliffs, New Jersey 07632

Printed in the United States of America

10 9 8 7 6 5 4 3 2 1

ISBN 0-13-463092-0 01

Prentice-Hall International, Inc., *London*
Prentice-Hall of Australia Pty. Limited, *Sydney*
Editora Prentice-Hall do Brail, Ltda., *Rio de Janeiro*
Prentice-Hall Canada Inc., *Toronto*
Prentice-Hall of India Private Limited, *New Delhi*
Prentice-Hall of Japan, Inc., *Tokyo*
Prentice-Hall of Southeast Asia Pte. Ltd., *Singapore*
Whitehall Books Limited, *Wellington, New Zealand*

Contents in Brief

Contents

PART I   INTRODUCTION

Psychology is the study of human behavior, but in contrast to most disciplines, it has two faces. One face, that of research, is sometimes called the *science* of psychology. The other, the application side, is called the *profession* of psychology. The profession is similar to that of physicians, engineers, and others concerned with the application of knowledge of some field to the practical problems of the real world.

The scientific aspect of industrial-organizational psychology is rooted in research that provides the knowledge that is a prerequisite for any practical applications. This knowledge can be in the form of theories or in the form of empirically determined relationships. In either case, such knowledge frequently can be applied by organizations to minimize some of the human problems that inevitably arise in the operations of all kinds of organizations.

The first part of the text includes an overall introduction to industrial psychology, a discussion of some of the factors that influence job-related behavior (the "bases" of such behavior), and an overview of behavioral research.

PART II   JOB–RELATED BEHAVIOR AND ITS MEASUREMENT

There are two primary purposes for the "measurement" of job-related behavior. First, virtually all psychological research in industrial-organizational psychology depends on the measurement of various aspects of behavior in the working environment. Second, certain personnel management functions (such as personnel evaluation) require the measurement in quantitative terms of work-related behavior, such as job performance.

The measurement of job-related behavior has its roots in the nature of the work activities that people perform. Chapter 4 consists of an overview of the field of job analysis. Chapters 5 and 6 deal with the circumstances in which the measurement of job-related behavior is useful, the type of job-related behaviors for which measurements can be developed, the methods of developing or obtaining such measurements, and some of the pitfalls that can be encountered in their development and use.

PART III   PERSONNEL SELECTION

One of the most important roles of some industrial-organizational psychologists is that which is related to personnel selection. Although some psychologists become directly involved in day-to-day personnel selection operations (including interviewing, testing, and appraisal), usually they are behind the scenes carrying out research to establish selection standards, developing and validating tests, and providing related consulting services to those responsible for personnel selection operations.

This part of the text deals with the various aspects of personnel selection with which psychologists become involved, including the development of general practices in personnel selection; the use of personnel tests, biographical data, and interviews in personnel selection. It also addresses the implications of the Equal Employment Opportunity Act and other legislation related to personnel selection.

PART IV   PERSONNEL TRAINING AND DEVELOPMENT

The personnel training provided by an organization should fulfill three broad objectives: (1) it should be compatible with the goals and objectives of the organization; (2) the job-related training should be rooted in an analysis of the job activities that are to be performed; and (3) the training should provide for fulfilling the training needs of individuals, considering their previous experience and training and their potential for further development in the organization.

Although the primary focus of most programs is that of training people to be able to perform their present jobs effectively, there is a trend toward placing additional emphasis on the career development of individuals. Such efforts can be of mutual benefit to the organization and the individual. Chapter 13 reflects this trend.

PART V   THE ORGANIZATIONAL AND SOCIAL CONTEXT OF HUMAN WORK

Working relationships are an important part of a person's life. Motivation and commitment to work and the satisfactions from it, are the mutual concern of the organization and the individual. Thus, the interaction of motivation factors, value systems, attitudes, and the like with the working situation is part of the study of human behavior in industry. In recent years, there has been increasing concern that many workers express dissatisfaction with their work situations. Much of the current interest of industrial-organizatioal psychologists is with regard to this problem.

This part of the text covers some of the personal and situational variables that, in combination, create the organizational and social context within which people perform their work activities. First, individual issues of motivation and job satisfaction are addressed. This is followed by interpersonal issues of power and status differences, leadership, and the communication and execution of work roles in the social context.

PART VI   THE JOB AND WORK ENVIRONMENT

For approximately forty hours a week most people in the labor force perform work activities that are assigned to them within certain predetermined working conditions and environments. In recent decades there has been increased attention to the "design" of the jobs people are expected to perform and the conditions and environments in which they are to work. Chapters 17 and 18 deal with two approaches to job design, namely human factors and job enrichment. The nature of the jobs people perform leads logically to the consideration of the rates of pay for jobs; thus, Chapter 19 deals with job evaluation, a procedure used to establish pay scales. Chapter 20 deals with working conditions (illumination, noise, atmospheric conditions, and work schedules). In turn, Chapter 21 deals with accidents and safety which are integrally related to the nature of the job and to the working conditions.

Preface

This text is intended as a survey of the field of industrial-organizational psychology. The field addresses a wide spectrum of human problems that arise in the production and distribution of goods and services. The dynamic nature of the technological, cultural, and economic environments in which goods and services are produced and distributed has brought about changes in the nature and importance of various human problems associated with these processes. The result has led to some major changes in the field of industrial-organizational psychology. Changes are reflected in a general broadening of the entire field, the development of new measurement and statistical methods and techniques, and the addition of new theories directed toward the explanation of human behavior at work. These changes have even led to a modification in the name of the field: a change from industrial psychology to industrial-organizational psychology. The new name is meant to stress that the field is concerned with the behavior of people at work in all kinds of organizations—state, local, and federal governmental units, schools, the military services, as well as industrial organizations. It also reflects the fact that concerns for human behavior at work must look to characteristics of the organizational context such as its size and the nature of its technology for explanations of behavior. Titling this edition of the book, *Industrial and Organizational Psychology* was done to reflect the present orientation of the field.

The rapid expansion of the scope of industrial-organizational psychology and the concurrent development of research related to the discipline is reflected in this edition. While still maintaining the classical research, theory, and practice reported in the previous edition, the present text incorporates substantial amounts of new material. Some of the major changes in this edition are the following.

Personnel staffing issues have been significantly revised to reflect recent conditions in two areas. One of these is the constantly changing legal environment that influences personnel policies and practices as corporations attempt to maintain a highly qualified workforce in a way that allows equal access and opportunity for individuals of all races, ages, and genders. The other area of rapid advancement is in the conduct of personnel research. Here the influence of selection models stressing validity generalization and the application of utility analyses to many personnel practices and procedures has introduced a different perspective from the approaches of the past.

Work environments have also received increased attention in the current edition. Here the implications of human factors for the design of work spaces and integrated networks of employees linked through video display terminals rather than face-to-face interaction is treated in detail. In addition, the chapter on job enrichment addresses many of the recent concerns and controversies in that area. The quality of work is also discussed under other topics as we explore the impact of work group structures and participation in decision making in such programs as quality circles and other quality of work life programs.

An entirely new chapter on careers has been added to the present edition. There is a concern in modern organizations for employee development in order to utilize more effectively those employees who have devoted years of their lives to the organization. In this chapter, career development is discussed from both the standpoint of the events in an employee's working life that influence career development and from the standpoint of age-related proclivities that change over the course of a lifetime. Some of the ways companies have tried to more fully develop the career lives of their employees are introduced.

Since it is not possible within the scope of a single text to bring together all, or even most, of the literature in a field as large as industrial-organizational psychology, we have selected research that is representative or illustrative of important problems and issues in the field. We have also attempted to identify and report what we feel are the most important and significant research contributions to the field. Although much of the content of the text consists of summaries of such research, it was also our intent to include information about various methods and techniques that are used in research and in personnel management, and to discuss current theories of behavior in work settings that influence both research and practice.

The field of industrial-organizational psychology includes both the *science* of psychology and the *profession*, or practice, of psychology. The latter deals specifically with the application of knowledge from the theories and methods of psychology as a science to the practical problems faced by people at work. In writing this text, it has been the objective of the authors to bridge the theoretical and applied aspects of the field of industrial-organizational psychology.

This text could not have been accomplished without the support, both direct and indirect, of a large number of people. We have relied heavily upon our colleagues in universities and other institutions for the research that we discuss. We take this opportunity to express our appreciation to them collectively. Acknowledgment of their individual contributions is given in the body of the text, with completed references at the end of each chapter. We also want to express our appreciation to those who reviewed copies of this text and the previous edition to provide us with useful comments for improving this edition.

- J. Marshall Brown, Lafayette College
- Cyril J. Sadowski, Auburn University at Montgomery
- David C. Gilmore, University of North Carolina at Charlotte
- Stephen Knouse, The Pennsylvania State University
- Patrick A. Knight, Kansas State University

Special thanks are due to Edie Riker and Marcy Schafer for their excellent help in preparing the manuscript for publication.

Finally, for specific recognition, we want to express our deep appreciation to Joseph Tiffin who began this text in the 1940s and authored the first three editions of it. With the fourth edition, Ernest J. McCormick joined him on the text. Although Dr. Tiffin has not been directly involved in the last two editions, his earlier contributions have influenced our present writing directly in the form of some of the research reported and indirectly as we attempt to continue to convey the mix of science and practice that his texts did so well.

Ernest J. McCormick
West Lafayette, Indiana
Daniel R. Ilgen
East Lansing, Michigan

About the Authors

Ernest J. McCormick is Professor Emeritus Purdue University and President of PAQ Services, Inc. After receiving his Ph.D. from Purdue University in 1948 he joined the faculty of the Department of Psychological Sciences at Purdue. His research in job analysis methods resulted in the development of the Position Analysis Questionnaire (PAQ), which is a structured, computerized job analysis questionnaire that is used for operational and research purposes. As President of PAQ Services, Inc. he has continued his interests in job analysis methods and in the application of job analysis data to various aspects of the management of human resources in business, industry, and public administration. He is the author of *Job Analysis: Methods and Applications* and co-author of *Human Factors in Engineering and Design* with Mark S. Sanders. He has served on various advisory boards and committees including the Army Scientific Advisory Panel, the Navy Advisory Board on Human Resources, and the Committee on Occupational Classification and Analysis of the National Academy of Sciences. He is a Fellow of the American Psychological Association and the Human Factors Society, and an Honorary Member of the Ergonomics Society. His awards include: the James McKeen Cattell Award of the Society of Industrial and Organizational Psychology; the Franklin V. Taylor Award of the Division of Applied Experimental and Engineering Psychologists (American Psychological Association); and the Paul M. Fitts Award of the Human Factors Society.

Daniel R. Ilgen is John A. Hannah Professor of Organizational Behavior at Michigan State University. He received his B.S. degree from Iowa State University and his M.S. and Ph.D. from the University of Illinois' Urbana-Champaign campus. He has taught at the University of Illinois, the U.S. Military Academy, Purdue University, and Michigan State University. From 1972 through 1983 he was a member of the Department of Psychological Sciences at Purdue University. While there he served as the area coordinator for the Industrial and Organizational Psychology area from 1977 through the spring of 1983 with the exception of one year. During that year, 1978–1979, he was a Visiting Associate Professor in the Department of Management at the University of Washington. He has served as Acting Editor for the journal of *Organizational Behavior and Human Performance* and now serves as its associate editor. He is a Fellow of the American Psychological Association and is serving or has served as a member of the editorial boards of the *Journal of Applied Psychology, Academy of Management Review,* and *Organizational Behavior and Human Performance.* He is author of numerous articles and book chapters and is a co-author of *A Theory of Behavior in Organizations* with J. C. Naylor and R. D. Pritchard.

1

Introduction

The decade of the 1980s is an exciting time for those who are concerned about the development, utilization, and well-being of human beings in organizations. Both social and technological accomplishments of the last two decades set the stage for acceptance and utilization of social-science knowledge and practice in work settings. The 1960s were characterized by dissatisfaction and disillusionment with the ability of large organizations to meet the needs of people and society. The sheer sense of frustration led some to retreat to small farms in the country to avoid completely the limitations of organizations; it led others to demonstrate in the streets against political leaders or manufacturers of products they saw as contributing to some of the social ills. Regardless of the reasons, there was a clear realization that bigger and bigger organizations and greater and greater technological sophistication were not sufficient to guarantee and develop the standard of living of a society. Implied in the acceptance of this re-alization was the belief that if organizations were to meet the needs of the constituencies they served, greater attention would have to be paid to the development, utilization, and welfare of the human beings who were associated with them.

In the 1970s, large organizations attempted more consciously to function effectively for all constituents—employees as well as employers and clients/customers served. Considerable effort was expended to try to improve conditions for all employees. Attempts were made to insure that policies and practices were fair to all employees regardless of race, age, sex, religious preference, or national origin. Safety procedures were scrutinized as never before. Much experimentation took place to attempt to discover ways to improve the quality of work life of employees. Such practices as having flexible times for beginning and ending work to allow people more freedom to schedule their own work days (called flexitime), creating small work teams with greater responsibility for their work processes, establishing committees of employees whose purpose it was to discuss and suggest ways that work quality might be improved (called quality circles) were just a few of the experimental procedures of the 1970s.

The 1980s are exciting because of what has gone before and because of what lies ahead. From the recent past, two things are clear: There are real, finite limits to the extent to which advances can be made when concentration is entirely upon technological factors, and improvements in the quality of working life can be made when attention is focused upon the human element of work as well. Demonstrated improvements in the past indicate clearly that such improvements can continue in the future. Along with an acceptance of the need for more concern for the human element in work are social and technological changes that challenge all of us to learn more about human behavior in general in order to deal with these changes. In particular, the continuing change in the composition of the labor force in the United States and other countries must be understood. Women continue to enter careers previously dominated by men and to remain in these careers through the child-bearing years. Work and careers play a larger part in the self-concepts of women than ever before. Technologically, major changes are occurring in both the workplace and the office as the computer imposes itself in the form of robotics, management information systems, and office network systems which no longer are physically limited to one building, one community, or even one nation. A recent television commercial illustrates some effects of the latter quite vividly. An individual in New York is shown meeting with several staff members, discussing the contents of a report that he must deliver at a board meeting in Paris. The person then leaves to catch his flight to Paris. At the same time several persons working with a networked computer system prepare the report by working at their own terminals and "communicating" and coordinating with each other. They finish the report as the person for whom they are preparing it arrives at his office in Paris. He calls up the report on his system, prints it, thanks the others for their good work, and walks into the meeting with the report in hand. It is clear that the technology is already available for such behaviors; it is less clear that the managers and staff in the offices of corporations are ready for it. Getting them ready for it is just one of the interesting tasks ahead—tasks to which we believe that industrial-organizational psychology can contribute significantly.

INDUSTRIAL–ORGANIZATIONAL PSYCHOLOGY

Psychology is the scientific study of behavior. Although the field as a whole is interested in the behavior of any organism either human or nonhuman, industrial-organizational psychologists limit their concerns to human behavior. In addition to the scientific emphasis, psychology also has a professional focus. This part of psychology is interested in putting to work knowledge generated by the science. The profession is similar to those of physicians, engineers, and others concerned with the application of knowledge generated in some field to practical problems relevant to that field.

Industrial-organizational psychology includes both scientific and professional concerns. Its scientific aspect is rooted in research that provides the knowledge that is prerequisite for any practical application. This knowledge can be in the form of theories or in the form of empirically determined relationships. In either case, such knowledge can frequently be applied by organizations to minimize some of the human problems that inevitably arise.

Even when the emphasis is upon the practical (professional) side of industrial-organizational psychology, the practice needs to be firmly rooted in psychological research; indeed, in many instances, practitioners themselves do research relating to the problems with which they are dealing, such as analyzing the factors associated with accidents, conducting an attitude survey, or studying the factors that influence people's willingness to accept promotions that involve transfers.

Industrial-Organizational Psychology as a Science

The solution of most of the human problems in organizations requires knowledge of human behavior. Such knowledge can be derived, in part, through experience. It would be a poor observer of human behavior who did not, through observation and experience, develop some useful insights into the reasons behind behaviors observed. Insight derived from experience, however, has its limitations. This is particularly true when that being observed is someone's behavior rather than the presence or absence of some physical event. Both in terms of the complexity of the observed property and the nature of the observer, it is often easier to judge whether some chemical solution turned a piece of litmus paper a particular shade of blue than it is to judge whether the person whose behavior is being observed is "trying hard." Hence, psychology as a science has to overcome some of the limitations of causal observation developed throughout everyone's life.

All scientific endeavor is predicated on the assumption that events and phenomena are the consequences of precipitating factors. Applied to the study of human behavior in organizations, this means that behavior is based on a complex assortment of variables existing within the person, that person's situation, and the unique interaction between that person and his or her situation. Bandura (1978) called the latter condition *reciprocal causation* to emphasize that a person serves as his or her own environment because as he or she behaves, the situation changes as a function of that behavior, and the changed situation serves as a stimulus for future behaviors. The cycle just goes on; there is no clear-cut boundary between cause and effect.

Psychological research aims to identify the variables associated with different aspects of behavior, such as the relationship between illumination and the ability of people to make visual discriminations or the effect of early job experiences on later career success. Beyond the objective identification of such relationships, some psychological research is primarily aimed at determining the underlying reasons for people's behavior—at "explaining" such behavior by developing theories of the behavior. Such research typically is initiated after the development of speculations about the cause of some aspect of behavior. Empirical observations (data) are generated to explore relationships among variables that are predicted by the theory. To the extent that the observations of the data are consistent with the theoretical explanations for certain relationships, the theory is said to be "supported." To the extent that they are not consistent with the predictions of the theory, either the theory or the nature of the "test" of the theory which the data represent is called into question. Over time, through the accumulation of empirical findings, confidence in a particular theory is either strengthened or weakened. Typically, the theory is neither supported nor rejected by any one data set but is rather supported or modified a bit to fit the new observations. Since it can never be known whether all aspects of a theory have been tested under all possible conditions, theories are never "proved." They simply vary in the extent to which people have confidence in them. Industrial-organizational psychologists, when operating in the scientific mode, work from some theoretical perspective to gather empirical data designed to aid in the understanding of behavior at work.

Industrial-Organizational Psychology as a Profession

As was mentioned before, psychology as a profession is concerned with the application of knowledge to some practical problem. Some industrial-organizational psychologists concentrate almost exclusively on solving practical problems. This can include consulting, program development, and individual evaluations. Typically, a psychologist in consulting activities advises in some area of expertise, such as management development, equipment or job design, or training methods. A psychologist in program development would be responsible for developing and installing some program such as a training program or a personnel-selection system. In individual evaluation, psychologists function much like clinicians in assessing the potentialities of individuals for specific positions, promotions, and so forth, or in counseling individuals themselves. In the latter capacity, they typically use interviewing techniques, tests, and related techniques as the basis for evaluation. Psychologists in organizations may also use their psychological backgrounds to deal with individuals in connection with other functions in an organization, such as helping to resolve individual or organizational conflicts. In sum, the industrial-organizational psychologist functioning as a practitioner applies his or her knowledge of psychological phenomena and research methods to conditions in organizations that depend on or impact on the behavior of people.

Combining Science and Practice

It is a mistaken assumption that theory and practice must remain separate. Some people think that the theory or the scientific part of a field is that which goes on in the "ivory towers" of universities and has nothing to do with the day-to-day practical concerns of the "real world." Granted, the scientist and the practitioner often operate in their own worlds with little concern for the other. But this condition is not a necessary one or even a desirable one. Science contributes to practice, and vice versa. A well-known social psychologist, Kurt Lewin, captured the relationship between science and practice very succinctly. He said, "There is nothing so practical as good theory." Lewin demonstrated the usefulness of theories about persuasion and commitment for changing people's willingness to alter their diets during times of food shortages created during World War II. Other examples abound. In the natural sciences, we have a vivid recent demonstration of the interaction of theory and science in the space program. Scientists working for the National Aviation and Space Administration (NASA) have made many major discoveries that have practical impacts far beyond the exploration and understanding of conditions in space.

Industrial-organizational psychology attempts to emphasize both theory as represented by the scientist and practice. The practitioner functions best when he or she is very much aware of what is going on in the science side of the field. Likewise, the scientist benefits from an awareness of the practical problems faced by the practitioner. As a result, industrial-organizational psychologists are trained in both science and practice, although at any one time they tend to emphasize one more than the other.

PAST AND FUTURE

Early Development

The field of industrial-organizational psychology has developed largely since the turn of the century. From its inception until around 1970, it was known only as industrial psychology. The first major books in the field were Walter Dill Scott's *The Theory of Advertising* (1903) and *The Psychology of Advertising* (1908), and Hugo Münsterberg's *Psychology of Industrial Efficiency* (1913). The early industrial psychologists were concerned with personnel selection, advertising, accidents, and, to a limited degree, employee-rating processes. To some extent the authors were rather timid and apologetic about the possibilities of the new field. Psychology itself was just trying to establish itself as a science so it was suffering somewhat from the need to show the world that it deserved being considered a full-fledged discipline and science. Against that background, suggestions of "practical" or "applied" interests were almost heretical.

As with many applied fields, the most rapid advancement of industrial psychology came when major problems needed to be solved. Many of the major problems resulted from the induction and utilization of large numbers of people in the military service during World Wars I and II. Coinciding with World War I was Binet's work in the development of intelligence tests that were able to predict quite well the performance of French school children. Psychologists were very interested in this work; the application of testing to the problem of assigning large numbers of individuals about whom little was known to jobs in the military service was immediately apparent. Much of the work in test development and selection and placement practices came out of the war effort.

During World War II interest in the utility of tests for selection and placement continued. In addition, human-factors techniques, which attempt to match the characteristics of machines to the people who use them, were developed and used at that time. The practical problem that served as the stimulus for much of this work was the large number of airplane accidents in the Army Air Corps that were attributed to "human error." Studying a number of accidents attributed to human error identified such problems as failure to correctly read the altimeter, activating the wrong control during an emergency, and so on. This led to work designing equipment that could help reduce the chances for human error. One such piece of equipment provided multiple cues about a control. This particular knob was placed in the same location on all aircrafts, but it also had a unique shape (for example, triangular) so that, without looking, pilots would know if it did not feel right to them. Simple changes like this greatly reduced the number of accidents due to human error. The result was the establishment of a whole subdiscipline of psychology: human factors. More is said about this later in this book.

During World War II there was also a heightened interest in the applied social-psychological aspects of industrial psychology. Some of the first controlled research on leadership styles by Lewin, Lippitt, and White (1939) explored the effects of democratic versus autocratic leadership on the productivity of groups and on the willingness of group members to work when it was not possible for the leader to provide close supervision. Other research investigated the effects of group cohesion on the ability of groups to resist stress (Stouffer, Suchman, DeVinney, Star, & Williams, 1949). Some of the concern for groups arose from the criticality of the problems of combat groups.

This work with groups was a continuation of interest in such topics that was generated in an industrial setting in the late 1920s and early 1930s by the much-publicized *Hawthorne Studies.* No research in industrial psychology has been so widely publicized as this work. In the late 1920s Elton Mayo of Harvard University began a series of studies at the Hawthorne plant of Western Electric. The employees were all involved in assembling units for the Bell Telephone System. The first studies were designed to look at the effects of changes in working conditions—primarily the temperature of the room and the amount of light on the work surface—on employee performance. Later the researchers experimented with different supervisory styles, the arrangement of work groups, the length and types of work breaks, and the length of the work day. Although changes in performance did result from changes in working conditions, the interesting conclusions related to several unexpected findings. One of these was that performance was affected less by the physical changes made than by the fact that *any* change was made. For example, to the surprise of the researchers, performance *improved* as the light on the work surface became dimmer and dimmer, even to the point at which the light was not much better than bright moonlight. It was concluded that the workers were responding not so much to the light as to the fact that managers and experimenters were paying attention to them. This effect has now become known as the *Hawthorne Effect*: an effect on behavior that is due to getting any treatment and not necessarily to the nature of the treatment per se. Secondly, the investigators found a work environment much richer in social relationships than they had expected. Informal organizational structures influenced work and nonwork behaviors as well as leadership styles. Up to that time, little or no attention had been paid to the social factors of work. Although the actual conduct of the studies has frequently been criticized for a lack of scientific rigor, one cannot deny the important role they played in stimulating interest in the social psychology of behavior at work.

In the last 20 years there have been two major influential forces that have impacted upon the field of industrial-organizational psychology. The first of these was the passage of the Civil Rights Act of 1964 and specifically Title VII of that act. Title VII stated that it was illegal to discriminate in hiring or other personnel decisions against people on the basis of race, sex, religious preference, or national origin. Since that time, almost all major organizations in the United States have carefully scrutinized their employment practices in order to guarantee treatment to all employees and potential employees that is fair and unbiased. Establishing such practices is not easy. Work on these issues is still going on, and industrial-organizational psychologists are actively involved in the attempt to design human resource-management practices that protect the rights of all individuals affected by these practices.

The second major recent influence on the field cannot be traced to any specific time or event: the effect of the changing societal view of the nature of work and the responsibility of work organizations toward the people that staff their organizations. We briefly alluded to changing work values in the opening paragraphs of this chapter. Clearly there is a greater belief in the responsibility of work organizations to contribute to the quality of work life of their employees. This has led to a greater focus upon the needs of these people. The specific responses to this value orientation vary considerably from a focus on safety, to implementation of quality circles, flexitime, or maternity leave for women or men. Regardless of the specific way responses to a concern for the quality of working life are manifested, the fact remains that the value orientation itself has impacted upon the types of concerns that involve industrial-organizational psychologists.

Looking Ahead

To date, the efforts of industrial psychologists have largely been directed toward the study of the independent relationships between specific variables on the one hand and various aspects of work-related behavior on the other. There have been numerous independent investigations of such specific variables as individual differences, organizational characteristics, incentives, group structure, equipment design, and working conditions. But studies of *combinations* of these and other variables are relatively few and far between, as was pointed out by Uhlaner (1970). According to Uhlaner, effective behavior and work performance are not always the *additive* effects of whatever variables may be involved, for the different variables *interact* in this process and may be complicated by different types of jobs. For example, one type of incentive might be appropriate for some kinds of people and jobs but not for others. Uhlaner's argument is that more behavioral research relating to human work should be carried out in the framework of its total context in order to explore the possible interactions. His own generalized conceptualization of the various possible interactions is illustrated in Figure 1.1, in which he depicts the various sets of variables that may interact to contribute to effective work and work performance. It seems reasonable that the same illustration can be applied to criteria of var-

ious human values (such as health, safety, and satisfaction) as well as to criteria of effective work and work performance. For this reason one should not view system "design," personnel selection, and training as separate, isolated facets of work-related functions, but rather as an integrated package. Related research should be approached accordingly.

Although, as Uhlaner implied, this multifaceted, interactive approach is not commonly used, it has not been entirely neglected. In fact, paralleling the development of human-factors engineering has been the development of the *systems concept*. In this specific frame of reference, the intent is to develop a "system" that provides an optimum blend of people, equipment, procedures, and operations in order to capitalize on the relative capabilities of human beings and of physical equipment in performing different functions. Although the systems concept is most obviously applicable to circumstances in which human beings are to interact with items of physical equipment, it is also applicable to processes or operations in which little physi-

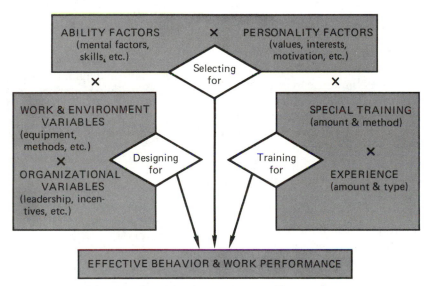

FIGURE 1.1 Conceptualization of interactions of human-factor system variables as related to human performance effectiveness. (Adapted from Uhlaner 1970)

cal equipment is used, such as office operations, service and distribution processes, and communication processes. Even a complete organization can be viewed as a system.

In the past, most of the behavioral research related to systems has been carried out in connection with military "man-machine" operations, as discussed by Parsons (1972). Some of this work has employed the type of integrated framework discussed previously, and some of it has been carried out in laboratory settings, in some instances using very elaborate experimental facilities and procedures.

PLAN OF THE BOOK

The remainder of this book addresses specific topics in industrial-organizational psychology. Some of these topics require the reader to have some background in basic statistical concepts and also a general feel for the purposes and structures of research design. It is not assumed that the reader has the background for all of the material presented. Therefore, before getting into topics particular to industrial-organizational psychology, we introduce the reader to some of the general approaches to studying human behavior, a few statistical considerations, and an overview of the logic behind research on human behavior. These topics are addressed in Chapters 2 and 3. Any additional information needed on research-related issues is either explained in the text as the issue is addressed or appears in the Appendices. If the material is in an appendix, the text refers the reader to it at the appropriate time.

Following the introductory chapters, which lay the groundwork for understanding the material of industrial-organizational psychology, are eighteen chapters arranged in five sections:

• Job-Related Behavior and Its Measurement
• Personnel Selection

• Personnel Training and Development
• The Organizational and Social Context of Human Work
• The Job and Work Environment

These sections are organized to flow from concerns with the fit between the individual and his or her job, to the social context in which work occurs, and then to the context in which both the job, the person, and the social context reside. To understand the fit between a person and his or her job it is necessary that we first know what the job is all about and also that we have some ways to describe and measure characteristics of people. Chapter 4 deals with measuring the job and Chapters 5, 6, 9, and 10 address the measurement of people. Assuming that the characteristics of jobs and people are relatively well understood, the next step is to address the match between these two. Chapters 7, 8, and 11 discuss the issue of the match in a static sense when the job and the characteristics of people are considered relatively constant. Chapters 12 and 13 move on to considerations of ways to improve the fit of people to jobs by developing the skills and abilities of the people in the jobs. That is, rather than consider people as relatively constant, these chapters assume that people change over their career lives and that some of the changes can be facilitated through training and other work experiences.

Our discussion so far has tended to downplay the social context of work. This does not mean that this context is ignored. Certainly, any description of a job must take into account the social nature of that job and the interpersonal skills and abilities needed to perform the work. It does mean that attention is not focused directly on social factors. In Chapters 14, 15, and 16 attention shifts more to the interpersonal nature of work as well as to the attitudes and motivation of people in that context. Finally, the last five chapters turn to contextual issues that are less social in nature but no less important in influencing behavior at work. In this last section attention is turned to the design of equipment and jobs and to the establishment policies and practices that create the conditions under which work is accomplished.

Note that in all the topics addressed our orientation is psychological—that is, we are interested in the behavior of *individuals* in organizations. When we look at that behavior and try to understand it, we can go to the job, the work environment, the people in the work environment, or the characteristics of the people themselves (such as abilities, skills, needs, or attitudes) to try to understand the behavior. In all cases, regardless of where the level of explanation is sought, the target remains the same: *individual beahavior*. Such a psychological point of view is, of course, not the only one that can be taken, but it can be a very effective one for dealing with problems related to human resource development and mangement in organizations. We trust that when you finish this book, you will agree.

REFERENCES

Bandura, A. (1978). The self system in reciprocal determinism. *American Psychologist, 33,* 344–358.

Lewin, K., Lippett, R., & White, R. K. (1939). Patterns of aggressive behavior in experimentally created social climates. *Journal of Social Psychology, 10,* 271–301.

Münsterberg, H. (1913). *Psychology and industrial efficiency.* Boston: Houghton Mifflin.

Parsons, H. M. (1972). *Man-machine systems experiments.* Baltimore: Johns Hopkins Press.

Scott, W. D. (1903). *The theory of advertising.* Boston: Small Maynard.

Scott, W. D. (1908). *The psychology of advertising.* New York: Arno Press.

Stouffer, S. A., Suchman, E. A., DeVinney, L. C., Star, S. A., & Williams, R. M. (1949). *The American soldier: adjustment during army life.* Vol. I. Princeton, NJ: Princeton University Press.

Uhlaner, J. E. (October 1970). *Human performance, jobs, and systems psychology: The systems measurement bed.* U.S. Army, Behavior and Systems Research Laboratory, Tech. Rep. S–2 (AD 716 346).

2

Bases for Job-Related Behavior

A fundamental assumption of industrial-organizational psychology is that individuals in organizations who are effective in their particular jobs make a positive contribution to the effectiveness of the total organization. There are, of course, some exceptions to this. In the microelectronics industry in the early 1970s companies with very ineffective employees could still do very well simply because the market was expanding so rapidly that it was almost impossible to do poorly. Similarly, steel workers in an outdated steel mill may do their job as well as is humanly possible and still the company may not be able to be effective if the technology of the industry has advanced far beyond the company's capability to compete. Nevertheless, all other things being equal, it is well-accepted that the behavior of people who populate an organization contribute to its effectiveness.

A corollary of this assumption is that there is a strong need to understand the behavior of people in work settings. This understanding requires, at a minimum, the description and measurement of the behaviors that are important on the job and then the development of some knowledge about the relevant variables that affect these important behaviors. In order to decide what behaviors on the job are important, a value judgment must be made that a behavior is of interest to the extent that it has some impact on the accepted goals and objectives of the organization. With such a value judgment, it should be obvious that such behaviors as attendance, tardiness, performance, and quitting are very important. The attention paid to these behaviors in the past attests to their perceived importance. Yet many would argue that *too much* attention has been paid to these behaviors; we agree. There are many other behaviors that are also relevant in organizations. From an organizational perspective, such behaviors as employee theft, loyalty, and willingness to transfer are also very important. More individually referenced behaviors are work over-load (and the stress that may develop from it) or the freedom to make job-relevant decisions. Certainly there is a need to expand the domain of behaviors that are considered as relevant at work, and there is a trend in that direction. Nevertheless, there are limits to the set of behaviors imposed by some general notion of importance to performing the job. Doodling on a note pad while attending a meeting is certainly an observable behavior but it is unlikely to be worthy of study given the relevance criterion.[1]

Once a behavior has been identified as important in work organizations, there is a need to understand the causes of that behavior. A causal focus is necessary if one desires to create conditions that will facilitate the display of desired behaviors. These situations may be created by designing jobs or company policies in such a way as to encourage and facilitate the occurrence of the desired behaviors, or by matching persons who possess the skills and abilities needed to show the behaviors desired to jobs that require their skills and abilities. In practice some mix between structuring situations and matching people to jobs is used. Regardless of the approach taken, an understanding of what causes the behaviors should precede attempts to deal with them.

BEHAVIOR IN ORGANIZATIONS

To approach the problem of understanding behavior in organizations, think about the

---

[1]Note that we use the term *behavior* rather loosely. At the most concrete level, it refers to overt actions on the part of individuals that can be observed by other people either directly by seeing the behavior, or indirectly by observing the products of the behavior. An example of the latter would be observing the number of pages typed by a secretary rather than actually seeing the secretary type the pages. We also stretch the word *behavior* to cover covert, less observable manifestations of work, such as the attitudes or opinions of people about their jobs and job situations, as well as the physiological or physical effects of work.

possible factors that might influence a person's behavior. Since there are a wide variety of possibilities here, it is best to cluster or group these factors into general sets. A view of behavior in organizations presented by McGrath (1976) offers some initial guidelines for identifying such clusters.

General Model

McGrath (1976) identified three conceptually independent systems, the interaction or intersections of which represent what is meant by behavior in organizations. Figure 2.1 is a graphic representation of these three systems. Following is a brief description of the figure:

- System A: The physical and technological environment in which the behavior takes place;
- System B: The social medium, or patterns of interpersonal relations, within which the behavior occurs; and
- System C: The "person system" or "self-system" of the person whose behavior is to be understood (p. 1367).

Behavior Settings

As depicted in Figure 2.1, these systems overlap or intersect two at a time, as well as all three at once. According to McGrath, the intersection of the physical-technical with the social-interpersonal systems (AB) represents the "behavior setting" in which the person displays the behavior of relevance to the organization. The boundary between AB and ABC emphasizes that, although the physical-technical and social-interpersonal systems define the setting in which the behaviors of individuals take place, the setting is not completely defined for any specific individual until that individual is in it and behaving. Through the individual's own behavior, the setting is modified due to his or her own idiosyncratic contribution to it.

To illustrate this point, consider for a mo-

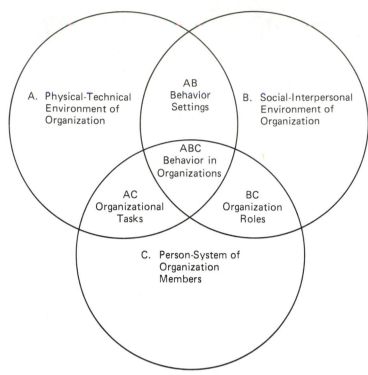

FIGURE 2.1 The systems in which behaviors in organizations are embedded. (From McGrath, 1976, Figure 4, p. 1368.)

ment the work by Barker and his students (e.g., Barker & Wright, 1955). They found that the degree to which high-school students are involved in the conduct of the school through participation in extracurricular activities, clubs, athletic teams, bands, orchestras, and the like is an inverse function of the size of the school: The larger the school, the smaller the proportion of students involved and the smaller the number of students who show an active interest in school activities. The activities perceived as necessary for running a high school, such as the band or football team, characterize the physical-technical system of the school (A of Figure 2.1). The student body of the school represents the social-interpersonal environment (B of Figure 2.1) which, when combined with the defined set of extracurricular needs, specifies the behavior

setting that influences a particular student either to accept or refrain from accepting responsibilities in some extracurricular activity.

As described so far, the influence is from the behavior setting to the student. But the influence goes both ways. The student's personal values, expectations, and beliefs, as well as his or her own skills and abilities, are part of the social setting that creates the norms for individual participation in extracurricular activities. Likewise, the student's special skills may influence the physical-technical environment in terms of those activities perceived as important components of a successful high school. For example, the proportion of time and effort devoted to music groups, as compared to team athletics, will vary as a function of the type of students who attend the school. To some extent, any particular individual determines the distribution of time and talent to these two activities by possessing characteristics on which the decision to define the "proper" mix of the two is based.

The net result is that the individual in an organization responds to an environment that he or she has helped to create. In addition, from a dynamic perspective that views the individual's behavior over time, the behavior alters the setting such that, at any given time, the past behaviors of that individual will affect the nature of the setting in the future. This idea, labeled *reciprocal determinism* by Bandura (1978), emphasizes that while environments influence behaviors, behaviors also create or influence environments.

Weick (1979) goes one step beyond reciprocal determinism in describing what he calls *enactment processes*. With enactment, the individual actively influences his or her own environment, just as described with reciprocal determinism. But the enactment notion emphasizes one additional fact: The individual responds to a world that he or she constructs rather than to an actual or objective world. In addition, the meaning of behavior is often constructed after the fact, not before behaving. Consider the character Goldie in *Fiddler on the Roof*. When asked by her husband, Tevya, if she loves him, at first she seems uncertain. Then she considers her behavior over the past 25 years—she lived with him, raised his children, kept his house, shared his bed. Finally, says Goldie, "Do I love him? . . . I guess I do." The feeling, love, follows from a consideration of the behaviors in this example of enactment. In a similar manner, Staw (1980) suggests that employees may not consider all the things that their jobs do or do not offer to them to "decide" how satisfied they are with the jobs. Instead, when asked how satisfied they are, they may reflect on the fact that they are still in the jobs and that the jobs offer certain kinds of conditions that most people consider satisfying; they may then conclude that they too must be satisfied.

Organizational Roles

The dual intersection of the person (C) and the social-interpersonal (B) environments form organizational roles (BC). These roles are patterns of expected behaviors for the person, in part self-determined and in part determined by others. The role of dental assistant differs for someone who has been on the job for 2 years from that of one who has been there 2 days. The expectations of others with regard to a certain role generally take into account the person for whom the set of behaviors is prescribed.

The intersection of the physical-technical system with the person system (AC) is characterized by the tasks that individuals perform. Here again, these are defined not only by the technical demands of those tasks (A) but also by the skills, abilities, and other characteristics the person brings to the job.

By now, it should be apparent that Figure 2.1 is deceptively simple. However, the incongruence between its simplicity and the complexity of behavior in organizations should not lead to the conclusion that the model depicted is not useful. Its usefulness is in the descriptions of general concepts and elements of the process of interest—behavior in organizations. Even though the regions of the model are, indeed, oversimplifications, they can be supplemented when we try to get a better understanding of behavior in organizations.

Conclusions about Behavior in Organizations

From our discussion of behavior in organizations, we are now prepared to draw some conclusions about both the setting and the nature of the behavior itself. First, with respect to the setting, three major sets of factors interact to influence the behavior of individuals in organizations. Figure 2.1 dealt with these in a general sense; Figure 2.2 gives

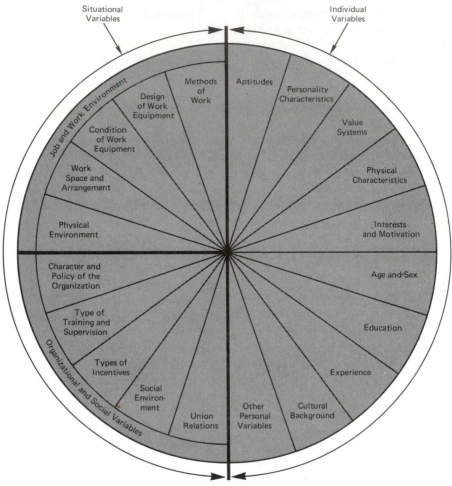

FIGURE 2.2 Graphic representation of some of the individual and situational variables that may be associated with job performance. The representation for any given job might include only some of these variables, and their relative importance as influencing factors might be unique to the job in question.

some more specific factors from each of the three regions. Because all three regions occur together simultaneously, there is some question about how much can be learned about any two of them in the absence of the other (Schneider, 1983). That is, one might not be able to learn much about the effects of individual variables such as experience on work-task performance if the task that is performed is studied in a setting that lacks some of the crucial social-interpersonal conditions present on the job. It may be that the social-interpersonal conditions define the task in a way that differs from what is created in a setting that lacks the social dimension.

Behavior itself occurs as a result of interaction among conditions from all three regions—that is, behavior is a function of individual, social, and task conditions. The exact nature of that function is impossible to define in the abstract, but it does become more specifiable as one looks closely at a particular individual or individuals in settings with known social and physical/task conditions. In the remainder of this chapter, we consider some examples of possible influences on work behavior arising from each of the three major regions of Figures 2.1 and 2.2. But we must first address the nature of variables from any of the three regions and discuss assumptions about causation with respect to human behavior.

THE NATURE OF VARIABLES

Two Primary Dimensions of Variables

Behaviors can generally be construed as varying along two dimensions. The first of these is *quantitative*. Most job-related behaviors can be quantified (that is, they can be measured) in some units appropriate to the behavior under consideration. For example, job performance can be quantified using such variables as the number of units produced, the number of errors or units that fail to pass inspection, the accuracy of performance, or the time to complete a particular job. Other quantifiable behaviors on the job might be tenure (measured by the number of days, months, or years on the job), number of absences, or an individual's attitude toward his or her supervisor (as reflected by scores on an attitude scale).

Behavior can also vary along a *qualitative* dimension. Clearly the behavior of typing is different from the behavior of speaking into a dictaphone even though both behaviors can be quantified and even quantified in the same units, such as words per minute. Therefore, any measurement system must take into account the qualitative difference between behaviors. Because (when talking about job-related behaviors) the units for quantification are rarely the same across qualitative dimensions, we usually quantify a behavior variable and then make quantifiable comparisons only within that qualitative dimension. The examples of typing and dictating were unusual in that both of these activities could be measured with the same quantitative variable. Comparing the performance of a baseball player as indicated by his or her batting average to the performance of a lobster trapper quantified by the number of pounds of lobster trapped per day is impossible unless something is done to transform hits per time at bat into units comparable with pounds per day. There are ways to make such comparisons; we discuss them later.

Although our discussion has been limited to variables that are all considered behaviors, quantitative and qualitative differences apply to variables in any domain. We can speak of the qualitative differences in the social/interpersonal domain by addressing groups composed of managers and others composed of union stewards. In the task/physical environment qualitatively different variables would be the degree to which a machine represented the latest design or the color of the walls of the room. Likewise, for each of these variables a quantitative dimension can be constructed, such as the number of group members, the age of the machine, or the amount of light that reflects off the walls.

Use of Variables

From the standpoint of addressing human behavior at work, both the qualitative and the quantitative dimensions of variables are important. However, from the standpoint of the relationship between particular variables and human behavior at work, we usually deal with the quantitative dimensions of the variables of interest. This requires that we identify the variables that are important for the behavior in question and then measure them using measuring instruments that meet our standards for acceptability of measures. Once measures are available for the variables of interest, we are in a position to assess the relationship of the variables to the behavior of interest.

Evaluative Dimension

Let us discuss for a moment one general dimension of behavioral variables: the mapping of quantitatively measured units onto some *evaluative* dimension which varies along some goodness-to-badness scale. Given the measurement of some behavior on a *quantitative* scale, one can then determine on an *evaluative* scale whether the behavior is good, bad, or about average. For example, the per-hour production of pepperoni pizzas by a pizza maker (a quantitative measure) can be evaluated as to whether it is up to standard, how that person's production rate compares to other pizza makers' production rates, and so on. In this regard, a given level of production might be very good for a beginner, but not good for an experienced pizza maker. Other behavioral measures can be similarly evaluated along an evaluative continuum—variables such as job satisfaction, heart rate,

absenteeism, and so forth. Such evaluation is frequently based on comparisons with measurements of other people's behavior, rather like comparisons of one person's score on a test with the scores of others.

FACTORS INFLUENCING HUMAN BEHAVIOR

Sources of Influence

For any given type of behavior, the variability along the quantitative continuum is assumed to be the consequence of some combination of factors. Consider, for example, employees on a particular type of job who differ in levels of performance. Differences in performance sometimes (but not invariably) form a normal distribution such as is illustrated in Figure 2.3. Assuming some criterion (such as productivity in units per day or sales in dollars), one would find that individuals fall at different points (*A*, *B*, and *C*) along the performance continuum. If our assumption of multiple causation is valid, then we must infer that individuals *A*, *B*, and *C* fall at their

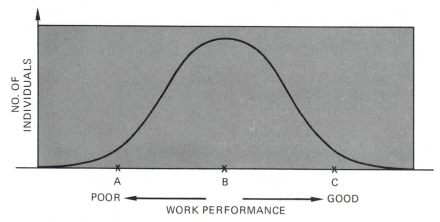

FIGURE 2.3 Distribution of differences in work performance of a hypothetical group of workers on a job. Positions *A*, *B*, and *C* represent three hypothetical individuals within the distribution whose performances are, respectively, generally below average (*A*), average (*B*), and above average (*C*).

respective positions of below average, average, and above average for some combination of reasons unknown to us at this point.

If we were not to speculate about some of the factors that might be associated with the relative performances of these three individuals, and workers in general, certain kinds of factors would almost inevitably be suggested. The list would include a variety of factors from any one or some combination of all three of the regions identified in Figure 2.1 and illustrated in more detail in Figure 2.2. Which specific variables would be represented would depend upon a variety of factors. Perhaps most important would be the nature of the job itself, which would likely have a strong influence on the skills and abilities as well as the attitudes and values of the persons on the job. This would also influence the nature of the social environment in which the work was done.

It should be clear from what we have said so far that the exact identification of the variables that are likely to cause most of the differences in performance in any given setting is dependent on the particular setting and the people in it. We cannot state with certainty what these variables will be for all conditions. Furthermore, even if we were to know the specific situation, identifying the variables that are most important is not that simple. There is a lot of subjective judgment required to explore the empirical relationship between a given set of variables and the behavior of interest. For example, the orientation of the investigator will influence the selection of variables. When faced with behavior on the same job, a mechanical engineer is likely to look at how design features of the equipment influence behavior, a psychologist will likely explore the effects of abilities, attitudes, and values, and a sociologist will investigate the effects of roles and group norms. Neither would be entirely right nor entirely wrong.

Causation

As you may have noticed we speak of factors that influence behavior at work but we have been somewhat reluctant to state that these factors *cause* behavior. This reluctance is real. It develops because of known limitations in our empirical analyses that do not allow researchers to draw causal conclusions directly from observed covariation. Simply because there is a statistical relationship between two variables does not mean that one variable necessarily "causes" the other. Although tall people may generally be better lumberjacks in forest operations than short people, it is not necessarily their height that causes them to be so. Their greater proficiency may well be due to another factor related to height, such as muscular strength or endurance. Thus, we find ourselves in the ambiguous situation of considering behavior *as if it were caused* by the variables we identify and investigate in some empirical study, but, at the same time, we realize that it is extremely difficult—in fact in most cases impossible—to state without question that one variable causes variation in another. Nevertheless, we can frequently build up a sufficient body of circumstantial evidence to be able to make reasonably good judgments of cause and effect. Furthermore, these judgments can be extremely useful for structuring job settings as well as for selecting people for particular jobs.

DISCUSSION

A primary objective or research in industrial-organizational psychology is to determine the relationship between specific individual and situational (both task-physical and social-interpersonal) variables on the one hand, and relevant job-related behaviors on the other. The results of such research can hopefully be used as the basis for taking some action to bring about improvement either in the job-related behaviors or in the conditions that lead to those behaviors.

With regard to taking action or establishing personnel policies and practices, matching people to jobs has probably been the most frequently used strategy of industrial-organizational psychologists to obtain more desirable job-related behaviors. Matching persons to jobs has generally operated according to one of two strategies, each of which is predicated on a different set of assumptions. One assumes that jobs (and other situational factors) are relatively "fixed"—relatively unchangeable and, therefore, not likely to be tampered with—and that the variability in relevant job-related behaviors on any given job arises mainly from differences among the individuals on that job. The strategy followed in such a case would focus on personnel selection of those individuals most suitable for the job, considering relevant personal characteristics (for example, aptitudes, physical characteristics, personality factors, education, or experience). In choosing individuals without the specific job-related experience or training that would be required, selection would focus on identifying individuals who seem to have the potential for learning the particular job.

The second strategy followed in many circumstances is predicated on the general assumption that the primary source of variability in relevant job-related behaviors is more a function of the job (and other "situational" factors). The strategy based on such an assumption leads to designing jobs and job situations so they are in some respects suited to the types of people likely to be on those jobs. Here the concern is less with the differences among people than it is with knowing what people who are likely to be on that job would generally be like.

Perhaps the most common application of such a strategy is reflected in job simplification which, carried to the extreme, would result in jobs that virtually anyone would be able to perform. The stereotype of this approach is the repetitive assembly-line job. Reaction against job simplification has contributed to developing job-enlargement or job-enrichment programs aimed at creating jobs more intrinsically satisfying than the simplified ones. Yet, even this approach operates under the same generalization—that is, that people are relatively fixed and that the job is changeable. Rather than assuming that people are fixed, with rather low levels of skills and abilities—as is the case for the simplification strategy—the job-enrichment approach assumes that people all possess a need to be more involved in what they do at work so that they can realize their human potential to grow and develop with respect to their skills and abilities. Although the latter approach certainly reflects a more human view of people than does the former, it is nonetheless similar to the job-simplification perspective in that it still places the emphasis for change on the job rather than on the person.

We have intentionally exaggerated the distinction between the two sets of assumptions underlying the two strategies for addressing the fit between people and their jobs. In practice, the distinctions between the assumptions and their associated strategies are by no means as clear cut as we have made them. At the same time, they do represent somewhat different frames of reference with respect to the person-job fit.

The world of human work cannot be viewed exclusively from either of these points of view. Rather, there are interactions between people and their job situations. Within reasonable bounds, both people and jobs are amenable to change. The implied strategy of such a frame of reference would be to optimize the combination of people and jobs so as to increase the probability that effective human involvement in producing goods and services will result while, at the same time, desirable human values will be enhanced. Actually, current theory tends to emphasize such an interactive frame of reference. The practical implementation of such a point of view on a broad scale is still in the future. However, there has been increased interest in interactionist positions that combine individual, social, and task factors to develop a strategy for approaching human behavior at work. In particular, the work of Schneider (1983) stresses this position. Others, such as McGrath and Rothford (1983) or Katz (1980, 1982), have stressed that we must not only take into account these three domains of influence, but that we must also consider the interaction of these three over time as people progress through their lives with an organization. From what we know from other fields, as theoretical and basic research develops in an area, practical, implicational results tend to follow, albeit rather slowly. Nevertheless, there is good reason to be encouraged about the possibilities for major advances in the interactive perspectives in organizations in the next few years.

In spite of our interactionist position, we should stress that much of the work in the past, done from a more simplistic perspective, has still made worthwhile contributions to the understanding of human behavior in organizations. Simple correlational studies of the covariation between some job characteristic and the behavior of people on the job have and still do provide useful cues about the extent to which jobs may affect behavior, and vice versa. From these simple empirical relationships, we can build more complex models and theories that are useful for guiding our understanding and our ability to design jobs and/or develop people in order to provide working conditions that meet the needs of organizations and the people who reside in them.

REFERENCES

Bandura, A. (1978). The self system in reciprocal determinism. *American Psychologist, 33,* 344–358.

Barker, R. G., & Wright, H. F. (1955). *Midwest and its children.* New York: Harper & Row.

Katz, R. (1980). Time and work: Toward an integrative perspective. In B. M. Staw & L. L. Cummings (Eds.), *Research in organizational behavior* (Vol. 2). Greenwich, Conn.: JAI Press.

Katz, R. (1982). The effects of group longevity on project communication and performance. *Administrative Science Quarterly, 27,* 81–104.

McGrath, J. E. (1976). Stress and behavior in organizations. In M. D. Dunnette (Ed.), *Handbook of industrial and organizational psychology.* Chicago: Rand McNally.

McGrath, J. E., & Rothford, N. L. (1983). Time and behavior in organizations. In L. L. Cummings & B. M. Staw (Eds.), *Research in organizational behavior* (Vol. 5). Greenwich, Conn.: JAI Press.

Schneider, B. (1983). Interactional psychology and organizational behavior. In L. L. Cummings & B. M. Staw (Eds.), *Research in organizational behavior* (Vol. 5). Greenwich, Conn.: JAI Press.

Staw, B. M. (1980). Rationality and justification in organizational life. In B. M. Staw & L. L. Cummings (Eds.), *Research in organizational behavior* (Vol. 2). Greenwich, Conn.: JAI Press.

Weick, K. E. (1979). *The social psychology of organizing* (2nd ed.). Reading, Mass.: Addison-Wesley.

3

Behavioral Research

We said earlier that in this text we deal with research related to the behavior of people at work. The various topics include examples of such research, with implications for applying relevant research findings to certain practical personnel and organizational problems. Although this text is not intended as a study of research methods, it will be helpful to the reader who is not already familiar with such methods to have at least a brief overview of some of the relatively basic research methods, statistical concepts, and procedures used in behavioral research. That is the aim of this chapter.

TYPES OF VARIABLES USED IN BEHAVIORAL RESEARCH

Most behavioral research is aimed at making "predictions" of relevant behavior. Such predictions typically require the use and measurement of two types of variables. One type

of variable, that which is being predicted, is usually called the *criterion*, and most typically characterizes some type of "behavior" (such as job performance, job satisfaction, absenteeism, or heart rate). The other type of variable is used in predicting the criterion and is usually called the *predictor*. In some instances, predictors are individual variables (such as test scores, measures of physical characteristics, or measures of other personal characteristics); in other instances, they are measures of situational characteristics like the size of the work group, method of training used, or noise level.

Frequently the criterion is also called the *dependent* variable and the predictor the *independent* variable. These terms are used especially in those studies in which there is some possible "control" of the predictor and in which the measure of the criterion (dependent variable) is viewed as being attributed to the effect of the predictor. Thus, one might study the effects of noise on hearing, of work schedules on productivity, of organizational climate on employees' attitudes, or of intensity of sound signals on the time it takes to react to an alarm.

In some research, the investigator is primarily interested in the criterion as it reflects the problem at hand, such as work performance, poor employee morale, or high accident rates. In such instances, the investigator is concerned with trying to identify possible causative factors (that is, predictors) of the criterion values. The predictors that might be investigated could be either individual, task-physical, or social-interpersonal variables, or any combination of all three. In other circumstances, however, the primary interest of the investigator might be that of the predictor, as in the case of studying the effects of noise, of work schedules, or of the aging process.

There are circumstances in which one variable can be used as either the predictor or the criterion. For example, job satisfaction might be used to predict work performance, or work performance might be used to predict job satisfaction. (Such an example reinforces the point made in Chapter 2 that we need to be cautious in inferring cause and effect from an observed relationship between two variables.)

TYPES OF MEASUREMENT SCALES

Virtually any type of behavioral research requires that the variables, both the predictors and the criteria, be measured. Measurement is basic to any statistical treatment of research data. It is also essential if any type of description and summarization of what is observed is to be carried out.

There are four basic types of *scales* that are used for measurement. A scale is a measurement system in which each observed unit is described. These four scales are described in detail shortly. Notice as you read about them

that these scales vary in the degree of precision offered to the variables of interest and the limits they create with respect to the types of comparisons that can be made among measured units. For example, a very primitive measuring system may simply attach labels or names to the variables measured. A small engine-producing company may measure its products by simply labeling the engines as "lawn-mower" motors, "compressor" motors for spray painters, and so on. This system identifies a unit as being in one class or another, so in a very basic sense each unit is measured by being classified into one of a set of mutually exclusive categories of engines. At a more precise level, all the engines may be measured in terms of the horsepower they produce. This measurement scale again gives a classification to each unit, but now the classification allows for some comparison among the units—that is, a 6 horsepower engine is more powerful than a ½ horsepower one. As a measuring system, horsepower still sorts each engine into some mutually exclusive category (an engine cannot be both a 6 horsepower motor and also a ½ horsepower one), yet it provides more because we know something about the differences between the categories in the horsepower measurement system; the simple labeling system could not do this.

The four common types of measurement scales ordered from low to high in terms of the amount of information they yield about comparisons among units on the scale are described next.

Nominal Scale

A nominal scale is one that has two or more mutually exclusive classes or categories of the general type of variable in question. Sex is a nominal scale when it classifies each individual as either male or female. Another common nominal scale used in industrial-organizational psychology is one of occupations: carpenter, plumber, electrician, waitress, manager, or college professor. In both these examples, any particular person could be classified or measured as belonging to one of these categories on the nominal scale but not more than one. It is the latter condition that makes the categories mutually exclusive. Note also that in the first example the nominal scale is complete; every observation could be sorted into one of the two categories on the scale. The second scale is not; there are many occupations that we have omitted from the scale. In this case, if we were to use such a scale and we wanted to measure every case on it, we would either have to limit our sample to people from the occupations on the scale, add more occupations to cover all possible conditions (a task that would be really impossible), or include some broad scale category into which all observations that did not fit the ones listed could fit. Labeling one category "Other" and sorting everything that does not fit elsewhere into it is a frequent solution to this problem.

Finally, it should be pointed out that occasionally variables which could perhaps be ordered in some fashion are treated as nominal scales. In this case, the ability of ordering is beyond the capabilities of a scale that has only nominal characteristics. An example of this would be a scale for communities with nominal labels of urban, suburban, small city, small town, and rural. Here we have nominal groups that are mutually exclusive, but they could also be ordered along a dimension based on the population density of the area being considered. Strictly speaking, this scale belongs in the next group considered.

Ordinal Scale

An ordinal scale is used to characterize the rank order on some variable, such as the rankings of individuals in a group of employees according to job performance or the ranking of jobs according to skill requirements. With an ordinal scale, the points on the scale can be ordered in some fashion. Thus, we can say that something with a lower rank is less than something higher on the scale, but we cannot say how much less. Consider the case of a supervisor who is asked to rank the five employees who work for him or her in terms of their performance on the job. With such a ranking, we can say that the person who is ranked second is seen as performing less well than the person who was ranked first. We cannot say that this same person is about as far below the person who is ranked first as the person ranked fifth is below the person ranked fourth. It may be that there is a big gap between the first and second, but that the fourth and fifth persons perform almost equally well. An ordinal scale has no information about the distances between entries on the scale.

Interval Scale

With an interval scale, the individual cases have numbers associated with them, and these numbers are significant in that any given numerical difference, anywhere along the scale, theoretically represents an equal difference in the underlying variable. However, the scale has no absolute zero; it is not possible, with such scales, to claim that there is none of the quality defined by the variable. One of the most common measures with interval-scale properties is an intelligence test. You may think you have an example of a person who has absolutely no intelligence, but such a conclusion could not be reached from an interval-scale intelligence test.

Many tests of human attributes and abilities are examples of interval scales, at least theoretically. With a properly developed test of arithmetic ability, for example, the difference between a score of 70 and a score of 75 would represent the same difference in arithmetic ability as the difference between 80 and 85. The absence of the zero point is apparent from the fact that even the lowest possible score on the arithmetic test would not be able to lead to the conclusion that the person has absolutely no arithmetic ability. Furthermore, it could not be said that someone with a score of 70 on the test is only half as smart as someone with a score of 140. In order to talk about ratios such as half or three times as much, it is necessary that the zero point be known.

Various types of tests are often treated *as if* their scores represented interval scales when the differences in score values across the range of scores on the variable really are not equal. The effect of violating the interval-scale characteristics and then operating as if the scale were an interval scale is hard to say. Certainly, it is a risky procedure. The size and nature of the effect, however, depend on the degree to which the data vary from interval properties, the range in scale values, the amount of variance in the scale, and other things. For now, we only point out that such violations occur frequently, and warn that one should be very cautious when they do.

Ratio Scales

Ratio scales preserve the equal intervals of interval scales and add one more feature: a true zero point. Ratio scales are best illustrated by variables of physical measurements—for example, height, weight, energy expenditure in calories, or speed of hand movements. Because a zero point exists for such scales, one can speak of ratios with respect to the scale—Mortimer weighs twice as much as Archibald or Henrietta operates the mail sorter twice as fast as Agnes.

STANDARD SCORES

In personnel practices, it is often useful to compare scores between different scales that may both have had at least interval qualities. For example, a district sales manager who is evaluating one of his or her subordinates on (1) product knowledge and (2) sales volume may have the following information: The person's sales volume last month was 380 units and her score on a product-knowledge test given at a recent training program was 136. In both cases, let us assume that the scales were good ones, with the volume calculated on a ratio scale and the product knowledge on an interval scale. In spite of the knowledge about scale properties, what do these numbers mean? How can they help the district sales manager judge the sales person's performance? As they now stand, the numbers do not mean much. Comparing across dimensions is meaningless because we have no idea about the similarities and differences between sales volume and product knowledge. This is a classic case of comparing apples to oranges. Even within the same dimension, more information is needed to judge the meaning of the score. For example, it is impossible to tell whether 380 units per month is good or bad. If the job is selling new cars, performance is outstanding; if it is selling soft pretzels from a street cart, we hope that the salesperson can eat a few on the side to make it through the month.

Since a large number of the traits and behaviors in which psychologists are interested are distributed normally in the population of people we deal with at work, the problem of lack of meaning within and across scales can be resolved. This is done by converting (or transforming) the obtained scores on a particular variable. This transformation converts raw scores into *standard scores*. The standard scores represent individuals' scores on the variable in units of the standard deviation based on all the persons in the sample.

To help interpret what we have just said, refer to Figure 3.1. At the very top of the page there is a normal distribution of scores on some test. The x_i placed along the horizontal axis represents a particular score on the test. This could be the salesperson's score of 136 in our example. The height of the curve immediately above x_i represents the number of persons who scored x_i on the test.

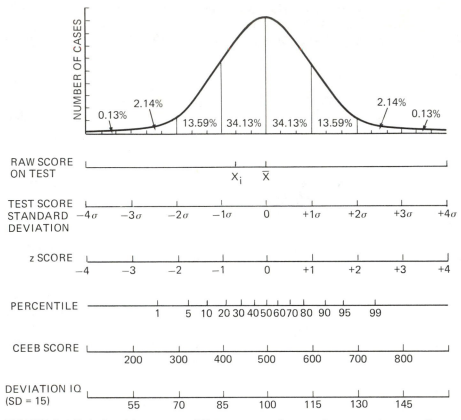

FIGURE 3.1 Relationships among different types of tests when a test is normally distributed.

With the data from all the people who took the test, it is possible to calculate the mean test score, $\bar{x}$, and an index of the degree of variation, or spread of scores, around the mean. This measure of variation is called the *standard deviation*. The estimate for the standard deviation in the population of possible persons who will take the test is:

$$\sigma = \sqrt{\dfrac{\displaystyle\sum_{i=1}^{n}(x_i - \bar{x})^2}{n-1}}$$

where:

σ is the standard deviation
x_i is each individual's score
$\bar{x}$ is the mean score for the sample
n is the number of people in the sample.

The first row below the normal distribution in Figure 3.1 shows points on the raw-score scale, in whole units of standard deviations. Notice two very useful characteristics about these standard deviation units. The first is that they are symmetrical around the mean—that is, -1 standard deviation is the same number of raw-score units below the mean as +1 standard deviation is above it. Even more important, given a normal distribution, we know what percent of people who took the test scored in any given range on the test. For example, we know that 34.13% of the people scored between the mean and +1 standard deviation; we also know that 13.59% scored between −2 and −1 standard deviations (see Figure 3.1).

Using the preceding information, it is now possible to gain some meaning for the raw scores in our example. Let us assume that we converted both sales volume and the product-knowledge test score to standard deviations based on the two separate distributions, and that we found that a sales volume of 380 represented +2 standard deviations and the test score was −1 units. This information allows us to conclude that the salesperson's sales volume is better than that of approximately 98% (all but 2.14 plus 0.13%) of the salespersons who were observed, and that product knowledge is better than that of approximately 16% (0.13 plus 2.14 plus 13.59%) of them (see the top scale in Figure 3.1). With this information, the sales manager is in a much better position to make sense out of the numbers. The manager can now conclude that the salesperson is far above most others in sales, but far below most of them in product knowledge. The numbers now have some "meaning."

All standard scores rely on the information gained by converting raw scores to standard-deviation units. However, standard deviation units are cumbersome to deal with and often misunderstood. Therefore, other standard scores are often calculated in order to remove some of the awkwardness. For example, intelligence-test scores in standard deviation units usually add 100 to the mean and use a standard deviation of 15 instead of 1. This transformation has *absolutely no effect* on particular individuals' standings in the group or on the meaning of this standing with respect to the number who score higher or lower than the individual. It does, however, get rid of the need to use negative numbers, and it converts the score to a range that is pretty well understood by a large number of people. The lower half of Figure 3.1 shows examples of some common standard score scales. Note how the scores on these scales could all be converted to other units as indicated by their relationships to the normal curve.

BASIC RESEARCH STRATEGIES

The most important fact to remember when conducting research is that research is done in order to answer some question. The question can be very simple—"What is the *real* length of the fish he caught?"—or it can be very complex—"Why do some executives turn down important promotions?" The next most important fact to remember about research is that, no matter what method is used, a number of alternative explanations for the results obtained are always possible. This is not to say that some ways to answer the question are not better than others. Obviously they are. For example, our best check on the angler's honesty would be to measure the fish with a ruler. Even this might result in an error, if the person measuring or the ruler were not very accurate. We could also "measure" the fish from a photograph by comparing the ratio of the size of the fisherman's hand in the picture to the fish's length and then multiplying this by our measurement of the actual length of the angler's hand. Obviously this approach is less suitable than the former *unless*, at the time the question was asked, we have nothing but an old photograph and a plateful of bones! If the question is an important one, it may be worthwhile to use research methods that are less precise than the ideal or not the best possible, if the best way cannot be accomplished.

The need for research arises when some questions must be answered. The first step in any research is to structure the questions so that some data can be gathered to answer the questions. This seems so basic that we really should not need to bring it up. Unfortunately, many research projects are undertaken before the questions are clearly stated. As a result, hours of time of both the researchers and the people who provide the data are wasted because they did not outline the questions of interest in a way that will lead to an adequate answer.

As a starting point, let us assume that a thoughtful question has been formulated and that we want to select a research strategy to answer it. From this point, the research strategy selected can be developed on the basis of the answers to three basic questions:

1. What variables need to be studied?
2. How should these variables be treated?
3. In what setting should the research be undertaken?

Once all three of these are answered adequately, the research design should be well formulated. The questions are complicated, however, because they are not independent. For example, the selection of a given variable of interest may severely limit the treatments available and/or the selection of settings. Nevertheless, it is instructive to consider these three as classes of questions to be asked. Note that a heavy debt is owed to the work of Runkel and McGrath (Runkel & McGrath, 1972; McGrath, Martin, & Kulka, 1982) for our thinking on the following issues.

Selection of Variables

The variables to be considered in research depend on *theoretical* and *practical* issues. By theory we simply mean that they depend on the issues outlined in the questions to be answered. Consider, for example, the question

of why some people turn down important promotions. Obviously, one of the variables that must be measured is the behavior of accepting or not accepting a promotion. Yet, even the decision about how to deal with this very obvious variable has some problems associated with it. One could offer people promotions and see who does or does not accept them, or one could describe a promotion and ask people if they would or would not accept it. Conceptually, these may be very similar, although the former may be closer to what is actually of interest. From a practical standpoint, these two methods are widely discrepant. It is almost always easier, and it costs considerably less, to ask the people than to offer promotions and observe the responses to the offers. Therefore, the choice of the variable would be affected by practical as well as by theoretical concerns.

Treatment of Variables

Table 3.1 describes several ways in which variables can be treated. These descriptions closely resemble those used by Runkel and McGrath (1972) with some modifications in description and labels. Let us consider each one.

For both practical and theoretical reasons, there are an indefinite number of variables which are *not* of interest in any given research. If there is no reason to believe some

TABLE 3.1 Treatments of variables in research

I. Do not measure:
  a. Ignore (Treatment 1)
  b. Randomization (Treatment 2)
II. Measure under the following conditions:
  a. With no manipulation (Treatment 3)
  b. Manipulated by
    1. Holding constant (Treatment 4)
    2. Matching (Treatment 5)
    3. Creating specific levels or categories (Treatment 6)

variables are interesting or could affect the results, they are usually *ignored* (Treatment 1). There is always the chance, however, that a particular variable may have an effect even though the researchers can think of no reason for such an effect. If the variable is simply ignored under such conditions, its effect will still show up. For example, suppose a person was interested in comparing two dentists' chairs in terms of their judged comfort. The researcher may very legitimately consider the chair's color to be unimportant. Yet, if the color did happen to influence people's judgments of comfort, ignoring it and comparing two chairs of different colors would be a problem. A better way to deal with such an uncontrolled variable would be to use *randomization* (Treatment 2). In this way the ignored variables are assumed to affect only the variable(s) of interest by chance alone. Over many observations with different mixes of treatments and chair colors, the chance effects should cancel out.

It is necessary to both measure variables of interest to research and to decide whether or not to manipulate them in some fashion. The simplest strategy is to measure the variables as they exist *with no manipulation* (Treatment 3). In this case, the variable is allowed to vary freely and is observed. For example, we might be interested in the relationship between age and job satisfaction. If so, both variables could be measured and allowed to take on whatever values the respondents had for them.

In any research, one may treat one or more variables by simply allowing them to vary freely and then measuring them, but *at least one variable must be allowed to vary freely*. If all were controlled, there would be no gain in information. If we wanted to see how age is related to job satisfaction and controlled levels of age and of satisfaction by selecting only older workers who were very satisfied and younger ones who were not, we would learn nothing about the relationship between age

and satisfaction; all we would be able to say is that we were successful in selecting the types of people we wanted. Only when at least one of the variables is uncontrolled can we find out the possible relationship. With age and job satisfaction, we could select some older workers and some younger workers (that is, control for age) and allow job satisfaction to assume whatever value the workers had for it. This could tell us if age and job satisfaction were related in our sample. Likewise, we could select some very satisfied workers and some very dissatisfied workers (control job satisfaction) and measure the ages of the workers selected (let age vary freely). This would also tell us something about the relationship between age and job satisfaction. Finally, we could select a sample of workers randomly and measure their age and job satisfaction (letting both variables vary freely) to see the degree of relationship between the two variables of interest. Each of these methods would yield some information because each has at least one variable that varied naturally without external control. Variables handled according to Treatment 3 are called *dependent variables* when related to variables using Treatment 6, explained later.

Treatments 4 and 5 represent ways of control in which the variable cannot have an effect on the observed conditions. The first, *holding constant* (Treatment 4), means making every case of interest the same on one variable. The effect of color in the dental-chair study could be controlled by using chairs of only one color. In this case, color could still affect the judgment of comfort, but, if chair A is compared to chair B for comfort and both are the same color, then color is "controlled" in the sense that it can have no influence on the *difference* in ratings between the two chairs; it has a constant effect and therefore cannot show up in the difference.

Variables can also be controlled by *matching* (Treatment 5) to eliminate possible effects of the variable. Here we might have dental chairs of Type X and Type Y and, for each type, one red, one white, and one blue chair. Color is not constant for each type in the sense that it is the same for the type, but all colors are represented equally in both types. Thus, any difference in rating of comfort between the two types should not be due to differences in color. Another illustration of holding a variable constant versus matching might be to compare two training programs in which the sex of the participants is controlled. Sex could be controlled either by having all participants in both training programs be of the same sex (Treatment 4) or by having the proportion of males and females be the same in both groups (Treatment 5). Note that this does not mean that there must be 50% males and 50% females in each treatment; it means that the proportion of males and females in each training program must be the same.

The final method of control is to *create specific levels or categories* of the variable (Treatment 6). Here the researcher could vary the levels of illumination, noise, or the size of work groups, for example. The researcher selects the levels of the variable to present in the research. When this is done, the variable so controlled is often called the *independent variable*. In any true experiment, one or more variables are manipulated in this fashion, persons are assigned *randomly* to levels of the manipulated variable, and at least one variable is allowed to vary freely while being measured (Treatment 3).

Research Settings

Research settings vary along a continuum from contrived to natural. Usually we refer to studies done in very contrived and artificial settings created by the researcher as *laboratory* studies and those done in natural settings as *field* studies.

Although, within these settings, variables can be treated in any of the six ways already described, the treatment of variables tends to be associated with the setting used. In the laboratory, variables with unknown effects or variables that are of no interest are normally treated by randomization (Treatment 2), and specific levels are created on some variables (Treatment 6) to observe their effects on the dependent variable (Treatment 3). Field research tends to ignore many variables (Treatment 1) because of the difficulty of being able to obtain randomization. Typically field research also requires collecting data that make it possible to analyze the covariation of several unmanipulated variables (Treatment 3). We call the latter a *field study*.

Experimental and Correlational Strategies

Experimental designs. In research strategies there is sometimes a distinction made between *experimental* and *correlational* studies. The experimental approach usually involves some form of "manipulation" of the independent variables, such as by holding them constant (Treatment 4), by matching (Treatment 5), or by creating specific levels of the variables (Treatment 6). The experimental strategy is used most commonly in laboratory studies but it is sometimes used in field studies when some form of control is possible. It lends itself most readily to investigation of task/physical environment variables such as incentive systems, temperature, job designs, or work methods. It also fits for manipulation of social/interpersonal factors such as group size.

Correlational designs. In the correlational strategy, data are obtained on the predictor and the criterion variables for each case or individual in the sample without any manipulation or control. For example, for each person in the study, the researcher might obtain information on age (the predictor) and job satisfaction (the criterion). This strategy is most frequently used for investigating the effects of individual variables on behavior. It is used most frequently in field studies but it is also used at times in the laboratory. The data themselves can be obtained at places of work, from company records, from surveys, or from a variety of other sources.

Comparisons of experimental and correlational designs. The major difference between experimental and correlational research strategies lies in the degree of confidence that can be placed in statements about causality—the extent to which condition A causes condition B. Philosophically, the notion of whether anything causes anything else has been debated for hundreds of years and is not now, nor ever will be, completely resolved. These arguments go far beyond our purpose here. Yet, when comparing experimental to correlational designs, we can say that more confidence in causal relationships arises from experimental than from correlational research. In correlational studies, it is much more difficult to eliminate alternative explanations for observed events. If we find that younger executives are more willing to accept transfers than older ones, we may think that growing older causes a drop in the willingness to transfer. Perhaps it does. But there are many other variables that are associated with age that may be affecting the relationship—number of children in high school, investment in housing with lower interest rates, and so forth. Experimental studies, especially when random assignment to experimental conditions is used, can eliminate many of these other explanations.

Recently there has been an increased interest in developing research models that use correlational designs but gain some additional confidence in the extent to which one variable causes another. These procedures are labeled "causal correlational analyses" (James, Mulaik, & Brett, 1982). Causal correlational analyses use mathematical models, most of which are based on multiple regression procedures (discussed later in the chapter). These approaches hold a great deal of promise for research done in organizational settings and should be used a lot more in the future. However, users of these procedures must study them carefully, especially when making assumptions about the nature of the relationships among the variables used in the causal models. These assumptions can be quite limiting at times. Furthermore, although the procedures increase the degree of confidence one can have in causal relationships in correlational settings, this confidence can never be perfect and will never be able to match that gained from a true experiment.

Quantitative versus Qualitative Research

Lately there has developed a certain degree of dissatisfaction and distrust of quantitative data that are generated in organizational settings. The reasons for this are complex but center around the belief that data generated by methods such as interviews and questionnaires fail to capture what is really going on. They fail because (1) the measures are so obtrusive that they get in the way of allowing people to accurately express what is happening; and (2) behavior in organizations is too complex and too temporary to really be observed and recorded by typical quantitative methods.

This dissatisfaction has led to the development of *qualitative* methods (Van Maanen, Dabbs, & Faulkner, 1982). These methods stress observing bits and pieces of behavior in organizations by much less systematic and numerically oriented procedures. For example, Van Maanen (Van Maanen, 1975; Van Maanen et al., 1982), who is interested in the socialization of police officers into the police force, actually joined the police force as a new recruit, went through the training program, and worked on the street for several months once he graduated from the training class.

The data that he collected are subjective, descriptive data seen from the point of view of a social scientist who is also a police officer. Another researcher interested in quantitative data takes snapshots of people interacting and analyzes these pictures.

The use of such qualitative data would appear to be a great source of ideas and hypotheses about behavior in organizations. However, for these data to have scientific value and to contribute to a cumulative data set leading to the understanding of work behavior, the methods must meet standards of replicability, reliability, and validity that have held for the more quantitative research data in the past. At present, the concern for these characteristics with respect to qualitative data is, in our opinion, less than it should be.

Discussion of Research

As indicated earlier, decisions about research strategies need to be based on considerations of the combination of the variables to be investigated, the treatment of those variables, and the setting in which the research is to be carried out.

Laboratory versus field research. Various advantages and disadvantages have been attributed to laboratory versus field settings for conducting behavioral research. For example, it is usually easier to control experimental variables in the laboratory than in the field; however, it has been argued that laboratory studies lack the reality of field studies. Schneider (1983) goes even farther than this. He argues that laboratory studies simply fail to account for all the other types of variables that must occur naturally in the field—for example, with the same people over a long period of time.

In part, because of the aspect of realism present in field studies, there is a rather common belief that such settings provide far more generalization of research findings than do laboratory settings. Certainly there is a bias

in industrial-organizational psychology toward field settings. Whether this bias is justified is questionable. On the basis of an analysis of numerous studies from both types of settings, Dipboye and Flanagan (1979) concluded that greater ability to generalize from the field to other field settings rather than from the laboratory to these same field settings was not necessarily the case.

It seems fairest to conclude that the extent to which one can generalize from either setting to the field depends on the nature of the problem being investigated and on the quality of the consideration that was given to the constructs of interest in the research, regardless of the setting in which it took place. For example, laboratory experiments are particularly relevant for investigating the effects of physical stimuli on sensory, perceptual, or psychomotor responses. Considering the effects of temperature on the ability to use small hand tools in cold climates can be accomplished in the laboratory without too much worry about a lack of generalization to field settings requiring the use of the same types of tools under the same conditions of temperature. Yet, due to the typically short time period for laboratory studies, research designed to investigate the effects of leadership style, participation in decision making in groups, and interpersonal communication may be less valid for organizations (Schneider, 1983). This limited validity is not necessarily inherent in the laboratory, but is certainly difficult to deal with there.

In very general terms, laboratory experiments are most relevant in circumstances in which the results of short periods of experimentation would be reasonably predictive of long-term performance or other behavior. If the investigation deals more with problems in which *long-term* motivational and attitudinal variables would be important, however, the real-life field setting is usually preferable; in some instances, it is virtually mandatory. The results of a short laboratory experiment would not necessarily predict the long-term results of a day-in–day-out routine. You might find from a laboratory study that people report that they like a particular type of music while performing a laboratory task, but in practice such music might drive them up the wall if they listened to it month after month. Or the interest in a challenging laboratory task might make it possible to perform the task well in that setting, but the same task might be so boring over a period of months that interest (and performance) would suffer.

Although there are certain types of behavioral research projects that should be conducted in laboratory settings, and others in field settings, there are still others that might lend themselves to either. In this regard, Dipboye and Flanagan (1979) argue for coordinated strategies in both types of settings on the grounds that laboratory and field research may be veiwed as complementary rather than as conflicting strategies.

Quasi-experimental design. In carrying out experiments either in the laboratory or in field settings, one should follow commonly accepted research practices. But there are circumstances in which it is simply not possible or practical to conform rigorously to ideal experimental practices. This is especially so in field settings, such as industrial or business organizations. For example, there may not be enough eligible subjects to use in both experimental and control groups. In this regard, Cook and Campbell (1976, 1979) discussed what they called *quasi-experimental designs.* Quasi-experimental designs depart in some manner from the ideal or "true" experimental design. Cook and Campbell asserted that although quasi-experiments do not allow for as strong a degree of confidence in the results as do true experiments, in some cases they can still provide useful information. Given the alternative of gathering no information versus gathering some with known limitations, the latter is usually preferred. Quasi-experiments offer ways to gather such data.

STATISTICAL ANALYSES IN RESEARCH

Although this text does not require understanding or use of very complex statistical concepts or methods, the reader should have at least passing acquaintance with certain basic concepts and methods. Certain statistical concepts are discussed in Appendix A, including graphic representations of data (such as frequency distributions and frequency polygons), measures of central tendency (the mean, median, and mode), measures of variability (particularly the standard deviation), correlations, standard scores, and percentiles. The reader who is not already familiar with these should begin to develop such familiarity by referring to Appendix A. For now, the reader should become familiar with graphic representations of data and measures of central tendency. When the text first refers to the other concepts, we make further references to Appendix A. One statistic, however, the correlation coefficient, is so common that it is described here.

Correlations

Correlation coefficient. A coefficient of correlation (usually called a correlation) is a statistical index of the degree of linear relationship between two variables. It ranges from $+1.00$ (a perfect linear relationship with a positive slope to the line), through intermediate positive relationships, down to 0.00 (the absense of any linear relationship), through intermediate negative values to -1.00 (a perfect linear relationship with a negative slope). Figure 3.2 illustrates the concept of correlations, and shows different *scattergrams* that reflect varying degrees of relationships.

It usually takes a bit of experience to be able to evaluate the magnitude of correlations, since the evaluation depends, in part, on the nature of the data. In some cases, a

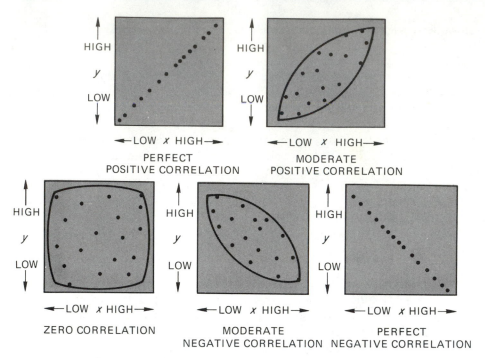

FIGURE 3.2 Illustration of scattergrams of several hypothetical correlations between two variables, ranging from a perfect positive correlation ($r = +1.00$) through a zero correlation ($r = 0.00$) to a perfect negative correlation ($r = -1.00$). Lines around dots depict the scatter or concentration of cases. Each dot represents one case.

correlation between two variables of .60 may be considered quite good and in other cases not very good at all. If this .60 is the degree of relationship between the amount of batting training a baseball player is given and his or her batting average after the training, this would indicate a pretty strong relationship between the two. On the other hand, if this represents the relationship between the decision of the umpire that the player is either out or to be walked and whether or not the player goes to first base, we would consider the relationship too low. Because every time the player is declared out, the player should not go to first base, and every time the player is walked he or she should, the correlation should be +1.00 for this example.

We should caution the reader that a coefficient of correlation cannot be interpreted directly as a proportion. In statistical terms, a correlation of a given magnitude accounts for the percentage of "variance" represented by the *squared* value of the correlation coefficient; thus, a correlation of .60 indicates that 36% (.60 × .60) of the variance in one variable is shared in common with the other.

Regression. A concept very similar to correlation is regression. In fact, when a regression coefficient is calculated for two variables, the resulting coefficient is exactly the same as the correlation coefficient and can be interpreted the same way. The difference between regression and correlation is that a regression analysis calculates the formula for the line that best represents the scatterplot between two variables. Consider the data in

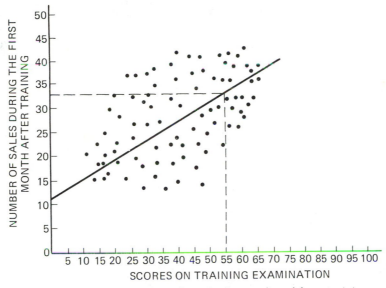

FIGURE 3.3 Regression of number of sales predicted from training examination scores.

Figure 3.3. Notice that the X axis represents scores at the end of a training program on a test designed to measure product knowledge for life-insurance salespersons. The scores on the Y axis represent the number of sales in the first month after the training course. Each dot in the scatterplot represents a person with a test score at the point over which the dot is located on the X axis and sales at the level parallel to the dot on the Y axis. The line running through the graph represents the "best linear fit" of a line to the data. Think of trying to find the location for a line such that the distance of each dot from the line for the whole set of dots in the scatterplot is as small as possible. The regression procedure does this by applying what is called the least-squared approach.

More important than how this is done is what results from it. The end result is an equation for the line that represents the best fit to the data. This equation is in the form of:

$$\hat{y}_i = a + Bx_i$$

where

$\hat{y}_i$ = the predicted value on the criterion
a = the value of the criterion at the point at which the line intercepts the criterion (Y) axis (In Figure 3.3, the value of a is approximately 12.)
B = the slope of the line
x_i = the value of the predictor.

The equation for this line can be very useful. It provides a way to predict the value of the criterion from the predictor. Consider, for example, the data of Figure 3.3. Assume that a group of salespersons was given the test and that the criterion data were collected for a group who had taken the test. Then for that group, suppose the regression equation illustrated was computed. If you now had a new person, i, whose score on the predictor was 55, then the best guess with respect to how well that person would do on the criterion is 33—that is, the regression line represents the point that best represents the predicted score for a person on the criterion, if we know the predictor score.

One word of caution must be interjected here: The process of fitting a line to the data as was shown in Figure 3.3 capitalizes on chance. Because each person's score on both the predictor and the criterion includes some error due to any number of factors that cause a measure to be an imperfect estimate of the person's true score on the variable, the regression equation based on fitting the data perfectly will be somewhat inflated. That is, the correlation between Y and Ŷ across all persons will be higher than could be expected with some new sample of people. There are statistical ways to correct for the bias that is likely to be present in the estimate of the regression equation and regression coefficient. The exact nature of these correction procedures is not addressed here. However, note that the regression coefficient obtained from a sample will usually be an *overestimate* of the true degree of relationship between the variables and that you should correct for the possible overestimation.

The final point about regression procedures is that more than one predictor can be used to predict a criterion. In fact, in most cases, several predictors are used. Consider the task of predicting the success of college students. Typically some criterion like the students' grade-point averages at the end of the first semester of the first year is used as the criterion and the predictors used are students' grades in high school and their scores on some standardized national tests like the Scholastic Aptitude Test (SAT) (or the College Entrance Examination Board, CEEB). In this case, the two predictors—high-school grades and SAT scores—can be entered into the prediction equation, which now becomes:

$$\hat{y}_i = a + B_1 \text{ (HS grade)}_i + B_2 \text{ (SAT)}_i$$

In an analogous fashion, the number of predictors can be expanded to any number that is reasonable from a logical and practical standpoint and that is sufficiently smaller than the size of the sample of people used to produce reliable statistical relationships.

Statistical Significance

Any discussion of statistical methods should include reference to the concept of *statistical significance*. In a general sense, statistical significance deals with the possible error associated with a statistic. In the results of political polls, for example, you may have heard that a given candidate was preferred by, "53% of the respondents and that this was 'accurate' within + or − 3 points." The ability to estimate the range in which the results are likely to occur uses concepts like statistical significance. The notion of statistical significance can be applied to virtually any type of statistic such as percentages, means, percentiles, correlation coefficients, or to differences between them.

To illustrate the notion of statistical significance we consider the difference between two arithmetic means with the data of Figure 3.4. The figure represents two hypothetical groups from the effects of two methods of training employees on a particular job. The independent variable is the training method. The two methods are referred to as I and II. Let us assume that the dependent variable or criterion is the production of the employees during a specified week. Example A of Figure 3.4 represents the distributions of production units produced per week by employees trained according to each method. The horizontal axis is the number of units produced and the vertical axis is the number of persons who produced at the level represented by the horizontal value. Given these two distributions, the question that the research would ask is if these two groups are different enough from each other to be considered different. There are really two parts to this question. The first part deals with whether or not these differences are reliably different in the sense

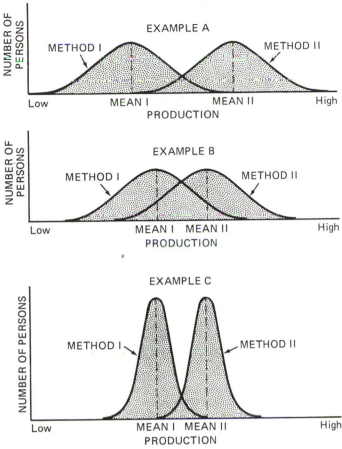

FIGURE 3.4 Hypothetical distributions of production records of employees trained by method I and method II.

that we can be confident that the difference is not just a chance difference. To judge whether the effect is likely to be due to chance, it is first necessary to know what size differences would occur by chance alone and then to compare the difference that was found to the chance distribution. Once this comparison is made, it is possible to state probabilistically the chances that the observed difference was or was not due to chance. For example, if we compared the difference between the means of the two methods in Figure 3.4, Example A, and found that a difference that large would occur by chance

alone only one time in 100, we would say that our results were significant (implying *statistically* significant) at the .01 level. The actual calculation of statistical difference is beyond the scope of this text. For our purposes, it is sufficient to know that statistical significance depends on the *number* of cases in the sample or samples used (the number of employees who received the two training methods in our example), the *variability* of the scores on the variable or variables of interest, and the numerical *values in question* (in our example, the size of the overlap between the two methods). Figure 3.4 shows differences in the amount of overlap between the distributions when Example *A* is compared to Example *B* and differences in the variability when Example *B* is compared to Example *C*.

Statistical significance is normally expressed in probability units such as .05, .01, or .001, respectively. These units mean that a particular result would occur by chance alone only five times out of 100, one out of 100, or one out of 1000. What is the "proper" or correct level of significance to use cannot be determined in any absolute sense. Typically, for psychological research, we tend to use levels of significance of .05 or smaller. Yet, this is only a convenient convention. If one were dealing with some new exploratory issue, the researcher might be willing to accept something at the .10 level of significance as worthy of further study. On the other hand, if one were dealing with some highly important issue like testing cans of soup for the presence of botulism, one would want to be much more confident than a chance of five times out of 100 that the conclusion about a clear batch could be wrong.

One important point is that statistical significance does not mean the same thing as *practical* significance. Something can be statistically significant and still not be of any practical significance. Practical significance refers to the extent to which statistically significant results have possible practical utility taking into account such things as cost, amount of possible benefit, and so forth. Refer again to Figure 3.4. The practical significance of method II is likely to be greater in Example A than in the other two examples, all other things being equal, because the size of the difference is greater in that case than in the other two cases. On the other hand, without knowing the costs of the treatments and the gains that can be expected from one training program as compared to the other, it is impossible to draw any conclusions about practical significance in the examples we have presented.

Just as we can determine the statistical significance of the difference between two means, we can also determine the statistical significance of the difference between other statistical relationships. One of the most common other cases is to ask questions about the degree of confidence that we can have about the fact that an observed relationship is significantly different from no relationship at all. For example, we frequently ask the degree to which an observed correlation between two variables in a sample is significantly different from zero.

One final twist to the concept of statistical significance is to establish *confidence intervals* around any given individual statistic. This interval indicates the possible limits of error at a specified probability level. Thus, a political pollster may report a result in terms of a specific percent of the vote and then also report that there is 95% confidence that the results will be between plus or minus a certain number of percentage points, such as 3, around that percentage point.

DISCUSSION

The result of any behavioral research consists of data. These data may be used as the basis for formulating theories, or they may be used directly for some specific problem. In any event, the data from a research investigation are simply data. The interpretation and application of research findings depend on the sound judgments of the investigators and on those who are in a position to apply such findings. Certain statistical methods, research designs, and analytical procedures have developed as a common language among researchers to aid in the interpretation process. To the extent that the users of these methods share a common understanding of the strengths and weaknesses of the procedures and to the extent that they agree on the conventions about what is and is not reasonable to do with data, the interpretations of data and the sharing of knowledge can be and are facilitated. It is to this end—facilitating a common understanding—that the statistical procedures and research methods have been established. To use them wisely, even while recognizing their strengths and weaknesses, is a real asset to understanding. To abuse them, either by blindly adhering to common practices without recognizing the implications of these practices for the problem at hand or by ignoring the assumptions, strengths, or weaknesses of the procedures, is perhaps the greatest danger of all with respect to effectively utilizing empirical data in organizations.

REFERENCES

Cook, T. D., & Campbell, D. T.(1976). The design and conduct of quasi-experiments and true experiments. In M. D. Dunnette (Ed.), *Handbook of industrial and organizational psychology.* Chicago: Rand McNally.

Cook, T. D., & Campbell, D. T.(1979). *Quasi-Experimentation: Design and analysis issues for field settings.* Boston: Houghton Mifflin.

Dipboye, R. L., & Flanagan, M. F.(1979). Research settings in industrial and organizational psychology. *American Psychologist, 34,* 141–150.

James, L. R., Mulaik, S. A., & Brett, J. M.(1982). *Causal analyses: Assumptions, models and data.* Beverly Hills, Calif.: Sage Publications.

McGrath, J. E., Martin, J., & Kulka, R. A.(1982) *Judgment calls in research.* Beverly Hills, Calif.: Sage Publications.

Runkel, P. L., & McGrath, J. E.(1972). *Research on human behavior: A systematic guide to method.* New York: Holt, Rinehart & Winston.

Schneider, B.(1983).Interactional psychology and organizational behavior. In L. L. Cummings & B. M. Staw (Eds.), *Research in organizational behavior.* Greenwich, Conn.: JAI Press.

Van Maanen, J.(1975). Police socialization. *Administrative Science Quarterly, 20,* 207–228.

Van Maanen, J., Dabbs, J. M., Jr., & Faulkner, R. R.(1982). *Varieties of qualitative research.* Beverly Hills, Calif.: Sage Publications.

4

Job Analysis

The operations of an organization are carried out with a combination of: (1) physical facilities; (2) organizational features (organizational structures, policies, procedures, and so on); and (3) human resources. This text focuses on the human-resources aspects of organizations, which are rooted in the jobs people perform. Knowledge of the jobs people perform is central to effectively managing the human resources of an organization, including recruiting, selection, training, and personnel development, performance evaluation, and wage and salary administration. Job analysis is the process of developing job-related information, and can serve as the cornerstone of an integrated human-resources program. This chapter deals with job-analysis processes and the uses of job-analysis information in human-resource programs.

The basis for the creation of jobs is tied in with the objectives of the organization. Presumably any job is brought into being in order to fulfill some function that is considered necessary to achieve the objectives of the organization. Thus, individual jobs might be created to fulfill such functions as receiving raw materials, assembling parts, maintaining equipment, serving hamburgers, adding up prices of groceries at a checkout counter, and so on.

WHY JOBS ARE LIKE THEY ARE

The nature of jobs can be influenced by many factors, but in general we can think of jobs as ranging from those whose features are predetermined for the worker (as in highly repetitive assembly work) to those in which the incumbent (i.e., the worker) virtually makes the job what it is (as might be the case with some research or planning activities in which the incumbent may decide what to do, and how to do it). In the case of jobs that are reasonably well crystallized for workers we could speculate about some of the factors that have caused the jobs to be what they are. Such factors could include: the stage of technology; the design of the equipment, tools, or devices used; the physical arrangement of the workplace; the specified procedures; the working conditions; seasonal and cyclical factors; and the timing of work demands (such as rush hours in restaurants). Some of these factors are pretty much outside the control of the organization (such as the types of machines that are available), whereas others are well within the control the organization may have (such as the arrangement of the workplace and the specific procedures to be followed). The latitude for incumbents to influence the nature of their own jobs is greatest in the case of professional, technical, scientific, managerial, and staff types of jobs.

Although some jobs are performed the same way now as they were in the past, other jobs are subject to gradual change, or dramatic change, as the consequence of technological developments. As we look ahead to the increased use of robotics and computers we can envision major shifts in the kinds of work people will be doing in the future.

USES OF JOB INFORMATION

There is hardly any aspect of the management of human resources that does not depend in some way on job information—the information obtained by job analysis. Some of these purposes are illustrated in Figure 4.1. In general terms these purposes fall into three categories: (1) organizational decisions (such as developing the organization structure); (2) work and equipment design; and perhaps most important (3) human-resources management. Job information can also serve other purposes outside the framework of organizations, such as in vocational counseling and in planning educational and training curricula. (You might speculate about the effect on your vocational objectives of whatever oc-

cupational information you have picked up over the years.)

In the past, job analysis has mostly been considered as a fairly mundane kind of activity, and has been something of a stepchild of personnel administrators, psychologists, and other behavioral professionals. However, the impact of relevant job information is of major consequence on individuals (as in the choice of vocations and in the jobs held during their working careers), and also on the effectiveness with which personnel-related functions are carried out in organizations.

The *Uniform Guidelines on Employee Selection Procedures*

A development in the United States in recent years has brought job analysis out of the doldrums into the limelight. The adoption of the *Uniform Guidelines on Employee Selection Procedures* (1978) has brought job analysis to the foreground in personnel management because the *Guidelines* require that job specifications be supported by information obtained by relevant job-analysis methods. Although the *Guidelines* do not require any specific type of job-analysis method, they do indicate that the analyses should include descriptions of job behaviors and, to the extent appropriate, work outcomes and measures of their criticality and/or importance. On the basis of a review of certain court cases that dealt with job information as related to the validation of personnel tests, Thompson and Thompson (1982) concluded that the most important types of job information in validation cases are: tasks, duties, skills, knowledge, and abilities.

TERMINOLOGY

Although terminology in the field of job analysis is used rather loosely, some terms have fairly well-accepted meanings. Definitions of

FIGURE 4.1 Some of the uses of job information. The first three columns represent the uses within an organization's human-resources program. The fourth column represents other uses, especially in vocational counseling and in planning educational curricula.

Uses within an Organization			Other Uses
Organizational Decision Processes	Work and Equipment Design	Human-Resources Management	
Organizational structure	Engineering design	Personal recruitment selection, and placement	Planning educational curricula
Organizational planning	Methods design	Training and personnel development	Vocational counseling
Organizational policies	Job design	Performance measurement and evaluations	
	Safety	Job-classification systems	
		Wage and salary administration	
		Labor relations	

a few terms are given here (adapted in part from the U.S. Employment Service, *A Guide to Job Analysis*, 1982).

Position: The work activities performed by one worker in one establishment.

Job: A single position or group of similar positions in one establishment, in which the work activities and objectives are similar in terms of worker actions, methodologies, materials, products, and/or worker characteristics, and in which the array of work activities differs significantly from those of other positions.

Occupation: A group of somewhat related jobs in different organizations. Thus, one can refer to the occupation of carpenter, accountant, or tight-rope walker wherever people engage in these activities.

Element: The term *element* has at least three meanings: (1) the smallest step into which it is practical to subdivide or describe work activities; (2) the physical (elemental) motions involved in work (used in industrial engineering practice); and (3) generally, virtually any level of work activity or other features of jobs, including those related to working conditions, work demands, and so on.

Task: A work activity that has a reasonably definitive purpose, and that can usually be clearly identified as a segment of the work of a particular job. Typical examples are: repairs automobile tires; takes X-rays of hospital patients; and directs traffic at street corners.

Duty: A general term that is sometimes used loosely to cover a broad group of related tasks, such as: repairs household appliances; prepares construction cost estimates; and cooks meals for patrons in restaurants.

Work activities: A general term that refers to virtually any of the physical actions or mental processes by which workers achieve intended job objectives.

ASPECTS OF JOB–ANALYSIS PROCESSES

Although this text is not intended to make a job analyst out of each of you, some overview of what is involved in job-analysis processes is in order. Planning a job-analysis program involves decisions about the five following aspects: (1) the type(s) of information to be obtained; (2) the "form" in which the information is to be obtained or presented; (3) the sources of information; (4) the agent (the individual who makes the analysis); and (5) the method of job analysis. These are discussed next.

Types of Job-Analysis Information

The types of information one can obtain about jobs goes on and on. Levine (1983), for example, enumerates fourteen different classes of job information. For our purposes we discuss only four.

Work Activities. Work activities can be described in various ways, but there are two basic sides of this coin. Job-oriented work activities characterize work in "job" terms that usually reflect end results or outputs (such as galvanizing, weaving, and cleaning). In turn, worker-oriented work activities refer to the types of human behaviors involved (such as sensing, decision making, performing physical activities, and communicating).

Equipment Used. This includes machines, tools, various types of devices, work aids, and so on, that are used to perform the job.

Working Environment and Conditions. This covers descriptions of the work space and the physical and social environment of the work situation.

Personal Requirements. These refer to any of the many types of human characteristics that are required for performing jobs, including: various types of sensory, mental, and physical abilities; physical characteristics; personality traits and interests; education and training; previous experience; job knowledge; and so on.

Form of Job-Analysis Information

The form of job-analysis information refers essentially to the distinction between qualitative and quantitative features. Qualitative information is typically descriptive (such as narrative descriptions of work or general statements about working conditions, social context, personnel requirements, and so forth), whereas quantitative information is typically characterized by the use of "units" of job information expressed in numerical terms (such as ratings of job characteristics, time required, or oxygen consumption).

Sources of Job-Analysis Information

Job-analysis information is most commonly obtained from incumbents (by observation, interview, or in some written form). However, such information can be obtained from other sources: supervisors; "experts"; available records (such as maintenance records); training manuals and materials; and blueprints and drawings of equipment and facilities.

Agent Used in Job Analysis

Typically job analysts serve as the agents for carrying out job analyses, but in some instances other persons are used: the job incumbents themselves, supervisors, industrial engineers, members of the personnel staff, and other individuals who may be assigned to serve as job analysts on a temporary basis.

Job-Analysis Methods

Just as there are many ways of skinning a cat, so there are many ways to analyze jobs. For our purposes we discuss the following in detail:

- Conventional job analysis
- Structured job-analysis questionnaires
    Task inventories
    Position Analysis Questionnaire (PAQ)
    Functional Job Analysis (FJA)
- Critical Incident Technique (CIT)

Conventional job-analysis methods are basically qualitative in nature in that they result in written, narrative descriptions of job activities and other job-related information. Over the years, however, the need for more quantitative information about jobs has resulted in the development of more systematic methods of job analysis. Some of these are structured job-analysis methods, of which three examples are included in the preceding list.

CONVENTIONAL JOB ANALYSIS

This method involves the observation and/or the interview of job incumbents and the subsequent preparation of a job description. Part of a job description is shown in Figure 4.2. A major criticism of conventional job descriptions revolves around the ambiguity that can arise from verbal descriptions of job activities and the lack of quantification of job-related information. (For example, a person with a writing flair can make the responsibilities of the position of the third assistant vice president sound like those of the president.) Although there are serious problems in writing conventional job descriptions, it is possible to write them in a useful way.

One approach that results in the writing of good job descriptions is a sentence-analysis technique used by the U.S. Employment Service. This is illustrated in Figure 4.3, which shows how a sentence can be written to provide information on what a worker does (using a verb and a direct object), why the worker does it or what gets done (using an infinitive), and what is the final result (using an object of the infinitive). Other practices and guidelines (which cannot be described here) can help to prepare useful job descriptions.

A major advantage of well-written job descriptions is that they reflect the roles and functions of jobs as related to the objectives of the organization and present something of an overall concept of what the incumbent does to fulfill such roles and how. (A commonly used frame of reference in describing jobs is to include specific information on the "what," the "why," and the "how" of jobs.)

STRUCTURED JOB–ANALYSIS QUESTIONNAIRES

Granted the usefulness of conventional job descriptions for some purposes, their lack of quantification has led to the development of structured job-analysis procedures that do lend themselves to quantification. These typically take the form of questionnaires that provide for analyzing jobs in terms of "units" or "items" that describe some type of job characteristic; there is then provision for the analyst to indicate if the item does or does not apply to the job in question, or more typically to use a rating scale to indicate the relevance of the item to the job. The items can represent various types of job characteristics. However, in most instances the items reflect work activities of a job-oriented or worker-oriented nature as described previously. As discussed next, task inventories consist of job-

FIGURE 4.2 Portions of a job description for an information-desk clerk. This includes a job summary and descriptions of five of the tasks. (From U.S. Employment Service, *A Guide to Job Analysis,* 1982, pp. 54, 55.)

Job Summary:

Answers inquiries and gives directions to customers, authorizes cashing of customers' checks, records data on lost charge cards, sorts and alphabetizes new credit applications, and requisitions supplies, working at information desk in department store Credit Office.

Description of Tasks:

1. Answers inquiries and gives directions to customers: Greets customers at information desk and ascertains reason for visit to Credit Office. Directs customer to Credit Interviewer to open credit account, to Cashier to pay bills, to Adjustment Department for correction of billing errors, or to other store departments on request, referring to store directory.

2. Authorizes cashing of customers' checks for payment to credit account: Requests identification, such as driver's license or charge cards, from customers, and examines check to verify date, amount, signature, and endorsement. Initials checks to authorize cashing, and directs customer to Cashier. Refers customer presenting Stale Date Check (more than 30 day-old) to bank.

3. Sorts and alphabetizes new credit applications daily: Separates regular charge-account applications from budget accounts. Sorts charge-account applications into local and out-of-town applications and arranges applications alphabetically within groups. Counts number of applications in each group and records totals into daily record book. Binds each group of applications with rubberband, and places a basket for routing to tabulating room.

4. Prepares requisitions for supplies: Copies amounts of supplies requested by Credit Department personnel onto requisition forms. Submits forms to Purchasing Officer or Supply Room.

5. Stores supplies: Places supplies on shelves in department store storeroom.

oriented work-activity items, whereas the Position Analysis Questionnaire (PAQ) and Functional Job Analysis (FJA) consist of worker-oriented work-activity items.

Task Inventories

Task inventories (also referred to as job inventories) typically consist of lists of the tasks pertinent to some occupational area, such as health services or automobile mechanics. In completing an inventory for any given position within the occupational area, each task is either checked or rated as it applies to the position. The rating may be in accordance with any of several possible rating factors, such as the *frequency* with which a task is performed, the *time* spent on the task, its judged *importance* or *significance*, its judged *difficulty*, the degree of *delegation* to others, or the estimated *time to learn*.

Task inventories have been used exten-

What Does the Worker Do?		Why Does the Worker Do it? What Gets Done?	What is the Final Result or Technological Objective?
		Infinitive Phrase	
Verb	Direct Object	Infinitive	Object of the Infinitive
Sets up	various types of metal-working machines	to machine	metal aircraft parts.
Persuades	customers	to buy	automobiles.
Interviews	clients	to assess	skills and abilities.
Drives	bus	to transport	passengers.

FIGURE 4.3 Illustration of the sentence-analysis technique used by the U.S. Employment Service in its job-analysis procedures. (From U.S. Employment Service, *A Guide to Job Analysis,* 1982, Figure 2, p. 8.)

sively by the U.S. Air Force, as described by Christal (1974). The Air Force method typically has the inventories completed by the incumbents themselves, either airmen or officers. A part of one inventory is shown in Figure 4.4 to illustrate the nature of the tasks, a typical format, and one type of rating scale.

Because the basic data for individual jobs are expressed in quantitative terms, the results of the analyses can be used for various statistical analyses. For example, a computer program can be used to group together those jobs that have reasonably similar combinations of tasks, such as hospital attendants that deal largely with patient-care tasks versus housekeeping tasks.

Position Analysis Questionnaire (PAQ)

A task inventory contains essentially "job-oriented" tasks, and thus its use is restricted to positions that fall within the occupational area for which it was developed. In contrast, a questionnaire that lists more "worker-oriented" job elements can be used more broadly, because it tends to cover more generalized worker behaviors. One such questionnaire is the Position Analysis Questionnaire (PAQ), developed by McCormick, Jeanneret, and Mecham.[1] The PAQ consists of 187 job elements in six divisions. The divisions are listed here with an example of a job element from each:

DIVISION	EXAMPLE OF JOB ELEMENT
1. Information input	Use of written materials
2. Mental processes	Coding/decoding
3. Work output	Use of keyboard devices
4. Relationships with others	Interviewing
5. Job context	Works in high temperature
6. Other job characteristics	Performs repetitive activities

[1]The Position Analysis Questionnaire (PAQ) is copyrighted by the Purdue Research Foundation and is available from the University Bookstore, 360 West State Street, West Lafayette, Indiana 47906.

	Check	TIME SPENT Present Job
1. Check tasks you perform now (√). 2. On the back of the book, write in any unlisted tasks which you do now. 3. In the "Time Spent" column, rate all checked (√) tasks on time spent in present job.	√ IF DONE NOW	1. Very small amount. 2. Much below average. 3. Below average. 4. Slightly below average. 5. About average. 6. Slightly above average. 7. Above average. 8. Much above average. 9. Very large amount.
DUTY H. REPAIRING AND MAINTAINING JET ENGINES		
1. Adjust afterburner nozzles		
2. Adjust maintenance trailers		
3. Apply safety wire to engine components		
4. Assemble engine sub-assemblies		
5. Assemble inner races of bearings on mating shafts		
6. Assemble main engine sections		
7. Clean engine parts and flush out cleaning fluids		
8. Clean or inspect oil filters		
9. Collect and forward oil samples for lab testing		

FIGURE 4.4 Portion of the United States Air Force task inventory for a jet engine mechanic. The basic inventory was developed for the Air Force by Lifson, Wilson, Ferguson, and Winick, Houston, Texas. The "time-spent" scale is currently used by the Air Force.

The first three divisions of the PAQ parallel a conventional model of behavior in which behavior is viewed as consisting of a stimulus (S) acting upon an organism (O) to bring about a response (R). Human work is one manifestation of this model but it might be expressed in different terms, as follows:

Information → Information → Action or
input(S)   processing   response (R)
              and
              decision (O)

The individual job elements within each of the six classes can either be checked if they apply to the position being analyzed or rated on an appropriate rating scale (such as importance, time, or difficulty).

Functional Job Analysis (FJA)

As one phase of its job-analysis program, the U.S. Employment Service provides for the analysis of jobs in terms of what are referred to as worker functions (also called functional job analysis or FJA). Worker functions are activities that identify worker relationships to *data, people,* and *things.* These are shown in Figure 4.5. Each function depicts a broad action that summarizes what the worker does in relation to data, people, or things. Although the arrangement of worker functions within each of the three categories is structured to suggest an upward progression from less complex to more complex functions, there are instances in which the implied hierarchical relationships are limited,

DATA		PEOPLE		THINGS	
CODE	DESCRIPTION	CODE	DESCRIPTION	CODE	DESCRIPTION
0	Synthesizing	0	Mentoring	0	Setting Up
1	Coordinating	1	Negotiating	1	Precision Working
2	Analyzing	2	Instructing	2	Operating-Controlling
3	Compiling	3	Supervising	3	Driving-Operating
4	Computing	4	Diverting	4	Manipulating
5	Copying	5	Persuading	5	Tending
6	Comparing	6	Speaking-Signaling	6	Feeding-Offbearing
		7	Serving	7	Handling
		8	Taking Instructions-Helping		

FIGURE 4.5 The worker functions of the functional job-analysis system as used by the U.S. Employment Service. (From U.S. Employment Service, *A Guide to Job Analysis*, 1982, p. 95.)

imprecise, reversed, or nonexistent. Thus, they should be interpreted as reflecting the nature of the worker's relationship to data, people, and things, and not to indicate rigid levels of job complexity.

In the use of the worker functions, the U.S. Employment Service assigns a relevant code to each job for each of the three categories. In fact, these three codes are part of the job-code system of the *Dictionary of Occupational Titles* (U.S. Department of Labor, 1977), which is a major job-information reference source.

Certain modifications and elaborations of functional job analysis have been developed by Fine (1973), including specific guidelines for writing task statements that crystallize the worker functions involved in work activities.

CRITICAL INCIDENT TECHNIQUE (CIT)

This procedure, developed by Flanagan (1954), provides for the collection of anecdotes (i.e., incidents) of job behavior that generally characterize especially good or especially poor job performance of individuals on a given job or group of jobs. In the usual use of this method, hundreds or thousands of incidents are collected from incumbents, fellow workers, former incumbents, supervisors, and others, using individual or group interviews, questionnaires, diaries, or other means. The incidents are then abstracted and classified into relevant categories. These categories, in effect, represent a composite picture of essential job characteristics.

This technique is especially used in connection with performance-evaluation systems. In some instances supervisors record critical incidents they observe on the part of their subordinates, and they usually classify these incidents in predetermined categories. In other cases, the incidents are used to develop behavioral rating scales. This is discussed further in Chapter 6.

COMPARISON OF JOB-ANALYSIS METHODS

No job-analysis method can serve all possible purposes, but most individual methods can serve certain purposes better than some of the others. This is not the place for a thorough discussion of the methods that can best serve specific purposes, but it is relevant here to summarize certain of the results of a survey dealing with the evaluation of various methods. Following a procedure developed by Ash and Levine (1980), Levine, Ash, Hall, and Sistrunk (1981) arranged for ninety-three experienced job analysts to rate seven job-analysis methods in terms of the following factors:

- Purposes of job analysis: job description; job classification; job evaluation; job design/restructuring; personnel requirements/specifications; performance appraisal; worker training; worker mobility; efficiency/safety aspects of jobs; manpower/work force planning; and legal/quasi-legal requirements.
- Practical considerations of job analysis: occupational versatility/suitability; standardization; respondent/user acceptance; job analyst training required; previous operational testing; sample size required; "off-the-shelf" availability; reliability; cost; quality of outcome; time to completion.

The seven methods included task inventories, the Position Analysis Questionnaire, Functional Job Analysis, the Critical Incident Technique, and three other methods not previously described here. Note that conventional job analysis was not included. In summarizing the major findings, the investigators reported the following:

- For job description and classification, task inventories and Functional Job Analysis were rated highest.
- The Position Analysis Questionnaire and task inventories were rated most standardized and most reliable.
- The Position Analysis Questionnaire was rated highest in terms of being ready for use right "off-the-shelf." In fact, it was rated highest on ten of the eleven "practical considerations."

A few additional results are summarized here:

- For job-evaluation purposes the Position Analysis Questionnaire was rated highest, and Functional Job Analysis and task inventories were also rated significantly higher than the others.
- For performance appraisal the Critical Incident

Technique was rated significantly higher than all other methods.
- For legal/quasi-legal requirements the task inventories, Functional Job Analysis, and the Position Analysis Questionnaire had the highest ratings.

STATISTICAL TREATMENT OF JOB-ANALYSIS DATA

The availability of data from structured job-analysis methods has made possible the use of statistical methods for processing and analyzing job data that were previously not possible. The results of such analyses have contributed immensely to the practical use of job data for various purposes. Two aspects of such analyses are discussed here—namely, the development of job dimensions and the development of job families or classifications.

Job Dimensions

The analysis of jobs in terms of the dozens or hundreds of items of a structured job-analysis method results in a rather indigestible mass of data for a single job, let alone for many jobs. However, some job activities or other specific features tend to go together or coexist in jobs. In statistical terms they are correlated with each other. By a statistical treatment called factor analysis it is possible to identify those combinations of job variables that tend to go together. The combinations of such interrelated variables are called factors or, more commonly in the field of job analysis, job dimensions. If the job variables used in the structured job-analysis questionnaire are descriptions of work activities (such as tasks or human work behaviors) the resulting job dimensions can be thought of as reflecting the "structure" of work.

In addition, by subsequent statistical manipulations we can add together (with appropriate statistical weights) the data on the individual job elements that characterize each job dimension for any given job, so that we have, for that job, a job-dimension score for each of the several dimensions. We then have a more comprehensible description of each job in terms of a more basic profile—namely, a set of job-dimension scores.

One example of the process of identifying job dimensions involves the use of the PAQ described earlier. In a study carried out by Mecham (1977), a relatively representative sample of 2200 jobs that had been analyzed with the PAQ was subjected to a series of factor analyses (technically, principal components analyses). Analyses of the data for the job elements within each of the six PAQ divisions resulted in the identification of thirty-two "divisional" job dimensions. In another analysis, the job elements from all divisions were pooled together, resulting in thirteen "overall" dimensions. Each dimension is characterized primarily by certain job elements. (Statistically, these are the ones that have the highest "loadings" or correlations with the dimensions.) Each dimension is named and described in terms of what is considered to be the concept or factor that is common to these dominant job elements. Since a title cannot always be clearly descriptive of the underlying common denominator of the dominant job elements, the titles of job dimensions need to be interpreted loosely. Recognizing this, the titles of the thirteen "overall" job dimensions resulting from Mecham's factor analysis of the PAQ are listed here:

1. Having decision, communicating, and general responsibilities;
2. Operating machines and/or equipment;
3. Performing clerical and/or related activities;
4. Performing technical and/or related activities;
5. Performing service and/or related activities;
6. Working regular day versus other work schedules;
7. Performing routine and/or repetitive activities;
8. Being aware of work environment;
9. Engaging in physical activities;
10. Supervising and/or coordinating other personnel;
11. Public and/or customer and/or related service;
12. Working in an unpleasant/hazardous/demanding environment;
13. Having a nontypical schedule.

The job-dimension profile of one job—that of mail clerk—is shown in Figure 4.6.

Although in some instances the nature of job dimensions identified by statistical analyses may seem simply to confirm "common-sense" impressions of the dominant features of jobs, a couple of points should be made. First, because "common sense" is not necessarily valid, statistical confirmation is certainly comforting. Second (and more important), by using statistically identified job dimensions, it is possible to convert job information into quantitative terms, such as job-dimension scores.

Job Classification

Sometimes it is useful to bundle together into specific classifications those jobs that share certain common characteristics. The development of such job classifications or families can be carried out with job data based on structured job-analysis procedures, using some form of statistical analysis. Such classifications serve various purposes, such as: personnel selection (considering candidates for jobs within each group); personnel evaluation (using a separate evaluation procedure for incumbents on all the jobs within each group); and job evaluation (such as assigning the same wage rate to all the jobs within a given group, or determining if jobs are sufficiently similar as to represent "equal work" under the provisions of the Equal Pay Act). Job-classification systems (sometimes called taxonomies) are also used for other purposes, such as for census information, reporting employment and unemployment data, and so on.

In developing job classifications or families

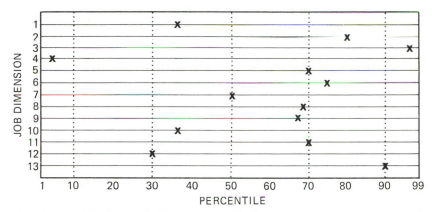

FIGURE 4.6 The PAQ job-dimension profile for a mail clerk. The position of the score for a given dimension is represented as the percentile of the raw score of the dimension for this job as compared to the scores of a sample of 2200 other jobs. The dimensions given here are the thirteen "overall" dimensions.

from data based on structured job-analysis procedures, two major decisions need to be made. One of these concerns the statistical method for grouping jobs, and the other concerns the type of job-analysis data to use. The type of data used (based on tasks, worker-oriented behaviors, skills, and so on) are sometimes referred to as descriptors.

Although various statistical methods are available (Pearlman, 1980), the most widely used is a hierarchical clustering procedure that is used by the U.S. Air Force in its job-analysis program using task inventories (Christal, 1974). This is a procedure in which a statistical index is derived for each possible pair of jobs in the total sample in question. In the Air Force job-analysis program, the index is based on the similarities of the ratings of the time spent on the tasks for all the jobs in question. By a procedure that need not be described here, the total sample of N jobs is reduced from N classifications (with one job in each classification) to $N - 1$, $N - 2$, and ultimately to one classification. A determination is then made as to the number of clas-

sifications that would best serve the intended purpose.

The development of job classifications or families by this method is illustrated in a simplified manner in Figure 4.7. This shows the PAQ job-dimension profiles for four hypothetical jobs for five hypothetical dimensions. In this illustration jobs A and B are very similar in their profiles, as are jobs C and D in theirs. With large samples of jobs the profiles of those within a given classification might not be as clear cut as the similarities of jobs A and B, and separately of C and D. However, the degree of similarity of the jobs within individual classifications would depend on the number of classification categories that one would choose to form.

The second consideration in developing job-classification systems deals with the type of descriptor (i.e., the type of job-analysis data) to use. The nature of the job classifications that result from a statistical analysis would, of course, depend on the type of descriptor used, and also in part on the sample of jobs involved. In addition, the purpose of devel-

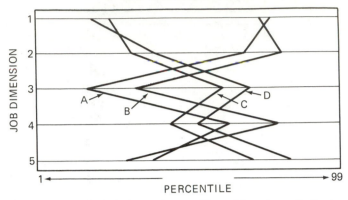

JOB - DIMENSION SCORE

FIGURE 4.7 The job-dimension profiles of four hypothetical jobs on five PAQ job dimensions. These illustrate how job classifications or job families can be formed on the basis of the similarities of such profiles. In this instance jobs A and B represent one job family, and jobs C and D represent another.

oping a classification system would influence the decision about the type of descriptor to use. A couple of examples may illustrate this point.

If all of the jobs in question fall within the same general occupational area, a task inventory of the job-oriented tasks within that area could be used. Thus, tasks would be the descriptors used, and the resulting classifications would consist of groups of jobs with reasonably similar profiles of tasks. However, if one is dealing with a wide variety of jobs—from various walks of life—a task inventory could not be used because the task inventories are typically restricted to separate occupational areas. In such an instance a generic job-analysis method would be necessary—one with descriptors that are applicable on an across-the-board basis, such as those of a worker-oriented nature. Thus, a system such as the PAQ or FJA could be considered. Some discussions of job classification have not dealt clearly with this critical distinction (Cornelius, Carron, & Collins, 1979; Levine et al., 1981; Pearlman, 1980; Sackett, Cornelius, & Carron, 1981).

In discussing the development of job-classification systems this point should be added: One can use, as the descriptors, the smallest "units" of job information provided for in a structured job-analysis questionnaire (such as tasks or PAQ job elements), or one can use broader groupings of such descriptors (such as scores on job dimensions).

Although job classifications have been based on data from structured job-analysis procedures, they have also been based on subjective judgment of the "overall" or "global" nature of jobs. Certain investigators have concerned themselves with a comparison of these two approaches (Pearlman, 1980; Sackett et al., 1981). They have concluded that classifications of jobs based on subjective judgment can serve reasonably well for combining jobs into families that can then be used for developing valid predictors for personnel selection. Such job classifications usually include jobs within some general occupational area, such as office jobs, craft jobs, or health-service jobs. In such instances the similarities tend to be reflected in the combinations of tasks (i.e., the job-oriented activities) involved. In the case of jobs that are spread across various technological areas, however (for which the common denominators are of a more worker-oriented nature), it is our conviction that statistical procedures based on data from an appropriate structured job-analysis procedure (a worker-oriented questionnaire) would have a distinct advantage over job classifications based on subjective judgment.

DISCUSSION

The field of job analysis has made significant strides during recent years, most notably in the development of structured job-analysis procedures that provide for the quantification of job-analysis information. These developments have had two primary applications—namely, contributing to systematic research dealing with the world of work, and contributing to various operational objectives in the management of human resources in business and industry. Certain specific applications are illustrated in later chapters.

Although job analysis has its mundane aspects, it provides data that can serve a variety of personnel-management functions. Optimally, such data can serve as the "core" of an integrated human-resources program. An example of such a program is the Career Dimensions Job Analysis Program of the Continental Bank of Chicago (Stahl, 1982). This program has involved the analysis of 2500 jobs with the PAQ in combination with a task inventory. The objectives of the program were to use the basic job-analysis data for personnel selection, job evaluation, performance appraisal, training and personnel development, career counseling, and human-resources planning. A significant feature of the program consisted of feeding back to the employees information about their jobs that resulted from the job-analysis process. Such

feedback contributed materially to the acceptance of the program. In the words of Elizabeth Carlson, Second Vice President who directed the program, "Workers everywhere are concerned about those things that affect their jobs, and the Career Dimensions Program provides the opportunity to involve bank employees more fully in the processes that affect them directly."

REFERENCES

Ash, R. A., & Levine, E. L. (1980). A framework for evaluating job analysis methods. *Personnel*, 57(6), 53–59.

Christal, R. E. (January 1974). *The United States Air Force occupational research project* (AFHRL–TR–73–75). Brooks Air Force Base, Texas: Air Force Systems Command.

Cornelius, E. T., III, Carron, T. J., & Collins, M. N. (1979). Job analysis models and job classification. *Personnel Psychology*, 32(4), 693–705.

Fine, S. A. (April, 1973). Functional job analysis: A desk aid. Washington, D.C.: W. E. Upjohn Institute for Employment Research.

Flanagan, J. C. (1954). The critical incident technique. *Psychological Bulletin*, 51, 327–358.

Levine, E. A. (1983). *Everything you always wanted to know about job analysis.* Tampa, Fla.: Mariner Publishing.

Levine, E. L., Ash, R. A., Hall, H. L., & Sistrunk, F. (February 1981). *Evaluation of seven job analysis methods by experienced job analysts.* Tampa, Fla.: Center for Evaluation Research, University of South Florida.

Mecham, R. C. (February 1977). Unpublished study. PAQ Services, Inc., Logan, Utah 84321.

Pearlman, K. (1980). Job families: A review and discussion of their implications for personnel selection. *Psychological Bulletin*, 87(1), 1–28.

Sackett, P. R., Cornelius, E. T., III, & Carron, T. J. (1981). A comparison of global judgment vs. task oriented approaches to job classification. *Personnel Psychology*, 34(4), 791–804.

Stahl, P. (November–December 1982). What's the price tag on your job? Quantitative job analysis: How one bank did it. *Journal of the National Association of Bank Women*, 14–18.

Thompson, D. E., & Thompson, T. A. (1982). Court standards for job analysis in test validation. *Personnel Psychology*, 35(4), 865–874.

U.S. Department of Labor (1977). *Dictionary of occupational titles* (4th ed.). Washington, D.C.: Government Printing Office.

U.S. Employment Service (March 1982). *A guide to job analysis*. Washington, D.C.: U.S. Employment Service, U.S. Department of Labor.

Uniform guidelines on employee selection procedures (August 25, 1978). *Federal Register*, 43(166), 38290–38309.

5

Behavioral Measurement: General Considerations

The field of industrial-organizational psychology is rooted in the measurement of human behavior and characteristics. This chapter and some of the following chapters deal with various aspects of such measurement. This chapter deals with some of the general considerations in the measurement of human behavior (especially job-related behavior). Chapter 6 covers various aspects of personnel rating and evaluation processes. Then, Chapters 7 through 11 deal with the measurement of personal characteristics, particularly within the framework of personnel selection.

For semantic convenience, in discussing measures of job-related behavior we use the term *behavior* in a very broad sense to include not only people's overt performances but also their subjective reactions and responses, such as their attitudes or beliefs.

The measurement of human behavior generally can serve at least two broad purposes—namely, administrative and research purposes. For administrative purposes, for example, the measurement of job-related behavior (such as job performance) can be useful as the basis for pay raises, promotions, and separations. Attendance records may also be used for such purposes. Likewise, results of attitude and opinion surveys may be used for revising organizational policies. The analysis of errors made by individuals might point to the need for changing work methods or modifying the equipment used, or it might indicate the need for improved employee selection or further job training. Accident and related injury records may be used to improve the safety conditions of a work situation.

In research undertakings behavioral measures are used very extensively as criteria, but in some instances they are also used as predictors of other criterion measures. Although there may be some differences in the specific measures of the same aspect of behavior for administrative versus research purposes, the basic problems of measurement for these two purposes are much the same, and the approaches or methods of measurement that might be used may also have much in common. Although most of the discussion in this chapter is in the framework of research "criteria," much of such discussion applies equally to behavioral measures used for administrative purposes.

TYPES OF BEHAVIORAL MEASURES

Many types of behavioral measures are used in various fields of psychology. However, our interest in this text is largely with measures that have direct or indirect relevance to the behavior of people in working situations. Some relevant research is, of course, carried out in controlled laboratory situations in which the nature of the behavioral measures depends on the type of study in question. However, most measures that are of concern to us are job-related. These can be grouped into six categories; performance criteria; job-withdrawal (or attendance) criteria; accident and injury criteria; physiological criteria; status criteria; and subjective rating criteria. (Job-attendance criteria and accident and injury criteria are almost always job-related; the other categories could also apply to laboratory investigations.)

Performance Criteria

In laboratory studies such criteria could reflect performance on a laboratory task (such as simulated assembly jobs) or performance on a laboratory test of some basic human ability (such as reaction time, finger dexterity, or visual acuity).

In the case of job-related performance criteria, the measures normally would be intended to reflect the extent to which individuals fulfill certain job objectives. Many such criteria vary along two dimensions: quantity and quality. The quantity dimension is based on the number of "units" produced or other-

wise fulfilled, such as the number of zippers produced, the dollar volume of a salesperson's sales, or the number of insurance claims processed. Usually such measures are related to a specified time period, such as units per hour, day, or month. Conversely, some such measures may be expressed in terms of time, as the average time required by an individual to process an insurance claim.

The other dimension, quality, is usually related to some type of human error. In fact, what we might think of as good performance is performance characterized by few or no errors. Although the consequences of some human errors in job situations are of minor importance, with little more than nuisance value, the consequences of others may be of major proportions in terms of human safety, effectiveness of operations, time, physical damage, economic loss, and others. Notions of "error-free" performance and zero defects are probably will-o'-the-wisp. Nevertheless, efforts to reduce errors can usually be justified, especially when the possible consequences of error are major.

The nature of human error. Human error obviously takes many forms, but it can generally be considered as a deviation from a required or expected standard of performance that results in an unwanted or undesirable consequence, such as time delays, damaged products, malfunctions, or losses of times.

Error analysis. The interest in the systematic analysis of errors as a criterion has come mainly from the ranks of engineers and others concerned with the human-factors aspects of equipment and system design. However, the error-analysis procedures developed by engineers also have relevance for psychologists and personnel managers who are concerned with the measurement of human performance. In theory (if not in practice) errors can be attributed to situational or individual variables or to a combination thereof. Situational variables are especially relevant when a job involves using some physical equipment (as tools or machines), engaging in physical work activities, or working in undesirable physical work environments (as noisy, poorly illuminated, cold, and so on).

The individual variables that contribute to errors can cover almost the entire gamut of human characteristics and attributes. However, in any given situation certain human attributes might be more important than others; for example, proofreading errors might be primarily associated with visual or perceptual deficiencies, while errors in a soldering task might be attributed primarily to deficiencies in psychomotor control.

Our primary interest in error analysis is to emphasize that errors can result from either situational or individual variables, and perhaps most commonly from a combination of them. The situational variables "set the stage" or provide the environment within which individual variables operate. Thus, the error rate in typing, for example, might be higher in a very noisy environment than in a quiet one. A simplified representation of the relationship between situational and individual variables as related to error rate is shown in Figure 5.1. In particular this illustrates how both types of variables might affect the probabilities of errors.

Analysis of errors. A primary objective in efforts to reduce errors should be to trace their sources. Toward this end various error classification systems and methods of data collection are used, especially in connection with the human-factors aspects of system design. Without going into the details of such procedures, a couple of examples may illustrate the objectives and the types of actions that might follow such error analysis. In the years gone by an analysis of accidents and near accidents with aircraft indicated that a major contributing cause was errors in reading the altimeters. The solution in this case was to redesign the altimeters to improve the accuracy of reading altitude. Another situation involves error rates in entering data into

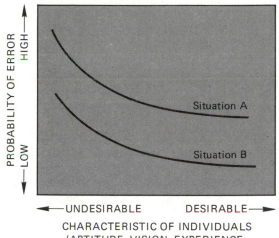

FIGURE 5.1 Generalized relationship of situational variables and individual characteristics as related to error rate (probability of error). Situations *A* and *B* might be differences in equipment design, methods, work periods, environments, and so on. (Adapted from Rook, 1962, Figure 1.)

computer terminals. If these rates are significantly higher for some people than for others, the solution would presumably be to do a better job in selecting candidates for the job, or possibly to provide further training for those whose work performance is deficient.

Reliability in error analysis. In some error-analysis programs the "reliability" of performance is measured. In other sections of this text, including the discussion later in this chapter of the reliability of criterion measure, the term *reliability* refers to the reliability of *measurement* of variables (as of a criterion or a test). In the framework of error analysis, reliability refers to the consistency of "performance," either of an item of equipment or of an individual. Since this usage comes from engineering, let us call it *engineering reliability*.

In this framework there are two basic indexes of reliability. One of these is the probability of successful performance. This index is used for activities that represent separate, independent (that is, "discrete") events (such as starting an automobile, inspecting individual bottles on a conveyor, or sorting letters into alphabetical piles). In such instances reliability is the probability of successful performance expressed as a proportion, such as .92 or .99, or in some instances as more precise values, such as .9936 or .9974. Such values are the *obverse* of the probabilities of errors and in effect represent the "odds" of successful or satisfactory performance. The other index of engineering reliability applies to *continuous* (as opposed to *discrete*) activities and is called the mean time to failure (MTF)—such as the mean time aircraft engines function until they break down, or (in the case of human performances) the mean time radar operators can monitor radar scopes before their performance falls below acceptable levels.

In summary, some measures of job-performance criteria are quite objective in that they are based on some method of measurement minimizing human judgment or involvement. Thus, in actual job situations, measures of units produced per hour or per day might be obtained, or in laboratory experiments one might measure reaction time to a given stimulus or time to complete a given task. In many, if not most, circumstances, however, one must use ratings of performance, either because it would be difficult or impossible to obtain objective measures, or because the performance criterion in question is essentially subjective (as in the case of persons in most artistic activities, in certain types of interpersonal-relations activities, etc.). The next chapter covers various types of rating systems, some of which are relevant for rating work performance.

Job-Withdrawal Criteria

At least three kinds of criteria can be lumped together under the heading of withdrawal criteria (also called job-attendance criteria) because they all relate to some aspect of the tendency of employees to "withdraw from" or "attend to" their jobs. These are: (1) job tenure (how long people remain on their jobs); (2) absenteeism; and (3) tardiness. Although one might assume that such criteria would be relevant as measures of job-related behavior, certain conceptual and measurement aspects argue for caution in their use.

Turnover. It has generally been assumed that most turnover is undesirable and costly to organizations, in large part because of the costs of replacing people (Dalton, Krackhardt, & Porter, 1981); lately, however, certain benefits of turnover have been discussed. There also has been a tendency to assume that most people who leave their organizations are better employees, although the evidence relating to this is somewhat conflicting (Martin, Price, & Mueller, 1981).

In the handling of turnover data it has been a common practice to differentiate between voluntary turnover (when employees voluntarily resign) and involuntary turnover (when employees leave for unavoidable reasons, such as health, family commitments, or the completion of temporary employment). In addition, employees who are fired are usually considered in a separate category. Dalton et al. (1981) argue for the classification of voluntary turnover as follows:

Dysfunctional turnover: The individual wants to leave the organization, but the organization prefers to retain the individual.
Functional turnover: The individual wants to leave the organization, and the organization is unconcerned. The organization has a negative evaluation of the individual.

Dalton et al. propose that a program to reduce turnover may be shortsighted for organizations with relatively large portions of functional and/or involuntary (i.e., unavoidable) turnover; arguably, functional turnover should not be reduced, and efforts to reduce unavoidable turnover would be futile. In other words, an organization should focus its efforts on reducing dysfunctional turnover, if that is possible. Such efforts, however, would require that "voluntary" separations be categorized as dysfunctional or functional. If such a categorization would indicate that those two groups are predictably different, the two groups might respond to different types of "intervention" on the part of the organization. Thus, an organization might be able to prevent desirable employees from quitting (dysfunctional turnover) without preventing undesirable employees from quitting (functional turnover). Thus, as one considers possible turnover criteria, the distinction between dysfunctional and functional categories should be recognized.

There has been a spate of papers on the determinants of turnover, and various theories or models have been proposed. These formulations have usually dealt with such variables as job expectations, job satisfaction, perceived job security, organizational commitment, and demographic variables such as age. Without digging deeply into such theories and models, we present one such model as an example, that of Arnold and Feldman (1982). This model, shown in Figure 5.2, shows that age, job satisfaction, and organizational commitment contribute to the "intention" to search for alternatives, and that tenure and perceived job security are signif-

icant factors in influencing actual turnover decisions. A more complex model is discussed in Chapter 14.

Absenteeism. As for turnover, criteria of absenteeism are also fraught with conceptual and measurement problems. In connection with the measurement aspect, it usually is the practice to differentiate between voluntary absenteeism (uncertified, unauthorized, unexcused) and involuntary absenteeism (illness, injury, death in a family, etc.). Although there are many possible indexes of absenteeism, the primary ones are frequency and duration (as number of hours, days, etc.). In connection with whatever indexes are used, however, Hammer and Landau (1981) point to the problems of errors in classification of absences (especially short-term absences) and to certain statistical problems in the analysis of absenteeism data (especially those resulting from the form of the statistical "distribution" of data and the limited reliability of data). As a partial (though far from perfect) solution to the problem of measuring absences, Hammer and Landau suggest that the classification of instances of voluntary versus involuntary absenteeism be based on the provisions of any formal contractual agreement between employers and employees. This requires detailed archival records, research assistance from the record keepers, and knowl-

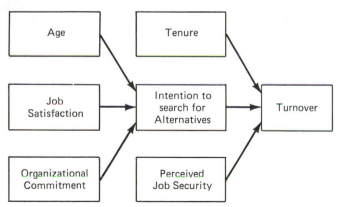

FIGURE 5.2 Model of the turnover process. (From Arnold & Feldman, 1982, Figure 2, p. 359.)

edge of union contracts and personnel policies that usually define legitimate involuntary absences such as illness, death or illness in the family, or medical leave. Even such a careful analysis, however, would not preclude the possibility of errors made (purposefully or unwittingly) by the employee. On the basis of their own analysis of absenteeism data Hammer and Landau conclude that frequency indexes (number of times absent) appear to be preferable to duration (lost-time) measures.

Because of some of the problems of measurement of absenteeism Latham and Pursell (1975) proposed using "attendance" as a substitute for absenteeism, indicating that the reliability of attendance records is higher than the reliability of typical absenteeism records. However, as Ilgen (1977) found, there are some logical and statistical arguments against the general use of attendance as a substitute for absenteeism criteria (although there may well be some circumstances in which this might be appropriate). The moral of all this is that, in developing a criterion of absenteeism, one should carefully consider the possible variations on this theme and choose the particular basis for the criterion that would best serve the purpose at hand.

On a more theoretical level, Steers and Rhodes (1978) developed a model of employee attendance based on a review of 104 empirical studies. This model differentiates in particular between the motivation of employees to attend to work and their ability to attend. It was postulated that motivation to attend is influenced by several variables including certain personal characteristics, job-situation factors, and job satisfaction. The results of an investigation of those variables by Watson (1981), however, indicate that they did not account for a major portion of the variance of lost-time absence of employees in a metal manufacturing plant. More specifically, job satisfaction was not found to be a major influence in explaining variance of lost-time absence. Thus, we seem to be left with

considerable ambiguity about the factors that contribute to employee absenteeism.

Tardiness. Of the three types of withdrawal criteria, tardiness is probably the easiest to measure, especially if time cards are used. However, although tardiness criteria might well serve administrative purposes, they have not been used very much for personnel research.

Discussion of withdrawal criteria. Every form of withdrawal criterion we have discussed so far has some drawbacks. The ambiguity about the factors associated with withdrawal criteria is increased by an analysis by Clegg (1983) of many studies dealing with such criteria and by the results of a study in a large engineering plant in England. In essence, Clegg criticizes the research methods used in many studies, in particular on the grounds that they are based on hypotheses that "affect" (specifically job satisfaction and organizational commitment) influences behavior (turnover, absenteeism, and tardiness) without considering the possible *reverse* effect (of *behavior* influencing *affect*).

In a recent study Terborg, Lee, Smith, Davis, and Turbin (1982) hypothesized that one of the reasons that absenteeism is often not correlated with satisfaction may be the use of unstable data—for example, data based on small samples of employees. To correct for this possibility Terborg et al. conducted research in six retail stores, and then combined the data for the six samples using a technique known as metaanalysis. They found significant correlations between three criteria (pay satisfaction, satisfaction with the work, and commitment to the organization) and the frequency of absences. These authors suggest that perhaps the relationship between absenteeism and dimensions of satisfaction is stronger than had been previously assumed. This suggests that combining data from several studies might reveal relationships that do not surface from the results of single investigations.

In summary, it must be acknowledged that the use of withdrawal criteria is fraught with problems—those of practical problems of measurement and those of a theoretical nature dealing with the causal relationships between attitudinal variables and various aspects of attendance behavior. Nevertheless, these behaviors are extremely important for the effective functioning of organizations. Therefore, much attention will continue to be paid to them.

Accident and Injury Criteria

These criteria are used when the inquiry in question is concerned with matters of safety, such as in industry or in driving. Such criteria can be useful either in analyzing the relative safety of two or more circumstances (such as different designs of equipment) or in analyzing the personal variables related to accident or injury occurrence.

Physiological Criteria

Physiological criteria include such measures as heart rate, blood pressure, electrical resistance of the skin, and oxygen consumption. Such criteria typically are used in studying the effects of environmental variables, physical work load, work periods, methods of work, and so forth.

Status Criteria

Occasionally the "status" of individuals with respect to some factor is used as a criterion. This "status" may be some indication of group "membership," such as occupation (nurse, police officer, or computer programmer), or education (elementary-school diploma, high-school diploma, B.A. or B.S. degree, etc.). In other instances the "status" may be based on relevant recorded information about individuals, such as number of promotions (one, two, three, or more in the past ten years), or duration of job tenure (less than 1 year, 1 to 4 years, 5 to 9 years, etc.).

Subjective Rating Criteria

As discussed previously, many performance criteria are based on subjective judgments of raters. Other types of subjective criteria used in industrial psychology include measures of attitudes and opinions obtained by questionnaires. In addition, in certain special circumstances other types of subjective responses are used as criteria, such as the ratings of jobs, the ratings of job applicants, or the preferences of people for different types of work equipment or working conditions. (The subjective judgments of the previously discussed types of criteria, especially job performance, should be considered as falling in their appropriate categories.)

SELECTION OF CRITERIA

The selection and development of behavioral measures are critical to whatever purpose they may be used, whether for a research program or for some administrative purpose. In this connection, three basic considerations should be taken into account: *relevance, freedom from contamination*, and *reliability*.

Relevance of Criteria

The relevance of a criterion refers to the extent to which criterion measures of different individuals are meaningful in terms of the objectives for which such measures are derived. Every job exists for some purpose, or complex of purposes, whether formally stated or not. Relevance, then, relates to the adequacy of criterion measures as indexes of the relative abilities of individuals in fulfilling such purposes. Because most jobs have various objectives (rather than just one), the issue of whether to use a single overall criterion, or to use separate criteria (subcriteria) for the individual objectives must be considered. This question is discussed later.

Freedom from Contamination

The criterion values for the individuals in any given situation should reflect as accurately as possible the true relative positions of the individuals along a scale of the construct the criterion is supposed to measure. Any factor that distorts the criterion values for individuals is a source of criterion contamination. Some examples of contamination are: production records of loom operators using different types of looms that vary in production capacity; sales records of sales representatives in different territories that differ in their sales potential; production records of personnel on the same job but for whom there are differences in the quality of material used, working conditions, conditions of machines or equipment used, or incentives provided; performance records of personnel on the same job but who have had different amounts of training; and performance records of personnel who have been subjected to pressure from other employees to restrict their output.

The ever-present possibility of many forms of criterion contamination should not cause us to throw up our hands in despair, for there are ways of minimizing, if not eliminating, their influence. One approach is selecting those individuals for whom the contaminating variables are equal or nearly so. Another method is making statistical adjustments for the influence of the contaminating variables. These adjustments can be made, for example, by using what are called partial correlations that can statistically "partial out" the influence of the contaminating variable. Another scheme is adjusting for differences in the mean values (and the distributions of values) of individuals in groups known to be different in terms of contaminating variables, such as individuals working on different types of machines or individuals with different lengths of experience. This sometimes can be done by converting the original criterion values of individuals in each such group to some type of "standard score." (More is said about this in the next chapter.)

Note that these various schemes do not necessarily eliminate the influence on the contaminating variable on the criterion, although they would at least tend to reduce its effects.

Reliability of the Criterion

Earlier in this chapter we discussed the concept of reliability in the frame of reference of error analysis, referring to it as *engineering reliability*. Now when we discuss the reliability of criteria, we are concerned with the *reliability of measurement*. Reliability of measurement applies to the measurement of virtually any type of variable, such as criteria, tests, and ratings. Unfortunately there is no simple, pat definition of such reliability, but in a very general sense we can think of it as the stability or consistency of measures of whatever variables we are using.

Measures of criterion reliability deal with variability such as: differences for individuals over time (as from day to day or week to week) of such variables as job performance, error rate, heart rate, reaction time, attitudes, and job satisfaction; and differences in ratings of employees by different raters. Some criteria do not have high reliability, and any research investigator should at least have some inkling of the reliability of the criterion being used. There are certain rather sophisticated statistical procedures that can be used in reliability analysis (such as a procedure called analysis of variance), but for our purposes we generally use coefficients of correlation.

For most job-related criteria (such as job performance) a rather straightforward approach to the measurement of reliability is determining the extent to which individuals

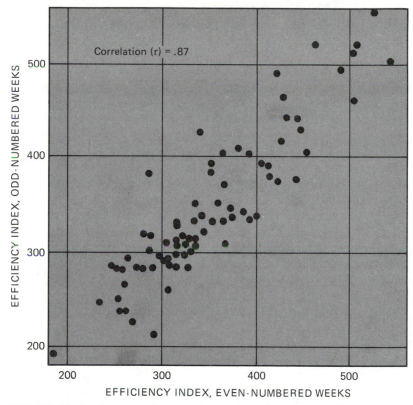

Correlation (r) = .87

EFFICIENCY INDEX, ODD-NUMBERED WEEKS

EFFICIENCY INDEX, EVEN-NUMBERED WEEKS

FIGURE 5.3 Scattergram showing the relationship between efficiency indexes of a group of seventy-nine unit wirers for two 5-week periods (5 even-numbered weeks and 5 odd-numbered weeks). (Courtesy Tetronix, Inc. and Dr. Guyot Frazier.)

tend to maintain the same level on the criterion over time. Sometimes such a time-related measure of reliability is determined by comparing the criterion values for individuals for two periods of time, as illustrated in Figure 5.3, which shows the consistency (in other words, the reliability) of production records of seventy-nine unit wirers for two 5-week time periods. The correlation between these two sets of data is .87, which reflects a fairly high degree of stability. The figure shows along the base line the efficiency index of the wirers during the 5 even-numbered weeks of the 10-week period (that is, weeks 2, 4, 6, 8, and 10), and on the vertical axis the index for the odd-numbered weeks (1, 3, 5, 7, and 9).

Each point represents the two values for a given individual—that is, the index for the even- and for the odd-numbered weeks. The similarity between these is quite apparent. Generally speaking, a reliability coefficient of .90 or higher would be considered exceptionally good, and those between .80 and .90 normally would be very acceptable.

Note that the more detailed discussion of different types of reliability in Chapter 8 (which deals with the reliability of tests) is also applicable to the reliability of criteria. At this point the reader should simply be aware that criteria should have high levels of reliability, that no criterion is perfectly reliable, and that the reliability sets limits on the extent to which other measures can be expected to be related to the criterion.

Stability of job performance. Realizing that reliability of job performance is frequently measured by comparing criterion measures for different time periods, such as shown in Figure 5.3, it is natural to be curious about the stability of performance over time. Some data regarding this are reported by Rambo, Chomiak, and Price (1983) for two groups of workers in a garment factory. These data cover weekly production records for 3½ years. One group included sewing-machine operators and the other "nonsewing" jobs such as folding, packing, and labeling. All were paid on a piece-rate basis.

The production records were correlated for each pair of consecutive weeks (as weeks 1 and 2, 2 and 3, etc.), for weeks 1 year apart, and for weeks 3½ years apart. The median correlations for these three time-interval differences were as follows:

GROUP	TIME INTERVAL		
	1 WEEK	1 YEAR	3½ YEARS
Sewing operators	.94	.69	.59
Nonsewing operators	.98	.86	.80

The correlations for consecutive weeks are remarkably high, and although they tend to be reduced for longer time intervals, the stability is still very respectable for intervals of a year and up to 3½ years. The investigators did note, however, that the stability was greater for the nonsewing operators than for the sewing operators. They attributed this difference to the fact that the relatively more complex psychomotor skills required by the sewing operations make production rates more vulnerable to unsystematic changes in the motivational climate and to interference from technical problems that occur in the workplace.

Other data on the stability of job performance came from a series of studies by Rothe, including one dealing with production rates of employees on ten production-type jobs (Rothe, 1978). For each job Rothe correlated production rates of employees for each of several pairs of consecutive weeks; there were 169 such correlations. The median of the several correlations for each study was derived, and the ten medians ranged from .48 to .85. An examination of these ten medians indicated, however, that there was a systematic difference in the correlations, depending on whether the employees were paid on the basis of an incentive system or not, as shown here:

INCENTIVE SYSTEM?	CORRELATIONS
No	.48; .52; .53; .64
Yes	.67; .68; .72; .78; .82; .85

These data suggest two conclusions. First, it seems that the nature of incentives can influence the consistency of job performance because the production rates for jobs paid on an incentive basis were more consistent than those on nonincentive pay jobs. And second, Rothe's results suggest that the output rates for some jobs are less consistent than for other jobs. This inference was also suggested from the study by Rambo et al.

Note, however, that low correlations of production for consecutive weeks must be carefully analyzed because of the statistical nature of correlations. If there is not very much difference in the production of different employees (as might well be the case with certain machine-controlled jobs), a low correlation would not be very meaningful. In such instances it would be advisable to accumulate production data for a period of several weeks in order to derive more reliable criterion values.

In discussing the variability of job performance over time Ronan (1971) suggested that there are individual differences in "performance stability" itself—in other words, that some people tend to remain on an even keel in terms of job performance whereas others tend generally to wobble around, sometimes performing well and at other times performing poorly. An analysis by Klemmer and Lockhead (1962) somewhat supported this contention. In analyzing about a billion responses by more than 1000 card-punch and bank proof-machine operators, Klemmer and Lockhead found that errors made by such operators varied from day to day to a much greater extent for some operators than for others.

Discussion of reliability. Although criterion data for different time periods are frequently used in deriving indexes of criterion measures, possible differences in the stability of job-performance data for different jobs and in the performance stability of different individuals can complicate the lives of researchers and administrators who use such data for personnel actions. Although "quick-fix" solutions for such problems may not be available, both researchers and administrators should be aware of any such complicating variables that can affect criterion values.

DEALING WITH CRITERION DATA

Certain administrative practices should be followed in obtaining and handling criterion data. For one thing, employees should be fully informed of the purposes in obtaining criterion data relating to them. If the data are to be used exclusively for research purposes, the employees should be assured that the data will not be used for administrative purposes. If, on the other hand, such data (such as personnel appraisals) are to be used for some administrative purposes (such as for personnel development or promotion decisions), the individuals should be fully advised of the intended use and usually should be provided

feedback about the results. Further, employees should be assured of the confidentiality of such data.

CRITERION DIMENSIONS

In many contexts in which criteria are to be used, there may be no single criterion that is obviously the one and the only one to use. Rather, two or more possible criteria might be relevant. In human work, for example, most jobs have various facets that typically give rise to what one might call criterion dimensions. When this is the case, an individual might do well in one aspect of a job (such as producing a large quantity of items) but less well on another aspect (such as the quality of the items produced).

Examples of Multiple Dimensions of Criteria

Following are a couple of examples that illustrate the multidimensional nature of criteria. One example comes from a study by Seashore, Indik, and Georgopoulos (1960) of 975 delivery men for whom several different criteria were available, including productivity (based on established time standards), effectiveness (ratings on overall quality of performance), accidents, absences, and errors (based on "nondeliveries" of packages). The correlations of these five criteria are given in Table 5.1. The generally low correlations indicate that these five aspects of job performance are relatively independent; the highest correlations (.28, .26, and .32) are among the variables of productivity, effectiveness, and errors. These and other results were interpreted by the investigators as contradicting the validity of "overall job performance" as a unidimensional construct and as a refutation of the practice of combining job-performance variables into a single measure having general validity.

TABLE 5.1 Intercorrelations among five criterion variables for 975 delivery men

	EFFECTIVENESS	ACCIDENTS	ABSENCES	ERRORS
Productivity	+.28	−.12	+.01	+.26
Effectiveness		+.02	+.08	+.32
Accidents			+.03	−.18
Absences				+.15
Errors				

Source: Adapted from S. E. Seashore, B. P. Indik, & B. S. Georgopoulos, (1960), "Relationships among Criteria of Job Performance," *Journal of Applied Psychology, 44,* 195–202. The signs of certain correlations (+ or −) have been changed so that a + sign indicates a positive correlation between "desirable" values of the two variables, and a − sign indicates a negative correlation between the "desirable" values. Copyright 1960 by the American Psychological Association and adapted with permission.

Another example comes from Cascio and Valenzi (1978), with criterion data for 952 police officers from a large metropolitan police department. Cascio and Valenzi reported the correlations between eight objective criteria and a criterion based on the subjective ratings made by supervisory officers. The objective criteria were the numbers of: personnel complaints; internal reviews; use of force reports; exonerated cases; recommendations and awards; physical-force allegations; injuries; and average number of times sick per year. Since separate data were reported for both minority and nonminority subjects there were correlations for fifty-six combinations of the eight objective criteria. These tended to be fairly low, with only nine being .50 or above, and nineteen being .40 or above.

The data in Table 5.1 for the delivery men and the data for police officers indicate that, at least in some situations, various possible criteria reflect relatively different aspects of job performance. Other indications regarding the multiple dimensions of job performance come from analyses of job dimensions as discussed in the preceding chapter.

Possible Treatment of Multiple Criteria

From the just-described and other studies it is evident that in many circumstances various criterion dimensions can be used in personnel research. When such criteria are highly intercorrelated, there is no particular problem selecting which criterion to use; in such a circumstance any given criterion, or an "overall" criterion, could be used for the purpose at hand inasmuch as the other criteria are highly related to it. The snag comes when the two or more criteria are not correlated. In such instances the investigator is faced with various alternatives, such as:

1. To select one of the criteria and use it;
2. To use each criterion independently;
3. To combine the various criterion dimensions into a single "composite" criterion, using some weighting scheme;
4. To develop an "overall" criterion, usually ratings (such as supervisor's ratings of overall job performance).

Since this question has generated quite a bit of controversy, we should explore at least certain aspects of the issues in using either separate (independent) criterion dimensions or some composite or overall criterion.

Arguments for multiple criteria. When various criteria for a job are not highly correlated with each other it can be argued that each criterion then represents a separate facet of job behavior. Schmidt and Kaplan (1971) refer to such separate criteria as *behavior* constructs on the grounds that the personal characteristics of individuals who perform well on one criterion may be very different from the characteristics of those who perform well on another criterion. Because of this Schmidt and Kaplan believe the use of separate criteria contributes to the understanding and to the prediction of performance on the different aspects of a job. In turn, they argue that the use of a single or composite criterion muddies the waters because any given value on a composite or overall criterion scale can be produced by different *combinations* of performance. Thus, two or more individuals might have equal criterion values on a composite or overall criterion, but they could have those same values for different reasons. For example, one person could be high on a quantity criterion dimension and low on a quality criterion dimension, a second person could have the reverse pattern, and a third person might be intermediate on both. Continuing with this line of argument, one could not reasonably expect to identify a common set of personal factors that would aid in identifying (predicting) individuals who might have the same composite criterion level but who achieve it by highly varied job-behavior patterns. Rather, one might reasonably expect to identify a combination of personal characteristics associated with one subcriterion (say, personal relations) and another combination associated with another subcriterion (say, numerical computation).

Arguments for composite or overall criteria. The basic contention of the advocates of a composite or overall criterion of job performance is that such a criterion should provide a measure of the individual's overall "success" or "value to the organization." Insofar as this is so, such a criterion is more an *economic* construct than a behavioral construct. In this connection, a significant concept was proposed by Brogden and Taylor (1950). If one is interested in criteria for individuals within an organization, Brogden and Taylor suggested that the criterion should measure the overall contribution of the individual to the organization. Toward this end, they proposed the construction of criterion measures in cost-accounting terms—the "dollar criterion." This proposal is predicated on the proposition that (when possible) the dollar provides a common denominator or a common metric for combining quite different subcriterion measures. More recently Cascio (1982) has expanded on the dollar or, more broadly, utility view of criteria by providing several suggestions for calculating "dollar values" of the performance of individuals based on their combined performance on the different aspects of their jobs.

Discussion of multiple and composite criteria. As we have seen, the use of multiple criteria in a research project makes it possible to identify the human characteristics that presumably are required for performance on the different aspects of a job. However, in developing criterion information about individuals in most personnel-research programs we need somehow to consider employees as complete individuals, and to evaluate their "total" performance on the job—considering their strengths and weaknesses in performing different aspects of the job. This, in turn, requires the determination of the relative importance (specifically the weights) of the different aspects of the job as they contribute to some concept of "overall" job performance. (This would reflect the total value of individuals to the organization in terms of the "economic" construct discussed previously.) The weights for various criterion dimensions should preferably be in statistical terms (discussed later). In some instances, however, people who make employment decisions use their own subjective weightings of the importance of various job dimensions when evaluating the potential qualifications of individuals for a job. They may not be aware that they are "cranking in" their own weights when making such decisions, but this is really what they do.

Weighting of Multiple Criteria

The weights for individual criterion dimensions would actually be applied to data about individual job candidates—in particular data about the characteristics that are relevant for performing the activities of the individual dimensions. Without worrying about how such data are derived, let us assume we have "ratings" for three job candidates (X, Y, and Z) that reflect their potential for performing on each of two dimensions (A and B) which represent "dealing with people" and "numerical computation." The ratings can range from 0 to 10. Let us now see how different weightings of the individuals on the two dimensions could influence the composite ratings of the three candidates. Table 5.2 shows the ratings of the three individuals (X, Y, and Z) on each of the two dimensions (A and B). In addition it shows the (predicted) composite criterion values (C) for the three individuals based on three weighting systems. With equal weights for the two dimensions, the three candidates end up in a dead heat, with each having a composite value of 500. For the two differential weighting systems, however, the rank order of the three individuals based on their composite ratings (C) is reversed. This particular illustration is "rigged" to amplify the effects of the different weighting systems. Although the effects of different weighting systems in actual circumstances would not usually be as marked as they are in this illustration, they can still have some influence on the composite ratings that are developed.

The weights for the individual dimensions can be derived from the judgments of knowledgeable persons or on the basis of some statistical procedure. Probably the most valid basis is a statistical procedure (specifically, regression analysis) that results in the statistical determination of optimum weights as related to some "overall" criterion. This procedure requires that a sample of individuals be "ordered" along a predetermined overall criterion scale, that values on the various specific subcriteria or criterion dimensions be derived for each individual, and that a statistical operation be performed to determine the appropriate weight for each of the subcriteria.

CRITERIA IN EVALUATING SITUATIONAL VARIABLES

The preceding discussion of criteria has generally focused on criterion measures for individuals (either for use in personnel research or for administrative purposes). When using criteria for evaluating situational variables (such as equipment design or working conditions), however, one is usually more interested in average (rather than individual)

TABLE 5.2 Illustration of the development of composite criterion values (C) from different weighting values for two criterion dimensions (A and B) for three individuals (X, Y, and Z)

| INDI-VIDUALS | RATINGS GIVEN ON CRITERION DIMENSIONS | | VALUES OF WEIGHTED DIMENSIONS AND OF COMPOSITE | | | | | | | | |
| | A | B | 1. EQUAL WEIGHTS | | | 2. DIFFERENT WEIGHTS | | | 3. DIFFERENT WEIGHTS | | |
			A(50)	B(50)	C	A(25)	B(75)	C	A(75)	B(25)	C
X	8	2	400	100	500	20	150	350	600	50	650
Y	2	8	100	400	500	50	600	650	150	200	350
Z	5	5	250	250	500	125	375	500	375	175	500

criterion values; thus, one might compare the average performance of people when using two different designs of computer keyboards or the average heart rate when carrying different loads. Chapter 17 includes a number of examples of criteria used in human-factors research.

In using criteria for such purposes, however, there can be instances in which certain independent criteria are incompatible with each other. For example, in designing a machine, it might be that a design conducive to a high rate of productivity by the employees might also be conducive to a high incidence of accidents. In such cases some tradeoff must be made—that is, some degree of one advantage must be given up for the other. In such a case, one would try to develop a design that would be most nearly optimum in terms of the two or more criteria in question. Such an optimum incorporates a weighting of the relative importance of the separate criteria in terms of the overall objectives.

DISCUSSION

In large part industrial-organizational psychology is directed toward exploring and understanding individual and situational variables that are associated with different aspects of human behavior. Critical requirements of any such effort include the selection of appropriate criteria of behavior and the development of reasonably adequate measures of such criteria.

REFERENCES

Arnold, H. J., & Feldman, D. C. (1982). A multivariate analysis of the determinants of job turnover. *Journal of Applied Psychology, 67*(3), 350–360.

Brogden, H. E., & Taylor, E. K. (1950). The dollar criterion—Applying the cost accounting concept to criterion construction. *Personnel Psychology,* 1950, 3, 133–154.

Cascio, W. F. (1982). *Costing human resources: The financial impact of behavior in organizations.* Boston: Kent.

Cascio, W. F., & Valenzi, E. R. (1978). Relations among criteria of police performance. *Journal of Applied Psychology, 65*(1), 22–28.

Clegg, C. W. (1983). Psychology of employee lateness, absence, and turnover: A methodological critique and an empirical study. *Journal of Applied Psychology, 68*(1), 88–101.

Dalton, D. R., Krackhardt, D. M., & Porter, L. W. (1981). Functional turnover: An empirical assessment. *Journal of Applied Psychology, 66*(6), 716–721.

Hammer, T. H., & Landau, J. (1981). Methodological issues in the use of absence data. *Journal of Applied Psychology, 66*(5), 574–581.

Ilgen, D. R. (1977). Attendance behavior: A reevaluation of Latham and Pursell's conclusions. *Journal of Applied Psychology, 62*(2), 230–233.

Klemmer, E. J. & Lockhead, G. R. (1962). Productivity and errors in two keying tasks: A field study. *Journal of Applied Psychology, 46*(6), 401–408.

Latham, G. P., & Pursell, E. D. (1975). Measuring absenteeism from the opposite side of the coin. *Journal of Applied Psychology, 60*(3), 369–371.

Martin, T. N., Price, J. L., & Mueller, C. W. (1981). Job performance and turnover. *Journal of Applied Psychology, 66*(1), 116–119.

Rambo, W. W., Chomiak, A. M., & Price, J. M. (1983). Consistency of performance under stable conditions of work. *Journal of Applied Psychology, 68*(1), 78–87.

Ronan, W. W. (April, 26, 1971). Personal communication to the authors.

Rook, L. W., Jr. (June 1962). *Reduction in human error in industrial production.* Albuquerque, N.M.: Sandia Corporation (Tech. Memorandum SCTM 93-62 [14].

Rothe, H. F. (1978). Output rates among industrial workers. *Journal of Applied Psychology, 63*(1), 40–46.

Schmidt, F. L., & Kaplan, L. B. (1971). Composite vs. multiple criteria: A review and resolution of the controversy. *Personnel Psychology, 24*(3), 419–434.

Seashore, S. E., Indik, B. P., & Georgopoulos, B. S. (1960). Relationships among criteria of job performance. *Journal of Applied Psychology, 44,* 195–202.

Steers, R. M., & Rhodes, S. R. (1978). Major influences on employee attendance: A process model. *Journal of Applied Psychology, 63*(4), 391–407.

Terborg, J. R., Lee, T. W., Smith, F. J., Davis, G. A., & Turbin, M. S. (1982). Extension of the Schmidt and Hunter validity generalization procedure to the prediction of absenteeism behavior from knowledge of job satisfaction and organizational commitment. *Journal of Applied Psychology, 67*(4), 440–449.

Watson, C. J. (1981). An evaluation of some aspects of the Steers and Rhodes model of employee attendance. *Journal of Applied Psychology, 66*(1), 188–189.

6

Personnel Rating

The preceding chapter referred to the need to measure human behavior (especially job-related behavior) for various purposes. The discussion in this chapter is focused primarily on the use of ratings in personnel administration, but the discussion is equally applicable to the use of ratings for research and employee counseling purposes.

In virtually any work situation each person makes some type of judgment about the other persons involved. For example, supervisors almost inevitably make judgments about their subordinates (and vice versa). Although most such judgments are made informally, some organizations set up formal, systematic procedures for making and recording them. The resulting ratings are then used for such purposes as making decisions about: personnel promotions, transfers, and demotions; salary or wage determinations; employee counseling; and other personnel actions. These rat-

ing programs are called by different names—performance ratings, performance appraisal, personnel assessment, employee evaluations, and so on—but in a broad sense they can all be thought of as personnel ratings. In some circumstances a distinction is made between personnel evaluation (the rating of performance on employees' present or past jobs) and personnel assessment (the rating of individuals in terms of their potential for promotion to higher-level jobs). Note, with regard to this distinction, that the ability to perform well on a particular job provides no assurance of the potential to perform at a higher level or on a different type of job. The "Peter Principle," enunciated by Peter (1969) in his light-hearted book, characterized the unfortunately rather common practice of promoting people to their "level of incompetence" because of their demonstrated ability to perform well on lower-level jobs. Peter cites many instances of individuals who have been promoted to their "level of incompetence," and flub the jobs to which they have been so promoted.

RELIABILITY AND VALIDITY OF RATINGS

The concepts of reliability and validity apply to virtually all types of measurements, including personnel ratings. More is said about reliability and validity in later chapters, especially in Chapter 8, which deals with personnel tests.

Reliability

The reliability of ratings refers to the consistency with which ratings are made. The concept is essentially the same as that discussed in Chapter 5 with regard to the criterion. There are three primary methods for determining the reliability of ratings, each of which applies to a different aspect of reliability. The first and third methods parallel rather well two of the three basic types of reliability of tests discussed later in Chapter 8.

Comparison over time. This method, sometimes called the rate-rerate or test-retest method, applies when one person rates the same group of people at two different times. Usually the two sets of ratings are spaced several days or more apart in order to minimize the possibility of memory of the first ratings' influencing the second. The reliability is usually measured by computing a correlation between the two sets of ratings. Latham and Wexley (1981) express the opinion that the correlation of such reliability should be .70 or higher (and preferably higher!).

Interater reliability. This method can be used if the same personnel are rated independently by two raters. Such ratings can also be measured by computing a correlation between the two sets. Since different raters usually have somewhat different perceptions of

ratees, the correlation between them might be somewhat lower than in the case of two ratings by the same rater. Latham and Wexley (1981) suggest that the interrater correlations should be at least .60 (and one would hope for higher correlations).

Internal consistency. This method would be applicable when several or many items in a rating system are intended to measure the same basic factor (for example, items intended to measure "dependability"). One method of measuring such reliability is by deriving separate "total" scores based on the ratings for the odd-numbered items and for the even-numbered items. For this type of reliability Latham and Wexley (1981) recommend a minimum acceptable correlation of .80.

Discussion of reliability of ratings. The reliability of ratings can be influenced by several factors—the type of rating method, the familiarity of the rater with the ratees, and the rating abilities of the raters. Thus, generalizations about the reliability of ratings are hard to come by. However, the reliability of some ratings does not come up to the minimums recommended by Latham and Wexley.

To the extent that ratings are unreliable one cannot regard small differences (as between two ratees) as reflecting "true" differences. However, by a statistical procedure it is possible to derive what is called the standard error of measurement of a set of ratings. Unless two ratings differ by more than three standard errors of measurement it is unsafe to assume they reflect true differences. (This is why the results of election polls report the possible range of error, such as 3% error.)

Validity of Ratings

The validity of ratings is associated with the extent to which they reflect the "true" variable being evaluated, such as some aspect of job performance or some type of behavior. There are generally three types of validity of measuring instruments—namely, *content va-*

lidity, criterion-related validity, and *construct validity.* These are discussed in more detail in Chapter 8. As applied to personnel ratings they can be described briefly as follows: The determination of content validity is generally made on the basis of judgments of experts with regard to the relevance of the rating system to the "content" it is intended to measure, usually some aspect of job performance as confirmed by a job analysis. Criterion-related validity refers to the extent to which the ratings are correlated with some separate "true" criterion of what the rating system is supposed to measure, such as job performance. Construct validity generally applies to ratings that are intended to measure some human quality or "construct" (such as creativity). Generally it must be inferred from several performance measures that are logically considered to measure the same construct (for example, creativity).

Discussion of validity of ratings. Although the concepts and procedures for determining the validity of personnel ratings have been thus set forth, in practical terms hard data about such validity have often not been reported. Probably the most feasible form of validity is content validity, because it is usually based on a judgment of the relevance of the ratings to some specific job behavior. Criterion-related validity is often not feasible because separate "true" criteria of, say, job performance, usually are not available and cannot be obtained. And the process of establishing construct validity is often very complicated and time consuming.

THE RATER AS AN INFORMATION PROCESSOR

A person making a judgment about another person—whether informally or as part of a formal rating process—is actually serving as an information processor (Carroll & Schneier, 1982; Ilgen & Feldman, 1983). Such information processing involves a series of stages including observation, storage (memory), organizing information, and combining and integrating information to form a judgment. The theories and intricacies involved in these processes need not be discussed here. Basically the rater makes inferences about individuals from observations. Such inferences are much easier to make if there is some obvious relevant behavior or output or consequence of such behavior that can be judged. For example, it is easier to judge the driving ability of a lift-truck operator in a warehouse or the quality of work of a typist than to judge the job performance of a night security guard or a research chemist.

Several factors can influence ratings in addition to the opportunity to observe relevant behaviors or behavioral outputs. Such factors include characteristics of the rater (such as perceptual skills, ability to make judgments from observations, experience, personality, attitudes, etc.), and the nature of the rating system to be used.

PERSONNEL-RATING FACTORS

Rating systems provide for ratings to be made in terms of one or more rating factors (i.e., concepts, constructs, or frames of reference). The factors in most personnel-rating systems tend to be of two classes, as follows:

1. Personal qualities, characteristics, or traits. Some examples are dependability, creativity, verbal ability, and leadership.
2. Job-related behavior. Some factors of this type are very general, such as quality of work, quantity of work, and overall work performance; others provide for evaluating performance on particular aspects of jobs, such as tasks (discussed in connection with task inventories in Chapter 4) or job dimensions of worker-oriented work behavior (also discussed in Chapter 4).

Job-Relatedness of Rating Factors

A cardinal principle in developing or selecting personnel-rating systems is that the factors should be those that are relevant for the job(s) in question. It is patently inappropriate to rate the night security guard we mentioned previously on "ability to work with others" or to rate an assembler on "leadership." It is fairly standard practice to provide different combinations of rating factors for broad classes of jobs, such as for salary versus hourly paid jobs, or for exempt versus nonexempt jobs. (In the United States nonexempt jobs are those that are subject to the Fair Labor Standards Act in terms of minimum wage and overtime pay requirements; exempt jobs are not subject to that Act, and include executive, administrative, professional, and outside sales jobs.)

Such broad classes, however, can include jobs of rather varied nature. It may thus be appropriate to provide different combinations of rating factors for smaller groups of related jobs or even for individual jobs. One scheme that can be used is to have a basic set of factors in a rating system, but to make it possible to select—for any given job or group of jobs—those factors that are relevant.

Grouping jobs for rating purposes. There are two general methods for grouping jobs together for personnel-rating purposes. One procedure is to use an appropriate structured job-analysis procedure for analyzing all jobs, followed by a statistical procedure for identifying different job classifications or families, as discussed in Chapter 4. Such a procedure was followed by Cornelius, Hakel, and Sackett (1979) in their analysis of the jobs of 2023 enlisted personnel in the U.S. Coast Guard. Using a special form of factor analysis, these authors identified five groups of related jobs, as follows: I Aviation; II Service and Clerical; III Electronics; IV Engineering; and V Deck and Watch. A separate rating form was developed for each of these classes, and each form provided for rating incumbents on a different combination of factors.

The second method is to develop job classifications on the basis of the collective judgments of people who are familiar with the jobs. There are indications that, in some circumstances, the job groupings based on such judgments correspond reasonably well with those based on statistical analyses (Pearlman, 1980; Sackett, Cornelius, & Carron, 1981).

In certain cases a separate, unique rating form is developed for each specific job. In such instances, of course, there is no need to establish separate groups of jobs.

Selection of Rating Factors

In the years gone by rating systems tended to provide for ratings on various personal qualities or traits. In recent years, however, there has been a greater emphasis on the use of more job-related factors. Most typically the selection of such factors is based on judgments. However, selection of the factors can be based on some statistical analysis of job-related data. An example of such an analysis is reported by Rhode in the *Development of the Retail Checklist Performance Evaluation Program* for store managers of a large retail chain. Rhode started by developing a checklist of 113 job-related behaviors such as: effectiveness in dealing with problem employees; skill in communicating with others; and initiation of change. These were rated in terms of their relevance to twenty-four different jobs. The fifty-one most important behaviors were then used in rating 407 employees. The results of these ratings were then used in a factor analysis, with the following factors identified: (1) technical knowledge; (2) knowledge application; (3) administrative effectiveness; (4) work relations; (5) response to supervisors; (6) directing subordinates; and (7) personal commitment. In the actual use of the rating system employees are rated on the fifty-one individual items, but the ratings are then consolidated into scores on these seven factors.

Rating of Job Performance

In some rating systems direct ratings are made on job performance as such, rather than on various "factors." In effect such ratings provide for making judgments on "how well" an individual is performing the job activity in question. (Various rating methods can be used; some of these are described later.) When direct ratings of job performance are to be made a central question arises as to whether the "job activity" to be rated should be the "job as a whole," or specific components of the job (such as individual tasks, duties, etc.). In this regard strong evidence suggests that personnel evaluations based on components of a job are generally more adequate than those based on ratings of "overall" job performance.

This practice was utilized in a study dealing with Naval personnel (Vineberg & Taylor, 1976). These authors provided for rating the performance of enlisted personnel on the basis of each of the following aspects of job content:

1. Overall job performance;
2. Worker-oriented job elements (based on a modified form of the Position Analysis Questionnaire, or PAQ);
3. Tasks (as included in appropriate task inventories).

Basically, they found that the ratings based on worker-oriented job elements and on tasks were generally more satisfactory than those based on overall job performance. Worker-oriented job-element ratings had a slight edge over task-related ratings. Despite these findings (and inklings from other sources), however, there are circumstances in which ratings

based on overall job performance would be most appropriate. This matter is discussed further toward the end of this chapter.

Job components to be rated. When performance is to be rated on the basis of job components the components can vary in both their nature and their level of specificity. In the study by Vineberg and Taylor cited earlier, worker-oriented job elements and tasks were used. However, to simplify the rating chore for raters it may be useful to ask for ratings on clusters of related elements, such as job dimensions. Such a procedure was used by Dickinson (1977) in the rating of sales representatives of a wholesale food company. Dickinson asked twelve sales representatives to describe their jobs with the PAQ. On the basis of these analyses job-dimension scores were derived for the job. (Such scores are derived by a computer program on a service basis by the Computer Processing Division, PAQ Services, Inc.)

The most important job dimensions (those with the highest job-dimension scores) were used as the rating factors in a personnel-evaluation procedure that was then developed. (The particular rating method used was a variation of the behaviorally anchored scales, discussed later in this chapter.) Dickinson concluded that the PAQ provides an adequate analysis of jobs in terms of identifying the relevant job dimensions and their relative importance, and that the procedure can be used with jobs having few incumbents.

Discussion of Rating Factors

The critical issue involved in this discussion is that personnel ratings should be job-related, and thus have their roots in appropriate job analysis of the jobs in question. In many circumstances structured job-analysis procedures can be useful in tying rating systems to the content of the jobs in question.

We now turn our attention to various types of rating methods.

TYPES OF RATING METHODS

Certain basic types of rating methods, and numerous variations on the themes of the basic methods, are used in personnel ratings. Some of the basic methods and their variations are listed here:

1. Rating scales (RS)
   a. Graphic scales
   b. Multiple-step scales
   c. Numerical rating scales
2. Personnel-comparison systems (PCS)
   a. Rank-order system
   b. Paired-comparison system
   c. Forced-distribution system
3. Critical incident technique (CI or CIT)
4. Behavioral checklists and scales
   a. Forced-choice checklist (FCCL)
   b. Behaviorally anchored rating scales (BARS)
   c. Behavioral-observation scales (BOS)
   d. Mixed-standard scales (MSS)
5. Other rating methods

These five categories are all based on essentially different rating procedures. Because each method has certain inherent advantages and disadvantages there is no single "best" method; rather, one method may best serve one purpose, but not another.

Rating Scales (RS)

Many variations of conventional rating scales are used in personnel rating. For example, a graphic rating scale consists of a line with numerical or adjectival benchmarks; the rater simply marks the position that represents the rating judgment. A multiple-step scale provides for ratings on any of several rating categories, usually from five to nine; these categories may be identified by numbers, adjectives, or brief descriptions. In turn, numerical rating scales provide for recording a number that represents the rating. The feature that characterizes such scales is that they require the rater to judge "how much" of the rating factor applies to the individual being rated.

A few variations of rating scales are shown in Figure 6.1.

Personnel-Comparison Systems (PCS)

Whereas conventional rating scales provide for rating the absolute level of the rating factor, personnel-comparison systems allow individuals to be rated in comparison with each other. With conventional rating scales there is a tendency for the raters to pile up the ratings at one end of the scale, frequently at the higher end. If this occurs, the results have limited value, for they do not differentiate adequately among the individuals. Personnel-comparison systems avoid this problem completely, because individuals are rated relative to each other. There are three principal variations in the methods of comparing people with each other.

Rank-order system. With this method the rater simply ranks the individuals. Each person's rating is then determined by position in rank.

Paired-comparison system. This method provides for rating each person in comparison with every other person on the rating factor. The rating can be done with cards or slips, each with the name of a separate pair of raters, or with a list of all pairs. The rater marks the ratee considered best on the rating factor. The total number of choices for the ratees can be used to determine their rank order, or can be converted to some type of scale value.

One problem with this procedure occurs when there is a large number of ratees, because the number of pairs increases tremendously with the number of ratees. The number of pairs is determined by the equation

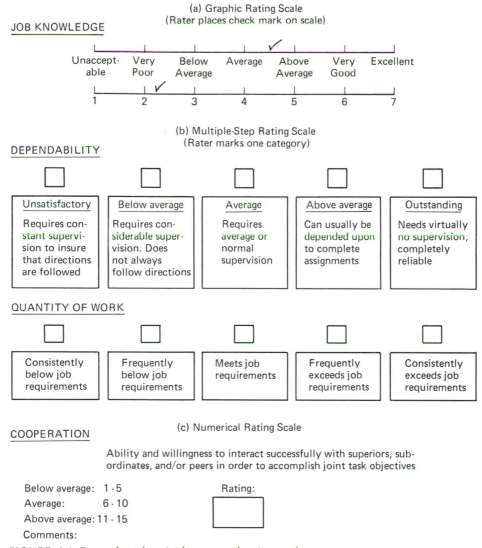

FIGURE 6.1 Examples of typical personnel-rating scales.

$$\text{No. of Pairs} = \frac{N(N-1)}{2}$$

in which N is the number of individuals to be rated.

There are two ways to use the paired-comparison system with large numbers of subjects. One is to divide the total group randomly into two subgroups and to rate the pairs in each subgroup separately. The other is to extract from a complete matrix of pairs a "patterned" sample of pairs, as illustrated by McCormick and Bachus (1952).

Forced-distribution system. This method is particularly useful when rating large numbers of individuals. The rater is asked to distribute the individuals into a limited number of categories (usually five) according to a predetermined and specified percentage distribution, such as the following:

Lowest 10%	Next 20%	Middle 40%	Next 20%	Highest 10%
☐	☐	☐	☐	☐

This procedure reduces the tendency to concentrate the ratings in one or a limited number of rating categories. In some situations, the percentages are used more as guideposts than as rigid requirements.

Critical Incident Technique (CI or CIT)

The critical incident technique, developed by Flanagan (1954), has had various uses in the framework of employee rating and job analysis. In the original form of the CIT, supervisors are usually asked to record employees' "critical behaviors"—that is, behaviors that are considered to be critical to the job in that they reflect especially desirable or especially undesirable job behaviors. Records of such behaviors are generally classified into certain categories, such as judgment or dealing with people.

The use of the critical incident technique in this fashion never became very common, but in recent years the technique has been adapted for use in connection with certain other behaviorally based rating methods. In particular these methods involve the development of statements of behavioral incidents that are used in any of various ways as the basis for eliciting rating judgments. In developing statements of behavioral incidents for such purposes people who are familiar with a given job or job type (supervisors, incumbents, peers, etc.) are asked to describe incidents they have observed or experienced that they consider as representing effective, intermediate, or ineffective job behavior. Records

of many such incidents are obtained. These are reviewed by eliminating duplicates, and are then edited to clarify the wording. This results in the development of a final pool of relevant incidents.

For certain purposes these statements need to be scaled by judges to derive a scale value for each. Examples of these scaled items are shown later, but at this stage let us describe one manner in which such statements are scaled: The pool of statements is given to several or many judges who are familiar with the job(s) in question. They are asked to rate the statements along a scale (such as a nine-point scale) in terms of the degree to which they think each statement would reflect favorable or unfavorable job behavior if it actually were true of a job incumbent. The results of the scaling of three hypothetical examples are shown in Table 6.1, which illustrates the distribution of ratings of ten judges using a nine-point scale. The intent of this scaling is twofold. First, statements with low reliability are eliminated; in this example statement B would be eliminated. Second, the "surviving" statements are given scale values, usually based on their mean scale values; thus, statement A would have a scale value of 4.0, and C a scale value of 2.1 (the mean $= [2 \times 1 + 2 \times 5 + 3 \times 3] \div 10 = [2 + 10 + 9] \div 10 = [21] \div 10 = 2.1$).

Behavioral Checklists and Scales

Another basic method of personnel rating uses some type of behavioral checklist or rating scale. The rater is given descriptive statements of job-related "behavior" and is asked to indicate, in one way or another, those statements which are (or might be expected to be) descriptive of the individual in question. Thus, the rater tends to be more a *reporter* of *the work behavior* of individuals than an evaluator of their performance or of their personal characteristics.

Because these methods are difficult and

TABLE 6.1 Hypothetical examples of the ratings by ten judges regarding the favorability-unfavorability of three job-behavioral statements[a]

	RATING CATEGORY								
	UNFAVORABLE						FAVORABLE		
STATEMENT	1	2	3	4	5	6	7	8	9
A				10					
B		1	2	1	3	2	1		
C	2	5	3						

[a]The number entered under each category is the number of judges who placed the statement in that category.

time-consuming to develop, they usually can be justified only if they are to be used widely. They offer some advantages, however, that warrant their serious consideration for circumstances in which they would be widely used. Most behavioral checklists and scales are developed for use in rating personnel on separate, individual jobs.

Forced-choice checklist (FCCL). This rating system usually consists of several groups of four or more behavioral statements. The rater is asked to mark one or two of the statements in each group that he considers to be most descriptive of the person being rated. The nub of the system lies in developing the statements and forming them into groups. The grouping of the statements is based on two indexes that are based on previous research with the statements. One of these indexes is a *preference* or *favorability* index. This index is derived by asking judges to rate the statements on their "social desirability"—that is, on how desirable, nice, or good it is (i.e., how "desirable" it would be) to use the statement in describing someone. This might be done with, say, a seven-point rating scale. In turn, a *discrimination* index is derived by having raters rate a sample of workers on the job in terms of how well each statement "describes" each worker. The sample rated includes those who are clearly "good" workers and those who are clearly "poor." A statistical index is then derived for each statement that indicates the extent to which the ratings discriminate between the "good" and "poor" workers.

Each group of statements is formed on the basis of the two indexes so derived. In the first place, statements are grouped together on the basis of their preference indexes, and those with reasonably similar indexes are put together. Of those with reasonably similar preference indexes, a further selection is made on the basis of the discrimination indexes. Usually a group of, say, four statements would include two statements with relatively high discrimination indexes, and two with low indexes. An example is given in Figure 6.2 with the indexes of the statements, although the indexes are not shown on the actual rating form. The rater cannot select the most "favorable" statement because all those in a group are about equal in their preference indexes. However, the statements selected for a group do differ in their discrimination indexes, and one or two are more descriptive of good workers than of poor workers. In the example in Figure 6.2 items 1 and 4 have higher discrimination indexes than do 2 and 3. A person's rating is based on the extent to which the rater selects the statements that have the highest discrimination indexes—those that are most descriptive of good workers.

A major advantage of this method is that the rater, who may attempt (consciously or unconsciously) to rate a person higher or lower than the person's "true" worth has no

FIGURE 6.2 An example of a block of statements in a forced-choice rating scale for police dispatchers. In this scale a rater marks the two statements considered to be most descriptive of the person being rated. The indexes are not shown on the actual rating form. (From Carroll & Schneier, 1982, Figure 5–12, p. 122.)

	Discrimination Index	Preference Index
_____ 1. Has excellent knowledge of all console equipment and can diagnose problems quickly.	1.95	6.1
_____ 2. Makes it a point to learn how to make minor repairs on the equipment.	.18	6.4
_____ 3. Changes tapes every day at 2400 hours.	.22	5.9
_____ 4. Obtains all pertinent information from caller before advising officer.	2.30	6.6

way of knowing which of the statements to check to raise (or lower) the rating from what it should be. There is, however, a major disadvantage to the method. Since the rater does not (and should not) know how the final rating values are derived, he may resent the system as a whole and therefore may not give it wholehearted support.

Behaviorally anchored rating scales (BARS). In recent years behaviorally anchored rating scales (BARS) have received considerable attention, including experimentation, research, and actual use. The basic nature of those scales was originally developed by Smith and Kendall (1963) in a study dealing with nurses. (The original term for those scales, behavioral expectation scales or BES, has been largely replaced by BARS.)

BARS provide for rating the incumbents on each of several dimensions. An example of such a scale is shown in Figure 6.3; the dimension in this example is motivation. Note that the statements range from those that reflect undesirable behavior (at the bottom) to those that reflect desirable behavior (at the top). These statements represent benchmarks for the scale of the rating factor in question (usually a job dimension). The scale values of the benchmarks are derived by a scaling process such as described earlier.

In the use of BARS the rater assigns a rating at the point on the scale at which the ratee would be "expected" to perform. That rating may be a whole number (for example, 3, 4, or 5) or a value in between whole numbers (such as 3.5).

The development of a BARS for a particular job is time-consuming. The procedures include the following:

1. Obtaining critical incidents. This procedure, described previously, results in a pool of incidents to use in the subsequent processes.
2. Developing performance dimensions. The statements of incidents are then clustered into groups representing different job dimensions. This is usually done on the basis of judgments of experts, but could well be based on statistically identified dimensions. Each dimension is defined or labeled by a description that best outlines the items included in the cluster.
3. Scaling of incidents. The scaling process is usually the same as that described previously.
4. Developing the final instrument. The final instrument consists of a subset of incidents that represent various positions along the scale for each of the dimensions (usually six to ten) that define the dimension.

Although BARS are usually developed for rating people on a specific job, Goodale and Burke (1975) suggest that the procedure may well lend itself to use across a number of jobs.

FIGURE 6.3 An example of a behaviorally anchored rating scale (BARS) for the job dimension of motivation. The rater assigns a ratee a score representing the level of behavior that would be "expected" of the ratee. (From Latham & Wexley, 1981, Table 3.7, p. 53.)

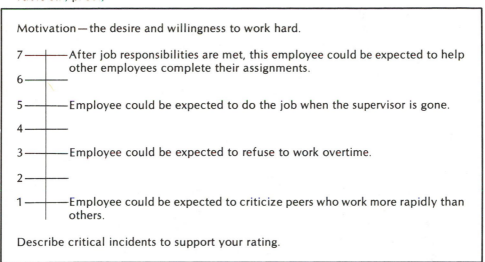

Motivation — the desire and willingness to work hard.

7 ——|—— After job responsibilities are met, this employee could be expected to help other employees complete their assignments.

6 ——|——

5 ——|—— Employee could be expected to do the job when the supervisor is gone.

4 ——|——

3 ——|—— Employee could be expected to refuse to work overtime.

2 ——|——

1 ——|—— Employee could be expected to criticize peers who work more rapidly than others.

Describe critical incidents to support your rating.

Such a broader application would require the use of more general dimensions, with critical incidents of a broader nature to serve as benchmarks for various levels of the dimensions. The dimensions Goodale and Burke used experimentally were: interpersonal relationships; organizing and planning; reaction to problems; reliability; communicating; adaptability; growth; production; quality of work; and teaching.

Various criticisms have been leveled at BARS. One of these deals with the problems in rating incumbents because of the very specific behaviors represented by the benchmark incidents of the scales. The behavioral incidents that have been observed for a ratee may not be (and usually are not) represented by such benchmarks; thus the rater needs to compare or equate the behavior of a ratee with the benchmark examples. One practice that can help minimize this problem is to supplement the benchmark incidents in the scale with those that are actually observed on the part of incumbents and that can be reliably equated to those on the scale.

Bernardin and Smith (1981) make the point that certain aspects of the BARS approach that distinguish it from other methods have been ignored or misinterpreted. For example, they emphasize that the original procedure was designed to encourage raters to observe employee behavior more carefully, and to record critical incidents throughout the appraisal period. This emphasis is intended to enhance the observational skills of raters and the abilities of raters to interpret the observed behavior of those being rated. Bernardin and Smith claim that it is this emphasis of the approach (as a method for enhancing future observations of behavior) that distinguishes it from other rating approaches, such as forced-choice and simple graphic scales.

Some of the barbs that have been aimed at BARS might be attributed to the fact that they have not always been used in the manner originally proposed and subsequently emphasized by Bernardin and Smith (1981). In evaluating BARS, the observations of certain reviewers may be relevant. Jacobs, Kafry, and Zedeck (1980), for example, conclude that results of various studies show that BARS are not better or worse than alternative performance-evaluation methods. In turn, Kingstrom and Bass (1981) express disappointment that BARS have not fulfilled the goal of reducing rating errors. They report that comparative studies of various rating systems have not revealed the clear superiority of BARS, and they stated, in back-handed fashion, that it is appropriate to conclude that BARS are not superior to tradidional rating methods. Neither, however, were BARS viewed as inferior to other methods.

Behavioral-observation scales (BOS). Behavioral-observation scales (BOS), like BARS, have their roots in critical incidents.

Although the BARS provide for rating in terms of how the ratee would be "expected" to perform relative to the scaled benchmarks of each dimension, the BOS provides for the rater to record the frequency with which specific behavioral incidents have been observed on the part of the incumbent. Figure 6.4, an example from a BOS for rating managers, lists several specific behaviors for the criterion or performance dimension of overcoming resistance to change. The rater uses the five-point scales to indicate the relative frequency with which the specific behaviors have been observed, and those ratings in turn are added together to derive a total rating.

The development of BOS generally par-

FIGURE 6.4 Example of a behavioral-observation scale (BOS), in particular for the criterion or performance dimension of overcoming resistance to change, for use in evaluating managers. The rater records the frequency with which the specific behaviors have been observed on the part of the ratee. (From Latham & Wexley, 1981, Table 3.8, p. 56.)

1. Overcoming Resistance to Change

  (1) Describes the details of the change to subordinates.

     Almost Never   1   2   3   4   5   Almost Always

  (2) Explains why the change is necessary.

     Almost Never   1   2   3   4   5   Almost Always

  (3) Discusses how the change will affect the employee.

     Almost Never   1   2   3   4   5   Almost Always

  (4) Listens to the employee's concerns.

     Almost Never   1   2   3   4   5   Almost Always

  (5) Asks the employee for help in making the change work.

     Almost Never   1   2   3   4   5   Almost Always

  (6) If necessary, specifies the date for a follow-up meeting to respond to the employee's concerns.

     Almost Never   1   2   3   4   5   Almost Always

Total = _____

Below Adequate	Adequate	Full	Excellent	Superior
6–10	11–15	16–20	21–25	26–30

allels that of BARS with regard to the identification of behavioral incidents and their grouping into dimensions. However, BOS incidents are not assigned scale values. The example in Figure 6.4 provides a five-point scale for rating frequency, ranging from "Almost Never" to "Almost Always." Another variation is given here (Latham & Wexley, 1977):

"Knows the price of competitive products"

Never Seldom Sometimes Generally Always

1   2   3   4   5

In some variations percent-of-time guidelines are provided for the five-point scale values; an example would be 20% class intervals. (Latham & Wexley, 1981, p. 59, suggest the following percent intervals for the five-point scale values: 0% to 64%; 65% to 74%; 75% to 84%; 85% to 94%; and 95% to 100%. Those generally correspond to the five points of the Likert-type scale usually used with BOS.)

The behaviors used in BOS instruments can be grouped into categories based either on judgments of the similarity of their content or on a factor analysis of ratings of frequency of observed occurrences.

Mixed-standard scales (MSS). As with most behaviorally based rating scales mixed-standard scales are developed for rating incumbents on a particular job (Blanz & Ghiselli, 1972). The usual format consists of a number of triads (groups of three) of behavioral statements. Various types of statements can be used. The statements in most scales describe either general traits, such as initiative or enthusiasm, or behavioral styles, such as the following triad from a rating scale for computer programmers (Carroll & Schneier, 1982, p. 123):

ITEM		SCALE VALUE
___ 1.	Is rude to customers; makes sarcastic remarks	1.8
___ 2.	Carefully considers customers' needs, problems, and financial constraints	6.8
___ 3.	Makes frequent, sometimes unnecessary changes in existing programs	3.9

Rosinger, Myers, Levy, Loar, Mohrman, and Stock (1982) propose the use of specific tasks in the triads. The following tasks were suggested for a rating scale for highway-patrol personnel, specifically to deal with the actions involved in stopping vehicles for violations:

- Stops vehicles for a variety of traffic and other violations.
- Concentrates on one or two kinds of violations and spends too little time on the others.
- Concentrates on speed violations, but stops vehicles for other violations as well.

In general each triad includes statements for a particular trait, behavioral style, duty, or job dimension.

The scales are predicated on the development of a pool of behavioral statements of the type to be used, and the derivation of scale values based on the judging process previously described (and used with BARS and BOS rating methods). A critical feature of the method is the process of selecting the statements for each triad. The three statements are selected to represent, respectively, good, average, and poor performance as reflected by their scale values. The statements are randomized within the triad, and the scale values are not included on the form as presented to the rater.

When rating an incumbent the rater is usually asked to indicate, for each statement, whether the person's performance is "better than", "the same as", or "worse than" that represented by the statement. In rating any ratee there are only seven logical response combinations for the good, average, and poor behavioral statements as follows: (B = Better than; S = Same as, and W = Worse than; the first letter stands for the rating of the first item in the triad, the second for the second, and the third for the third):

$$BBB \quad SBB \quad WBB$$
$$WSB \quad WWB \quad WWS \quad WWW$$

Other response patterns are illogical—for example if a rater rates person X better than Y ($X > Y$), Y better than Z ($Y > Z$), but Z better than X ($Z > X$). There are, however, scoring procedures for adjusting for such illogical ratings (Saal, 1979).

A variation in the form of rating response is proposed by Rosinger et al. (1982), specifically for use with statements that are descriptive of tasks. In particular, these authors propose the use of a seven-point rating scale of proficiency, from 1 (very poor) to 7 (outstanding), to replace the "better than", "same as", and "worse than" rating categories usually used. (This particular rating procedure would presumably have to be used with task-like statements.) The results with this variation were considered to be quite satisfactory for evaluating highway-patrol personnel.

The mixed-standard scale must probably still be viewed as an experimental method because it has not yet been subjected to extensive research or operational use. However, it seems to offer reasonable promise as another rating method.

Other Rating Methods

Other methods of personnel rating are sometimes used. One is a group-evaluation plan in which each person is evaluated by a group of supervisors during a conference. In certain situations a "free-written" rating pro-cedure is used; in this procedure the evaluator (usually a supervisor) "describes" the person in question by writing a "word picture" of that person. In other circumstances those being evaluated participate in some type of group problem, discussion, or "game," and the evaluation is made by observers.

SOURCES OF POSSIBLE DISTORTIONS IN RATINGS

Our discussion of personnel ratings included some suggestions of undesirable distortions in the ratings. These possible distortions can arise from various sources, including certain raters' tendencies and contamination from extraneous sources.

Raters' Tendencies

Some of the distortions in personnel evaluation arise from rather common tendencies by raters, in particular the halo effect, the constant error, what we call rating restriction, the contrast effects, and the personal characteristics of ratees (for example, sex and race).

The halo effect. The halo effect is the tendency on the part of some raters, when rating individuals, to assign somewhat the same ratings on various factors—either high, average, or low. In other words, the rater presumably does not differentiate in the ratings for the different rating factors. The usual explanation for this tendency is that the rater has formed a definite impression of the ratee on one factor (such as personality or initiative) and permits that impression to influence the ratings on other factors (such as productivity, quality of work, etc.). In general, the result of the halo effect is that the ratings or various factors tend to have higher correlations with each other than otherwise would be the case.

Some implication of the halo effect comes from a study by DeCotiis (1977) in which twenty-eight police supervisors rated police officers using the following three types of rating scales with the indicated numbers of rating factors: (1) a behaviorally anchored rating scale (BARS) with six dimensions; (2) a rating scale with eleven traits; (3) and a rating scale for rating on ten job-performance factors. For each scale a correlation was computed between each pair of rating factors. The median correlations and their ranges are given here:

| | CORRELATIONS | |
SCALE	MEDIAN	RANGE
BARS	.73	.27
Trait-rating scale	.91	.15
Performance- rating scale	.85	.28

These correlations are all quite high, reflecting a strong tendency by the raters to assign ratings to individuals across the several rating factors at somewhat corresponding levels. This suggests the possible influence of the halo effect. In another example Landy, Vance, and Barnes-Farrell (1982) report an average intercorrelation of .60 among sixteen rating factors used in rating management personnel.

The problem of halo in rating has led to attempts to develop rating methods that would be less sensitive to this tendency. The forced-choice and mixed-standard scales were designed for this purpose; they keep the rater in the dark about the scale values of the items. Another approach to the halo problem is based on statistical procedures; these involve the "partialing out" of the effects on total ratings of the intercorrelations between the rating factors. Both of these approaches have their disadvantages. Rating scales that reduce halo (such as the forced-choice and mixed-standard methods) are usually not well accepted by raters. Statistical controls remove not only invalid halo, but also the effects of valid in-

terrelationships between rating factors. In this regard Hulin (1982) calls attention to the fact that human traits and abilities are *not* independent of one another, but that many are actually correlated with each other. Our everyday observation of friends, acquaintances, and others tends, in a common-sense fashion, to support this contention. In job-related situations such observations strongly suggest that many desirable human traits and characteristics are related to (and therefore correlated with) job-related performance and behavior.

In general, then, it can be concluded that the correlations between rating factors can be the consequence of the *combinations* of "true" correlations and of halo rating errors. It is admittedly difficult to sort out the influence of these two factors, although certain statistical procedures have been suggested for this purpose (Harvey, 1982; Hulin, 1982; Landy, Vance, Barnes-Farrell, & Steele, 1980; and Murphy, 1982). A procedure proposed by Bartlett (1983) offers some promise of being able to differentiate between what he calls "invalid" halo from "valid" halo. However, it involves the use of the forced-choice method, which generally is not well accepted by raters. Perhaps the most practical method presently available for minimizing the possible "invalid" halo effect is to train raters so they are aware of it and can, to some degree, guard against it. However, even this is not a sure cure because there are some indications that such training might cause raters to avoid valid as well as invalid halo (Bernardin & Pence, 1980).

The constant error. The constant error is a tendency to concentrate the ratings in one section of the rating scale, such as toward the upper end of the scale (sometimes referred to as the *leniency tendency*), in the center of the scale (the *error of central tendency*), or toward the lower end of the scale. These tendencies were all reflected in the ratings obtained from different raters in one company. One supervisor's ratings averaged 405 points out of a possible 600, whereas another's averaged 295 points. Probably the most common type of constant error is the leniency tendency.

If various raters within an organization do demonstrate different raters' tendencies (as reflected by significant differences in their average ratings), and if the purpose of the ratings requires the comparison of ratings across raters, one cannot compare equitably the actual rating values of individuals rated by different raters. Rather, it is necessary to convert the different sets of ratings to a common numerical scale—in particular, some type of standard score system. Such procedures are discussed later.

Rating restriction. Another type of raters' tendency, somewhat tied to the constant error, is rating restriction. This is the tendency to use only a restricted range of the rating scale when assigning ratings to individuals. This restriction sometimes occurs in combination with the leniency tendency since the leniency tendency is frequently characterized by a clustering of most of the ratings near the top of the scale. Rating restriction is usually reflected by a small standard deviation of the ratings or by a narrow range of ratings across those who are rated.

A word of caution needs to be added about the possibility of a restricted range of ratings. A restricted range is not necessarily an indication of raters' tendencies, because on some jobs the "true" range of performance is limited. This can occur if, for example, the poor workers have fallen by the wayside and are no longer on the job. Or it may even be the consequence of intentional restriction of work output on the part of workers.

The contrast effect. This is the tendency for a rater to evaluate a person relative to other individuals rather than in terms of the requirements of the job. Latham and Wexley (1981) point out that such errors occur most frequently in personnel selection when an interviewer might judge a single applicant in comparison with other applicants rather than in terms of job requirements. Such a person might be rated lower if the other applicants are very good than if the other applicants are very poor; thus, the applicant's rating is influenced by the "contrast" with the others. Similarly, in a job situation, one worker's rating on job performance might be influenced by the fact that the other workers are either particularly good or particularly poor. The contrast effect could, of course, not apply in the use of personnel-comparison systems because such methods actually provide for rating individuals in comparison to others.

Personal characteristics of ratees. There are reasons to believe that some raters' ratings may be influenced by the personal characteristics of the ratees—for example, sex and race. Unfortunately, most evidence about such effects comes from simulated laboratory studies rather than from actual work situations (Schmitt & Lappin, 1980; Terborg & Ilgen, 1975; Wendelken & Inn, 1981). Some such studies show that ratings are somewhat influenced by the sex and/or race of the ratees, although at least one study indicated that such effects were negligible (Wendelken & Inn, 1981).

Until more adequate data based on ratings from actual work situations are available, it is probable that the best strategy for personnel administrators is to provide adequate training for raters, emphasizing the desirability of minimizing the influence of personal biases when rating individuals.

The control of bias in ratings. In connection with bias in ratings Wherry (Wherry & Bartlett, 1982) developed a rating theory and crystallized a number of theorems and corollaries stemming from the theory. The theory is far too complex to deal with here. However, the implications of certain of the theorems and corollaries are summarized next, each expressed in terms of some variable or factor that would be expected to minimize the bias in ratings.

Ratings would be expected to be more accurate when:

- Performance is controlled by the ratee rather than by the work situation. Examples: self-paced work; constant working conditions; no restrictions by union.
- The rating scales or items have as behavioral referents tasks controlled by the ratee rather than by the work situation.
- Raters' contacts with ratees have been more relevant and frequent rather than less relevant and frequent.
- The rating-scale items refer to easily observed behaviors rather than to hard-to-observe behaviors.
- The rater has been properly instructed concerning the types of activities to rate.
- The rater is provided with a checklist of objective cues to refer to when evaluating ratees.
- The rater keeps a written record of critical incidents between rating periods.
- The ratings are obtained soon after the "observation" period.
- The behavior to be rated can more readily be classified into separate categories than when the job involves a complex pattern of behaviors.
- The rating scale has several homogeneous items to measure each specific rating dimension.
- The rating scale is composed of items dealing with several independent dimensions.

Ratings would be expected to be more reliable when:

- Reliability is measured by the test-retest method rather than by the interrater method.
- Several items are used to measure any given unidimensional variable rather than when a single item is used.

Certain of these points are amenable to some type of corrective action (such as training raters). Other points, however, may not lend themselves to corrective action (for example, those dealing with the nature of the job activities to be rated).

Contamination of Ratings

In the previous chapter the possible contamination of various types of criteria was mentioned. Contamination can likewise occur in personnel ratings—for example, when raters are influenced, perhaps unknowingly, by various factors extraneous to whatever is being rated, such as the organizational unit or the job of the ratee.

Organizational unit. Frequently the ratings reported from one organizational unit (such as a department) are different from those from other units. Although such differences may be due in part to "true" differences in the performance of individuals in the various units, they may also result from differences in the standards or rating "policies" of raters in the different units. Figure 6.5 illustrates the actual differences in ratings of three departments in one company. From this example, we can see that a rating of 350 would be very low for a man in the engineering department, approximately average for a man in the maintenance department, and very high for a man in the plant-protection department.

Job differences. Sometimes somewhat similar differences occur in the ratings of people on various jobs. In a steel mill, for example, the average ratings of people on various jobs ranged from about 385 for tinners to about 275 for openers and examiners. The same tendency was reported by Klores (1966, p. 416) for professional personnel in various job levels, as shown here:

JOB LEVEL:	A (LOW)	B	C	D	E	F (HIGH)
Mean rating (1 = high; 5 = low):	4.0	3.6	3.4	2.3	2.3	2.5

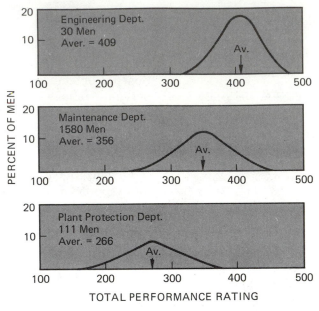

FIGURE 6.5 Differences in performance ratings among departments in a steel mill.

Discussion of Distortions in Ratings

In some circumstances some personal (or other) factor that is related to the ratings of a group of employees may be viewed as a source of distortion in the ratings, but may actually reflect a "true" relationship. For example, a summation of the ratings of the 9000 personnel in the steel mill just mentioned showed that the average ratings decreased with length of service on the present jobs (perhaps because the better workers were promoted to other jobs, leaving the poorer workers with long service still on the job). The data also showed that average ratings varied somewhat with age, and that younger and older workers received lower average ratings than those in the intermediate age range (perhaps because the younger workers were less experienced and older workers were "slowing down").

Such relationships as these, and others, would not necessarily be found in other situations. The point we are leading up to is that an organization should know what such relationships are, and should try to figure out the basis for them, in order to judge whether they represent "true" differences or whether they represent some form of unintended rating influence, based on the personal characteristics of the workers, contamination, and so on.

WEIGHTING FACTORS IN RATING SCALES

Most rating systems provide for ratings to be made on various factors: personal traits, job dimensions, types of behavior, and so on. This practice immediately raises two questions: (1) What weight should each factor have? and (2) How can one provide for giving each factor its intended weight?

Let us start with the assumption that all factors are to have equal weight. In such instances it is the usual practice to develop scales for the several factors that are identical—for example, from 1 (low) to 50 (high). The use of identical scales, however, does *not* insure equal weighing of the factors as reflected in the total rating scores that are derived by adding the scores on the individual factors. This possible differential effect arises from the fact that, when one combines scores, the scores in part weight themselves automatically in proportion to their respective *variabilities* (in particular, their standard deviations; the standard deviation was discussed in chapter 3 and is also described in Appendix A).

Let us consider the hypothetical case of two factors (say "judgment" and "initiative") that are to have equal weights: Each is to be rated on a scale from 1 to 50. Let us assume that the ratings for many ratees on judgment range from 20 to 30, and on initiative range from 10 to 40, and that the distributions of the ratings are relatively normal. In this instance the actual influence of the total ratings on the two factors would *not* be equal; rather the factor of initiation (which ranges over thirty points from 10 to 40) would have approximately three times as much influence on the combined ratings as the ratings on judgment (which vary over a range of only ten points—from 20 to 30).

If two or more factors are to have differential weights it is common practice to incorporate the intended weights into the scales, as illustrated here:

FACTOR	INTENDED WEIGHT	RANGE OF SCALE VALUES
A	1	1 to 30
B	2	1 to 60

Let us assume that the actual distribution of the ratings for many ratees are as follows (with normal distributions):

- A 1 to 30 (with an actual range of thirty points)

- B 15 to 45 (with an actual range of thirty points).

In this instance the *actual* influence of the two factors would be the same and not the intended weights of 1 and 2.

The practical implication of all of this is that one should examine the distribution of ratings on the various factors. If ratings on certain factors are much more restrictive, or more variable, than those on other factors, one needs to do something about the ratings to adjust for what would otherwise be unintended influences on the combined ratings. Although the maximum numbers of points that it is possible to assign to individual factors may reflect the *intended* relative weights, this is no assurance that the *actual* weight will correspond to those that are intended.

The determination of the weights that are to be applied is usually made on the basis of the judgments of those responsible for the development of the rating system. There are, however, statistical methods that can be used for determining what these weights should be. One such procedure involves a large sample of ratees, the availability of a very good "overall" criterion of their job performance, and the use of a regression analysis procedure. This produces the factor weights as they have contributed to overall criterion values.

Adjusting Ratings for Raters' Tendencies or Distortion

We have seen that personnel ratings can be affected adversely by certain raters' tendencies, or by some form of contamination. If there is evidence of any form of distortion, the ratings cannot be accepted as the "true" evaluations of the individuals in question. One may be able to tolerate the distortion if the ratings are to be used entirely *within the context of the group* from which they come (such as the ratings of one rater, or those for people on the same job). However, if the ratings are to be compared *between* or *among* *groups* of ratees, they should *not* be used *unless* they are adjusted for whatever distortions may exist. There are at least two ways of doing this.

Adjusting for differences in means. Let us use, as an example, a situation in which the ratings given by different raters differ significantly. One solution is to determine the average of the ratings given by each rater and to compute the difference between *each rater's* average and the average of *all raters*. This difference can then be added to or subtracted from the ratings given by a particular rater, in order to bring them into alignment with those of other raters. This simple adjustment is satisfactory if the *variabilities* of the ratings given by the different raters are about the same. The variability in the distributions of ratings can be compared by comparing their standard deviations.

Adjusting for differences by standard scores. A more systematic method of adjusting for such differences is to convert all ratings to a common numerical scale. Some type of *standard score* (comparable score) may be used for this. There are various types of standard scores; one is *z*-scores. Standard scores, including *z*-scores, indicate the *relative* position of individual cases in a distribution. Such scores are based on deviations of individual cases from the mean and are expressed in *standard deviation units*. A "standard deviation" (SD) is a statistical index of the degree of variability of the cases within a distribution. It is expressed in terms of the numerical values of the original distribution. In a relatively normal distribution, two-thirds of the cases fall within 1 SD above and below the mean, about 95% are within 2 SD above and below the mean, and about 99% fall within 3 DS. Thus, regardless of what the mean of a distribution is, or what the magnitude of its SD is, it is possible to express the deviation of any given numerical value in terms of the number of standard deviation units it is above or below the mean. A *z*-score is simply the deviation of a given raw score from the mean expressed in standard deviation units.

Let us now see how this helps us compare the ratings produced by a "tough" rater with those produced by a "lenient" rater. Suppose that distributions A and B of Figure 6.6 represent, respectively, the total ratings given to their respective groups by rater A and rater B. Clearly a rating of 110 by itself is meaningless unless it is related to the distribution of which it is a part. (It means a very high rating by rater A and a very low rating by rater B.) These two distributions can both be

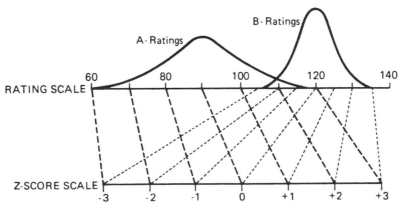

FIGURE 6.6 Conversion of two sets of ratings (*A* and *B*) to a common scale of *z*-scores.

converted to z-scores, as illustrated at certain points on the distributions by the broken lines and dotted lines from the basic rating scale to the z-score scale below it. We can now see that a rating of 110 by rater A would mean a z-score of *plus* 2, but by rater B it would mean a z-score of *minus* 2, and that a rating of 100 from rater A would correspond to a rating of 125 from rater B, since both convert to z-scores of plus 1. Similar conversions can be made with other groups of ratees for which some form of contamination is apparent, as for employees on different jobs or in different departments.

Adjusting for Unintended Weights of Factors

In the previous discussion of weights for factors in a rating system, it was pointed out that the *effective* weights of factors may be different from their *intended* weights if the distributions of the ratings (i.e., the variabilities) for the various factors are markedly different (as compared with the ranges of the scales to be used). When this is the case, basically the same statistical procedures discussed with regard to raters' tendencies and distortion can be used, as follows: (1) convert the ratings on each factor to standard scores (such as z-scores); (2) multiply the standard scores for each factor by the intended factor weight; and (3) add these weighted scores to derive a total rating for each ratee.

DEVELOPING AND ADMINISTERING PERSONNEL-RATING SYSTEMS

The development of effective personnel evaluation systems and the effective administration of personnel-evaluation programs depend on several important aspects: the selection or development of an appropriate type of rating system for the purpose(s) in mind;

the selection of raters; the training of raters; and in some instances the "conversion" of the original ratings given by the raters into summated ratings.

Selection of Type of Rating System

The first step in establishing a personnel-evaluation program, or for carrying out any type of program for which ratings are to be obtained, is to select the rating system that best serves the intended purpose. The various types of rating systems have their own advantages and limitations. The pros and cons for the various systems, in turn, influence their suitabilities to various uses.

Following are a few general comments about the various types of systems, including those that point up certain individual characteristics and that reflect certain advantages and limitations:

- Rating scales: The most commonly used type of rating. Susceptible to raters' tendencies such as constant error and halo.
- Personnel-comparison systems: Avoid the constant error by forcing raters to spread out their ratings. Depend on relative judgments rather than on absolute judgments and tend to have respectable reliability. Limited in some uses (such as personnel counseling) because they reflect only order of merit and are not "analytical" in showing specific strengths and weaknesses of ratees.
- Critical incident technique: Tends to be burdensome for routine use. Does not lend itself readily to quantification. Its major strength is that it provides a record of specific incidents for use in employee counseling.
- Forced-choice checklist: Time-consuming to develop. Not readily accepted by raters as they do not know what responses are used to derive a person's final rating. Tend to minimize the constant error. Probably should be used only when it is feasible to hide final ratings from raters.
- Behaviorally anchored rating scales (BARS). Time-consuming to develop. Probably relatively simple for raters to use because of job-related nature. Participation by employees in

their development probably contributes to their acceptability. Evidence of susceptibility to constant error and halo is mixed but generally seem to be no better in these regards than conventional rating scales are.

- Behavioral-observation scales (BOS): Time-consuming to develop. Seem to represent a relatively promising development in personnel rating when two conditions can be fulfilled: (1) adequate sample of ratings is available for use in development; and (2) continuous opportunity for raters to observe ratees in order to rate frequency of behaviors. Some raters consider BOS more "practical" than BARS. Reliability seems acceptable.
- Mixed-standard scales (MSS): Still experimental but may be less susceptible to constant error and halo effects. May help identify inconsistent (less competent) raters (who could then be eliminated or given further training). Time-consuming to develop.

Suggested uses of various rating methods. Each of the different rating methods has advantages and disadvantages for various purposes. Table 6.2 recommends the possible uses of the various methods just discussed. This table is based in part on a similar table

presented by Barrett (1966) for the first five methods. Barrett suggested either to use a particular method (*Yes*), or not (*No*). The current authors have incorporated into Table 6.2 suggested uses for the methods developed since then—namely, the BARS, BOS, and MSS methods. In addition some modifications have been made to Barrett's suggestions, and another category was introduced—namely *D*, which identifies a use that would "depend" on the specific nature and content of the rating form in question, and in some instances on the administrative and legal aspects relating to the use in question. The suggestions in Table 6.2 should be interpreted with caution because special circumstances might justify departure from the specific suggestions proposed.

Training Raters

Most of the data relating to the training of raters come from simulated studies. The results of such studies are admittedly ambiguous (Borman, 1979; Fay & Latham, 1982).

TABLE 6.2 Suggested uses of various personnel-rating methods

SUGGESTED USE	TYPE OF METHOD[a]						
	RS	PCS	CI	FCCL	BARS	BOS	MSS
Pay increase	Y[b]	D	N	Y	Y	Y	Y
Promotion: higher jobs	D	D	N	D	D	D	D
Job transfer	D	D	N	D	D	D	D
Discharge, demotion	D	D	N	D	Y	Y	Y
Administrative control	Y	Y	Y	D	Y	Y	Y
Personnel development	Y	N	Y	Y	Y	Y	Y
Research	Y	Y	Y	Y	Y	Y	Y

Source: Adapted in part from Barrett, 1966, Table 5, p. 61.

[a]Legends (type of scale): RS = Rating Scale; PCS = Personnel-Comparison Systems; CI = Critical Incident; FCCL = Forced-Choice Checklist; BARS = Behaviorally Anchored Rating Scale; BOS = Behavioral-Observation Scale; MSS = Mixed-Standard Scale.

[b]Legends (table entries): Y = Yes; N = No; D = Depends (depends on the specific nature and content of the scale).

However, the general implication of such studies is that relevant training can minimize some rating errors such as the halo, constant error, and contrast effects.

The nature of the training to be provided, however, is a matter of considerable concern. Latham and Wexley (1981), for example, are critical of certain approaches to such training on various grounds: teaching inappropriate behaviors, such as encouraging raters to give ratings to form normal distribution (when in fact the "true" distribution might be skewed); forcing the use of the entire range of ratings (when the ratees actually represent only a portion of that scale); failing to provide opportunities to practice the rating skills that are learned; and failing to provide feedback to the raters. Rather, they urge that rater training programs should concentrate on such matters as: enhancing the accuracy of ratings through discussion of the multidimensionality of work performance; recording objectively what is seen; developing specific examples of effective and ineffective performance; and emphasizing rating in terms of actual job requirements. They go on to describe a workshop type of training program that involves, in part, a videotape of job candidates being evaluated by managers during an interview type of situation, followed by group discussions and brainstorming aimed at identifying specific practices that would minimize specific types of errors.

Administrative Aspects of Rating Programs

If an organization is going to embark on a personal evaluation or assessment program, a number of administrative aspects need to be considered. This is not the place to cover these in detail, but generally they would include: developing rating materials and instructions; determining which individuals are to be rated; designating raters; publicizing the program; scheduling training programs for the raters; scheduling the actual ratings; providing for the collection and recording of the ratings (and in some instances the derivation of summary ratings from ratings on specific rating factors); and compiling and analyzing ratings (such as for different raters, organizational units, jobs, etc.). The results of the ratings can then be used for whatever purposes the organization wants. In some instances this may include arrangements for feedback to the ratees from their supervisors. (Feedback of ratings is discussed in Chapter 13, *Careers.*)

DISCUSSION

The critical ingredient in a personnel-rating program is the rater, whose judgments serve as the basis for the ratings. Thus, it is important that the raters understand the purposes of the rating program and that they be committed to it. In addition they should be thoroughly familiar with the rating scale to be used and with how it is to be used. In this regard there is no rating scale that can compensate for incompetent or untrained raters. However, an appropriate, well-designed rating system can indeed facilitate the process of eliciting satisfactory ratings from competent raters.

The most typical use of rating systems provides for evaluating performance on the present jobs of incumbents. For such a purpose a rating system should insure that the ratings are specifically relevant to the job(s) in question. If one can afford the luxury of developing a separate system for each job, one of the recently developed types of scales might well be considered; these include behaviorally anchored rating scales (BARS), behavioral-observation scales (BOS), and mixed-standard scales (MSS). These methods have the potential advantage of providing for the rating of performance in terms of specific job-related behaviors. If a rating system is to be used for groups of jobs (instead of for individual jobs), the three primary considerations are: (1) grouping the jobs into relatively homogeneous categories; (2) rating the jobs in each group on factors that are relevant for the jobs in each category; and (3) selecting or developing a rating method that is appropriate for eliciting ratings on the factors in question. In certain circumstances it may be possible to use such methods as BARS, BOS, and MSS for this purpose, if they are specifically developed for the rating factors and jobs in question.

REFERENCES

Barrett, R. S. (1966). *Performance rating.* Chicago: Chicago Science Research Associates.

Bartlett, C. J. (1983). What's the difference between valid and invalid halo? Forced-choice measurement without forcing a choice. *Journal of Applied Psychology, 68*(2), 218–226.

Bernardin, H. J. & Pence, E. C. (1980). Effects of rater training: Creating new response sets and decreasing accuracy. *Journal of Applied Psychology, 65*(1), 60–66.

Bernardin, H. J., & Smith, P. C. (1981). A clarification of some issues regarding the development and use of behaviorally anchored rating scales (BARS). *Journal of Applied Psychology, 66*(4), 458–463.

Blanz, F., & Ghiselli, E. E. (1972). The mixed standard scale: A new rating system. *Personnel Psychology 25*, 185–199.

Borman, W. C. (1979). Format and training effects on rating accuracy and rater errors. *Journal of Applied Psychology, 64*(4), 410–421.

Carroll, S. J., & Schneier, C. E. (1982). *Performance appraisal and review systems.* Glenview, Ill.: Scott, Foresman.

Cornelius, E. T., III, Hakel, M. D., & Sackett, P. R. (1979). A methodological approach to job classification for performance appraisal purposes. *Personnel Psychology, 12*(2), 283–287.

DeCotiis, T. A. (1977), An analysis of the external validity and applied relevance of three rating formats. *Organizational Behavior and Human Performance, 19*(2), 247–266.

Dickinson, A. M. (1977). *Development of a systematic procedure for the evaluation of employees: Job performance based on a standard job analysis questionnaire.* Master's thesis, Fairleigh Dickinson University, Madison, New Jersey.

Fay, C. H., & Latham, G. P. (1982). Effects of training and rating scales on rating errors. *Journal of Applied Psychology, 35*(1), 105–116.

Flanagan, J. C. (1954). The cricital incident technique. *Psychological Bulletin, 51,* 327–358.

Goodale, J. G., & Burke, R. J. (1975). Behaviorally based rating scales need not be job specific. *Journal of Applied Psychology, 60,*(3), 389–391.

Harvey, R. J. (1982). The future of partial correlation as a means to reduce halo in performance ratings. *Journal of Applied Psychology, 67*(2), 171–176.

Hulin, C. L. (1982). Some reflections on general performance dimensions and halo rating error. *Journal of Applied Psychology, 67*(2) 165–170.

Ilgen, D. R., & Feldman, J. M. (1983). Performance appraisal: A process focus. *Research in Organizational Behavior, 5,* 141–197.

Jacobs, R., Kafry, D., & Zedeck, S. (1980). Expectations of behaviorally anchored rating scales. *Personnel Psychology, 33*(3), 595–640.

Kingstrom, P. O., & Bass, A. R. (1981). A critical analysis of studies comparing behaviorally anchored rating scales (BARS) and other rating formats. *Personnel Psychology, 34*(2), 263–289.

Klores, M. S. (1966). Rater bias in forced-distribution performance ratings. *Personnel Psychology, 4,* 411–421.

Landy, F. J., Vance, R. J., & Barnes-Farrell, J. L. (1982). Statistical control of halo: A response. *Journal of Applied Psychology, 67*(2), 177–180.

Landy, F. J., Vance, R. J., Barnes-Farrell, J. L., & Steele, J. W. (1980). Statistical control of halo error in performance ratings. *Journal of Applied Psychology, 65*(5), 501–506.

Latham, G. P., & Wexley, K. M. (1977). Behavioral observation scales for performance appraisal purposes. *Personnel Psychology, 30*(2), 255–268.

Latham, G. P., & Wexley, K. N. (1981). *Increasing productivity through performance appraisal.* Reading, Mass.: Addison-Wesley.

McCormick, E. J., & Bachus, J. A. (1952). Paired comparison ratings: I. The effect on ratings of reductions in the number of pairs. *Journal of Applied Psychology, 36,* 123–127.

Murphy, K. R. (1982). Difficulties in the statistical control of halo. *Journal of Applied Psychology, 67*(2), 161–164.

Pearlman, K. (1980). Job families: A review and discussion of their implications for personnel selection. *Psychological Bulletin, 87*(1), 1–28.

Peter, L. J. (1969). *The Peter principle*. New York: William Morrow.

Rhode, R. H. (undated). *Development of the retail checklist performance evaluation program*. Chicago: Sears, Roebuck.

Rosinger, G., Myers, L. B., Levy, G. W., Loar, M., Mohrman, S. A., & Stock, J. R. (1982). Development of a behaviorally based performance appraisal system. *Personnel Psychology, 35*(1), 75–88.

Saal, F. E. (1979). Mixed standard rating scale: A consistent system for numerically coding inconsistent response categories. *Journal of Applied Psychology, 64*(4), 422–428.

Sackett, P. R., Cornelius, E. T., III, & Carron, T. J. (1981). A comparison of global judgment in task oriented approaches to job classification. *Personnel Psychology, 34*(4), 791–804.

Schmitt, N., & Lappin, M. (1980). Race and sex as determinants of the mean and variance of performance ratings. *Journal of Applied Psychology, 65*(4), 428–435.

Smith, P. C., & Kendall, L. M. (1963). Retransla-tion of expectations: An approach to the construction of unambiguous anchors for rating scales. *Journal of Applied Psychology, 47*(2), 149–155.

Terborg, J. R., & Ilgen, D. R. (1975). A theoretical approach to sex discrimination in traditionally masculine occupations. *Organizational Behavior and Human Performances, 13*, 352–376.

Vineberg, R., & Taylor, E. N. (1976). *Performance of men in different mental categories: 1. Development of worker-oriented and job-oriented rating instruments in Navy jobs*. Alexandria, Va.: Human Resources Research Organization.

Wendelken, D. J., & Inn. A. (1981). Nonperformance influences on performance evaluations: A laboratory phenomenon. *Journal of Applied Psychology, 66*(2), 149–158.

Wherry, R. J., & Bartlett, C. J. (1982). The control of bias in ratings: A theory of rating. *Personnel Psychology, 35*, 521–551.

7

Staffing Organizations: Selection and Placement

The discussion of job analyses in Chapter 4 described procedures for determining *what* people do on their jobs: the discussion of performance appraisal in Chapter 5 dealt with *how well* these jobs are done. Although these are important issues in the effective use of human beings in organizations, one critical element is missing: *Who* should do the work on any particular job? In this and the following four chapters we devote considerable time to the issues directly related to matching individuals with jobs in organizational contexts. This matching process is typically labeled selection and placement. *Selection* refers to the specific condition of an organization's having some number of positions to be filled and at least one more individual to fill them than there are positions (Cronbach & Gleser, 1965). Also, the persons applying for the jobs are, at the time, not employees of the organization. *Placement,* on the other hand, refers to the situation in which there are at least two positions and there are the same number of

candidates for the positions as there are positions to be filled (Cronbach & Gleser, 1965); everyone is sorted into a position and no one is left without a position. Typically, the placement process occurs after hiring and is a continually ongoing process as current employees are transferred to openings throughout the organization when old jobs become open and new positions are created.

MATCHING ASSUMPTIONS

Beneficial for All Concerned

Underlying the use of selection and placement practices is the assumption that a good match between the nature of the job and the personal characteristics of the jobholder is to the benefit of both the organization and the person. From the organization's standpoint, the job should be performed more effectively if the person holding the position in question possesses the skills and abilities to accomplish the task and also finds the job compatible with his or her interests and needs. Likewise for the individual; if the job is compatible with the person's skills, abilities, and needs, the person should find the quality of working life on that job higher than on one for which there is not a good match between personal characteristics and job demands.

Stability of Job and Person Characteristics

A second assumption underlying the use of selection and placement is that the set of jobs and their respective requirements are relatively stable over time. Similarly, it is assumed that individual characteristics are relatively stable. The "relative" part of the last two statements means that it is well recognized that the nature of jobs do change and so do people. However, these changes are not so rapid as to create total instability in either work settings or people.

Available Labor Pool

The final assumption is less of an overall assumption than an operating strategy. When choosing to use selection and/or placement to achieve a good match, the implicit assumption is that the match between person characteristics and job demands can best be achieved by locating people to put into jobs as the jobs currently exist. Selection and placement attempt to create good matches by treating the job as fixed and people as pretty much constant in terms of the characteristics they bring to the job. Both strategies then attempt to find the right people for the job.

There are, of course, other strategies that could be considered to create the match. For example, characteristics of people could be treated as fixed and jobs could be changed to fit their characteristics. This is done in job design; the nature of the tasks and equipment

is fit to the characteristics of the people who are most likely to hold the job. Another strategy is that of training; for it, the job requirements are treated as fixed and people as changeable. Training builds into people the skills needed to accomplish the job. Clearly, none of these strategies is reasonable to the exclusion of the others; each one is preferred for some types of conditions.

INTERNAL AND EXTERNAL DEMANDS

Internal

The primary determination of what is needed with respect to the selection and placement of personnel in an organization comes from the needs of the organization for staff members. These needs are assessed by considering both the present staff in terms of the extent to which they are able to perform their jobs effectively and by anticipating future needs. The process of attempting to take into account both the present and future needs is termed *Human-Resource Planning* (HRP). Within the organization itself, as it presently exists, HRP relies heavily upon information gained from job analyses about the nature of jobs and their requirements for individuals as well. HRP also uses performance appraisals for information about how well current employees are performing their jobs. We deal with HRP in more detail in the following section.

External

In addition to the internal needs of the organization, external demands also affect staffing decisions. Many of these deal with the nature of the labor supply available to the organization. For example, the decision whether to select skilled workers for a particular job or to train them will depend, in part, upon the extent to which people with such skills exist in the pool of people from which job applicants are obtained. If no qualified persons are available, it may be necessary to train people for the job rather than to use selection to fill the position. The other external demand placed on organizations is that of society's beliefs about the proper treatment of personnel. These beliefs are translated into laws that regulate organizational practices with respect to the hiring, firing, and promoting of individuals. The most significant set of legal requirements involves issues related to the treatment of minority group members, women, and older workers. Clearly, it is not sufficient for an organization to look only at its internal demands and ignore the societal needs for fair employment opportunities for people regardless of race, sex, religion, age, or national origin. Since the legal responsibilities of organizations play a major part in the conduct of personnel practices relevant to selection and placement, we devote considerable space to these issues in the latter part of this chapter.

Systems Perspective

Due to the need to consider multiple requirements both within and outside the organization when addressing issues of selection and placement, these two processes are best seen from a *systems perspective*. A systems perspective stresses that there are multiple influences on any part of the system and that it is not possible to focus entirely within any one function. A change in one part of the system will impact on all others. Thus, no one can afford to focus entirely upon internal organizational demands or to let the external demands so tie up the selection and placement processes as to disturb the internal functioning of the organization such that the organization can no longer function competitively in its own field. Keeping this in mind, we now turn to specific concerns that set the stage for

effective use of selection and placement in organizations.

HUMAN-RESOURCE PLANNING

Needs Analysis

The starting point for any attempt to select new employees or to relocate present employees within an organization is to assess the present employment situation. This requires a thorough understanding of the nature of all the different jobs within the organization and an assessment of the level of performance of current employees on these jobs. These are best accomplished with good job-analysis practices and performance appraisals, both of which were described in earlier chapters.

At the simplest level, with only knowledge about the nature of the job and about performance levels in that job, it is possible to develop selection procedures for filling openings that exist in a particular job and then to develop practices to make such selections. However, responding only to present needs as they arise is likely to be limiting in the long run. Such practices fail to anticipate future changes in jobs and/or in the labor-force composition. For example, technological changes in many industries are shifting production staffing needs from heavily labor-intensive conditions with manual skill requirements but little technical knowledge to conditions that require more technical skills and demand knowledge about maintenance and monitoring of very sophisticated machinery. This fact, coupled with the fact that it is always painful to release present employees when their jobs are replaced by other jobs, argues strongly for selection strategies for filling present jobs that emphasize the flexibility to change to the anticipated demands of future jobs. Thus, a needs analysis goes beyond the initial step of describing the present situation by making some assumptions about anticipated future states and then choosing a course of action for the present that appears to be best for meeting present *and* future needs.

The aspect of HRP that addresses the future-oriented part of a needs analysis is labeled *needs forecasting* by Walker (1980) and others. Figure 7.1 displays an overall view of the elements that Walker considered in needs forecasting. Note two characteristics of this analysis: First, note that conditions external to the organization are addressed, because human resources have to be supplied by the society and more specifically the community in which the organization operates. Next, note that within the organization, factors that influence future needs are clustered into those conditions that establish the needs (requirements) and those that are created by the work force as it exists now and is anticipated to exist based on knowledge about the flow of people into and out of positions within the organization. All of these factors lead to a forecast that establishes guidelines for pres-

ent practices with respect to hiring, layoffs, transfers, training, and long-term career development.

Computer Models

Significant strides have been made recently in computerizing personnel data (Niehaus, 1979). The effect of this is twofold. First it means that it is now possible to have large amounts of data available on many aspects of the personnel function. These data can then be used to better describe the nature of the work force and to analyze the effects of past policies and practices on issues relevant to staffing. This allows not only for looking at particular conditions but also for plotting data over time and analyzing trends. Thus, a large corporation can study the extent to which it has been able to attract women to positions that had previously been reserved primarily for men and can check to see which jobs, divisions, or offices have been able to show the greatest change in composition by sex over

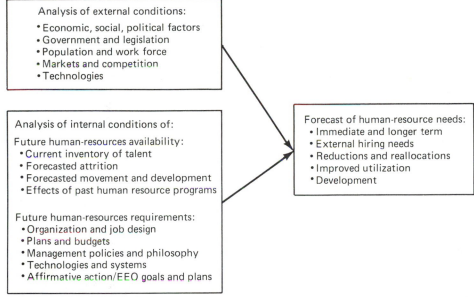

FIGURE 7.1 Needs forecasting: A necessary process in Human-Resource Planning. (Adapted from Walker, 1980.)

the last 5 years. Prior to the existence of computerized personnel data bases such analyses were possible but terribly time-consuming. Today they are much easier, and therefore allow us to study the personnel process in much more detail.

The second major impact of computer-based personnel systems is their use in conjunction with computerized forecasting models (Niehaus, 1979). These models are sophisticated computer programs that use information gained from past personnel conditions along with assumptions about the nature of future conditions to make forecasts or predictions about future states. These predictions, of course, are no better than the assumptions on which they are based, and, like any assumptions, the assumptions may be wrong. Nevertheless, they do allow for the generation of some very useful information about possible future conditions.

Ironically, most of these computer-based forecasting models are not in the public domain. They have been developed by personnel specialists, systems analysts, and management science personnel within particular corporations to model the flow of personnel through their own organizations, taking into account their own unique needs and requirements. Few systems have received use across a large number of organizations. There are, however, some such systems being developed by consulting firms. One of them is "Journey," developed by Personnel Technology, Inc. (Hawkins, 1983). The system simulates the flow of people into, through, and out of an organizational hierarchy. Assumptions about promotions, transfers, losses, recruitment, growth, and the organization's structure can be made and fed into the Journey model. The model then yields estimates of future salary costs, the costs of recruiting, selection, and transfers, the number and nature of employees that will be needed, and so on. By changing the assumptions, one can play the "what if . . ." game and get estimates of

the effects of certain kinds of conditions or changes on the variables of interest. Although only time will tell how effective these computer models are, it is likely that they will be playing a larger and larger role in HRP in the next few years.

EMPLOYMENT PRACTICES AND THE LAW

As we have already seen, one of the most prevailing external influences on personnel selection and placement is the societal demand for equal access to jobs regardless of race, sex, age, religion, or national origin. In the United States, increasing attention has been paid to the fact that employment in many occupations is not proportionately representative of the number of persons in various subgroups (sexual, racial, or ethnic minority groups, for example). The employees in certain occupations are either predominantly males or females. And, in certain occupations, there are disproportionate numbers of whites or blacks, or members of other groups. This unequal distribution of subgroups to jobs is problematic particularly because lower-level jobs in both status and pay tend to have a greater proportion of minority-group members and women whereas the reverse tends to be true for higher-level jobs.

Such disproportionate representation in some occupations and/or organizations has served as a basis for charges of unfair discrimination in employment. Undoubtedly, in several cases, racial, ethnic, and sexual biases did lead to employment practices that were intentionally discriminatory against certain subgroups. However, in many cases, unequal distribution of jobs across subgroups was either due to unintentional discrimination and/or to a complex mixture of causes. For example, word-of-mouth recruiting in organizations originally employing primarily white males unintentionally excluded minority group members. In other cases, the proportions of subgroup members were affected by cultural and other preference patterns. Women tend to enter the field of nursing more than men whereas the reverse is true for logging. It has been argued that these distributions are due, in part, to discrimination and adaptation to such discrimination. For example, it is likely that some women attracted to a career in medicine gravitated toward nursing rather than toward becoming medical doctors because they believed that they had little chance to become doctors. Indirect evidence to support this conclusion is that as medical schools have attempted to attract more women, the number of women has increased. Although opportunities for women to become doctors may have restricted their entry into this field, such an interpretation is less likely for logging. In the latter case, attempts to attract women to jobs as loggers have not met with much success. This implies that preferences, cultural patterns, or a number of other factors other than discrimination against women tend to maintain unequal distributions of men and women in logging.

In the United States by the early 1960s public concern over apparent discrimination against minority group members and women had grown. This culminated in a series of legislative and executive actions and court decisions designed to ensure equal employment opportunity for all. These actions of the 1960s and 1970s have affected all aspects of employment from recruiting, screening, and selecting employees, to placement, evaluation, training, compensation, and promotion. The impact of these actions has been such that, in less than 15 years, legal issues have become a dominant concern of personnel management.

In the remainder of this chapter, we first address the legal developments in the United States which have shaped recent employment practices with respect to subgroup mem-

bers. We attempt not only to describe the laws and court decisions which have evolved but also to place these in perspective by describing the social ends they were designed to attain. We then turn our attention to the impact of the laws upon personnel practices in organizations.

LEGAL CONSIDERATIONS

General Positions and Assumptions

In the United States two major foci guided development and implementation of public policy designed to insure the development of fair employment practices. First and foremost was a desire to protect any individual minority group member or woman from unfair discriminatory practices. This led to descriptions of what constituted fair treatment and to the development of procedures to follow for those who believed they were unjustly treated. If these individuals were judged to be correct, various actions against the offending organization could be taken. The assumption underlying these actions was that if the legal framework protected each member of the groups in question, then the societal goal of an equal right to jobs for all individuals who were qualified for the jobs would be met.

A second, less-explicit aim was to right past wrongs to minority groups and women in regard to employment. This concern was directed toward groups as a whole rather than toward individuals. Starting from the observation that there exist differential distributions of subgroup members in job categories and/or organizations, it was often assumed that these unequal distributions were due to past or present discriminatory practices (regardless of whether they were intentional or unintentional). The assumption that this condition represented unfair discrimination against the group in question led to attempts to insure that the ratio of the number of subgroup members to the number of white males on the job (or in the organization) in question was approximately equal to the ratio of these groups in the appropriate comparison population. In many instances, the appropriate population is considered to be the group of potential employees in the locale who could reasonably be expected to consider employment at the organization under consideration.

Regardless of the causes of disproportionate representation in some occupations, the efforts to establish policies to correct for presumed injustice to the group or groups in question have led to many gains for minority groups and women over the last two decades in the United States. However, efforts to equalize employment in various occupations on an across-the-board basis have had at least two major drawbacks when attempts were made to implement them. First, as we have already indicated, disproportionate representation arises for many reasons. In some cases, subgroup members may prefer to be underrepresented in a given career or job. Clearly women are not clamoring to be loggers, even though the opportunity is there. Second, although the concern for minorities and women both at the individual and the group levels led to legislative and court actions to establish equal employment opportunity, these actions have also had to be compatible with constitutional guarantees for *all* individuals. In theory, the individual and group aims are compatible with all individuals' rights. In practice, the government's decisions and policies and the organizations' responses as they focus on minority groups and women may actually deny majority groups' rights, also guaranteed (see *University of California Regents v. Bakke*, 1978).

Accompanying the belief in individual rights is the general acceptance that our society needs strong, healthy organizations in which the goods and services of the society are produced. To maintain this strength, it is assumed that organizations must be able to evaluate the qualifications of applicants and employees and to judge who will be hired, promoted, or placed on jobs.

With this assumption, along with the issue of individual rights, it is obvious that there will be some conflicts and that there will have to be compromises in order to meet all these requirements. One can only conclude that it is not easy to accomplish social goals through public policy. If one realizes that there are two overall goals (protect individuals and right past wrongs) and that the guarantee of individual rights and organizational needs for survival may conflict with these, in practice if not in theory, then it is easier to understand the recent problems in personnel management. As public policy and organizational practices have evolved, often in an atmosphere of confrontation, it has been difficult for organizations to reach the goal of equal employment opportunity for all individuals in organizations and at the same time to remain competitive by selecting, training, and promoting competent employees.

Legal Bases for Nondiscrimination

An overview of the legal process in the United States is beyond the scope of this book, but four areas of jurisdiction are particularly important to the requirement for nondiscriminatory actions by organizations. Each of these is discussed with descriptions of the laws, orders, or decisions of that group which affect personnel practice.

Federal legislative branch. The legislative branch of the U.S. government enacts statutes which are the laws of the land. For personnel decisions, Title VII of the Civil Rights Act of 1964, as amended by the Equal Employment Acts of 1972, is by far the most significant legislation. Other acts, such as post-Civil War legislation on civil rights, the Equal Pay Act of 1963, and the Age Discrimination in Employment Act of 1967 have helped define and clarify fair employment, but none has had the impact of Title VII.

The central tenet of Title VII as amended is its declaration that it is illegal for employers to discriminate on the basis of race, sex, religion, or national origin. It states:

It shall be an unlawful employment practice for an employer—

(1) to fail or refuse to hire or to discharge any individual or otherwise to discriminate against any individual with respect to his compensation, terms, conditions, or privileges of employment, because of such individual's race, color, religion, sex, or national origin; or

(2) to limit, segregate, or classify his employees or applicants for employment in any way which would deprive or tend to deprive any individual of employment opportunities or otherwise adversely affect his status as an employee because of such individual's race, color, religion, sex, or national origin.

Of most interest to us is the statement that employment may not be "designed, intended, or used" to discriminate against the five classes mentioned. In addition, the act describes some special conditions when race, color, sex, or national origin may be legitimate (for example, actors or actresses playing male or female parts) and addresses several other issues.

Similar statements outlawing discrimination apply to apprentice programs. The law affects private employers and labor organizations with fifteen or more employees (members), private employment agencies, and public organizations.

The second major tenet of Title VII is the establishment of the Equal Employment Opportunity Commission (EEOC), which in the EEO Act of 1972 was given considerable enforcement power. The commission is an independent regulatory agency which monitors compliance with Title VII by public and private employers and by labor organizations. It sets policy and determines whether there is reasonable cause to believe that discrimination has occurred in individual cases. These individual cases may either be brought to the commission by individuals or they may be initiated by the commission itself. By the mid-1970s the EEOC was processing approximately 70,000 such cases annually (Ash & Kroeker, 1975).

Federal executive branch. Presidential executive orders directed at the discriminatory behavior of government contractors and federal employers (Executive Orders 11246, 11478, 11375) duplicate many of the Title VII regulations. For contractors, the Office of Federal Contract Compliance (OFCC) was established in 1965 under the Department of Labor to handle discrimination issues (now the Office of Federal Contract Compliance Programs, OFCCP). Before the EEO Act of 1972, the OFCC had considerably more power than the EEOC because it could terminate or limit employers' contracts. Since approximately one-third of the labor force works for federal organizations or organizations having some form of government contracts, the OFCCP had considerable influence.

Almost all companies with government contracts are subject to both the EEOC and the OFCCP. They must comply with the executive orders (OFCCP) because of the contract and to Title VII (EEOC) simply because all national companies are subject to federal law. Given the number of organizations having government contracts, it should then come as no surprise that there was and is considerable pressure for the EEOC and the OFCCP to agree on practices related to fair employment. In 1978, there was a major step toward this goal when common guidelines, described later in this chapter, were accepted.

Fair employment practices. In the United States, Fair Employment Practice (FEP) statutes are state rather than federal laws and date back to 1945. Well over one-half of the states now have such laws. Although the laws vary from state to state, their existence is important with respect to the total response of the government to alleged discrimination. Where they exist, state FEP commissions are the offices to which employees bring their initial complaints, or to which the EEOC refers cases. These complaints are reviewed at the state level and then are either acted on or referred to the appropriate federal agency. If there are discrepancies between state and federal statues, the federal ones take precedence.

Judicial branch. The legislative and executive branches write laws and establish ways to enforce them, but the judicial branch interprets them and also determines how to enforce them. For issues of discrimination, the courts have interpreted the meaning and intent of Title VII and have specified actions to be taken for noncompliance with the law. Much current policy has come from court decisions and the process is continuing with new cases being added every day.

The role of the courts is best understood by considering an example. Assume that some group or individual feels that there has been discrimination by a private company with no federal contracts and that he or she wants to file a complaint. After the complaint is filed at a regional office of the EEOC, the EEOC refers the complaint to a state or local FEP commission, if it exists. The state agency may act or may refer the complaint back to the EEOC. If it does not act after 60 days, the EEOC can begin its own investigation. From the EEOC investigation, decisions are made on whether there has been an infraction and, if it appears that there has been, on what should be done about it. At this point, the most desirable conclusion is that the government, the company, and the one(s) who filed the complaint will agree on the conclusion, and the parties will voluntarily comply with the decision. If so, a mechanism for monitoring the compliance is established, and the case is closed. If either the one who filed the complaint or the company does not accept

the decision, the case will go to court. Assuming that the case is not settled out of court, an eventual decision is reached by some court. Although this decision is for the particular case, it also provides a precedent for later decisions. This means that it may be necessary to change some of the EEOC guidelines to incorporate these decisions. In this way, the courts are essential for evolving policy.

UNIFORM GUIDELINES

It was mentioned earlier that the EEOC and the OFCCP were established to set policy and to enforce laws or executive orders. Policies are prescribed by each agency as well as by the U.S. Office of Personnel Management guidelines developed by each agency. In 1972, in order to decrease confusion caused by each agency having its own guidelines, efforts were initiated to develop a single set of guidelines. After much deliberation, the most recent Uniform Guidelines on Employee Selection Procedures were accepted in mid-1978 (Equal Employment Coordinating Council, 1978). These guidelines supercede all previous guidelines for employee selection and generally incorporate court decisions, previous guidelines, practical experience of the agencies, and test standards of the American Psychological Association. For the near future, the Uniform Guidelines will be the standards for fair employment. Remember, however, that these are only guidelines and do not have the force of law. Also, as we have seen, decisions by the courts can always lead to modifications of these guidelines. In practice, however, the courts have given considerable weight to the guidelines.

FAIR EMPLOYMENT ISSUES

In the United States, through the interaction of the federal legislative and executive branches, state FEP acts, and the courts, fair employment practices have evolved. Although the overriding desire is to create conditions of equal employment opportunity for all, progress has been spotty. Often court decisions are made, policy is established, and laws are written by those who have had little direct experience with personnel practices. At other times, the issues are so complex that no firm solutions can be accepted by everyone. The result is that a whole set of issues and terms pertaining to fair employment have been born that were certainly not central to personnel practices before 1964. The most important ones are discussed next.

Adverse Impact

Adverse impact refers to the effects of employment practices on members of groups protected by Title VII. The Uniform Guidelines state:

The use of any selection procedure which has an adverse impact on the hiring, promotion or other employment or membership opportunities of any racial, ethnic, or sex group will be considered discriminatory and inconsistent with these guidelines, unless the procedure has been validated in accordance with the guidelines. . . . (Sec 3.A of the Uniform Guidelines, *Federal Register,* August 25, 1978, p. 38297, by the Equal Employment Coordinating Council)

A selection rate for any race, sex, or ethnic group which is less than four-fifths (4/5) (or eighty percent) of the rate of the group with the highest rate will generally be regarded by the Federal enforcement agencies as evidence for adverse impact. Smaller differences in selection may nevertheless constitute adverse impact, where they are significant in both statistical and practical terms or where a user's actions have discouraged applicants disproportionately on grounds of race, sex, or ethnic group. Greater differences in selection rate may not constitute adverse impact where the differences are based on small numbers and are not statistically significant, or where special recruiting or other programs cause the pool of minority or female candidates to be atypical of the normal pool of applicants from the group. . . . (Sec. 4.D of the Uniform Guidelines, *Federal Register,* August 25, 1978, 38297–38298 by the Equal Employment Coordinating Council)

The Uniform Guidelines demonstrate that regulatory agencies seldom question selection procedures unless adverse effects on protected groups are suspected. This means that organizations may use procedures with little or no validity as long as there is no adverse effect. Guion (1976) best described this as follows: ". . . organizations have the right even to be fairly stupid in their employment practices as long as they are stupid fairly" (p. 818). It also explains why, in the short run, organizations fearful of litigation may turn to a quota-dominated selection procedure even though firm quotas are illegal (*University of California Regents* v. *Bakke,* 1978) and they limit the organization's options in selection decisions.

The "eighty percent" definition of adverse impact is new to the Uniform Guidelines. Previously, it had been left undefined. It should be noted that the exceptions listed to the "eighty percent" rule simply recognize that there may be extenuating circumstances making it an unreasonable standard. For example, without one of the exceptions, efforts to recruit more minority members would increase the denominator of the selection ratio and increase the probability of adverse impact. This, in turn, should decrease the incentive to recruit minorities actively—an effect obviously not desired by those who developed the guidelines. Therefore, several exceptions are listed. The extent to which exceptions will be tolerated in practice remains to be seen as the EEOC interprets and applies the guidelines and the courts react to these interpretations.

Testing

The use of tests for making hiring and promotion decisions has become one of the most troublesome issues of Title VII (Miner & Miner 1978).[1] Testing is another issue on

[1]By test we mean any standardized sample of behavior collected under standardized conditions, scored, and quantified.

which most people agree in principle, but on which many disagree in practice. Title VII as amended accepts the use of tests as legitimate when the tests are related to performance on the job. Several Supreme Court decisions have also been made which explicitly deal with tests (such as *Griggs* v. *Duke Power Company* [1971], *Albemarle Paper Company* v. *Moody* [1975], and *Washington* v. *Davis* [1976].) Although the latter cases place many restrictions on the test-to-performance relationship and the performance measure used, none denies that tests can be used or that they can be useful.

Job analysis. On the use of tests, government policy and psychologists agree that the essential first step is a job analysis. The job analysis is necessary (1) to define the kind of test to be used; and (2) to decide how to judge the adequacy of criteria in a predictive validity study. The latter is critical from the psychologists' standpoint of developing good criteria. It is even more important as judges with limited experience in test validation must decide whether the criteria used are valid measures of job performance.

Validity. The Uniform Guidelines specifically state that tests or other selection procedures may rely upon three methods of validation: criterion-related, content, and construct validity. In most cases criterion-related validity refers to predictive validity. Although these forms of validity are not described in detail until the next chapter, the remainder of the discussion here demonstrates that considerable complexity exists with respect to the validity of tests.

Without question, predictive validity, if feasible, is the preferred form of test validation. Government policy is difficult to understand, however, on several issues. One is the size of the validity coefficient. Psychologists have recognized for years that the usefulness of a test for making personnel decisions is directly related to the size of the validity coefficient, but that the *absolute* value

of the coefficient depends upon the importance of the decision (Cronbach & Gleser, 1965). For example, a low validity coefficient (e.g., .25) might be quite useful if it improves our ability to identify the best candidates on extremely important jobs when other procedures cannot identify such people at all. On the other hand, such a low coefficient would be of no value on a simple job when most people selected without tests could handle the job. In spite of this fact, government policy tends to use a specific number on rather doubtful bases. At one time this was .30 or greater. Fortunately, more flexibility is beginning to be recognized as necessary.

A second issue is that government policy states that the criteria predicted by the test must be valid, job-related measures, but the judgment of whether criteria meet this requirement is very subjective. As a result, the judgment must often be made on a case-by-case basis, which can be very frustrating for those trying to meet a changing standard.

Issues of content and construct validity primarily concern the subjective judgment of the extent to which each is present. Unlike predictive validity, the techniques are less accepted for these two forms. Recently, psychologists have made some progress in specifying more precisely the nature of content validity (see Guion, 1978; Lawshe, 1976; Tenopyr, 1977), but construct validity still remains equivocal. As a result, when judges, lawyers, government officials, and psychologists address a particular case, it is not surprising that they often disagree.

Linn (1978) raised another validity issue. He correctly stated that the emphasis on criterion-related validity has placed too great an emphasis upon the validity coefficient. We have already mentioned the need to consider the importance of the decision. We shall see in the next section that decisions on the presence or absence of discrimination depend on much more than the validity coefficient itself.

Although reasonable persons who are conscientiously trying to make a correct decision are bound to disagree at times, it is no wonder that there are conflicts in test validation. It is obvious from our description that, despite which form of validity is used, there are several subjective decisions that must be made. There are many opportunities for disagreement. When the stakes are as high as they are both for the individuals (loss of jobs, back pay, etc.) and for the organizations (settlements frequently cost thousands or millions of dollars), it is not surprising that the situation creates considerable anxiety.

In part because of these uncertainties, many organizations have stopped using standardized tests (Miner & Miner 1978). If this is done, two options are available. The first is to use some other source of information about job candidates. This has two drawbacks. First, all alternative methods are required to meet the same standards as tests. Yet, past research indicates that it is extremely unlikely that most alternatives will be as valid as the tests. The second option is to relinquish the organization's right to make decisions, by adopting a strategy that ensures the absence of adverse impact. Such a strategy concentrates almost exclusively upon keeping the proportions of subgroups in line to avoid adverse impact by using relatively rigid quotas. Although there may be short-term gains for this, in the long run it is not wise.

Unfair discrimination. To many readers the subtitle, "unfair discrimination," may seem redundant. The fact that it is not has been one of the major problems related to testing.

Any effective predictor of job performance or behavior must discriminate in a *statistical* sense (Guion 1976). If the predictor is to be useful, it must be able to identify those who are likely to be successful and those who are likely not to be. To those concerned with testing, this means that the predictor must

discriminate among those for whom predictor scores are available. For example, a test designed to measure color blindness must discriminate between those who are color-blind and those who are not. The test discriminates fairly if the differences between the groups defined by it (color-blind and normal color vision) are not caused by irrelevant factors associated with subgroup membership. Consider the case of the individual's sex and the color blindness test. If the color blindness test discriminates fairly, it should sort males and females into two groups—color-blind and normal color vision—regardless of the individual's sex. The test might discriminate unfairly if it used the technique of hiding colored numbers in a series of dots and if men were more likely to see numbers in the hidden figures than women were. In this case the "score" on the test would differ across sex groups for reasons totally unrelated to color blindness. The fact that the test will identify more men as color blind than women obviously does not mean that the test discriminates unfairly. It is well known that color blindness is a sex-linked characteristic which appears much more frequently among men than women. A fair test of color blindness should find many more color blind males than females.

Although to those familiar with testing, discrimination is a neutral term, to lay persons and to judges it is not. In a legal sense, to discriminate automatically implies unfairness (Guion 1976). Therefore, a major stumbling block in interpreting court cases and developing strategies of implementation is language. We use unfair discrimination as we have defined it, but we appreciate the fact that often "discrimination" is interpreted as *unfair* discrimination.

At a more technical level, the definition of unfair discrimination is not clear. This creates a second major problem for fair testing. Scholars have offered several different definitions of unfair discrimination, all of which seem reasonable at first glance, but many of which have very different implications. In spite of the intuitive appeal of all of these definitions, their application has proven difficult. When the definitions are quantified through the application of measurement and statistical procedures appropriate to each, major differences result between them. These differences can lead to personnel decision strategies that result in the selection of a subset of minority group members in one case and the rejection of these same individuals in another. The selection or rejection of some of the individuals will depend, in part, upon the assumptions of the definition of fairness that is used.

Fortunately, the Uniform Guidelines on Employee Selection Procedures recognizes that there is no specific definition of test fairness that is acceptable to all test experts or in all situations. In the guidelines, test fairness is described as a "developing concept" that is not firmly delineated at the present time. With this recognition, it is possible to apply reasonable procedures to meet relatively well-accepted criteria for fairness without having to demonstrate that the procedure is fair according to every possible definition.

Differential validity. Concern about differential validity arose out of a commonly held belief that standardized tests unfairly discriminated against minority group members. It was assumed that tests either were predictive for majority group members but not for minority group members, or that they predicted each group's performance but in a different way. In the first case, if the test were used with minority group members, it would be unfair because the test simply did not relate to performance for them. In the second case, decisions using the test could be made if different cut-off scores were used for each group. In either case, majority and minority group members should not be treated the same; different decision rules were needed for each group.

Differential validity exists when the valid-

ity coefficient for one subgroup differs significantly from that for another (Humpreys, 1973). In most cases in which differential validity exists, decisions based upon predictors which do not take into account group membership will produce unfair discrimination against members of one of the groups. The intuitive appeal of the belief that groups probably differ in their validities led the EEOC to state in their 1970 guidelines that, when feasible, organizations should validate their selection procedures for subgroups as well as for the whole group.

After a thoughtful analysis of differential validity, Linn (1978) concluded that to focus solely upon differences in validity coefficients is a mistake. He concurred with Bobko and Bartlett (1978) who stated that the real interest should be upon the differences in prediction systems between groups. That is, we should look at a number of different things which could differ when we try to predict performance from tests or other predictors. (For a discussion of the specific factors on which differences might exist, see Linn [1978]. Most of these are of a statistical nature beyond the scope of the present text.) Although we agree with this conclusion, we hasten to add that there is no reason to suspect that the direction of errors in predictive systems will be any different than it was for validity coefficients. Minority group members more than likely are being overpredicted as frequently as underpredicted.

By now sufficient data are in to reach two conclusions. First, differential validity is far less common than was originally assumed (Schmidt, 1977). Second, when differential validity does exist, the direction of the differences is such that the selection system is detrimental to the majority group approximately as often as it is to minority groups. Therefore, the failure in the past to carry out differential validity studies should have had little impact upon denying minority group members equal access to jobs.

We can only conclude from the extensive

research on differential validity that it is a much less common phenomenon than originally expected by most people. When it does exist, its effects are beneficial to minority group members as frequently as they are detrimental. As a result of currently available data, the latest version of the Uniform Guidelines is less adamant about the need of employers to do differential validity studies than was the 1970 form of the EEOC guidelines. In fact, some individuals (Schmidt, 1977) are questioning the utility of searching for differences in the face of what has been demonstrated by the research.

Technical feasibility. With regard to criterion-related validity, the Uniform Guidelines often refer to actions that employers should take where "technically feasible." Technical feasibility is defined as, ". . . conditions permitting the conduct of meaningful criterion-related validity studies." (See 16.V of the Uniform Guidelines, *Federal Register*, August 25, 1978, p. 38308 by the Equal Employment Coordinating Council.) Conditions mentioned specifically as influencing technical feasibility are: (1) adequate samples; (2) sufficient ranges of scores on predictors and criteria; and (3) unbiased, reliable, and relevant measures of job performance or other criteria of employee adequacy.

All three dimensions of technical feasibility involve some degree of subjectivity among professionals as to what is or is not sufficient. However, the issue of sample size has come under particular scrutiny in recent years. Schmidt, Hunter, and Pearlman (1982), focusing upon the statistical power of tests to detect differences in criterion scores, concluded that personnel psychologists have severely underestimated the size of the samples that were needed for meaningful criterion-related validity research. They point out that, in general, it has been assumed that samples of from thirty to fifty are adequate for criterion-related research. Schmidt and others show that this is a rather severe underestimate of the number needed for the research,

and they provide tables to guide researchers in the selection of an adequate sample size. In the past, technical feasibility has been overestimated. The impact of this conclusion on future action is not clear at this time, but it should lead to a restriction in the number of situations in which criterion-related validity can be used and an expansion in the use of less direct and more inferential validation procedures such as content, construct, and job-component validation. This position is strongly advocated by Schmidt and Hunter (1980), who question the future of criterion-related validity in the traditional form.

Business necessity. The Uniform Guidelines recognize that, at times, the use of race, sex, color, religion, or national origin for selection may lead to adverse impact but that it may also be a requirement of the job. For example, it is legitimate to specify the sex and perhaps the race of applicants for a specific part in a play. Nevertheless, the government agencies and the courts have tended to define business necessity very narrowly. It is not legitimate to argue a business necessity on the basis of customer demands or on the decision that certain groups of individuals will fit better into an organization.

Secure testing. Ethical standards for psychologists have long stressed the need to keep scores on tests secure. Only those who need to know the scores and who are qualified to interpret the scores correctly should be given the scores on tests. Furthermore, if the test is a standardized one that will be used in the future by job applicants, the exams should be carefully protected.

In a landmark case, *Detroit Edison v. NLRB*, the need for secure tests was challenged (Sparks, 1980). Local union 223 of the Utility Workers of America protested the selection of six employees for a position of Instrument Repairman at Detroit Edison. The position was advertised both within and outside the company. The decision was challenged by union members who were current employees of the company. Selection for the position was based, in part, upon the Instrumentman Aptitude Test Battery. When several current employees failed to be selected for the position, the union argued that the union should have the right to copies of the aptitude test, item sheets for the test, and employees' scores. The company argued they should not. The company position was that to reveal such information without the consent of all who took the tests would be unethical, and, furthermore, to release all items and scoring sheets would jeopardize the use of the test at any future time. The National Labor Relations Board agreed with the union, and several lower courts supported the union's position. Detroit Edison appealed up to the U.S. Supreme Court, where the decision was made in favor of secure testing. Thus, for the time being, companies have the right to keep such information secure. However, such security does not allow them to use test information without demonstrating that the information is being used in a manner that is fair to all employees. The right to keep scores confidential may not interfere with the rights of employees to be treated fairly.

Affirmative Action

We began the chapter by stating that the goal of equal employment opportunity was societal. We also stated that to accomplish the goal of equal employment opportunity for all, government policy had focused on specific individuals and on specific subgroups in our society, which have been termed "protected classes" in reference to the protections guaranteed them by Title VII.

Affirmative action is an attempt to reach this goal by focusing on the protected groups rather than on individuals. It is also aimed at the future and is proactive rather than reactive (Cascio, 1982). That is, affirmative action is an attempt by the organization to create conditions that will offer equal employment opportunity to all, and will, over the long run, distribute members of protected groups among positions in the organization in approximately the same proportions as majority group members are distributed.

Guidelines have been developed for organizations to adopt these affirmative action plans. The guidelines have required extensive analyses of the current labor force and of the labor market from which employees are drawn. Based on the race, ethnic background, and sex of current employees, the numbers of protected class members in an organization's labor market, and several other factors, goals are established for hiring and promoting members of protected classes. These goals have had substantial impact on recruiting, selecting, training and promoting employees. Also, to form these goals and to evaluate progress toward them, the organization must keep extensive records. The reader is referred to other sources (such as Miner & Miner, 1978) for a detailed description of what is needed to establish what is known as an Affirmative Action Plan.

Affirmative Action Plans must be filed by organizations subject to the OFCCP if they have government contracts. The EEOC or the courts may also require plans of organizations which have been found to be in violation of adverse-impact guidelines. Finally, organizations may voluntarily set up such plans.

EEO IN PERSPECTIVE

This presentation has had three goals. First, we discussed the implications of EEO for personnel practice by briefly describing the U.S. government agencies involved in EEO issues, how they evolved, and their jurisdiction. Second, we selected what we consider to be the major problems in personnel practice that have developed out of the EEO emphasis. Finally, we attempted to give a sufficient background of the development of EEO for the reader to realize its complexity.

The third goal is essential to remember. As should be apparent by now, one needs to be able to tolerate ambiguity in today's personnel management. This is not likely to change in the next few years, as the United States attempts to meet the needs of protected groups as defined by Title VII, to maintain the right of individuals as defined by the U.S. Constitution, and at the same time to allow organizations the flexibility to make personnel decisions necessary to remain competitive.

Sound personnel practices can be applied and developed to meet staffing needs in organizations if we realize that (1) there will be differences in opinion about how best to reach the goals of equal employment opportunity for all, at least in the short run; (2) for any specific situation, conflict between group, individual, and organization needs is likely; and (3) procedures developed for establishing the validity of personnel practices have a judgment component to them. The first step in dealing with complex problems is to recognize their complexity. Once this occurs, complex solutions are acceptable. Simple solutions, although appealing on the surface and often appealing to those who do not understand the problem very well, are not going to solve both organizational and societal needs for effective human resource management.

DISCUSSION

Selection and placement approaches the staffing problem by attempting to match the needs of an organization with the needs and abilities of individuals in such a way that both the individuals and the organization benefit. Although this matching process may seem straightforward at first—to simply learn the nature of the jobs and the nature of the peo-

ple and then to put the two together—we have seen that it is not. To appreciate the complexity, selection and placement must be put into a systems perspective. Many factors interact with these processes and the interaction is reciprocal: Selection and placement practices are influenced by these factors and, in turn, influence the factors themselves.

The demands of internal organizational needs as identified by a needs analysis through human-resource planning procedures will identify obvious needs and will guide the development of selection and placement policies and practices. However, the organization does not exist in a vacuum. It is dependent upon and responsible to the society from which its members are drawn. As a result, that society sets certain guidelines for what are and are not acceptable practices. There are few places in the personnel function where these societal demands are felt more strongly. Only by being sensitive to the legal requirements of the society as well as to the internal demands of the organization for successful matching of personnel with positions can an organization develop effective selection and placement practices. The exact nature of some of these practices is addressed in the next few chapters.

REFERENCES

Ash, P., & Kroeker, L. P. (1975). Personnel selections, classification, and placement. *Annual Review of Psychology, 26,* 481–508.

Bobko, P., & Bartlett, C. J. (1978). Subgroup validities: Differential definitions and differential predictions. *Journal of Applied Psychology, 63,* 12–14.

Cascio, W. F. (1982). *Applied psychology in personnel management* (2nd ed.). Reston, Va.: Reston Publishing.

Cronbach, L. J., & Gleser, G. C. (1965). *Psychological tests and personnel decisions* (2nd ed.). Urbana: University of Illinois Press.

Dunnette, M. D., & Borman, W. C. (1979). Personnel selection and classifications systems.

Annual Review of Psychology, Palo Alto, CA: Annual Reviews, Inc.

Equal Employment Opportunity Coordinating Council (August 25, 1978). Uniform guidelines on employee selection procedures. *Federal Register,* 38290–38315.

Guion, R. M. (1976). Recruiting, selection and job replacement. In M. D. Dunnette (Ed.), *Handbook of industrial and organizational psychology.* Chicago: Rand McNally.

Guion, R. M. (1978). Scoring of content domain samples: The problem of fairness. *Journal of Applied Psychology, 63,* 499–506.

Hawkins, M. D. (1983). Personal communications.

Humphreys, L. B. (1973). Statistical definitions of test validity for minority groups. *Journal of Applied Psychology, 58,* 1–4.

Lawshe, C. H. (1976). A quantitative approach to content validity. *Personnel Psychology, 28,* 563–575.

Linn, R. L. (1978). Single-group validity, differential validity, and differential prediction. *Journal of Applied Psychology, 63,* 507–512.

Miner, M. G., & Miner, J. B. (1978). *Employee selection within the law.* Washington, D.C.: Bureau of National Affairs.

Niehaus, R. J. (1979). *Computer-assisted human resources planning.* New York: Wiley-Interscience.

Schmidt, F. L. (October–December 1977). Are employment tests appropriate for minority group members? *Civil Service Journal, 18,* 10–11.

Schmidt, F. L., & Hunter, J. E. (1980). The future of criterion-related validity. *Personnel Psychology, 33,* 41–60.

Schmidt, F. L., Hunter, J. E., & Pearlman, K. (1982). Two pitfalls in assessing fairness of selection tests using the regression model. *Personnel Psychology, 35,* 601–608.

Sparks, P. C. (1980). Open versus secure testing. *Personnel Psychology, 33,* 1–2.

Tenopyr, M. L. (1977). Content-construct confusion. *Personnel Psychology, 30,* 47–54.

U.S. Supreme Court (1975). *Albermale Paper Company v. Moody, United States Reports,* 422, 405.

U.S. Supreme Court (1971). *Griggs v. Duke Power Company, United States Reports,* 401, 424(a).

U.S. Supreme Court (1978). *University of California Regents v. Bakke. United States Supreme Court Reports: Lawyer's Edition,* 57, 750–853.

U.S. Supreme Court (1976). *Washington v. Davis, Supreme Court,* 96, 2040(c).

Walker, J. W. (1980). *Human resource planning PS.* New York: McGraw-Hill.

8

General Practices In Personnel Selection

A critical function of personnel management is making decisions about assigning individuals to specific jobs or positions. This is the process of matching individuals to jobs taking into account the actual or potential qualifications of the individuals on the one hand, and the requirements of the jobs on the other. At the most basic level, to achieve a good fit, it is necessary to assess the relevant characteristics of the job and of the persons, to assign persons to jobs, to allow them to work on the jobs long enough to assess their performance, and then to evaluate the quality of the person-to-job match. The development and implementation of all phases of this general process is called selection and placement.

TYPES OF PERSONNEL ACTIONS

Definitions of Terms

Let us digress for a few moments to discuss certain distinctions often made among personnel actions related to matching people to jobs. Some of these terms are reviewed from the preceding chapter; others are new.

Personnel selection. Personnel selection, in a technical sense, refers to choosing from a number of available candidates one or more who are to be employed. Typically the selection decision is made with the view of assigning an individual to a given job or to training for a job such as a management-training program for all newly hired managers. In all cases, there is at least one more candidate than there are jobs or positions to be filled; thus, in every selection-decision condition, there is the possibility of rejection as well as of selection. In addition, selection decisions are typically made among candidates who are not presently employed by the organization but who are seeking employment. The exception to this would be the case of selecting employees to attend a training program from a pool of current employees, not all of whom will be selected to attend the program.

Placement. Placement is viewed more from the individual's perspective and focuses on choosing, from a number of possible positions, the one presumably best suited to a given candidate. In such instances, the individual is usually already employed in the organization and the placement decision is then made to assign the employee to that job for which he or she is considered best qualified. In all cases, the number of persons being placed is equal to the number of positions or jobs into which the persons are to be placed.

Classification. The term *classification* is closely related to placement, with only a slightly different twist. In contrast to placement, where the assignment process is viewed from the perspective of the individual being assigned, classification looks at the problem from the perspective of the whole pool of persons being considered. For classification, there is a pool of individuals and a pool of jobs to which the individuals are all to be assigned. The objective of the assignment process is to optimize, *collectively*, by assigning persons to jobs such that the final set of assignments is the best for the whole pool. Within a pool of N persons who are to be assigned to N jobs, rarely is one person best for each job and the same job best for that person. Thus, optimizing for the pool does not mean that each person in the pool will necessarily be assigned to the job that is best for him or her.

After making the distinction between selection, placement, and classification, we should point out that many, including ourselves, often blur this distinction. Because all three processes share the common matching process and because many of the procedures and practices necessary to carry out each of the three processes are identical, the label *personnel selection* is often used to refer to all three. We tend to use personnel selection to refer to any of the three and then make a specific distinction for cases in which actions in one of the domains would differ from those in the others so that the distinction between them would be important.

Assignments. Often we label the types of personnel assignments on the basis of the move that they represent for the person who is awarded an assignment. These labels are familiar, so little explanation is needed. *Hiring* refers to matches between jobs and individuals who are not currently members of the organization. *Promotions* are advancements to positions of higher status or at a higher level in the organization than the position currently held by the person. *Transfers* are less precisely defined. The term is often used to refer to assignments to positions within an organization that require the employee to move from his or her community of residence to another community. Almost always, transfers also involve promotions to higher-level positions. In addition, transfers within the same organization often describe assignments to new positions that may not be of any higher status or responsibility than the one the employee currently holds. When transfer is used in this fashion, it is termed a *lateral transfer* to connote a reassignment that did not involve a promotion.

JOB REQUIREMENTS AND PERSONNEL SPECIFICATIONS

Personnel selection should be directed toward identifying those individuals who stand the best chance of success in the job in question. This means that one should try to identify those characteristics of individuals that are the most likely to contribute to success on the job. In selecting individuals for any given job, there is (or should be) some set of what are variously called *personnel specifications* or *job specifications*. These are frequently written, although sometimes they exist partly or entirely in the minds of those responsible for personnel selection.

One way to view personnel specifications is to focus on the underlying source of those specifications. Such a focus creates two general classes of specifications. The first set is composed of those specifications that are *intrinsic* to the job itself—those that are required for effective performance on the job (for example, visual acuity and hand steadiness to saw lumber or physical strength to load moving vans). Intrinsic requirements generally include aptitudes and sensory (e.g., visual acuity), physical (e.g., grip strength), and mental (e.g., arithmetic reasoning) abilities.

The second class of specific requirements is associated with *labor-market conditions*. These conditions may influence the types of people who work best on the job but they are not inherent to the nature of the task. In other settings with other conditions, the specifications may be different. An example of labor-market conditions is that facing many retail establishments today. As a result of the long number of hours that most stores are open, combined with the nature of the retail task that requires employees in zones within the stores at all times and, in many cases, involves them in tasks that are not terribly demanding, the work force of large retail establishments is primarily composed of part-time workers. These employees work only a limited number of hours each week. Many stay with the store for years as part-time personnel. This has led to a new labor-market classification: permanent part-time workers. Many such employees are attracted to these jobs because of the part-time nature of the work, which allows them to go to school, be home when the children are home, or hold down other full-time jobs somewhere else. As a result some of the personnel specifications for these jobs may be less a function of the intrinsic nature of the work itself than of the

nature of the people who are most likely to be attracted to such jobs.

To the extent that labor-market conditions change, the kinds of people available as job candidates may also be expected to change, thus suggesting the need to modify the personnel specifications accordingly, as far as the aspects related to the "labor market" are concerned.

Intrinsic requirements vary from job to job, some being rather clear cut and obvious, and others being rather vague and hard to pin down. A bookkeeper's job clearly requires basic arithmetic abilities such as adding and subtracting. On the other hand, the requirements for a laboratory technician, city planner, or detective are not quite as obvious.

By now it should be clear that job requirements are not absolute and inviolate; they "depend." They depend, for example, upon value judgments of acceptable standards of performance and the extent to which certain values can be sacrificed for others. Granting this, however, the realities of personnel-administration processes necessitate some sort of guidelines for personnel selection.

OBJECTIVES IN ESTABLISHING PERSONNEL SPECIFICATIONS

The objective of setting up personnel specifications is to state those items of personal data that are "valid" for selecting individuals for a job. We discuss validity later in this chapter, but for the moment let us say that a set of personnel specifications would be valid to the extent that the individuals who meet the specifications have a significantly better chance of performing effectively than those who do not. For example, if individuals who meet some minimum height and weight specifications are generally better at performing the physical activities of the job of warehouse loader than those who do not meet those standards, it could be said that these specifications are valid. Actually, the personnel-selection process is essentially one of predicting job success on the basis of relevant information about the candidates. Relevance is defined in terms of the match to the job specifications. The remainder of this chapter is devoted almost entirely to determining what the standards are, assessing the extent to which people possess the standards, and then evaluating the extent to which those who meet the standards actually do perform their jobs better than those who do not or those who only meet them to a minimum extent. Note that all three of these topics require measurement. The focus of the measurement varies from the job, to the people, and finally to the effectiveness of job performance. However, regardless of the focus, all demand that the measures and measurement processes be of sufficient quality to draw accurate conclusions. Therefore, before turning to the ways that job specifications are established, we first address the criteria that are used to judge the quality of measures.

Standards for Measures and Evaluations

The standards used to judge the quality of measures are often labeled *psychometric properties* when they refer specifically to psychological tests. On the other hand, these standards are relevant for a wide variety of measures, many of which may not appear to be very psychological in nature. Specifically, the standards are grouped under two topics: (1) reliability; and (2) validity. As you will recall, reliability refers to the extent to which the measure can be counted on to produce the same score if the conditions being measured remain the same. Validity refers to the extent to which the measure measures what it is supposed to. Thus, whether one is measuring a person's mathematical ability or the length of a 2 × 4 before sawing it, the mea-

suring instrument should possess these qualities.

RELIABILITY

We have already discussed the notion of reliability, as related to criteria and performance evaluations. In person-job matching, reliability is relevant to at least three contexts—namely, the reliability of criteria, of judgments of personnel specifications, and of measurements of individuals. In all of these, it refers to the consistency or stability of whatever measurements are in question.

For measurements of human variables, the American Psychological Association has published the *Standards for Educational and Psychological Tests*, which sets forth guidelines for the use of "tests," and which describes various types of test reliability. Note that the term *test* is used in a very broad sense. According to the *Standards*, "tests include standardized aptitude and achievement instruments, diagnostic and evaluative devices, interest inventories, personality inventories, projective instruments and related clinical techniques, and many kinds of personal history forms" (1974, p. 2).

Types of Reliability Coefficients

The American Psychological Association *Standards* recognize three classes of reliability, all expressed in terms of different types of "coefficients" associated with them: coefficient of stability, coefficient of equivalence, and coefficient of internal consistency.

Coefficient of stability. A coefficient of stability is based on the use of the same type of measurement instrument administered at two points in time to a sample of people; the results of these two administrations are usually correlated. The resulting correlation is called a *coefficient of stability*. This approach is frequently called the *test-retest method*.

For conventional types of tests, the same test is administered twice to the same subjects at different times. This method should not be used for tests in which practice or memory associated with the first administration might influence performance on the second. This influence might apply, for example, to tests of knowledge (with questions such as "Who commanded the French forces at the battle of Waterloo?), or to tests that require practice in some task (such as converting yards to meters). This method can be used with tests of sensory, psychomotor, or cognitive skills that cannot be improved with brief practice, nor influenced appreciably by memory from the first administration.

A coefficient of stability is sometimes used to estimate the reliability of various types of ratings, such as performance evaluations or ratings of job requirements. It can also be used with other sets of data (such as criterion data) obtained at different times. For example, in one company injury indexes of employees in a given department were derived for two periods, one based on injuries during odd-numbered weeks and the other on even-numbered weeks. These two indexes were correlated. (In this instance the correlation was .69.)

Coefficient of equivalence. A coefficient of equivalence index of reliability is based on data from two "samples" of the "universe" of the behaviors or events being measured. The most clear-cut circumstance to which this applies is a conventional test for which alternate and comparable forms are available. This approach to reliability is sometimes called the *alternate-* or *parallel-forms method.* The two alternate forms should be developed so that they are matched in style, content, and statistical characteristics. In effect, each form should have about the same number of each kind of item, the means of the two forms should be about the same, and the standard deviations of the scores of the two forms should be about the same. The use of parallel

forms of tests evades the problem of the test-retest approach that can arise if memory from the first administration influences performance on the second administration. It cannot, however, deal with the problem of practice.

The coefficient of equivalence can sometimes be used with ratings made by supervisors or interviewers. In such an instance it would be necessary to have two "equivalent" rating forms, each with many different items that provide collectively for ratings on the same attributes or qualities but that are worded differently.

The same approach can sometimes also be used with certain other types of personal or personnel data, such as measures of learning during training, productivity, and absenteeism, by viewing data obtained at different times, as long as the time periods can be considered relatively equivalent.

Coefficient of internal consistency. The various parts or items of a test of some behavior or attribute should usually all measure essentially the same thing. In other words, the various parts or items should be internally consistent. There are two methods for deriving coefficients of internal consistency. Both are based on data obtained from a single administration of the measuring instrument. One of the methods is called the *split-half method.* When the test is "scored," two scoring keys are used, each covering only half of the items. The two halves may be chosen randomly or they may consist of alternate items, with one scoring key used on all the even-numbered items and the other used on all the odd-numbered items. The correlation between scores made on the two halves is then computed. This provides a reliability measure of a test half as long as the original test. By using a commonly accepted statistical procedure, the correlation is corrected by the Spearman-Brown prophecy formula to provide an estimate of the reliability of the total test.

The other method is based on some type of *analysis of variance,* the results of which reflect estimates of the average of the correlations between and among the items of the test. Probably the most common examples of this method are Kuder-Richardson formula 20 (K-R 20) and Cronbach's *alpha.* This formula yields essentially an average of all the split-half correlations that could have been obtained using all possible ways of dividing the test.

It should be pointed out that a coefficient of internal consistency is *not* appropriate for what are called speed tests. A speed test is one in which all of the items are the same or virtually the same—for example, a finger-dexterity test putting pegs into holes. The scoring of such tests is based on how many "items" a person completes within a stated time period or how long it takes to complete a specified number of items.

General reliability issues. There are variations and refinements of the reliability theme that we do not discuss here (Campbell, 1976). Which of the three basic approaches just discussed is most appropriate depends on the circumstances in question and on the type of "data" in question. There is no such thing as *the* reliability of any test or other measurement instrument. Rather, reliability is, in part, a function of the individuals or events (or of whatever units of measurements are used) and of the approach used in deriving the reliability estimate. When using virtually any measurement instrument, however, it is desirable to determine the reliability in the situation in question unless there already are substantial reliability data that would provide reasonable confidence and comfort in using the instrument. For many published tests, at least some reliability data are usually reported in the accompanying manuals.

How important is the reliability of a test or other measurement instrument? Respectable reliability does lend confidence in the use of the measures or scores in question. Conversely, low reliability virtually precludes the possibility of obtaining any meaningful results from using the data. For example, a criterion with poor reliability is not worth trying to predict, and a predictor with poor reliability cannot predict any criterion.

VALIDITY

Validity is difficult to define in a single statement. In its *Standards for Educational and Psychological Tests* the American Psychological Association stated that questions of (test) validity are "questions of what may properly be inferred from a test score" and that validity refers to the "appropriateness of inferences from test scores or other forms of assessment" (1974, p. 25).

The *Standards for Educational and Psychological Tests* set forth three basic types of validity for tests. (Remember that the concept of a "test" in this frame of reference is a very broad one.) These include *content* validity, *construct* validity, and *criterion-related* validity. Dunnette and Borman (1979) caution that the implication that validities come in different types is confusing and often leads to oversimplification. On the other hand, the official recognition of various types of validity argues for familiarity with them. Let us describe these three types of validity, but with a warning of the danger of oversimplification.

Content Validity

The *content validity* of tests or other measurement instruments has traditionally been viewed as referring to the extent to which the instrument provides for the measurement of a reasonably representative sample of the behaviors or other kinds of responses considered to comprise the "domain" the test is supposed to cover. In the most straightforward examples, it applies to various types of achievement tests—that measure the level of achievement in some relatively definitive domain of knowledge or performance. Job-knowledge or job-performance tests typically would be considered to be content valid if, based on the judgments of experts, the items or questions are judged to be representative of whatever the test is supposed to measure.

Questions have been raised about this concept of content validity. Tenopyr (1977), for example, made the point that content validity has usually been considered an indication of how well the content of a test samples a larger universe of content, and that it therefore is based on inferences about test *construction* and not about test *scores*. Since validity typically is concerned with inferences about test scores (that is, with making predictions on the basis of test scores) Tenopyr stated that what has been called content validity is not validity at all. Guion (1978) echoed this view, commenting that when one is constructing an ability test by content sampling, the issue is the validity of the *sample,* or its representativeness of the defined job-content domain. But, to describe the validity of a test as the basis for drawing inferences, one needs to deal with test *scores,* as these might be relevant to making predictions. It is difficult, if not impossible, to establish a meaningful (cut-off) score on an employment test unless one uses a predictive framework (Tenopyr, 1977).

Although Guion and Tenopyr argued that there is no such thing as content validity, the American Psychological Association and the *Uniform Guidelines on Employee Selection Procedures* both recognize such validity for personnel-selection purposes. In light of this disparity, it is suggested that those who tread the murky waters of content validity try to establish the predictability of any test in question by determining the relationship between test scores and relevant criteria.

Construct Validity

Construct validity is concerned with the extent to which a test measures the underlying phenomenon (termed *construct*) that it is supposed to measure. Cronbach and Meehl (1955) originally defined a construct as a postulated (that is, assumed or hypothetical) attribute of people that underlies and determines their overt behavior. The construct itself cannot be observed but rather is inferred from the way that people respond to a number of tests or situations.

The construct validity of a test is the extent to which the test tends to fit into a pattern of relationships with other tests and measures of behaviors in the way that the "theory" about the construct says it should. Consider the following example: Assume that we believe that intelligence is some notion about the mental ability of persons and that we have just developed a new test of intelligence. In this case, intelligence is the construct of interest. We cannot actually see it, but we have some general ideas about what it means to have high intelligence and what it means to have low intelligence. Now assume that we give our new intelligence test to a group of college students for whom we have the following four measures in addition to their scores on our new intelligence test: (1) undergraduate grade point average (GPA); (2) overall score on the Scholastic Aptitude Test (SAT), a standardized measure of ability to do intellectually oriented behaviors typically experienced in college; (3) scores on a classroom examination of American history; and (4) the time taken to run a 10 kilometer race. With this information, we now attempt to determine the construct validity of our new intelligence test. To do this we have to make some assumptions about what we mean by intelligence as a construct of mental ability; in other words, we must have a theory about the construct of intelligence. This theory would say that intelligence should be most relevant to activities that require a lot of mental activity and concentration. Also, it should be a general level of mental ability such that it relates more strongly to all types of mental activity than to a single narrow type. Given these very vague assumptions, it would seem reasonable to say that, if our test measures intelligence, then, given the measures we have, we would expect it to be more strongly related to grade point average and SAT scores than to running speed. Finally, a score on a classroom exam should be less related to intelligence than either GPA or SAT and yet more so than running speed. To construct validate our test we would then look at the actual relationships between scores on our new test and the other scores to see if the *pattern* of relationships supports the "theory" we have for our construct. The more the pattern fits the theory, the more confident we can be that our test measures the construct we say it measures.

Specific methods do exist for inferring the degree of construct validity possessed by a test. The best known of these is the Multi-Trait Multi-Method (MTMM) matrix method of Cronbach and Meehl (1955). This involves a strategy for arranging a series of tests of various constucts and then inferring the quality of the measures in a construct-validation sense from the pattern of interrelationships of the data. The exact procedure goes beyond what is needed to understand the general notion of construct validity so it is not covered here. However, the end result is a complex pattern that does not yield any single index that would imply high or low validity. Also, there is no way to get a direct estimate of the relationship between scores on the test and the underlying construct that is being measured. However, a method that does offer some promise for doing the latter is the use

of the *fidelity coefficient* (Drasgo & Miller, 1982). This coefficient reflects the correlation between the scale or measure and the underlying construct that scale is designed to measure. Yet, even this index is not an easy or automatic answer to construct validiation. It depends on the ability of the researcher to sample items appropriately for both the test being evaluated and the other tests to which it is related, as well as other specific restrictions. Nevertheless, it does offer a promising advance in our ability to deal with some of the complexities of construct validity.

Criterion-Related Validity

Criterion-related validity is determined by comparing test scores with one or more independent criteria. In personnel selection the criterion is usually a measure of individual job performance.

There are two common types of criterion validity: *predictive validity* and *concurrent validity*. Predictive validity is by far more common and more preferred in personnel selection. It is determined by investigating the relationship between a test score and performance on the criterion when test scores are obtained at some time before the criterion is measured. For example, test scores may be obtained from job applicants, then related to the performance of those who were selected for the jobs after they have been on the jobs 6 months or so. Concurrent validity obtains measures of the predictor (test, etc.) and criterion at approximately the same point in time. Both of these forms are discussed in more detail later in the chapter.

ASSESSING PERSONNEL SPECIFICATIONS

Having discussed the standards by which measures are judged, we are now ready to turn to the issue of measuring job specifications. This is the process of establishing personnel standards. To establish personnel standards it is necessary to focus on the nature of the job. There are various procedures that have been established to do this. We discuss these procedures under three categories: those based on judgments, structured job-analysis procedures, and statistical analysis.

Specifications Based on Judgments

In some instances personnel specifications are established on the basis of judgments, considering each job as a complete entity. In the past (and probably even today) many personnel specifications were based on off-the-cuff guesses. Such guesswork does not necessarily mean that the judgments are invalid; one simply does not know whether they are valid or not.

Judgments of personnel specifications need not be willy-nilly. They can be based on knowledge and understanding of the job activities. This is essentially an inferential process, because the job requirements are inferred from someone's beliefs about the work activity.

Establishing personnel specifications in this manner receives mixed blessings from the psychological fraternity, in part because there are so many variations on this theme and in part because of the varied backgrounds of the practitioners making the judgments about specifications. In the hands of a professional who is familiar with a given job, however, the method can result in personnel specifications in which one can place reasonable confidence. Such inferences can be fairly straightforward. For example, the requirement for a reasonable level of arithmetic-computation ability can be inferred with considerable confidence for an account clerk who needs to add and subtract numbers. The inferences of the requirements for many job activities, however, are not at all obvious, such as the requirements for learning to perform a

complicated chemical laboratory task. At the same time inferences must frequently be made in such circumstances.

Various procedures have been used for judging the specifications of jobs, ranging from completely unsystematic schemes to those using standardized systematic procedures. One such procedure is used by the United States Training and Employment Service for setting forth the worker trait requirements for jobs as given in the *Dictionary of Occupational Titles* (U.S. Department of Labor, Employment and Training Administration, 1977). For the various jobs in the *Dictionary*, ratings are made by job analysts on each of the following worker traits: G (Intelligence); V (Verbal); N (Numerical); S (Spatial); P (Form perception); Q (Clerical perception); K (Motor coordination); F (Finger dexterity); M (Manual dexterity); E (Eye-hand-foot coordination); and C (Color discrimination). The ratings are made according to a rating scale which expresses the amount of each trait possessed by various segments of the working population, as follows:

1. The top 10% of the population;
2. The highest third exclusive of the top 10% of the population;
3. The middle third of the population;
4. The lowest third exclusive of the bottom 10% of the population;
5. The lowest 10% of the population.

Reliability of judgments. Some indication of the reliability of ratings of jobs in terms of aptitudes comes from a study by Trattner, Fine, and Kubis (1955) in which the authors had ten jobs rated on ten different aptitudes by two groups of job analysts. One group of eight analysts rated the ten jobs on the basis of their job descriptions, and the other group rated corresponding jobs by direct observation. The reliability coefficients of the ratings (as based on all eight raters) were very respectable, especially for the mental and perceptual aptitudes (coefficients ranging from

.87 to .96). In the case of the physical aptitudes, the reliability coefficients were generally lower (from .08 to .87, mostly from .57 to .87).

Thus, we see that the reliability of judgments of job requirements made by trained raters is reasonably high, although some attributes can be rated more reliably than others. Interrater reliability by itself, however, is not necessarily an indication of the validity of such judgments.

Validity of judgments. Even though personnel specifications have been established on the basis of judgments in millions of situations, there is actually little quantitative evidence on the validity of such judgments. Some data relating to the validity of such judgments come from the study by Trattner, Fine, and Kubis (1955). They had available test data for about sixty workers on each of the ten jobs; the data included a test score for each person on a test of each of the ten aptitudes. For those workers on each job the mean test score was computed for each of the ten aptitude tests. In turn, the mean aptitude rating was computed for each aptitude from the ratings given by the eight analysts in each of the two groups. Through a procedure that need not be described here, correlations were computed for the two "groups" of aptitudes, as follows:

	BASED ON JOB DESCRIPTION	BASED ON OBSERVATION
Mental and perceptual aptitudes	.60	.71
Physical aptitudes	.01	.27

The results of this rather modest study need to be accepted with some caution, but they tend to indicate that judgments of the mental and perceptual aptitude requirements of jobs may be better (that is, more valid) than judgments of physical aptitudes.

Specifications Based on Structured Job-Analysis Procedures

A somewhat more analytic approach than judgments is based on the use of job data from structured job-analysis procedures. These procedures typically provide for the analysis of jobs in terms of specific "units" or components. The personnel requirements for these components are then established either on the basis of judgments or of statistical analysis. In turn, the total requirements for any individual job are derived by first analyzing the job in terms of these components and by then "building up" the total requirements by consolidating the requirements of the individual components that apply to the job.

This more analytical approach was used, for example, by Bouchard (1972), who urged using the critical incident technique to identify "job dimensions" as discussed in Chapter 4. Given such dimensions for a job, Bouchard suggested that they be used as the "units" of job behaviors about which inferences of job requirements can be made. Thus the ratings of the importance of the dimensions can give cues to the relative importance of the requirements inferred from them. Table 8.1 illustrates the concept of job dimensions based on critical incidents and the nature of the inferences about the abilities required for satisfactory performance of the behaviors associated with the dimensions. The table also lists potential tests to measure those abilities.

An additional and rather different example of this general approach is the "generic skills" program of what is now the Canadian Employment and Immigration Commission (Kawula & Smith, 1975). This study focused on identifying "generic skills" that would be relevant to training people for various occupations. For this purpose generic skills were considered to be those behaviors fundamental to many tasks performed in a wide range of occupations. Five classes of generic skills were covered in the study. These are listed

TABLE 8.1 Illustration of job dimensions for a hypothetical job based on the critical incident technique and the ability requirements inferred from them.

JOB DIMENSION	IMPORTANCE RATING[a]	ABILITIES INFERRED	POTENTIAL TESTS
1. Planning (coordination of information and projection to future)	1.2	Intelligence	WAIS Watson-Glaser Wessman
		Verbal comprehension	Terman Concept Mastery Quick Word Test.
2. Supervision of subordinates	1.6	Leadership Dominance	Fleishman Leadership Opinion Questionnaire California Personality (CPI)
3. Communication with higher-level personnel and other agencies	2.5	Verbal fluency Self-confidence	SRA Verbal Fluency Guilford Fluency Test California Personality (CPI)

[a]The ratings in this illustration are based on a five-point scale of importance, with 1 = extremely important and 5 = hardly important at all.
Source: Adapted from Bouchard, 1972, Table 1.

next, along with a few examples of specific skills within each class:

CLASS	EXAMPLES
1. Mathematic skills	Multiplying whole numbers Adding fraction Solving single-variable algebraic equations
2. Communication skills	Reading to determine job requirements Recording data on forms Writing technical reports
3. Reasoning skills	Scheduling work Diagnosing problems Making decisions
4. Interpersonal skills	Giving rewards and discipline Using attending behaviors Using group-maintenance skills
5. Manipulative skills	Using eye-hand coordination Using proper body posture for lifting and carrying

A total of 192 such skill items were identified and grouped into two "core" clusters, one at the nonsupervisory level and the other at the supervisory level.

Although the focus of the study was on developing broad-based occupational training programs, the study has interesting implications for some aspects of establishing job requirements. First, it provides a reasonably well-formulated inventory of "generic" skills which could be considered "units" of job requirements. Second, it includes a potentially useful procedure for determining the relevance of such "units" of job requirements, specifically an interview using employees and supervisors as respondents.

The survey by Kawula and Smith encompassed seventy-six occupations with 820 worker interviews and 1130 supervisor interviews; a major aspect of the interviews was identifying the specific skills judged to be required in individual positions. For each occupation it was possible to tally the frequency with which specific skills actually were used.

These frequencies were converted to a common metric, specifically the "number of skill users out of 10." If this was three (out of ten) or more for a particular skill, that skill was considered to be "significant." One result was an occupational matrix that showed, for each occupation, the number of "significant" skill users (that is, the number of skill users of three out of ten, or above). A partial matrix is shown in Figure 8.1.

Specifications Based on Statistical Analysis

The use of statistical analysis to establish personnel specifications is directed toward determining the relationship between measures or indications of differences in some human characteristic (that is, a predictor) and a measure of a relevant criterion (such as job performance). This is an oversimplification, as we see later, but for the moment let us look at this process in this oversimplified manner. The predictors used can represent individual differences of virtually any human characteristic or attribute that might be related to job effectiveness. In practice such indications include biographical data (age, marital status, education, work experience, etc.), test scores, ratings (such as by interviewers), and other data. The indications of job effectiveness can consist of any relevant criteria, such as those discussed in Chapter 5. The methods for analyzing the data on the interrelationships between the predictor and the criterion are elaborated later; they can range from very

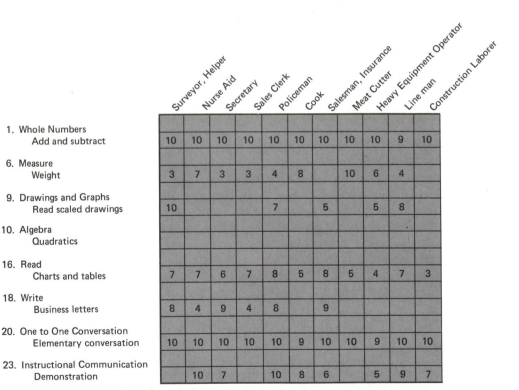

	Surveyor, Helper	Nurse Aid	Secretary	Sales Clerk	Policeman	Cook	Salesman, Insurance	Meat Cutter	Heavy Equipment Operator	Line man	Construction Laborer
1. Whole Numbers / Add and subtract	10	10	10	10	10	10	10	10	10	9	10
6. Measure / Weight	3	7	3	3	4	8		10	6	4	
9. Drawings and Graphs / Read scaled drawings	10				7		5		5	8	
10. Algebra / Quadratics											
16. Read / Charts and tables	7	7	6	7	8	5	8	5	4	7	3
18. Write / Business letters	8	4	9	4	8		9				
20. One to One Conversation / Elementary conversation	10	10	10	10	10	9	10	10	9	10	10
23. Instructional Communication / Demonstration		10	7		10	8	6		5	9	7

FIGURE 8.1 Partial matrix of "generated skills" for a sample of nonsupervisory occupations. The numbers in the cells represent the "significant" skills, in particular the numbers of positions (out of ten) for which the skill was reported. (Adapted from Kawula & Smith, 1975, Chart 6, pp. 120–125.)

simple summarization and presentation of data to very sophisticated statistical analyses.

Such an analysis is usually carried out for a sample of people on a particular job in order to determine what predictors are significantly related to the criteria in that sample. In turn, these predictors are then used, in the case of candidates for a job, as the basis for predicting the criterion values of the candidates.

Example of statistical analysis. One example of a statistical approach to establishing personnel specifications was reported by Fleishman and Berniger (1960). They used a sample of 120 women office employees who had been employed over a 2-year period. This sample was divided into a long-tenure group, who had stayed on the job for 2 years or longer, and a short-tenure group, who had stayed less than 2 years. A comparison was then made between these two groups for each of certain items of personal data; some of these comparisons are given in Table 8.2. The magnitude of the differences in the percentages of long-tenure versus short-tenure personnel for individual items of data served as the basis for deriving a weighting system, with

the weights ranging from +3 to −3. Note that age did differentiate but that previous salary did not. The "corrected" weights shown were derived by the authors of this text in order to illustrate how negative values can be avoided. Specifically, we have added a constant of 3 to each category and have shown the weight that results. Although this procedure increases the ultimate numerical values of all weighted scores (by 30), it has no effect on the form of the distribution of scores.

The investigators then took another sample of 100 cases hired during the same period. This sample served as a so-called "holdout" sample for "cross-validation" purposes. Each individual in the second sample was scored using the weighted scoring scheme given. This holdout group was also divided into a "short-tenure" and a "long-tenure" group, and the weighted scores were then related to tenure, as shown in Figure 8.2, which illustrates the percentage of both groups who had weighted scores below 34 (based on the "corrected" scoring procedure). The scores tend to differentiate reasonably well between the two tenure groups.

TABLE 8.2 Example of analysis of two items of personal data of female clerical employees as related to job tenure

	CRITERION GROUPS[a]		WEIGHT ASSIGNED TO CATEGORY	
	SHORT-TENURE PERCENT	LONG-TENURE PERCENT	"ORIGINAL"	"CORRECTED"
Age				
Under 20	35	8	−3	0
21–25	38	32	−1	2
26–30	8	2	−1	2
31–35	7	10	0	3
35+	11	48	+3	6
Previous salary				
Under $2000	31	30	0	0
$2000–$3000	41	38	0	0
$3000–$4000	13	12	0	0
Over $4000	4	4	0	0

[a]Some percents do not add up to 100 because of omissions, rounding off, and so on.
Source: Fleishman & Berniger, 1960.

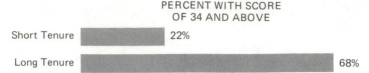

PERCENT WITH SCORE
OF 34 AND ABOVE

Short Tenure   22%

Long Tenure   68%

FIGURE 8.2 Relationship between weighted scores based on several items of personal data and tenure of a sample of female office employees. (Adapted from Fleishman & Berniger, 1960.)

ASSESSING INDIVIDUAL CHARACTERISTICS

Measuring Person Characteristics

Once the specifications for a job have been defined in terms of the human characteristics demanded by the job of the people who hold that job, it becomes necessary to make a judgment about the extent to which people possess the characteristics specified. This means that the people being considered for a job must be assessed or measured with respect to the specifications in question. The form of measurement required depends to some extent on the nature of the characteristic(s) specified by the job and to some extent on the types of measuring instruments that exist for that characteristic. If, for example, one is selecting astronauts who must ride in space capsules that cannot handle persons over 5 feet 10 inches tall, the issue of how to measure this characteristic is straightforward: We measure height with a ruler or tape. We do not interview candidates and ask them to tell us their heights.

There are many ways to measure individual characteristics: letters of recommendation, transcripts from schools attended, application blanks, interviews, and personnel tests. In a sense, all of these are "tests" because all must be evaluated in terms of the extent to which they produce reliable and valid measures of the characteristics of interest. We have already discussed the standards for reliability and validity. Since all of these methods require the same standards for judging their value and since personnel tests are the most frequently considered for gathering information about characteristics of people, we limit our discussion here to such tests. However, keep in mind that most of what we have to say applies equally well to other ways of measuring individual characteristics.

Personnel Tests

Properly used personnel tests can serve as an integral part of an organization's personnel-management program. They can be very useful aids to decision making but, obviously, they should be used only when there is reasonable evidence that they can serve their purpose—that is, when they have reasonable validity. In addition, tests should not be used if they unfairly discriminate against protected classes. Remember from the discussion of fairness and validity in Chapter 7 that tests can be extremely valuable for assessing individual characteristics, but that test users are obligated to insure that the tests, as used, do not unfairly discriminate against members of any group. Indeed, test users are legally obligated to insure fairness to members of groups protected by Title VII of the Civil Rights Act of 1964 and the legislation related to it.

Personnel tests are not infallible. Although personnel tests can be very useful for personnel selection (and other decisions involving personnel management), the advocate of such tests should never forget that they are not infallible; in personnel selection, for example, some persons who score high on a test that actually is valid might not perform satisfactorily on the job. Any new procedure, whether in employment, production, or whatever, should be evaluated not as to whether it achieves perfection but as to whether it results in some improvement over methods that have preceded it. For example, let us consider a company that has been selecting candidates for a particular job but finds that only 60% of those selected turn out to be successful on the job. If the company finds that by using tests 70% of the applicants hired are successful, it might consider the test worthwhile even though 30% of the applicants hired do not turn out to be successful on the job.

Types of tests[1]. Tests that have been and are being used for employee selection may be classified in several different ways. They may be *group* or *individual* tests. The group variety may be given to almost any number of persons simultaneously, the only limitation being the number that can be seated and provided with writing facilities and an adequate opportunity to hear the instructions given by the group examiner before the test is begun. Individual tests, on the other hand, are given to one person at a time and usually call for the undivided, or nearly undivided, attention of the examiner while the test is being administered.

Tests can also be classified by content. In content, most of the tests used in industry are of three types. The first includes tests of basic human abilities, such as mental abilities and psychomotor skills. These tests are generally used as *aptitude* tests to determine whether individuals have the capacity or latent ability to learn a given job if they are given adequate training. The second type of test measures job-specific abilities, such as typing skill and

knowledge of machine-shop practices. Some such tests are called *achievement* tests because they measure the level of achievement in some job-related area. The third class of tests measures personality and interest; such tests are usually named *personality and interest inventories*. These are intended to measure personality characteristics or patterns of interests of individuals, on the assumption that such characteristics or interests may be related to performance on various kinds of jobs. When such tests are used as employment tests, they predict job performance in essentially the same manner as aptitude tests do. There are certain serious limitations to the usefulness for employment purposes of currently available personality and interest tests; these are discussed in Chapter 10.

EVALUATING THE PERSON-JOB MATCH

At this point assume that we have been able to measure the job specifications and also the person characteristics with respect to the specifications. The next step is to evaluate the effectiveness of matching individuals with the characteristics of interest on the job. This evaluation can be done either directly or indirectly. In both cases, the process is labeled *test validation*.

Before we discuss specific forms of test validation, we should note the possibility for confusion between test validation and the validity of a test (or any measure). The validity of a test, discussed earlier in the chapter, is concerned with the extent to which any test measures what it is supposed to measure. Thus, if a test is designed to measure mechanical ability, the validity of that test is based on the extent to which it actually does measure mechanical ability. In contrast, test validation, with respect to personnel selection, addresses the question of the extent to which the test relates to organizationally rel-

---

[1]A list of some of the commonly used tests is given in Appendix D.

evant criteria. Although a test of mechanical ability might be a valid measure of mechanical ability, it may not be a valid measure of job performance. This could occur if the job in question really did not require any mechanical ability. In this case, from the test-validation perspective, the selection system would not be valid if this test were used as the basis for selection.

The methods discussed for test validation are in some cases similar and in other cases dissimilar to the methods of test validity. The following gives a brief preview of the two sets of methods. The discussion following elaborates on the methods of test validation.

METHODS OF TEST VALIDATION	METHODS OF TEST VALIDITY
Concurrent validation ⎫ Predictive validation ⎬	Criterion-related validity
Content validation	Content validity
Construct validation	Construct validity
Job-Status validation	No corresponding method

Concurrent Validation

The concurrent validation of a test for a particular job is derived by what is sometimes called the *present-employee method* of test validation, since it is based on the use of a sample of incumbents who at the time in question are on the job. The procedures are as follows:

1. *Select battery of experimental tests.* An early step in a test-validation project is the selection of a battery of tests to be tried. These tests should be chosen in accordance with the extent to which they are considered to measure attributes judged to be important to job success. This selection should be made on the basis of information obtained from a job analysis.
2. *Administer tests to present employees.* The tests selected are then given to employees presently on the job. When an organization plans to carry

out a test-validation research project that will include the experimental testing of present employees, the organization should make such participation voluntary and should give full assurance that the tests are being given only for experimental purposes and that the results will not in any way affect the employees' relationships with the organization.
3. *Select appropriate criteria.* At some early phase of a test-validation project it is necessary to determine what criterion of job performance to use. Appropriate criteria were discussed in Chapter 5.
4. *Obtain criterion information on present employees.* After determining what criterion or criteria to use, it is then in order to obtain criterion information on the individual employees now on the job. Depending on the criterion in question, this may involve the accumulation of available records (such as production records, sales volume, and the like), or it may consist of obtaining ratings from supervisors on job performance of the employees, or other appropriate processes.
5. *Analyze results.* After the test scores and criterion information have been obtained, the results may be analyzed in several different ways. One method has three steps. First, the total group of employees is divided into a high-criterion group and a low-criterion group, as mentioned previously. Next, the employees are divided on the basis of test scores into two test-score groups, those scoring in the top half on the test and those scoring in the lower half. Then the percentage of high-criterion employees in each test group is determined. If there is a higher percentage of high-criterion employees among the employees in the top half on the test than there is among those in the lower half on the test, the difference is subjected to a statistical check to determine whether it is "significant."

When a test has been found to be acceptable on this basis, employees can then be split into smaller groups by test scores, such as fifths—that is, the highest fifth on the test, the second fifth, the third fifth, the fourth fifth, and the lowest fifth. The percentage of high-criterion employees is then computed for each of these test groups, and the resulting data are then plotted in an expectancy

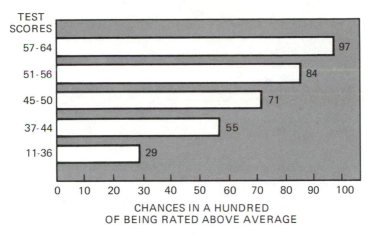

TEST SCORES

Test Scores	Chances in a hundred
57-64	97
51-56	84
45-50	71
37-44	55
11-36	29

CHANCES IN A HUNDRED
OF BEING RATED ABOVE AVERAGE

FIGURE 8.3 Expectancy chart showing the relation between scores made on the Minnesota Paper Form Board and rated success of junior draftsmen in a steel company.

chart such as the one shown in Figure 8.3.[2] The chart shows the "odds" of being a superior employee for employees in each test-score bracket.

The most common method of determining the relationship between test results and job performance is to compute a coefficient of correlation between the test scores of the employees and their criterion values. This has certain advantages over the expectancy-chart method just mentioned. First, it more accurately indicates the *amount* of the relationship between test scores and job performance. Second, it enables the employment manager to take advantage of the all-important selection ratio (see p. 132) in using the test. Third, it enables computation of the relative importance of several tests in an employment battery. Finally, the use of the correlational method makes it possible to offset, statistically, whatever influence such factors as experience on the job or age may have had both on the test scores and on job performance of

the employees. These possible influences are mentioned later.

Although the correlational approach has certain advantages over the expectancy-chart method, these are largely statistical advantages. In terms of understanding by nonstatisticians, the expectancy-chart method is probably superior.

Predictive Validation

The predictive validation of a test is determined by what is called the *follow-up* method of test validation. It consists of administering tests to individuals at the time they are candidates for the job in question. The tests, however, are *not* used as the basis for selection. Rather, the individuals are selected just as they normally would have been selected if the test had not been administered, and the test scores are later related to whatever criterion is appropriate. The steps in this method are:

1. *Select battery of experimental tests.* This step is essentially the same as with the present-employee method.

[2]The procedure for constructing a five-bar expectancy chart such as the one shown in Figure 8.3 is given in detail in C. H. Lawshe & M. J. Balma (1966). *Principles of Personnel Testing.* New York: McGraw-Hill.

2. *Administer tests to applicants*. The tests are administered to applicants who are to be employed for the job in question, but the applicants should not know at the time that a decision has been made to employ them. The test results are then filed until a later date.
3. *Select appropriate criterion*. This determination is made in the same way as with the present-employee method.
4. *Obtain criterion information on the new employees*. The criterion information on the new employees should not be obtained until after sufficient time has elapsed for them to demonstrate their actual abilities on the job. Usually this would be after completion of training, or at least after completion of most of the training.
5. *Analyze results*. This step is carried out in the same manner as with the present-employee method.

Comparison of Concurrent and Predictive Validation

Both the concurrent and predictive test-validation strategies have advantages and disadvantages. In using concurrent validity with aptitude tests, for example, it is possible that the test scores achieved by present employees may reflect, in part, the improvement in some ability resulting from experience on the job. In other words, the test scores may represent some combination of the original level of attribute measured by the test when the incumbents began work on the job plus whatever improvement the individuals have achieved through experience on the job. (Some abilities are more influenced by additional experience than are others.) In validating aptitude tests by this method, it is necessary to insure that the tests, besides differentiating between employees according to a criterion of actual job performance, do *not* show a significant correlation with length of experience on the job.

A direct way of getting around the problem of having the relationship between test scores and job performance be influenced by experience on the job is by using a predictive-

validity strategy. In this case the test scores are obtained *prior* to any experience on the job and therefore cannot be influenced by job experience.

The concurrent-validity approach has certain other possible disadvantages. In some instances, the present employees on a job may be a highly select group, inasmuch as most of those who were *not* satisfactory either may have been dismissed or may have left of their own accord. In such a case, the correlation between test scores and criterion values would *not* represent the relationship that one would expect with the predictive-validity approach.

Further, the "mental set" of present employees toward taking tests on a voluntary "experimental" basis may be different from the "mental set" of applicants. This difference can influence performance on some types of tests, especially personality and interest tests. When this influence is of some consequence, it would be preferable to use a predictive-validity approach. If this is done, the test is then validated in the same type of situation as the one in which it will later be used.

Another disadvantage of the concurrent-validity strategy is that the arrangements for testing present employees are sometimes difficult to work out, especially because it is necessary to take people away from their jobs in order to test them. For all these reasons concurrent validity is *not* one of the methods recommended or accepted as evidence for or against unfair discrimination against protected classes.

The predictive method is clearly preferable for validating tests, except for the possible disadvantage of the time required. Fortunately, it is possible in some cases to use the concurrent method for developing a battery of tests for immediate use and still plan on later "follow-up" of those selected. Although the range of test scores (and of criterion values) for those so selected usually would be restricted (thus bringing about a lower correlation), it is sometimes possible to adjust for this restricted range statistically. Such an adjustment makes it possible to obtain an estimate of what the predictive validity coefficient *would* have been had the tests *not* been used for initial selection. This adjustment procedure would not be appropriate, however, if some nontest basis (for example, membership in a minority group) had been used for excluding some applicants.

Content Validation

As indicated earlier, content validity is controversial. Basically it should be viewed as an attribute of the test itself, in particular the extent to which the test consists of a representative sample of the tasks or knowledge domain it is intended to measure, such as knowledge of electrical practice, typing ability, driving ability, or law practice. Such validity is frequently based on a combination of thorough job analyses and the judgments of experts of the adequacy of the content sample of the test to the domain in question. There are, however, certain fairly systematic sampling procedures that can contribute to the development of a representative sample.

Given a test that is an adequate representative sample of the domain in mind, the question then is whether it predicts what one wants to predict, such as level of performance on a job. Here we need to determine the relationship between test scores and the criterion. Tenopyr (1977) proposed to do a thorough job of content-oriented test construction followed by a token criterion-related study, indicating that such an approach would support construct interpretations and would also solve the problem of setting a meaningful critical score to use in personnel selection. Such an approach would seem to offer a reasonable solution to what is otherwise a bit of an enigma.

Construct Validation

Construct validity is a bit like content validity in that it must be considered from two aspects. The first deals with the extent to which a test measures the construct it is intended to measure. The second deals with the extent to which the construct is a requirement of whatever job is in question. This, the relevance of the construct to the job, must be supported by job analysis that shows the work behavior(s) required for successful job performance, the critical or important work behaviors, and the construct(s) believed to underlie (or to be required for) successful performance of the behaviors in question. Such a demonstration is complicated and has not often been carried out in the field of personnel selection.

Job-Status Validation

This method is generally based on the assumption that people tend to gravitate into, and remain in, those jobs that are compatible with their abilities, interests, and other characteristics. It can be thought of as a "natural-selection" position. It is postulated that those who do not have the basic characteristics required for a job fall by the wayside, either leaving of their own accord or being separated for inadequate performance. In other words, "survival" on jobs for a reasonable period of time is assumed to be evidence that individuals are successful on their jobs. The use of this strategy typically consists of the following steps: (1) identifying individuals on a given job who are considered to be successful (such as those who have "survived" on the job for a reasonable period of time); (2) identifying or measuring the characteristics of such individuals (depending on the circumstance, such characteristics can consist of patterns of responses to interest inventories, biographical data, physical characteristics, or mean scores on relevant tests); and (3) establishing those characteristics as the basis for the selection of future candidates for the job. In some instances comparative data are obtained for individuals in two or more distinct job categories (such as in comparing the interests or biographical backgrounds of people in different occupations).

Historical basis for the job-status method. Historical documentation of the relationship between test scores and occupations goes back over half a century, and was summarized and discussed by Tyler (1965). The first major set of relevant data was obtained from U.S. Army personnel during World War I. Mean test scores on the Army Alpha test (a mental-ability test) were derived for men classified by their previous civilian occupations. Similar data were summarized for one sample of World War II personnel by Harrell and Harrell (1945), and for a larger sample by Stewart (1947). As Tyler points out, the hierarchy of occupations by mean test scores was virtually the same in all of these studies. A few examples illustrate the results of these studies. The following mean scores on the Army General Classification Test by occupation were reported by Harrell and Harrell:

OCCUPATION	MEAN TEST SCORE
Engineer	127
Chemist	125
Pharmacist	121
Clerk-Typist	117
Printer	115
Machinist	110
Carpenter	102
Cook	97
Barber	95
Farm hand	91

The fact that the ordering of occupations was essentially the same in all three data sets referred to previously and in certain other studies cited by Tyler is consistent with a natural-selection position. Tyler points out that consistency of occupational differences in in-

tellectual level are not confined to one sort of test material—they also occur with both verbal and performance tests, and with both vocabulary and nonverbal reasoning. Some indication of this generality is given here—in particular the mean test scores on a clerical test (*Manual for the USTES General Aptitude Test Battery*, U.S. Department of Labor, 1970, Table 9–2):

OCCUPATION	MEAN TEST SCORE
Librarian	122
Stenographer	112
Bookkeeper	111
Sales clerk	99
Automobile service-station mechanic	93
Sewing-machine operator	88
Laborer, steel mill	77

Discussion of the job-status method. The consistency in the ordering of jobs in terms of their incumbents' mean test scores is well documented. Data on the characteristics of successful job incumbents represent very stable criteria for use in validating tests. Given such stability, the investigator can then identify or measure the personal characteristics of successful workers in their respective jobs (such as mean test scores) and use such data as the basis for establishing the requirements of future candidates for the jobs in question.

In the use of job status for this purpose, two points should be kept in mind. Tyler points out that the variability (that is, the standard deviation) of scores tends to be somewhat greater for incumbents on occupations with lower means; if the demands of the occupation are high, individuals with low scores on a relevant test probably would not succeed. On the other hand, a person on a lower-level job might have scores that are considerably higher on certain abilities than are really needed when factors other than job performance have operated to keep him or her on the job.

The second point is that if admission to particular jobs has been restricted for some reasons unrelated to the nature of the job and job performance, currently successful employees could possess different abilities than would be present in the absence of such restrictions. Although we have no reason to believe that this condition is widespread, prior to the use of job-status validity, the investigator should assure himself or herself that such restrictions are unlikely to have occurred.

FACTORS AFFECTING THE FUNCTIONAL VALUE OF PERSONNEL TESTS

Several practical and theoretical factors determine the functional utility of personnel tests. These include the *reliability* and *validity* of the tests used, the *selection ratio,* and the *percentage of present employees who are "satisfactory" on the job.* Our discussion of these factors is primarily in the frame of reference of criterion-related validation (concurrent and predictive validity). In a general sense, the discussion also applies to circumstances in which other types of validation are used.

Reliability

As stated earlier, a test must have an acceptable level of reliability if it is to be useful. The fact that a test has high reliability, however, provides no assurance of its criterion-related validity. A test might have *high reliability* but *low validity,* or even no validity at all. The converse is not true, for if a test has *low reliability* it cannot be expected to have any appreciable degree of validity as related to a criterion. (This is not only a rational conclusion but is also based on the principles of statistical theory. The coefficient of reliability of a test imposes a theoretical maximum on its possible coefficient of validity.)

Validity

Recognizing the potential "ceiling" of validity imposed on a test by its reliability, it is logical for us to ask: How high must the concurrent- or predictive-validity coefficient of a test be for the test to be worthwhile in actual use?

The answer to this question depends on the use being made of the test. The user of a test is nearly always interested in one of two objectives but is seldom interested in both at the same time. He or she is interested in either making a careful and accurate analysis of *each person tested,* which is to be used for individual prediction or vocational guidance, or in selecting from a large group of individuals a smaller group that, *on the average,* will surpass the larger group in some particular respect. In individual counseling work, which deals with vocational aptitude and guidance, psychologists are interested in the former objective. Their work will stand or fall on the accuracy of their predictions of individual clients. They therefore have little use for tests that do not have a validity sufficiently high to justify their use in individual prediction. The exact value of the validity coefficient that meets this requirement is not completely agreed upon by all students of the subject, but it is uniformly agreed that the higher the validity of the test the better, and that *there is no substitute for high validity for individual prediction.*

On the other hand, one may be interested in segregating from a large group of persons tested a smaller group that, on the average, will surpass the larger group in whatever trait is being tested. This is, in fact, the situation that confronts employment managers. On the basis of tests, they are willing to accept a few individuals who will fail on a given job and to reject (or place upon some other job) a few who, had they been placed on that job, would have succeeded, *if* on the whole *their percentage of successful placements is higher with the tests than it is without them.* Under these circumstances the acceptable validity of the tests can be somewhat lower. But one may still ask: How low can it be? This question can be answered but not for all situations. The answer depends on the size of the *selection ratio*, which we discuss next.

The Selection Ratio

Given a personnel test with a validity coefficient indicating *some* relationship with the criterion and given more candidates than can be placed on the job in question, the functional value of the test depends on the ratio of those placed to those tested who are available for placement. This has been referred to as the *selection ratio*. An example will clarify the operation of this principle.

If a certain test is given to a large number of employees for whom a criterion of successfulness as employees is available and if the scattergram of test scores against the criterion is plotted, the points ordinarily will fall into an oval-shaped area somewhat similar to the oval in Figure 8.4. The higher the coefficient of validity, the narrower the oval will be; and the lower the validity, the more nearly the oval will approach a circle. A validity coefficient of approximately .60 will result in a scattering of scores approximately covering the oval area shown in Figure 8.4. Now, if candidates are placed without regard to test scores, their criterion scores will usually be the average of all individuals falling within the oval. If only those placed in this job have test scores as high as or higher than T1, those not placed on the job will clearly have, on the average, lower criterion scores than the group as a whole, and those placed will accordingly be higher in their criterion scores, on the average, than the group as a whole. A still higher average criterion score for the group placed

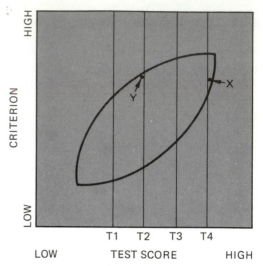

FIGURE 8.4 Effect of shifting the critical score required of applicants on average criterion score of employees hired.

can be achieved by setting the critical test score at T2. By moving the critical score to T3, T4, or even higher, still more favorable placements, according to average criterion score, can be made.

If a given number of persons, say sixty, are to be placed, any one of the conditions mentioned previously may exist. Which one exists will depend on the selection ratio that is utilized—that is, the ratio of the number placed to the number tested. Suppose we work with a ratio of 1.00—that is, all those tested are placed. In this case, the distribution of test scores will be over the whole range of possible test scores; the criterion scores will be over the whole range of possible criterion scores, and the test will contribute nothing whatsoever to the efficiency of the placement procedure. Now suppose that we test eighty individuals and place the sixty who score highest on the test, either not hiring the twenty who score lowest or placing them on some other job. We thus reduce those placed to 75% of those tested, or reduce the selection ratio to .75. Under these conditions, we will place on this job only individuals who test at least as high as T1, and the average criterion scores of those so placed will clearly be higher than the average of the group as a whole. By testing 120 persons and placing the sixty who score highest on the test, the selection ratio will be reduced to .50 and only individuals to the right of T2 will be placed. The average criterion score of this group will not only be higher than that of the whole group but it will also be higher than that of the group placed when the critical test score was at T1. In turn, if the selection ratio could be decreased to .10, only those testing at least as high as T4 would be placed on the job, and the average criterion score of the group placed under these circumstances would be much higher than the score of those placed under any larger selection ratio.

The foregoing discussion is based on the assumption that the placement of employees is successful in proportion to the average success of the employees placed. Anyone can readily see that even working with a selection ratio of .10, some individuals (like X in Figure 8.4) will be placed who will be poorer according to the criterion than a few other individuals (like Y in Figure 8.4) who have not been allocated to this job. But if one is willing to measure the success of the testing program by average results rather than by individual cases, the results will be more and more favorable as the selection ratio is decreased.

The main argument of this discussion is that—in *group* testing—one can effectively use a test with a relatively low (statistically significant) validity coefficient if the selection ratio is sufficiently low. There is, however, one drawback. As the selection ratio drops, more people who are not selected must be tested to find those who are successful. This means that the cost per person selected increases as the selection ratio decreases. Therefore, economic conditions, among other things, limit our ability to manipulate selection ratios.

Percentage of Present Employees Considered Satisfactory

Another factor that affects the efficiency of a personnel test in a given employment situation is the percentage of present employees who are considered satisfactory. This factor may be clarified by Figure 8.5. Suppose we are working with a test having a validity coefficient such that the employees tested fall into the oval-shaped area. Suppose, further, that we are working with a selection ratio of .50—that is, only persons falling in the oval-shaped area to the right of T2 will be placed on the job. If 50% of the present employees are satisfactory (that is, C2 in Figure 8.5 represents the line separating those who are successful from those who are not), any increase over this amount in the percentage of satisfactory employees placed that can be achieved by using the test is a gain. Under these conditions, the ratio of satisfactory employees among those placed to the total of those placed would be the ratio of the number of individuals falling to the right of line T2 and above C2 to all persons to the right

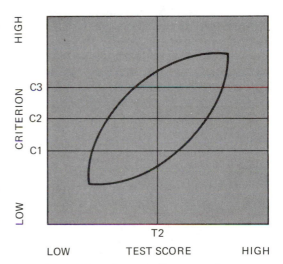

FIGURE 8.5 Variation of efficiency of an employment test with differences in percentage of current employees considered satisfactory.

of line T2. This ratio would clearly be higher than .50, and the amount by which it exceeds .50 would be indicative of the functional value of the test under the conditions discussed.

If all the conditions just named remain the same except that previous employment methods have resulted in 75% satisfactory employees, then the criterion separation line of the successful and unsuccessful employees would be C1 and the percentage of satisfactory employees placed by means of the test would be the ratio of the individuals to the right of line T2 and above C1 to all persons to the right of line T2. In the latter case, a larger percentage of employees hired will be satisfactory than in the former case, even though the test, selection ratio, and other controlling factors remain the same. In other words, if everything else is equal, the *smaller* the percentage of present employees who do well (score highly on the criterion) ignoring the test scores, the larger will be the percentage increase of satisfactory employees when employees are placed using test results.

This may be illustrated by an example. Suppose we have available a test with a validity coefficient of .50 and that we are using a selection ratio of .50. Table 8.3 shows the increase in the percentage of satisfactory employees after using the text over the percentage prior to using the test. The values in Table 8.3 were obtained from the Taylor-Russell tables (Taylor & Russell, 1939) shown in Appendix B. If only 5% of employees placed by traditional means are successful, then the expected increase to 9% represents an 80% increase in the number of satisfactory employees placed by the test, under the specified conditions of test validity and selection ratio. If larger percentages of satisfactory employees have been achieved without the test, the percentage of increase achieved by using the test will become increasingly smaller. If 90% of employees placed by traditional means have been successful, the increase of this percentage to 97% by the test, used under the specified conditions, results in an improvement of only 8% in the number of employees satisfactorily placed.

TABLE 8.3 Increases in percentage of satisfactory employees placed on a job over various original percentages of satisfactory employees when a test with a validity coefficient of .50 is used with a selection ratio of .50

	A	B		
	PERCENTAGE OF SATISFACTORY EMPLOYEES PLACED ON THE JOB WITHOUT THE TEST	PERCENTAGE OF SATISFACTORY EMPLOYEES PLACED ON THE JOB WITH THE TEST	DIFFERENCE IN PERCENTAGE BETWEEN COLUMNS A AND B	PERCENTAGE OF INCREASE OF VALUES IN B OVER VALUES IN A
	5	9	4	80
	10	17	7	70
	20	31	11	55
	30	44	14	47
	40	56	16	40
	50	67	17	34
	60	76	16	27
	70	84	14	20
	80	91	11	14
	90	97	7	8

Source: Taylor-Russell Tables, Appendix B.

The general conclusion is that, other things being equal, the more difficult it has been to find and place satisfactory employees without using test procedures, the greater the gain one may expect from a suitable testing program.

Use of the Taylor-Russell Tables

The foregoing discussion pointed out that the four factors mentioned earlier—reliability, validity, percentage of present employees considered to be satisfactory, and selection ratio—operate to determine the functional value of a personnel-selection test. Assuming that the reliability of a test is reasonably satisfactory and knowing the values of the other three factors, we can predict the improvement in personnel placement that would result from using the test. What is more, we can also estimate the further improvement that would result from reducing the selection ratio on changing any other parameter.

Figure 8.6 is a chart that shows how the percentage of employees selected who will be successful is estimated from the validity of the test and the selection ratio. This chart represents an employment situation in which

50% of present employees are considered satisfactory. The base line in this figure gives the selection ratio, and each of the curves plotted indicates a different test validity. By using a test with a validity of .90 and by reducing the selection ratio to .60, the percentage of satisfactory employees placed will be raised from 50% to 77%. Also a corresponding increase to 77% in the number of satisfactory employees will be achieved by a test with a validity of only .50 if the selection ratio is decreased to .20.

The Taylor-Russell tables make it possible to determine what percentage of employees hired will be satisfactory under different combinations of test validity, selection ratio, and percentage of present employees considered satisfactory.

These tables may be clarified by an example. Suppose an employment manager with a test with a validity coefficient of .40 has twice as many applicants available as there are jobs to be filled and is hiring for a department in which 30% of the present employees are considered satisfactory. Looking in the upper half of the table on p. 455 (entitled *Proportion of employees considered satisfactory = 30%*), we find in the row

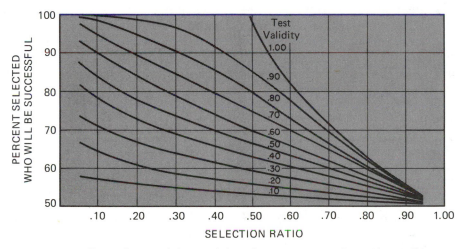

FIGURE 8.6 Effect of test validity and the selection ratio on the working efficiency of an employee-selection test.

representing a validity coefficient of .40 and in the column representing a selection ratio of .50, the value .41 where the indicated row and column cross. This means that under the conditions specified, 41% of the employees placed will be satisfactory, instead of the 30% attained without the test. If conditions are such that the selection ratio may be reduced still further, the same test will place a still higher percentage of successful employees. For example, if only the highest 10% of the persons tested are placed on the job, the percentage of satisfactory employees will be raised to 58%, or nearly double the percentage of satisfactory employees placed without the test.

Limitations of Taylor-Russell Tables

Smith (1948) made several warnings about using the Taylor-Russell tables. He pointed out that the tabled values do not apply to triangular distributions of test scores plotted against a criterion. Figure 8.6, which was used to explain the operation of the Taylor-Russell tables, assumes that every increase in average test score is associated with an increase in average criterion measure. The tables further assume that the criterion measure in relation to test score is a linear function. Under certain conditions, however, neither of these assumptions is fulfilled. For example, it is sometimes found that success on a job increases with test scores up to a certain point, but that above this point, further increases in test scores have no relation or even (in rare cases) have a negative relation to job success. An inspection of the scattergram between test scores and criterion is usually sufficient to determine whether the relation is essentially linear, but there are several methods available if it seems desirable to test the linearity of the plot. If it is decided that the scattergram represents a definitely nonlinear function, the Taylor-Russell tables should not be used to predict the proportion of successful employees that will be obtained by using the test.

Although there is a definite theoretical point to Smith's warning, some work by Tiffin and Vincent (1960) suggested that one can usually safely assume that the relationship shown by a correlation coefficient is sufficiently linear to justify the use of the Taylor-Russell tables. Using fifteen independent sets of predictor-criterion data, the theoretical expectancies obtained from modified Taylor-Russell tables (which are known as the Lawshe Expectancy Tables; see Appendix C) were compared with the empirical expectancies determined directly from the raw data. The data of each sample were split into fifths on the test-score continuum, and the percentage of satisfactory employees in each test-score category was computed directly. These percentages were then compared with the theoretical percentages predicted from the Lawshe tables. In none of the fifteen sets of data did the empirical percentages differ from the tabled percentages more than could be accounted for by chance, and in the majority of cases there was rather remarkable agreement between the empirical and the theoretical expectancies. Figure 8.7 gives examples of one of the worst fits from the fifteen studies and of one of the better fits. On the basis of these results, the authors concluded that, in the majority of instances, it is advisable to use theoretical instead of empirical expectancies in constructing expectancy charts.

LIMITATIONS OF CRITERION-RELATED TEST VALIDATION

The underlying theme of test validation is the need to demonstrate that scores on the tests are related to effective performance on the job. Such demonstrations are usually accomplished with criterion-related test-validation procedures, and should preferably be done with predictive validation approaches rather

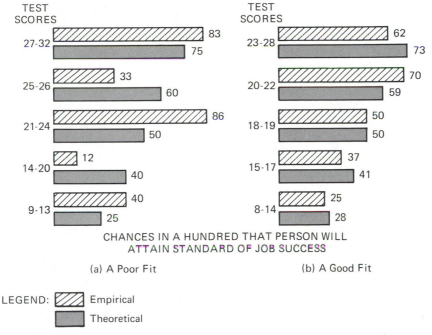

FIGURE 8.7 An example of one of the poorest "fits" (a) and of one of the best "fits" (b) of empirical to theoretical expectancies. (From Tiffin & Vincent, 1960.)

than concurrent validation. There are, however, limitations to criterion-related validation procedures.

One major limitation is the size of the sample needed to make reliable estimates about the strength of the relationship between tests and job performance. There are differences of opinion about how large a sample should be used in a validation study, but it is clear today that the problems of small samples are greater than was once believed (Schmidt & Hunter, 1980). It was once thought that samples of thirty to fifty people would be minimally acceptable. Most people today would argue that 150 to 200 is about as small a sample as one should risk and even that may be too small if there are a number of predictors being used to predict a criterion.

There are other limitations to criterion-related validation procedures, such as the administrative problems of using tests, dif-

ficulties with obtaining criterion information from employees, certain statistical problems, and the time needed to conduct a good validity study. It is not uncommon for such a study to span several months and sometimes years.

Three approaches have been developed to provide the basis for addressing some of the limitations of the predictive-validity study. All deal with the overall problem of generalizing findings about test validities. The three approaches are: *validity generalization, job-component validity,* and the *J-coefficient.* Each is discussed and then all are compared.

VALIDITY GENERALIZATION

Validity generalization (Pearlman, Schmidt, & Hunter, 1980; Schmidt & Hunter, 1977) addresses the condition in which there is a need to estimate the predictor-criterion relationship in situations that are similar to ones in which validity studies have already been conducted. This would apply to cases in which the same job has had a validity study done on it in some different division of an organization or in a different organization, to cases in which an earlier study has been done on the same job but some time has passed since the study was done, or to any other situation in which validity information exists for the same or similar jobs.

A well-established empirical fact is, that, even when jobs and tests are similar or essentially identical, there is a lot of variability in validity coefficients obtained across a number of criterion-related validity studies. Figure 8.8 illustrates just one example of the type of variability that is typically observed for almost any job. Schmidt, Gast-Rosenberg, and Hunter (1980) obtained validity coefficients from forty-two studies that used the Programmer Aptitude Test (PAT) total score to predict the job proficiency of computer programmers. Across these forty-two studies (of 1299 computer programmers), the mean validity coefficient was .38 and the standard deviation among the validity coefficients was .23. This means that in 68% of the studies, validity coefficients fell between .15 and .61.

Clearly this represents a wide range of values. The issue at hand is how to interpret the range of observed validity coefficients—why is there so much difference between the way tests predict in one situation and the way they predict in another when the test and the job in question remain the same?

Traditionally the differences in ability to predict job proficiency were believed to be due to subtle but important differences between specific situations. Thus, it was thought that computer programmers in one setting might need different skill combinations to perform their jobs than in another setting. The result of this belief was the conclusion that a new validity study should be done in every setting where such studies were "technically feasible" (*Uniform Guidelines* for *Employment Selection Procedures,* 1978).

Schmidt and Hunter (1977) suggested that although some of the variance in observed validity coefficients across studies may be due to the unique situational demands, much of it is probably due to limitations in each of the studies that reduce the size of the possible validity coefficients that could be observed. In particular, four common problems are likely to reduce the size of validity coefficients:

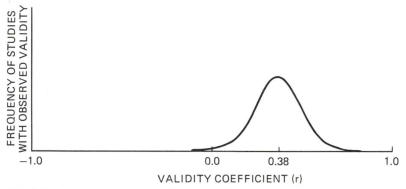

FIGURE 8.8 Distribution of validity coefficients illustrating a sample of forty-two validity studies using the total score on the Programmer Aptitude Test (PAT) to predict job proficiency. (Adapted from Schmidt et al., 1980.)

- *Sampling error.* In any correlation between a predictor and a criterion, it is unlikely that all the possible people for which the validity study is to apply can appear in the validity study. Only a small number of people are used in the sample to estimate what would be the case for the whole group or population to which one wants to generalize the findings. As a result, obtained data only approximate the population; they do not match it completely. The extent to which samples do not match populations is sampling error. Sampling error increases quickly as sample sizes become smaller. It is because of sampling error that we recommended the use of samples of 150 or more in validity studies.
- *Criterion reliability.* As the reliability of the measure used as a criterion drops below 1.0, the potential magnitude of the validity coefficient drops. The reliability of the criterion sets an upper limit on the size of the validity coefficient.
- *Predictor (test) reliability.* This has the same effect as criterion reliability.
- *Range restriction.* To the extent that the possible range in scores on either the test or the criterion is restricted, the size of the possible validity coefficient is restricted. This effect was discussed earlier when we presented the correlation coefficient.

Schmidt and Hunter (1977) argue that all of these sources of problems plus several more are likely to be present in all validity studies. Furthermore, these are all going to influence the size of the validity coefficients observed by reducing them below what they really should be. More importantly, they believe that these sources of error are more likely to be contributing to the variability in validity coefficients across studies than is the contribution of performance demands specific to any particular setting. Therefore, if the magnitude of the contributions of these various sources of error could be estimated, it should be possible to estimate the extent to which validity coefficients between particular tests on particular jobs generalize across situations. The process of estimating these effects to arrive at a judgment about the size of a validity coefficient for a given job using a known set of predictors is called *validity generalization.*

The actual conduct of a validity-generalization study is beyond the scope of this presentation, because it requires procedures for estimating the size of errors believed to be contributing to reduction in the validity coefficients. However, to the extent that one accepts the assumptions necessary to arrive at the estimates needed for the analyses, the results are very impressive. For example, regarding the computer programmers, Schmidt et al. (1980) concluded that the best estimate of the true validity coefficient between the PAT and job proficiency was .73. A validity coefficient of this magnitude would be extremely useful to an organization interested in selecting computer programmers.

Once an estimate of the size of the validity coefficient has been made for a particular job, the validity-generalization information can be used to decide whether or not it is necessary to do another validity study in a different setting for the same job. If one knows the likely size of the errors that will be present in the study to be conducted, it is possible to estimate the likelihood that the new study would yield information that would be different from the conclusions based on previous studies. If, for example, there are only a limited number of people available for the sample on which to do the new study and, therefore, the sampling error will be relatively high, it may not be worth doing a new study. Validity-generalization procedures offer a way to judge whether it seems worthwhile to do such a study.

The contribution of Schmidt and Hunter's validity-generalization research to personnel selection has been substantial. The implications of the methods are just beginning to be recognized. However, it is not without its problems. In particular, the strength of the method relies upon the quality of the estimates of the major types of errors that are hypothesized to affect validity coefficients. Controversies that have arisen with respect to the method primarily involve disagreements about the ways in which the estimates are made.

JOB-COMPONENT VALIDITY

The basic concepts of job-component validity, first introduced by Lawshe (1952), were termed *synthetic validity*. The procedure is predicated on the assumption that those jobs that have particular activities in common also share similar job requirements: They require people with the same general skills and abilities to carry them out. Therefore, if one could identify a test that is valid for predicting performance on a given job activity (component) that is common with components of other jobs, that test could be used to predict performance of people on the component in jobs for which the test has never been related to job performance.

For example, assume that one wanted to select mechanics to work in a service station. If it is known that the job consists of two components—mechanical work and customer relations—and that the job is approximately 75% mechanical and 25% customer relations, it might be possible to put together a selection battery consisting of one or more tests that measure mechanical ability and one or more that measure the ability to relate to other people. If data were available from various job situations about the validity of tests for each of these components, it would be possible to piece together a test battery for the job even though, more than likely, the corner-station operator could never hire enough mechanics to do a reasonable predictive validation study in the usual manner. The process of inferring the degree of validity in one setting for which the basic components of the job are known from information about the relationship between those components and certain predictors from other jobs is known as job-component validity.

There are several forms of job-component validity. Most of these involve the use of systematic, structured job-analysis procedures. The most generalizable and most widely used procedure involves the use of the Position Analysis Questionnaire (PAQ), which was described in detail in Chapter 4. Recall that the PAQ measures job elements that characterize behaviors and that these behaviorally oriented dimensions are used to describe jobs.

The general logic of the procedure is as follows: The PAQ is used to assess and describe a job in terms of a profile based on the dimensions measured by the instrument. Thus, the job will be described as high on some dimensions and low on others. Using a large data base built up over many years and many jobs, the next step is to locate other jobs in the PAQ data bank that have job activities similar to the one of interest. Finally, this information is combined with other data in the data bank on the ability tests used for people in the other similar jobs. From this, inferences are made about the tests to use on the new job as well as estimates about cut-off scores on these tests.

In our example of the gas-station mechanic, the PAQ would identify components like mechanical behaviors and customer relations and the search through the data base would locate ability tests that predicted these behaviors on other jobs with similar behavior requirements. Then the tests most likely to be good predictors of job success would be identified. The estimated cut-off scores would be used to determine those more likely to be successful on the job (those who scored above the cut-off) as opposed to those who would not (those who scored below the cut-off).

The primary job-component validity analysis of this type was done by Mecham (1977) with a sample of 163 jobs for which the U.S. Employment Service had published test-validity data for each of nine ability-test dimensions. The nine tests were part of a commonly used ability-test battery called the General Aptitude Test Battery (GATB). The data available to Mecham were the descriptions of a job as well as the means and standard deviations on each of the nine dimensions of the GATB for persons on each of the 163 jobs.

The mean test score of the job incumbents on each of the 163 jobs was used as the major criterion of the relative importance of the attribute measured by each test for the jobs in question. The justification for this is the assumption that, over time, those who lack the needed attributes for a job will either quit, be let go, or be transferred to another job.

The following examples illustrate the test data used in connection with the job-component validity strategy and the PAQ. These examples involve two ability constructs from the GATB—specifically, Intelligence (G) and Numerical ability (N). Tables 8.4 and 8.5 include the mean test scores of incumbents on each of several jobs. For the moment refer only to the data for actual incumbents, identified by I. The jobs illustrated in Table 8.4 are ordered from high to low on intelligence as measured by the test, and this order is pretty much in line with our common-sense knowledge of the intelligence demands of the jobs on the list. If one accepts gravitational or natural-selection assumptions, the data could be interpreted as follows: The jobs with high mean test scores presumably require a substantial level of the characteristic measured by the test (Intelligence or Numerical, as the case may be). On the other hand, since workers on jobs with low mean test scores have "survived" on those jobs despite their low scores, the characteristic measured by the test is presumably not required for the jobs in question. In turn, the jobs with intermediate mean test scores presumably require intermediate levels of the characteristic measured by the test. (Note that if two tests have a substantial correlation with each other in the population at large, one of them might have higher mean test scores for certain jobs than would be the case if they were not so corre-

TABLE 8.4 Mean test scores on the GATB intelligence (G) test for selected occupations based on actual incumbents and predictions from PAQ job-dimension scores

OCCUPATION	MEAN TEST SCORE	
	I: INCUMBENTS	P: PREDICTED
Mathematician	143	
General practitioner (M.D.)	135	130
Pharmacist	127	
Surveyor		118
Forester	124	117
Sales agent, insurance		116
Clothes designer	110	
Teller, bank	109	103
Stenographer	106	107
Power-plant operator	105	107
Sheet-metal worker	100	99
Barber	96	100
Plasterer	93	95
Grounds keeper		93
Custodian, school	88	93
Riveting-machine operator		88
Yarn winder	80	78
Shirt presser	76	
Tomato peeler	55	

Source: I: *Manual for the USTES General Aptitude Test Battery,* U.S. Department of Labor, 1970, Table 9–3. P: PAQ Services, Inc.

lated, since such scores might be influenced in part by the correlation of that test with the other one. Thus, the "unique" attribute measured by the one test may not be as strong a requirement of the job as the attribute measured by the other test. Even so, to the extent that high scores on such a test are characteristic of successful workers on the job, the test could be useful in the selection of candidates for the job.)

It would seem, then, that an ordering of jobs from high to low in terms of mean test scores of successful incumbents reflects the approximate level of the attribute (i.e., the

TABLE 8.5 Mean test scores on the GATB numerical (N) test for selected occupations based on actual incumbents and predictions from PAQ job analysis dimensions

OCCUPATION	MEAN TEST SCORES	
	I: INCUMBENTS	P: PREDICTED
Mathematician	135	
Programmer, engineering	131	122
Insurance underwriter	125	116
Accountant	121	119
Computer operator	116	
Surveyor		112
Bookkeeper	112	110
Teller	107	102
Room clerk, hotel	105	
Keypunch operator	100	104
Meat cutter	99	95
Barber	95	97
Grounds keeper		90
Box maker		90
Coil assembler	88	
Sewing machine operator	86	88
Farm hand		86
Food service worker	80	
Nut sorter	69	

construct) measured by the test that is characteristic of successful workers on various jobs. Such mean test scores were then used by Mecham (1977) as one criterion in the study of job-component validity with the PAQ. The other criterion was the test score representing 1 standard deviation (SD) below the mean on the test. Mecham considered this to be an index of minimumly acceptable levels of job requirements.

In his study, Mecham used PAQ analyses for jobs that matched the 163 jobs for which PAQ test data on job incumbents were available. The PAQ job-dimension scores of the 163 jobs were then used in a regression anal-

ysis (one for each of the nine GATB tests) as predictors of the two test-related criteria, the mean test scores and the scores 1 SD below the mean. The results of that analysis, given in Table 8.6, show the multiple correlations of combinations of job-dimension scores with the two test-related criteria. A multiple correlation can be interpreted in much the same fashion as a regular correlation, except that it reflects the relationship between an optimally weighted *combination* of predictors (in this case job-dimension scores of jobs) and the criterion (in this case mean test scores and scores 1 SD below the mean). Most of these correlations are quite respectable; the median correlations for the two criteria are .73 and .71. In only two of the tests were the correlations below .60: Finger Dexterity (*F*) and Manual Dexterity (*M*). These data strongly suggest that quantitative data from a structured job-analysis procedure can be used statistically to identify attributes relevant to selecting candidates for individual jobs (as

TABLE 8.6 Shrunken multiple correlations of combinations of PAQ job-dimension scores as predictors of GATB test-related criteria (number of jobs = 163)

GATB TEST	CRITERION	
	MEAN TEST SCORES	1 SD BELOW THE MEAN
G: Intelligence	.79	.78
V: Verbal Aptitude	.83	.84
N: Numerical Aptitude	.77	.73
S: Spatial Aptitude	.69	.71
P: Form Perception	.61	.60
Q: Clerical Perception	.78	.75
K: Motor Coordination	.73	.67
F: Finger Dexterity	.41	.41
M: Manual Dexterity	.30	.24
Median	.73	.71

Source: Mecham, 1977.

such attributes are identified by predictions of high mean test scores) and to derive approximations of test cut-off scores that might be used.

Use of the PAQ Job-Component Validity Strategy

The actual use of the job-component validity strategy involves two basic stages. The first consists of the analysis of the job(s) in question with the structured job-analysis procedure that is used. The second consists of statistical analyses to derive estimates of the personnel requirements that have been determined to be relevant for the "job components" identified or measured by the job-analysis method. In using the PAQ, the statistical analyses are usually carried out by computer. For any given job, the analyses include the derivation of job-dimension scores and the use of such scores to derive a prediction of the mean test score that would be expected on the part of a sample of incumbents on the job. An estimate of the score 1 SD below the mean is also derived (this is reported as a possible lower bounds cut-off score for personnel selection).

A few examples of the predicted mean test scores of a few actual jobs for the Intelligence (G) and Numerical (N) tests of the GATB test battery were included in Tables 8.4 and 8.5 presented earlier. The jobs for which predicted mean test scores are given are identified by P, and are inserted in their respective positions relative to the other jobs in that table for which actual mean test scores are given. The "ordering" of the jobs with predicted mean test scores appears to be compatible with the jobs for which actual test scores are shown.

One other illustration of data based on the PAQ job-component validity procedure is in order—namely, portions of a table of actual computer outputs for the job of mail clerk. Table 8.7 shows, for this job, the predicted

TABLE 8.7 Portions of a computer printout of predicted test data for the job of mail clerk as based on PAQ data

TEST	MEAN TEST SCORES	POSSIBLE CUT-OFF SCORES[a]	BEST COMBINATION OF TESTS
G: Intelligence	89	76	
V: Verbal Aptitude	92	82	
N: Numerical Aptitude	94	79	
S: Spatial Aptitude	96	78	
P: Form Perception	104	87	*
Q: Clerical Perception	106	91	*
K: Motor Coordination	101	84	*
F: Finger Dexterity	102	84	
M: Manual Dexterity	109	90	

[a]The possible cut-off score is the score 1 SD below the mean.

mean test score, a possible cut-off score (the score 1 SD below the mean), and an indication (with an asterisk) of the three tests considered best for use in selection. (These three tests are identified by a statistical procedure that identifies the best combination of tests; it does not necessarily identify the tests with the highest mean scores, since it takes into account the correlation between them.) Given data from such an analysis, a personnel manager would be in position to establish the test-based aptitude requirements for most typical jobs in industry and business.

J-COEFFICIENT

Primoff (1955a, 1955b) developed a formula for synthetically estimating the validity of a test for predicting overall job proficiency. The formula yields an index, called the J-coefficient, that is similar in many respects to a Pearson product-moment correlation (Urry, 1978). It represents the estimated correlation between scores on a test and overall performance on the job that is of interest.

In order to use the J-coefficient it is necessary to have the following information:

1. Several jobs belonging to the same class or family that share many behavior requirements. That is, each of the jobs in the set has several behaviors (job components) that are needed to perform the job, and each job has in common with the other jobs in the set several, but not necessarily all, of the behaviors.
2. Data on the correlation between individual characteristics (that is, scores on ability or other tests) which have been correlated with on-the-job behaviors.
3. Data on the correlation among the behaviors on the job. These correlations indicate the extent to which performance on one or more of the job behaviors is related to performance on the others.

With the just-listed information available, it is possible to estimate the validity of a test for a new job with only two pieces of infor-

mation about the new job. First, we must be confident that the new job belongs to the same class or family of jobs as the ones for which we have the information. Next, we need to obtain information about the importance of each job-dimension behavior in the new job for successful performance on that job. From the importance weights for the behaviors, and the validities of the test for predicting the behaviors for other jobs in the same job class or family, the J-coefficient can be calculated as an estimate of the validity of the test. Since importance weights can be obtained quite easily from raters familiar with the job, the procedure is quite easy to apply and, at least in principle, meets many of the conditions that the courts have desired for such procedures (Trattner, 1982).

EVALUATION OF VALIDITY GENERALIZATION, JOB-COMPONENT VALIDITY, AND THE J-COEFFICIENT

Validity generalization, job-component validity, and the J-coefficient strategies that have just been discussed attempt to deal with some of the limitations confronting criterion-related validity studies. In many respects, each has made some major strides in dealing with a problem that only a few years ago seemed overwhelming. Yet, each also has its limitations. All three procedures are restricted, to some extent, by the nature of the problems that each can address. Recall that validity generalization deals best with generalizations to jobs that are the same as the ones for which data are available. It is also the only strategy that offers a direct link to utility analysis by suggesting what the corrected validity relationship should be. Both job-component validity and the J-coefficient are useful for jobs that share some similar dimensions (behaviors) with jobs for which data are available, but for which not all dimensions are the same. Furthermore, job-component validity can handle more dissimilarity than can the J-coefficient, which requires that the new job belong to the same job family or class as the other jobs.

Limiting Assumptions

Validity generalization. The Achilles heel of all three techniques is the assumptions underlying each procedure. The most vulnerable is validity generalization simply because of the number of assumptions necessary. Many assumptions must be made about the contributions of each of several factors to the error in estimation of the validity coefficient. In addition, the corrections for these errors require estimations that are not agreed upon by all.

One of the weaknesses of the estimation process is that it leads to results that are too robust. That is, it leads to the prediction of high validity coefficients across such varied jobs that one might conclude that the tests are valid for almost everything. In one of several studies, Schmidt, Hunter, and Pearlman (1981) looked at over 360,000 workers in various clerical jobs which were grouped into five job families. Test-validity data for eight aptitude tests were generated from 3368 validity coefficients. The average generalized validity coefficients for the eight tests across the five job families differed only slightly. In another set of data dealing with thirty-five different types of jobs for army personnel, there were only small differences in validity coefficients across the thirty-five jobs.

Hunter (1982) obtained validity data from the nine tests of the General Aptitude Test Battery (GATB) of the U.S. Employment Service for a set of 515 jobs and 12,000 employees. The jobs were grouped into five categories varying in complexity. Within each category containing a large number of different jobs, a specific combination of tests was

equally valid for all of the jobs in that category.

The implication of all this research is that test validities can be generalized across broad groups of jobs that differ markedly in their nature and content. Hunter's (1982) work implied that validity generalization is so broad that almost all jobs can be grouped into just five categories based on complexity and that the same combination of tests can be used with all jobs within a category so defined. Although it is undoubtedly true that there is a great deal of generalizability in validity across jobs (especially jobs in the same job family), we remain somewhat skeptical about the extent to which the generalizations can be made to such a diverse set of jobs with a wide variety of individual characteristics. At some point the assumptions on which the procedure is based and the techniques for estimating parameters of generalizability become too robust and raise questions about the extent to which we may need to look more closely at them and be cautious about their application. These cautions, however, should not imply that there has not been nor does not continue to be great value in the procedure.

Job-component validity. Job-component validity requires the assumption that the most qualified people for a particular job are those who tend to remain on it. Therefore, the skills, abilities, and other characteristics of people on any job are assumed to be those that would be needed for anyone to do well on that job. This is in a sense a natural-selection view of job behavior.

There is empirical support for this position, as summarized by Tyler (1965) and discussed and illustrated earlier in this chapter in the section dealing with the job-status method of test validation. From the data presented there and the data of Mecham (1976) also presented earlier in this chapter, the assumption that people gravitate to jobs in which they are successful and that data from these people can be used to identify skills and abilities important on the job appears extremely reasonable.

A major criticism of this position is that it relies entirely upon past employment practices (Trattner, 1980). If these past practices restricted the access of people with particular skills to the same jobs (such as skills brought by women or minority-group members) new jobs validated on these samples could perpetuate these problems. Although we cannot deny this possibility, it does seem unlikely that such practices would control much of the variance in the differences between jobs on ability measures. To observe such tendencies would have required both severe restrictions in hiring, and, more importantly, quite high correlations between mean ability levels and membership in groups. The overlap in ability distributions between groups defined by sex, race, religion, or ethnic background is sufficiently high to decrease considerably the possibility of such an effect.

J-coefficient. The major assumptions of the J-coefficient are that the job in question falls within the job family or category from which the data are obtained and that estimates of the importance of the various job-performance dimensions are reliable and valid. Indeed, job-clustering procedures, such as those described in Chapter 4, have been quite successful in clustering jobs. Ratings of the importance of job dimensions are also reasonably accurate. They do, however, rely on past conditions but perhaps to a lesser extent than is the case for job-component validity. That is, the importance ratings rely on judgments based on current employees obtained statistically or from experts. To the extent that the current applicant pool contains people who accomplish the task by emphasizing certain job behaviors that are different from those a new group of employees might emphasize, the method would perpetuate the past. Nevertheless, most jobs do not allow a great deal of fluctuation in the types of tasks

that must be done well, so this problem does not seem to be a major one.

HOW TO USE TESTS FOR EMPLOYMENT

When a test has been found to be valid for a certain job, the next question is how the test should be used in the employment situation. What critical score (cut-off score) on the test should be required? Is it necessary, or desirable, to change the critical score from time to time?

The critical score to be used at any given time depends on the test norms and the selection ratio used for hiring. An example in which both of these data were used can clarify this point. First, the validity of the Adaptability Test for first-line supervisors was determined. This investigation resulted in the institutional expectancy chart shown in Figure 8.9. It is clear from Figure 8.9 that there were ninety-four chances in 100 that individuals making scores of 18 or higher would survive as supervisors for a period of 6 months. Figure 8.9 also shows the percentage of "survivors" among those making successively lower critical scores. Obviously, the higher the Adaptability Test scores of individuals placed in the supervisory jobs, the greater the chances are that those selected will be able to handle the new assignments. However, to decide without regard to the pool of eligible candidates that only those making a score of 18 or higher will be placed on the jobs is quite unrealistic.

At this point, therefore, we should look at norms on the test derived from the eligible candidates. These norms, shown in Table 8.8, illustrate the percentile ranks equivalent to various raw scores for the group with whom we are concerned. As Table 8.8 shows, 100% of the individuals scored 27 or below, 95% scored 26 or below, 90% scored 21 or below,

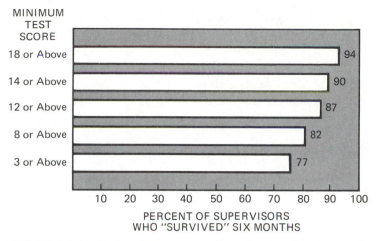

MINIMUM
TEST
SCORE

Minimum Test Score	Percent
18 or Above	94
14 or Above	90
12 or Above	87
8 or Above	82
3 or Above	77

PERCENT OF SUPERVISORS
WHO "SURVIVED" SIX MONTHS

FIGURE 8.9 Institutional expectancy chart showing the percent of new supervisors who "survived" 6 months as a function of minimum scores on the Adaptability Test.

80% scored 17 or below, and so on down the table. In other words, 80% scored 17 or below, and only 20% scored 18 or above. This means that to find twenty individuals scoring 18 or above, we would need a pool of 100 from which to select, and we would therefore need to use a selection ratio of .20. Because a pool of 100 individuals might not be available, we would have to reduce our critical score in order to fill the vacancies. If we needed twenty individuals and there were only fifty to choose among, we would be op-

erating with a selection ratio of 20:50 or .40, which means that we would have to reduce the critical score to 13. The reason for this change in the critical score is that, as Table 8.8 shows, a score of 12 is at the sixtieth percentile, which means that 60% of the group scored 12 or below, and only 40% of the group scored 13 or higher. If we refer again to the expectancy chart in Figure 8.9, we can see that a lower percentage of individuals would survive on the supervisor's job for 6 months if we use the critical score of 13 than when we used the critical score of 18.

The point is that the critical (cut-off) score on a test must be varied with the tightness or looseness of the labor market. The tighter the market, the lower the critical score. The looser the market, the higher the critical score can be.

COMBINING TESTS INTO A BATTERY

No single test will measure all of the capacities or abilities required on any job. Even the simplest of jobs is complex if one considers

TABLE 8.8 Percentile norms on the adaptability test for supervisors in one plant

PERCENTILE RANK	SCORE ON TEST
100	27
95	26
90	21
80	17
70	15
60	12
50	11
40	10
30	9
20	7
10	5
5	4
1	3

the combination of capacities or abilities required of a person who is to remain on the job and do it well. The aptitudes for any job consist of a syndrome of abilities, and one needs all of these to be successful. This makes it desirable, and in some cases necessary, to use a battery of tests rather than a single test. There are two basic methods of using tests in a battery—the *multiple cut-off* method and the *composite-score* method. With both methods, it is assumed that the validity of each test in the battery has been established for the job in question.

Multiple Cut-Off Method

The multiple cut-off method involves establishing a minimum standard on *each* of the tests administered to the job candidates and not accepting an applicant unless he or she scores above the minimum on *all* tests. The procedure is used for jobs in which having a high score on one dimension will not compensate for having a low score on another. Consider the task of selecting students for pilot training and those for attendance at a particular university. In both cases, assume that two tests were used. For the pilots we could use a test of mental ability and a vision test. For the college students we could use grades in high school and scores of the Scholastic Aptitude Test (SAT). In the case of pilot selection, we would use a multiple cut-off method because the applicant would have to score above a minimum on both exams. For pilots, having high mental ability will not compensate for being nearly blind and neither will excellent eyesight make up for being stupid. On the other hand, the student-selection battery could combine scores in such a way that high grades in high school could compensate for low test scores, and vice versa. This situation would not require the use of multiple cut-offs.

Multiple hurdles. When the tests are given one at a time and the next test is not given unless the applicant passes the earlier test(s), this represents a special case of the multiple cut-off called *multiple hurdles*. Using this procedure, by the time an applicant takes the last test only that group of applicants that has passing scores on all tests to that point is tested. As a result, multiple cut-off examination batteries are often given in a sequence using multiple hurdles, because it is more economical than giving all tests to all applicants.

Composite-Score Method

The composite-score method is usually based on the use of multiple correlations and regression analysis. A multiple correlation can be thought of as the correlation of a combination of two or more predictors (in this case, tests) with another variable (in this case, a criterion such as job performance). The predictors are combined by weighting them in such a way that the linear combination of all of the predictors predicts the criterion as well as possible. The regression analysis provides the statistical procedure for determining the weights to assign to each predictor so as to obtain the highest correlation possible between the weighted combination of the predictors and the criterion. Once the weights are determined from one sample, they can be applied to applicants in another sample to select persons in the new sample.

One word of caution should be mentioned with respect to multiple regression as a technique for determining the weights for composite scores. The procedure capitalizes on chance. Recall that every person's score on a test and on the criterion can be thought of as the sum of that person's true score plus some error; therefore, every score has some error component to it. The multiple regression technique, as we mentioned, optimally fits scores on the predictors to the criterion so as to maximize the prediction of the criterion from the predictors. Yet, because all of the scores that are fitted together statistically contain some error, the next time the weights are used the error scores will change and the weights will be less than optimal. To estimate how much less, normally *cross validation* is used. In this case, the sample is divided into two groups. One sample is usually about one-third of the total sample, and the other is the rest. The weights are determined using the larger sample and then the weights are applied to the smaller one. It is then possible to compare the size of the multiple correlation in the larger sample to the size of the regression coefficient between the weighted composite score and the criterion in the smaller one. Due to errors in measurement, the latter coefficient will almost always be somewhat smaller than the former. How much smaller depends on the size of the error and the size of the samples; the larger the sample for which the weights were determined, the less the change. The change is known as *shrinkage*. The magnitude of the shrinkage can also be estimated from a statistical formula. In fact, Murphy (1982) presents several convincing arguments for always using a shrinkage formula rather than cross validating by splitting the sample when using multiple regression for estimating weights in selection.

Composite scores can also be created using procedures other than multiple regression. For example, experts might judge the importance of each test, and then the experts' ratings might be used to weight the test scores. More commonly unit weights are used; each test is simply weighted by 1.00 and all test scores are added together. When this method is used, it is usually necessary to convert all test scores to equal units—that is, to standardize each test—otherwise the test with larger units would be weighted more heavily. For example, unit weights used to combine high-school grade point averages figured on a 4.0 scale would be grossly underweighted if raw scores were combined with SAT scores, where the mean for the exam is

500 and the standard deviation is 100. However, if both were converted to standard score units with a mean of 0.0 and a standard deviation of 1.0 (see discussion of standard scores in Chapter 3), unit weights would give each equal weights.

At first glance it would appear that almost any weighting system would be better than equal weighting. After all, equal weights treat all tests as equally important for predicting performance. Intuitively it seems that some would just have to be more important than others. A large body of research has been done comparing various ways to weight tests and to establish a composite score. Interestingly, unit weights fare quite well (Campbell, 1974). In fact, when the sample sizes are small—less than 150 to 200 people—using unit weights is almost always superior to using any other weighting scheme.

TEST ADMINISTRATION AND CONFIDENTIALITY

The use of personnel tests should be mutually advantageous both to the organization and to the individuals being tested. Toward this end, the tests should be administered under conditions that help place the individual at ease, for some people tend to become nervous and apprehensive at the prospect of being tested. In order to insure reasonably adequate test results, the following guidelines should be followed:

1. The test room should be light, roomy, and quiet.
2. Each person should have a comfortable chair and table or desk.
3. The test administrator should follow whatever instructions there are for administering the test, including adherence to any specified time limits.

Once tests have been administered to individuals, they should be used in a professionally ethical manner. This means that individuals' test scores should be available only to those persons who have a legitimate use for them and that the scores and tests should be considered entirely confidential by those persons who do have access to them. That they will be kept in confidence should be stated by the test administrator before the tests are given to the candidates to help allay their apprehensions.

DISCUSSION

So much attention was devoted to personnel selection for two reasons. First, many of the issues that are necessary to understand for selection also apply to other personnel functions. For example, job analysis, an absolutely critical feature in selection, is important for training, placement, salary and wage administration, and other job-related factors; performance appraisal, necessary as the criterion in selection, is also valuable for counseling and career development, motivation, and so on. Thus, many of the topics that were introduced in this chapter come up again and again throughout the text.

Selection is also important because several major changes are going on in current selection research. Title VII of the Civil Rights Act of 1964 protects specific groups against unfair selection practices. As a result, much emphasis is placed on developing selection practices that are fair. We have learned much in this regard in the last 20 years, and are still learning more. Finally, new procedures to estimate the likelihood of successful selection practices have led to some major changes in selection processes. In many cases, these processes are still being evaluated. In some cases, the data look quite promising, but the courts are somewhat reluctant to accept these new procedures. Hopefully, in the not-too-distant future, as more data accumulate, these

procedures will receive the support they deserve.

For all of these reasons, much space has been devoted to personnel selection. In the chapters that follow, we build on many of the concepts and procedures introduced here.

REFERENCES

American Psychological Association (1974). *Standards for educational and psychological tests.*

Bouchard, T. J. (1972). A manual for job analysis. Minneapolis: Minnesota Civil Service Commission.

Campbell, J. P. (1974). A Monte Carlo approach to some problems inherent in multivariate prediction: With special reference to multiple regression. TR. 2002, Personnel Training Research Program, Office of Naval Research, Washington, D.C.

Campbell, J. P. (1976). Psychometric theory. In M. D. Dunnette (Ed.), *Handbook of industrial and organizational psychology* (Chap. 6). Chicago: Rand McNally.

Cronbach, L. J., & Meehl, P. E. (1955). Construct validation in psychological tests. *Psychological Bulletin, 52,* 281–302.

Drasgow, F., & Miller, H. E. (1982). Psychometric and substantive issues in scale construction and validation. *Journal of Applied Psychology, 67,* 268–279.

Dunnette, M. D., & Borman, W. C. (1979). Personnel selection and classifications systems. In J. Rosensweig and L. Porter (Eds.), *Annual Review of Psychology.* Palo Alto, CA: Annual Reviews, Inc.

Fleishman, E. A., & Berniger, J. (1960). One way to reduce turnover. *Personnel, 37,* 63–69.

Guion, R. M. (1978). "Content validity" in moderation. *Personnel Psychology, 31*(2), 205–213.

Harrell, T. W., & Harrell, M. S. (1945). Army general classification test scores for civilian occupations. *Educational and Psychological Measurement, 5,* 229–239.

Hunter, J. E. (1982). Test validation for 12,000 jobs: An application of job classification and validity generalization analysis to the General Aptitude Test Battery (GATB), East Lansing, MI: Unpublished paper, 1982.

Kawula, W. J., & Smith, A. De W. (1975). *Handbook of occupational information.* Prince Albert, Saskatchewan, Canada: Manpower and Immigration, Training Research Station. (Note: The generic skills program is now being carried out by the Occupational and Career Analysis Branch, Canadian Employment and Immigration Commission, Ottawa, Ontario.)

Lawshe, C. H. (1952). Employee selection. *Personnel Psychology, 5,* 31–34.

Mecham, R. C. (February 1977). Unpublished report. Logan, Utah: PAQ Services, Inc., P. O. Box 3337.

Murphy, K. J. (1982). Cost-benefit considerations in choosing among cross-validation methods. Presentation at the Annual Meetings of the American Psychological Association, Washington, D.C.

Pearlman, K., Schmidt, F. L., & Hunter, J. E. (1980). Validity generalization results for tests used to predict job proficiency and training success in clerical occupations. *Journal of Applied Psychology, 65,* 373–406.

Primoff, E. S. (1955a). *Basic formulae for the J-coefficient to select tests by job analysis requirements.* Washington, D.C.: U.S. Civil Service Commission, Standards Division.

Primoff, E. S. (1955b). *Test selection by job analysis: The J-coefficient, what it is, how it works.* Technical Series No. 20, Washington D.C.: U.S. Civil Service Commission, Standards Division.

Schmidt, F. L., Gast-Rosenberg, I., & Hunter, J. E. (1980). Validity generalization results on computer programmers. *Journal of Applied Psychology, 65,* 643–661.

Schmidt, F. L., & Hunter, J. E. (1977). Development of a general solution to the problem of validity generalization. *Journal of Applied Psychology, 62,* 529–540.

Schmidt, F. L., Hunter, J. E., & Pearlman, K. (1981). Task differences as moderators of aptitude test validity in selection: A red herring. *Journal of Applied Psychology, 66,* 166–185.

Smith, M. (1948). Causations concerning the use of the Taylor-Russell tables in employee selection. *Journal of Applied Psychology, 32,* 595–600.

Stewart, N. (1947). AGCT scores of Army personnel grouped by occupation. *Occupations, 26,* 5–41.

Taylor, H. C., & Russell, J. T. (1939). The relationship of validity coefficients to the practical effectiveness of tests in selection: Discussion and tables. *Journal of Applied Psychology, 22,* 565–578.

Tenopyr, M. L. (1977). Content-construct confusion. *Personnel Psychology, 30*(1), 47–54.

Tiffin, J., & Vincent, N. L. (1960). Comparisons of empirical and theoretical expectancies. *Personnel Psychology, 13,* 59–64.

Trattner, M. H. (1982). Synthetic validity and its application to the uniform guidelines validation requirements. *Personnel Psychology, 35,* 383–397.

Trattner, M. H., Fine, S. A., & Kubis, J. F. (1955). A comparison of worker requirement ratings made by reading job descriptions and by direct job observation. *Personnel Psychology, 8,* 183–194.

Tyler, L. E. (1965). *The psychology of individual differences.* New York: Appleton-Century Crofts.

Uniform guidelines on employment selection procedures (August 25, 1978). *Federal Register, 43* (166), 38290–38309.

U.S. Department of Labor, Employment and Training Administration (1977). *Dictionary of occupational titles* (4th ed.) Washington, D.C.: Superintendent of Documents, Government Printing Office.

U.S. Department of Labor (1970). *Manual for the USTES general aptitude test battery.*

Urry, V. W. (1978). Some variations on deviations by Primoff and their extensions. (TN–78–3.) Washington, D.C.: U.S. Civil Service Commission, Personnel Research and Development Center, NTIS No. PB 287–298.

9

Human Abilities and Their Measurement

This chapter and the next deal primarily with the use of tests to measure human characteristics and the application of these tests for personnel measurement. This chapter covers what we refer to as human abilities, and the next chapter deals with personality and interest factors.

BASIC HUMAN CHARACTERISTICS

We start with a very simple observation—people are different. Although there are thousands of adjectives to describe people, we cannot deal with thousands of types of human differences. This problem has led to research to identify what might be thought of as the "basic" human characteristics (what are sometimes called *constructs*). There is still some question as to whether the identified "basic" characteristics are actually discrete, underlying human qualities, or whether they simply represent our "conceptualization" of

the nature of human characteristics. In either case, however, the characteristics so identified are those for which many tests have been developed and used in personnel selection.

The Identification of Basic Human Characteristics

The identification of basic human characteristics is typically carried out by factor analysis. As used for this purpose factor analysis typically consists of the following processes: (1) administering a variety of tests to a sample of people; (2) correlating each test with every other test: (3) identifying the various factors by means of statistical manipulations (essentially, this step is based on the identification of the several tests that tend to form individual "groups" or "clusters" on the basis of their correlations with each other); and (4) naming each factor on the basis of subjective judgment of the "common denominator" that characterizes those tests with high statistical "loadings" on the factor. A high loading of a test represents a high correlation of the test with the factor. Thus the tests with the highest loadings on a particular factor presumably are measuring somewhat that same basic characteristic. It is assumed that the underlying characteristic producing the high intercorrelations of the tests with the factor is the common denominator that has resulted in their high correlations. The investigator gives the factor a name or label that captures the meaning of the underlying construct that is shared with all the tests.

An Inventory of Basic Human Characteristics

There have been numerous factor-analytic studies aimed at identifying the basic human characteristics within each of certain rather broad classes. We consider Peterson and Bownas' (1982) to be the most comprehensive analysis of these studies. They have grouped the studies into the following categories:

• Cognitive abilities (mental abilities);
• Psychomotor abilities and physical proficiencies;
• Personality;
• Vocational preferences (interests).

For each of these categories they present a taxonomy that they consider to be the best representation of the structure of the basic human characteristics (i.e., the constructs) of the category. These are referred to later in this and the next chapter.

TEST CONSTRUCTION

This is not intended as a text on test construction. However, because we are dealing in part with personnel tests, we do mention certain aspects of test construction—in particular, item analysis. In developing a test, the test developer must first select the content of items that are judged to treat the construct, field of knowledge, or whatever the test is supposed to measure. The next stage is to develop items to incorporate into what is usually an experimental form of the test. Selecting the material to be included in test items and the actual development of items are important phases of test development and should be carried out on the basis of sound professional practice.

In developing tests there are two aspects of item analysis, both of which are directed toward selecting those items for the final form of the test that would be most useful (meaning most valid) for measuring whatever is to be measured. One of these is the notion of internal consistency, and the other concerns the relationship of items to some independent criterion considered to reflect the "thing" the test is intended to measure.

Internal consistency within a test is concerned with the extent to which the individual items measure the same thing that the total pool of items tends to measure. Internal consistency of the items can be measured in various ways. One of these is deriving a statistical index for each item that shows its relationship to the *total scores* on the experimental test of a sample of individuals. There are many indexes that can be used; one is called a D (for discrimination) value as presented by Lawshe (1942). In using the D value to determine internal consistency, a sample of subjects is divided into two groups on the basis of their total scores on an experimental form of the test—namely those with high scores and those with low scores (such as those above and those below average). For each item, the percent who gave a correct response (or in some instances some specified response) is determined for those in each of the two criterion groups (high and low). These two percents are then used with a nomograph to derive a D value. The higher the D value is, the greater the discrimination of the item is in terms of the criterion. Following are a few hypothetical examples:

| ITEM NO. | PERCENT OF CORRECT RESPONSES | | D VALUE |
	IN HIGH GROUP	IN LOW GROUP	
1	90	60	1.1
2	60	60	0.0
3	65	40	.7
4	75	65	.3
5	95	85	.6

The D value is influenced by the difference between the two percentages and by the difficulty of the item (that is, the combined percentage of those who give correct answers). The selection of items with high D values tends to "purify" the test—that is, to form a final test with relatively homogeneous items. But internal consistency tells us nothing about the extent to which the test measures what it is intended to measure, other than whatever inferences can be drawn from a subjective evaluation of the items. To determine this one needs to administer the test to one or more groups for whom some external criterion can be obtained or inferred, a criterion considered to reflect variations in the quality that the test is intended to measure. Such a criterion might consist of scores on another test recognized as measuring the quality in question, or perhaps of groups of people considered to differ on the quality. For example, for a test that is supposed to measure arithmetic ability, one might use as criterion groups high-school students who have high grades in arithmetic courses and those who have low grades, or one might use a group of bookkeepers (who are considered to have substantial arithmetic ability) and a group of, say, receptionists (who would be expected on the average, to have less arithmetic ability). With "high" and "low" criterion

groups so formed, it is then possible to administer the experimental form of the test to them and then carry out an item analysis to identify those items that discriminate adequately between the two groups. One could use the D value for this purpose.

The two-stage process of analyzing items against an internal criterion and then against an external criterion helps assure that the items that survive both of these processes will comprise a reasonably adequate test of the quality the test is intended to measure. Repetition of these operations can sometimes contribute to even further "purification" of the test. After developing a final form of a test using such procedures, it is then usually sound practice to try the test out as a total procedure with one or more additional groups of subjects as an additional validation step for developing test-score norms.

COGNITIVE ABILITIES AND TESTS

Interest in cognitive or mental abilities goes back to the early research of Sir Francis Galton (1883) and the development of the early tests by Binet (Binet & Henri, 1895), specifically those for identifying mentally deficient children in schools. Subsequently Spearman (1927) came forth with a postulated concept of a "g" (for general) factor of *mental energy*, plus a variety of specific factors. The next major stage of mental testing was the monumental work of Thurstone (1948), who, by factor analyses, identified what he called the seven primary mental abilities. In turn, Guilford (1967) postulated the notion of 120 factors to depict the "structure of intellect." The evidence to support the validity of such an array of distinct cognitive factors has not been forthcoming, however.

At present, we believe that the analysis by Peterson and Bownas (1982) represents an excellent inventory of the basic cognitive abilities. It is based in large part on the earlier work of Eckstrom (1973) as reviewed later by Dunnette (1976), but also includes three other factors suggested on the basis of subsequent research. The complete proposed taxonomy of cognitive abilities includes the following thirteen factors:

1. Flexibility and speed of closure (the ability to "hold in mind" a particular visual percept and find it embedded in a distracting background);
2. Fluency;
3. Inductive reasoning;
4. Associative (rote) memory;
5. Span memory;
6. Number facility;
7. Perceptual speed;
8. Deductive (syllogistic) reasoning;
9. Spatial orientation and visualization;
10. Verbal comprehension;
11. Verbal closure (ability to solve problems requiring the identification of words, as when some letters are missing, disarranged, or mixed with other letters);
12. Figural fluency (the ability to produce a response quickly by drawing a number of examples, elaborations, or restructurings based on a given visual descriptive stimulus);
13. Visual memory.

Tests of Cognitive Abilities

Thousands of tests of cognitive or mental abilities have been developed. Many such tests (along with others) are described in *The Eighth Mental Measurements Yearbook* by Buros (1978), which also gives information about the source of each test, references of relevant research, and usually some evaluation of the test and data on validity and reliability. (Appendix D of this text lists several tests that are in reasonably common use in industry.)

The tests that are available represent a wide variety; many are used with children in clinical-psychology practice, in schools, for vocational counseling, as well as in personnel work in industry. Although some tests are intended to measure the specific basic characteristics just listed, many tend to be broad

gauge in nature, and cover material that represents several of the basic characteristics. The use of such broad-gauge tests probably can be justified on the grounds that certain of the basic cognitive (i.e., mental) characteristics are in fact correlated with each other. Furthermore, there are indications in connection with validity generalization that various tests of the same general type can serve equally well for personnel selection.

Recognizing some of the limitations of criterion-related studies (such as the problems associated with small samples and the growing indications of validity generalization), following are the results of a couple of validity studies with mental-ability tests.

Clerical Jobs. In one study the Adaptability Test was administered to clerical employees in several departments of a paper company. The correlations of scores on the test with supervisors' ratings ranged from .40 to .65 in the various departments. The individual expectancy chart for the department in which the correlation was .65 is shown in Figure 9.1.

Supervisors. Mental-ability tests frequently have substantial validity as the basis for selecting supervisors. This was illustrated by the results of a study of seventy employees of a rubber company who had been promoted to supervisory jobs. During the first session of a training program these men were given the Adaptability Test. The test results were filed for 6 months, at which time a follow-up analysis was made in relation to a criterion of being "still on the job." Approximately one-fourth of the men had not "survived" as supervisors for that period; they had either quit voluntarily or had been demoted, transferred, or dismissed. Figure 9.2 shows the percentage of men still on the job after these 6 months, in relation to their test scores. Interestingly, not a single man with a score of 4 or below was still on the job, and of those with scores between 5 and 9 only 59% had

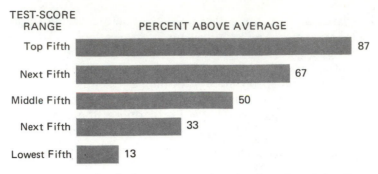

TEST-SCORE
RANGE   PERCENT ABOVE AVERAGE

Top Fifth   87

Next Fifth   67

Middle Fifth   50

Next Fifth   33

Lowest Fifth   13

FIGURE 9.1 Individual expectancy chart for the Adaptability Test as a predictor of job success for clerical jobs in a paper company. This chart is based on a correlation of .65 between test scores of job incumbents and supervisors' ratings of job performance.

survived (as contrasted with 90% or more for those with higher scores).

MECHANICAL ABILITY

Various tests used in personnel selection are commonly called mechanical-ability tests. These vary in their nature and content, but some tap certain cognitive abilities of a perceptual nature that are considered to be relevant for various types of mechanical and related work. Of the cognitive abilities listed previously, perceptual speed and spatial orientation and visualization would be particularly applicable. Such perceptual skills are useful in jobs that require the visualization of physical relationships, such as putting a carburetor back together, or drafting or interpreting blueprints. A few mechanical-ability tests tend to measure some aspects of mechanical experience—that is, familiarity with, and understanding relating to, mechanical equipment and tools and mechanical principles and practices.

Tests of Mechanical Ability

A few of the most common tests of mechanical ability are listed in Appendix D. Ex-

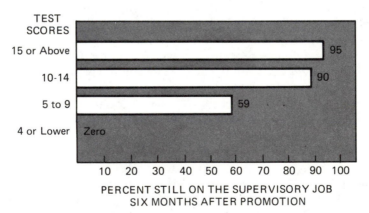

FIGURE 9.2 Percent of men promoted to supervisory jobs in a rubber company who were still on the job 6 months later, as a function of score on the Adaptability Test.

amples of certain of these, or items from them, are shown in Figures 9.3 and 9.4. The Purdue Mechanical Adaptability Test, in particular illustrates the processes used in developing standardized tests of this type.

The Purdue Mechanical Adaptability Test was developed to aid in identifying men or boys who are mechanically inclined and who, therefore, are most likely to succeed on jobs or in training programs calling for mechanical abilities and interests. The test measures one's experiential background in mechanical, electrical, and related activities.

The questions comprising Form A of the Purdue Mechanical Adaptability Test were selected by statistical methods designed to achieve maximum reliability of the final test and as low a correlation as possible with general intelligence. The effort to develop a mechanical-ability test that would not depend very much on the general intelligence of the persons being tested payed off quite well, for the correlations of scores on this test with scores on various mental-ability tests are generally rather low.

Figure 9.5 is an expectancy chart based on a validation study with the Purdue Mechanical Adaptability Test for airplane engine mechanic trainees. The criterion used was instructor ratings. This figure illustrates the relevance of mechanical-ability tests to successful performance in job activities of the type represented.

PSYCHOMOTOR AND PHYSICAL ABILITIES

Human beings have a wide repertoire of psychomotor abilities and physical proficiencies. The most extensive research relating to the nature of these abilities has been carried out by Fleishman and his associates (Fleishman & Hogan, 1978; Theologus, Romashko, & Fleishman, 1970). Their inventory of nine-

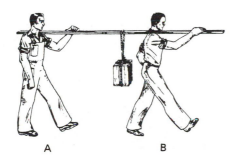

X

Which man carries more weight?
(If equal, mark C.)

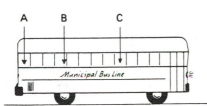

Y

Which letter shows the seat where a passenger will get the smoothest ride?

FIGURE 9.3 Two items from Forms S and T of the Bennett Test of Mechanical Comprehension. (Reproduced by permission. Copyright 1940, renewed 1967; 1941, renewed 1969; 1942, renewed 1967; © 1967, 1968 by The Psychological Corporation, New York, N.Y. All rights reserved.)

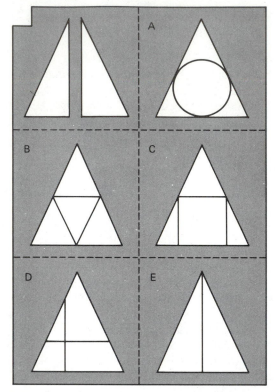

FIGURE 9.4 An item from the Minnesota Paper Form Board Test. The person tested is asked to select the set of lettered parts (A, B, C, D, or E) which may be formed by the parts shown in the upper-left square.

teen such abilities falls into two broad classes, as follows:

Psychomotor abilities:

1. Choice reaction time;
2. Reaction time;
3. Speed of limb movement;
4. Wrist-finger speed;
5. Multilimb coordination;
6. Finger dexterity;
7. Manual dexterity;
8. Arm-hand steadiness;
9. Rate control;
10. Control precision.

Physical abilities:

11. Dynamic strength;
12. Trunk strength;
13. tatic strength;
14. Explosive strength;
15. Extent flexibility;
16. Dynamic flexibility;
17. Gross body coordination;
18. Gross body equilibrium;
19. Stamina.

Psychomotor Tests

The most common tests of psychomotor ability deal with such skills as finger and manual dexterity. Examples of these are shown in Figures 9.6, 9.7, and 9.8. (See Peterson &

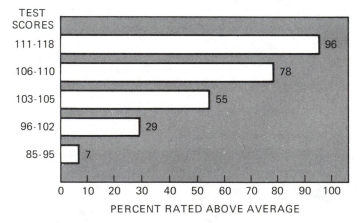

FIGURE 9.5 Relation between scores on the Purdue Mechanical Adaptability Test and ratings of thirty-four airplane engine mechanic trainees.

FIGURE 9.6 Bennett Hand-Tool Dexterity Test. (Photograph courtesy of The Psychological Corporation.)

FIGURE 9.8 Stromberg Dexterity Text. (Photograph courtesy of The Psychological Corporation.)

Bownas, 1982, pp. 80, 81, for tests of the specific psychomotor abilities just listed.)

Measuring Physical Abilities for Jobs

Tests that measure individuals' physical abilities naturally require relevant physical performance, usually involving some physical apparatus. (Tests that measure most of the abilities are listed by Peterson & Bownas, 1982, pp. 80, 81). Sometimes, however, the assessment of individuals' physical abilities is made by physicians on the basis of physical examinations, especially in the case of physically handicapped persons.

The physical requirements of jobs can be ascertained by conventional test-validation procedures, although such procedures are usually not very practical because of the time involved to administer physical-ability tests. Because of this various alternative procedures have been explored. One such procedure has been developed by Fleishman and his associates (Fleishman & Hogan, 1978). The procedure is based on extensive research in which experienced people use a seven-point scale ranging from very, very light to very, very hard to rate many types of job ac-

FIGURE 9.7 Purdue Pegboard.

tivities in terms of their requirements for each type of physical ability. For any given ability the activities that are rated most consistently by the raters are then used as benchmarks to represent different "levels" on a scale for that ability. An example for the ability of stamina is shown in Figure 9.9. Any other work activity can also be rated on this scale, using the benchmarks as guidelines. Such ratings have respectable levels of reliability and validity.

VISUAL SKILLS

Most jobs require at least moderate visual skills, but for some jobs, visual skills are especially important.

The Nature of Visual Skills

Following are descriptions of some of the more important visual skills, along with comments regarding their measurement:

Visual acuity. This is the ability to make discriminations of black and white details in the visual field. The basic measurement of acuity is the visual angle subtended at the eye of the smallest features of a visual target that a subject can discriminate—for example, the letters on a chart in the doctor's office. Visual acuity usually should be measured separately at near and far distances.

Depth perception (stereopsis). We use various visual cues to judge distance or depth, such as the relative sizes and positions of objects in the visual field. "True" depth perception or stereopsis, however, is based on the fact that the two eyes see slightly different views of objects because of their different positions.

Color discrimination. Absolute color blindness is very rare. However, certain aspects of color deficiency are somewhat more common, such as the inability to discriminate between the reds and greens or between the blues and yellows.

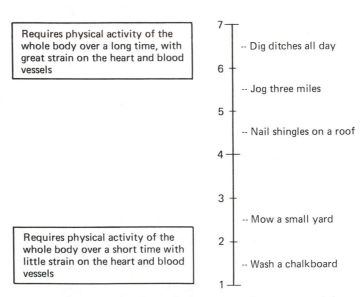

FIGURE 9.9 Example of a scale for rating jobs in terms of their physical-ability requirements. This example is for stamina. (From Fleishman & Hogan, 1978, Appendix B.)

Postural characteristics of the eyes (phorios). Under normal seeing conditions the two eyes move in relation to each other so that both converge symmetrically upon an object. This convergence gives us a clear, single image of the object when it is viewed binocularly. However, in some individuals, the muscles that control these movements are not properly "balanced." This imbalance needs to be measured under testing conditions in which the eyes are not required to converge on a specific object and can therefore assume independent "postures." Such imbalances are called phorias, and they may be either vertical or lateral. Most people with phorias have learned to overcome phoria conditions by controlling the muscles that direct both eyes to the point of visual regard, but in so doing they may have to maintain the eyes in a "strained" posture, thereby running the risk of muscular fatigue if the postures have to be retained for some time.

Vision Tests

Ophthalmologists (physicians who specialize in visual problems) and opticians have various sophisticated devices for measuring certain visual abilities and characteristics. Because of the complexity of such devices, however, they are not used extensively in personnel selection. When employment offices require vision tests they usually use a chart with letters of decreasing size, or one of a few vision-testing instruments that lend themselves to easy use.[1] The letter-type test determines separately for each eye the smallest letters the subject can read. The resulting acuity score is in the form of a fraction. The standard is 20/20, which means that the subject can read at 20 feet what the "standard

[1]See Appendix D for a list of certain vision-test instruments.

eye" could read at twenty feet. In turn, a score of 20/15 means that the person can read at 20 feet what the "standard eye" could read at fifteen feet.

Some limitations of the usual letter-type vision test are: It only measures visual acuity; it measures only far acuity (and not near acuity); and the visual targets used—namely, letters—vary in their level of perceptual difficulty. Because of these limitations, some of the other types of vision tests are usually more suitable for use in personnel selection, especially if the jobs in question have special visual requirements.

In this regard, Dr. Joseph Tiffin carried out extensive research relative to the visual requirements of jobs in industry. Tiffin's research used the Ortho-Rater, and resulted in the identification of several visual "job families," each of which had a different profile of visual skill requirements. An example of the profile for one job family—that of vehicle operator—is shown in Figure 9.10. Individuals whose scores on the various tests fall in the shaded areas are considered to fulfill the visual-profile requirements, and those with scores in the white areas do not.

Some evidence of the validity of such profiles is based on data for 2420 individuals on forty-three different jobs categorized by job family. The individuals on each job were divided into those whose visual skills "passed" or "failed" the visual-performance profile for their job family. Because job-performance criteria were also available for each individual, it was possible to determine the percentage of "high-criterion" employees on the jobs among those who had "adequate" and among those who had "inadequate" vision, as measured by whether they passed or failed the vision-profile standards. These results are summarized on page 162.

There is generally a higher percentage of high-criterion employees among those whose vision met the specified profiles than among

VEHICLE OPERATOR

Visual Performance Profile

FAR

Phoria	Vertical	1	x	1	2	3	4	5	6	7	8					9	
	Lateral	2	x	1	2	3	4	5	6	7	8	9	10	11	12	13	14	15
Acuity	Both	3	0	1	2	3	4	5	6	7	8	9	10	11	12	13	14	15
	Right	4	0	1	2	3	4	5	6	7	8	9	10	11	12	13	14	15
	Left	5	0	1	2	3	4	5	6	7	8	9	10	11	12	13	14	15
	Unaided																	
	Depth	6	0	1	2	3	4	5	6	7	8	9	10	11	12			
	Color	7	0	1	2	3	4	5	6	7	8	9	10	11	12	13	14	15

NEAR

Acuity	Both	1	0	1	2	3	4	5	6	7	8	9	10	11	12	13	14	15
	Right	2	0	1	2	3	4	5	6	7	8	9	10	11	12	13	14	15
	Left	3	0	1	2	3	4	5	6	7	8	9	10	11	12	13	14	15
	Unaided																	
Phoria	Vertical	4	x	1	2	3	4	5	6	7	8'					9	
	Lateral	5	x	1	2	3	4	5	6	7	8	9	10	11	12	13	14	15

FIGURE 9.10 Visual-performance profiles for an illustrative job family based on the Ortho-Rater. An individual "passes" the visual requirements of a given profile if all scores fall in the shaded areas, and "fails" if one or more scores fall in any white area.

those whose vision did not meet the profile standards.

VISUAL JOB FAMILY	PERCENT OF "HIGH CRITERION" EMPLOYEES AMONG THOSE WITH:	
	ADEQUATE VISION	INADEQUATE VISION
Clerical and administrative	71	37
Inspection and close work	62	50
Vehicle operator	59	45
Machine operator	63	45
Laborer	67	34
Mechanic and skilled tradesmen	69	57
Total	65	46

JOB-SPECIFIC ABILITIES AND TESTS

Job-specific abilities are those that are unique to individual jobs or to groups of jobs. Tests of such abilities are used for two general classes of purposes: to measure the present level of proficiency or achievement in some job-related area of those individuals who have had related job experience or training or to select individuals who can begin working on the job in question with little or no additional training. Such tests can also be used to evaluate individuals in training programs, for maintaining and updating performance levels (as with airline pilots), and, in some instances, for certifying or licensing individuals (to practice various occupations). Some job-specific tests are used more to measure aptitudes to identify those likely to become successful workers. Usually such tests are simulations of certain job tests or activities that do not require extensive training or experience.

The validity of job-specific tests is usually based on content validity, meaning that experts judge the relevance of the content of the test to the job in question. However, in some circumstances they are validated against some appropriate criterion. Sometimes this is done by using two or more job groups—for example, a group of journeymen in a trade and a separate group of nonjourneymen (possibly apprentices)—as the criterion groups.

Types of Job-Specific Tests

Some types of job-specific tests are: performance tests, written tests, and in-basket tests. Some job-specific tests are referred to as work-sample tests because they measure samples of job activities, knowledge, or skills.

Performance tests. Performance tests require individuals to perform specific job operations in controlled testing situations using actual or simulated equipment. Depending on the nature of the test, the scoring may be based on a checklist by observers, ratings of performance by observers, or evaluations of the work completed by the person being tested.

An example of a performance work sample for fork-lift operators, Figure 9.11, shows the driving course used for the test. The person giving the test has a checklist that consists of forty-two poor operating techniques such as "Did not start in low gear," "Started jerkily," "Scraped side walls of tires," "Lowered load too quickly," and "Number of pallets displaced." Scoring is based on the number of errors recorded in the checklist.

The most common work-sample tests are probably those for typists, secretaries, and other office jobs. Part of the Thurstone Typing Test is shown in Figure 9.12. This particular test requires that the person being tested type material from a corrected copy.

Written tests. These usually consist of items that measure a person's knowledge of some relevant area, or judgments about the application of knowledge to some practical situation. The following example is an item from the Information Test of Engine Lathe Operation, one of the Purdue Vocational Tests:

Instructions. In each of the multiple-choice statements to be listed below, there are four possible answers, but only one is correct. Read each state-

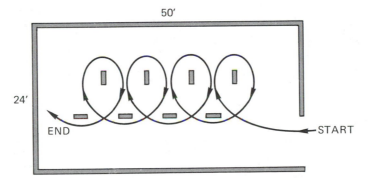

FIGURE 9.11 Standard driving course diagram for performance test for fork-lift operators. (Test prepared by U.S. War Department, Office of Quartermaster General, Philadelphia Quartermaster Depot, Testing Station.)

The typical business man is an optimist. For him, the future
is full of possibilities that have never been realized in the past.
He is not, however, a dreamer, but one whose imagination is used in
setting up purposes which lead to immediate action. His power of
execution and planning often surpass that of his imagination, and
he is often surprised to have (realized) his vision in less time
than he had even dared hope.

FIGURE 9.12 Part of the Thurstone Typing Test (included in the Thurstone Employment Tests). The person tested is required to copy this material, making the indicated corrections.

ment carefully before making your choice of answers:

When grinding a tool bit:

(A) It should be moved back and forth across the face of the tool

(B) It should be held on the wheel until the tool is blue

(C) It should be ground the same shape to cut all metals

(D) A tool rest should never be used

In-basket tests. In-basket tests have received a fair amount of attention in recent years for management training, but they can also be used for personnel selection. The name comes from the fact that the test consists of an assortment of items such as a manager might find in an in-basket: letters, reports, memoranda, notes, and related materials. Each subject taking such a test is confronted with these and must "do" something with each of the items or note down what action he would take about them if in a manager's job. For example, the subject may "answer" a letter, and in some instances may be asked to indicate the reason for the "action." There is a standard procedure for scoring such tests. Examples of items from an in-basket test described by Meyer (1970) are shown in Figure 9.13. In scoring this test, three different approaches were used:

1. The *content* of the behavior (such as "referred it to a subordinate" or "decided to change the production schedule").

2. The *style* of behavior (such as "involves subordinates" or "makes a concluding decision").

3. Rating on *overall performance* by the scorer.

In this particular study, scores were given on twenty-seven specific categories. The split-half reliability of these scores ranged from .50 to .95. For a sample of forty-five managers there was a correlation of .31 between a composite score (based on certain in-basket test items) and criterion ratings made by their superiors on "planning-administrative" performance.

Work-Sample Tests in Use

An example of a personnel-selection test program based on work-sample tests is reported by Cascio and Phillips (1979). This program involved developing and using twenty-one tests to evaluate candidates for jobs for the city of Miami Beach. The tests were developed on the basis of job analyses of the twenty-one jobs. Eleven tests were primarily motor tests involving simulated tasks for such jobs as air-conditioning mechanic, utility worker, and plumber. The other ten were verbal in nature, for such jobs as library assistant, parking-meter checker, and concession attendant. Certain tests, to assess developed skills, consisted of actual work samples. Other tests, to assess aptitudes for development, consisted of more simulated tasks. An interesting aspect of this program was that

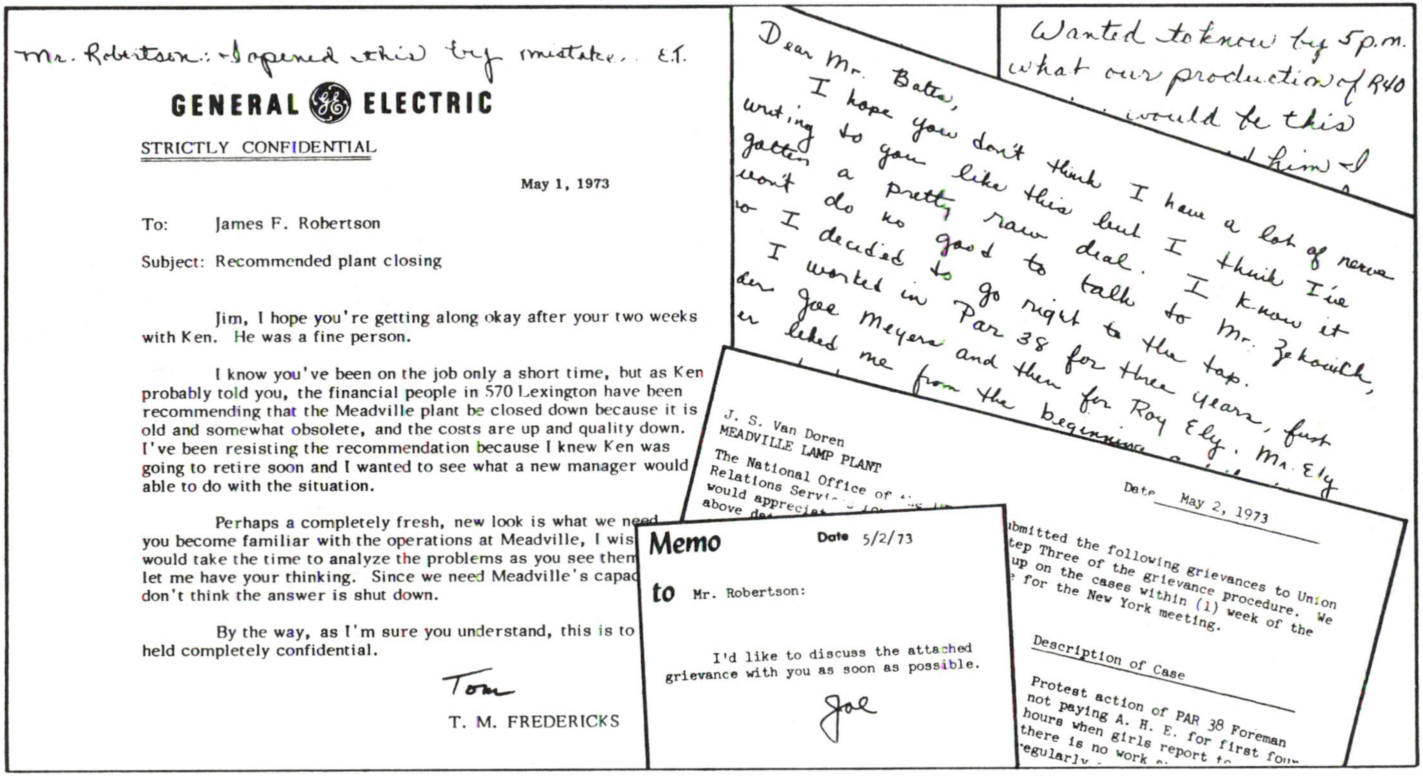

GENERAL ⚡ ELECTRIC

May 1, 1973

STRICTLY CONFIDENTIAL

To: James F. Robertson

Subject: Recommended plant closing

Jim, I hope you're getting along okay after your two weeks with Ken. He was a fine person.

I know you've been on the job only a short time, but as Ken probably told you, the financial people in 570 Lexington have been recommending that the Meadville plant be closed down because it is old and somewhat obsolete, and the costs are up and quality down. I've been resisting the recommendation because I knew Ken was going to retire soon and I wanted to see what a new manager would be able to do with the situation.

Perhaps a completely fresh, new look is what we need you become familiar with the operations at Meadville, I wis would take the time to analyze the problems as you see them let me have your thinking. Since we need Meadville's capac don't think the answer is shut down.

By the way, as I'm sure you understand, this is to held completely confidential.

Tom

T. M. FREDERICKS

Mr. Robertson: depend this try mistake.. E.f.

Wanted to know try 5 pm.
what our production of R40
would be this ...

Dear Mr. Bates,
I hope you are
writing to you you don't think I
gotten a pretty little this I
want do ho like this but I have a lot of news
I decided good now deal. I think I'a
I wanted to to talk to Mr. Fehnrich
in Joe Meyers and then Par 38 for three years, first
field me from the to the top.
... for Roy Ely, Ma. Ely
... the beginning ...

J. S. Van Doren
MEADVILLE LAMP PLANT

The National Office of ...
Relations Servi...
would appreci...
above da...   Date May 2, 1973

Memo   Date 5/2/73

to Mr. Robertson:

I'd like to discuss the attached
grievance with you as soon as possible.

Joe

mitted the following grievances to Union
ep Three of the grievance procedure. We
up on the cases within (1) week of the
for the New York meeting.

Description of Case

Protest action of PAR 38 Foreman
not paying A. H. E. for first four
hours when girls report to work
there is no work ...
egularly ...

FIGURE 9.13 Partial examples of some "items" of an in-basket test—letters, memoranda, and the like—with which an individual is to deal. (Courtesy H. H. Meyer and General Electric Company.)

the ratings of the candidates' test performances were carried out by many local business and government personnel who donated their services.

One of the criteria used in evaluating the program consisted of a comparison of turnover rates for the twenty-one jobs before and after the introduction of the testing program. The results were as follows:

TIME PERIOD	TURNOVER RATE
Before introduction of test program	40%
After introduction of test program	3%

In part the marked reduction in turnover rates was, of course, based on the selection of the best candidates. But some of the reduction was also attributed to the fact that the tests gave candidates a realistic preview of what the jobs would be like. Research in other contexts has strongly supported the notion that realistic previews of jobs (that is, information about what jobs are really like) tend to reduce subsequent turnover, either because those selected do not have false, unrealistic expectations about the jobs, or because those who believe the jobs would not be suitable for them eliminate themselves from further consideration. In connection with the testing program for the city of Miami Beach it was estimated that the reduced turnover resulted in savings of over $336,000 during a 9 to 26 month period.

Survey of validity of work-sample tests. Asher and Sciarrino (1974) summarized published validity data about work-sample tests. They divided the studies into two groups based on whether the tests were "motor" tests requiring physical manipulation of things (such as tracing a complex electric circuit, operating a sewing machine, making a tooth from plaster, or repairing a gear box), or "verbal" tests, either language-oriented or people-oriented (such as a test about farming, a test of chemical information, an in-basket test, or a test relating to police work). The summarized results are shown in Figure 9.14. By and large the motor work-sample tests had higher validity coefficients than did the verbal tests as related to the job-proficiency criteria, whereas the verbal tests tended to have higher validity coefficients as related to the training criteria. (Verbal tests generally have higher correlations with training criteria than with job-performance criteria.)

THE CONCEPT OF BEHAVIORAL CONSISTENCY

Wernimont and Campbell (1968) suggested the notion of *behavioral consistency* as a general frame of reference for personnel selection. This means essentially the same as the familiar bit of conventional wisdom, "the best indicator of future performance is past performance." Wernimont and Campbell proposed that one should rely less on "signs" of future job performance than on "samples" of relevant behavior. "Signs" refer to the relatively conventional predictors such as aptitude tests and biographical data. They argued for the use of "samples" of behavior—that is, behaviors similar to the actual behaviors to be performed on the job.

Such an approach requires a systematic study of the job. The first step in this process is to identify the critical dimensions of job performance. This is followed by a thorough search of each applicant's previous work experience and educational background to determine if any behaviors (for example, "samples") relevant to these dimensions have been required of the applicant or have been exhibited by him in the past. The adequacy of such "behaviors" could then be used as the basis for predicting performance in corresponding aspects of the job. If the person's

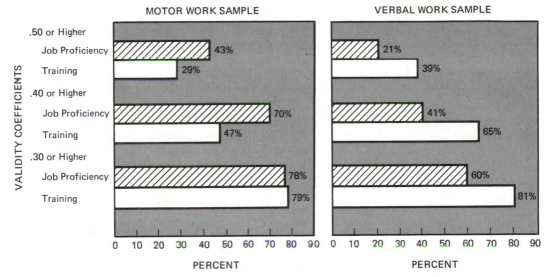

FIGURE 9.14 Proportions of motor work-sample and verbal work-sample tests having validity coefficients of various magnitudes when validated against job-proficiency versus training criteria. (From Asher & Sciarrino, 1974, Figures 4 and 5, pp. 526, 527.)

past repertoire has not included such behaviors, one might then obtain a measure of such behaviors by using work-sample or simulation exercises.

Support for the Behavioral-Consistency Model

Although the systematic application of the behavioral-consistency model has not taken on epidemic proportions, there is some support for its use in personnel selection. For example, Asher and Sciarrino (1974) cited some evidence that background information about people reveals that their previous experience can better predict job performance than can various tests. On the basis of such evidence they postulated a point-to-point theory which stated that the more features there are in common between the predictor and the criterion, the higher the validity will be.

Although the behavioral-consistency model would usually be used by comparing the activities of a person's previous work ex-

perience with the activities of a job for which the person is being considered, job-sample tests can also be used to get some indications of a person's repertoire of abilities. In this regard, for example, Campion (1972) used a performance test with a sample of maintenance mechanics. From an analysis of the job, a work sample of four tasks was developed: installing pulleys and belts, disassembling and repairing a gearbox, installing and aligning a motor, and pressing a bushing into a sprocket and reaming to fit a shaft. These tests and a battery of paper-and-pencil tests were administered to the mechanics and paired-comparison criterion ratings of the mechanics were obtained from the supervisors. Scores on the work-sample test had a correlation of .46 with the criterion, but none of the five paper-and-pencil tests had a significant correlation.

In still another instance Gordon and Kleiman (1976) found that a work-sample test for police officers with both "motor" and "verbal" components better predicted a criterion of trainability than did an intelligence test.

Collectively, there appears to be substantial support for the behavioral-consistency theory, which suggests that the closer one can come to getting some measure or indication of performance on *samples* of the work activities people might be expected to perform in a job, the better the predictions one would be able to make of the actual performance of individuals on the activities in question.

VALIDITY OF VARIOUS TYPES OF ABILITY TESTS

This chapter has included a few examples of test-validation studies for certain ability tests used with specific jobs. Let us now take an overview of the validity of various types of ability tests for selecting people for various occupations and occupational groups as reported before the recent focus on validity generalization.

The most extensive overviews are reported by Ghiselli (1966, 1973) and Asher and Sciarrino (1974). Ghiselli summarized data from many specific test-validity studies. Some of his results, in Figure 9.15, show the mean validity coefficients for five types of tests, for several occupation categories, for both training criteria and proficiency criteria. Scanning this figure reveals the following patterns: The mean coefficients of the tests show at least some validity for most occupation categories; the coefficients for the intellectual-ability tests are generally higher than those of other tests; the coefficients for the different types of tests are rather different for certain occupation categories but are quite similar for others; the coefficients for training criteria are generally higher than for job-proficiency criteria; but the general level of the coefficients is not particularly high, with most falling in the range from .15 to .35 or .45.

Figure 9.16 shows a partial comparison of the test-validity data summarized by Ghiselli with that for work-sample tests and biograph-

ical data presented by Asher and Sciarrino (1974). These are summarized for all occupation categories for proficiency criteria. The systematically highest correlations for biographical data are discussed further in Chapter 11, but such data, along with the good showing of motor work-sample tests, also support the potential relevance of the concept of behavioral consistency already discussed. Note that the validity data referred to are for individual tests. Usually combinations of two or more tests add at least a bit to the prediction of job performance.

The historical data summarized by Ghiselli and by Asher and Sciarrino can be interpreted as precursors of the more current interest in validity generalization, because most types of tests have some validity for various types of jobs, and because of the dominance of intellectual (i.e., cognitive) tests for various types of jobs.

GENERALIZED VALIDITY OF BASIC ABILITY TESTS

The preceding chapter introduced the topic of validity generalization. Here we discuss it in somewhat more detail, in particular in relation to the results and conclusions of a study by Hunter (undated), which are summarized in a report by the U.S. Department of Labor (1983).

Validity Generalization as Based on 515 jobs

Hunter's (undated) study was based on an intensive analysis of test-validity data published by the U.S. Employment Service of the U.S. Department of Labor. However, Hunter extrapolated his results to apply to the 12,000 jobs of the *Dictionary of Occupational Titles*. The validity data for the 515 jobs were based on the nine tests of the General Aptitude Test Battery (GATB) of the U.S. Employ-

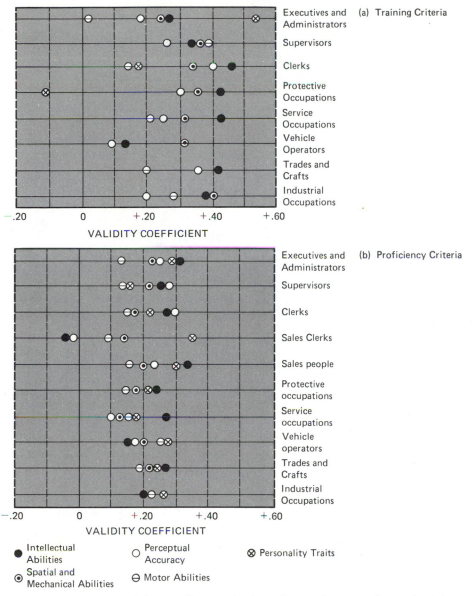

FIGURE 9.15 Mean validity coefficients for five classes of personnel tests for jobs in various occupation categories. Part (a) shows validity coefficients for training criteria and part (b), for proficiency criteria. This figure represents hundreds of validity coefficients covering thousands of individuals. (Adapted from Ghiselli, 1966.)

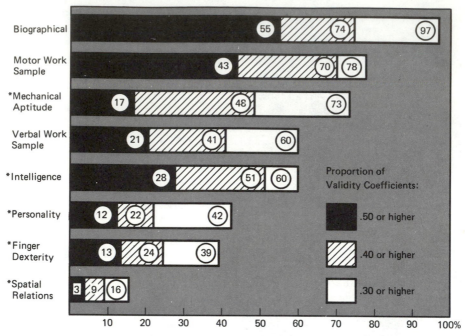

FIGURE 9.16 Proportions of validity coefficients of various magnitudes with job-proficiency criteria for eight types of predictors. (Adapted from Asher & Sciarrino, 1974, Figures 1, 2, and 3. Data for items with* are from Ghiselli, 1966.)

ment Service. These nine tests are referred to in the next section and are also listed later in Table 9.2. From his analysis Hunter concluded that all major ability tests meet the scientific standards for validity without validation studies for specific jobs. However, as discussed in the previous chapter, Hunter reported that, for validity-generalization purposes, jobs could be divided into five major categories reflecting various levels of "complexity" and he proposed that a somewhat different combination of cognitive, perceptual, and psychomotor tests be used for each of these categories.[2]

Summary of Hunter's validity data. After dividing the jobs into these five categories,

Hunter summarized the test-validity data for each category by separating the data into three classes: Cognitive (Intelligence-G; Verbal-V; Numerical-N); Perceptual (Spatial-S; Form-F; Clerical-Q); and Psychomotor (Motor coordination-K; Finger dexterity-F; Manual dexterity-M). Table 9.1 summarizes certain of Hunter's data for the five complexity levels, in particular:

• Average "true" validity for each of the three types of tests: These coefficients are corrected for certain sources of error, such as sample size and unreliability; thus, they are higher than those usually found in actual practice.
• "Weights" for tests: These are statistical weights proposed for the weighting of the three types of tests for reasonably optimum prediction; they are used in deriving multiple correlations.
• Multiple correlations: These are the multiple correlations that would be expected by applying the weights for the three types of tests.

[2]The five categories are based in part on an intensive analysis of data from the functional job-analysis procedures of the U.S. Employment Service that provide for analyzing jobs in terms of their involvement with data, people, and things.

TABLE 9.1 Validity data for three types of ability tests for jobs in five levels of complexity (decimals omitted)

	COMPLEXITY LEVEL					
	1	2	3	4	5	MEAN
AVERAGE "TRUE" VALIDITY						
Cognitive tests	56	58	51	40	23	45
Perceptual tests	52	55	40	35	37	37
Psychomotor tests	30	21	52	43	48	37
"WEIGHTS" FOR TESTS						
Cognitive tests	40	58	45	28	07	
Perceptual tests	19					
Psychomotor tests	07		16	33	46	
MULTIPLE CORRELATIONS (R)	59	58	53	30	49	53

Source: Hunter, undated, Tables 18b and 20a.

Implications of results. Hunter draws the following implications from these and other results:

For predicting criteria of *job performance*:

- General cognitive, perceptual, and psychomotor ability are valid predictors of job proficiency for all jobs.
- The validity of ability tests changes only with very large changes in job content.
- Cognitive-ability tests predict job performance for all jobs to a useful extent.
- However, the validity of cognitive tests drops off sharply for low levels of job complexity.
- Psychomotor-ability tests have their highest validity for jobs with the lowest levels of job complexity (levels 4 and 5).
- Adding psychomotor tests to cognitive tests increases validity by appreciable amounts for the three lowest levels of complexity (levels 3, 4, and 5).

For predicting criteria of *training success*:

- The validity of cognitive-ability tests is uniformly high across all levels of job complexity.
- The validity of psychomotor-ability tests varies sharply across levels of jobs complexity; it is lower than for job-performance criteria, especially for the highest levels of complexity.

Data from Hunter's study and elsewhere strongly suggest that the validity of ability tests is indeed very general, and that some modest differences do exist in the validity of such tests in relation to job complexity (in particular, five levels of complexity).

Discussion of Generalized Validity

As stated in the preceding chapter we are inclined to the view that there is, indeed, substantial generalized validity across jobs, but not as sweeping or as broad as is implied by the results of studies such as Hunter's. In this regard, for example, Gutenberg, Arvey, Osborn, and Jeanneret (1983) report the results of additional, more analytical, statistical analyses of the USES job data for 111 of the 515 validity studies used in Hunter's study. Although Hunter concluded that cognitive tests had generalized validity for all jobs, the research of Gutenberg et al. suggests that cognitive tests may demonstrate negative or near-zero validities for jobs with low complexity levels. These results raise questions about the extent to which generalized validity applies across jobs.

There is, however, another issue regarding the implications of validity generalization. Given a validity coefficient of a test for a given job, it is generally assumed that the expected levels of candidates' job performances increase with test scores, even if the validity coefficient is small. (In fact, this point was made in the previous chapter.) This would argue for using as high a cut-off score as possible (considering the selection ratio that may be dictated by the available labor supply and the number of individuals required for the job). However, some of the data relating to the natural-selection or gravitational theory show that people on various jobs tend to be clustered around different levels on certain tests (such as general intelligence, numerical aptitude, and reasoning ability). The assumption underlying this theory is that people tend to gravitate into jobs that are compatible with their own abilities and other characteristics. There still are genuine differences of opinion about the validity of this assumption. However, the fact that there are differences in the mean test scores of incumbents who have "survived" on various jobs strongly implies that the *level* of certain abilities required varies across jobs, and that some jobs require more, say, general intelligence or numerical aptitude than others. Thus, it would seem that, in addition to knowing if a test is valid for a given job, it would also be useful to know something about the approximate level of scores that are characteristic of people who have held the job and presumably have been successful at it.

A Validity Strategy Between Specificity and Generalization

What seems to be needed is a validity approach that avoids, on the one hand, the Scylla of having to validate tests and other predictors for each and every job and, on the other hand, the Charybdis that seems to be implicit in an overly broad validity-generalization approach. A strategy that seems to offer substantial promise of striking a happy medium between these two extremes is the job-component validity approach discussed in the preceding chapter. It is predicated on the principle of validity generalization (but generalization based on job components rather than on complete job entities), but at the same time identifies the combinations of levels of basic abilities that arise because of the many unique combinations of job components in the world of work.

Tables 8.4 and 8.5 illustrated certain aspects of the job-component approach with the PAQ by showing, for the Intelligence (G) and Numerical (N) constructs, the predicted mean test scores for incumbents for several jobs, based on data from their PAQ job-dimension scores, along with the actual scores on intelligence and numerical tests of incumbents on the same jobs and on a few other jobs. The predicted mean test score for a particular test for a given job is based on a statistically derived equation using scores for the job dimensions that best predict scores for the test in question. Table 9.2 shows the predicted mean test scores for a few illustrative jobs for all constructs represented by the GATB tests.

With the PAQ job-component system there is provision for indicating the best combination of three tests. Because some tests are correlated with each other the best combination does not necessarily consist of the three tests that have the highest correlations. Also, for any given construct, the score 1 SD below the mean is also derived by computer and is presented with the other test-related data as a possible cut-off score as illustrated in Table 8.6. (This would normally eliminate only the lowest 16% of possible successful incumbents.)

The smoke has not yet settled over the opposing frames of reference of job-specific validity versus validity generalization, but it is proposed that the job-component validity

TABLE 9.2 Predicted mean scores for incumbents on nine ability constructs for selected jobs as derived from job-dimension scores for the jobs based on the position analysis questionnaire (PAQ)

CONSTRUCT	TYPIST	RIVETING-MACHINE OPERATOR	TOOL AND DIE MAKER	MAIL CLERK
G:Intelligence	106	88	105	89
V:Verbal Aptitude	106	89	99	92
N:Numerical Aptitude	106	89	100	94
S:Spatial Aptitude	104	93	111	96
P:Form Perception	111	98	102	104
Q:Clerical Perception	115	99	99	106
K:Motor Coordination	111	101	100	101
F:Finger Dexterity	105	99	101	102
M:Manual Dexterity	106	107	109	109

Source: PAQ Services, Inc., 1983.

strategy may capitalize on the advantages of both frames of reference.

REFERENCES

Asher, J. J., & Sciarrino, J. A. (1974). Realistic work sample tests: A review. *Personnel Psychology*, 27(4), 519–533.

Binet, A., & Henri, V. (1895). La psychologie individuelle. *Année psychologie*, 2, 411–465.

Buros, O. K. (Ed.) (1978). *The eighth mental measurements yearbook* (Vols. 1 & 2). Highland Park, N.J.: Gryphon.

Campion, J. E. (1972). Work sampling for personnel selection. *Journal of Applied Psychology*, 56(1), 40–44.

Cascio, W. F., & Phillips, N. F. (1979). Performance testing: A rose among thorns? *Personnel Psychology*, 32(4), 751–766.

Dunnette, M. D. (1976). Basic attributes of individuals in relation to behavior in organizations. In M. D. Dunnette (Ed.), *Handbook of industrial and organizational psychology*. Chicago: Rand McNally.

Eckstrom, R. B. (1973). *Cognitive factors: Some recent literature* (Tech. Rep. No. 2, ONR contract N00014-71-C-0117, NR 150-329). Princeton, N.J.: Educational Testing Service.

Fleishman, E. A., & Hogan, J. C. (June 1978). A taxonomic method for assessing the physical requirements of jobs. Washington, D.C.: Advanced Research Resources Organization.

Galton, F. (1883). *Inquiries into human faculty and its development*. London: Macmillan.

Ghiselli, E. E. (1966). *The validity of occupational aptitude tests*. New York: Wiley.

Ghiselli, E. E. (1973). The validity of aptitude tests in personnel selection. *Personnel Psychology*, 26(4), 461–477.

Gordon, M. E., & Kleiman, L. S. (1976). The prediction of trainability using a work sample test and an aptitude test: A direct comparison. *Personnel Psychology*, 29(2), 243–253.

Guilford, J. P.(1967). *The nature of human intelligence*. New York: McGraw-Hill.

Gutenberg, R. L., Arvey, R. D., Osborn, H. G., & Jeanneret, P. R. (1983). Moderating effects of decision-making/information-processing job dimensions on test validities. *Journal of Applied Psychology*, 68(4), 602–608.

Hunter, J. E. (undated). *Test validation for 12,000 jobs: An application of job classification and validity generalization analysis to the General Aptitude Test Battery (GATB)*. Unpublished report, Michigan State University.

Lawshe, C. H., Jr. (1942). A nomograph for estimating the validity of test items. *Journal of Applied Psychology*. 26(6), 846–849.

Meyer, H. H.(1970). The validity of the in-basket test as a measure of managerial performance. *Personnel Psychology*, 23(3), 297–307.

Peterson, N. G., & Bownas, D. A. (1982). Skill, task structure, and performance acquisition. In M. D. Dunnette & Fleishman, E. A. (Eds.), *Human performance and productivity: Human capability assessment* (Vol. 1). Hillsdale, N.J.: Lawrence Erlbaum Associates.

Spearman, C. E. (1927). *The abilities of man*. New York: Macmillan.

Theologus, G. C., Romashko, T., & Fleishman,

E. A. (January 1970). *Development of a taxonomy of human performance: A feasibility study of ability dimensions for classifying tasks.* Silver Spring, Md.: American Institutes for Research, Tech. Rep. 5 (R70–1).

Thurstone, L. L. (1948). *Primary mental abilities.* Chicago: Psychometric Laboratory, University of Chicago, Report No. 50.

U.S. Department of Labor (1983). Overview of validity generalization for the U.S. Employment Service. Washington, D.C.: U.S. Department of Labor, Employment and Training Administration, USES Test Research Rep. No. 43.

Wernimont, P. F., & Campbell, J. P. (1968). Signs, samples and criteria. *Journal of Applied Psychology, 52*(5), 372–376.

10

Personality and Interest

It is widely accepted that people's personalities and interests can influence their work performance and their adjustments to their jobs. Assuming for the moment the validity of this statement, we can postulate two bases for it. First, it is reasonable to believe that such factors influence people's work performance and job adjustment via motivation. Hence one could expect that individuals with certain interest and personality patterns might be more inclined to look for certain types of jobs and that once on such jobs they would adjust better to them and perhaps gain greater satisfaction from them than would people with other interest and personality patterns. Certainly vocational guidance pays much attention to such factors.

Second, it is reasonable to assume that, in *some kinds* of jobs, personality factors have a direct bearing on the adequacy with which people can fulfill the functions of their jobs. This is particularly true for jobs that require

substantial amounts of personal contact with other people, as in some sales work, public-relations work, some supervisory and management activities, interviewing, and the like. Even some politicians' success depends on how well they interact with people.

Even if we accept the implications of the effects of personality and interest factors on job behavior, the fact remains that success with using measures of these factors has been pretty bleak. We discuss the problems associated with such measures later, but first we discuss briefly the "structure" of personality and interest factors and we describe certain personality and interest tests.

PERSONALITY FACTORS

In our everyday lives we describe people in terms of various personality qualities or traits: sociability, dominance, and introversion, for example. Although thousands of words are used to describe people, the number of relatively distinct personality factors or constructs is relatively limited. Probably the most adequate inventory of such constructs is that developed by Browne and Howarth (1977) on the basis of factor analyses of a comprehensive pool of personality-type test items. Browne and Howarth identified the following fifteen factors:

1. Social shyness;
2. Sociability;
3. Mood-swing readjustment;
4. Adjustment-emotionality;
5. Impulsiveness;
6. Persistence;
7. Hypocondriac-medical;
8. Dominance I (being easily downed, submissive, etc.);
9. Dominance II (taking command, exerting leadership, etc.);
10. General activity;
11. Trust versus suspicion;
12. Superego;
13. Social consideration;
14. Inferiority;
15. Cooperativeness-considerateness.

In the case of most constructs, individuals can vary along a scale ranging from one extreme (that implied by the label of the construct) to the other. Typical personality tests measure constructs such as these, although the specific factors measured by some such tests by no means correspond with these. Rather, some measure more specific aspects of personality, in some instances they measure concepts that represent figments of the test developers' imaginations.

TYPES OF PERSONALITY TESTS

There are generally two types of personality tests—those that use *projective techniques* and *questionnaire inventories*.

Projective Techniques

Examples of tests that use projective techniques are the Rorschach Ink Blot Test and the Thematic Apperception Test (TAT). In these tests, subjects are presented with intentionally ambiguous stimuli (such as ink blots or pictures) and are asked to tell what they "see" in them. In other words, they "project" themselves into the stimuli. A trained administrator interprets the individual responses and patterns of responses and assesses the subjects. These tests are not used very commonly in industry, although they are used more for selecting executives than for other types of personnel. They are used rather widely in clinical practice.

Personality Inventories

The second class of personality tests consists of paper-and-pencil questionnaires. Although such questionnaires are commonly called tests, they are in a sense not really "tests" inasmuch as there are no right or wrong answers; the term *inventory* is more accurate.

Conventional format and scoring of inventories. Conventional personality inventories usually contain statements or questions relating to behavior, attitudes, feelings, or beliefs. Subjects are asked to respond to these as they apply to them. Following is an example of such an item:

I feel uncomfortable with other people.
(a) Yes
(b) Don't know
(c) No

The responses to individual items are usually scored on each of several personality attributes or traits, such as dominance, sociability, or impulsiveness. Responses are scored for a particular attitute or trait after they have been identified—either by statistical analysis or on rational grounds—as the responses characteristic of individuals who possess that attribute or trait.

Forced-choice personality inventories. Because of the possibility of what is labeled "faking" with conventional personality inventories, some inventories are based on the forced-choice technique. In the final forms such inventories include blocks of two or more statements from which subjects are asked to select the one that is "most" or "least" like themselves. The items within any given block have been combined into that block because they are about equal on their "favorability." (This is an index of the "social desirability" of the individual items, based on the responses of a sample of subjects who were asked to indicate whether, or to what extent, the items were characteristic of themselves.) Of those with equal favorability within a block, however, one will have been selected because it has been found to discriminate statistically between a couple of criterion groups (for example, between introverts and extroverts). Because individuals cannot select the "best" response (all responses being "equal" in favorability), they would presumably tend to select the one that really is most like themselves. Such a response "adds" to their score on the dimension on which the item has been found to discriminate.

EXAMPLES OF PERSONALITY INVENTORIES

A number of personality inventories used in personnel selection are listed in Appendix D. Two of these are described briefly here.

California Psychological Inventory (CPI)

This inventory is essentially a spinoff of the Minnesota Multiphasic Personality Inventory (MMPI), except that whereas the MMPI was designed for use with "abnormal people," the CPI was developed for use with "normal individuals." It provides scores on eighteen components in four classes, as follows:

- Class I. Measures of poise, ascendancy, and self-assurance.
  Components: 1. Dominance; 2. Capacity for status; 3. Sociability; 4. Social presence; 5. Self-acceptance; 6. Sense of well-being.
- Class II. Measures of socialization, maturity, and responsibility.
  Components: 7. Responsibility; 8. Socialization; 9. Self-control; 10. Tolerance; 11. Good impression; 12. Communality.
- Class III. Measures of achievement potential and intellectual efficiency.
  Components: 13. Achievement via conformance; 14. Achievement via independence; 15. Intellectual efficiency.
- Class IV. Measures of intellectual and interest modes.
  Components: 16. Psychological-mindedness; 17. Flexibility; and 18. Femininity.

Edwards Personal Preference Schedule

This inventory is based on the forced-choice technique discussed earlier; the pairs of items in the inventory were matched with respect to their social desirability values (i.e., favorability indexes) as much as possible. However, the items within each pair differentiate in terms of the personality constructs the inventory is intended to measure. An example of a pair of items is given here. The respondents are asked to choose one item with this question in mind: Which of these two statements is more characteristic of what you like?

A. I like to talk about myself to others.
B. I like to work toward some goal that I have set for myself.

The responses to the 225 items are used to derive scores on fifteen personality factors.

INTEREST FACTORS

The most widely accepted basic taxonomy of job-related interests is that developed by Holland (1966).

Holland's Taxonomy of Interests

Holland's taxonomy consists of six factors in terms of which the interest patterns of individuals can be characterized. The six constructs (to which Holland refers as personality types) are:

R: Realistic
I: Intellectual
A: Artistic
S: Social
E: Enterprising
C: Conventional

On the basis of responses to Holland's Vocational Preference Inventory (VPI) individuals typically are characterized in terms of the three classifications that are dominant in their interests, using the letter codes that represent the six factors.

Holland has also found that occupations can be characterized in terms of the same six classifications. In practice most occupations are coded with the letters of the three most relevant factors, with the first letter representing the dominant classification. Some examples are:

RAI: Painter
IAR: Physicist
AIS: Commercial artist
SRI: Guide
ESI: Manager, retail store
CSE: Secretary

The hexagonal model. Using these codes to represent specific occupations makes it possible to determine the relationships between these six categories and the interests of people as measured by the Vocational Preference Index. For a sample of about 1200 people, the correlations between all possible pairs of the six categories triggered the development of Holland's hexagonal model, shown in Figure 10.1, in which the values on the lines between the various pairs are the

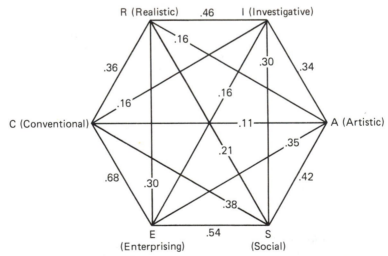

FIGURE 10.1 Holland's hexagonal model of six interests (to which he refers as personality types). The numbers on the intersecting lines are correlations between the classifications. (From Holland, Vernstein, Kuo, Karweit, & Blum, 1970, Figure 1.)

correlations between them. The six categories are so ordered that those with the highest correlations are adjacent to each other; the correlations of the pairs of categories opposite each other are generally the lowest.

EXAMPLES OF INTEREST INVENTORIES

Interest inventories usually require the person being tested to indicate the strength of his interests in such things as hobbies, recreation, leisure-time activities, jobs, and other activities. Sometimes this is done by presenting groups of activities and asking the individual to indicate which one is liked most and which least, or by indicating for each stated activity how much it is liked. Brief descriptions of several interest inventories follow.

Vocational Preference Inventory (VPI)

As previously discussed, this inventory was developed by Holland (1966) and served as the basis for the development of six interest factors. The responses for an individual are scored in terms of these six factors. An interesting twist with the inventory is that it is also possible to assign individual occupations to the six categories or to combinations of them. For example, advertising agents and sales representatives are in a category designated ESC (Enterprising, Social, Conventional).

Strong-Campbell Interest Inventory (SCII)

This inventory has been developed primarily for vocational guidance and counseling. A person's responses are scored in three ways, as follows:

1. General occupational themes: The person is scored on each of six "themes," which are the same as Holland's six categories. That score is shown in comparison with the scores of general samples of men and women.
2. Basic interest scales: The person is scored on each of twenty-three basic interests—for example, agriculture, science, social service, and sales. These are also organized into Holland's six classifications. The person's score is shown in comparison with those of general samples of men and women, as are the basic occupational themes.
3. Occupational scales: The person is scored for each of eighty-two occupations, in such a way as to show how the person's interests compare with happily employed men and women in each occupation. The use of this score is based on the hypothesis that, other things being equal, a person choosing an occupation is more likely to be happy and successful if the person's basic interests are similar to those of persons actually in the occupation.

Part of one person's interest profile is shown in Figure 10.2. Notice the six specific occupational scales for which the person's interests were most similar, and the five for which they were least similar.

Kuder Interest Inventories

The items of the Kuder inventories consist of triads of activities, from each of which the individual chooses the most preferred and the least preferred. Of the different forms of these inventories, the main one is the Kuder Preference Record (KPR)—Vocational (Form C). This form assesses interests associated with ten broad occupational areas: mechanical, outdoor, computational, scientific, persuasive, artistic, literary, musical, social service, and clerical. The Kuder Occupational Interest Survey (KOIS) (Form DD) provides for scoring on the basis of the interest patterns of people in various occupations who are satisfied with their work choices; in this respect it is much like the Strong-Campbell Interest Inventory. The Kuder Preference Record can also be scored in terms of the six

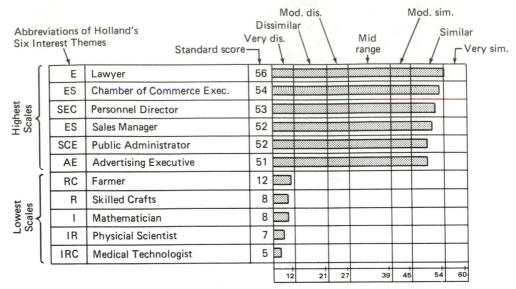

FIGURE 10.2 One person's scores based on the Strong-Campbell Interest Inventory. This shows the six highest and the five lowest scores for the Occupational Scales for the person (a male). A score of 50 is the mean for males in each occupation; thus scale categories above and below 50 represent varying degrees of similarity and dissimilarity between individual interests and those of males in the occupation. (Adapted with the permission of Stanford University Press from Campbell & Hansen, 1981, Table 10-C, p. 106.)

factors of Holland's Vocational Preference Inventory.

Work Activity Questionnaire, Form I (Interests) (WAQ, Form I)

The WAQ, Form I (Interests) is an interest inventory rooted in the Position Analysis Questionnaire (PAQ). As discussed before, the PAQ provides for the analysis of jobs in terms of many basic human behaviors. The WAQ, Form I allows individuals to indicate the level of their interest in each activity or situation that could be part of any job they might consider. Following are a few examples:

¹The Work Activity Questionnaire, Form I was originally called the Job Activity Preference Questionnaire (JAPQ).

How much would you like to engage in each of the following activities?

Reading
Using precision tools
Performing repetitive activities

Individuals use a six-point scale in responding to each item. An individual's responses are then scored in terms of several job dimensions. An example for one individual is shown in Figure 10.3, which illustrates the interest profile of the individual for four job dimensions, along with the job-dimension scores for two jobs, A and B. The degree of match of the individual's interest profile is much greater for job A than for job B. A statistical index of the degree of match can be derived for many different jobs. Following are such indexes for the individual represented

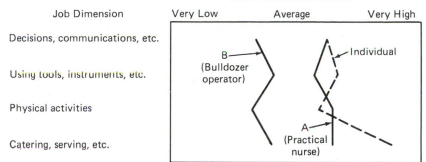

JOB-DIMENSION SCORE

Job Dimension   Very Low   Average   Very High

Decisions, communications, etc.

Using tools, instruments, etc.

B — (Bulldozer operator)

Individual

Physical activities

Catering, serving, etc.

A — (Practical nurse)

FIGURE 10.3 A partial job-interest profile for an individual based on the Work Activity Questionnaire, Form I (Interests) and the partial PAQ job-dimension profiles for two jobs. The WAQ interest profile matches the profile for job A much better than for job B.

in Figure 10.3 for four jobs, including jobs *A* and *B* shown in that figure:

JOB	INDEX OF DEGREE OF MATCH
A Practical nurse	96
Physical therapist	96
B Bulldozer operator	60
Truck driver helper	58

The possible advantage of the WAQ, Form I, as contrasted with other inventories, is that individuals express their interests in terms of the same PAQ job elements that are used to describe jobs, and they are scored in terms of similar job dimensions. Most other interest inventories provide for scoring individuals in terms of some "intervening" variables (for example, broad areas of interests or interest profiles of people in various occupations). The direct comparison with the WAQ, Form I (Interests) would seem to minimize the amount of "slippage" between individuals' measured interests and the nature of job activities.

LIMITATIONS OF PERSONALITY AND INTEREST INVENTORIES

As one might imagine, personality and interest inventories have rather serious limitations for personnel selection. The most critical is the possibility of what is called "faking" by the individual taking the test.

Faking Personality and Interest Inventories

People taking a personality or interest inventory for personal counseling or for vocational guidance are usually motivated to give relatively truthful answers, for it is in their interest to find out all they can about themselves. If they are applying for a job, however, their motivation to get the job might consciously or unconsciously induce them to give responses that they *think* will make them appear to be the kind of persons for which the employer is looking. Various studies of faking have been carried out, some in simulated situations (such as classrooms) and others in real-life situations.

Faking in simulated situations. The studies of faking in simulated situations have typically been carried out by asking subjects (usually students) to take a personality or interest inventory in a simulated employment situation and to respond as though they were applying for a job. They are also asked to take the same inventory in a simulated guidance situation and to respond as though they were being counseled. Such studies generally indicate that people can (and do) give somewhat different responses when given instructions for the frame of reference they should assume when responding to the inventory.

Faking in real situations. The more critical question, however, relates to the extent to which people fake their responses in real-life situations—for example, when applying for jobs. There is little hard evidence on this, and what there is reflects something of a mixed bag. Years ago, Gordon and Stapleton (1956) compared scores on the Gordon Personal Profile for 121 high-school students who first took the inventory for their regular guidance program and later when applying for summer employment. There were significant differences in the scores on certain factors measured by the inventory and in the total scores.

However, the extent of faking in actual employment situations may not be as widespread and pervasive as it has generally been assumed to be. Evidence of this comes from circumstances in which two sets of scores on interest or personality inventories were available for the same individual—once administered under conditions in which people might be expected to fake, and once under conditions in which people would not be under pressure to fake. Such studies are reported by Abrahams, Neumann, and Gilthens (1971) and Schwab and Packard (1973). The differences in the two sets of scores in both of these studies were relatively small implying that there was no evidence of major distortion by applicants seeking employment.

Discussion. The evidence regarding faking in actual employment situations is, then, still somewhat ambiguous. However, there is no strong evidence of a generalized, pervasive, universal tendency for people to distort their responses in real-life situations in which they have (or think they have) something to gain by so doing. Perhaps such a tendency varies from individual to individual.

Methods of Minimizing Faking

Although the extent of faking of personality and interest inventories is not actually known, it behooves employment personnel to be aware of the possibility of its occurrence and, when appropriate, to take steps to minimize that possibility and its effects. Following are some means of doing this.

Forced-choice technique. Even though it has been shown that some forced-choice inventories are vulnerable to faking, it is probably not possible to indicate the extent of this vulnerability in real-life situations. Although some unspecified amount of faking may be possible, it still seems that such inventories are somewhat preferable to conventional inventories that do not use this method.

Identification of fakers. Some inventories have special scoring procedures for identifying individuals who tend to give faked responses. These scores are based on the responses to items which are seldom chosen by persons responding honestly but which are frequently chosen by those who deliberately try to fake the inventory. Such scores are provided for in the Minnesota Multiphasic Personality Inventory, the California Psychological Inventory, and the Kuder Preference Record. In fact, such scores themselves are sometimes predictive. For example, Ruch and Ruch (1967) found that such a score on the Minnesota Multiphasic Personality Inventory (the K score) had a correlation of .39 with rated performance of 182 sales representatives. The correlations of scores on the five scales of the inventory ranged from −.10 to

−.41. Thus the K score was more predictive than all but one of the regular scores.

Use of special scoring keys. Another scheme that can help to minimize the effects of faking is the development of a special scoring key for use in each circumstance, using the follow-up (that is, predictive) validation procedure. The steps are:

1. Administer a personality or interest inventory to a group of applicants for a particular type of job.
2. Select candidates in the usual way (*without* reference to the inventory).
3. Later obtain relevant criterion data for the personnel selected (such as measures of job performance, tenure, etc.).
4. Item-analyze the responses to the inventory against the criterion in order to identify those responses which differentiate in terms of the criterion.
5. Incorporate these into a special scoring key.

In this procedure the responses that were given by individuals when they were candidates would have been influenced by whatever mental set they had at the time. If some such responses—whether honestly given or not—do differentiate, they could be used in an empirically based scoring procedure.

The study that best illustrates this approach goes back many years (Tiffin & Phelan, 1953). The procedure just described was used in a metal parts factory where applicants for hourly paid jobs had been given the Kuder Preference Record. However, the inventories had not been used in the employment process. In a follow-up item analysis with one sample of employees, certain items of the inventory were identified that collectively discriminated reasonably well between a "long-tenure" group and a "short-tenure" group. A scoring key based on these items was used to score the inventories of a second sample of the original group of employees, who were also divided into long-tenure and short-tenure groups. The results of this cross validation, shown in Figure 10.4, indicate rather

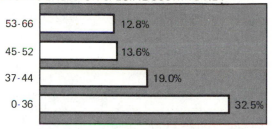

SCORES BASED ON SPECIAL SCORING KEY

PERCENT OF SHORT-TENURE EMPLOYEES

FIGURE 10.4 Percent of short-tenure employees by test-score categories based on special scoring key used with Kuder Preference Record. (Adapted from Tiffin & Phelan, 1953.)

clearly that the special scoring key would be useful in identifying candidates most likely to remain on the job.

VALIDITY OF PERSONALITY AND INTEREST INVENTORIES

Remembering the reservations about personality and interest inventories, let us refer to a few studies dealing with the validity of such inventories.

Personality and Interest Characteristics Related to Occupations

It has been shown that some people in particular occupations tend to have certain personality and interest characteristics. Such relationships have sometimes been viewed in the framework of construct validity. In a strict sense, however, it can stretch the concept of construct validity to use it in this manner, because the pattern of characteristics of people in a given occupation may not necessarily be *required* for success in that occupation. (For example, although many landscape architects have "artistic"' interests as measured by an interest inventory, there could well be some who do *not* have such interests.)

Some partial relevant data about the interest patterns of people in certain occupations come from a study by Gottfredson (1980). Gottfredson started her study by using procedures developed by Holland for coding 437 jobs in terms of the six factors based on Holland's Vocational Preference Inventory. Although these factors reflect people's personality types, Gottfredson used the same factors to characterize jobs, thus making it possible to classify the jobs according to their resemblance to the six types of work implied by the factors.

With the jobs so classified Gottfredson then related them to the following sets of job-related data: the prestige ratings of occupations; the census occupational classification system; various sets of data from the jobs in the *Dictionary of Occupational Titles* (DOT) of the U.S. Employment Service; and data on twenty-one "occupational reinforcers" that are used with the Work Adjustment Project (Borgen, Weiss, Tinsley, Dawis, & Lofquist, 1968). The results of the analyses provided what Gottfredson considers the most comprehensive evidence available on what she referred to as the construct validity of Holland's occupational classification typology.

Some further inklings about the relationship between people's personality and interest characteristics and the occupations they hold comes from a study by Borman, Rosse, and Abrahams (1980). (They also discussed their study in terms of construct validity.) These authors identified certain personality and interest "constructs" of *job incumbents* that could serve as links with *criterion* "constructs" (that is, measures of specific aspects of job performance).

Discussion. As discussed early in this chapter, it is reasonable to believe that, for *some kinds* of jobs, certain personality factors have a *direct* bearing on job performance. The nailing down of such relationships would indeed constitute construct validity of whatever personality measures would be used.

Such evidence, however, is illusive. In the absence of hard evidence, a more realistic objective would be to identify the factors measured by personality and interest inventories that have some modest relationship to performance of certain types of jobs or job activities, even though such factors are not absolute requirements. Information about such relationships could at least improve the odds of selecting suitable candidates. Certain inventories seem to be useful in establishing the links between personality or interest characteristics and performance on specific types of jobs or job activities. For example, Holland's Vocational Preference Inventory can be used to measure individuals' interests in terms of the same six factors that can be used to classify jobs. Likewise, the Work Activity Questionnaire, Form I (Interests) provides for measuring individuals' interests in terms of the same job dimensions that are used to characterize jobs.

Criterion-Related Validity of Inventories

Following are a couple of specific examples of the criterion-related validity of inventories, along with a summary of validity data for several types of jobs.

Managers. One such study is reported by Munson and Posner (1980), in which they administered two inventories to a group of managers and to a group of nonmanagers. The investigators used the England Personal Values Questionnaire and the Rokeach Value Survey. They used the job-status validity strategy because they compared the responses of the managers with those of the nonmanagers. For one sample of each group they first identified the subtests of each inventory that discriminated between the managers and nonmanagers; they then used scores on those subtests to predict, for a holdout sample of each group, whether individuals would be "classified" as managers.

The results for the Rokeach Value Survey, summarized here, show the percent of individuals in each group (managers versus nonmanagers) who were predicted to be in each group on the basis of their scores:

ACTUAL GROUP MEMBERSHIP	PREDICTED GROUP MEMBERHIP	
	MANAGERS	NONMANAGERS
Managers	74%	26%
Nonmanagers	33%	67%

Such results suggest that the scoring procedure for the inventory would help to improve the odds of selecting individuals who would be successful managers.

Police officers. Another criterion-related validity study is reported for police officers by Mills and Bohannon (1980). The California Psychological Inventory was administered to police cadets during their first few months at the police academy, and was scored on the eighteen scales of the Inventory. At this point a special "police performance equation" was used that provided for the differential weighting of four of the personality factor scales. This equation had been developed by Hogan (1971) in connection with an earlier validation study with police officers in another state.

After a year of service the officers in the study by Mills and Bohannon were rated by two supervisors on two criteria: leadership and suitability. The composite scores based on the police performance equation were then correlated with the mean ratings, with the following results:

CRITERION	CORRELATION
Leadership	.43
Suitability	.45

The fact that the police performance equation, developed in one study of police officers, "held up" in another study implies that the four personality factors in question are fairly stable aspects of successful police performance.

General Predictiveness of Inventories

Chapter 9 referred to summarizations by Ghiselli (1966, 1973) of the validity of various kinds of tests for many different jobs. Although Ghiselli's summaries were primarily of aptitude tests, they also covered personality and interest inventories. Figure 9.15 shows the mean validity coefficients for all five types of tests for jobs in various categories. In that figure the mean validity coefficients for personality tests (as measured against proficiency criteria) were highest for sales clerks and salespersons, and next highest for executives and administrators. The predictiveness of personality tests for sales occupations is shown in greater detail in Figure 10.5, which gives the mean validity coefficients of personality and interest inventories for each of six more specific sales occupations.

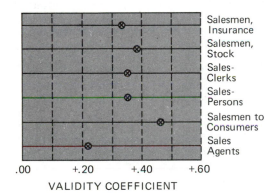

FIGURE 10.5 Mean validity coefficients of personality and interest inventories for seven sales jobs in each of certain sales occupation categories. (Adapted from Ghiselli, 1966, Figure 4-4, p. 79.)

DISCUSSION

Although personality and interest variables are related to job performance in some situations, the use of personality and interest tests is fraught with problems that might preclude such tests having any practical utility. In view of this, the most defensible use of such tests is only after their validity has been clearly demonstrated. This can best be done with a predictive validity strategy, which utilizes the responses to such inventories given by candidates *at the time they are applying for a job* as the basis for the prediction of future job-related behavior. Using this procedure one can develop special scoring keys that may be more predictive than are the standard scoring keys.

REFERENCES

Abrahams, N. M., Neumann, I., & Gilthens, W. H. (1971). Faking vocational interests: Simulated versus real life motivation. *Personnel Psychology*, 24(1), 5–12.

Borgen, F. H., Weiss, D. J., Tinsley, H. E. A., Dawis, R. V., & Lofquist, L. H. (1968). The measurement of occupational reinforcer patterns. *Minnesota Studies in Vocational Rehabilitation*, 25, Bulletin 49.

Borman, W. C., Rosse, R. L., & Abrahams, N. M. (1980). An empirical construct validity approach to studying predictor-job performance links. *Journal of Applied Psychology*, 65(6), 662–671.

Browne, J. A., & Howarth, B. (1977). A comprehensive factor analysis of personality questionnaire items: A test of 20 positive factor hypotheses. *Multivariate Behavioral Research*, 12, 399–427.

Campbell, D. P., & Hansen, J. C.(1981). *Manual for the SVIB-SCII Strong-Campbell Interest Inventory*. Stanford, Calif.: Stanford University Press.

Ghiselli, E. E. (1966). *The validity of occupational aptitude tests*. New York: Wiley.

Ghiselli, E. E. (1973). The validity of aptitude tests in personnel selection. *Personnel Psychology*, 26(4), 461–477.

Gordon, L. V., & Stapleton, E. S. (1956). Fakability of a forced-choice personality test under realistic high school employment conditions. *Journal of Applied Psychology*, 40, 258–262.

Gottfredson, L. S. (1980). Construct validity of Holland's occupational typology in terms of prestige, Census, Department of Labor, and other classification systems. *Journal of Applied Psychology*, 65(6), 697–714.

Hogan, R. (1971). Personality characteristics of highly-rated policemen. *Personnel Psychology*, 24, 679–686.

Holland J. L. (1966). A psychological classification scheme for occupations and major fields. *Journal of Counseling Psychology*, 13, 278–288.

Holland J. L., Vernstein, M. C., Kuo, H. M., Karweit, N. L., & Blum, Z. D. (November 1970). *A psychological classification of occupations*. Baltimore: The Johns Hopkins University Center for the Study of Social Organization of Schools, Report No. 90.

Mills, C. J., & Bohannon, W. E. (1980). Personality characteristics of effective state police officers. *Journal of Applied Psychology*, 65(6), 680–684.

Munson, J. M., & Posner, B. Z. (1980). Concurrent validation of two value inventories in predicting job classification and success for organizational personnel. *Journal of Applied Psychology*, 65(5), 535–542.

Ruch, F. L., & Ruch. W. W. (1967). The K factor as a (validity) suppressor variable in predicting success in selling. *Journal of Applied Psychology*, 51(3), 201–204.

Schwab, D. P., & Packard, G. L. (1973). Response distortion on the Gordon Personal Inventory and Gordon Personal Profile in a selection context: Some implications for predicting employee turnover. *Journal of Applied Psychology*, 58(3), 372–374.

Tiffin, J., & Phelan, R. F. (1953). Use of the Kuder Preference Record to predict turnover in an industrial plant. *Personnel Psychology*, 6, 195–204.

11

Nontest Methods of Personnel Selection

Personnel decisions can be made on the basis of various types of information about job candidates. The preceding two chapters dealt with personnel tests. This chapter deals with other types of information about job candidates, such as biographical data (obtained from application forms and questionnaires), self-assessments, references, and information obtained by interview.

BIOGRAPHICAL DATA

Biographical data can cover a wide variety of information about job candidates and their backgrounds, including age, sex, place of birth, place(s) of residence, family background, numbers of brothers and sisters, education, work experience, marital status, number of children, physical characteristics (such as height and weight), medical history, hobbies, reading habits, use of leisure time, and sometimes history of the parents. Al-

though most biographical data are factual in nature, some are subjective in that they deal with attitudes, feelings, value judgments, and enjoyment of leisure activities.

Sources of Biographical Data

Biographical data (we call them *biodata*) are usually obtained directly from job candidates on application forms or special questionnaires, such as biographical information blanks (BIB). Such data might also be obtained directly from individuals by an interviewer, or from outside sources, such as former employers or educational institutions. These latter sources sometimes merely confirm biodata obtained previously.

Biodata items

When job candidates complete application forms and other questionnaires they may give responses to biodata "items." The nature and format of individual biodata items should be particularly suitable to the content, and their construction should follow acceptable professional practice. Owens (1976) and Asher (1972) offered certain guidelines for constructing such items. Owens, for example, listed the following rules (along with others) for constructing biodata items:

1. Brevity is desirable.
2. All response options or alternatives should be provided.
3. Items, particularly item stems, should have a neutral or a pleasant connotation for the respondent.

Following are some examples of items from Owens (1976, p. 613):

Continuum, Single choice

What is your weight?
    (a) under 135 pounds
    (b) 136 to 155 pounds
    (c) 156 to 175 pounds
    (d) 176 to 195 pounds
    (e) over 195 pounds

Non-continuum, single choice

What was your marital status at college graduation?
    (a) single
    (b) married, no children
    (c) married, one or more children
    (d) widowed
    (e) separated or divorced

Continuum, plus "escape option"

What was your length of service in your most recent full-time job?
    (a) less than 6 months
    (b) between 6 months and 1 year
    (c) 1 to 2 years
    (d) 2 to 5 years
    (e) more than 5 years
    (f) no previous full-time job

Non-continuum, plus "escape option"

When are you most likely to have a headache?
    (a) when I strain my eyes
    (b) when I don't eat on schedule
    (c) when I am under tension
    (d) January first
    (e) never have headaches

Common stem, multiple continua

Over the past 5 years, how much have you enjoyed each of the following? (Use the 1 to 4 scale shown.)
    (a) loafing or watching TV
    (b) reading
    (c) constructive hobbies
    (d) home improvement
    (e) outdoor recreation
    (f) music, art, or dramatics, etc.

Scale

(1) very much
(2) some
(3) very little
(4) not at all

The most comprehensive assortment of items has been compiled by a committee under the auspices of the Division of Industrial and Organizational Psychology of the American Psychological Association.[1]

Accuracy of Biodata

It is natural to be curious about the accuracy of the biodata reported by job candidates. In considering such accuracy we need to differentiate between verifiable items (such as previous employment records, previous wages, and marital status) and unverifiable items (such as opinions, attitudes, and beliefs). Data on the accuracy of verifiable items are skimpy and somewhat inconsistent. Goldstein (1971), for example, found substantial differences between responses given by applicants for unskilled labor jobs and data later verified. In a much earlier study, however, Keating, Paterson, and Stone (1950) reported

[1] *A catalogue of life history items.* Prepared by Scientific Affairs Committee, Division of Industrial and Organizational Psychology (Division 14), American Psychological Association (June 1966). Greensboro, N.C.: Creativity Research Institute, The Richardson Foundation.

remarkably close agreement on wages and duration and duties of jobs as reported by applicants during interviews and by previous employers. Following is a summary of their findings:

| | INDEX OF AGREEMENT | | |
ITEM	TYPE	MEN	WOMEN
Wages	Correlation	.90	.93
Duration of employment	Correlation	.98	.93
Duties of job	Percent	96%	96%

In another early study Weiss, Dawis, England, and Lofquist (1961) compared information reported by 325 physically handicapped individuals who were interviewed in their homes, and information obtained from their previous employers. The information included job title, job duties, dates of employment, hours, pay rates, and so on. The percentage of agreement for the eleven items ranged from 38 to 83, with only two below 60. For items for which numerical values were reported, correlations were computed in addition to the percentage of agreement. The four items with the lowest percentage of agreement (final pay, length of job, starting pay, and pay increases) still had high correlations between interview and employer data. These differences can be largely attributed to the distinct tendency of individuals to report "upgraded" or "inflated" information about themselves. To the extent that this is a general tendency, it is possible for a percentage of accuracy to be low but for the correlation to be high.

Although responses to verifiable items fall somewhat short of perfect accuracy, they have nonetheless generally been considered adequate for use in most circumstances (Cascio, 1975; Keating, et al., 1950; Owens, 1976). Responses to unverifiable items, however, have generally been viewed with more skepticism. In this regard, of course, the possibility exists that people could fake their responses to unverifiable items in order to make themselves "look good." However, evidence regarding possible faking is very limited.

Scoring of Biodata Items

Biodata items can be "scored" either individually or by groups.

Scoring individual biodata items. This scoring procedure subjects the responses to the individual items to item analysis against a job-related criterion such as tenure or job performance. Those responses found to discriminate significantly in terms of the criterion are then incorporated into a special scoring key that is then used in selecting future candidates. The individual items may be given equal or differential weights to the extent to which they contribute to the prediction of the criterion.

One example of a differential weighting system comes from a study conducted by Mitchell and Klimoski (1982) using a ninety-eight biodata questionnaire with real-estate salespersons. The criterion used was whether or not the individuals in the sample had attained real-estate licenses (which is considered a mark of the calibre of salespersons). Following is an example of the analysis and the resulting scoring of one item. The scoring procedure used is described by England (1971). It is based on the magnitude and direction of the difference in percentages of the two criterion groups.

| | LICENSE? | | | |
DO YOU	YES	NO	DIFFER-ENCE	WEIGHT
Own your home?	81%	60%	21%	5
Rent home?	3	5	−2	−1
Rent apartment?	9	25	−16	−4
Live with relatives?	5	10	−5	−2
	100%[a]	100%[a]		

[a]The "yes" responses do not add up to exactly 100% because of rounding.

A person's total score is based on the sum of the weights of the responses to the various items.

This method of scoring was used by an industrial organization in a study of retail outlet dealers. The dealers completed biodata questionnaires, and the results were analyzed in the manner just illustrated. The dealers were then divided into high and low criterion groups based on ratings made by regional management officials. Using this approach, there were nine items that differentiated significantly in terms of the criterion groups. These items were then used to develop a scoring key that was cross validated with another sample of fifty-five dealers. The results of this study, shown in Figure 11.1, indicate quite clearly that the scores derived by this process could be used very effectively to select potentially successful dealers. The odds of success for those with low scores (especially 8 and below) are quite limited. (Cross validation is important to analyses of this type because some personal-data items might be related to a criterion simply by chance and thus will not really be differentially discriminating in terms of the criterion.)

Scoring groups of biodata items. A growing body of data suggests that groups or clusters of biodata items tend to reflect relatively basic patterns of previous experience. Owens (1976) suggested that such data can be regarded as presenting an historical view of an individual's development. If we adopt this view of biodata as a measure of prior experience, we can gain some insight into the rationale for its possible use in predicting job-related criteria. This rationale is based on the axiom that what a person has done in the *past* is the best predictor of what the person will do in the *future*. (This is the concept of behavioral consistency discussed in Chapter 9.)

There are two methods for developing groups of biodata items, or what are sometimes called dimensions. The most common method uses factor analysis. Owens and his associates have made the most significant contributions in this area (Brush & Owens, 1979; Owens, 1976; Owens & Schoenfeldt, 1979). In the study by Brush and Owens, for example, a biographical inventory was completed by 1987 nonexempt employees of an oil company. The responses were subjected to a factor analysis, and nine factors were identified:

1. Trade skills;
2. Family relationships;

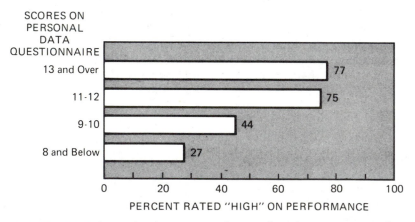

FIGURE 11.1 Relationship between total scores based on nine items of personal data and successful performance of retail outlet dealers. (Reproduced with permission of the company.)

3. Achievement motivation/self-confidence;
4. Academic success;
5. Athletic and extracurricular interests;
6. Socioeconomic level;
7. Personal work-related values;
8. Introversion;
9. Organized-institution affiliation.

Each factor is dominated or characterized by the biodata items that have the highest correlations with the factor. An individual's score on a factor (whether high, average, or low) is especially influenced by responses to the items that dominate the factor.

The second approach to the formation of groups of biodata items is on the basis on subjective judgments of item content made by a selected group of judges. Such a procedure was followed by Matteson, Osburn, and Sparks (1970) using data from a biodata questionnaire completed by 2590 applicants for employment in a large company. Thirteen clusters of items were thus formed, and a scoring key was developed to derive a score for any individual on each cluster.

In a subsequent application of the scoring keys to another sample of 168 men who were actually employed (but without the use of the biodata), a correlation of .43 was found between scores on a combination of the thirteen clusters and ratings on overall performance at the end of 6 months of employment.

Discussion. Although arguments have been made for the use of individual versus group scoring of biodata items, there is only one reported study that involved a comparison of these two strategies (Mitchell & Klimoski, 1982). As discussed earlier, this study involved the experimental use of a biodata questionnaire with real-estate salespersons. Mitchell and Klimoski found that the individual-scoring approach predicted success in selling real estate slightly better than did the group-scoring method. Despite this one study, however, we are inclined to believe that the group-scoring strategy probably has

more general, across-the-board, long-range relevance than does the scoring of individual items. At the same time, in certain specific situations, the individual-scoring approach could probably "tease out" a modest degree of criterion-related validity over and above the group-scoring approach.

Grouping People with Similar Biodata Profiles

With the group-scoring strategy discussed each individual would have a score for each group or cluster of items. In addition to grouping biodata *items*, one can also group *individuals* on the basis of the similarity of their biodata profiles. For this purpose, one can use either the responses to individual items or the scores for groups of items. In either case the end result consists of several groups of individuals, each consisting of people with relatively similar biodata profiles. (The usual procedure is some form of hierarchical grouping technique, which we need not describe in detail.) Owens and his associates have been major proponents of such a procedure, and their work has resulted in what Owens refers to as a classification of persons (Brush & Owens, 1979; Owens & Schoenfeldt, 1979).

It is not feasible here to describe the classifications of people that have resulted from such analyses, and labels for such groups are not fully satisfying. However, following are a few labels that reflect the "flavor" of certain groups. These labels are based on data from a study of university students (Owens & Schoenfeldt, 1979):

- Female biodata subgroups
    Well-adjusted achievers
    Scholarly bookworms
    Active, conventional social leaders
- Male biodata subgroups
    Bright, achieving leaders
    Humanitarian underachievers
    "Jocks"

The biodata items that serve as the basis for each group represent a unique profile or constellation of experiences.

The Assessment-Classification Model

The underlying assumption of behavioral consistency (discussed in Chapter 9) is that the best indicator of future performance is past performance. Similarly, one could suggest that the use of classifications of people based on biodata might well serve to predict the match of individuals with various types of jobs. The assessment-classification model is predicated on such a matching process.

The model, as set forth by Schoenfeldt (1974, 1982), is described briefly here and is illustrated in Figure 11.2:

1. Formation of biodata subgroups (S). These are groups of individuals (I) with similar biodata profiles, based on statistical analysis of responses to a biodata questionnaire.
2. Formation of job families (F). These are clusters of jobs (J) with similar profiles of job activities,

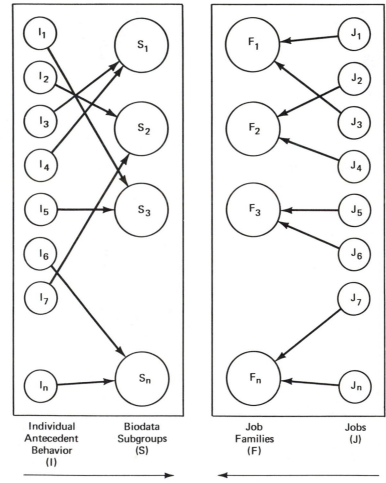

FIGURE 11.2 Illustration of the assessment-classification model. See text for discussion. (Adapted from Schoenfeldt, 1982, Figure 4.)

based on data from a structured job-analysis questionnaire such as the Position Analysis Questionnaire (PAQ).

3. Analysis of relationships. An analysis is carried out to determine the probability of some job-related criterion (performance, tenure, satisfaction, etc.) given the following: that an individual (*I*) is a member of a given biodata subgroup (*S*) and is performing a given job (*J*) which is a member of job family (*F*). The result of this analysis would be the identification of the statistically significant relationships between biodata subgroup (*S*) and job families (*F*).

4. Use of model. In actual practice, candidates for jobs would complete the biodata questionnaire and would then be classified in the biodata group they most closely resemble. An individual (*I*) would be recommended for jobs in the job family or families (*F*) for which significant relationships have been found with his or her biodata subgroup (*S*).

An example of the assessment-classification model. An example of such an approach, reported by Brush and Owens (1979), involved about 2000 office and clerical employees on 939 jobs in an industrial organization. Data from a biodata questionnaire were used in a factor analysis to identify nine biodata factors (these are listed earlier in this chapter). Factor scores for the individuals (*I*) were then used to formulate eighteen biodata subgroups (*S*). Separately, the jobs (*J*) of the individuals were analyzed with a structured job-analysis procedure, and the results were used to identify nineteen job families (*F*).

The statistical analysis of the relationships between the biodata subgroups (*S*) and the job families (*F*) consisted of determining the percentage of the 2000 employees in each combination of biodata subgroups (*S*) and job families (*F*). The intent was to identify relationships whose percentages were significantly higher than the "base rate" (or average). Eleven of the eighteen subgroups (*S*) manifested clear departures from the base rates, some of them exceeding the base rate by 15% to 25%. This analysis indicates, then, that persons with certain patterns of back-ground (reflected by their scores on biodata factors) tend to gravitate into occupations that have certain patterns of characteristics. This lends support to the assessment-classification model discussed.

Validity of Biodata in Personnel Selection

Data from certain specific studies of biodata were given earlier in this chapter. Perhaps the most comprehensive data on the validity of biodata for personnel selection, however, are those in Figure 9.16, summarized by Asher and Sciarrino (1974). That figure represents the average validity coefficients from eleven previous studies (summarized by Asher, 1972) in comparison with average validity coefficients for various types of tests, and shows that, in general, biodata have been more predictive of job-proficiency criteria than various types of tests are. Note that the eleven studies summarized by Asher used cross validation with a second group, thus supporting these results. Schwab and Oliver (1974) pointed out, however, that some studies with biodata have not been cross validated and that some studies with "negative" results do not find their way into published journals. Thus, the results given in Figure 9.16 may not be entirely representative of the overall utility of biodata for personnel selection. Any organization using such data should therefore cross validate them before using them for actual personnel selection.

Biodata and the *Uniform Guidelines*

The *Uniform Guidelines on Employee Selection Procedures* (1978) prohibit discrimination in employment practices on grounds of race, color, religion, sex, or national origin. Because of this, it is illegal in the United States to use biodata items relating to these factors in personnel selection.

Discussion of Biodata

Although biodata have been used in personnel selection for several decades, they have never had a major role in this process. In fact, Dunnette and Borman (1979) admitted that such data have acquired a bad reputation among scientific-industrial psychologists. However, the work of Owens (1976) and Brush and Owens (1979) and the introduction of the assessment-classification model (Schoenfeldt, 1974, 1982) may change that image. Although data to support the assessment-classification model are still rather skimpy, the concept seems to make sense. It remains for future investigators, however, to provide the research base to support—or conversely, to pull the rug out from under—this possible approach for using biodata in personnel selection.

As an attempt to account for some of the conflicting evidence on the use of biodata personnel selection we would like to suggest a distinction that might account for some of the inconsistencies that have plagued their use; biodata can be considered as falling into two general classes, *job-related* and *labor-market related* (although there undoubtedly would be substantial overlap between these two classes).

The job-related class contains those items that fit into the assessment-classification model and that have some stable implications (direct or indirect) for the human qualities required for successful performance on a job or group of jobs.

The second group of biodata items are more reflective of labor-market conditions and the effects thereof on the kinds of people who present themselves as job candidates. (For example, in some communities more married women are available as job applicants than in other communities.) Labor-market conditions are, of course, transitory, and as they change they can cause changes in the kinds of people who are available for work.

We have no substantiative evidence to support this distinction. (Indeed, even if such a distinction does in fact exist, it would not be a neat dichotomy.) We have elaborated on this theme, however, in the hope that it may have some validity, or that it could at least lead to some further clarification of the sources of apparent inconsistency and ambiguity in dealing with biodata.

SELF-ASSESSMENTS

A few investigators have explored the possibility of using self-assessments of such factors as ability, skill, and knowledge in personnel selection. The results of these investigations are admittedly mixed. Primoff (1980) and Ash (1980), for example, report modestly encouraging results from studies of self-assessment of such office skills as spelling, arithmetic ability, and typing. On the basis of a review of several studies, however, Reilly and Chao (1982) conclude that self-assessments cannot be recommended for use in personnel selection because of the potential for overrating by job candidates.

Although present evidence regarding the potential of self-assessments is rather bleak, further research efforts might help pinpoint the types of circumstances in which such assessments could be used with confidence. It might be, for example, that self-assessments could be useful for career planning and vocational counseling (when the individual has no reason to distort an assessment) even if not for personnel selection (when an individual might be motivated to over rate personal abilities).

REFERENCES

References are sometimes used in personnel selection, especially in the case of higher-level positions. However, many people view references with skepticism, probably with some justification. For references to be useful, at least four conditions must be fulfilled by those who give them: (1) they must have had adequate opportunity to observe the individual in relevant situations (such as on the job); (2) they themselves must be competent to make the necessary assessments and evaluations; (3) they must be willing to give frank opinions; and (4) they must be able to express these opinions so that the recipient interprets them as they were intended. All of these factors can be stumbling blocks to using references in personnel selection, but the willingness to convey one's real opinions is probably the most serious. There is abundant evidence that many people do not like to say negative things about others and thus tend to mention only their good sides.

Validity of references. Although there are not many studies dealing with the validity of references for personnel selection, Reilly and Chao (1982) summarized such data for seven studies for which ten correlations were available. Eight of these involved ratings as criteria and two involved turnover as criteria. The results are summarized here:

CRITERION	NO. OF CORRELA- TIONS	NO. OF INDIVIDUALS REPRESENTED	AVERAGE CORRELA- TIONS
Ratings	8	2022	.08
Ratings and turn- over	10	5718	.14

Although these data indicate that references have some predictive value, the average level of prediction is obviously very meager. On the basis of another review of references, Muchinsky (1979) concluded: "Most of the available evidence suggests that they are not particularly valuable as selection devices, although some notable exceptions have been reported."

Discussion. Muchinsky's comment about "exceptions" seems to suggest the following

recommendation: References should be used in personnel selection in those specific circumstances in which there is supporting evidence or strong arguments in favor of doing so. For example, references should be used:

- When a validity analysis of references has demonstrated their validity;
- When the recipient of a reference knows the person who wrote the reference and has confidence in that person's integrity;
- When specially designed reference procedures minimize distortion, as with the forced-choice procedure;
- In special circumstances in which it can reasonably be expected that the value of references would be above the "run-of-the-mill," as in the selection of some professional and management personnel. Previous experience of the organization (or of other organizations) may provide inklings about the value of references for certain types of jobs.

THE INTERVIEW

The interview is used as a communication process, for various purposes in industry, such as employment counseling, attitude and opinion surveys, and market and consumer surveys. Our interests are focused on the employment interview for personnel selection, although certain phases of our discussion may also be relevant to other contexts. The employment process is aimed at deciding whether or not to offer employment to individual job candidates.

Various people within an organization may interview job candidates, including employment interviewers, recruiters, personnel managers, executives, department heads, and supervisors. In some instances candidates may be interviewed by two or more individuals.

Those who serve as interviewers (whatever their positions in an organization) can make three general types of judgments about candidates: (1) judgments about specific aspects of the candidates, such as their personal qualities, work experience, or motivation (in some instances the interviewer is asked to make formal evaluations or ratings of such factors); (2) recommendations (such as to hire or not); and (3) final decisions to hire or not. All interviewers make at least informal judgments about some aspects of candidates (item 1). The "outcome" of an interview may consist of recorded evaluations or ratings of candidates (item 1), recommendations (item 2), or employment decisions (item 3).

The interview has been raked over the coals by many knowledgeable people, primarily on the grounds that it has limited reliability and validity. On the other hand, it has been defended as an essential aspect of the employment process. Granting its limitations, however, there are few who would scrap it completely. Because the interview appears to be a fixture in personnel selection, it behooves us to do whatever is possible to contribute to its improvement. This chapter summarizes some of the research that has been directed toward understanding some of the variables that impinge upon the interview process, with the view toward improving it.

Variables Involved in the Interview

Some of the variables and processes that are involved in the interview process and that can affect its outcome are shown in Figure 11.3. This model groups the variables into four categories: (1) applicant characteristics; (2) the interview situation; (3) interviewer charactacteristics; and (4) the interview process itself, leading up to the interview outcome. Most of the interview research has involved specific aspects of these categories. The discussion later in this chapter deals with only a few of these variables.

Interview Research Strategies and Settings

Two principle strategies have been used in interview research: the *microanalytic* and *macroanalytic* approaches. In the microanalytic

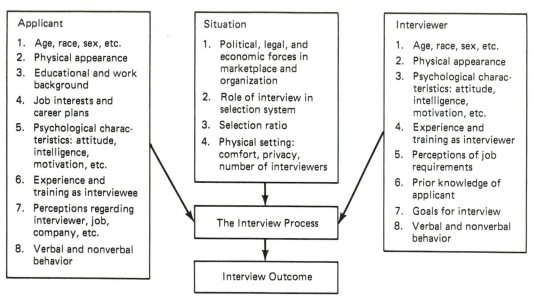

FIGURE 11.3 A model of an employment interview showing some of the variables and processes that influence it. (Adapted from Arvey & Campion, 1982, Figure 1, p. 283.)

strategy the interview is "dissected" into some type of units for investigation—for example, specific types of information about candidates. The macroanalytic strategy treats the interview more as a complete entity and tends to focus on the variables that influence decisions based on the "overall" interview.

Another important distinction in interview research concerns the research setting. Some research has been carried out in simulated situations, in which subjects are asked to behave or respond "as if" they were actual interviewees or interviewers; frequently such subjects are college students, but in some instances they are people who are responsible for employment decisions but who are asked to evaluate hypothetical job candidates. Other research has been carried out in the real world, with actual interviewees and interviewers. Most research has probably been carried out in simulated situations, in which college students frequently serve either as the "interviewers" or the "candidates." Based on a review of a number of studies, Bernstein, Hakel, and Harlan (1975) conclude that "no important findings that would limit generalizability have been discovered, except that students are lenient relative to (actual) interviewers," and that ". . . interview decision-making processes appear to be similar to samples composed of students and employment interviewers." These conclusions suggest some generalizability of research results to real-life interview decisions based on research with college students. However, one would receive more comfort if more of the interview research had been carried out in actual interview situations.

Accuracy of Information Obtained from Interviewers

An initial question about the interview is the extent to which the information obtained is accurate. (This can be thought of as a form of validity—that is, the validity of the information. Another aspect of interview validity is the extent to which interviewers make judgments and decisions about job candidates that are correlated with the ultimate performance of the individuals.) Although actual information on the accuracy of interview data is rare (and most of what is available is not current), Kahn and Cannell (1956) suggested that there are persistent and important differences in interview data and corresponding data obtained from other sources. Some support for this pessimistic view was provided by a study by Weiss and Dawis (1960). On the other hand, as we discussed earlier certain reasonably accurate verifiable biodata can be obtained by interview (Keating et al., 1950; Weiss et al., 1961). The implications of the somewhat conflicting bits of evidence and opinions on the accuracy of data obtained from interviews are the following: that some types of data are probably more accurate than others; that interviewers should sharpen their interviewing techniques in order to elicit as accurate information as possible; and that, when particularly important, data obtained from candidates should be verified, if possible.

The Applicant

Employment interviews are directed toward obtaining information and impressions about applicants that can serve as the basis for employment decisions. Such information and impressions fall into two broad classes: those which are relevant and those which are not.

Applicant characteristics that influence decisions. Although the line between relevant and irrelevant information is thin, it is probable that in many employment situations irrelevant information does influence decisions. This is especially the case with regard to applicants' sex, race, and sometimes appearance, and the "impressions" the applicants give (when such characteristics are not relevant for the job).

Following are the results of a few studies of the characteristics that have been reported to influence interview decisions. Unfortunately, most such studies have been carried out in simulated situations.

In one study Dipboye, Fromkin, and Wilback (1975) had thirty college recruiters rate the résumés of twelve hypothetical applicants for the position of head of the furniture department of a department store. The twelve résumés were systematically varied in terms of three dimensions of information: applicant's sex (male and female); scholastic record (high, average, and low); and physical attractiveness (attractive and unattractive). Photographs of the applicants were included (the photographs of the "attractive" versus "unattractive" applicants were selected according to previous judgments of people not otherwise involved in the research).

The results of the study are summarized in Figure 11.4, which shows the average ratings (on a nine-point scale with nine being high) given by the college recruiters who served as raters. Scholastic standing was clearly the most important determinant of the ratings. Assuming that scholastic standing was the most rational basis for the ratings, we can see rather systematic influences on the rat-

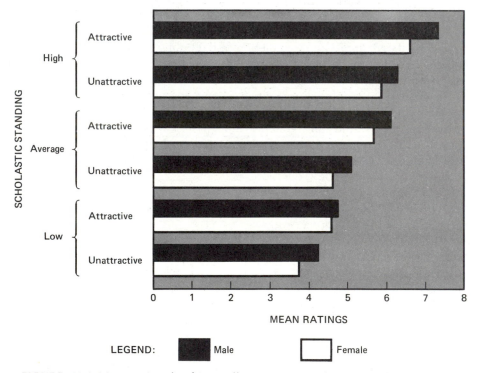

FIGURE 11.4 Mean ratings by thirty college recruiters of résumés of twelve hypothetical applicants (six males and six females) with various combinations of scholastic standing and personal appearance. (Adapted from Dipboye et al., 1975, Table 1, p. 41. Copyright 1975 by the American Psychological Association. Reprinted by permission.)

ings of appearance and sex, with appearance being the more dominant. These influences suggest the possibility of unfair discrimination, since persons with equal qualifications fared differently in the ratings depending on their sex and appearance. In a somewhat comparable investigation, Cann, Siegfried, and Pearce (1981) also found that applicants' sex and attractiveness influenced the "hiring decisions" of the students who made the ratings on the basis of simulated résumés and photographs of the applicants. The applicants' sex, however, apparently influenced the hiring decisions much more than their appearance.

In still another study Hollandsworth, Kazelskis, Stevens, and Dressel (1979) asked seventy-three college recruiters to rate 338 applicants on six factors, including personal appearance. The recruiters also responded to this question: "Would you hire this candidate?" In this study personal appearance only had a fairly modest influence on the hiring decisions, as contrasted with the other studies.

Discussion. Evidence on the effects of personal characteristics on hiring decisions is admittedly conflicting. Recognizing this, the following tentative conclusions can be suggested: (1) that the perceived competence of applicants by interviewers is probably the dominant factor in the interviewers' decisions; (2) that applicants' verbal and communication skills influence the decisions of at least some interviewers (however, the pervasiveness of this influence is not known; neither is there much evidence to indicate whether interviewers' judgments about applicants' verbal and communication skills are, or are not, relevant to the jobs for which they are being considered); and (3) that the decisions of at least some interviewers are influenced by the applicants' sex or appearance (although the pervasiveness of this is not known either).

Situational Aspects of the Interview

As would be expected, various aspects of the situation can have an impact on the interview—aspects such as the physical setting, the role of the interviewer, and the selection ratio (which influences the extent to which interviewers can be "choosy" in selecting candidates). Another aspect, which is specifically discussed next, is contrast effects.

Contrast effects. The concept of contrast effects as applied to interviews refers to the possible effects on an interviewer's judgments of one candidate of the impression of the preceding interviewee(s). Thus, what might be a good or "average" candidate might be judged as being a better candidate if interviewed after a very *poor* candidate than if interviewed after a very *good* candidate. Although there is something of a controversy over these effects, the evidence seems to indicate that there is such a tendency, as shown by the results of a study by Wexley, Yukl, Kovacs, and Sanders (1972). The subjects who served as raters of "applicants" watched videotaped interviews of applicants for the job of office-system salesperson. Each applicant was role played by a graduate student who gave predetermined responses to each of ten questions. From the information incorporated into the responses, each applicant was categorized in terms of his suitability to the job as high (H), average (A), or low (L). Each rater watched three interviews and rated the applicant in the third interview. By planning for the first two applicants to be high or low in terms of suitability, it was possible to determine the effects of those applicants on the ratings of the third applicants (who were high, average, or low in their suitability).

Some of the results are shown in Figure 11.5. High-suitability applicants were systematically rated lower following high-suitability applicants than when following low-suitability applicants. The same general pattern was also

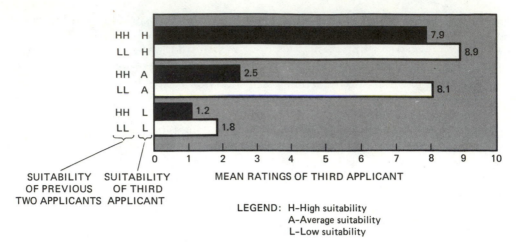

FIGURE 11.5 Mean ratings of third applicants (who varied in their "suitability" for a job following observed interviews with two previous applicants who were high (*H*) or low (*L*) in their job suitability. This demonstrates the contrast effect. (Adapted from Wexley et al., 1972, Table 1, p. 46. Copyright 1972 by the American Psychological Association. Reprinted by permission.)

evident for average- and low-suitability applicants. The general findings, then, tended to support the contrast-effects theory.

The Interviewer

Many features of interviewers can affect the interview process and outcome. The following discussion covers interviewer stereotypes, interviewer "set," and interviewer training.

Interviewer stereotypes. There is evidence that many interviewers have stereotypes of "ideal" candidates that they use as their "standard" in assessing actual candidates. One phase of a major research program of the Life Insurance Marketing and Research Association dealt with this matter (Mayfield & Carlson, 1966). (This program is an example of the microanalytic research approach.) A number of life insurance managers were asked to list the types of information about candidates they considered when making employment decisions. An edited list of these items was then sent to another sample of managers, who were asked to

rate how favorable or unfavorable it would be if each item were true of an applicant (the ratings were to be done on a seven-point scale from "extremely favorable" to "extremely unfavorable," plus an eighth category "I would no longer consider this man." As one would expect, the agreement on certain items was very high—for example, "Earned all college expenses" was consistently rated favorably. Other items were consistently rated intermediate or low. A more surprising result was that the ratings on some items showed marked disagreement—for example, "The applicant says he feels he's gotten nowhere for the last five years and it's change jobs now or never."

In the next phase of the research, seven "hypothetical" applicants were constructed, each consisting of six items of information. The items used were those on which there had been substantial disagreement, on their favorability or unfavorability. An example of such an hypothetical applicant follows:

• Has a net worth of $3000.
• Received a C average in college.

- Is more satisfied than dissatisfied with his present job.
- Owns $8000 of life insurance (face value).
- Has seven close friends in the community.
- His favorite hobby is listening to music.

Sixty-nine managers then ranked these "applicants" in order of their suitability for the job of a life insurance agent. The result was that *each* applicant was ranked *best* by one or more managers, and *worst* by one or more, and at *each intervening rank* by one or more! Following are three examples:

APPLICANT NO.	NUMBER OF RATERS RANKING APPLICANT AS:						
	BEST	2ND	3RD	4TH	5TH	6TH	WORST
1	10	5	12	8	8	13	13
4	16	17	12	7	9	7	1
7	8	8	10	9	10	12	14

In interpreting their results, Mayfield and Carlson concluded that interviewers do have stereotypes of ideal candidates, but that the stereotypes have two parts. The first is the common stereotype of the ideal candidate which most interviewers share. The other is a "specific" stereotype that is different for different interviewers. These specific stereotypes are represented by those items on which different interviewers disagree as to favorability. The notion of there being a rather common stereotype of the ideal applicant seems to be fairly well accepted. If, in addition, individual interviewers tend to have their own individual stereotypes, this could account for at least a share of the inconsistencies characterizing decisions made by different interviewers.

Interviewer "set." Some years ago Springbett (1958) concluded that interviewers tend to approach appraisal of candidates with a "set" of caution that he described as a search for negative information. The implication of this conclusion is that interviewer judgments are influenced more by negative information about candidates than by positive information. In discussing this matter, however, Webster (1982) refers to certain subsequent studies that (as he puts it) "further sharpened our knowledge of the conditions under which unfavorable information is likely to affect impressions and decisions" (p. 62). In effect, Webster confirms the existence of such a "set," but he indicates that it does not apply to all employment interviews—in other words that such a set tends to be situational. (One could speculate that some interviewers have such "sets" in order to minimize the possibility of referring or recommending potentially undesirable candidates, since they might later be criticized if too many of their referred candidates turned out to be poor employees.)

Interviewer training. It has been an article of faith that some of the problems associated with the interview can be minimized by appropriately training interviewers. In summarizing certain studies, Webster (1982) reports that training interviewers can minimize certain types of errors in the rating of candidates—for example, the halo effect, the contrast effect, the effect of first impressions, and the "similarity to self" influence. However, Webster also makes the point that we have no information as to whether reducing such errors has any effect on the final decisions made by interviewers. In discussing this depressing conclusion, he goes on to state (Webster, 1982) that it is unreasonable to expect that a 3- to 5-day training program "will permanently change well-established, emotionally colored attributions, stereotypes, illusory correlates and other non-rational aspects of implicit thought and feeling triggered by making a new acquaintance: the applicant" (p. 88). The implication of such a point of view is that it is critical to *select* interviewers who have the basic qualifications to make good decisions. Yet, the data on the selection of interviewers are limited.

The Interview Process

Interviews take on many shapes and forms. Some features of the manner in which interviews are conducted can influence the information obtained and the judgments of the interviewers who conduct the interviews.

Interview format. Most employment interviews conform to one of the following three formats:

1. Free interviews. The content of the interview and the sequence of topics are not planned, but depend on the interaction of the interviewer and interviewee.
2. Semistructured interviews. The interviewer systematically covers certain background areas, and tailors questions to obtain as much relevant information as possible. There may be provision for the interviewer to rate different aspects of the candidate's background.
3. Structured interviews. The interviewer follows a specific set of preplanned questions. There is usually also provision for the interviewer to rate the candidate on various background areas.

Following are examples of a few questions from a structured interview. These are from a Selection Interview Blueprint used by the Life Insurance Marketing and Research Association (Mayfield, Brown, & Hamstra, 1980), and deal with work experience:

A.1 How did you happen to go with this company?
Did you consider other companies at that time?

A.2 Briefly, what did you do on this job?
Nonsales job: Did you have any contacts with the public on this job?
How did this come about?
Sales job: (a) How did you locate your customers? What kind of people were they (e.g., age, education, income)? (b) How did you handle an actual sale?
What was your sales record? How did yours compare with the others?

A.3 How was your work schedule determined?
What hours did you work?
Did you ever have to work extra hours?

Under what circumstances? How often? How did you feel about it (p. 729)?

A variant of the structured interview, the situational interview, was developed by Latham, Saari, Pursell, and Campion (1980). This format is based on the critical incident technique of job analysis. The incidents are turned into interview questions and job applicants are asked to indicate how they would behave in a given situation. Following is an example:

Your spouse and two teenage children are sick in bed with a cold. There are no relatives or friends available to look in on them. Your shift starts in 3 hours. What would you do in this situation (p. 424)?

Various responses are scaled in the same manner as the "behaviors" in behaviorally anchored rating scales (BARS) described in Chapter 6. The responses of candidates are then compared with those scaled examples, and scale values are assigned accordingly.

Janz (1982) reports some encouraging results with the situational interview (which he calls the behavior-description interview). On the basis of data from critical incidents regarding the job in question (teaching assistants in a university), Janz identified five "behaviorally defined" job dimensions, and developed patterned questions to use during interviews of persons who had already been selected for the job. The interviewees were interviewed by both the behavior-description interview (BD) and by a conventional, unstructured interview, and ratings were then made of the predicted performance of the teaching assistants. These ratings were later correlated with criterion ratings of the teaching assistants given by their students at the end of the semester. The ratings based on the BD interviews were much more predictive of the later criterion ratings (with a correlation of .70) than were those based on the unstructured interview (with a correlation of .07).

Discussion of interview formats. The situational (or behavior-descriptive) interview thus seems to offer substantial promise for certain circumstances. However, the time required to develop the critical incidents and to develop the interview procedure based on them would warrant its use only if there were many candidates for a single job. Of the more common interview formats, most of the evidence suggests that structured or semistructured interviews are superior to the typical unstructured interview. Schwab and Heneman (1960), for example, report the following correlations of interrater consistency for individuals who were interviewed with three types of interviews:

INTERVIEW METHOD	INTERRATER RELIABILITY COEFFICIENT
Structured	.79
Semistructured	.43
Unstructured	.36

Some additional, moderate support for structured interviews comes from a study that deals with data used in the real-life selection of candidates for life insurance sales jobs (Mayfield et al., 1980). The Selection Interview Blueprint (SIB) referred to previously provides for the rating of candidates on items such as their ability or tendency to:

- Give careful thought to the future;
- Participate in outside activities;
- Work without close supervision.

The ratings of 163 previous candidates in one insurance agency were dredged up and used in an analysis of the employment decisions made regarding the candidates. Of thirty-nine items for which ratings had been obtained, fourteen were significantly related to the decision to hire or not hire. A multiple correlation was computed for these fourteen items as related to the hire versus not-hire deci-

sions. This correlation was .36, indicating that the actual ratings made in connection with a structured-interview procedure had at least moderate validity in terms of the employment decisions.

Although there is some conflicting evidence about the advantages of structured and semistructured interviews (Heneman, Schwab, Huett, & Ford, 1975), we feel that some form of patterned interview is preferable to the usual unstructured interview of most employment situations. We also believe that the situational interview should be considered when it is feasible. Although the advantages of patterned interviews seem well supported, Webster (1982) is probably correct when he says that the free (unstructured) interview will continue to be used, especially by the thousands of small employers and by many supervisors who make final decisions about many candidates. However, perhaps over time such practices will change.

The Interview Outcome

The outcome of interviews can consist of evaluations or ratings of candidates, recommendations about employment, and final employment decisions.

Interviewer judgments about candidates. Information about the validity and reliability of judgments about various aspects of candidates is relatively sparse, and most such data are of early vintage. Wagner (1949), for example, made a thorough survey of available data on the judgments reported for ninety-six human traits or characteristics. The results for twelve traits appear in Table 11.1. Note that the validity refers to the accuracy with which ratings were made (not the validity for predicting job performance or other criteria). There are obviously marked differences in the reliabilities and validities of the various traits and characteristics. For example, the reliability of ratings for "alertness" was .36, whereas for "sociability" the reliabilities (in two situ-

TABLE 11.1 Reliability and validity of judgments of selected human traits and characteristics in interviewlike situations

TRAIT OR CHARACTERISTIC	RELIABILITY			VALIDITY		
Ability to present ideas	.42					
Alertness	.36					
Background, family and socioeconomic				.20		
Energy	.64					
Initiative	.57					
Intelligence or mental ability	.96	.87	.77	.58	.82	.45
	.62	.90		.94	.51	.70
				.21		
Personality						
Self-confidence	.77					
Sociability	.87	.72		.37		
Social adjustment				.22		
Tact	.26					
Overall ability	.71	.48	.24	.27	.21	.16
	−.20	.26	.43	.87	.23	
	.68	.61	.85			
	.55					

Source: Adopted from Wagner, 1949.

ations) were .87 and .72. The validities ranged from .20 for "background," to the .80s and .90s for "intelligence or mental ability."

Some other data on interviewers' ratings of various traits of interviewees comes from a study by Moore and Lee (1974). Their data are the ratings by twenty-four bank managers of videotaped interviews; the interviewers were experienced bank interviewers, and the "candidates" were graduate students in business school. Coefficients of consistency between raters on twelve specific traits ranged from .16 to .60 with a median of .42. The traits with the highest coefficients were: leadership (.60); self-expression (.51); and interest (.51). Those with the lowest coefficients were: motivation (.16); intelligence (.25); and attitude (.31). The coefficient on "overall" was only .10.

In general, then, it seems that interviewers probably would be best able to judge qualities that are overtly obvious in the behavior of interviewees or that can be inferred from such behavior. On the other hand, interviewers should not be expected to make judgments about traits or characteristics that cannot be observed during the interview or inferred from interview observations—characteristics such as motivation, creativity, dependability, industriousness, punctuality, or dexterity.

The studies by Wagner and by Moore and Lee dealt with ratings of human "traits." In a study of a different type, Mayfield et al. (1980) had 270 life insurance managers rate a job candidate on each of thirty-nine items that were more "behavioral" in nature (these were items of the Selection Interview Blueprint—SIB—referred to previously). The ratings, made on the basis of a taped interview with the candidate, consisted of judgments of how well the candidate would be expected to perform the behaviors reflected by the items. The raters used a five-point scale (definitely yes; yes, to a degree; ?; no, not really; and definitely not). In general the ratings fell into two groups, those with high interrater reliability and those with low reliability. The ratings for two items from each group are given in Table

TABLE 11.2 Ratings of a job candidate on illustrative items with high and low reliability.

RATING ITEM	YES	RATING ?	NO
HIGH RELIABILITY ITEMS:			
Have direct contact with customers	246	6	18
Keep charge accounts etc. under control	241	11	18
LOW RELIABILITY ITEMS:			
Take over increasing responsibilities	128	28	114
Have realistic plans for future change	130	15	125

Source: Mayfield, Brown, & Hamstra, 1980, Table 2.

11.2. (In the table the ratings are collapsed into three categories: yes; ?; no.

In discussing their results Mayfield et al. make the point that the behavioral items with low interrater reliability are those which are less directly observable and more "future oriented." Considering these results along with those dealing with ratings of traits discussed earlier, it seems reasonable to conclude that interviewers could be expected to make reasonably adequate judgments about traits or behavior tendencies that are observable in the behavior of interviewees—or that can be reasonably inferred from such behavior—but not about those that are not so observable or that involve too much prediction into the future.

Information used in interview decisions. The types of information used by interviewers in making employment decisions or recommendations should depend on their relevance to the jobs in question. However, it is possible, in any given situation, to identify the types of information interviewers actually do use in making decisions. This was done in another phase of the research reported by Mayfield et al. (1980). These authors carried out a factor analysis of the ratings of candidates on the thirty-nine items of the SIB and identified five factors (groups

of related items). These were labeled: (1) ability to plan; (2) past sales-related work experience; (3) ability to keep financial situations under control; (4) interest in people-related activities; and (5) knowledge and experience with life insurance. Although only fourteen of the thirty-nine items were of major consequence in the actual decision process, these fourteen items tapped the same factors.

As another example Grove (1981) reports that five statistically derived factors were found to be important for effectiveness in beginning-level production work in plants producing soaps, detergents, and related items. These five factors were: (1) stamina and agility; (2) willingness to work hard; (3) ability to work well with others; (4) ability to learn the work; and (5) initiative. A structured-interview procedure was developed to guide interviewers in eliciting information from candidates that could be used as the basis for rating the candidates on these factors. This process was viewed as being in the behavioral-consistency model because it provided for obtaining behaviorally oriented pictures of applicants that would be relevant in evaluating their suitability for the jobs in question.

These examples illustrate the potential utility of systematically identifying the types of information about candidates that would be useful in making employment decisions.

Favorable and unfavorable information. A few investigators have been concerned with the influence of favorable versus unfavorable information about candidates on interviewers' decisions. Most such studies have been carried out in simulated situations, so the results need to be accepted with a few grains of salt.

One such study is reported by Constantin (1976), who had 112 students in a management course rate an interviewee whose interview had been taped. The interviewee was an "applicant" for the job of laboratory assistant. Into the part of the tape dealing with academic achievement was inserted one of four, 1-minute segments that varied in favorability and "normativity," as follows:

| FAVORABILITY | NORMATIVITY (GRADES OF OTHER STUDENTS) | |
	NORMATIVE	DEVIANT
Favorable: Grade of A	As and Bs	Cs and Ds
Unfavorable: Grade of D	Cs and Ds	As and Bs

The normativity aspect reflected the degree to which the interviewee's grades were "normative" or "deviant" as compared with those of other students.

The mean ratings of the four interview tapes were as follows:

	NORMATIVE	DEVIANT
Favorable: Grade of A	4.39	5.18
Unfavorable: Grade of D	4.07	3.68

The favorable-deviant and unfavorable-deviant information, respectively, resulted in the most favorable ratings (5.18) and the most unfavorable ratings (3.68). These data suggest that not only does the favorableness of information about applicants influence interview decisions, but that the extent to which that information (favorable or unfavorable) deviates from norms tends to accentuate interviewers' judgments.

This tendency—to permit one's ratings of others to be influenced by a comparison with corresponding information about others—is presumably a manifestation of the contrast effect discussed previously.

In addition, the influence of various types of information on decisions must be considered in light of whether the information (fa-

vorable or unfavorable) is, or is not, relevant for selection for the jobs in question. It appears that favorable information of any kind—even if irrelevant to the job in question—tends to enhance the ratings of candidates (Constantin, 1976; Weiner & Schneiderman, 1974). There is, however, some dangling question about the extent to which unfavorably irrelevant information might tend to reduce ratings.

Temporal order of interview information. Closely related to the issue of the impact of favorable versus unfavorable information on decisions is the matter of the temporal order of information. As discussed before, Springbett (1958) concluded that at least some interviewers have an attitude of caution and a "set" to search for negative information. In addition, he reported that some interviewers tend to make decisions early, within the first 4 minutes of a typical 15-minute interview.

In this regard Webster (1982) refers to the "bolstering" hypothesis (also called "gating"), which deals with the influence of new information on (tentative) decisions. Webster (1964) suggests that, as applied to the interview, this phenomenon implies that the effect of a particular item of information on a decision depends on the time of the item's occurrence in the decision sequence. Thus, if "unfavorable" information bobs up early in the interview, it might lead to an early negative decision, and vice versa. In other words, the "first impression" may tend to persist, even to the extent of causing a later disregard of conflicting information.

An illustration of this effect is based on an investigation by Peters and Terborg (1975), who offered various items of favorable, unfavorable, and neutral information in a simulated interview and asked student judges to make two types of ratings of the "applicants" represented by the information. The various items of information were given in two sequences, one with the unfavorable information (U) presented early in the interview and the other with the favorable information (F) presented early. Certain items of neutral information (N) were also introduced. The two sequences were as follows:

1. Unfavorable information early:
   UUUFNFNF
2. Favorable information early:
   FFFUNUNU

Although the information presented collectively was the same, the judges tended to give lower ratings in terms of hiring decisions and salary recommendations to the interviewees for whom the unfavorable information was presented first. This confirmed the "first-impression" theory. Note, however, that the generality of this effect is still somewhat questionable.

Summary. The interview research sponsored by Webster (1982) at McGill University undoubtedly represents the most comprehensive program of this type. Following is Webster's summary of research findings. Most of these points have already been discussed, but his summary helps to crystallize a vast amount of research:

1. Interviewers who select staff for plant or clerical positions usually reach decisions within a few minutes. They quickly know whether or not they want an applicant and then seek supporting evidence. It is easier to change an early favorable impression than an early negative one.

2. Unfavorable information almost always carries more weight than favorable data.

3. The effect of unfavorable information about an applicant depends both on when it is perceived and when the judge records impressions.

4. Once a judge is committed to accept an applicant, additional information increases confidence in the decision but does not improve its quality.

5. Nonverbal as well as verbal interactions influence decisions.

6. Training and experience have minimal effects on the quality of judgment.

7. Training may reduce interviewer error but there is no evidence that reduction of error improves judgment.

8. One uses a different mental process to describe an individual from that used to pass judgment.

9. If several really promising or very unpromising applicants have been evaluated in succession, one who is "average" will be under- or overrated.

10. Interviewers develop a stereotype of the good applicant and seek to match applicant to stereotype (pp. 13–14).

DISCUSSION

The specific procedures that should be used to select candidates for any given job or group of jobs should obviously be those that would be expected to be most appropriate for the job or jobs in question. In other words there is no single "best" way. However, now that we have discussed personnel tests and a few nontest methods for selection, an overview is in order. Such an overview has been presented by Reilly and Chao (1982), based on an extensive survey of published studies. Reilly and Chao evaluate each of several methods in terms of the validity, adverse impact, fairness, and feasibility of eight alternatives to tests. They strongly support the use of standardized personal tests and also believe that job-related miniaturized training tests and unassembled examinations hold some promise (if they do not depend on specific previous job experience).

Without going into details, these authors conclude that—of the methods we have discussed—biodata is the only one that by-and-large is equal to tests in terms of validity. They take a dim view of self-reports, references, and interviews. (However, as we indicated before, the interview is probably with us to stay.) Other methods they reviewed (which we have not discussed) include: peer evaluations; academic-performance measures; expert judgment; and projective techniques. Of these they consider peer evaluations to be particularly promising in terms of validity, although there are features that might limit their feasibility in use. The other methods do not receive very high marks.

In reflecting about the evaluations of Reilly and Chao, we should, of course, reiterate that a particular method may not be appropriate for some jobs, or even for most jobs, but it might still be appropriate in specific job situations.

REFERENCES

Arvey, R. D., & Campion, J. E. (1982). The employment interview: A summary and review of recent research. *Personnel Psychology*, 35(2), 281–322.

Ash, R. A. (1980). Self-assessment of five types of typing skills. *Personnel Psychology*, 33(2), 273–281.

Asher, J. J. (1972). The biographical item: Can it be improved? *Personnel Psychology*, 25(2), 251–269.

Asher, J. J. & Sciarrino, J. A. (1974). Realistic work sample tests: A review. *Personnel Psychology*, 27(4), 519–523.

Bernstein, V., Hakel, M. D., & Harlan, A. (1975). The college student as interviewer: A threat to generalizability? *Journal of Applied Psychology*, 60(2), 266–268.

Brush, D. H., & Owens, W. A. (1979). Implementation and evaluation of an assessment classification model for manpower utilization. *Personnel Psychology*, 32(2), 369–383.

Cann, A., Siegfried, W. D., & Pearce, L. (1981). Forced attention to specific applicant qualifications: Impact on physical attractiveness and sex of applicant biases. *Personnel Psychology*, 34(1), 65–75.

Cascio, W. F. (1975). Accuracy of verifiable biographical blank responses. *Journal of Applied Psychology*, 60(6), 767–768.

Constantin, S. W. (1976). An investigation of information favorability in the employment interview. *Journal of Applied Psychology*, 61(6), 743–749.

Dipboye, R. L., Fromkin, H. L., & Wilback, K. (1975). The importance of applicant sex, attractiveness, and scholastic standing in evaluation of job applicant résumés. *Journal of Applied Psychology*, 60(1), 39–43.

Dunnette, M. D., & Borman, W. C. (1979). Personnel selection and classification systems. *Annual Review of Psychology*, 30, 477–525.

England, G. W. (1971). *Development and use of weighted application blanks*. Minneapolis: Industrial Relations Center, University of Minnesota, Bulletin 55.

Goldstein, I. L.(1971). The application blank: How honest are the responses? *Journal of Applied Psychology*, 55, 491–492.

Grove, D. A. (1981). A behavioral consistency approach to decision making in employment selection. *Personnel Psychology*, 34(1), 55–64.

Heneman, H. G., III, Schwab, D. P., Huett, D. L., & Ford, J. J. (1975). Interviewer validity as a function of interview structure, biographical data, and interview order. *Journal of Applied Psychology*, 60, 748–753.

Hollandsworth, J. G., Jr., Kazelskis, R., Stevens, J., & Dressel, A. E. (1979). Relative contributions of verbal, articulative, and non-verbal communication to employment decisions in the job interview setting. *Personnel Psychology*, 32(2), 354–367.

Janz, T. (1982). Initial comparisons of patterned behavior description interviews versus unstructured interviews. *Journal of Applied Psychology*, 67(5), 577–580.

Kahn, R. L., & Cannell, C. F. (1956). *The dynamics of interviewing*. New York: Wiley.

Keating, E., Paterson, D. G., & Stone, H. C. (1950). Validity of work histories obtained by interview. *Journal of Applied Psychology*, 34, 6–11.

Latham, G. P., Saari, L. M., Pursell, E. D., & Campion, M. A. (1980). The situational interview. *Journal of Applied Psychology*, 65(4), 422–427.

Matteson, M. T., Osburn, H. G., & Sparks, C. P. (April 1970). *The use of non-empirically keyed biographical data for predicting success of refinery operating personnel*. Washington, D.C.: Experimental Publication System, American Psychological Association, Issue No. 5, Ms. No. 118C.

Mayfield, E. C., Brown, S. H., & Hamstra, B. W. (1980). Selection interviewing in the life insurance industry: An update of research and practice. *Personnel Psychology*, 33(4), 725–739.

Mayfield, E. C., & Carlson, R. E. (1966). Selection interview decisions: First results of a long-term research project. *Personnel Psychology, 19*(1), 41–53.

Mitchell, T. W., & Klimoski, R. J. (1982). Is it rational to be empirical? A test of methods for scoring biographical data. *Journal of Applied Psychology, 67*(4), 411–418.

Moore, L. F., & Lee, A. J. (1974). Comparability of interviewer, group, and individual interviewer ratings. *Journal of Applied Psychology, 59*(2), 163–167.

Muchinsky, P. M. (1979). The use of reference reports in personnel selection. *Journal of Occupational Psychology, 52,* 287–297.

Owens, W. A. (1976). Background data. In M. D. Dunnette (Ed.), *Handbook of industrial and organizational psychology* (Chap. 14). Chicago: Rand McNally.

Owens, W. A., & Schoenfeldt, L. F. (1979). Toward a classification of persons. *Journal of Applied Psychology, 65*(5), 569–607.

Peters, L. H., & Terborg, J. R. (1975). The effects of temporal placement of unfavorable information and attitude similarity on personnel selection decisions. *Organizational Behavior and Human Performance, 13*(2), 279–293.

Primoff, E. S. (1980). The use of self-assessment in examining. *Personnel Psychology, 33*(2), 283–290.

Reilly, R. R., & Chao, G. T. (1982). Validity and fairness of some alternative employee selection procedures. *Personnel Psychology, 35*(1), 1–62.

Schoenfeldt, L. F. (1974). Utilization of manpower: Development and evaluation of an assessment-classification model for matching individuals with jobs. *Journal of Applied Psychology, 59,* 583–595.

Schoenfeldt, L. F. (1982) Intra-individual variation and human performance. (Chap. 4). In M. D. Dunnette & E. A. Fleishman (Eds). *Human performance and productivity: Human capability assessment.* Hillsdale, N.J.: Lawrence Erlbaum Associates.

Schwab, D. P., & Heneman, H., G., III (1969). Relationship between interview structure and interviewer reliability in an employment situation. *Journal of Applied Psychology, 53*(3), 214–217.

Schwab, D. P., & Oliver, R. L. (1974). Predicting tenure with biographical data: Exhuming buried evidence. *Personnel Psychology, 27*(1), 125–128.

Springbett, B. M. (1958). Factors affecting the final decision in the employment interview. *Canadian Journal of Psychology, 12,* 13–22.

Uniform guidelines on employee selection procedures. (August 25, 1978). Federal Register, 43(166), 38290–38309.

Wagner, R. (1949). The employment interview: A critical summary. *Personnel Psychology, 2,* 17–46.

Webster, E. C., (1982). *The employment interview.* Schomberg, Ontario, Can.: S.I.P. Publications.

Webster, E. C. (1964). Decision making in the employment interview. Montreal, Canada: Industrial Relations Centre, McGill University.

Weiner, Y., & Schneiderman, M. L. (1974). Use of job information as a criterion in employment decisions of interviewers. *Journal of Applied Psychology, 59*(6), 699–704.

Weiss, D. J., & Dawis, R. V. (1960). An objective validation of factual interview data. *Journal of Applied Psychology, 40,* 381–385.

Weiss, D. J., Dawis, R. V., England, G. W., & Lofquist, L. H. (September 1961). *Validity of work histories obtained by interview* (Minnesota Studies in Vocational Rehability: No. 12). Minneapolis: University of Minnesota.

Wexley, K. N., Yukl, G. A., Kovacs, S. Z., & Sanders, R. E. (1972). Importance of contrast effects in employment interviews. *Journal of Applied Psychology, 56*(1), 43–48.

12

Personnel Training

People bring to their jobs their individual assortments of previously learned skills, knowledge, temperaments, interests, motivation, and attitudes. The additional learning people acquire after they become employees can take place in either of two ways: through on-the-job experience or through training. Although actual day-to-day work experience is probably the most effective method for developing expertise in some jobs, for many jobs well-planned and executed training programs provide the most practical method for people to develop such expertise. This chapter deals with some of the aspects of personnel training.

Certain theoretical and practical issues, however, presently limit the extent to which psychological science can contribute to the development and execution of effective training programs. Some of these limitations are referred to in the following discussion.

THE NATURE OF LEARNING

Since training is essentially the management of learning, we look first at the nature of learning and at some of the conditions that sometimes help people to learn. As we discuss learning, however, let us keep in mind that it is impossible to observe directly the process that we call learning. The fact that a person has "learned" something can be inferred only from a comparison of the individual's behavior before and after experiences of one kind or another—for example, a person's driving a car as the result of driving lessons.

The Instigation of Behavior

Behavior of whatever form (starting a motor, dispatching a taxi, calling a meeting, or kicking a cat) is instigated; it is not fortuitous, even though it sometimes looks as though it is. In characterizing human behavior it is conventional to talk in terms of a stimulus (S) acting upon an organism (O) to bring about a response (R). The stimuli are frequently external to the individual (a part coming down a conveyor belt, the change in a traffic light, or instructions from a supervisor), but they may be internal (the completion of one operation that triggers another, as in a sequence of bookkeeping operations). Some external stimuli are very definite—for example, a traffic light; others are very subtle and might be picked up only by those especially attuned to them—for example, the tone of a supervisor's voice, or slight differences in the appearance of tobacco leaves as perceived by a tobacco buyer.

In the job context there usually is, for each stimulus or syndrome of stimuli, some behavior or range of behaviors (that is, responses) that would be optimal (that is, most appropriate) for the objectives at hand. The purpose of training generally is to "establish the connection" between given stimuli and their optimum responses. This is a fairly straightforward proposition in the case of, say, routine assembly work, but it is a very complex affair in the case of jobs requiring complex decision making.

In many jobs, as well as in many circumstances in personal life, the "stimuli" are not identifiable individual stimuli; rather, they may be combinations of stimuli, such as one finds in complex traffic conditions. In turn, the response is not always a single discrete act, but may be composed of many separate acts, in some instances forming a predetermined routine and in other instances consisting only of behaviors generated on the spot.

Types of Learning

We all recognize that learning to drive a car is a different "kind" of learning than is learning about the genetics of cells. Gagné (1977) characterized the types of learning (what he called catagories of learning outcomes) as follows:

- Verbal information;
- Intellectual skills;
- Cognitive strategies;
- Motor skills;
- Attitudes.

Conditions for different types of learning. There are many types of conditions that can contribute to learning (what Gagné calls events of learning). These include: the presentation of written or verbal materials, pictures, and so on; demonstrations; practice; "modeling"; conditioning; and using various principles of learning (discussed later). However, the conditions that facilitate different types of learning may be very different. For example, the learning of concepts depends in part on the presentation of relevant material in oral or printed form, whereas the learning of motor skills depends more on demonstrations, practice, and appropriate feedback, and the acquisition of attitudes depends in part on modeling (having other people in one's environment to use as a "model") and in part on reinforcement (Gagné, 1977).

We might back up a moment to distinguish between two types of conditioning. *Classical* conditioning is the process of causing a *new* stimulus to bring about a natural or unconditioned response. Pavlov's early studies of conditioning a dog to salivate to a bell, by simultaneously presenting the dog with two stimuli—the bell and food—dealt with classical conditioning. On the other hand, *operant* conditioning is somehow causing people or animals to make a response not in their "natural" repertoire of unconditioned responses—for example, to operate the keyboard of a calculating machine while reading the numbers on a price list. When such responses are "reinforced" by some reward, the responses tend to be repeated later when the same stimuli are presented. When conditioning is dominant in learning job activities, it is typically operant conditioning.

LEARNING THEORIES

Various theories have been proposed to "explain" the learning process. A learning theory can be thought of as a way to explain in conceptual terms what takes place when learning occurs, how the learning takes place, and what conditions aid the learning process. To date no single theory has been generally accepted as explaining the learning process. It is not within the province of this book to describe the various learning theories. From the welter of studies on learning, however, certain learning "principles" have emerged. These are discussed next.

PRINCIPLES OF LEARNING

The various principles of learning that have evolved from research and experience have received mixed reviews. Hinrichs (1976), for example, made a caustic comment about the frequent reference to "the same tired list" of such principles. At the same time these principles have had such widespread acceptance that they cannot be ignored. Certain of the principles have solid theoretical roots, and most of them have at least some empirical support. Because of the many types of training situations, no single principle can be applied on an across-the-board basis. Rather, the specific principles should be considered for use in those training contexts for which they are specifically appropriate.

Goal Setting

The goal-setting theory, as formulated by Locke (1968), is postulated on the notion that individuals' behavior is, in part, influenced by their conscious goals. Corollaries of the the-

ory are that hard goals usually result in better performance than easy goals, and that specific goals are better than general goals. The application of the theory has relevance in at least certain work situations (Latham & Locke, 1979). Wexley and Latham (1981) suggest that goal theory has three important implications for motivating trainees: (1) learning objectives should be conveyed clearly to trainees at the beginning of training and at strategic points during the training program; (2) the goals should be difficult enough to challenge the individuals, but not so difficult as to discourage them; and (3) the ultimate goal of "finishing the program" should be supplemented with periodic subgoals during training—for example, trainer evaluations and praise, work-sample tests, and periodic quizzes. Goal setting generally is considered to contribute to trainees' motivation.

Reinforcement

Reinforcement in learning consists of some type of reward following the performance of an activity that increases the likelihood of the activity's being performed again. As shown by Goldstein (1974), there is a distinction between primary and secondary reinforcers. Primary reinforcers are considered to be innate or unlearned—for example, food for a hungry person and water for a thirsty person. In turn, secondary reinforcers are those that have been learned (as by operant conditioning) to have some value to individuals. In job-learning situations most reinforcers are secondary. Some examples are praise, attention, prestige, money, or the satisfaction of fulfilling one's goals.

A few points should be added about reinforcement: (1) the trainee should know what specific behaviors are expected of him or her and any reinforcement should be related to these behaviors; (2) reinforcement should be prompt and continuous when the trainee begins to learn a new behavior, but as the behavior becomes better established, the schedule of reinforcement can be stretched; (3) the types of reinforcements that are effective can vary from individual to individual, so the person providing the reinforcement should try to identify those forms that are most effective for the particular individual.

Feedback (Knowledge of Results)

Feedback about the results of one's behavior can serve either of two functions in learning. The first is a *directional* function—providing information about the behaviors necessary to perform the job successfully. A crane operator, for example, simply cannot learn to manipulate the controls without knowing how the crane responds to the handling of the controls. The second is a *motivational* function in that it provides information about the outcomes of behaviors that are associated with possible rewards.

Because feedback that serves the directional function is necessary for learning (and for subsequent continuous performance), there is no question about its relevance for training. The relevance of feedback that serves the motivational function, however, is somewhat controversial, as discussed by Ilgen, Fisher, and Taylor (1979).

Sources of feedback. Following are the primary sources of feedback, and a few examples of each:

- Internal: Based on internal cues, such as: body balance; sensing by touch; feel of steering wheel; pressure level on pedal.
- External: Based on stimuli external to the individual.
- Direct: Based on observing or otherwise sensing and evaluating the results of one's own actions, such as: observing a meter or gauge when pumping gasoline; hearing clarity of sound when tuning a radio; observing a video display scope after entering data with a computer keyboard.
- Indirect: Based on comments from, or observation of, others, such as: supervisors, trainers,

coworkers, subordinates, clients, customers, and so on. Also based on other indications of consequences of actions, such as: acceptance or rejection of products by inspectors, performance evaluations, and so on.

Discussion of feedback. Internal feedback and external direct feedback generally serve the directional function discussed earlier. In some circumstances the nature of feedback can be modified by appropriate human-factors design principles in order to enhance its effectiveness in learning and in subsequent ongoing work activity. On the other hand, most external indirect feedback serves the motivational function. Such an effect is illustrated by the results of a 45-week study of the observed safety practices of vehicle-maintenance mechanics in a large city (Komaki, Heinzmann, & Lawson, 1980). The 45 weeks were divided into five experimental phases including a "baseline" phase (before any training or feedback), two periods of training only, and two periods of training plus feedback. The feedback consisted of slides, discussions of safety rules, setting goals, and presenting information on the frequency of observed safety practices. The results for preventive maintenance mechanics are given here (high safety-level indexes reflect desirable safety practices):

PHASE	NO. OF WEEKS	SAFETY-LEVEL INDEX
1) Baseline	10	49
2) Training only	6	61
3) Training and feedback	9	76
4) Training only	10	64
5) Training and feedback	10	75

Various factors can influence the effectiveness of the feedback (Ilgen et al., 1979). A few of these are: the credibility of the person who is the source of feedback; the frequency and timing of the feedback; the positive or negative nature of the feedback information (positive feedback is usually more effective); the specificity of the feedback (specific feedback is usually more effective than general feedback); the relevance of the feedback to appropriate goals; and individual differences among recipients.

There are still many dangling questions about the implications of these and other factors related to the learning process. Thus, it is not now feasible to provide trainers with a complete, well-documented set of guidelines to follow in providing feedback to trainees. Realizing this, however, the trainer needs to take advantage of the admittedly fragmentary guidelines that are available to enhance the learning of trainees.

Behavior Modeling

Behavior modeling has its roots in the conventional wisdom that people tend to pattern their behavior from that of their associates—parents, friends, teachers, acquaintances, and so on. For a teenage person such modeling may be for the better or the worse depending on the role model the person tends to follow: Compare the inspiring effects of an exceptional teacher with the degrading effects of the members of a street gang with whom the youth is associated.

The theoretical foundations of such influences were crystallized by Bandura (1977), who postulated that much human behavior is learned by observing others. By observing others an individual forms an idea of how behaviors are formed and what effects they produce. The theory tends to explain human behavior in terms of a continuous reciprocal interaction among cognitive, behavioral, and environmental determinants. In Bandura's (1977) view, "—in the social learning view, people are neither driven by inner forces nor buffeted by environmental stimuli. Rather, psychological functioning is explained in

terms of a continuous reciprocal action of personal and environmental determinants" (p. 11). In recent years organized training programs have been developed to take advantage of the tendency for people to model their behavior after that of others.

Features of behavioral modeling in training. Moses (1978) describes these programs as having four features: modeling; behavior rehearsal; feedback; and transfer of training. These features are described next.

- **Modeling.** This is the foundation of the program. A short film or videotape is presented to participants. The modeling display typically shows a supervisor-subordinate interaction dealing with a management problem (poor work quality, excessive absenteeism, discrimination complaints, etc.). The supervisor models a number of key behaviors which result in a successful resolution of the problem. Although the modeling display is necessary for learning to occur, it is not sufficient.
- **Behavior rehearsal.** Each participant is provided an opportunity to rehearse and practice the behaviors demonstrated by the model. Although often confused with role playing, behavior rehearsal does not require the participant to play a role. Rather, he or she rehearses the actual behaviors which will be used on the job, by following the action steps demonstrated by the trainer.
- **Feedback.** This is provided by the trainer and other participants for applying the principles modeled. Social reinforcement plays an important role in the initial acceptance on the part of participants. As the participant becomes confident with his or her new skills, considerable feedback is received from subordinates, and as importantly, by the participant as well.
- **Transfer of training.** A variety of strategies are used to facilitate transfer. The term *applied learning* is an apt description. The problem situations selected reflect real problems with real solutions. Training schedules, job aids, and management support systems all facilitate transfer of skills from classroom to the job. Although modeling approaches vary depending on program intent, the following features enhance transfer (Moses, 1978):

  1. A pretraining needs analysis to identify real problem situations; 2. Sequencing of training

from simple to complex problems; 3. Training schedules designed for distributed rather than massed practice; and 4. Follow up and reinforcement of acquired skills (p. 226).

Examples of behavior modeling. An evaluation study of the effectiveness of behavior modeling is reported by Moses and Ritchie (1976). These authors compared and evaluated the performance of ninety supervisors of the AT & T company who participated in a behavior-modeling program with that of ninety-three supervisors in a control group. The evaluations were made by specially trained individuals who played the roles of the subjects' subordinates in an assessment-center situation. The evaluators rated the supervisors on how well they could transfer and apply training concepts to discussion problems not specifically covered in training. (The evaluators did not know which supervisors had been through the training.) The mean performance ratings of the two groups are shown in Figure 12.1. Notice the higher ratings for the trained group on all three discussion problems. The distribution of overall performance ratings for the two groups also shows the superior performance of the trained group, as shown here:

OVERALL RATING	TRAINED GROUP	CONTROL GROUP
Above average	84%	32%
Average	10	35
Below average	6	33

Another example, reported by Latham and Saari (1976), also dealt with supervisors. Forty supervisors were randomly assigned to a behavior-modeling training group and a control group. The training was designed to improve supervisors' interpersonal skills in dealing with their employees. Various criteria were used to evaluate the behavior-modeling training, including special ratings by superintendents a year after training and performance appraisals. Following is a comparison for the two groups on these criteria:

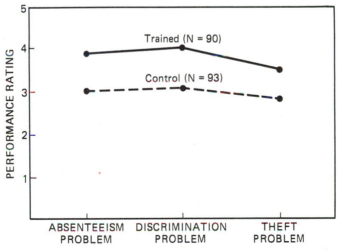

FIGURE 12.1 Mean performance ratings of two groups of supervisors in three simulated problem-solving discussions with role-playing subordinates. The trained group had been through a behavior-modeling, training program 2 months before. (Adapted from Moses & Ritchie, 1976, Table 3.)

GROUP	MEAN RATING	MEAN PERFORMANCE APPRAISAL
Training group	3.5	3.8
Control group	2.5	2.7

Some questions have been raised about the effectiveness of behavioral modeling as a training method (McGehee & Tullar, 1978). Although the research evidence in actual training situations is still rather skimpy, it nonetheless seems that behavior modeling does offer considerable promise for certain aspects of personnel training.

Distribution of Practice

This principle pertains to the scheduling of training sessions over time. In the lingo of the experimental psychologists, the scheduling of learning sessions can be either "massed" or "distributed." If one has 8 hours to train machine operators, should the 8 hours be concentrated in 1 day, or should they be split up into two 4-hour sessions on different days, or even spread out over 8 days with a 1-hour session each day? Although a commonly accepted notion is that, for any given training situation, there is some "optimum" schedule, there are actually few data to support such a contention. Unfortunately, most of the research dealing with distribution of practice comes from laboratory studies rather than from job-training situations.

From the available evidence, however, the following generalizations can be suggested (adapted in part from Bass & Vaughan, 1966):

- Distribution of learning is more beneficial to learning motor skills than to verbal learning or other complex forms of learning.
- The less meaningful the material to be learned and the greater its difficulty and amount, the more distributed practice will be superior to massed practice.

- Material learned by distributed practice tends to be retained longer than that learned in concentrated doses.

In addition, in scheduling learning sessions the following practices are desirable:

- Each training session should cover some cohesive segment of training content.
- Boredom can be minimized by interspersing breaks in the training sessions.
- Even short breaks frequently facilitate the learning process.

Whole versus Part Learning

Most jobs consist of several parts or tasks. When such is the case, one of various learning strategies can be used, including what are called whole training (training for the job as a complete entity) and part training (training for each part separately). These are illustrated here:

	STAGE			
	1	2	3	4
Whole training	A+B+C	A+B+C	A+B+C	A+B+C
Part training	A	B	C	A+B+C

The preferable strategy for any given training situation depends on the *complexity* of the tasks (essentially their difficulty) and on their *organization* (the extent to which the tasks are interrelated, as opposed to comprising separate, independent job activities) (Naylor, 1962). For jobs with highly organized and well-coordinated tasks, the whole method tends to be more effective, especially as task complexity increases. Conversely, for jobs with low task organization the part strategy tends to be superior; again, the difference is most apparent on complex tasks.

Examples can clarify the distinction between whole versus part learning. Driving a tractor involves coordinating several activities, including steering, shifting gears, braking, accelerating, and so on. Because these activities are so interrelated in the actual driving operation, the basic training should be by the whole method (perhaps preceded by brief instruction about the individual activities). On the other hand, the job of secretary involves several quite independent activities, such as typing, filing, duplicating, and answering the phone. These could be learned and practiced separately, so the part method would be most suitable.

Transfer of Learning

The circus tight-rope walker probably has a better chance of getting safely to the other end of an I-beam on a new skyscraper than you or I do. A pretzel twister probably could do a better job of tying bows on Christmas packages than the proverbial man on the street. These are examples of transfer of learning, and such transfer is essentially what industrial training is. Much of the training in industry is carried out in "simulated" situations with the expectation that it will, in effect, transfer to the "real job" as such. Besides its relevance to training, the question of possible transfer of learning also comes up when an individual changes from one job to another, especially if there is some kind of similarity between the two jobs.

Psychologists have given a great deal of attention to the study of transfer of learning, beginning with the early work of Thorndike and Woodworth (1901). Long ago Thorndike (1924) concluded that transfer in a general way does not occur at all and that what is often regarded as transfer is simply the result of *identical elements* common to the two activities. The identical elements might be overt activities as such (for example, the operation of a spray painter, whether in painting automobile bodies or railroad cars), or methods or approaches (for example, the procedures used in balancing accounts, whether the accounts deal with girdles or dog whistles). In connection with this explanation of transfer of learning, some nagging questions have led to other possible explanations, some of which are predicated on the assumption of much more generalization than Thorndike implied.

The persisting ambiguity about the factors associated with transfer of learning raises a question about the degree of fidelity of the "simulation" provided during training. Although this question applies to virtually every facet of training, it is particularly relevant to the development of various types of training devices, equipment, and other physical facilities used in some training programs. In this connection, one needs to distinguish between the degree of *physical* fidelity and that of *psychological* fidelity. Psychological fidelity refers to the degree of similarity of the human operations and activities. Psychological fidelity is critical to the transfer-of-learning context.

Discussion of Principles of Learning

With these principles of learning two points alluded to previously should be emphasized: (1) Any given principle probably is pertinent to certain *types* of learning situations rather than being applicable on an across-the-board basis; and (2) there are conflicting opinions (and evidence) on the relevance of learning principles to industrial training situations.

PRINCIPLES OF TRAINING DESIGN

Aside from the principles of learning discussed above, McGehee (1979) has formulated a set of principles of training design. These deal with specific practices that may be useful in developing training programs. They are listed here:

1. Each subject to be learned or behavior to be acquired must be broken into small steps.
2. These steps must be defined in terms of outcomes expected in behavioral terms.
3. The learner must emit responses or otherwise actively engage in the learning sequence.
4. Contingencies of reinforcement of the desired responses must be established.
5. Cues must be used in instruction to elicit the desired responses, and then gradually fade out.
6. The concept of *shaping* must be used, involving the initial reinforcement of responses which approach the desired terminal responses and the gradual reinforcement of only the desired terminal behavior.

LEARNING CURVES

Although there still are many theoretical questions about the learning process and the principles relevant to learning, the fact is that people do learn. Job-related learning is depicted with learning curves that show the cumulative changes in criteria that occur over time. The form and length of learning curves vary considerably from one situation to another. The total period of training on some jobs, for example, may be months or even years, whereas on other jobs it may be only days or weeks. The shape of the curve may also vary.

Generally the *relative* degree of improvement in learning is greater for more difficult jobs than for easier jobs. This is illustrated by the comparisons shown in Figure 12.2. Each part of this figure shows the production throughout training of employees on two pairs of related jobs in the manufacture of oscilloscope accessories; in each pair, one job had been judged by management representatives as "most difficult" and the other as

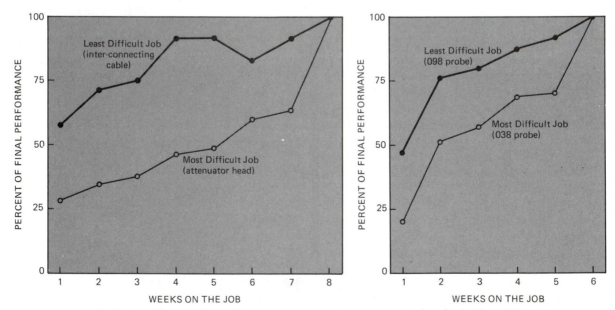

FIGURE 12.2 Comparison of learning curves of two pairs of related jobs that differ in difficulty level. In each, productivity is shown relative to the productivity during the last week (equated to 100%). Note that the *relative* improvement is greater for the more difficult jobs (and, in fact, on those jobs was continuing to rise at the end of the period shown). (Courtesy of Tetronix, Inc., and Dr. Guyot Frazier.)

218

"least difficult." The greater relative improvement in the most difficult job is evident in each pair. This difference generally can be attributed to the fact that an "easy" job is one for which most people already have the basic acquired skills and knowledge in ready-to-use form requiring little adaptation; thus they start out closer to their ultimate ceiling. For more difficult jobs, initial performance is much lower relative to final performance, which leaves more "room" for improvement.

TRAINING NEEDS

In his forthright manner McGehee (1979) stated that an organization should commit its resources to a training activity only if, in the best judgment of the managers, the training can be expected to *achieve some results other than modifying employee behavior*. It must also support some *organizational end goal*, such as more efficient production or distribution of goods and services, reduction of operating costs, improved quality, or more effective personal relations. In other words, McGehee said that the modification in employee behavior effected through training should be aimed at supporting organizational objectives.

In this regard Goldstein and Buxton (1982) discuss what they call instructional development systems (IDS) or instructional technology. The first, and major, step in such a program is the assessment of instructional need. Goldstein and Buxton argue that this stage should consist of three complementary analyses: (1) organizational analysis; (2) job or task analysis; and (3) person analysis. These three serve very different purposes in an integrated training program.

Organizational Analysis

As envisioned by Goldstein and Buxton (1982) organizational analysis should include an examination of the goals of the organiza-tion, its resources, and the organizational environment. The intent of such a process is to insure that the training program is designed to meet organizational needs and that it is matched to organizational reality. However, as these authors point out, there is a paucity of information on how to go about such an analysis. Although a broad, comprehensive strategy for organizational analysis does not yet exist, Wexley and Latham (1981) help to crystallize an important objective of such an analysis with this question: "*Where* is training and development needed and *where* is it likely to be successful within an organization?" In this regard they propose, in part, the use of employee attitude surveys that deal with job satisfaction, perceptions of personnel utilization, attitudes toward the administration, and so on. In addition, inklings of organizational training needs can sometimes be obtained from personnel records (for example, turnover, absence, and training records), employee-skills inventories, and manpower planning data (Craig, 1976).

Because there are no comprehensive strategies available for organizational analysis, any procedures that can be developed that would fill in at least a few chinks of information could aid somewhat in developing training programs to serve organizational needs.

Job and Task Analysis

Some form of job or task analysis is basic to the development of job-training programs. Such training programs are intended to help individuals acquire the knowledge, skills, and attitudes required for a job. The training content, then, must be rooted in a detailed study of the job. Job and task analysis were discussed in Chapter 4. For training purposes a conventional job description usually serves as a starting point, but a detailed task analysis is usually necessary for developing specific training-course content. Various task-analysis methods can be used for this purpose, including task inventories (discussed in Chapter 4) and the critical incident technique (discussed in Chapter 6). Certain other methods can also be considered. Following are some examples.

Stimulus-Response-Feedback analysis. This approach to task analysis, developed by Miller (1962), provides that task-activity statements specify the *indication* or *cue* which calls for a response, the *object* to be used (such as a control device that is to be activated), the *activation* or *manipulation* to be made, and the *indication of response adequacy* or feedback. Thus, such a task description would specify *when* individuals are to do something, *what* they are to do it with, what *action* they are to take, and what *feedback* will indicate that the action has been performed adequately. As a simple illustration consider opening an automatic garage door. An analysis of this task in the terms might be something like the following:

- *Task:* opening automatic garage door by individual in garage
- *Indication or cue (when):* sound of automobile horn outside garage entrance
- *Object (what):* push-button control
- *Activation or manipulation (action):* press push button
- *Indication of response adequacy (feedback):* observe door raised to overhead position and hear motor stop

Miller's approach is most suitable for jobs that consist of simple, structured tasks for which there are relatively clear-cut stimulus-response-feedback relationships. It is not suitable for unstructured and complex jobs.

Task-sequence analysis. Another procedure that is most suitable for relatively structured jobs consists of analyzing the steps in tasks and the sequence in which they are carried out. The following example lists the job elements for the task of cleaning and replacing spark plugs (Mager & Beach, 1967):

1. Note plug location relative to the cylinder; remove plug cover leads.
2. Remove all spark plugs.
3. Identify the type of plugs.
4. Decide whether to clean, adjust, and/or replace plugs.
5. Adjust and clean plugs, if appropriate.
6. Reinsert plugs in engine.
7. Connect ignition wire to appropriate plugs.
8. Check engine firing for maximum performance.
9. Clean and replace equipment and tools.

A variant of the task-sequence analysis that is relevant for some jobs involves the use of a decision flow chart that indicates decision points and the alternative actions that would be appropriate for each possible decision. The following chart illustrates one step in the collection of plant fossil specimens (Carlisle, 1982):

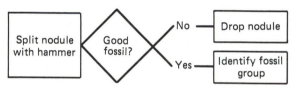

Such an analysis may be expanded to incorporate the stimulus-response-feedback features of Miller's procedures, and other elaborations on the specific aspects of the job elements.

Work sampling. In industrial-engineering practice work sampling is sometimes used to determine the time devoted to various tasks or other work activities. This usually involves the initial development of a list of relevant job activities (as tasks). A work sampling can be carried out either by observers who, at randomly specified times, observe and record the work activities of people, or by cameras set to take pictures at random times. The frequencies with which individual activities are thus "observed" provides the basis for estimating the time spent on each.

Discussion of task analysis. These various methods of task analysis have their own advantages and limitations. Task inventories and work sampling have the advantage of identifying the tasks that are most important in terms of time. The critical incident technique serves to identify the "critical" tasks (regardless of time); however, task inventories can also serve this objective by providing for workers to rate tasks on "criticality" or "difficulty" as well as time. The stimulus-response-feedback and task-sequence procedures serve well for structured jobs, especially those involving physical activities, but are less suitable for more complex jobs.

The analysis of the tasks involved in some jobs brings to attention the body of knowledge that is required to perform the job, which in some instances is very extensive. Once that body is identified, the focus of the trainer would, of course, be to analyze the specific content to be incorporated in the training program.

Person Analysis

Person analysis is largely focused on identifying the specific training needs of people, most typically people who are now working on their jobs. (In some instances this might also apply to job candidates). The training needs of present employees might be analyzed for *individuals* (such as department-store complaint clerks who ruffle the feathers of customers) or for *groups* of employees (such as supervisors who are generally inept in interpersonal relationships with their subordinates).

Training needs of individuals. Some of the methods for analyzing the training needs of individuals are: observations, as by supervisors; performance evaluations; quality control records; and performance tests. The next chapter deals with the related topic of career development.

Training needs of groups. The training needs of groups of workers can sometimes be

predicated on the informal judgments and observations of supervisors or managers. However, various types of survey questionnaires can be used to elicit judgments more systematically. They can be completed by supervisors or managers, or by the incumbents themselves. An example of such a questionnaire for office supervisors is shown in Figure 12.3. In this particular instance the incumbents and their supervisors reported their judgments of the incumbents' level of "need" for training in each of the areas listed. A simple scoring system was used to score the responses: great need = 2; some need = 1, and little need = 0. Adding up the scores for several individuals gave a total weighted score, as shown in Figure 12.3. These weighted scores, in turn, could be used to establish priorities in a training program.

Another procedure utilizes the critical incident technique. This method was used in a program reported by Folley (1969) for determining the training needs of department-store sales personnel. The "critical incidents" were based on actual reports by regular customers who volunteered to prepare statements about the sales personnel who had served them in three department stores in a large city. The 2000 resulting incidents were then categorized by content analysis into seven categories of effective behavior and six of ineffective. Figure 12.4 shows the percentage of incidents in these categories. Although these percentages do not necessarily represent the relative importance of the categories, they do provide the trainer with some basis, during training, for insuring that the sales personnel know the implications of these behaviors from the customers' point of view and that they know how to avoid the undesirable behaviors.

Other procedures that can be used to assess the training needs of groups of individuals include performance evaluations and tests (paper-and-pencil tests for measuring

	OFFICE SUPERVISORS (Possible Subjects for First Line Supervisors and Foremen)				

	Please put an "x" after each topic to indicate the need as you see it.		Column Weights		
			2	1	0
			Great Need	Some Need	Little Need
Rank		Weighted Score			
3	1. The Supervisor's Job (Objectives, Activities, Authority, Responsibility)	48	20	8	2
3	2. Communication Principles & Approaches	48	16	16	2
9	3. Oral Communication	48	17	12	6
9	4. Written Communication (memos, reports)	48	15	12	7
12	5. Listening	45	17	11	6
16	6. Interviewing (employment, appraisal, etc.)	42	14	14	5
33	7. Conducting Departmental Meetings	28	9	10	12
1	8. Understanding & Motivating Employees	50	21	8	2
22	9. Selecting New Employees	36	11	14	8
22	10. Inducting New Employees	36	9	18	7
6	11. Training New Employees	47	16	15	3
28	12. Understanding the 20–30 year olds	32	11	10	11
14	13. Appraising Employee Performance	44	16	12	7
16	14. Preventing & Handling Complaints & Grievances	42	14	14	6

FIGURE 12.3 Partial list of topics in a questionnaire used to survey the training needs of office supervisors showing the weighted scores and rank orders of topics based on responses of one group of supervisors. (Adapted from Kirkpatrick, 1977, Form 2, p. 24. Reproduced by special permission from the February 1977 *Training and Development Journal.* Copyright 1977 by the American Society for Training and Development Inc.)

knowledge and performance tests for measuring skills).

Developing Training Objectives

Organizational analysis, job and task analysis, and training analysis are aimed at determining training needs, and serve as the basis for developing specific training objectives. These should be set forth in behavioral terms—that is, in terms that specify the behaviors that the learner is expected to be able to do upon completion of training. Following are some guidelines regarding the characteristics of these behavioral objectives (adapted from Mager & Beach, 1967):

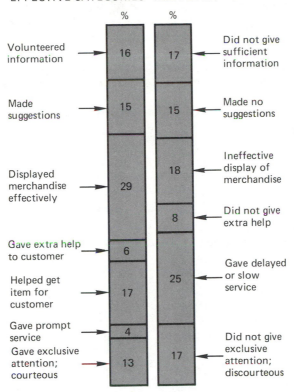

EFFECTIVE CATEGORIES   INEFFECTIVE CATEGORIES

Effective	%	%	Ineffective
Volunteered information	16	17	Did not give sufficient information
Made suggestions	15	15	Made no suggestions
Displayed merchandise effectively	29	18	Ineffective display of merchandise
		8	Did not give extra help
Gave extra help to customer	6		
Helped get item for customer	17	25	Gave delayed or slow service
Gave prompt service	4		
Gave exclusive attention; courteous	13	17	Did not give exclusive attention; discourteous

FIGURE 12.4 Percent distribution by categories of 2000 critical incidents regarding sales personnel as reported by customers. The critical incidents were divided into those representing effective performance and those representing ineffective performance. (Adapted from Folley, 1969.)

a. An objective is a statement about a student, not the text or teacher.
b. The objective refers to the behavior of the student. It does not just specify what a student is to know but instead further describes what you mean by *knowing* by indicating what the student will be doing to reflect the fact that he knows.
c. An objective is stated in terms of terminal performance. Thus, it is a description of the end product, not the method for reaching the end product.
d. An objective describes the conditions under which the student will perform. Thus, if the student is expected to perform with the use of a training aid (e.g., a calculator), the objectives specify its use.

e. An instructional objective further indicates the level of performance necessary to achieve that objective. Thus, statements related to the number of errors permitted and the speed of performances are included as part of the objective.

TRAINING METHODS AND TECHNIQUES

A wide spectrum of training methods and techniques, each with its own uses and constraints, is available for the various training programs sponsored by training organizations. Some of these are: lecture, audio-visual aids, simulators and training aids, conference methods, laboratory training, case method, role playing, management games, programmed instruction (PI), and computer-assisted instruction (CAI). It is not appropriate here to attempt an exhaustive analysis of the various methods and techniques and their uses.[1] Instead, we describe a few briefly and a few more extensively.

Lecture

The lecture has been severely criticized as a method of training, primarily because it normally does not allow for active participation by the trainees; this lack of participation, in turn, usually precludes any feedback. Although such criticisms argue against its indiscriminate use, there are various circumstances in which the lecture is an appropriate method of training.

For example, the lecture method can be used effectively in the following circumstances: when presenting completely new material to a group, when working with a large group, when introducing another instruction method, when classroom time is limited, and when summarizing material developed by another instruction method. It also can be useful in reducing anxiety about upcoming training programs or about job and other changes.

Audio-Visual Aids

Technology has enabled the use of a variety of audio-visual aids in training: motion pictures, slides, filmstrips, overhead and opaque projectors, and television, for example.[2] This equipment also enables the presen-

tation of a wide range of subject matter in audio and/or visual form. But how effective are these techniques in helping people to learn? Hollywood-type presentations may be very impressive but they are not necessarily instructive. Three points are relevant here.

First, certain kinds of presentations can be made more effective by the use of audio-visual methods than by any other. Cameras, for example, can sometimes be placed where a learner cannot be—for example, in demonstrations of surgical techniques or certain mechanical operations. In addition, audio-visual techniques facilitate demonstrations (as by animation) that otherwise might not be feasible. Second, there is no substantial evidence to suggest that such methods are *generally* more effective in presenting regular course material than other methods, but in some *individual* circumstances they have been found to be. Third, a disadvantage of some audio-visual methods is that they do not allow for participation by the trainees. Certain specific systems, such as those just discussed, are exceptions.

Simulators and Training Aids

Simulators and training devices can accustom trainees to physical equipment that resembles to some degree the equipment to be used on the job. Such devices are usually used when it is impractical, for some reason such as possible injury to the trainees or others, to use the actual equipment or when the cost of the actual equipment is excessive.

As indicated earlier, the transfer of training from some type of physical simulator to the actual job depends more on the degree of "psychological" fidelity than on the degree of physical fidelity. Psychological fidelity is the extent to which the various stimuli and responses in the simulation and in the intervening mental operations and decisions correspond to those of the actual job. Although there are undoubtedly some circumstances in which the degree of psychological

[1]The interested reader is referred to such sources as: R. L. Craig, (1976). *Training and development handbook*. New York: McGraw-Hill.

[2]For an excellent discussion of available audio-visual equipment and techniques, the reader is referred to C. P. Otto & O. Glaser (Eds.) (1970). *The management of training*. Reading, Mass.: Addison-Wesley.

fidelity depends on the degree of physical fidelity, Weitz and Adler (1973) found that the results of various studies suggested that much beneficial training can result from the use of devices with low physical fidelity.

It is generally accepted that training aids add to the effectiveness of training. There is, however, a danger in using training aids, for the instructor may become "training-aid happy," and rely on the aids to the detriment of the effectiveness of the training.

Conference Methods

In the training context the conference method allows for the participants to pool ideas, to discuss ideas and facts, to test assumptions, and to draw inferences and conclusions. This method, intended to improve job performance and personnel development, is most appropriate for such purposes as: (1) developing the problem-solving and decision-making faculties of personnel; (2) presenting new and sometimes complicated material; and (3) modifying attitudes.

Probably the most important psychological principle is the active participation of those taking part in a conference. In addition, a conference permits "reinforcement" of such participation by the trainer, as pointed out by McGehee and Thayer (1961). Reinforcement should be for the participation as such and should not be verbal rewards or punishments for the *nature* of the participation; otherwise the conference leader would lose his or her neutrality.

Laboratory Training

There are a number of variations of what is sometimes called laboratory training or sensitivity training. Some programs are called T-group training (T for training).

The most common applications of laboratory training in industry are to the development of supervisory and management personnel, but they have also been used to develop other groups of personnel. The trainees form a group with a trainer in which they interact in a very unstructured manner for a period of 2 or 3 days, or a week or more. There are no established agendas for the sessions, nor are there any established membership or leadership roles; this creates an environment in which anxieties and tensions almost inevitably arise. Within this unstructured, ambiguous, and tension-generating environment, the interaction among the participants is intended to bring about greater self-awareness of the individual participants, increased sensitivity to, and understanding of, others, and thus improved facilities in interpersonal relationship skills.

It should be noted that the experience of undergoing laboratory training is indeed traumatic for some individuals. There have been instances of breakdowns following such training, for example. In these cases, the leaders or members failed to protect the affected individuals from other, aggressive members of the groups.

Evaluation of laboratory training. The problem of evaluating the effectiveness of laboratory training is, to use a British phrase, a sticky wicket. One can use testimonials from the participants, as well as other measures linked directly to the content and processes of the training (such as measures of attitude change and performance in simulated problem-solving situations), to assess change. These are called internal criteria. Such changes are not themselves indicative of actual behavioral changes on the job. In one sense, the proof of the pudding should be in the changes in job behavior; such changes, which Campbell and Dunnette (1968) called external criteria, can be reflected by ratings from superiors, subordinates, or peers, by changes in production or other aspects of job performance, by turnover, or by other indexes.

In adding up the black and red sides of the ledger for laboratory training, let us paraphrase the observations of Campbell and

Dunnette: The assumption that such training has positive utility for organizations must necessarily rest on shaky ground, for it has been neither confirmed nor disproved; on the other hand, it should be emphasized that utility for an organization is not necessarily the same as utility for the individual.

Of those individuals who have undergone laboratory training, many have undoubtedly gained useful personal insight into and understanding of themselves. But such training programs have been criticized because some participants may feel pressured into participating when in fact they would rather not. Further, the traumatic aftermath of such training for some individuals must be considered as one of its liabilities.

Case Method

The case method is one in which an actual or hypothetical problem is presented to a training group—usually of supervisors or management personnel—for discussion and solution. The cases are usually human-relations problems and may be presented in writing, "live" (with individuals playing different roles), on film, or by recordings. There are a number of variations in the techniques and procedures, but they have the same constituent elements, including a case report (in some form), a case discussion (of some sort), case analysis (systematic or otherwise), and the current situation (the interaction of the group members and course director in learning to work together). The case method is intended to help the participants analyze problems and to demonstrate that because many problems have multiple causes and effects, simple answers are few and far between.

Role Playing

In role playing each participant plays the "part" (role) of someone in a simulated situation. There are many variations of role play-

ing, but generally they are either preplanned or spontaneous. In the preplanned format the (hypothetical) situation is structured by setting forth the "facts" of a situation: the job situation in question, the events that led up to the "current" situation, and other information. In these respects role playing resembles the case method. In role playing, however, individuals are designated to play the roles of persons in the "case." The cases can be built up around many different kinds of problems that can generate conflicting interests, such as unscheduled coffee breaks, work assignments, or vacation schedules. Once the case has been stated and the individuals assigned to their roles, they "play" those roles as though the situation were real. Thus, a supervisor might play the role of a subordinate, a salesperson the role of a customer, and a nurse's aide the role of a hospital patient. Having to put one's self in someone else's place and play the part of that person generally increases one's empathy for the other person and one's understanding of his behavior.

In spontaneous role playing, the participants play the roles of different individuals and discuss some problem without a prepared script.

Role playing can be used in any training situation involving interaction between two or more people, such as in counseling, interviewing, performance review, supervision, job instruction, or selling. In whatever context it is used, the intent of role playing is to teach principles or skills or to provide a tool for changing attitudes and behavior in interpersonal relationships.

Business Games

A business game (or management game) is a form of simulation in which separate teams of participants are presented with a typical management "problem"—one concerned with production scheduling, retailing operations, personnel assignments, or product development, for example. Whatever the problem the team is given appropriate information on such factors as assets, inventories, labor costs, storage costs, demand curves (the demand for a product as it varies with price), and interest charges. The team then organizes itself (perhaps by selecting a president and other officials) and proceeds to make decisions about its policies and operations. The effects of these decisions can be computed in quantitative terms, such as profits. At the end it is possible to determine which team "won." Whether the game takes hours, days, or even months, it represents a longer time span. The game is then followed by a critique in which the actions of the teams are analyzed.

Goldstein (1974) stated that such games provide practice in decision making and experience in interacting with others and that the feedback provisions and the dynamic quality of the play are intrinsically motivating to the participants.

Although business games have a certain intuitive appeal as a training method and are generally viewed favorably by participants, there is little hard evidence of their effectiveness as a management-training method. This is not to say that the method is not useful, but rather that there has been little rigorous evaluation of it.

Programmed Instruction (PI)

The concept of programmed instruction (PI) emerged in the late 1950s. In the 1960s and later it found its way into rather extensive use in education and into moderate use in personnel training. More recently the label *programmed instruction* has fallen by the wayside in some circles, though it has sometimes been replaced by *self-instruction* (Wilson, 1982). In fact, the use of PI as a specific training method has declined from the earlier years of its heyday.

Although PI as such is not now in common use in personnel training, however, it has contributed significantly to changes in the nature of such training (Craig, 1976). In a general sense the principles of PI have been incorporated in various aspects of training, especially in helping to make training more individualized and in encouraging more active participation on the part of trainees. In addition, the principles of PI are basic to the burgeoning development of computer-assisted instruction (CAI).

The nature of programmed instruction. In PI the material to be learned is presented in a series of steps or units that generally progress from simple to complex. At each step learners make a response and receive feedback in some way so that they know whether their responses were correct or not. If the responses were incorrect, the trainees back up and are guided in some way to learn the correct responses (and why they are correct) so that they can proceed further in the program.

The method has such advantages as: It teaches by small steps; it requires active responses by the learners; it provides feedback to the learners; and it permits the learners to proceed at their own pace. The principle of reinforcement through feedback is especially important.

The typical instructional program consists of a series of "frames" (also called items). Each frame contains a small segment of information that is intended to elicit some sort of response from the learners. The frames vary from one program to another; examples are given in Figure 12.5. The frames are ordered in sequence, and usually one frame builds upon the preceding frame. As the learners progress from frame to frame (receiving feedback in each case), they then build up, bit by bit, the complete subject matter of the program.

Certain variations in approaches to programming should be noted. First, the responses can be *constructed* or *multiple choice*. A constructed response is one in which the learner actually writes in the response; it requires recall, or the formation of an answer based on what the subject has learned. A

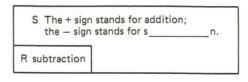

FIGURE 12.5 Illustrative programmed instruction frames from various programs. Only one frame is shown from each program; thus, these examples do not illustrate the sequence of frames within a single program. The correct response (shown as *R*) is not in view of the respondent until he or she has entered a response.

multiple-choice response is one in which the learner selects one of several possible responses; this requires recognition rather than recall. Evidence regarding the pros and cons of these two approaches generally has shown no systematic superiority of one over the other.

Another distinction is between *linear* and *branching* programs. With linear programs, each subject goes through all frames in sequence and must master each one in turn. A branching program is one that can be adapted to the level of achievement of the learner. This is done by providing, at specific frames in the program, "branches" to be followed by those who have not adequately mastered the material to the point in question.

Evaluation of programmed instruction. A general evaluation of the effectiveness of programmed instruction was carried out by Nash, Muczyk, and Vettori (1971). These researchers analyzed the results of over 100 empirical studies in which programmed instruction had been used either in academic or industrial circumstances. In about half of these, programmed instruction was reported to be of "practical effectiveness" (meaning that the differences in results between it and conventional instruction were statistically significant and exceeded 10% of the criterion values in question). Figure 12.6 shows a comparison among these for several industrial studies. This comparison and other data show that programmed instruction almost always reduces training time to a significant extent; the average saving in time is about one-third. Such a procedure, however, usually does not improve training performance in terms of immediate learning or retention, for the studies show no significant difference in favor of either method. Thus, the primary advantage of programmed instruction seems to be in training time. Economic comparisons—specifically between instruction costs and time of the trainees and the cost of developing programmed instruction materials (which can run into many thousands of dollars)—are important when considering whether or not to use programmed instruction.

Computer-Assisted Instruction (CAI)

As discussed earlier, computer-assisted instruction (CAI) is essentially a sophisticated descendant of programmed instruction. In

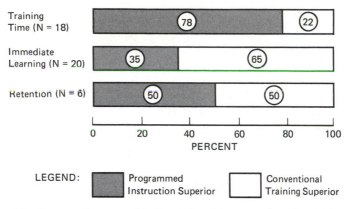

Training Time (N = 18): 78 | 22
Immediate Learning (N = 20): 35 | 65
Retention (N = 6): 50 | 50

PERCENT

LEGEND:
Programmed Instruction Superior
Conventional Training Superior

FIGURE 12.6 Percent of industrial-training programs in which programmed instruction (PI) was "practically superior" to conventional training methods for three criteria. (Adapted from Nash et al., 1971, Table 3.)

the last few years the confluence of programmed instruction principles and computer technology (especially microcomputers) has resulted in the rapid expansion in the use of CAI training programs in industry. Its applications, of course, are largely in the areas of relevant knowledge (as contrasted with the development of skills or the modification of attitudes). The range of coverage of such programs is varied; it incudes engineering, nursing, real-estate selling, management development, accounting, musical skills, biomechanics, banking, blueprint reading, machinery operation and repair procedures, language literacy, reading and writing skills, and even "computer literacy" for managers.

Effectiveness of computer-assisted instruction. A review of the effectiveness of CAI by Boettcher, Alderson, and Saccucci (1981) turned up no studies in which the comparison between CAI and any other method was based on the same actual content. These authors compared CAI and PI methods using the same actual content (psychopharmacological nursing); the subjects were nursing students. No significant differences in the results between the CAI and PI methods emerged.

Such results, along with fragmentary results from other studies, suggest that CAI

procedures generally tend to be as effective as other methods, and that in some instances they have a moderate edge over other methods. Thus, the decision to use CAI should be based on practical considerations, including cost effectiveness. Unfortunately, the development of CAI programs (like PI programs) is time-consuming and costly, and can usually be justified only if the programs are to be used with large numbers of people.

Discussion of Training Methods

Each of the individual training methods can serve certain objectives better than others. Carroll, Paine, and Ivancovich (1972) surveyed 200 training directors of major corporations to obtain their judgments about the effectiveness of nine training methods for achieving six training objectives. They used the following rating scale: highly effective (5); quite effective (4); moderately effective (3); limited effectiveness (2); and not effective (1). The mean ratings for four ranges of scale values are shown in Figure 12.7. Note, however, that because of serious qualms about the effectiveness of training programs in general, one needs to be a bit cautious in accepting outright the judgments of training directors about the types of programs for which they

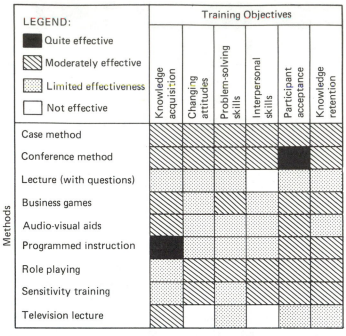

FIGURE 12.7 Training directors' ratings of effectiveness of alternative methods for various training objectives. The mean ratings are shown in four categories: quite effective (4.0 and above); moderately effective (3.0 to 3.9); limited effectiveness (2.0 to 2.9); and not effective (1.0 to 1.9). See text for discussion. (Adapted from Carroll et al., 1972.)

have been responsible. A few other comments are in order about the results of this survey. In the first place, mean values (as summarized in the figure) can mask over considerable variation in individual differences in ratings. In addition, the objectives given do not include developing skills, such as for many manual jobs. Further, some comments are in order about the use of the much maligned lecture method (which received low ratings). Granting that lectures can be dull, their effectiveness for knowledge acquisition generally is more effective than the ratings of the training directors indicate (Carroll, et al., 1972). In many situations in which the primary objective is to convey information the lecture is the most effective and economical (and maybe the only practical) method. (Incidentally, lectures need not be dull, and even if the context if fairly dry, the information conveyed can be very relevant.)

TYPES OF TRAINING PROGRAMS

After the foregoing overview of some principles of learning and of certain training methods, a brief discussion of some of the major types of training programs is in order. These generally fall into the following classes:

- *Orientation training.* Typically used to orient new employees to an organization by providing information about the organization, its history, products, policies, and so forth.
- *On-the-job training.* Used to help personnel learn new jobs; may be on an organized, systematic basis, or on a catch-as-catch-can basis.
- *Off-the-job training.* Covers a wide range of training activities given by an organization: ves-

tibule training (training for specific jobs), supervisory and management training and development, some apprentice training, and job-improvement training, among others. May be combined with on-the-job training, as in apprentice-training programs.

- *Outside training.* Training arranged with outside organizations, such as universities or trade and professional associations.

The training methods that would be most appropriate for a specific training situation would, of course, depend on the particular circumstance and its objectives.

THE EVALUATION OF TRAINING

Any discussion of the evaluation of training should be forthright in stating that the state of affairs of such evaluation is abysmal. The number of training programs that have been evaluated is indeed miniscule, and the results of some of the evaluations even leave much to be desired in terms of experimental rigor. Bunker and Cohen (1977) stated: "Training evaluation is one of the most under-researched and neglected areas of industrial/organizational psychology. Ironically, this trend toward continued avoidance of the evaluation issue comes at a time when measurement of training impact would appear to be increasingly important (pp. 525, 526).

As Goldstein and Buxton (1982) point out, the evaluation of training centers around two interacting concerns: (1) the establishment of measures of success (criteria); and (2) the experimental designs used in the evaluation.

Criteria of Training Effectiveness

The criteria used in training evaluation generally fall into four classes: (1) opinions; (2) learning; (3) behavior; and (4) results.

Opinion criteria. The opinions of trainees about training programs are sometimes obtained from questionnaires. Although favorable reactions from trainees does not necessarily insure that learning has taken place, obtaining such reactions can help trainees to assess the success of their efforts and to improve future programs (Wexley & Latham, 1981).

Learning criteria. Learning criteria can best be obtained by the use of tests—for example, paper-and-pencil tests to measure knowledge and performance tests to measure skills and abilities.

Behavior criteria. Behavior criteria are generally measures of actual job performance. Such measures can be obtained by various methods, as discussed in Chapters 5 and 6—performance evaluations, ratings, and so on.

Result criteria. Result criteria are usually reflected in terms of cost-related results or behavioral outcomes such as: reduced turnover; reduced absenteeism; increased productivity and quality of items produced; increased sales; and reduced accidents (Wexley & Latham, 1981).

Experimental Design in Training Evaluation

The evaluation of training is fraught with serious experimental-design problems. A procedure that is sometimes used is to obtain criterion measures after completion of training. Such a procedure, however, does not tell anything about what change may have occurred from the pretraining period. This deficiency would argue for obtaining criterion measures both before and after training: pretest and posttest measures. But this scheme has its limitations as well. Maybe the trainees would have improved anyway because of the intervening time. Or maybe the assignment to the training increased the trainees' motivation. Or maybe the process of obtaining the pretest criterion (such as with a test) improved the posttest criterion measures without bringing about a "real" improvement.

These and other variables can adversely affect the conclusions and inferences one can draw from a training-evaluation study, *unless* the design of the study has been carefully planned and executed. Although this book is not the place to discuss experimental design, we at least mention certain aspects relevant to training evaluation.

We illustrate what is called the Solomon design, which is based on the use of four groups of subjects, with individual subjects assigned randomly to the four groups. In this representation the following codes are used: T–1 represents a pretest, T–2 a posttest, and X the training given. The four groups are, then, as follows:

	Time ⟶		
Group 1	T–1	X	T–2
Group 2	T–1		T–2
Group 3		X	T–2
Group 4			T–2

Using a single group (as group 1) offers no assurance that the training (X) caused any difference between the pretest and the posttest, since other variables (such as those referred to previously) might have had an influence. Using a second group as a control group at least equalizes the possible effects of the pretest for the two groups but still leaves dangling the question of the possible effects of the pretest. Using three groups gets around the possible effects of the pretest (since there is none for the third group) but does not make it possible to compare what would have happened without either a pretest or the training. Using the fourth group helps to make that kind of comparison.

If one is interested in generalizing from the evaluation of one training program to other situations, however, even such a four-group design would not necessarily eliminate the in-

fluence of all possible extraneous variables (McGehee, 1979).

In reflecting about the status of training evaluation, Bunker and Cohen (1977) express the opinion that industry can no longer afford to bypass or conserve expenses in training evaluation because of their investments in training and the risks and costs associated with erroneous evaluations. We strongly endorse such an objective. At the same time the practical problems will undoubtedly continue to preclude the possibility of truly rigorous evaluation in many circumstances. It is urged that the evaluation be as rigorous as the circumstances permit.

A Survey of Evaluation Practices

Reflection of some companies' actual training-program evaluation practices comes from a survey by Catalanello and Kirkpatrick (1968). These authors queried 110 organizations known to be concerned with human-relations training about their training-evaluation practices. Of these, about 78% reported that they attempted to measure trainee *reactions* (i.e., opinions), and about half said they attempted evaluation in terms of *learning, behavior,* and/or *results*. More detailed questionnaires were sent subsequently to the latter "half," and forty-seven companies responded. Replies to certain questions are summarized in Figure 12.8. We can see that a large portion did attempt to measure learning both before and after the training programs but that less than half attempted to measure changes in behavior as such, and that about a third attempted to measure results. Those who did measure results reported that they did so on the basis of observation, interviews, analysis of production reports, turnover figures, and other indexes. It might be noted that the number using control groups was virtually negligible. Collectively, then, the companies would not

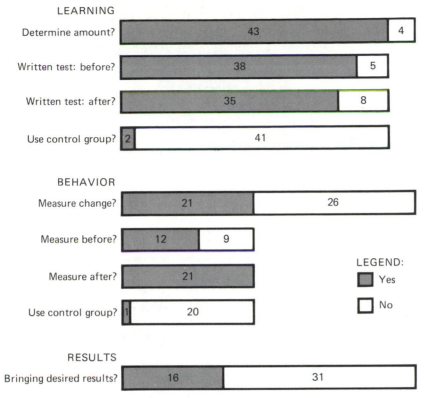

LEARNING

Determine amount? 43 | 4

Written test: before? 38 | 5

Written test: after? 35 | 8

Use control group? 2 | 41

BEHAVIOR

Measure change? 21 | 26

Measure before? 12 | 9

Measure after? 21

Use control group? 1 | 20

LEGEND:
Yes (shaded)
No (white)

RESULTS

Bringing desired results? 16 | 31

FIGURE 12.8 Responses of forty-seven selected companies to a questionnaire regarding their practices in measuring learning, behavior, and results in relation to human-relations training programs. (Adapted from Catalanello & Kirkpatrick, 1968.)

stack up very well in terms of acceptable standards of experimental design!

Examples of Training Evaluation

The following examples illustrate training evaluation studies that have been reported, but (as with most reported studies) these do not fulfill all the requirements of rigorous experimental design.

Skill Training. A comparison of the learning curves of employees in a cotton-weaving mill is shown in Figure 12.9. Both of these curves are expressed in wages earned (directly related to productivity on the job), but

one shows the average earnings for those who had no organized training, whereas the other shows earnings for those who went through a specialized training program. Those who received the specialized training reached the "shed average" within about 26 weeks, as opposed to the previous full year required to reach par.

Grocery-store clerks. Another example concerns a training program with clerks in a small grocery store. The objective was to improve performance in terms of three behavioral criteria (Komaki, Waddell, & Pearce, 1977): (1) remaining in the store; (2) assisting customers; and (3) stocking merchandise. The

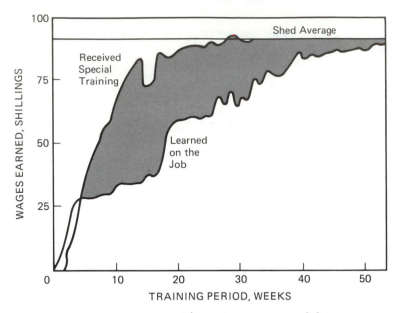

FIGURE 12.9 Learning curves (shown in wages earned) for two groups of employees in a cotton-weaving mill. One group learned "on the job" without any organized training effort; the other group went through a specialized training program. The study was carried out by the Cotton Board Productivity Centre, Ltd., of Great Britain. (Originally published by Fielded House Productivity Centre, Ltd., as presented by Singer & Ramsden, 1969, Figure 3.2.)

nature of the training and the method of obtaining the criterion measures need not be described, but the results are shown in Figure 12.10. The mean performance levels of the three criteria on a before-and-after basis were as follows:

CRITERION	BEFORE	AFTER
1	53	86
2	35	87
3	57	86

The results strongly suggest that the training resulted in improvement in the three criteria. However, the use of control groups would have strengthened the experimental design.

SPECIAL ASPECTS OF TRAINING

Our discussion of training has generally dealt with conventional personnel-training programs within organizations. There are, however, certain aspects of training whose implications extend beyond the walls of individual organizations, sometimes into the societal, economic, and technological environment in which we live. For illustrative purposes we only discuss occupational obsolescence, and training problems associated with disadvantaged persons and with the aged. The implications of these aspects of training extend into the educational and training programs that are offered by private and public schools at all levels, and special training programs sponsored by government agencies. In addition, some of the responsibility for deal-

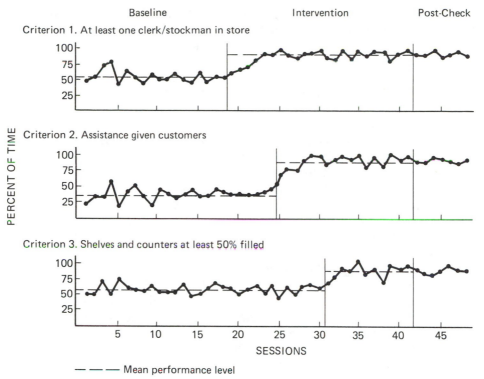

FIGURE 12.10 Results of the evaluation of a training program for grocery-store clerks in terms of three criteria. (From Komaki et al., 1977, p. 342.)

ing with such training problems resides with business and industrial organizations.

Occupational Obsolescence

One of the prices we pay for a fast-moving technology is an increase in the obsolescence of certain occupations, especially those of a technical, scientific, and professional nature. Indeed, the rate of obsolescence is rather dramatic in some occupations. The training implications are fairly obvious: we must provide a continual up-dating of educational curricula as well as opportunities for people in affected occupations to become "refurbished" by special training or educational programs.

Disadvantaged Persons

The problems of various disadvantaged groups (such as the hard-core unemployed, certain minorities, and the uneducated) have many dimensions—social, personal, economic, and so forth. These problems have important implications for training, inasmuch as opportunities for gainful employment are predicated on the development of relevant job skills. The training of such groups usually involves a scope of content that heretofore has generally been outside the baliwick of typical training activities: the need to teach prospective employees to be reliable, neat, and punctual; and in some instances the need to offer basic reading and arithmetic and to teach the moral obligations of citizenship. As for the skills contributing to "employability," Barbee and Keil (1973) found that a training program designed to enhance the interviewing skills of disadvantaged persons did in fact increase the chances of obtaining employment.

In an overview of training the hard-core unemployed, Goodman, Salipante, and Paransky (1973) surveyed a number of published studies on this topic, and Salipante and Goodman (1976) followed up the experiences of 130 programs directed toward hiring and training such individuals. The results of these overviews are admittedly somewhat mixed, and any generalizations need to be taken with some reservations. A few of the inferences drawn by Goodman and others are that trained individuals are more likely to value work, to have positive attitudes toward time schedules, and to show increased feelings of personal efficacy concerning achievement; and that, although training can have positive values, it can also have dysfunctional consequences, such as leading to greater expectations than the job situation can fulfill. Although they also reported that training was unlikely to affect the retention of trainees on their jobs, the later survey by Salipante and Goodman raised questions of the generality of this conclusion. In particular, Salipante and Goodman found a tendency for retention to be somewhat higher for training programs that emphasized job-skills content as contrasted with those that emphasized role playing (to sensitize trainees to themselves and others). They hastened to state that these results should not imply that training programs for the disadvantaged should be devoted completely to job-skills training (as opposed to "attitudinal" training), but rather that they implied that job-skills training should be a major focus of such programs. They also found that the longer the training program was, the less the trainees retained *unless* the program was accompanied by counseling to

provide direct reinforcements to strengthen beliefs in the desirability of coming to work.

There are no simple rules to insure success of training programs for the disadvantaged, but available materials suggest that the greatest emphasis on job-skills training with moderate emphasis on "attitudinal" training, accompanied by counseling, may enhance the likelihood of success. Petty (1974) provided evidence that the best way to present job-related information to disadvantaged trainees is orally; if written materials are to be distributed, they should be preceded by an oral version of the same material.

Aging Workers

The common stereotypes of older workers imply that they are "over the hill" in many respects. In reflecting about the older workers (those over 50) a few general comments are in order. To begin with, certain changes do tend to occur with age—changes in sensory skills, aspects of memory, physical abilities (after all, we do not have many octogenerian football players), and so on. However, the common stereotypes are undoubtedly grossly exaggerated and, furthermore, there are marked individual differences in the changes that do occur. And, although some changes do occur in some older workers, there are compensating factors on the other side of the coin. As Kaminski (1982) points out, for example, the differences between older and younger workers' productivity are generally fewer than those within the ranks of any specific age groups. Kaminski indicates that, once trained, older workers are more likely to be more dependable and to place information learning in the context of previous experiences. In addition, certain abilities tend to increase with age, as critical judgment, insight, patience, and recognition of an action's potential effect. Thus, as Kaminski concludes, older workers are a positive resource in the labor market.

Because of certain of the changes that do occur through time, however, Kaminski itemizes twenty-three special training considerations that should be taken into account in developing training programs for older workers. Some of these are: the use of large type sizes in visual aids; the use of as much self-paced learning as possible; the permission of more practice; and the use of constant positive feedback.

DISCUSSION

The general status of training in industry must be viewed as being relatively desultory, or at best as being spotty. Such an assessment seems warranted because of several factors: The systematic analysis of training needs is not practiced as often as it should be; there are deficiencies in the techniques for the systematic analysis of training needs; the extensive research on learning theories is not very relevant to personnel training; there is considerable disagreement about the relevance of various learning principles and training methods for specific training objectives; the training field has been beset by various fads over the years, most of which have failed to achieve their much-touted goods; and there has been limited hard-fisted evaluation of training programs.

Because of this state of affairs much of the training in industry has been based on faith and hope. This is not to say that all, or most of, such training has been ineffective in serving desired organizational goals, but rather it implies that there is no way of knowing how effective such training has been. However, it is undoubtedly true that massive amounts of money have been squandered on ineffective training.

On the other hand, there are certain signs and developments that offer some hope for future improvement: the sense of self-criticism appearing in some training publications; the development of certain training technologies, such as computer-assisted instruction; and the surfacing discussions of instructional design, instructional systems, and other similar concepts that have as their proposed frame of reference the development of a comprehensive, integrated approach to personnel training.

REFERENCES

Bandura, A. (1977). *Social learning theory*. Englewood Cliffs, N.J.: Prentice-Hall.

Barbee, J. R., & Keil, E. (1973). Experimental techniques of job interview training for the disadvantaged. *Journal of Applied Psychology, 58* (2), 209–213.

Bass, B. M. & Vaughan, J. A. (1966). *Training in industry: The management of learning*. Belmont, Calif.: Wadsworth.

Boettcher, E. G., Alderson, S. F., & Saccucci, M. (August 1981). A comparison of the effects of computer-assisted instruction versus printed instruction on student learning in the cognitive categories of knowledge and application. *Journal of Computer-Based Instruction, 3*(1), 13–17.

Bunker, K. A., & Cohen, S. L. (1977). The rigors of training evaluation. A discussion and field demonstration. *Personnel Psychology, 30* (4), 525–541.

Campbell, J. P., & Dunnette, M. D. (1968). Effectiveness of T-group experiences in managerial training and development. *Psychological Bulletin, 70*(2), 73–104.

Carlisle, K. E. (December 1982). The learning strategy technique of task analysis. *Performance and Instruction, 21*(10), 9–11.

Carroll, S. J., Jr., Paine, F. T., & Ivancovich, J. J. (1972). The relative effectiveness of training methods—Expert opinion and research. *Personnel Psychology, 25*, 495–510.

Catalanello, R. E., & Kirkpatrick, D. L. (May 1968). Evaluating training programs: The state of the art. *Training and Development Journal, 22*(5), 2–9.

Craig, R. L. (Ed.) (1976). *Training and development handbook* (2nd ed.). New York: McGraw Hill.

Folley, J. D., Jr. (July 1969). Determining training needs of department store sales personnel. *Training and Development Journal, 23*(7), 24–26.

Gagné, R. M. (1977). *The conditions of learning* (3rd ed.). New York: Holt, Rinehart & Winston.

Goldstein, I.L. (1974). *Training: Program development and evaluation.* Monterey, Calif.: Brooks/Cole.

Goldstein, I.L., & Buxton, V. M. (1982). Training and human performance. In M. D. Dunnette & E. A. Fleishman (Eds.), *Human performance and productivity: Human capability assessment* (Chap. 5). Hillsdale, N.J.: Lawrence Erlbaum Associates.

Goodman, P. S., Salipante, P., & Paransky, H. (1973). Hiring, training, and retraining the hardcore unemployed: A selected review. *Journal of Applied Psychology* 58(1), 23–33.

Hinrichs, J. R. (1976). Personnel training. In M. D. Dunnette (Ed.), *Handbook of industrial and organizational psychology* (Chap. 19). Chicago: Rand McNally.

Ilgen, D. R., Fisher, C. D., & Taylor, M. S. (1979). Consequences of individual feedback on behavior in organizations. *Journal of Applied Psychology, 64*(4), 340–371.

Kaminski, V. (December 1982). A team for the future: Industrial gerontology and training. *Performance and Instruction, 21*(10), 21–23.

Kirkpatrick, D. L. (February 1977). Determining training needs: Four simple and effective approaches. *Training and Development Journal, 31*(2), 22–25.

Komaki, J., Heinzmann, A. T., & Lawson, L. (1980). Effect of training and feedback. Component analysis of a behavioral safety program. *Journal of Applied Psychology, 68*(3), 261–270.

Komaki, J., Waddell, W. M., & Pearce, M. G. (1977). The applied behavior analyses approach and individual employees: Improving performance in two small businesses. *Organizational Behavior and Human Performance, 19*, 337–352.

Latham, G. P., & Locke, E. A., (August 1979). Goal setting: A motivational technique that works. *Organizational Dynamics*, 68–80.

Latham, G. P., & Saari, L. M. (1976). Application of social learning theory to training supervisors through behavioral modeling. *Journal of Applied Psychology, 64*(3), 230–246.

Locke, E. A. (1968). Toward a theory of task motivation and incentives. *Organizational Behavior and Human Performance, 3*, 157–189.

Mager, R. F., & Beach, K. M., Jr. (1967). *Developing vocational instruction.* Belmont, Calif.: Fearon.

McGehee. W. (1979). Training and development theory, policies, and practices. In D. Yoder & H. G. Honenman, Jr. (Eds.), ASPA *Handbook of personnel and industrial relations* (Chap. 5.1). Washington, D.C.: Bureau of National Affairs.

McGehee, W., & Thayer, P. W. (1961). *Training in business and industry.* New York: Wiley.

McGehee, W., & Tullar, W. L. (1978). A note on evaluating behavior modification and behavior modeling as industrial training techniques. *Personnel Psychology, 31*(3), 477–484.

Miller, R. B. (1962). Task description and analysis. In R. M. Gagné (Ed.), *Psychological principles in system development.* New York: Holt, Rinehart & Winson.

Moses, J. L. (1978). Behavior modeling for managers. *Human Factors, 20* (2), 225–232.

Moses, J. L., & Ritchie, R. J. (1976). Supervisory relationships training: A behavioral evaluation of a behavior modeling program. *Personnel Psychology, 29*(3), 337–343.

Nash, A. N., Muczyk, J. P., & Vettori, F. L. (1971). The relative practical effectiveness of programmed instruction. *Personnel Psychology, 24*, 397–418.

Naylor, J.C. (February 1962). Parameters affecting the relative efficiency of part and whole practice methods: A review of the literature. Port Washington, N.Y.: United States Naval Training Devices Center, Tech. Rep. No. 950–1.

Otto, C. P., & Glaser, O. (Eds.) (1970). *The management of training.* Reading, Mass.: Addison-Wesley.

Petty, M. M. (1974). Relative effectiveness of four combinations of oral and written presentations of job related information to disadvantaged trainees. *Journal of Applied Psychology, 59*(1), 105–106.

Salipante, P., Jr., & Goodman, P. (1976). Training, counseling, and retention of the hard-core unemployed. *Journal of Applied Psychology, 61*(1), 1–11.

Singer, E. J., & Ramsden, J. (1969). *The practical approach to skills analysis.* London: McGraw-Hill. (Published and distributed in the United States by Daniel Davoy & Co., Inc., Hartford Connecticut.)

Thorndike, E. L. (1924). Mental discipline in high school studies. *Journal of Educational Psychology, 15*, 1–22, 83–98.

Thorndike, E. L., & Woodworth, R. S. (1901). The influence of improvement in one mental function upon efficiency of other functions. *Psychological Review, 8*, 247–261, 384–385, 553–564.

Weitz, J., & Adler, S. (1973). The optimal use of simulation. *Journal of Applied Psychology, 58*(2), 219–224.

Wexley, K. N., & Latham, G. P. (1981). *Developing and training human resources in organizations.* Glenview, Ill.: Scott, Foresman.

Wilson, J. (1982). A look at programmed instruction from within the publishing industry. *Performance and Instruction, 21*(9), 16–20.

13

Careers

When jobs are scarce for long periods of time, as was the case during the Great Depression of the 1930s, people are relatively content with simply having a job—any job. Furthermore, little attention is paid to the sequence of jobs any given individual holds over a long period of time. Moving from one position to another often represents an unplanned shift depending on reductions in the work force, the whims of management, or any other of a large number of causes that are dominated by the short-term needs at a given time.

In better economic times, when jobs are more plentiful, individuals have more choice, and organizations must use human resources more effectively. Under such conditions closer attention is paid to the nature of the sequence of positions a person holds over his or her lifetime in the work force. Anderson, Milkovich, and Tsui (1981) mentioned several general factors that contribute to a longer time perspective with respect to the sequence of jobs held by individuals. Two of

these are particularly important. The first is the economy and the nature of jobs that need to be filled. Even when unemployment is high, as it was in the United States in the early 1980s, a large number of jobs remain unfilled primarily because they require higher-level skills than are available in the labor force. As the mean level of skill requirements for jobs increases, so does the time it takes to develop these skills in the individuals who make up the work force. Longer time periods require more prior planning to insure that skills are available in the work force when they are needed. The second general force comes from within members of the work force themselves; people are less satisfied with simply having jobs. They want jobs that match their skills, abilities, and interests. Furthermore, as they transition from one job to another, they want to build on the skills and abilities they developed in the past. Thus, both external pressures in the work environment and internal pressures within members of the work force lead to the same conclusion: Attention must be paid to developing a coherent pattern of jobs over the course of each individual's working life. This individual perspective over time forms the basis for what we call careers.

PERSPECTIVES ON CAREERS

Definition

In their annual review of the literature on careers, Super and Hall (1978) define a career as "a sequence of positions occupied by a person during the course of a life-time" (p. 334). A career is neither a profession nor an occupation. The latter two describe sequences and types of jobs, but they do not do so from the individual's perspective. The occupation of commercial airline pilot specifies a long series of jobs that must be held by all of those who are members of that occupation, but the career of any particular pilot is represented by all the specific jobs and experiences he or she has had since entering the work force.

Three Views

The definition of Super and Hall (1978) is the one we use here. Yet, there are many different views of careers that appear in the literature. Vardi (1980) describes three perspectives. Industrial sociologists tend to look at careers from the perspective of occupations. They are concerned with the practices used to socialize individuals into occupations and the similarities and differences among occupations in socialization procedures. Human-resource analysts focus upon labor markets and examine the movement of people to different jobs as a function of the availability of particular labor forces to fill certain types of jobs. Finally, organizational psychologists study variables related to career perceptions and the behaviors of people in organizations.

All three of these perspectives have contributed to what we know about careers. However, because this book has a psychological focus, our orientation is toward the individual view of careers, but we borrow from the works of sociologists and human-resource analysts when these latter points of view are useful for understanding individual behavior.

Overview

In the remainder of the chapter, we first examine three perspectives on careers. These orientations are general ways to view the careers of individuals and are helpful for understanding how careers unfold over the work life of an individual. From the foundation offered by these overall perspectives, we move to the problem of developing and managing careers. Here we are concerned with assessing individual characteristics and with using the information about these characteristics to aid in making good career decisions. These decisions may involve the types of jobs that individuals accept, or the training they receive to develop the skills necessary to meet their career objectives. We are also concerned with what motivates managers to be concerned about managing their own careers. Finally we look briefly at events in the career lives of individuals that may create difficulties for them. Specifically, we address the problems of job transfers and of dual-career couples.

ORIENTATIONS TOWARD CAREERS

One way to look at an individual's career is to focus upon the conditions encountered during his or her life at work. From this perspective the important concerns are the specific conditions encountered in organizational life and the way in which the individual adjusts and adapts to these conditions. Another approach is to begin with the individual and to address the changes that occur in him or her over the course of a lifetime. This developmental view pays less attention to the nature of the conditions in organizations than it does to the nature of people.

Both of the just-described orientations are prevalent in the literature on careers. We label the first of these the *organization* view of careers and the second the *individual* view.

Organization View of Careers

From the organization view, the process of building a career involves a person's being socialized into various roles over the course of a lifetime. The socialization process involves moving from being an outsider to being an insider in the role that is of interest. This process takes time and is indexed by benchmarks or hurdles that are crossed over time. As such, career success is seen in terms of the extent to which the individual adjusts to the demands of the role into which he or she is placed.[1]

The boundary spanning model of organizational socialization developed by Schein and his colleagues (Schein, 1978; Schein & Van Maanen, 1979) perhaps best represents the organization view of careers. Socialization is seen as a three-stage process. The first stage is labeled "anticipatory socialization" and contains conditions that are encountered before joining an organization. Thinking about the nature of jobs that would be encountered at work, training in the form of specific-skill training or general educational training, and observing others who do the type of work in which the person is interested are all forms of anticipatory socialization.

Once the person joins the organization, he or she passes from an outsider to an insider and attains "newcomer" status. The newcomer stage lasts from 6 to 10 months according to Schein and others (Louis, 1980) and involves "learning the ropes." This period can be very stressful; at the very least, it demands a lot of time and energy on the part of the new individual to learn how to behave in the new setting.

The final stage of the socialization process is that of becoming an "insider" and settling into the new role. Assuming that the newcomer learns the job and is accepted into the organization by others, the remainder of his or her career involves various types of changes and modification in behaviors, beliefs, and attitudes throughout an association with the organization. If, for some reason, the person moves from one organization to another, according to this view, the process recycles. However, the nature of each cycle may be somewhat different and may last a different amount of time depending on the amount of difference between the old organization and the new, as well as the nature of the new job compared to the old.

Schein's (1978; Van Maanen & Schein, 1979) specific model focuses upon the *boundaries* that are crossed as a person moves from outsider to insider and within an organization. Figure 13.1 illustrates the three major dimensions of the organization that create various boundaries for the individual to cross. The first of these are the functional areas of an organization. We have illustrated three types of functions; obviously there are many more that are common in most organizations—for example, marketing, research and development, finance, or purchasing.

The second dimension in the model is that of inclusion. Here the individual advances in the degree to which he or she is accepted into the groups that make up the social structure of the organization. Initially, the person, as a newcomer, is little more than an outsider; he or she is on the job but is not likely to be trusted with important, confidential information. For example, in the highly competitive, microcomputer industry where being the

---

[1]Much of the remaining part of this section appears in a text by Ilgen and Weiss (in press).

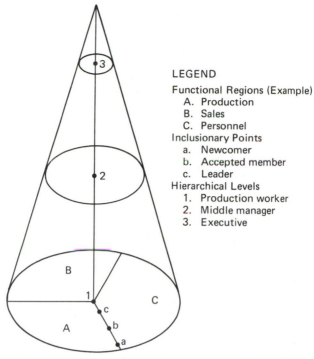

LEGEND

Functional Regions (Example)
  A. Production
  B. Sales
  C. Personnel
Inclusionary Points
  a. Newcomer
  b. Accepted member
  c. Leader
Hierarchical Levels
  1. Production worker
  2. Middle manager
  3. Executive

FIGURE 13.1 Schein's model of segments of boundaries important to socialization in organizations.

first to come out with a particular product can lead to a great market advantage, newcomers working in research and development may not be trusted with "state of the art" projects until they have proven themselves to be loyal employees who will neither resign quickly and take important information to a competitor nor talk too much to outsiders about the nature of their work. Note that regardless of the functional nature of the job, the person passes through the inclusionary dimension. Of course, the speed at which one transitions along this dimension may be affected by the function. Someone in sales might find it easier to be considered an insider than someone in production, for example.

The final boundary is that of hierarchy. Most organizations have fewer positions available at higher levels than they do at lower levels. Figure 13.1 illustrates this with a conal shape rather than a cylinder. Note that hierarchy is independent of function but is NOT independent of inclusion. The concentric circles become smaller as one goes up the hierarchy; this illustrates that persons higher in the organization are also included more.

Schein assumes that socialization is introduced into this model when individuals are most influenced in their career adjustments into the organization—that is, when they are preparing to or have just crossed some boundary between regions in the three dimensions of Figure 13.1. According to this view, when individuals are familiar with their jobs and are comfortable in them, they are not crossing boundaries between roles and are pretty well settled into their jobs. On the other hand, when they are changing jobs and moving across boundaries of any one of the three types just mentioned, they often feel the need to learn more about what is required in the new roles. The old practices are often not sufficient for the new roles. As a result, in the new positions the individuals are more open to pressures from others.

Frequently, individuals cross more than one boundary at a time. At these times, individuals are particularly sensitive to socialization pressures. The most demanding and, therefore, the most stressful time is usually when people enter new organizations. At this time, all three boundaries are crossed simultaneously. It is not surprising that the time of entry into a new job is very stressful, and it is a time when the individual is particularly sensitive to the socializing pressures of others around him or her. It is also not surprising that organizational practices are often developed to help socialize new members. Managerial training programs, apprentice pro-

grams, and other initial orientation practices spend as much or more time on teaching the norms and values of the organization as they do on teaching specific task-related skills.

A somewhat more complex socialization view of career adjustment is presented in Figure 13.2. Here Feldman (1981) is more specific about the types of events that occur at each of the three major phases of the socialization process as the person moves from outside to inside the organization. Feldman also goes beyond the stage of adjustment to suggest the types of results that emerge from successful (or unsuccessful) adjustment.

Individual View of Careers

In contrast to the organization view of careers, which focuses upon the organizational context, individual views look to the nature

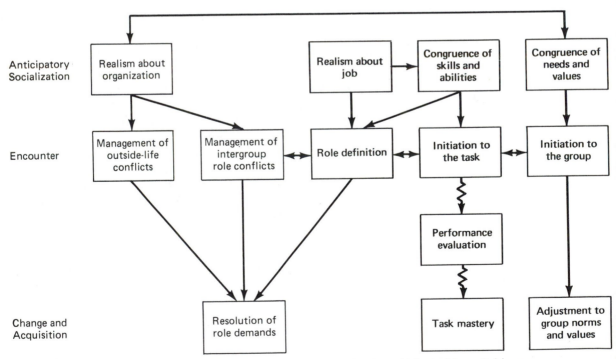

FIGURE 13.2 Stages of socialization into organizations. (Adapted from Feldman, 1981.)

of the people involved for explanations of career events. The explanatory framework for the observed changes in job-related behaviors over time is drawn from developmental changes in individuals that are part of the continually unfolding process of maturing and aging. Although recognized as a continuous ongoing process throughout the lifetime of an individual, maturation is usually broken down into stages. These stages are bounded chronologically and are labeled by the dominant behaviors present at those periods in one's life.

Daniel J. Levinson's The *Seasons of a Man's Life* (1978) exemplifies the individual orientation toward careers. Rather than describe all phases of Levinson's model in great detail, we limit ourselves to the initial phase because it illustrates the general adjustment/developmental view of all stages and because it is the phase that is of most interest to a college-age audience.

Levinson studied hourly workers in industry, business executives, university biologists, and novelists. Within each group, ten individuals were selected for study. All were males.

According to Levinson, all of us mature and develop by passing through a sequence of eras, each lasting about 20 years. In particular, there are four significant areas or stages in each of our lives:

1. Childhood and adolescence: Age 0 to 22
2. Early adulthood: Age 17 to 45
3. Middle adulthood: Age 40 to 65
4. Late adulthood: Age 60 plus.

Within the early-adulthood stage, Levinson includes three subphases: entering the adult world, age 30 transition, and settling down. In the first, the individual is faced with some major transitions. He or she begins by shifting from the role of a child in a family dominated by adult-defined conditions to the role of a "novice adult" with responsibility for his or her own life. The major decisions with long-term implications at this time revolve around the choice of a career, mate, and the other lifestyle issues that are often related to and accompany mate and career selection. Levinson argues that, at this time, it is necessary for the person to be able to explore alternatives that may be open to him or her, and to try out some of the possible roles to "see how they fit." During this exploratory phase, the person tries to keep his or her options open so that roles discarded temporarily are not necessarily closed off.

From the organization's standpoint, the implications of this phase are obvious; provision should be made for the person to explore and test the alternatives available to allow him or her to find a niche. There must also be some tolerance for the fact that the individual may discover, in the course of exploring alternatives, that the organization does not fit his or her needs. Specifically, turnover is a natural part of this process. Although organizations usually approach turnover as something that is costly and that should be eliminated, some turnover is necessary in order to allow young people the opportunity to reach the conclusion, on their own, that the particular organization and the nature of the job that they do for it are indeed what they feel they do or do not need.

The second and third subphases of early adulthood are periods in which the exploration of the early years slows down as the individual settles into a career and lifestyle. Upon reaching the age of 30, the individual begins to realize that life is for real and that the choices that have already been made are shaping his or her life. According to Levinson, the person begins to put down roots and begins to realize youthful ambitions. A sense of well-being is critical during this phase and is derived from a person's feeling that he or she is doing well in the roles that have been taken up to that time. For nearly a decade, the individual continues through this phase, emphasizing the successful accomplishment

FIGURE 13.3 Important features of business executives' lives during the early-adulthood stage. (Excerpted from Levinson, 1978.)

1. Forming a Dream: Unlike most of the occupational groups, the executive was less guided by a specific dream built and nurtured during this time. He did not have a specific dream that he strived for.*

2. Forming a Mentor Relationship: A mentor relationship developed with another person within the organization. Most mentors were about one-half generation older and relatively successful. These mentor relationships were seen as very important both to the executive and to his mentor.

3. Exploring Alternatives: The executive, like others in this age group, explored several alternatives for his career. In general, those that made a firm commitment to occupations very early without exploration, lived to regret it.

4. Marriage and Family: Concomitant with starting a career, the executives were selecting spouses and making decisions with respect to the size of family and the distributions of responsibilities within the family. For the most part, these decisions with respect to family responsibilities were quite traditional. (Note: although we would expect that executives' family patterns with respect to individual roles would follow traditional sex roles more closely than some other groups, the breakdown of sex roles is likely to be greater today than it was when Levinson's data were collected.)

* All participants in the research were male.

of his or her chosen roles and exploring alternatives only if success in the present role is missing and/or out of reach. Figure 13.3 describes some specific events in the early-adulthood phase of business executives in the Levinson study.

Career Stages: An Integration

Rather than focus primarily upon either the organization or the individual, Hall (Berlew & Hall, 1966; Hall, 1976; Hall & Schneider, 1973) combined the influences of both in his concept of *career identification*. The focus of this point of view is on the individual's self-concept. From the developmental models, we have already seen that the late teens and early 20s are a time of struggle with the identity crisis, as people try to discover who they are and what they want to be. During this time, choices of a vocation and of an organization in which to work are made. The experiences resulting from these choices impact on each individual's unfolding self-concept—the way in which the person sees himself or herself. The self-concept acts as a standard or frame of reference against which each of us judges our own actions. The amount of self-concept related to career depends on a person's experiences at work and in other domains of life.

According to Hall's career-identification model, the individual begins with little or no part of the self-concept related to a career. A teenager, for example, may be considering vocational choices but may have no real experience in any career so he or she really does not think of self in terms of the career. With experience at the workplace during the exploratory years of life, the person's career begins to take on an increasingly larger proportion of the total self-concept. At some point, an individual may begin to see himself or herself in terms of career labels—a lathe operator, a telephone repair person, a troubleshooter, an accountant, a Sears employee.

How much of the total self-concept is devoted to career-related phenomena depends, in large part, on the degree to which the person believes that he or she has been *successful* in the career and the degree to which the career is *valued*. If either of these conditions is not met, the self-concept will probably develop along other lines.

Figure 13.4 illustrates the career-identification model by describing two general types of persons outlined by Rychlak (1974, 1982), who attempted to summarize a large body of data on AT&T managers who participated in the Management Progress Study. Note that as both prototypical managers—enlargers and enfolders—advanced and matured from early to midcareer, the proportion of self-concept devoted to career-related factors increased. However, from midcareer onward, the pattern changed. The enlargers continued to expand the region of self-concept devoted to their careers. They increased their commitments to their professions and sought more challenging positions in the corporation. The enfolders, on the other hand, leveled off in their orientations toward their careers. They did not necessarily perform poorly in their present jobs, but neither did they devote large portions of their time and effort to career-related activities. For example, Rychlak found that in comparison to enlargers, enfolders were more likely to have strong family and community ties and to devote more of their time to off-job concerns.

Exactly what led to the divergences in orientation between the two groups is unclear. Some was due to experiences on the job and some to differences in personal values and orientations that were developed before coming to work at AT&T. According to the career-identification model, however, the general pattern of change in career orientation does seem to represent a combination of life experiences interacting with developmental proclivities within the individuals.

Before leaving the topic of career identification, we must reflect upon the relevance of the model for the work force of the 1980s and beyond. Paradoxically, the model that evolved, in part, from the all-male sample of AT&T managers and executives may be becoming less relevant for males and more for females. Extensive study of work values and lifestyles of people in general by Yankelovich and others (Kerr & Rosow, 1979) and of managers by Miner (Miner & Smith, 1982) shows a general trend away from the centrality of careers and work in the lives of males. According to Miner and Smith (1982), however, this downward trend in work motivation tended to level off by the late 1970s. The definition of individual success is no longer as narrowly defined as it once was, so it is possible for males to choose not to enter the traditional career path aiming for the top of the corporate or professional ladder. On the other hand, the trend is for women to have more of their self-concepts related to work than was the case in the relatively recent past. This is particularly true among college-educated women. Although it is not clear at the present time where the balance will be struck with respect to careers and the self-concepts of males and females, if we were to extrapolate beyond the present, it appears that both women and men will, in the future, be strongly influenced by the nature of their work with respect to how they view themselves. Thus, the career-identification model should be useful for attempting to understand career motivation for both males and females for some time to come.

CRITICAL TIMES

As defined here, a career is an individually referenced construct that reflects the sum total of jobs that a person has had over his or her working life. Although any particular segment of work-related time contributes to a career, all time periods are not equally critical either in describing a person's career or in

FIGURE 13.4 Partial descriptions of two managerial "types." (Adapted from Rychlak, J. A. 1974. In D. W. Bray, R. J. Campbell, & D. L. Grant, eds. *The formative years in business: A long-term AT&T study of managerial lives.* New York: Wiley.)

Two composite descriptions of general types of employees based upon interviews, psychological tests, and assessment center evaluations of a group of employees over the first seven years on the job.

I. Life Theme: Enfolders
   A. Joined the company in his mid-twenties after having spent three years in the service and then obtained a college degree.
   B. Presented ideas in small groups which showed that he was quite intelligent, but the ideas were not easily understood by the group members.
   C. Showed rather low organizational and decision-making ability.
   D. Problem oriented in group problem solving sessions.
   E. Technically competent and reliable.
   F. Interested in job early in career.
   G. Bored with early training courses.
   H. High interest and concern for immediate family and extended family.
   I. Disliked company transfer policy (frequent moves) and expressed this often to co-workers and superiors.
   J. Off-the-job interests in gardening and working in his woodworking shop.
   K. Missed early promotions he felt for making a couple of early mistakes although he was not too upset about this.
   L. Interest in work-related issues leveled off over time.
   M. Interest in family grew stronger over time.

II. Life Theme: Enricher
   A. Joined the company in his mid-twenties after having spent three years in the service and obtained a college degree.
   B. Presented ideas in small groups that were good but not above average.
   C. Showed high organizational and decision-making ability.
   D. Planned ahead at all stages of his career. For example, although an engineering major in college, he took many liberal arts electives to prepare himself as broadly as possible.
   E. Was very interested in reading and pushed himself to keep up, both on and off the job.
   F. Became an unquestioned leader in group situations.
   G. Had strong beliefs in family responsibility and worked hard to maintain the immediate family but realized that extended family ties were breaking down.
   H. Accepted transfers without concern.
   I. Obtained three good promotions early in his career.
   J. Became more and more involved with his career over time.
   K. Thoroughly enjoyed his career and the company but continued to keep open the possibility of making a major career change.

evaluating the time and effort required of the person to maintain the career. Some times are much more critical than others. Three time periods are particularly influential in the development of an individual's career.

Career Exploration and Planning

The exploratory phase in a career occurs before the person ever begins work. Much of the work in this area is done in career counseling and career education within the educational system—in high schools, colleges, and universities. In these settings, persons trained as career counselors attempt to make young people aware of vocational opportunities in the work force and to assess the skills, abilities, interests, and values of those making career decisions in order to provide useful data and advice with respect to these decisions.

The primary focus of career counseling is upon assessing the career objectives and vocational entry possibilities of those facing the prospect of entering the labor market in the not-too-distant future. Many of the assessment instruments are the same ones we discussed earlier: ability tests and interest tests. Others are geared specifically to career concepts. An example of the latter is Crites' Career Maturity Inventory (CMI) (1973). Career maturity is the extent to which adolescents are well prepared for making career decisions and seem to be making their career-related decisions in a rational manner. The CMI measures three group factors and eighteen more specific factors of preferences for various occupations. The group factors are: realism of career choices, career-choice competencies, and career-choice attitudes. The degree of career maturity can then be related to the types of choices the person makes with respect to vocational preferences. Crites postulates that career maturity should increase from grade to grade, and in general he finds this. He also found, however, that twelfth graders had lower scores on career maturity than did eleventh graders (Crites, 1973). Although researchers have criticized the specific factors of the CMI and strict adherence to the expectation that career maturity should increase across every grade (Super & Hall, 1978), it is well accepted that we need to understand more about what leads individuals to make mature career decisions. The need for career counselors and career-focused assessment aimed at aiding individuals make

important decisions related to their careers is also well accepted. Such practices can be useful for both the individual who is attempting to make career decisions that will best suit his or her own needs and for society, as we attempt to distribute members of the work force across jobs in a manner that best utilizes the skills, abilities, interests, and values of members of that labor force.

Organizational Entry

We have already stated that beginning a new job is a critical time in a person's career. It is a stressful time that requires considerable adjustment as the individual tries to make sense of the new job situation (Louis, 1980).

Aiding the adjustment of new employees to a job begins in the recruiting process. An apropos analogy for recruiting is that of courtship. The potential employee is seeking a position with a company and is concerned about two things: (1) gathering valid information about the company in order to make a good career decision; and (2) presenting himself or herself to company personnel in a way that will be attractive to them. Likewise, organizational representatives have the same two objectives (Porter, Lawler, & Hackman, 1975). Unfortunately, each side feels some inherent conflict in these two sets of like motives: In an attempt to appear as attractive as possible to the organization, the individuals tend to bias the information they share with the organization such that they often come across as more attractive than is actually the case. Similarly, company personnel are not likely to share information that they think will discourage the applicant from accepting a job offer. The result is that each party interferes with the other party's ability to gather valid data on which to make a well-reasoned decision.

Realistic Job Previews (RJPs). One of the ways to improve the match between an applicant and an organization and also to improve the applicant's initial adjustment to a new job is to provide the applicant with information about the job that is as close as possible to the real conditions to be encountered, even though this information may appear at first to be less than positive with respect to some job features. In other words, the organization should take a unilateral step and resist the temptation to favorably bias information given to applicants. The process of providing accurate information to job applicants has been termed Realistic Job Previews (RJPs) (Wanous, 1973, 1980).

Research on RJPs has demonstrated that they are beneficial for reducing turnover. The initial study by Weitz (1956) was conducted with insurance salespersons. Weitz constructed a booklet describing the job of an insurance salesperson that addressed the typical issues—possibilities for a good income, opportunities to set one's own work schedule, advantages of helping others, and so on. In addition, he also described some of the less attractive features of the job that were often overlooked during recruiting: such things as having to work evenings, frequently being turned down by persons contacted, making appointments with people and driving some distance to meet them only to find them not home or no longer interested, and living with the insecurity of an income based entirely upon commissions.

Weitz conducted a field experiment in which he gave half the applicants for positions as salespersons the booklet with its realistic preview and half the typical recruitment process. He then compared the two groups on two sets of data. First he looked at the number of days positions remained unfilled when the applicants received the realistic versus the standard recruitment procedure. There was no difference between the groups; it was no harder to fill the positions when people received realistic previews than when they did not. Next he compared the amount of turnover among those who accepted the job after getting the realistic preview with those who accepted it after the standard recruitment program. Those who received the realistic preview had *lower* turnover than those who did not.

Research on RJPs since that time has demonstrated positive effects in a variety of jobs and settings: telephone operators (Wanous, 1973); military academy cadets (Ilgen & Seely, 1974; Macedonia, 1969); and retail employees (Dugoni & Ilgen, 1981). On the other hand, there have been a number of studies in which the effects have been minimal (see Reilly, Brown, Blood, & Malatesta, 1981, for a review). To our knowledge, however, none of the studies to date has indicated negative effects of RJPs either on an organization's ability to attract qualified applicants to accept jobs when offered or on the adjustment of new employees to their jobs. Thus, it seems reasonable to conclude that RJPs are useful for an applicant's initial encounter with an organization.

One caution before we leave the topic of organizational entry: Whatever the positive effects of providing realistic initial information about some of the less positive features of a job, no one would suggest that telling people about these features will have nearly the positive effect of removing the negative features altogether. A recent study by one of the present authors (Dugoni & Ilgen, 1981) found that part-time checkers and baggers in a large retail store were most dissatisfied when their supervisors had to change their hours of work at the last minute. Even though we told job applicants that this would happen and the reasons why it happened prior to their employment, having such knowledge did not lessen their dissatisfaction with being told on Friday at 4:00 P.M. that instead of having Saturday off they were needed from 2:00 to 10:00 P.M. the next day. Only not changing their hours would have lessened their dissatisfaction with the situation.

Early job challenge. A classic study by Berlew and Hall (1966) with AT&T managers showed that later success in the organization was a function of the degree of challenge experienced on the first job assignment. Two common-sense "theories" exist with respect to the initial assignments of new employees. One is that new employees should be worked into their jobs gradually. The argument is that once the person has learned the job well and understands the way things are done in the organization, he or she will have a strong background and will be able to build upon it. In contrast, the early job-challenge position advocates placing the persons in challenging and demanding jobs which require them to learn a lot and to perform well in a relatively short period of time. According to this position, a person who is very involved in a demanding job early in his or her career and who then experiences success in that type of job internalizes the "sweet taste of success" (Berlew & Hall, 1966) and continues to seek jobs that provide him or her with similar challenges.

Researchers have compared later career success of those in challenging jobs with those in less challenging jobs for the following fields: auto employees (Dunnette, Arvey, & Banas, 1973); engineers (Kaufman, 1974); and Roman Catholic priests (Hall & Schneider, 1973). In general, they all reached the same conclusion: Early job challenge does have a positive effect on later career success as indexed by the rate of promotion, salary increases, and the nature of the types of positions held. Using laboratory data, Taylor (1981) did not refute this conclusion but she did suggest that the effect may be due to factors other than the internalization of the success norm. She also pointed out that more should be known about individual differences in responses to early job challenge because, in most initial-placement situations, some jobs are challenging and others must also be done but are less challenging. Since someone

must get the latter jobs, it is not reasonable to assume that everyone can be assigned a challenging job. Therefore, we should learn more about who can benefit most from challenging jobs.

Career Transitions

There are points in a person's career that require major changes from what was done in the past. These represent what we call *career transitions*. Recall Schein's model of careers, which stressed three dimensions of an organizational environment that affect a person's career: functions, interpersonal acceptance, and moving up the hierarchy. Career transitions are most apparent as a person crosses the major boundaries between regions of the cone in Figure 13.1. Consider, for example, a product engineer who worked in a staff function for 10 to 12 years and who is then promoted to a middle-management position requiring little or no actual conduct of technical work but rather supervising others who do that work. In this case, a whole new set of skills may need to be developed.

To facilitate career transitions, organizations often build systematic training programs around anticipated transitions that are needed. An excellent example of such a system is that used in the military for officers. All branches of the military service have four general schools for officers that are geared to aid them in their transition to different positions likely to share some functional characteristics not present in previous experience. The first school is for new officers and is designed to serve a socializing function for people moving from civilian status to military status as well as to introduce some specific skills and knowledge needed for entry-level jobs. The second school comes after the person has been with the organization for 3 to 5 years and is designed to give more in-depth knowledge and skills dealing with specific jobs that the person will encounter. Third is a school that focuses upon developing middle-level manager skills that are less tied to the nitty gritty of specific tasks. These skills focus on operating with superiors and subordinates within the organization in order to accomplish tasks by working across levels and co-ordinating the efforts of several groups. Finally, after nearly 20 years in the service a school is designed to aid transitions from middle-level managers to top-level ones. Here the focus is on a broader, "big-picture," view that introduces the officers not only to the functions of the particular organization but to the total system in which the organization operates. Katz and Kahn (1978) termed this a *systems perspective* to stress the need for seeing how the total organization fits into the total network of relationships with other organizations in which it operates.

In all cases just discussed, the goal of the training is to provide skills that are lacking in a person's past career experiences to allow him or her to assume new roles more effectively. To do this, it is necessary first to diagnose the skill requirements of jobs typically held by organizational members with similar career histories and then to assess the types of skills that will be necessary for the individual to move to the next phase in his or her career. The diagnosis can be aided by a thorough knowledge of the nature of jobs and the job families in which the jobs fit. Once this is known, the training assessment can be done and training can be developed. Previous chapters on job analyses and training have addressed these topics; here we only stress the relevance of job analyses and training for aiding career transitions.

CAREER ASSESSMENT

If a career were simply the sum total of the positions that an individual has held over a lifetime, we could do nothing more than wait until someone retired to describe the per-son's career by looking back at it. We are not satisfied with doing this because we assume that some changes might be possible in an individual's career path which could, in the long run, lead to a more useful and satisfying career for the person and for the organizations for which he or she works.

In order to initiate change, or at least evaluate whether or not some change seems desirable, it is first necessary to assess or measure relevant information about a person and then to evaluate that information in terms of its implications for the person's career. The types of assessment instruments used to generate career information are not necessarily unique to career assessment; often the distinction between career assessment and assessment for purposes of selection, placement, promotion, or other personnel actions is only in the use to which the data are put. Career information, for the most part, is shared with the person involved to aid him or her to make career-relevant decisions.

Career-relevant information is measured in one of two general ways. The first is some form of paper-and-pencil test, which has been discussed at length earlier in this book. Paper-and-pencil tests are used almost exclusively to gather information for early career decisions related to occupational choice. A second type of measure used to generate career data is the assessment center. This procedure is used almost exclusively to evaluate managers only because most centers developed to date have focused on the job of manager. The method itself if not necessarily restricted as to the nature of the job it can address. Assessment centers, in contrast to paper-and-pencil tests, present the individual with some particular situation and require the person to actually behave in response to the situation. The behaviors are then scored in some standardized fashion.

Because many of the paper-and-pencil measures useful for career assessment have already been covered, the rest of this section discusses assessment centers and one paper-and-pencil test that has received widespread attention with respect to career information.

Assessment Centers

Background. Assessment-center techniques initially developed from a need to select personnel for positions primarily in military organizations rather than from a concern for career development. Dissatisfaction with any single "testing" procedure—paper-and-pencil tests or the use of trained interviewers—led to the use of (1) multiple types of tests to assess any given individual characteristic; and (2) situational simulations as tests. In the latter, people were presented with situations that required the use of the behaviors they believed were important on the job. When these behaviors are relatively straightforward—for example, the ability to make certain kinds of welds—the development of the situational test is likewise straightforward. However, when the behaviors are concerned with showing leadership, showing good judgment, being decisive, and so on, the situational "test" becomes more complex. Assessment centers use both multiple assessment techniques and situationally oriented tests to evaluate individuals.

In an excellent discussion of the development of assessment centers Thornton and Byham (1982) trace present-day practices back to the German officer-selection program beginning in the 1930s. The general selection practices were known and modeled by the British War Office Selection Boards and then by the U.S. Office of Strategic Services (OSS) during World War II. In all cases, the need was to select large numbers of military personnel to be placed in demanding leadership assignments. Yet the individuals to be selected did not possess extensive past records and experiences to guide the selection decisions. Some form of evaluation was needed; the one developed placed the individuals in

contrived situations in which they were required to perform. For example, they were required to role play a member of a problem-solving group and actually work on solving the problem. Problem-solving skills, decisiveness, leadership in the group, and other behaviors were judged from observing their behavior.

The single most important contribution to the present-day popularity of assessment centers was the Management Progress Study at AT&T. Douglas Bray and others (Bray, Campbell, & Grant, 1974; Bray & Grant, 1966) began following a group of 442 managers who joined six Bell System companies in 1956 through 1960; they are still keeping track of their careers today. This is the most complete longitudinal study of managers ever attempted. From the beginning, Bray and the research team developed multiple assessment procedures to measure the characteristics of these managers that might be related to their successes and adjustments to their jobs at AT&T. The AT&T assessment process has become the model for the present-day assessment centers. A more detailed look at the assessment-center process follows.

Description. An assessment center is a procedure that uses several different techniques to evaluate individuals on a number of different work-relevant dimensions (Thornton & Byham, 1982). The "tests" that make up a center require the persons being assessed to respond either individually or as members of a group. Typical individual tests are the usual paper-and-pencil tests and an *in-basket* exercise. The in-basket exercise asks the person being assessed (called an *assessee*) to assume that he or she has just been assigned a new job, replacing a person who was transferred. The assessee's task is to go through what is now his or her in-basket and to deal with the materials that are in it. The in-basket items, which represent the "test" for the assessee, include memos, telephone messages, letters, and other types of things typically found in an in-basket and often needing some type of response, such as returning a phone call, writing a letter, or filling out an evaluation form on a subordinate. The items in the in-basket have been specifically developed to measure such individual characteristics as decision-making skills, decisiveness, written communication ability, or willingness to delegate responsibility. The assessee works on the in-basket exercise for a fixed amount of time (often 2 hours). At that time his or her responses are collected and scored by a member of the assessment-center staff who has been trained to score them. The staff member, called an *assessor*, then interviews the assessee to clarify any responses to the in-basket that were unclear.

Group exercises typically tend to be one of two types. In one, several assessees, usually six, are given some problem to solve as a group. The problem might be to develop a set of contingency plans for the people who would be involved if a plant that has been losing money for years had to be closed. The key feature of these problem-solving sessions is that no one in the group is assigned any particular role or is given any information that is not shared by all. The assessees have no particular roles with respect to the group; they are simply to work in the group to reach a solution to the problem in a given amount of time. While they work on the problem, the group is observed by several assessors. Each assessor is assigned to observe one or two assessees closely and to record their behavior on a standardized recording sheet. These records are used to evaluate each assessee's behavior in the group.

A second type of group exercise involves assigning specific roles to group members. For example, the group may be asked to role play a group of people who have been appointed as a commission to consider relocating the railroad lines that run through the center of a medium-sized community. Each assessee would be given a particular role with information specific to that role. For exam-

ple, in the problem just mentioned, some possible roles are a member of the Chamber of Commerce, a railroad representative, a representative of the farmers whose land is likely to be lost with relocation, a member of the largest industry in the community that is currently on the railroad line and also in the downtown area, and other people who are likely to have specific interests in the solution to the problem. In this problem, the role players have specific interests and expertise, and there is likely to be disagreement among them as to the solution that best fits the needs of the various members of the group. As with the previously described exercise, assessors observe and record behaviors during the interaction.

An assessment center normally consists of four to six exercises of the type just described and takes 2 to 3 days to complete. By the end of the session, each assessor has had the opportunity to observe each assessee, and each assessee has performed a variety of tasks requiring behaving alone and in the company of others, as well as completing a set of paper-and-pencil tests. Following the data collection, the assessors meet with members of the assessment-center staff to discuss each assessee. From these discussions, a report is prepared on each assessee. The exact nature of the report depends on the use to which the data are to be put. At the very least, scores are presented and interpreted on a series of behavioral dimensions assessed by the exercises. Figure 13.5 lists a set of behaviors typically assessed in an assessment center.

Evaluation. The typical assessment-center validity study obtains measures in a center and relates these data to indications of later success in the organization. "Success" is most frequently indexed by level to which promoted, number of promotions, salary level (adjusted for initial starting salary), and potential for promotion, and is rarely measured in terms of performance criteria. Considera-

FIGURE 13.5 Dimensions of individual characteristics typically measured by assessment centers.

DIMENSION	DESCRIPTION
Decision making	Extent to which conclusions reached reflect considerations of the evidence at hand, the alternatives available, and the potential ramifications.
Decisiveness	Readiness to make decisions and render judgments when necessary.
Initiative	Active efforts to influence events rather than passive acceptance.
Leadership	Effectiveness in bringing a group to accomplish a task and in getting ideas accepted.
Management control	Appreciation of need for controls and maintenance of control over processes.
Oral communications	Effectiveness of expression in individual (one-on-one) and group situations.
Planning and organization	Effectiveness in approaching, arranging, and relating work in a systematic and situationally appropriate manner.
Problem analysis	Effectiveness in identifying, seeking out, and relating data pertinent to the solution of a problem.
Responsiveness	Appreciation of and positive reaction to the needs and concerns of the various publics served.
Risk-taking	Extent to which calculated and logically defensible risks are taken.
Sensitivity	Awareness and consideration of the needs and feelings of others.
Stress tolerance	Stability of performance under pressure and opposition.
Tenacity	Tendency to stay with a position or line of thought until the desired objective is achieved or is no longer reasonably attainable.
Use of delegation	Effective assignment of decision-making authority and accountability.
Written communication	Effectiveness of expression in writing; correctness of grammar, syntax, and other basic English items.

ble research has been conducted in a number of major U.S. corporations. A few examples are: AT&T (Moses, 1972), IBM (Dodd, 1971; Kraut & Scott, 1972), and Standard Oil of Ohio (Finkle & Jones, 1970; Mitchell, 1975). In general, this research is supportive of predictive validity of the method for identifying management progress. Correlations between assessment-center measures and management-progress indexes (excluding job-performance ratings) tend to range from the mid-.30s to the mid-.50s, and when compared to the other predictors tend to be somewhat better.

An example of the latter is the data of Bray and Grant (1966) from AT&T. These data compared test scores with assessment scores for predicting the ratings of managers by members of a field review team that visited each manager. The multiple correlation of four paper-and-pencil test scores with the criterion was .33 and the correlation of the assessment-center rating with the same criterion was .51. Although the differences between the two types of measures is rarely this large, the general direction of the difference tends to be in favor of assessment ratings.

The early success of the procedure, its widespread use, and the visibility of some of the most successful assessment-center programs in major U.S. corporations have led to some very strong endorsements for the use of assessment centers. We would concur that assessment centers represent a very important addition to the human-resource management process. For a very supportive review of research on assessment centers by two strong advocates of the method, see Thornton and Byham (1982).

In spite of the generally positive response to assessment centers, some serious concerns have been raised. Klimoski and Strickland (1977) suggest that perhaps the assessors who provide the ratings in an assessment center have been able to learn the general stereotype of a person who is successful in the corporation, and they simply rate highly those people who fit that general stereotype. They suggest that implied support for this position is that assessment centers are better at predicting promotion and salary criteria than they are at predicting job-performance criteria. This criticism is tempered somewhat by data that show good predictability for a sample of women officers in the Israeli army (Tziner & Shimon, 1982), although this study rated performance in a training program rather than performance or progress measures on the job.

A second criticism is leveled at the ratings of the dimensions themselves. Recent work by Sackett and his colleagues (Sackett & Dreher, 1982; Sackett & Wilson, 1982) has raised serious questions about assessors' abil-ities to produce ratings of separate dimensions like those listed in Figure 13.5. One study (Sackett & Dreher, 1982) clearly shows that scores on dimensions are quite similar within any particular exercise. The major differences in dimension scores are predicted by the exercise in which the dimension scores were obtained, rather than by differences in the dimensions themselves. The logic of the argument is as follows: Assume that the three behavioral dimensions of leadership, oral communication, and problem analysis are measured on two different exercises. If these three dimensions are really different, then it would be expected that a person's leadership, oral communication, or problem-solving analysis across the two situations would be relatively similar and that there would not necessarily be a high degree of relationship among the three dimensions. The data show that the ratings of all three dimensions are similar *within* each exercise but are not very similar across exercises. This suggests that the assessors get some general impression of performance on each exercise and rate all dimensions in line with this general impression rather than appraise each separate dimension.

The questioning of the ability to measure specific behavioral dimensions' validity in an assessment center is less problematic for using assessment centers for selection purposes than it is for using them for career counseling and guidance. In the former case, if the overall assessment-center ratings are predictive of later management progress, then the data can be useful for making such predictions. On the other hand, career counseling has some interest in the global overall prediction but is more interested in specific strengths and weaknesses. The dimension scores are particularly important for this. It would, for example, be very useful to know that a person had very high leadership and planning and analysis skills but was weak in written communication. However, if the scores on the individual dimensions are suspect, the value of this information is decidedly decreased. Clearly Sackett's work deserves further attention to discover the limits of assessment-center data and to work on ways to improve it or modify our recommendations about its use.

Conclusions about assessment centers. All things considered, assessment centers do offer a source of information about individuals that has been demonstrated to predict later potential, particularly in managerial jobs. Like all other assessment procedures, however, they have their limitations. At present the limitations that seem most important are those related to the extent to which dimension scores represent underlying behavioral tendencies on those dimensions. More work is needed to explore the quality of such dimension scores.

Two final points should be mentioned which are not directly related to validity. First, the centers can also contribute to the development of those who serve as assessors in addition to those who are assessed. Assessors are often drawn from the ranks of managers in an organization. They are (or at least should be) given extensive training in the types of behaviors to be measured by the dimensions and in how to observe such behaviors. This training, plus the experience of watching others behave while attempting to rate the behaviors that are seen, sensitizes assessors to the types of behaviors that are important and may improve their abilities to appraise the behaviors of others. At the very least, training a large number of assessors over a period of time should create a group of people who share a common system for observing others.

Finally, assessment centers are expensive—*very* expensive. To go through a typical center requires 2 days from the person being assessed; it requires more of the assessors, who not only must observe the behavior but must also participate in the preparation of a report on each assessee. It is not uncommon for a cycle to last 4 to 5 days and to involve 2 days from twelve assessees, 4 to 5 days from six assessors, and at least 5 days from one or two permanent staff members at the assessment center. Regardless of the positions of the people involved, the amount spent simply in salaries can be substantial. As a result, assessment centers are usually not used for lower-level jobs and are frequently not used for hiring new employees at an early point in the interview process, when many more people might have to go through the center than are hired. If assessment centers are used for hiring, cost constraints often limit them to two or three exercises.

Holland's Self Directed Search

Holland (1966, 1976) developed a theory of vocational education and planning that stresses the match between characteristics of the person and those of the environment. An instrument was developed—the Self Directed Search (SDS)—to help vocational-guidance personnel and individuals assess individual characteristics and provide information for improving career-relevant decisions. The instrument has received widespread use in recent years not only in the typical samples of high-school and college students faced with occupational choices but with personnel already on the job who either voluntarily or involuntarily face prospects of career changes.

The theory itself assumes that most people can be classified into one of six general types which reflects their general orientation toward careers. The six types are outlined in Figure 13.6. Keep in mind that, as with any personality-type labeling system, there is a lot of variance within any given type. Thus, the labels are only useful to give a general impression; the exact mix varies from person to person. Also, often the specific descriptors within a category are not precise. They are meant only to provide a general impression of the types of traits that make up the category.

In addition to the person types, Holland's

FIGURE 13.6 Some sample descriptions of persons and environments according to Holland's theory.

TYPE	PERSON CHARACTERISTICS	ENVIRONMENT CHARACTERISTICS
Realistic	Aggressive Mechanically oriented Practical minded Physically strong Conventionally masculine Acts out problems Avoids interpersonal tasks Prefers concrete to abstract tasks	Requires explicit, concrete, physical tasks Outdoors Needs immediate behavior Needs immediate reinforcement Makes low interpersonal demands
Investigative	Think through problems Scientifically inclined Inventive Precise Achieving Shy Radical	Requires thought and creativity Task-idea oriented Makes minimum social demands Requires laboratory equipment but not high physical demands
Artistic	Original Asocial Dislike structure More conventionally feminine Emotional	Interprets and modifies human behavior Has ambiguous standards of excellence Requires intense involvement for long periods of time Works in isolation
Social	Responsible Humanistic Accepting of conventionally feminine impulses Interpersonally skilled Avoids intellectual problem solving	Interprets as well as modifies human behavior Requires high communications Helps others Emphasizes prestige Delays reinforcement
Enterprising	Verbally skilled Power and status oriented	Needs verbal responses Fulfills supervisory roles Needs persuasion Needs management behaviors
Conventional	Prefers structure High self-control Strong identification with power and status	Systematic, routine Concrete Makes minimal physical demands Indoors Makes low interpersonal demands

theory assumes that some types of job environments match these person types. These are also described in Figure 13.6. Given these two conditions, people and job conditions, the final assumption is that people search their environments for jobs that allow them to use their skills and abilities, to express their attitudes and values, and to perform work roles that agree with their general orientations toward work and people at work.

Much of the research on the theory uses the SDS to assess individual characteristics and then compares the nature of the people on jobs to the characteristics of the jobs themselves. Samples of men and women without college degrees working in transportation-related jobs (Benniger & Walsh, 1980), black women with college degrees (Bingham & Walsh, 1978), and employees representing five of Holland's six job types (Mount & Muchinsky, 1978) all tend to support the congruency between person and job types suggested by Holland.

The implication of the acceptance of the congruency hypothesis for occupations is that individuals should seek to develop careers that are congruent with their orientations. The SDS does seem to be a useful diagnostic instrument for those seeking additional information to aid in career-related choices.

CAREER DEVELOPMENT

Concern for career development is predicated on the assumption that an individual's career need not be some haphazard path from one job to another but that it can be planned and organized so that positions build on previous experience. A second assumption is that some changes can be made in jobs and/or people so that a more orderly career progression can be accomplished.

Three sets of information are necessary for career development. First it must be possible to assess the characteristics of people. Second, jobs must be described and analyzed in such a way that not only are they understood but so are their relationships with other jobs. The latter requires the use of job analyses, the clustering of jobs into job families, and the knowledge of the flow of people through an organization. The first two of these topics were discussed in Chapter 4, and the last was discussed under human-resource management in Chapter 8. The purpose of all of this information for career development is to be better able to assign positions to individuals

that will contribute to the growth and development of their careers. A third set of information necessary for career development is knowledge about the possibility of changing individuals through training or other types of experience in order to influence the directions of their careers.

Assuming the existence of these three sets of information, career-development practices are directed toward assessing individual characteristics, comparing these to job characteristics, impacting upon the assignment of individuals with career objectives in mind, and training and developing individuals so that they qualify for positions that fit into their career objectives. Although there is no difference between placement or career development for career-development purposes than for selection or human-resource management purposes, there is a difference in emphasis. The focus of career development is upon the individual. Placement and training are approached from the standpoint of their value to the person rather than to the effective functioning of the organization. The individual versus organizational perspectives are not necessarily in conflict, but the differences in orientation are likely to lead to different emphases at times.

There is a growing awareness of the need for career development in organizations. Corporations have specific career-development programs. These consist of career counseling and guidance, and assessment using such tools as assessment centers and such career/occupational assessment instruments as the SDS. Finally, training for development and for career shifts is part of career development. Unfortunately, in spite of the importance of such training for established employees, there is very little research in this area (Super & Hall, 1978). Such training does exist, but it is often unsystematic and rarely reported to a larger audience outside the organization. Published literature that does exist contains an overrepresentation of atypical employees compared to typical ones, primarily because of government support for programs designed to aid disadvantaged workers. A sample of some research is discussed next.

Rehabilitation Training

Robinault and Weisinger (1973) developed a series of audio tapes for disabled counsellees and compared those who used the tapes to those who did not. They found gains in decision-making, insightfulness, and general interpersonal growth for those who used the tapes, but not for those who did not. They recommended that the tapes be used as a supplement, not a substitute for vocational counseling with disabled workers.

Feldman and Marinelli (1975) addressed the problem of improving the vocational maturity of inmates at Massachusetts correctional institutions. Three groups were established: trained, attention but no training, and control. Results showed that the trained group scored significantly higher on the Vocational Development Inventory than did either of the other groups. Training consisted of providing career-planning experience, discussing test scores on career planning, and discussing realistic career opportunities with the participants.

Training for the Hard-Core Unemployed

A major national concern has been with those workers who are chronically unemployed due to a lack of education, low-level work skills, and negative or inappropriate attitudes and beliefs related to work. Several large-scale programs have been developed in an attempt to provide these individuals with the capacity to hold a job. Perhaps the best known of these are programs resulting from the Comprehensive Employment and Training Act (CETA) and from the National Alliance of Businessmen's Job Opportunities in the Business Sector (JOBS). The success of these programs has been very limited. For example, one study by Goodale (1973) compared an experimental group of 110 people participating in a JOBS program with a sample of employees and another of students in terms of changes in work values over an 8-week time period during the training. The two comparison groups, of course, received no training. The change in work values was no different for the group in training than for the two comparison groups, although, Goodale points out, the focus of the training was more on skills than on work values.

Triandis, Feldman, and Welde (1974) suggested that part of the problem with training hard-core unemployed may have been the failure of trainers to understand the subcultures of the trainees. Indirect support for this conclusion is that supervisors who showed support and understanding of subordinates who were selected from the ranks of the hard-core unemployed had lower turnover among these employees than did supervisors less supportive of the individuals (Beatty, 1974).

Career Flexibility

If changes are to occur in individuals' career plans, the persons themselves must be open to change. Unfortunately, experience with technological changes or shifts in economic conditions indicate that people are very reluctant to change careers even when the jobs they hold are no longer in demand. Therefore, from the standpoint of career development, it would be valuable to understand why some people are more open to change than others.

Morrison (1977) compared two groups of managers in the middle of their careers—one of which he labeled *adaptive* and the other *nonadaptive*. Adaptive managers performed better than nonadaptive ones on timed tests of mental ability but not on untimed ones. Adaptive managers continually engaged in more exploratory behavior than did nonadaptive ones. It was as if adaptive managers never really completed the exploratory phase of their development to the degree that the nonadaptive ones did. Remaining in the exploratory phase was functional for them if and when change was required.

Kaufman (1974), who reviewed the literature on obsolescence among professionals, identified three personal factors associated with low obsolescence in midcareer: high intellectual ability, high self-motivation, and personal flexibility. Kaufman concluded that obsolescence might be reduced if organizations were to select for long-term needs, assess and test individual characteristics looking for the three just mentioned, and counsel persons with respect to career needs. Given the rather rapid rate of change at present and the fundamental changes that are being made in the operation of many organizational jobs as computers play larger and larger roles in all aspects of organizational functioning, the need to plan for reducing obsolescence through career development seems more important now than ever.

CAREER MOTIVATION

London (1983) suggested that knowledge about work motivation in general could be directed toward understanding behaviors that are specifically related to a subset of behaviors important for careers. These include searching for and accepting a job, deciding to stay with an organization (often referred to as commitment to the organization), revising one's career plans, seeking training and new job experiences, and setting and trying to accomplish career goals. Specifically, London (1983) defined career motivation as ". . . the set of individual characteristics and associated career decisions and behaviors that reflect the person's career identity, insight into factors affecting his or her career, and resilience in the face of unfavorable career conditions" (p. 620).

The most interesting contribution of London's discussion of career motivation is the development of three variables—career identity, career insight, and career resilience—that are considered to be the primary factors that determine career motivation. All three are strongly influenced by personal experiences both on and off the job.

Career identity is the extent to which one's career is central to one's self-identity. We have discussed this notion earlier in the chapter when we described Hall's work. London (1983) sees career identity as composed of two general sets of factors; one deals with the extent to which the person is involved in the type of work that he or she does and the other with what London calls upward mobility. The latter includes the extent to which the person desires advancement, recognition, dominance, and money. Furthermore, London speculates that those who are very conscious of upward-mobility issues find delayed gratification difficult; they seek to be on jobs and to behave in a manner that provides them with advancement, recognition, and other rewards rather quickly after having accomplished something.

Career insight, according to London, is the extent to which the person accurately appraises his or her own ability and is able to select career goals and objectives that are realistic in light of personal limitations.

Finally, career resilience is the extent to which the person is able to cope with situations that are less than optimal for his or her career. Over the long haul of a career everyone is going to experience some times when conditions are not good for the development or even the maintenance of a given career. Perhaps the person happens to have a new supervisor whose behaviors thwart the careers of those around him or her. The scarcity of resources can mean that projects that everyone agrees really do need to be done must be put off for some time. All kinds of events can temporarily block career opportunities at any given time. Career resilience deals with the extent to which the person can effectively handle these disruptions, either by realizing that they are temporary and therefore being willing to "wait them out" while doing one's best under the circumstances or by rationally judging that the situation must be changed and then making the changes in a constructive fashion.

From an applied standpoint the contribution of London's career motivation is the identification of conditions that are likely to impact on career identification, insight, and resilience. Company policies and practices, leadership, group cohesiveness, career-development programs, compensation systems, and many other important aspects of organizational life can all be considered in terms of their impact on each of the three major factors in career motivation. London (1983) begins this process by suggesting several factors that influence each of the three although he provides no data to actually test the extent to which his propositions are or are not correct. Nevertheless, the perspective offered by this view of career motivation should be useful for guiding research and the structuring of career-development practices in the future.

OTHER CAREER-RELATED TOPICS

Transfers

In this day of large corporations with multiple divisions, plants, and offices widely distributed throughout the country and the world, remaining with the same corporation and advancing to positions of higher authority over the course of a career usually means being moved to several different locations. It has become very unlikely for individuals—especially managerial or professional personnel—to complete their entire careers while

residing in the same communities the entire time. Therefore, there is considerable interest in the effects of relocating or transferring personnel. This is of interest from the standpoint of understanding how to best meet staffing needs that may involve relocating individuals. It is perhaps even more important from individual employees' perspectives because transfers are often described as traumatic side-effects of our mobile society.

In an interesting study, Brett (1982) compared transferred employees and their families to samples of individuals who had not been transferred. The names of 3000 employees who had one or more transfers were obtained from ten large corporations. From this list 500 employees were selected and approximately 70% of these agreed to participate. The employees and their spouses each completed a survey questionnaire that addressed issues of satisfaction with work and nonwork issues, quality of friendships, adjustment of children, quality of family life, and physical health. This group's responses were compared to those of three other samples of persons who had not been transferred. The most interesting general conclusion from this research was that it refuted many commonly held beliefs about the negative effects of transfers. Other than less satisfaction with social relationships among those who had been transferred compared to those who had not been, differences that existed between the groups tended to favor the transferred group. For example, the transfers reported significantly fewer negative physical conditions—such as shortness of breath, dizziness, nightmares, and weight loss—than those who were not transferred. (The reverse was true for headaches, however.) The direction of effects tended to be the same for beliefs in the degree to which their lives were interesting, satisfaction with marriage and family life, and satisfaction with both intrinsic and extrinsic factors at work. The major differences that did exist between transferred families and the others related to friendship; in comparison to the others, both men and women in the mobile sample were less satisfied with opportunities to make friends at work, at nonwork activities, among neighbors, and in the community. Nevertheless, the data do raise serious doubts about the extent to which transfers are likely to have detrimental effects, either on those who are transferred or on their families. It appears that the popular press is overstating the degree to which individuals suffer as a result of being transferred.

Dual-Career Couples

As a result of the ever-increasing number of women who are pursuing full-time employment in careers that had, until recently, been limited primarily to men, there are large numbers of couples in which both people are equally committed to their own careers. This relatively recent phenomenon has major implications for both the development of careers and the structure of family relationships. It has impacted on job definitions, transfers, recruiting, child-care facilities, the family roles of men and women, and many other important issues both on and off the job. Unfortunately, our knowledge about dual careers is limited. The best-documented work on the subject has been done by Francine and Douglas Tim Hall (Hall & Hall, 1978, 1979). This work relies heavily upon self-reports from surveys and interviews with dual-career couples. Although these data are appropriate for the early stages of attempting to understand a recent social trend, and although they do provide advice for those experiencing the pressures of maintaining dual-career relationships, there is a strong need to go beyond this stage and gain a deeper understanding of the issues involved in dual careers. We have not yet gone very far beyond recognizing the unique difficulties of dual careers and recognizing that more must be provided in the near future to deal with this phenomenon.

DISCUSSION

As a field, industrial-organizational psychology is sometimes accused of being light on theory and heavy on practice; at times the practice procedures are developed with insufficient thought given to why people behave as they do or why the practices do or do not work. Careers and career development are topics that have a good mix of theory and practice. There is considerable theoretical development of the socialization process and its relationship to careers. Well-developed practices also exist for vocational counseling, training, and evaluating career progress and career needs. In the area of transfers and dual-career couples, however, there is a need for more theory development and more research, and the establishment of practices and policies consistent with the research findings to foster the career development of people at work.

REFERENCES

Anderson, J. C., Milkovich, G. T., & Tsui, A. (1981). A model of intra-organizational mobility. *Academy of Management Review, 6,* 529–538.

Beatty, R. W. (1974). Supervisory behavior related to job success of hardcore unemployed over a two-year period. *Journal of Applied Psychology, 59,* 38–42.

Benninger, W. B., & Walsh, W. B. (1980). Holland's theory and non-college degreed working men and women. *Journal of Vocational Behavior, 17,* 81–88.

Berlew, D. E., & Hall, D. T. (1966). The socialization of managers: Effects of expectations on performance. *Administrative Science Quarterly, 11,* 207–223.

Bingham, R. F., & Walsh, W. B. (1978). Concurrent validity of Holland's theory for college degreed black working women. *Journal of Vocational Behavior, 15,* 141–147.

Bray, D. W., Campbell, R. J., & Grant, D. L. (1974). *Formative years in business: A long-term AT&T study of managerial lives.* New York: Wiley.

Bray, D. W., & Grant, D. L. (1966). The assessment center in the measurement of potential for business management. *Psychological Monographs, 80*(17, Whole No. 625).

Brett, J. M. (1982). Job transfer and well being. *Journal of Applied Psychology, 67,* 450–463.

Crites, J. O. (1973). *The career maturity inventory.* Monterey, Calif.: McGraw-Hill.

Dodd, W. E. (August 1971). *Will management assessment centers insure selection of the same old types?* Paper presented at the 79th Annual Convention of the American Psychological Association, Washington, D.C.

Dugoni, B. L., & Ilgen, D. R. (1981). Realistic job previews and adjustment of new employees. *Academy of Management Journal, 24,* 579–591.

Dunnette, M. D., Arvey, R. D., & Banas, P. A. (May/June 1973). Why do they leave? *Personnel,* 25–39.

Feldman, D. C. (1981). The multiple socialization of organization members. *Academy of Management Review, 6,* 309–318.

Feldman, H. S., Marinelli, R. P. (1975). Career planning for prison inmates. *Vocational Guidance Quarterly, 23,* 358–362.

Finkle, R. B., & Jones, W. S. (1970). *Assessing corporate talent: A key to managerial manpower planning.* New York: Wiley-Interscience.

Goodale, J. G. (1973). Effects of personal background and training on work values of the hardcore unemployed. *Journal of Applied Psychology, 57,* 1–9.

Hall, D. T. (1976). *Careers in organizations.* Santa Monica, Calif.: Goodyear.

Hall, F. S., & Hall, D. T. (Spring, 1978). Dual career couples—How do couples and companies cope with the problems? *Organizational Dynamics,* 57–77.

Hall, F. S., & Hall, D. T. (1979). *The two-career couple.* Reading, Mass.: Addison-Wesley.

Hall, D. T., & Schneider, B. (1973). *Organizational climates and careers: The work lives of priests.* New York: Academic Press.

Holland, J. L. (1966). A psychological classification scheme for vocations and major fields. *Journal of Counseling Psychology, 13,* 278–288.

Holland, J. L. (1976). Vocational preference. In M. D. Dunnette (Ed.), *Handbook of industrial and organizational psychology.* Chicago: Rand McNally.

Ilgen, D. R., & Seely, W. (1974). Realistic expectations as an aid in reducing voluntary resignations. *Journal of Applied Psychology, 59,* 452–455.

Ilgen, D. R., & Weiss, H. M. (in press). *Organizational behavior: A psychological approach.* Englewood Cliffs, N.J.: Prentice-Hall.

Katz, D., & Kahn, R. L. (1978). *The social psychology of organizations* (2nd ed.). New York: McGraw-Hill.

Kaufman, H. G. (1974). Relationship of early work challenge to job performance, professional contributions, and competence of engineers. *Journal of Applied Psychology, 59,* 377–379.

Klimoski, R. J., & Strickland, W. J. (1977). Assessment centers: Valid or merely prescient? *Personnel Psychology, 30,* 353–363.

Kraut, A. I., & Scott, G. J. (1972). Validity of an operational management assessment program. *Journal of Applied Psychology, 56,* 124–129.

Levinson, D. J. (1978). *The seasons in a man's life.* New York: Knopf.

London, M. (1983). Toward a theory of career motivation. *Academy of Management Review, 8,* 620–630.

Louis, M. R. (1980). Surprise and sense-making: What newcomers experience in entering unfamiliar organizational settings. *Administrative Science Quarterly, 25,* 367–393.

Macedonia, R. M. (1969). *Expectation, press, and survival.* Unpublished dissertation, New York University.

Miner, J. B., & Smith, N. R. (1982). Decline and stabilization of managerial motivation over a twenty-year period. *Journal of Applied Psychology, 67,* 297–305.

Mitchell, J. O. (1975). Assessment center validity: A longitudinal study. *Journal of Applied Psychology, 60,* 573–579.

Mount, M., & Muchinsky, P. M. (1978). Concurrent validation of Holland's hexagonal model occupational workers. *Journal of Vocational Behavior, 13,* 348–354.

Morrison, R. F. (1977). Career adaptivity: The effective adaptation of managers to changing role demands. *Journal of Applied Psychology, 62,* 342–351.

Moses, J. L. (1972). Assessment center performance and management progress. *Studies in Personnel Psychology, 4,* 7–12.

Porter, L. W., Lawler, E. E., III., & Hackman, J. R. (1975). *Behavior in organizations.* New York: McGraw-Hill.

Reilly, R. R., Brown, B., Blood, M. R., & Malatesta, C. Z. (1981). Effects of realistic job previews: A study and discussion of the literature. *Personnel Psychology, 34,* 823–834.

Robinault, I. P., & Weisinger, M. (1973). Leaderless groups: A tape cassette technique of vocational education. *Rehabilitation Literature, 34,* 80–84.

Rosow, M., & Kerr, C. (Eds.) (1979). *Work in America: The decade ahead.* New York: Van Nostrand Reinhold.

Rychlak, J. F. (1974). Life themes: Enlargers and enfolders. In D. W. Bray, R. J. Campbell, & D. L. Grant (Eds.). *Formative years in business: A long-term AT&T study of managerial lives.* New York: Wiley.

Rychlak, J. F. (1982). *Personality and life-style of young male managers.* New York: Academic Press.

Sackett, P. R., & Dreher, G. F. (1982). Constructs and assessment center dimensions: Some troubling empirical findings. *Journal of Applied Psychology, 67,* 401–410.

Sackett, P. R., & Wilson, M. A. Factors affecting the judgment process in managerial assessment centers. *Journal of Applied Psychology, 67,* 10–17.

Schein, E. H. (1978). *Career dynamics: Matching individual and organization needs.* Reading, Mass.: Addison-Wesley.

Super, D. E., & Hall, D. T. (1978). Career development: Exploration and planning. In M. R. Rosenweig & L. W. Porter (Eds.), *Annual review of psychology* (Vol. 29). Palo Alto, LA: Annual Reviews, Inc.

Taylor, M. S. (1981). The motivational effects of task challenge: A laboratory investigation. *Organizational Behavior and Human Performance, 27,* 255–278.

Thornton, G. C., & Byham, W. C. (1982). *Assessment center and managerial performance.* New York: Academic Press.

Triandis, H. C., Feldman, J. M., & Welden, D. E. (1974). Designing pre-employment training for the hard to employ: A cross-cultural psychological approach. *Journal of Applied Psychology, 59,* 687–693.

Tziner, A., & Shimon, D. (1982). Validity of an assessment center for identifying future female officers in the military. *Journal of Applied Psychology, 67,* 728–736.

Van Maanen, J., & Schein, E. H. (1979). Toward a theory of organizational socialization. In B. M. Staw (Ed.), *Research in organizational behavior* (Vol. 1). Greenwich, Ct.: JAI Press.

Vardi, Y. (1980). Organizational career mobility: An integrative model. *Academy of Management Journal, 5,* 341–356.

Wanous, J. P. (1973). Effects of a realistic job preview on job acceptance, job attitudes, and job survival. *Journal of Applied Psychology, 58,* 327–332.

Weitz, J. (1956). Job expectancy and job survival. *Journal of Applied Psychology, 40,* 245–247.

14

Work Motivation

Why do people work? Work is so pervasive in our society that almost all people wrestle with this question at some time during their lives. If they have not asked it about others, they at least have wondered about their own work behavior.

Over a 7-year period, Studs Terkel interviewed hundreds of workers about their work. His book *Working* (Terkel, 1972) is a fascinating glimpse of what people see in their work. Figure 14.1 has some brief excerpts from the book. Reading through these, one immediately is struck by their diversity. People work for *many* reasons. Some work only for money; some work because they love what they are doing; others work because of the status they receive. The list goes on and on.

ABILITY VERSUS MOTIVATION

Understanding why people work is the domain of work motivation. To clarify what is meant by motivation let us start with an observed behavior and work backwards to possible causes of it. Assume that we have just observed a bank teller who has handled approximately 300 transactions a day for 5 days and, at the end of each day, his or her transactions check out perfectly the first time they are totaled. Two general classes of explanatory concepts are usually used to describe behaviors such as this. The first is *ability*. Abilities represent the individual's capability to handle the job at a certain time. For a teller, the ability to add and subtract as well as to operate the equipment for entering transactions certainly would be critical to being able to perform as well as was indicated. The abilities represent certain minimum conditions necessary for completion of the work. In a sense, we can think of them as the "can do" factors associated with the behavior. They are necessary but not sufficient precursors of the behavior.

The second set of explanatory concepts for

FIGURE 14.1 Selected quotes from Studs Terkel's *Working* (1972).

Hots Michaels, player at piano bar in New York hotel

". . . because I enjoy the action, I enjoy people. If I were suddenly to inherit four million dollars, I guarantee you I'd be playin' piano, either here or at some other place. I can't explain why. I would miss the flow of people in and out."

Cathleen Moran, nurse's aid

"I really don't know if I mind the work as much as you always have to work with people, and that drives me nuts. I don't mind emptying the bed pan, what's in it, blood, none of that bothers me at all. Dealing with people is what I don't like. It just makes everything else blah."

Nora Watson, editor

"Jobs are not big enough for people. It's not just the assembly line worker whose job is too small for his spirit, you know? A job like mine, if you really put your spirit into it, you would sabotage immediately. You don't dare. So you absent your spirit from it. My mind has been divorced from my job, except as a source of income, it's really absurd."

Elmer Ruiz, gravedigger

"Not anybody can be a gravedigger. You can dig a hole any way they come. A gravedigger, you have to make a neat job. I had a fella once, he wanted to see a grave. He was a fella that digged sewers. He was impressed when he seen me diggin' this grave—how square and how perfect it was. A human body is goin' into this grave. That's why you need skill when you're gonna dig a grave . . . I start early, about seven o'clock in the morning, and I have the part cleaned before the funeral. We have two funerals for tomorrow, eleven and one o'clock. That's my life . . .

I enjoy it very much, especially in summer. I don't think any job inside a factory or an office is so nice. You have the air all day and it's just beautiful. The smell of the grass when its cut, it's just fantastic. Winter goes so fast sometimes you just don't feel it."

the behavior is often labeled *motivation*. Motivation is the individual's *desire* to show the behavior and might be thought of as the "will do" factors influencing the display of work-related behaviors. Knowing that a teller can perform arithmetic operations flawlessly and can operate the machines by no means insures that he or she will perform as well as the teller in our example. He or she must want to perform accurately and efficiently and direct his or her effort toward doing a good job.

DEFINITION OF WORK MOTIVATION

In their text entitled *Motivation and Work Behavior* Steers and Porter (1983) identified three major components of motivation. The first is an *energizing* component. This is the force or drive present in an organism which leads to some behavior. Second, there is some *directing* function that guides the behavior in a particular direction. For example, for the person who is hungry, behaviors are likely to be directed toward obtaining food. Finally, motivation is *maintaining* or *sustaining* behavior once it has occurred. The latter is particularly important to work settings in which job incumbents once hired and placed on jobs are expected to maintain high attendance, good performance, and the like, as long as they remain with the organization.

Emphasizing these three factors, work motivation is defined as *conditions which influence the arousal, direction, and maintenance of behaviors relevant in work settings.* The inclusion of behaviors *relevant* to work settings emphasizes that not all behaviors at work are of interest. In the past, relevant behaviors were defined as productivity-oriented activities—absenteeism, turnover, and performance. Yet, other behaviors also are important, such as political maneuvering of executives for attractive positions in the organization or scientists' conflict and rivalry for scientific information. Behaviors such as leaning back in one's chair or writing with the left versus the right hand are irrelevant to most jobs and, therefore, are not of interest.

PROBLEMS FACING THE UNDERSTANDING OF WORK BEHAVIOR

To limit our search for reasons for work behavior to those labeled motivational influences would seem to simplify the task of understanding people's behavior. Unfortunately, it does not. At least four factors complicate our understanding of work motivation. The first has already been mentioned: the *diversity of reasons* for which people work. The others need to be examined.

A second stumbling block in understanding work behavior is that *stereotypes* abound. Everyone has his or her pet theory for why people do what they do on the job. Managers and workers alike have their own views and, without hesitation, can cite numerous examples which "prove" their "theory." Two of these "theories" are worth noting because they are so pervasive. The first assumes that motivation to work is a basic human characteristic. Some have it; some do not. Perhaps more accurately, it should be said, a few ("like me") have it and most do not. Motivation, according to this view, is a personal trait just as is height or weight. Since it is part of the person, individuals who hold this view tend to feel that having high work motivation on the job is a matter of finding the right people—those who possess this trait. We label this view the "internal state" view of motivation.

Another widely accepted stereotype of why people work emphasizes the conditions of the work environment and the job. Stress is placed upon pay, supervision, working conditions, geography of the area, and so on. It can be considered "carrot and stick" motivation. The emphasis is on "external states" which are assumed to influence most individuals, regardless of their personal orientations.

These two stereotypic points of view, held to various degrees by managers and workers, have some interesting twists. For example, people tend to attribute good performance to internal states if it is their own performance more often than if it is someone else's performance. Also, on some jobs, it is expected that people will be motivated by internal states more than by external conditions, and on other jobs the reverse is true. It is assumed, for instance, that college professors work because they love their work and that grave diggers work only because they need the money. Complaints among college professors about pay, teaching loads, class size, and publication pressures, and statements such as the one in Figure 14.1 from the grave digger vividly illustrate the fallacies of such theories. Nevertheless, these "theories" of motivation are well entrenched and cannot be ignored.

A third factor that complicates understanding why people behave the way they do is that there are *different reasons for behaviors at different times*. For example, the bank teller introduced earlier may have worked very hard to do well when he or she first took the job, in order to avoid being reprimanded by the supervisor and to improve his or her chances for promotion. After having done well during several months on the job, it would probably be apparent to the teller that he or she was very well respected by the supervisor and that his or her position was quite secure. At the same time, it may be equally apparent that there is no chance for any promotion in the job. Does this mean that the teller's performance will drop off? Perhaps, but also, perhaps not. In most banks, at the end of the work day, tellers must stay at their work areas until their daily transactions balance. When their records balance they may go home. The teller, in this case, may maintain high performance simply in order to be able to leave soon after the bank closes. The reasons for the same observed behavior may have changed.

Finally, work motivation is complicated because there are many *different behaviors* in the work setting that are of interest. Number of units produced per hour, attendance, quitting, drinking on the job, listening to a supervisor, taking night school courses, accidents, and so forth all are types of work behaviors considered relevant for various jobs. The causes or reasons for these behaviors may be very different. Their diversity attests to the difficulty of understanding work motivation.

APPROACH TO MOTIVATION

Vroom (1964) and others (for example, Naylor, Pritchard, & Ilgen, 1980) correctly concluded that work motivation does not differ extensively from other kinds of motivation. The focus is limited only because the subset of behaviors of interest are those relevant to

a work environment. Yet, these are still behaviors, and, if we can understand the reasons for behaviors in general, we shall be able to understand work behavior in particular.

The remainder of this discussion concentrates first on theories of work motivation. Some theories apply to all behavior, not just to work behavior. Others are adaptations of general theories of human motivation to behavior at work. In either case, the emphasis of the following section is not on specific applications of techniques to improve work performance, but rather on understanding why people do what they do in work settings. Following the theoretical views, we turn to practices within organizational settings which have motivational emphases. These practices either explicitly or implicitly have their roots in one or more of the theoretical positions.

THEORIES OF WORK MOTIVATION

The theoretical treatment of work motivation was a latecomer to the study of work behavior. Before the mid-1950s it was generally assumed that people worked for either economic or social reasons. Personnel practices and policies reflected these assumptions. Today the situation has changed. There now are several theories which have substantial impact on the way work behavior is conceived. In his 1979 chapter for the *Annual Review of Psychology*, Mitchell found that almost 25% of the articles on behavior in organizations were concerned with motivation. The proportion remains about the same today.

The upsurge of theoretical interest is both a blessing and a curse. On the one hand, the theoretical orientations do offer a better understanding of work behavior and an appreciation for its complexity. On the other hand, several very diverse theoretical orientations have evolved. Ideally, we would offer an integration and evaluation of all theories that lead to a single, accepted position on work motivation. Unfortunately, such a definitive conclusion is beyond the knowledge of work motivation at the present time. Several theoretical positions do provide some useful insights into why people behave as they do in work settings. With a good knowledge of the theories that do exist and the support or lack of support for them, intelligent decisions can be made about the design of jobs and the development of personnel practices to facilitate desirable job behaviors.

Need Theories

Motivational theories which emphasize needs posit the existence of some internal state of the individual, labeled a need or a motive. This internal state is usually described in terms of the conditions that will satisfy the need. Thus, a need for food is identified by the fact that individuals will seek out objects classified as food when they are hungry. The need for food, or hunger, is inferred from the behaviors of seeking food. Let us now describe several need theories relevant to work motivation.

Need hierarchy theory. Perhaps the most widely discussed theory of motivation is Maslow's (1954, 1970). Although Maslow did not develop the theory specifically for work motivation, the implications of the theory for work were quickly recognized and received extensive attention (see, for example, Porter, 1962).

Maslow proposed that sound motivational theory assumes that people are continuously in a motivational state, but that the nature of the motivation is fluctuating and complex. In addition, human beings seldom reach a state of complete satisfaction except for a short time; as one need or desire becomes satisfied, another rises to take its place. This never-ending sequence produces a hierarchy of needs. The theory has two goals. First, it is concerned with identifying the needs, which are the basis of motivation. These needs provide the content of the theory. The second goal is to explain how the needs are related to each other.

Maslow proposed that the needs are ordered in a hierarchical fashion with all needs lower in the hierarchy having *prepotence* over those higher. As lower needs are satisfied, the individual shifts his or her concern to higher-order needs. The hierarchy of needs is often misconstrued to mean that the lower level needs have to be satisfied before higher-order needs begin to operate. Maslow clarified this misinterpretation (Maslow, 1970); he stated that lower-order needs are, in general, satisfied to a greater extent than are higher-order ones. This did not preclude the possibility of more than one need operating at a time. Maslow also recognized individual exceptions to the theory—for example, individuals who would give up everything, including life, for their ideals (Locke, 1976).

Some modifications of Maslow's original categories (especially of labels) were made by McGregor (1957, 1960). Following are some brief descriptions of these categories.

Physiological needs are taken as the starting point and are conceived to be the most prepotent. These include the basic needs for food, water, and the like. These needs cannot be ignored for long and must be met before all others. To the person in a state of virtual starvation or water deprivation, matters other than food or water are of little concern.

Once the physiological needs are relatively well met, a new set of needs, categorized generally as *safety needs*, emerges. These are concerned with protection against danger, threat, and deprivation. Protection against physical dangers is of less consequence now, in our civilization, than it was in the past. On the other hand, in an industrial society the safety needs may be important to the dependent relationship between employees and employers. As pointed out by McGregor, the safety needs may serve as motivators in such circumstances as arbitrary management actions, behavior which arouses uncertainty of continued employment, and unpredictable administration of policy.

Once the physiological and safety needs are reasonably well fulfilled, the *social needs* become important motivators of behavior. These include needs for belonging, for association, for love, for acceptance by one's fellows, and for giving and receiving friendship.

Next in the hierarchy are the *ego needs*. McGregor distinguished two kinds: (1) those needs that relate to one's self-esteem—needs for self-confidence, for achievement, for competence, for knowledge; and (2) those that relate to one's reputation—needs for status, for recognition, for appreciation, for the deserved respect of one's peers. In contrast with the lower needs, the ego needs are seldom fully satisfied. These needs usually do not become dominant until the lower needs have been fulfilled.

Highest among the needs is that of self-fulfillment or *self-actualization*—the need for realizing one's own potentialities and for continual self-development. This need is seldom fully met by human beings.

Keeping constantly in mind that the just-described hierarchy represents the *general* order of relative potency of the various needs and that it does not apply invariably to all individuals, remember that Maslow (1970) believed that the hierarchy was characterized by some supporting aspects or features, a few of which are given here:

1. The higher needs are a later evolutionary development.
2. The higher the need, and the less imperative it is for sheer survival, the longer gratification can be postponed, and the easier it is for the need to disappear permanently.
3. Living at the higher need level means greater biological efficiency, greater longevity, less disease, better sleep, better appetite, and so forth.
4. Higher needs are less urgent, subjectively.
5. Higher-need gratification produces more desirable subjective results—that is, more profound happiness, serenity, and richness of the inner life.
6. Pursuit and gratification of higher needs represent a general trend toward good health.
7. Higher needs require better outside conditions (economic, educational, etc.) to make them possible.
8. Satisfaction of higher needs is closer to self-actualization than is the satisfaction of lower needs.

Maslow suggested that the various need levels are interdependent and overlapping, and that each higher-level need emerges before the lower-level need has been completely satisfied. In addition, he noted that individuals may reorder the needs. The latter obviously violates a strict adherence to the hierarchy.

Although widely accepted because of its intuitive appeal, the empirical support for the theory is less than impressive. For many years supposed tests of the theory relied upon cross-sectional data. Comparisons among work groups—such as workers versus managers—generally found that managers reported better satisfied lower-order needs and more concern for higher-order needs than workers did. These data were generally supportive of Maslow's position. However, such comparisons across groups do not represent strong tests of the theory. To adequately test it, longitudinal research must demonstrate that the same individual progresses through the hierarchy changing from one need level to the next as lower needs are satisfied. Two studies in which changes over time were addressed provided no support for the theory. Hall and Nougaim (1968) followed AT&T executives over several years and hypothesized that as a need became satisfied its importance should drop, according to Maslow's theory. In fact, just the opposite occurred for the executives; the more satisfied they were with a particular need, the more important it was seen to be. Similar findings by Lawler and Suttle (1972) using causal correlational analyses must lead us to conclude that the hierarchical nature of the theory simply does not hold.

In addition, Miner and Dachler (1973) concluded from their review that there is no support for the contention that Maslow's list of five needs is somehow inherent in or basic to humans. Factor-analytic research, as well as other research, fails to reproduce a set of five and only five needs that match Maslow's set. Finally, Locke criticized the theory on logical grounds. The most telling of his criticisms is that it is impossible to find an intelligible definition of self-actualization. Locke (1976) said:

For example, to "become more and more what one is" is self-contradictory. To become "everything one is capable of becoming" is impossible if taken literally, since every person is metaphysically capable of becoming almost an unlimited number of things. A person who tried to become self-actualized in this sense would probably become neurotic due to unsolvable conflicts among the thousands of choices open to him (p. 1308).

ERG theory. Alderfer (1969, 1972) offered an alternative theory closely related to Maslow's that addresses some but not all of the criticisms raised. He termed his the *Existence, Relatedness, Growth (ERG)* theory. The name reflects the three basic needs postulated by the theory:

1. *Existence needs:* These needs concern the physical existence of the organism. They include basics such as food, clothing, and shelter and the means provided by work organizations to attain these factors—for example, pay, fringe benefits, safe working conditions, and job security.
2. *Relatedness needs:* These are the interpersonal needs that are satisfied through interactions with others both on and off the job.
3. *Growth needs:* These are personal-development and improvement needs. They are met by developing whatever abilities and capabilities are important to the individual.

According to Campbell and Pritchard (1976) Alderfer's definition is "as slippery as ever and . . . represents no major conceptual breakthrough" (p. 77) for growth needs. A direct comparison of Maslow's needs to Alderfer's is presented in Figure 14.2.

Although Alderfer's list of needs may be neither more complete nor more conceptually clear than Maslow's, the processes he proposed do offer some definite improvements. First of all, ERG theory places less emphasis on the hierarchical order. More than one need may operate at one time, and satisfaction of a need may or may not lead to a progression to the next higher need.

The second major change in orientation is that frustration of higher needs may lead to *regression,* with an increased concern for lower-level needs rather than, as Maslow predicted, continued efforts to satisfy the frustrated need. The regression effect has some

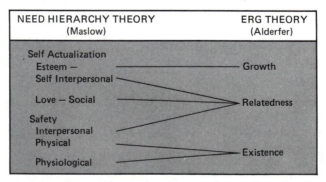

FIGURE 14.2 A comparison of Maslow's needs to those of Alderfer.

particularly interesting ramifications for work behavior. Alderfer (1969) suggested that if relatedness needs are frustrated and if individuals do not feel that they are able to make the close interpersonal associations they need from their jobs, rather than trying to obtain these factors, they may become more concerned with meeting their existence needs. Therefore, they may show more concern for salary, working conditions, vacations, and other fringe benefits as a result of frustrated social needs. Alderfer wondered if perhaps the high concentration of existence issues in union contracts may be due, in part, to frustrated social needs which have led to the regression effect. His original data suggested such an effect but, to our knowledge, this interesting hypothesis has not been properly tested to date.

A final process difference in ERG theory is the statement that some needs, specifically relatedness and growth, may *increase* in strength when individuals have been presented with relatively high levels of conditions to meet the need. For example, having a very challenging job may increase rather than decrease the growth needs of an individual. This is directly opposite to what Maslow predicted; yet it is consistent with results of Hall and Nougaim (1968) and others, who found satisfaction of a need positively related to its importance.

All in all, Alderfer's ERG theory appears to be the most promising version of the need-hierarchy theory available at this time (Miner & Dachler, 1973). Research is needed to explore it in more detail, but unfortunately, little has been done with it recently (Mitchell, 1979).

Need for achievement. In separate studies of one aspect of motivation, McClelland (1961) and Atkinson (1957) addressed achievement-oriented activity. McClelland formulated the concept of the need to achieve (n-Achievement, sometimes abbreviated *n-Ach*), postulating that this seemed to be a relatively stable personality trait rooted in experiences of middle childhood. McClelland's interest in this construct is related especially to entrepreneurial activities in developing countries (McClelland & Winter, 1969). The possible implications of this construct cover a wide range of occupations in industry and business.

The theory is concerned with predicting the behavior of those who have either high or low needs for achievement. It has been postulated that those who have high *n-Ach* tend to "approach" those tasks for which there is a reasonable probability of success and to avoid those tasks which either are too easy (because they are not challenging) or too difficult (because of fear of failure). Thus, the opportunity for success associated with a task can affect the tendency to "approach" it. These relationships have been worked into a theoretical formulation by Atkinson and Feather (1966). Their theory postulates that achievement-oriented activity is undertaken by an individual with the expectation that his or her performance will be evaluated in terms of some standard of excellence. Further, it is presumed that any situation which presents a challenge to achieve (by arousing an expectation that action will lead to success) must also pose the threat of failure (by arousing an expectation that action may lead to failure). Thus, achievement-oriented activity is influenced by the result of a conflict between two opposing tendencies: the tendency to achieve success (*n-Ach*) and the tendency to avoid failure (*n-AF*).

Achievement-oriented activities are also influenced by other extrinsic *motivational* tendencies. Atkinson and Feather proposed that the tendency to approach or continue a task depends both on the difficulty of the situation and on the individual's motivation. A generalized model of their predictions is presented in Figure 14.3. Those with high *n-Ach* are shown as having the strongest tendency to approach tasks of intermediate difficulty;

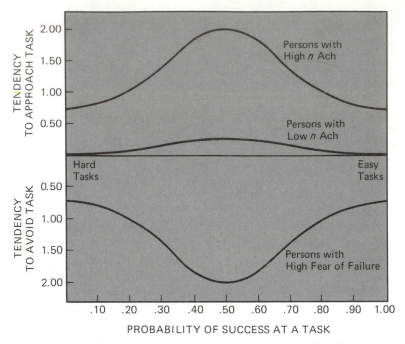

FIGURE 14.3 The interaction of type of motive and probability of success in influencing the tendency to approach or to avoid a task, as based on the theory of Atkinson and Feather (1966). (Adapted from McClelland & Winter, 1969, Figure 1–1, p. 17.)

those with low *n-Ach* also tend to approach tasks of intermediate difficulty, but the curve is much flatter. Those with high fear of failure (the *negative* aspect of *n-Ach*) tend to avoid such tasks, preferring either easier tasks, in which they are almost certain to succeed, or harder tasks (because failure at such tasks is clearly "not their fault").

Atkinson and Feather (1966) presented evidence from a number of studies that tends to support the basic premise of their theory. McClelland and Winter (1969) summarized the results of studies that reflect relationships between *n-Ach* and various indexes of entrepreneurial success. For example, Koch (1965) reported correlations ranging from .27 to .63 between the *n-Ach* scores of executives at fifteen Finnish knitwear factories and several indexes of business expansion (such as increase in number of workers and gross in-

vestments). Such data tend to suggest that the success of the companies is related to the high achievement motivation of their executives. McClelland and Winter also found that apparently achievement motivation can be learned and is not exclusively predetermined by childhood experiences. Such learning has been brought about through special training programs and, in some instances, presumably as a result of the person's being placed in a position in which achievement-motivated behavior is in some measure expected and rewarded.

The learned aspect of the need brings up the issue of whether staffing an organization with people who have high achievement needs leads to a highly competitive and successful organization, as McClelland suggested, or whether the placement of people in highly competitive jobs or organizations leads to achievement-related behavior. Obviously both occur, but McClelland implied that it is more the former than the latter. On the other hand, the weight of the data seems to be in favor of the reverse (Klinger & McNelly, 1969).

Regardless of the order of causation, achievement motivation does seem to be related to important work behaviors. For example, it has been found that high achievers stay on the job longer than do low achievers (Rhode, Sorensen, & Lawler, 1976). Also when criticized, high achievers tend to respond better and to improve their performance more than do low achievers (Greenberg, 1977). Finally, achievement-oriented managers tend to display the types of behaviors considered desirable for managers: being candid, open, and receptive to new ideas, offering subordinates more opportunity to participate in decisions, and having more respect for others (Hall, 1976).

With the continued concern about the access of women and minorities to high quality jobs in the work force has come an exploration of the affects and distribution of achievement motivation in these groups. Spence and Helmreich (1983) have compared men and women on achievement-related variables using the Work and Family Orientation Questionnaire (WFOQ). The self-report scale yields three achievement-oriented dimensions: mastery (a preference for challenging jobs and the opportunity to strive for excellence); work (the desire to work hard); and competitiveness (the enjoyment of competition with others). The Spence and Helmreich data show that the structure of men's and women's achievement motives are very similar, but that there are differences in the strength of the motives. Women tended to be somewhat higher on the work dimension whereas men were somewhat higher on mastery and considerably higher on competitiveness. Although data of this type always suffer from the limitations of the group sampled, the fact that differences were found points to the need to explore them further.

Less research has been done with achievement motivation and race than with gender. What has been done tends to be rather speculative and less directly related to work settings. For example, Boykin (1983) addresses the underlying cultural differences between the Euro-American culture of Whites and the Afro-American culture of Blacks. He then considers the effects of these differences on Blacks who are confronted with a school system that is dominated by a culture different from their own. He suggests that the problems Blacks face attempting to achieve successful performance in such school systems may be the result of a conflict of cultures and the Black students' need to reconcile differences between their primary culture and the culture to which they are expected to conform.

The search for reliable individual differences between subgroups in the work force with respect to achievement motivation continues. That so much interest in this particular motive or need has existed over quite a long time attests to the fact that the need is important in work-oriented organizations. It also results from the fact that some rather interesting relationships between achievement motivation and work behavior have been found.

Discussion of need theories. Several other need-oriented theories could be discussed at this point. We have chosen to conclude our treatment of the topic for several reasons. First, there is no end to the number of needs that can be conjured up to explain behavior. As a result, where one stops the search for new needs is arbitrary. We felt that those presented here were sufficiently representative to cease our search at this point.

Second, one rather telling criticism of need theories cannot be overlooked: Needs and other similar types of personality traits explain far less of the variance in behavior than do ability variables and situational characteristics. This may be partially because measures of needs tend to be less reliable and valid than measures of abilities and situational characteristics. Yet, weaknesses in the measures are not sufficient to explain the failure of individual needs to predict behavior in many situations; in many cases, these constructs simply do not add much.

The limited success of need approaches in work motivation has led some to question the utility of any need-oriented views. Relying heavily upon personality psychologists who have questioned the very existence of needs (see, for example, Mischel, 1973) and the interactionists who insist that all behavior is a complex interaction of person-situation interactions over time (Ekehammer, 1974; Schneider, 1983), some have questioned whether any attention at all should be paid to needs (Mitchell, 1979). Others have taken a less extreme position, coming down on the side of caution. Weiss and Adler (1984), for example, acknowledge the failure of internal-state variables like personality constructs or needs to add much to the prediction and understanding of behavior at work, but at the same time, they criticize the weak conceptual development of the need constructs and measures that have typically been used to address work motivation. They also argue strongly for longitudinal research that looks for consistency in behavior across time and settings. Most research has looked only at the connection between a need and behavior at one point in time. It shows that often behavior is not consistent with needs when only one behavioral observation is obtained. However, the support of individual differences is much stronger when we look at the trends in behavior for the same individual over several settings spread out across a number of occasions. We agree with Mitchell (1979) and others who are disappointed with the showing of needs in work motivation, but, at the same time, we share Weiss' and Adler's (1984) be-

lief that research to date has not provided a good evaluation of the potential for need effects and that more longitudinal research looking at a string of behaviors over time is needed.

Balance Theories

Throughout the late 1950s and most of the 1960s social-psychological research and thought was dominated by what is known as balance or consistency theories of behavior. The best known of these is Festinger's (1957) theory of cognitive dissonance; yet there are several others. A comprehensive collection of these theories is presented in the book by Abelson, Aronson, McGuire, Newcomb, Rosenberg, and Tannenbaum entitled *Theories of Cognitive Consistency* (1968).

Although the theories vary somewhat, they all share the following tenets: First, individuals are said to possess some set of beliefs. Beliefs can be about almost anything—oneself, friends, the physical environment, political candidates, and the like. In addition, these beliefs (or cognitions) are not isolated. They are often associated with each other, and the association can vary from being very consistent to being very inconsistent. An example of a consistent set of beliefs would be that you are a very ambitious and competent person and that you were promoted much more quickly than were others. Two inconsistent beliefs are the belief that you are ambitious and competent and the knowledge that you have just been fired because of laziness. According to balance theories, inconsistent beliefs are dissatisfying and create tension within the individual. The tension, in turn, leads to attempts by the individual to reduce the tension and to return to a consonant state. From a motivational standpoint, then, the tension is the source of the motivational force that pushes the individual to action. What action is taken is another matter. We address this issue in detail later.

For behavior in organizations, *Equity Theory*, originally formulated by J. Stacy Adams (1965), has been the most influential position. It is discussed next.

Equity theory. Equity theory as constituted by J. Stacy Adams (Adams, 1965; Adams & Jacobson, 1964; Adams & Rosenbaum, 1962) combines the notions of cognitive dissonance with those of social exchange to address issues of the effects of money on behavior in work settings. It has two major process emphases. According to Adams (1965), people hold certain beliefs about the *outputs* they get from their jobs and the *inputs* they bring to bear in order to obtain certain outcomes. The outcomes of a job situation include actual pay, fringe benefits, status, intrinsic interest in the job, or other factors that individuals perceive to have utility or value to them and that result from their job relationships. In turn, the inputs include any and all of the factors that individuals perceive as being either their "investment" in the jobs or something of value that they bring or put into their jobs. The inputs could include a person's general qualifications for a job, his or her skill, education level, effort, and other similar factors. The various specific outcomes and inputs as they are perceived by an individual are weighted according to his or her judgment of their relative importance to form a total outcome and a total input. These two totals combine to form an outcome/input ratio.

According to Adams' theory, a person is said to consciously or unconsciously compare his or her outcome/input ratio with that of other persons or other classes of persons whom he or she perceives as relevant to such comparative purposes. Equity is said to exist when an individual perceives his or her own outcome/input ratio to be equal to that of other persons; inequity exists if the person's ratio is *not* the same as that of other persons. All of these comparisons are subjective, not objective. Inequity can be in either direction

and of varying magnitudes. Let us use Pritchard's (1969) notation to illustrate these ratios and those combinations which, according to the theory, result in equity and inequity. Let *H* indicate that the individual perceives his or her input or outcome to be high and *L* mean that it is seen as low. The basic ratio is:

$$\text{Equity ratio} = \frac{\text{Outcome } (H \text{ or } L)}{\text{Input } (H \text{ or } L)}$$

In Figure 14.4, the first ratio is that of the individual himself or herself, the second (following *v* for *versus*) is that of the persons used for comparison. The comparisons are thus described by Pritchard (1969).

The dissonance formulation enters into the comparison process to explain the degree of affect (or tension) associated with a comparison. If a comparison is equitable, no tension exists; the individual is satisfied and should have little desire to change the outcome/input ratio. If, on the other hand, the comparison of the two ratios results in a perception of inequality between them, inequity results. The inequity creates tension and, with it, a desire by the individual to reduce the tension by altering one or more elements of the ratios to bring the comparison back to equality.

There can be two types of inequity with regard to pay. *Underpayment* is by far the more common. Here the individual believes that, in comparison to others, he or she is not receiving a sufficient amount of pay (the outcome) for the inputs invested in the job. In other words, the amount of money is not high enough. Dissatisfaction results, and the individual is motivated by a desire to improve his or her outcome/input ratio and bring it in line with the ratio of the comparison others.

Overpayment is less common, but more interesting for it predicts that the individual will be dissatisfied because he or she receives *too*

FIGURE 14.4 Equity relationships. (Adapted from Pritchard, 1969.)

EQUITY CONDITION	OUTCOMES/INPUTS OF SELF VERSUS OUTCOMES/INPUTS OF OTHERS		
Overreward Inequity	L/L v L/H H/L v H/H	H/L v L/L H/H v L/H	H/L v L/H
Equity	L/L v L/L H/H v L/L	H/H v H/H L/H v L/H	L/L v H/H H/L v H/L
Underreward Inequity	L/L v H/L L/H v H/H	L/H v L/L H/H v H/L	L/H v H/L

much money. Therefore, there is tension, and the individual is motivated to reduce it. Adams (Adams & Rosenbaum, 1962) did recognize that there was a much greater tolerance of overpayment inequity than of underpayment.

Equity theory generated considerable interest and research (see Campbell & Pritchard, 1976; Goodman, 1977; Goodman & Friedman, 1971; Miner & Dachler, 1973; and Pritchard, 1969, for major reviews of equity theory). Interest was piqued primarily because of the overpayment condition. The idea so opposed the accepted notion of economic people who seek to maximize rewards that many sought to research it carefully. Underpayment inequity, on the other hand, led to the same behavioral predictions as did already-existing theories.

Adams' and Rosenbaum's study (1962) is a good example of the equity phenomenon. The authors assumed that feelings of equity or inequity could be manipulated in a controlled setting by telling employees that they were either qualified or not qualified for a job. Presumably, those told that they were qualified for a job would use as their comparison group others like themselves. Those told they did not have the necessary qualifications would assume that other did have them and, therefore, that what they brought to the job in terms of qualifications was less than what others brought. The result would be that they would have lower inputs than those who were qualified.

Students who answered a newspaper advertisement conducted interviews for a company. Half were led to believe they were qualified for the job and half, unqualified. One of two bases for pay were established. Those employed in one condition were paid a fixed amount per hour (hourly pay). The others were paid a certain amount per interview that they completed (piece rate). The interview task itself allowed the individuals to vary performance on two dimensions, quantity and quality. Quantity was the number of interviews completed, and quality was the completeness and detail in each interview report turned in after a work session.

The two pay systems offered an excellent test of equity effects. Overpaid people who believed they were not qualified for the job and who were paid by the hour could increase their effort and do more interviews and/or increase the quality of their interviews. Both behaviors should increase their perceived inputs and produce a more equitable comparison. On the other hand, overpaid people who were paid on a piece-rate system could not increase quantity to bring their outcome/input ratio back into line because increasing the number of interviews also increased the amount of money received. Both numerator and denominator changed, leaving the ratio still inequitable.

For the most part, the data supported the theory. Overpaid employees conducted significantly more interviews than equitably paid ones only when paid by the hour. The quality of the interviews was higher for those overpaid as compared to those equitably paid when a piece-rate pay system was used. Quality was not as predicted under hourly pay, but this, more than likely, was because the nature of the job made it extremely difficult, if not impossible, to increase both quantity and quality.

The original research generated considerable interest and was supported in replications. However, it was pointed out that the results may have been caused by many factors other than equity. A number of studies eliminated most of the alternative explanations, save one. It was argued that underqualified people who had just been told they were unqualified might have worked in order to save face or prove themselves; the observed behaviors may not have had anything to do with a feeling of equity. In attempts to create overpayment inequity without threat or manipulation, the researchers found it extremely difficult to replicate the overpayment effect. Only one study was able to generate moderate support for it. In this case, employees were hired to do a catalogue-order task for one week (Pritchard, Dunnette, & Jorgenson, 1972). Overpaid employees tended to process more catalogue orders than equitably paid employees who received the same amount of pay.

With respect to equity theory, two conclusions seem justified. First, people do make social comparisons, and these comparisons are important. To understand why people behave as they do we must get outside the individual and look at how each individual compares himself or herself to others. Second, with respect to pay, an equity notion often does seem to operate. However, individuals' tolerance of overpayment inequities are *much* greater than of underpayment inequities. The effect of overpayment on behavior does not seem to be very significant in most settings. There are many reasons for this. It may be that in most organizational settings the range in possible amounts of inequity is so controlled because of salary schedules that it is seldom great enough to have an effect. It may also be that the types of conditions necessary to evoke equity concerns often do not exist. Finally, it may be that the individuals reduce inequity in ways other than altering performance.

The more interesting recent work has either expanded the equity-theory question or has applied it to issues other than performance. Vecchio (1981) introduced the notion of individual differences in susceptibility to equity norms. Using a measure of moral maturity, he found that those with more highly developed value systems were more likely to respond to overpayment by putting forth more effort and were more likely to be concerned with increasing work quality when overpaid than were people with less well-developed value systems. Greenberg and Ornstein (1983) hired undergraduate students to work on a proofreading task, and then changed the job responsibilities and the job title. They found that students who were given a higher status job and job title based upon past superior performance (equity) felt equitably paid and maintained their previous levels of performance. Those who got the new title and job without earning it felt overcompensated and worked harder than before, but only for a short time. Later on, their performance dropped off sharply, and they felt underpaid. This research and others points to a real need to understand how long feelings of inequity exist and how these feelings and the performance they influence change over time.

Discussion of balance theories. The evidence from social-psychological research as well as from the theory discussed here does support the notion that human beings do strive for some kind of balance or consistency among beliefs. They may also display behaviors designed to make previously inconsistent conditions more consistent. The role of others in the comparison process is important, particularly in organizational settings.

Despite this, there are some major questions about balance theories which greatly affect their use in understanding work behavior. In many cases, the questions place rather stringent limitations on the ability of the theories to explain work behavior. It is our conclusion, at this time, that because of several limitations, balance theories will play only a minor role in the understanding of work behavior in the near future. This is not to say that the concepts are not reasonable and do not influence behavior; they are and they do. But other motivational constructs seem to explain a greater proportion of the variance in work behavior over a wider variety of settings than do either equity or consistency constructs. A few of the issues are outlined here:

1. Do behaviors or cognitive distortions usually create balance? Exactly how balance will be restored has always been a problem. It may be through behaviors which change inputs and/or alter performance, but it may also be a simple cognitive distortion without action. It would be good if more guidelines could be offered for whatever resolution is chosen.
2. What conditions evoke comparisons? Some settings evoke comparisons more than others do. Both Korman (1976) and Pritchard (1969) pointed this out. Yet, we need to know more about when people will or will not be responsive to comparisons.
3. How are others chosen for comparison?
4. Can inputs and outcomes really be kept separate? For example, one person may consider a challenging job to be an outcome while another may see it as an input requiring more time and effort from him or her.

Two-Factor Theory

Herzberg (Herzberg, Mausner, & Snyderman, 1959) proposed a theory of job satisfac-

tion that was adapted to a motivational theory by Herzberg in his 1966 book. Its motivational implications have received the most attention, so we discuss them here. The theory has had considerable influence on job design. The following discussion summarizes the basic study from which the theory arose and then outlines the contributions and controversies related to the theory.

The original study (Herzberg et al., 1959) was an intensive analysis of the experiences and feelings of 200 engineers and accountants in nine different companies. During structured interviews, employees were asked to describe a few previous job experiences in which they felt "exceptionally good" or "exceptionally bad" about their jobs. Some of the most significant results are shown in Figure 14.5. High and low job-attitude events are those described as leading to feeling good or feeling bad about their work, respectively.

The major inferences of these and other data from the study relate to the distinction between what are called *motivator* factors and *hygiene* factors. The events that are associated with high job attitudes generally are linked directly or indirectly with *job activities*; these categories are achievement, recognition, the work itself, responsibility, and advancement. These factors are related to job content, which means that they are intrinsic to the job itself. Because positive expressions of these factors are generally associated with high job-attitude situations, they have been called *motivators, satisfiers, intrinsics,* or *content* factors. The events predominately associated with low job-attitude situations are those extrinsic to the work itself and are associated with the job context rather than with job activities. These have been called *hygiene factors, dissatisfiers, extrinsics,* or *context* factors.

From a motivational standpoint, Herzberg (1966) distinguished between two sets of human needs. One set of needs within this framework relates to the human drive toward

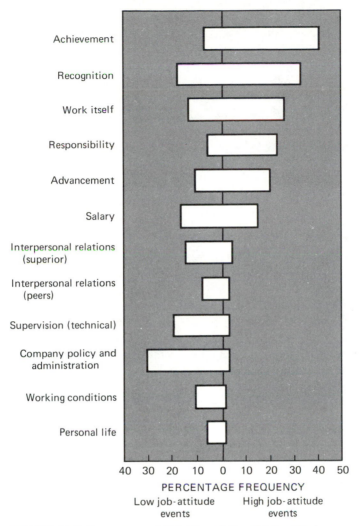

FIGURE 14.5 Percentage of ''high'' and ''low'' job-attitude sequences in which each of the categories appeared. (Adapted from Herzberg et al., 1959, p. 72.)

self-realization—that is, essentially the self-fulfillment need as postulated by Maslow. According to the theory, self-realization can be achieved only through the fulfillment of factors intrinsic to the work itself—in other words, the motivator factors. The second set stems from people's animal nature and their need to avoid pain; this set consists of the needs to which the hygiene factors are rele-

vant. Because these factors serve only to reduce pain, they cannot contribute to positive satisfaction but only to the avoidance of dissatisfaction according to Herzberg (1966).

From its inception, this theory has been surrounded by controversy. Throughout the 1960s and into the early 1970s, there were multiple attacks and sometimes even a counterattack, at least at the early stages. Most of the shots were directed at the theory as it relates to job satisfaction. We address these issues later, under job satisfaction. The distinction between satisfaction and motivation is often not clear, so there will be some overlap.

The major criticism of the theory was directed at the assumed independence of motivator and hygiene factors. According to the theory, the presence of hygiene factors led *only* to the absence of dissatisfaction rather than to satisfaction. Likewise only motivators could lead to satisfaction. Assuming a hedonic model of motivation in which individuals seek satisfaction, the implication of the theory was that true motivation could be obtained only through the provisions of motivators in work settings.

Neither the satisfaction nor the motivation conclusion following from it held up to empirical test. (For a review of the satisfaction data see King, 1970, and our discussion in the following chapter.) It suffices to say that work behavior can be maintained for extended periods of time with hygiene factors as well as with motivators.

Discussion of the two-factor theory. Although virtually every major tenet of the theory is unsupported, it did have and still does have a major impact on organizational psychology. When it appeared, the time was right for some fresh ideas, and the two-factor theory stimulated work in two major and interrelated areas. First, for many, it served as a basis for the design of jobs in order to provide more interesting and absorbing work. Concern for expanding the content of jobs led to several early quasi-experiments in large corporations—such as Texas Instruments (Myers, 1964) and American Telephone and Telegraph (Ford, 1969)—and formed the basis for what has become known as *job enrichment*. The early work in job enrichment used as its theoretical springboard Herzberg's two-factor theory. Although it has been argued that there certainly are more sound bases for

job enrichment than the two-factor theory (Hulin, 1971), it cannot be denied that the theory did provide the impetus for important research.

A second contribution of the theory was to create an interest in what has been termed intrinsic motivation. Those concerned with intrinsic motivation recognize that the features of a job itself can provide an environment in which the individual can gain satisfaction from doing the job, without receiving any external reinforcement such as money, praise, or recognition. It is said that individuals are motivated to do such jobs simply because of the characteristics intrinsic to the jobs themselves. Although the two-factor theory did not develop the notion of intrinsic motivation very well, the existence of the theory and the controversy surrounding it did create interest in intrinsic motivation.

Behavior Modification

Behavior modification (also termed operant conditioning or Skinnerian approaches in recognition of the monumental impact of B. F. Skinner on this theory) focuses upon the individual's environment. The tenets of behavior modification are few and clear. Simply stated, it posits that behavior is controlled by its consequences. The consequences of interest are *reinforcers*. A reinforcer is anything that follows a behavior and influences the probability that that behavior will be repeated in the future. Reinforcers can be positive, such as a raise, or negative, such as a verbal reprimand. For example, an employee who receives a warm smile and a friendly "Good morning" after saying "Good morning" to another employee is reinforced for the behavior and is more likely to repeat the friendly greeting in the future. The reinforcer, in this case, is the friendly response from the person greeted.

The second major variable is the *contingency* or degree of association between the response and the receipt of the reinforcement. The connection between a response and the receipt of the reinforcement varies on two dimensions. One dimension is *time*. The length of the time interval between the response and the reinforcement can vary from almost immediately to weeks or months. With few exceptions, the shorter and interval, the more likely it is that the reinforcer will influence behavior at least in rather simple tasks. The second dimension is the *ratio* of responses needed before the reinforcer is administered. For example, considering pay as a reinforcer, a salesperson may be paid by the company only after selling 100 cases of a product. Such a schedule would require 100 responses (assuming each sale is for only one case) before the reinforcer is administered. In this example, the time between sales of 100 cases may vary considerably. Therefore, the reinforcement schedule cannot be described in units of time.

With (1) the assumption that the behavioral response of interest can be made by the individual; (2) the principle of contingency; and (3) the notion of reinforcement, behavior modification proposes that all behavior can be understood. Internal characteristics of the individual such as needs, values, and beliefs are considered totally unnecessary for understanding behavior, according to this view. In fact, taken literally, internal states are not only unnecessary, they have no causal effect on behavior (Locke, 1977).

Use of behavior modification in organizations. The popularity of behavior-modification techniques in industry was given a real boost by the widely publicized work of Feeney at Emery Air Freight (*Business Week*, December 18, 1971; *Business Week*, December 2, 1972). Discouraged by the lack of success of sales-training programs based on testimonials from "super-salespeople," Feeney instituted a new program which emphasized programmed learning procedures with frequent feedback. Annual sales increases jumped from 11% to 27.8% and, rightly or wrongly, were credited largely to the application of behavior-modification techniques. Dramatic changes in customer service and shipping-container use were also associated with newly installed systems of feedback and positive reinforcement. Considerable improvements backed by a vocal and visable spokesperson has led to heightened interest in behavior modification in industry since the early 1970s. Although the effects observed at Emery Air Freight can be questioned because of the weaknesses in experimental design, the effects were so strong that it did appear that something was happening and that behavior-modification techniques deserved a further look.

Research conducted under more controlled conditions has been limited in scope, but its conclusions are generally as predicted by behavior modification: Reinforcement increases behavior more than nonreinforcement does (Jablonsky & DeVries, 1972; Komaki, Waddell, & Pearce, 1977), and schedules of reinforcement can influence behavior (Pritchard, Leonard, Von Bergen, & Kirk, 1976). Furthermore, feedback about the nature of behaviors and the consequences of the behavior increases the likelihood that the behavior will be repeated (Komaki, Collins, & Penn, 1982; Komaki, Heinzmann, & Lawson, 1980).

Discussion of behavior modification. It is clear that reinforcers influence behavior and so do the contingencies between behavior and reinforcement. What is not clear is the extent to which behavior modification adds anything to what already exists (Locke, 1977). Other theories stress rewards (reinforcements) and contingencies without denying or downplaying the importance of the organism's internal states as behavior modification does. Clearly, people think, hold values, and have different needs and feelings. Granted, these factors may have been overemphasized at times, but to deny their existence or relegate absolutely no importance to them flies in the face of what is known (Locke, 1977). Therefore, according to Locke, the tenets of the behavior-modification position appear to add little that is new and something that is false.

Another criticism of applied behavior modification has been from an ethical standpoint. It is argued that controlling the behavior of others denies them control over their own actions. Criticism has been particularly severe when the individuals involved are confined to total-control institutions such as prisons and hospitals and, to some extent, military organizations. In work organizations, the criticism is less justified because of the freedom to leave the organization. Even denying this, the attack on ethical grounds is rather weak. A wide range of behaviors by organizational members could be seen as attempts to influence others. Behavior modification represents just one of many ways in which one might attempt to influence others. The fact that it works better than many other more subtle attempts does not mean that it is unethical.

A final criticism of behavior modification is made on an empirical basis. Mawhinney (1975) remarked that much of the research purporting to apply behavioral modification procedures in organizational contexts had not done so because of a misunderstanding of behavior modification. As a result, some of the purported support remains to be demonstrated. Along a different line, there is some evidence that implies that when money is used as a reinforcer and is highly contingent upon performance, the frequency of the behavior may decrease instead of increase as would be predicted by behavior modification (Deci, 1972, 1975). According to Deci, linking external rewards too closely to behavior in jobs that are originally very interesting to the individuals can decrease motivation because these people no longer are doing the job out of interest; they are doing it for the pay. We

address this issue to a greater extent later, but it suffices to say at this point that, to the extent that this does occur, schedules of reinforcement with pay predictions made from a behavior-modification position may need to be modified.

In spite of the criticism, behavior modification makes at least two contributions to the understanding of human behavior in organizations. First, although its focus on the individual's environment rather than on internal states of the organism may be overstated, it does offer a healthy counterposition. Industrial-organizational psychologists and managers often tend to overemphasize individual characteristics to the exclusion of environmental ones. Behavior modification emphasizes the need to look outside the individual for explanation. Second, it offers a series of terms and technologies for dealing with individual behavior. Classes of reinforcers, schedules of reinforcement, and well-researched, descriptive terminologies relating to changes in behavior are useful. Applications of the techniques have been particularly useful in programmed learning for training. The procedures and technology have had some real benefits.

Expectancy Theory

The historical roots of expectancy theory go back to Tolman (1932), Lewin (1938), and Peak (1955), but Vroom's version of the theory presented in *Work and Motivation* (1964) introduced it to industrial-organizational psychology. Since that time, the theory has been modified and expanded by Campbell, Dunnette, Lawler, and Weick (1970), Dachler and Mobley (1973), Lawler (1971), and Porter and Lawler (1968), to name a few. Without a doubt, the theory has been extremely influential in the field over the last few years.

The theory is a cognitive one based upon a rational-economic view of people. It assumes that people are decision makers who choose among alternative courses of action by selecting the action that, at that time, appears most advantageous. The choice need not actually be the most advantageous one, however. It is recognized that individuals are limited in their rationality and their ability to recognize alternatives. They are limited also by habits and other factors which may inhibit decision making. Nevertheless, the theory assumes that individuals cognitively consider alternatives and make choices within the limits of their capabilities. The theory is concerned with (1) the elements of cognitions that go into the decision and (2) the way in which individuals process these elements to reach a decision. The exact nature of each of these factors depends on which particular version of the theory is considered. But they have much in common. We first address the elements of the theory and then the process by which they are said to combine.

Valence. An individual's "affective" orientation toward particular outcomes is called the valence of the outcome. Put another way, the valence is a person's desire for the outcome or the attractiveness of the outcome to him or her. When the outcome is actually received, it may or may not be as satisfying as anticipated. From the standpoint of the valence, at any one time the degree to which the actual and anticipated satisfaction agree does not matter. For example, consider the valence of a promotion to a specific position. An individual may find the possibility of receiving the promotion and working in the position very attractive, yet if he or she is promoted to it, the position may not look nearly as attractive. At a time before the promotion, the individual's behavior would be based not on what actually will be but on what he or she thinks will be. The term valence refers to this anticipation of the attractiveness of the position.

Valence does not exist in the abstract. It is associated with some object or state called an outcome. The outcomes may be tangible objects such as money or clean work settings, intangible factors such as recognition or feelings of accomplishment, or they may be levels of performance. Frequently, behaviors and performance levels are termed first-level outcomes and all others second-level outcomes (Campbell et al., 1970).

Theoretically, the number of second-level outcomes is almost limitless. However, within work settings, individuals share a relatively small set that really influences their behavior. In fact, Parker and Dyer (1976) found that a set of only eight outcomes did a better job than a set of twenty-five for predicting reenlistment decisions of naval officers.

Instrumentality. The outcomes we discussed before all are considered to have some degree of association with the individual's performance. Instrumentalities represent this association. Vroom defined instrumentalities as subjective correlations between two outcomes. Usually one outcome is performance. For performance, a positive subjective correlation means that the individual believes that as his or her performance increases so will the amount of the outcome in question. A negative subjective correlation is the reverse of this, and a zero subjective correlation means that the amount of the outcome received is unrelated to performance.

Expectancy. The final element in the theory links an individual's act to an outcome. Again the outcome in this link is usually considered to be performance. Vroom considered this link to be a subjective probability held by the individual that an act (a behavior) would lead to the outcome. As is the case with all probabilities, the values range from 0.00 probability to +1.00. A subjective probability of zero means the person is absolutely certain that the act will *not* lead to the attainment of the outcome; +1.00 is certainty that the act *will* lead to the outcome, and other levels of certainty lie between. Figure 14.6 shows the three terms.

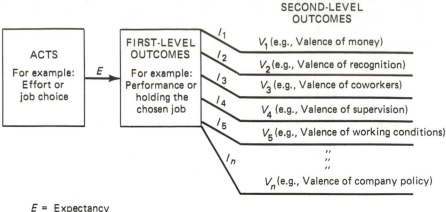

VALENCE OF
SECOND-LEVEL
OUTCOMES

V_1 (e.g., Valence of money)

V_2 (e.g., Valence of recognition)

V_3 (e.g., Valence of coworkers)

V_4 (e.g., Valence of supervision)

V_5 (e.g., Valence of working conditions)

V_n (e.g., Valence of company policy)

E = Expectancy
  = Subjective probability that an act will lead to an outcome
  $0.00 \leqslant E \leqslant + 1.00$

I_j = Instrumentatlity of the first-level outcome for the attainment
  of second-level outcome j
  = Subjective correlation between attainment of the first-level
  outcome and outcome j
  $-1.00 \leqslant I_j \leqslant + 1.00$

V_j = Valence of outcome j
  = Subjective judgment about the attractiveness of outcome j

FIGURE 14.6 Expectancy-theory terms.

Motivation model. Motivation is a function of the combination of the three elements—valence, instrumentality, and expectancy. Mitchell (1974) presented what is perhaps the most generally accepted of the models for the combination of valence, instrumentality, and expectancy. Note that, as presented, it treats the act of committing effort to work. It would function the same way for committing an act of choosing a job or engaging in any other behavior or act. The model is as follows:

$$W = E \left(\sum_{j=1}^{n} I_{ij} V_j \right)$$

in which

W = effort
E = the expectancy that effort leads to performance

I_{ij} = the instrumentality of performance level i for the attainment of second-level outcome j
V_j = the valence of second-level outcome j
n = the number of second-level outcomes

Look more closely at the model in the preceding paragraph. The summated product of the I_{ij}s multiplied by the V_js represents the valence of performance. If the sum of these products is very high, it means that the individual perceives a high degree of association between performance and the attainment of valued (that is, highly valent) outcomes. If the value is near zero, the individual does not perceive much of value to be associated with performance, and if it is negative, he or she believes that increases in performance lead to more and more undesirable conditions.

At first glance one might think that individuals would strive to attain high performance if they believed that performance led to valued outcomes. According to the model, this is true only if the expectancy term (E) is greater than zero. If it is zero, which means the individual does not believe that there is any connection between his or her effort and performance, then, according to the model, no matter how much more attractive higher performance levels are than lower ones, the individual should see no reason for putting out great effort.

Discussion of expectancy theory. Support for the model has been mixed but in general is positive (Mitchell, 1974; 1979). Nevertheless, the support of any one study is not particularly strong.

Criticisms of the theory have been leveled at the assumptions of the theory and at methodological issues. It is most severely criticized for assuming that humans are too calculative in their decision processes (Behling & Starke, 1973; Korman, 1977). We have already mentioned that the theory recognized that people are limited in their capabilities for making decisions on such a complex basis as the theory requires. The critics say such recognition is not enough. People simply cannot and do not use such a complicated process. All types of simplification strategies are used to process information according to people's cognitive limits. The theory does not give sufficient weight to these limits.

A second assumption of the theory which has been attacked is that people are basically hedonic—that is, they seek to attain more and more pleasant conditions and to avoid painful ones. Both Locke (1976) and Korman (1976) took issue with this assumption on both logical and empirical grounds. Although we may believe that these criticisms are valid at the extremes—that is, that hedonic principles are not sufficient for all people or, for that matter, for any one person all of the time—we still believe that for a vast majority

of behaviors under consideration at work, the assumption is better than any others.

Empirical results using the theory have raised several methodological issues. Many of these issues concern the measures used for the variables. A recent study by Ilgen, Nebeker, and Pritchard (1981) compared several different types of measures for each of the three major variables in the theory. The comparison looked at the validity and reliability of the measures. The study showed that very good measures of the three variables could be constructed.

Criticisms of the theory have led to a number of modifications and changes in it. One major change was to expand the theory to include possible causes for each of the variables. Figure 14.7 shows Lawler and Suttle's (1973) expansion of the theory to other variables that cause or influence the primary variables of the theory. More recently Staw (1977) expanded the theory in several dimensions and Naylor, Pritchard, and Ilgen (1980) introduced several different causes of the variables in addition to proposing that the theory itself be greatly expanded. The theory as expressed by Naylor et al., among other things, introduces the notion that behavior in organizations primarily involves decisions about the distribution of time and effort to tasks. They argue that time and effort are really the *only* commodities that the individual has to offer to the organization and that understanding work behavior is understanding how these two are allocated by the individual to tasks.

In summary, expectancy theory has generated high interest and considerable controversy. The result, in most cases, is modifications and extensions that have been incorporated into broader theories of work behavior. Clearly, the concepts introduced by expectancy theory are useful in understanding behavior. People do seem to weigh alternatives and select courses of action based on some judgment of the value of alternatives.

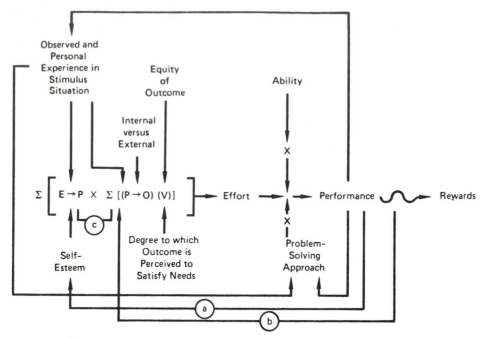

$$\Sigma \left[E \rightarrow P \; X \; \Sigma \left[(P \rightarrow O) \, (V) \right] \right]$$

FIGURE 14.7 An expanded expectancy theory of work performance. (From Lawler & Suttle, 1973.)

Yet, there is also more to behavior than can be predicted by such a rational decision model. Therefore, we conclude that the theory has contributed, and we believe will continue to contribute, when viewed as only part of how behaviors at work are chosen.

Intrinsic Motivation

Intrinsic motivation is not a "full-blown" theory on the same level of development as are the other theories. Yet, it is a topic that has recently received considerable attention in organizational behavior and, given the trends in work values and thinking about the role of organizations in the work lives of their employees, it will continue to receive more attention over the next few years.

In many ways, intrinsic motivation is not much different from the concern for higher-order needs in Maslow's hierarchy (1954) or for growth needs in Alderfer's ERG theory

(1969, 1972). Given the current interest and the "catchy" nature of the topic to date, we have decided to risk redundancy and present it separately.

Intrinsic motivation as currently conceived is championed by Deci (1975). His construal of intrinsic motivation stems from two sources. The first is White's (1959) notion of competence motivation. White assumed that in performance settings people are motivated to do well in order to experience a sense of competence. Experiencing a sense of competence is satisfying and, as a result, individuals will strive to attain it. The second concept of intrinsic motivation, according to Deci, stems from De Charms' (1968) notion of personal causation. This assumes that people need to feel responsible for their own actions. Responsibility for action is the freedom to choose among alternative courses of action. This occurs in the absence of pressure, either positive or negative, to select one course of action over another. Negative pressure to display some behavior could be created by the threat of punishment for not doing it; for example, the threat of losing one's job for not coming to work prevents absenteeism. Positive coercion is less intuitively obvious. Here, the individual loses freedom to choose to reject a behavior because of the positive inducements. "Golden handcuffs" created by pension plans with lucrative profit-sharing contributions from the organizations, new cars provided at company expense, and other benefits will restrict an executive's freedom to leave an organization just as surely as will punitive forces. In both cases, the individual loses control over his or her actions.

Combining competence motivation with personal control suggests that jobs should be designed to allow individuals to experience feelings of both competence and control over their actions. These conditions are considered necessary for intrinsic motivation. Under these conditions the individual can, in a sense, give himself or herself reinforcement by feeling a sense of accomplishment from doing the job.

To what exactly is intrinsic motivation related? Is it intrinsic to the individual or to the job? The best conclusion seems to be that it is a little bit of both. Jobs provide necessary but insufficient conditions for intrinsic motivation. If jobs provide personal control over behavior and a sense of competence, then it is likely that people placed in those jobs will be intrinsically motivated—that is, they will do the job because of the sense of accomplishment and enjoyment they feel while doing it. On the other hand, since individuals in a sense must give to themselves the rewards of accomplishment and enjoyment of the task, the task conditions alone are not sufficient for intrinsic motivation.

Most of the research on intrinsic motivation has concentrated on the interaction between intrinsic and extrinsic rewards. In a series of intriguing studies Deci (1975) concluded that money, an extrinsic reward, under certain conditions could *decrease* intrinsic motivation because it would decrease personal control. This led to the conclusion that perhaps interesting jobs would be less stimulating and enjoyable if one were paid too much to do them. Although the validity of this conclusion is uncertain because of some questions about Deci's methodology (Calder & Staw, 1975), there is some evidence that the phenomenon does occur when these problems are controlled (Pritchard, Campbell, & Campbell, 1977). Nevertheless, whether pay practices normally experienced in industrial settings can decrease intrinsic motivation is still uncertain (Fisher, 1978; Staw, 1977).

Mawhinney (1979) argued that to view intrinsic and extrinsic motivation as forces acting on the individual in some way that was not simply additive (total motivation was not the sum of the two) ignored the fact that individuals may differ in their degree of intrinsic motivation. Mawhinney suggested that individuals differed in the extent to which they would remain interested in a particular activity even when the activity itself was one that had some interest value. Likewise, activities themselves differed in the extent to which they could maintain interest. Put another way, there is an optimal time for each individual for any activity beyond which the activity is no longer interesting. If the activity and the period over which the activity is supposed to be observed are kept constant (for example, we require a person to solve problems in computer games for 2 hours), then differences in the amount of time individuals spend doing the activity over that time period is primarily a function of the individual's optimal time for that activity. Some people may consider it fun for the whole 2 hours; others may never consider it fun.

Using the notion of optimal time, Mawhinney argued that for any activity to be displayed for a fixed period of time, three groups of people could be defined. The groups were composed of people who are:

- Perfectly intrinsically motivated: People who really enjoy the activity and will work at it for the whole time period without needing any extrinsic reward to keep at it.
- Perfectly extrinsically motivated: Those for whom the task holds no interest and who will work on it only if forced to do so through the promise of extrinsic rewards.
- Imperfectly intrinsically motivated: Persons who enjoy the task for a while but not for the whole time that is allotted to it. Therefore, they will work only up to a point, after which they will have to receive extrinsic rewards for working on it any longer.

Using this classification system, Mawhinney reinterprets the data from previous intrinsic-motivation research and also collects some data of his own. He argues that extrinsic rewards do not decrease intrinsic motivation. They simply affect those people who are perfectly extrinsically motivated and those who are imperfectly extrinsically motivated. Extrinsic rewards keep the former group working on the task and as soon as they are withdrawn, these people cease working. For those who are imperfectly intrinsically motivated, the extrinsic rewards will stretch the point at which they would normally quit due to lack of continued interest to the point from which the extrinsic rewards are withdrawn.

Conclusion about Theories

After a review of the most prominent theories of work motivation, we have two general impressions. First, the theoretical positions are quite different. Diversity seems to be the rule with little convergence upon one global, all-encompassing theory. Second, none of the theories is without problems. All have been quite thoroughly researched but none has held up under all conditions.

Despite the diversity of the area in general and the moderate support for any theory in particular, there are several useful generalizations. First, the theories have identified three general processes which influence people's behavior. The first is some attempt by individuals to judge the value of courses of action and to select behaviors that seem to be most beneficial, based on their limited rationality. People think and in many instances try to do what they think is best for themselves. Expectancy theory addresses these issues most directly. Second, individuals compare themselves to others around them, and their behavior is based, in part, on the results of those comparisons. Finally, people may limit their desires, based on some judgment of what is a "proper" amount. More is not always better. Equity theory speaks most directly to these last two processes. Although no single one of the three processes is sufficient to explain all people's behavior or any one person's behavior all of the time, all three do seem to operate for various behaviors at any one time for all persons.

Besides the process of work motivation, we have learned something about its content. People do differ in what they desire or value from work. These differences occur among individuals and within individuals across time and across situations. During certain stages in a person's development, some factors are more important than others. For example, the social needs of adolescents may dominate all other needs, whereas older workers may be more concerned with security issues. Our review of motivation theories has identified several content issues. For example, achievement-oriented concerns and an individual's self-concept seem to be very important. We also have seen that environmental issues may influence content factors in the interaction between intrinsic and extrinsic outcomes. All of these issues illustrate that theories of motivation do offer some cues to issues to consider when attempting to understand behavior at work.

MOTIVATIONAL PRACTICES IN ORGANIZATIONS

The Place of Theory

The theories presented here are the major ones influencing industrial-organizational psychology today. Yet, as we have seen, all have their weaknesses as well as their strengths. There are no quick and easy answers to the question, "What motivates people to work?" Some may claim to have this answer but we, and now you, know better.

The absence of simple answers does not mean that the theories have nothing to offer. On the contrary, they have contributed the basis for the design and structure of work settings as well as guidelines for personnel practices. The link between theories and practice in motivation is illustrated in Figure 14.8 as a three-step process. The theories are the most general level of analysis. They provide a base for a second level which we have termed General Practices for Influencing Behavior in Organizations. Here, theoretical issues have identified important sets of variables related to work behavior. These variables have, for the most part, been researched extensively, and their impact on behavior has been relatively well understood. Finally, specific programs are developed and implemented within organizations which may incorporate one or more of the general procedures. An example of the latter is *Management by Objectives* (MBO). This rather popular management procedure incorporates goal setting into individual participation in decision making in order to establish individual work goals to which the employee feels reasonably committed.

A discussion of the specific programs is beyond the scope of this book; they are far too diverse and eclectic for our consideration. But, the general practices are very important to psychologists and others concerned with work behavior. Of the four general practices listed in Figure 14.8, we address three; the fourth is treated in a later chapter.

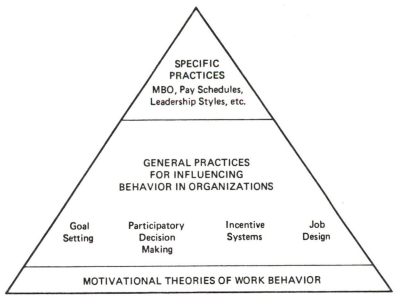

FIGURE 14.8 Levels of consideration for work motivation.

Goal Setting

According to Locke (1968), the most direct antecedent to performance-related work behavior is the employee's performance goal or goals. These goals represent what the employee intends to do at some time in the future. For example, the salesperson's goals may be to sell x number of units in the next 6 months, establish y number of new accounts, and/or decrease the number of customer complaints by z amount. Note that all these goals are related to the performance of a salesperson and pertain to future rather than to past or present behavior. Also note that, although the goals refer to the employee and are discussed in terms of the employee, others may have similar goals for him or her. In the just-cited example the salesperson's supervisor may have similar types of goals for him or her.

Our knowledge of the effects of goals on past behavior is well grounded in theory and in empirical research. The seminal work of E. A. Locke (see Locke, 1968, for a statement of his theory and his early research) provided a theoretical framework for understanding goal-setting effects, and research since that time has substantiated most of Locke's propositions. Latham and Yukl (1975) reviewed goal-setting research done only in the field and found over twenty-five studies, almost all of which substantiated Locke's earlier propositions. Locke, Shaw, Saari, and Latham (1981) provided a complete review of the goal-setting literature between 1970 and 1980 and found few surprises; goal setting works well to influence performance.

Functions of goals. Goals have two major functions: They provide a basis for motivation, and they guide behaviors. Motivationally, a goal offers guidelines for deciding how much effort to put into a job. If the individual receives feedback about how he or she is doing with regard to a goal, this provides in-

formation on whether the individual should work harder, continue at the same pace, or relax a bit. It also might persuade the individual to reject the goal by deciding it is just too difficult or easy and therefore not worth the effort. Either way, the effect is motivational.

Goals guide behavior in conjunction with feedback. By guiding the behavior we mean that they provide the individual with cues about the specific behaviors that need to be accomplished. For example, consider a goal of writing ten letters by tomorrow afternoon. This goal tells the individual that sitting at a desk is more appropriate behavior than talking on the telephone if the goal is to be met. Both behaviors may be relevant to the job, but the goal offers a cue to which behaviors are more appropriate if the goal is to be met.

Necessary conditions for goals. Goals are, to the individual, his or her intended behaviors. Yet, when it comes to goals which are set or held by others for a specific individual, we all know from experience that the other's goal for the individual may not be the behavior toward which the individual intends to work. Therefore, we must ask what the most basic conditions are that a goal must meet. We suggest that there are two conditions. First, the individual must be aware of the goal and know what it is that is supposed to be accomplished. The combination of awareness and knowledge of action can be considered the goal's *information value*. Second, the individual must *accept* the goal for himself or herself. Acceptance of it implies that the individual must intend to use the behavior(s) necessary to accomplish the goal. Most of our discussion of goals is on their effects on awareness or on acceptance.

Dimensions of goals. Goals can vary along several dimensions, but two of these stand out as by far the most significant. These are *specificity* and *difficulty*. The effects of these are quite clear; in general, work performance increases as goal specificity increases and as goal difficulty increases (Latham & Yukl, 1975; Locke et al., 1981; Steers & Porter, 1974).

The specificity of a goal provides information for the individual. The more specific the goal, the more the individual knows what is required of him or her. Therefore, the goal serves to route behavior in a specific direction (Terborg, 1977). In an informational sense, specific goals may also improve the value of performance feedback (Ilgen, Fisher, & Taylor, 1979). Often feedback from others is quite general, such as "You're doing a good job." Such feedback is of little value if the individual is not sure what is to be done. If the communicator of the general feedback has expressed specific goals, then the general feedback takes on specific meaning in terms of those goals.

There is no reason to expect that, under most conditions, the degree of acceptance of the goal is affected by its specificity. People should be just as committed to specific goals as to general ones. There is indirect evidence for this in a study of the production of logging crews (Ronan, Latham, & Kinne, 1973). Setting specific goals for the crews influenced the behavior only when the supervisors stayed around to encourage their crews to meet the goals. In this setting the specificity of the goal was not sufficient to influence performance. Only when acceptance or commitment was enforced by the supervisor did behavior improve with specific goals.

One study of truck drivers who drive loads of logs to lumber mills demonstrated the complexity of trying to understand how specific goals work. Latham and Baldes (1975) created two groups by randomly selecting truck drivers for one of two treatments. One group was told to do its best in loading its trucks. Another group was told to try to load its trucks up to 94% of the legal limit. (The closer to legal limit, the fewer trips needed, and the more economical per unit of logs.)

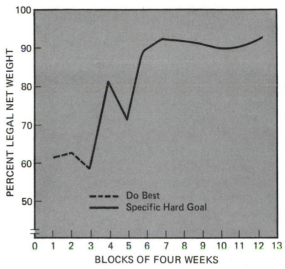

FIGURE 14.9 Percent legal net weight of thirty-six logging trucks across blocks as a function of a specific hard goal. (Latham & Baldes, 1975, p. 122.)

Figure 14.9 shows that specific goals were superior, but why? The most likely reason is informational—when the drivers received feedback about how close they came to the goal they learned how to load their trucks to their limits (Terborg, 1977). Commitment may also have been responsible. The authors reported that it became a "game" among the truckers to see who could do better. Therefore, the competition, not the specificity per se, may have fostered improved performance. Regardless of what was the actual cause, the data illustrate that specificity of goals can improve performance but that the nature of exactly how is often difficult to isolate.

Turning to goal difficulty, the effect seems to be through commitment more than through information increase. There is no reason to believe that the commitment to the easier goal of typing twenty words per minute would be any stronger than typing sixty words per minute. However, if rewards (such as pay, promotions, or supervisory approval) were associated with reaching the goal, we would expect greater commitment to the goal of sixty versus twenty words per minute.

The commitment effect is quite clear when the goal becomes too difficult—that is, when it becomes perceived as impossible. At that point, performance drops off to a point lower than with no goal at all. Stedry and Kay (1966) had supervisors set goals that were easy, difficult, or impossible with respect to production and to rework orders. Their data showed that performance under the impossible condition was significantly lower than under the other two conditions.

Group versus individual goals. Goals can be set for a given individual or for a whole group. Since most people in organizations function in groups, an interesting question is whether goals set for individuals or those set for groups are more effective. The effects depend on the information value of the goal and on commitment to the goal. For the first, group goals often dilute the information value of the goal. If the goal is stated in terms of group performance and if feedback is also in terms of the group, frequently the individual is not sure of his or her contribution to the group product and, therefore, is unsure of what the goal means to him or her. Similarly, commitment may be less to group goals, for there is some evidence that people tend to blame others rather than themselves for a group's failure to meet a goal and thus do not take responsibility for it (Johnston, 1967; Schlenker, Soraci, & McCarthy, 1976). On the other hand, commitment may be higher if there is strong group pressure for goal compliance.

The alternative possibilities just given suggest that to ask whether group or individual goals are better is to ask the wrong question. The data simply do not allow for a simple answer. It seems to us, if one were interested in choosing between setting group or individual goals, one would need to ask two questions: What is the effect of each type on the information about performance available to the

individual under each condition? And, what effect will each have on the individual's commitment to the goal? The answers will vary according to conditions, but they should be more constructive than remaining at the more global level of individuals versus groups.

Participation in Decision Making (PDM)

Participation in decision making is a highly complex and controversial topic because it is the *cause célèbre* of many, for reasons varying from the moral, to the political, to the pragmatic. The humanist argues that people must be allowed to decide about factors related to work because to do anything less is inhuman. Communist and socialist political philosophies see it as a way to avoid domination by a capitalist minority. Pragmatists support PDM, for they believe that employees who participate in making decisions will be more committed to their decisions and will work harder to accomplish them. The result is a widely diverse set of conditions, all of which are labeled PDM, but many of which have little in common. Therefore, we first consider what is meant by PDM and then turn to a description of some of its effects as well as to an evaluation of it.

Description of PDM. At the individual level, PDM means that the person participates in the decisions that need to be made about the work he or she does. This seems quite simple, but it is not, because the nature of the participation can vary along several dimensions. Locke and Schweiger (1979) pointed out that PDM can vary in *degree*, *content*, and *scope*. Degree refers to a continuum ranging from no participation to full participation. In the middle ranges PDM is more on the basis of consultation with those who have the power to either accept or reject the participant's inputs. The content of the issues on which one participates can vary in several respects, but Locke and Schweiger concluded that there are four categories usually encountered in organizations. These are: (1) routine, personnel functions (training, payment, etc.); (2) work itself (task assignments, work methods, speed of work, etc.); (3) working conditions (number and nature of rest pauses, lighting, placement of equipment, etc.); and (4) company policy (layoffs, profit sharing, general wage level, etc.).

The scope of PDM is the total system in which it occurs and the involvement of individuals in the issues faced by the system. High-scope PDM is exemplified by the workers' councils in Yugoslavia, where employees at the rank-and-file level of production in the company are elected and serve on a council responsible for all the major management decisions involving that company. Low-scope PDM might limit the decisions to issues of the specific job and work area of the individuals.

Effects of PDM. Possible psychological effects of PDM are best illustrated by Figure 14.10 from Locke and Schweiger (1979). Note that the initial impact of PDM on the individual can be classified into three major areas: values, cognitions, and motivation. At the motivational level, it is hypothesized that resistance to change is decreased if individuals participate in decisions regarding change and that individuals accept and are more committed to decisions in which they have participated. PDM borrows from many of the motivational theories discussed earlier in this chapter, but tends to have its roots more in the humanistic theories of Maslow and Alderfer. Cognitively, it is assumed that better ideas are generated by those who are closest to the task to be done.

Let us consider two field experiments in which the motivational effects of PDM were clearly demonstrated. A study by Coch and French (1948) found large decreases in resistance to change among production workers who were allowed to participate in decisions about production changeovers. Before Coch's and French's intervention, there was high turnover and severe production losses when-

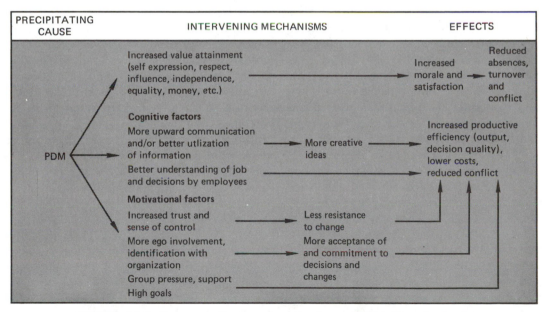

FIGURE 14.10 Proposed effects and mechanisms of PDM. (From Locke & Schweiger, 1978.)

ever the company, a pajama-manufacturing plant, changed procedures for jobs. Four groups were created by the experimenters. The first continued to use the old method of having managers inform the workers of needed changes and then implement them. The second group elected a representative to be on the management team that laid out the changeover procedures. The other two groups had total participation among all members in designing the changes. Results of the research impressively supported PDM. Production and other indicants of performance were superior in the PDM groups and were highest under the total-participation conditions.

In the Coch and French study, the PDM effects could have been from either motivational, cognitive, or value factors, and, most likely, were a combination of all three. For example, PDM groups may have discovered better ways to make the change, and the improved methods, not motivation, may have influenced production.

Lawler and Hackman (1969) eliminated the latter effect and still found improvements in attendance under PDM. A certain company had many small teams assigned to offices and businesses throughout the city to provide janitorial services. Absenteeism was high among these teams, so several were allowed to devise ways to handle absenteeism in their teams. The solution a team reached was then implemented for that team *and* for another team which did not participate in designing the procedure. In this way, the change was controlled. Any difference between the teams should have been due primarily to participation. The results showed much stronger effects on attendance in the participation groups than in the other groups.

An interesting follow-up to this study was reported by Scheflen, Lawler, and Hackman (1971). After implementing the changes for a short time, the company decided to withdraw them. The follow-up showed that once the old methods were restored, absenteeism in the participation groups dropped to a level well below the prechange conditions, whereas the control group's attendance varied little before, during, or after the changes. These two sets of data clearly indicated that PDM can affect behavior, but that its presence or absence cannot be taken lightly.

Much of the most recent PDM focus has been on the extent to which leaders should or should not involve their subordinates in decisions and on the role of participation in improving the quality of working life (QWL) for employees. The role of leadership is addressed in the next chapter. Jackson (1983) provides an interesting study of participation in the QWL domain. Nursing and clerical employees in a hospital outpatient facility either were or were not exposed to increased opportunity to participate in decisions about their jobs. Increases in participation were accomplished by increasing the number of staff meetings and also the quality of these meetings. To provide the latter, unit heads participated in a 2-day workshop in which they were trained on techniques for conducting group meetings with active participation and also were prepared on the types of topics likely to be of interest to their units. The training occurred 6 weeks before the increase in the number of staff meetings. After 6 months, those who had the opportunity for increased participation, when compared to those who did not, reported less role conflict, more confidence about what they were supposed to do on their jobs (lower role ambiguity), and more perceived influence on their jobs. Of particular interest in this study was the effects of participation on emotional strain. Participation reduced strain but only indirectly—through its effect on role conflict and role ambiguity. Figure 14.11 illustrates the relationships found by Jackson.

Evaluation of PDM'S Effectiveness. The euphoric reaction to PDM following the Coch and French experiment should have

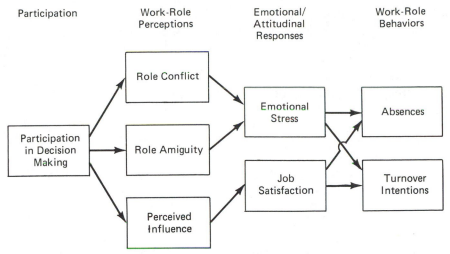

FIGURE 14.11 Some effects of participation in decision making on a sample of hospital employees. (Adapted from Jackson, 1983.)

been short lived. Yet, faith more than fact led to its continued advocacy. From very comprehensive reviews of PDM, first by Lowin (1968) and more recently by Dachler and Wilpert (1978) and by Locke and Schweiger (1979), there have been two general conclusions:

1. PDM usually has either a positive effect or no effect on the attitudes (satisfaction) of those who have the degree of their decision-making possibilities increased. Rarely does it decrease satisfaction.
2. Positive behaviors result from PDM at about the same frequency as do negative ones, and both of these occur less frequently than no observable effect of PDM on behavior.[1]

There are many explanations for the mixed support. Yet, all explanations lead to the conclusion that effective PDM depends upon many complex factors in the particular *setting,* the *nature of the decision,* and the *individuals* in the setting. These factors are too complex and numerous for us to outline here.

A few examples should illustrate some of these issues: The participants must possess knowledge of the topics or issues in which they are to participate. This seems obvious but is often ignored. Second, the decisions to be made must not have to be made quickly. We would not want a truckload of fire fighters to sit down and discuss the advantages and disadvantages of entering the front door versus a second-story window of a burning building upon arriving at the fire. Suffice it to say, PDM is no panacea for all ills facing organizational members. Yet, there are conditions in which it can be highly effective. Some of these conditions are addressed in the reviews we have cited as well as in a recent approach to leadership by Vroom and Yetton (1973) developed according to the description of conditions to which various forms of PDM should be applied.

Incentive Systems

Work for organizations is an exchange between the employee and the employer. The employee agrees to exchange time and effort to produce goods or services for the em-

---

[1]Our conclusions are based primarily on the summary tables in Locke and Schweiger (1979).

ployer. In exchange for the employee's inputs, the employer agrees to exchange various items or outcomes (either tangible or intangible) for his or her contributions. A subset of the total set of items in this exchange and the rules of the exchange form the incentive system of the organization.

Incentives are those items given to individuals that are designed to influence future behavior. The future orientation is important, for it means that an incentive serves as an anticipated reward for behavior to be accomplished. The individual may have received the reward in the past for some behavior, but it serves as an incentive for continued behavior only to the extent that he or she anticipates that continuing the behavior will lead to more of the reward.

Incentive systems are concerned with (1) identifying the items to be included as incentives and (2) establishing rules and procedures for disbursing the items to members of the organization. The motivational issues associated with these factors are most closely associated with the tenets of the expectancy theory, reinforcement approaches, and equity theory discussed earlier.

Importance of rewards. Identifying items valued by employees is extremely important to establishing effective incentive systems, but there has been surprisingly little good research on this, perhaps because most managers, union leaders, and industrial psychologists think they already know what people want. It stands to reason that people differ in what they want from work, and effective incentive systems should consider these differences.

The value of pay is an interesting case, and it illustrates the lack of understanding that can and does result from misunderstanding employees' views. For the most part, managers and union leaders view pay as the single most important reward, overshadowing all others. Psychologists, on the other hand, have conducted numerous surveys and find pay ranked from third to sixth in importance behind such items as having a steady job and being able to do the type of work wanted.

There is sufficient reason to believe that none of these estimates is very accurate for most groups. Pay is not the most important characteristic of work for many people, but it depends on how pay is treated. If by pay we mean pay or no pay at all, probably pay would be *the* most important. It is the incremental change or difference in pay level on which people differ in their evaluations and on which more pay is often not the most important issue.

Just as pay is probably not the most important item to employees, as managers and union leaders assume it is, it probably is not as low in importance as psychologists' ratings seem to indicate. Values frequently expressed which could be summarized by "money isn't everything" may make individuals who rate the importance of pay either reluctant to state its real importance when they feel it is very high or unwilling to admit to themselves that they value it so highly.

The research by Nealey (1964) was an exception to not fully studying the value of rewards to a group to which a set of rewards is to be applied. Nealey assessed the preferences of a large sample of electrical trade-union members for six benefit options. All options were approximately equal in cost to the employer. The six options were: (1) an additional $50.00 per month contribution to the retirement fund by the employer; (2) a 6% raise; (3) reduction in the work week from 40 to 37.5 hours with no drop in pay; (4) full hospitalization insurance for the employee and his or her family; (5) a union shop; and (6) an extra 3 weeks of paid vacation. Figure 14.12 shows the preferences of the employees. Figure 14.13 shows that employees of different ages had very different preferences. The differences across age groups clearly indicate that the application of one set of incentives and one incentive system to all employees in

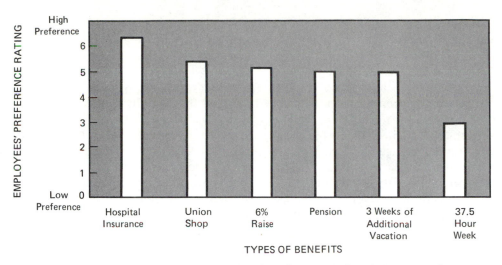

FIGURE 14.12 Relative preference for benefits equated to their cost to the organization. (Adapted from Nealey, 1964.)

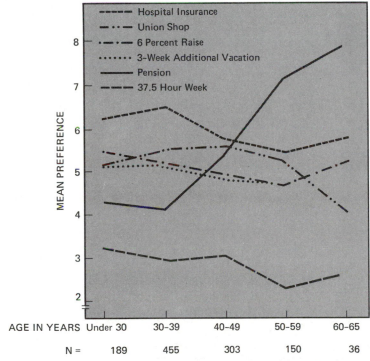

FIGURE 14.13 Benefit preference by age. (Adapted from Nealey, 1964.)

a given job class may not be best from a motivational standpoint.

Jurgensen (1978) capitalized on his position in a large metropolitan utility to gather data on over 57,000 job applicants from 1945 to 1975 to assess the preferences of men and women of various ages for different work-related factors. The data in Table 14.1 illustrate these preferences by age and sex. Not presented here were ranks over time. For the most part, preferences have stayed relatively stable over the last 30 years, but differences between age groups and sex are evident in Jurgensen's data.

Another way to analyze the value of rewards is to compare *amounts* of any particular reward with the importance of one reward relative to others. Intuitively we would expect that more of any particular reward that is valued by the individual is better than less of it. This is true, but only to a point—that is, the relationship between the amount of a reward and its attractiveness is not linear across amounts; there can be too much of a good thing. In an article entitled "More is Not Better: Two Failures of Incentive Theory," Korman and Glick (1981) found that people did not find enlisting in the Navy more and

TABLE 14.1 Ranks of employee preferences for various work conditions

	MEDIAN RANKS ASSIGNED JOB FACTORS IN RELATION TO AGE								
JOB FACTOR	UNDER 20	20–24	25–29	30–34	35–39	40–44	45–49	50–54	55 OR OVER
MEN									
Advancement	4.4	3.2	3.0	3.2	3.5	3.7	4.1	4.3	5.8
Benefits	7.9	6.7	6.5	6.5	6.6	6.6	6.9	6.9	6.9
Company	5.7	5.0	4.3	3.9	3.3	3.2	2.8	3.0	2.6
Co-workers	5.6	6.2	6.3	6.2	5.8	5.8	5.8	5.3	5.1
Hours	6.2	7.6	7.9	7.9	7.9	8.0	7.8	7.8	7.3
Pay	4.5	5.2	5.7	6.3	7.0	7.4	7.4	7.6	8.4
Security	3.8	2.7	2.2	2.0	1.9	2.0	2.1	2.1	2.1
Supervisor	6.1	6.5	6.5	6.3	6.0	5.8	5.4	5.5	5.0
Type of Work	2.7	3.0	3.3	3.6	3.9	4.0	4.4	4.3	4.5
Working conditions	7.1	7.8	8.2	8.2	8.3	7.9	7.9	7.5	7.0
No.	6,626	14,109	8,842	4,560	2,755	1,326	779	393	280
WOMEN									
Advancement	5.4	5.0	5.1	4.7	5.1	5.6	5.4	6.1	6.7
Benefits	8.4	8.0	7.7	7.5	7.6	7.1	7.0	7.0	7.8
Company	4.6	5.0	4.7	4.4	3.8	3.9	3.0	2.3	2.8
Co-workers	5.3	4.8	5.1	5.7	5.5	5.6	5.7	5.5	5.1
Hours	6.5	7.2	7.1	7.3	7.3	6.8	7.0	7.5	7.0
Pay	6.1	5.5	5.8	6.0	6.7	7.0	7.3	8.2	7.3
Security	4.8	5.2	4.9	4.1	3.4	3.7	3.5	3.5	3.6
Supervisor	5.6	5.1	4.9	5.0	4.9	5.1	5.2	4.9	5.0
Type of Work	1.5	1.4	1.6	2.1	2.4	2.3	2.5	2.3	2.8
Working conditions	5.9	6.8	7.0	7.2	7.3	7.2	7.1	7.1	6.9
No.	7,501	5,535	1,633	709	495	396	291	168	101

Source: Jurgensen, 1978, p. 271. Copyright 1978 by the American Psychological Association. Reproduced by permission.

more attractive as the size of the reward for enlisting increased.

Reward contingencies. To influence behavior, the rewards must be associated with the behavior of interest (Lawler, 1971). Both expectancy theory and reinforcement approaches emphasize the connection between behavior and reward. The degree of association can vary from none at all to a very strong connection. Some rewards, frequently labeled systems rewards, are available simply because an employee is a member of a particular organization. In this case, the rewards are contingent on behavior in only a very gross sense; they are basically contingent on remaining with the organization. Such rewards as medical insurance and the number of weeks of vacation, for example, usually cannot be influenced by behavior other than remaining with the organization.

At the other extreme are rewards that depend on very specific behaviors. An auto mechanic paid by the number and type of jobs completed exemplifies this type of reward system.

The solution for the development of sound incentive programs is obvious: Rewards must be made contingent on those behaviors the incentive systems are designed to influence. These behaviors may be performance, attendance, lack of turnover, low employee theft, or any other behavior. Unfortunately, although in principle the contingency notion is sound, it is too simplistic. The major reason for this is that changing one reward contingency often alters several other contingencies, because of the complex interrelationships in interpersonal systems. For example, shifting pay from an hourly pay system to a piece-rate system theoretically should lead pay to be more closely tied to behavior and should increase the influence of pay on performance. The individual piece-rate system, however, may increase tension among group members if it creates large differences in performance among group mem-

bers and makes these differences obvious. For example, older workers with more seniority may not be able to keep up with younger, less senior workers. The net result could be a decrease in performance across the group with the piece rate as compared to those in the hourly condition because of the tension it creates. Obviously, in this case, a simple change in pay procedures would not lead to the predicted results, because of the complexities of the pay and social system. Regardless of the reward under consideration, it is rare when a change in the contingency between that reward and a behavior does not influence other reward-behavior contingencies in the work setting. Often the effects on other contingencies are unexpected and work against the desired effects of the change in the reward under investigation.

Extrinsic rewards and intrinsic motivation. The contingency between pay and task performance has recently come under particular scrutiny because of its alleged effect on intrinsic motivation. Recall that intrinsic motivation is the extent to which an individual works on a job because of the intrinsic enjoyment he or she gets from doing it. Deci (1972, 1975) has argued that pay that is closely associated with (contingent on) performance *decreases* intrinsic motivation because the person is controlled by the pay and no longer can choose to do or not to do the task. The controlling nature of pay decreases the intrinsic motivation.

The ramifications of this effect for incentive programs are obvious. The practices of intrinsic motivation originally thought to be useful must be reevaluated. Absorbing and interesting jobs usually carry more responsibility *and pay more*. This implies that perhaps pay for these types of jobs should not be related very closely to performance.

Deci's findings have not gone unquestioned. They have been criticized methodologically (Calder & Staw, 1975), as well as for their limited ability to generalize the laboratory research from which most of these conclusions were drawn (Fisher, 1978; Staw, 1977). It looks as if this effect is not very likely in work settings in which pay is an integral part of the employment contract (Fisher, 1978). Nevertheless, the jury is still out on this issue; further work is needed. Until we know more, the effects of pay on intrinsic motivation should at least be considered when incentive systems are designed.

TRENDS IN OVERALL WORK MOTIVATION

For some time, John B. Miner has been interested in managerial motivation. Miner defines such motivation as a general interest and willingness to devote time and effort to the task of managing in organizations. Using an instrument called the Miner Sentence Completion Scale (MSCS), Miner has sampled the beliefs and attitudes of managers and management students several times over the last 20 years (Miner & Smith, 1982). Several interesting trends emerge. First, differences that once existed between men and women have now disappeared; women no longer show lower levels of motivation to manage. Second, a trend appeared across the 1960s and early 1970s in which managerial motivation dropped significantly from one time period to another. In the most recent samples—1980—the decrease has stopped but the level of motivation, as indicated by the survey, is not reversing—that is, it is not returning to the levels that were observed in the early 1960s.

DISCUSSION

Our treatment of work motivation has been long and extensive. It should be obvious that the topic of work motivation is complex and diverse. There are no panaceas. None of the theories incorporates all we need to know about work behavior. Each offers a perspective which can be useful for understanding why and how people work.

The general practices which were discussed (goal setting, participatory decision making, and incentive systems) all had as their basis one or more of the theoretical frameworks discussed in the earlier part of the chapter. These general practices are then incorporated into specific organizational policies and practices. We did not discuss this final step because of the diversity of ways to accomplish this. One cannot prescribe, a priori, a particular system without a thorough understanding of the particular organization and its functioning. We have tried to show that psychologists and others concerned about the behavior of individuals in organizations have considered the motivational bases for work behavior and have developed some general strategies with reference to a particular theory or theories.

REFERENCES

Abelson, R. P., Aronson, E., McGuire, W. J., Newcomb, T. M., Rosenberg, M. J., & Tannenbaum, P. H. (Eds.) (1968). *Theories of cognitive consistency: A source book*. Chicago: Rand McNally.

Adams, J. S. (1965). Inequality in social exchange. In L. Berkowitz (Ed.), *Advances in experimental psychology* (Vol. 2). New York: Academic Press.

Adams, J. S., & Jacobson, P. R. (1964) Effects of wage inequities on work quality. *Journal of Abnormal and Social Psychology, 69,* 19–25.

Adams, J. S., & Rosenbaum, W. E. (1962). The relationship of worker productivity to cognitive dissonance about inequities. *Journal of Applied Psychology, 46,* 161–164.

Alderfer, C. P. (1969). Effects of task factors on job attitudes and job behaviors. II. Job enlargement and the organizational context. *Personnel Psychology, 22,* 418–426.

Alderfer, C. P. (1972). *Existence, relatedness, and growth: Human needs in organizational settings.* New York: Free Press.

Atkinson, J. W. (1957). Motivational determinants of risk-taking behavior. *Psychological Review, 64*, 359–372.

Atkinson, J. W., & Feather, N. T. (1966). *A theory of achievement motivation.* New York: Wiley.

Behling, O., & Starke, F. A. (1973). *Some limits on expectancy theories of work effort.* Proceedings of the Midwest Meeting of the American Institute of Decision Sciences.

Calder, B. J., & Staw, B. M. (1975). Self-perception of intrinsic and extrinsic motivation. *Journal of Personality and Social Psychology, 31*, 599–605.

Campbell, J. P., Dunnette, M. D., Lawler, E. E., & Weick, K. E., Jr. (1970). *Managerial behavior, performance and effectiveness.* New York: McGraw-Hill.

Campbell, J. P., & Pritchard, R. D. (1976). Motivation theory in individual and organizational psychology. In M. D. Dunnette (Ed.), *Handbook of industrial and organizational psychology.* Chicago: Rand McNally.

Coch, L., & French, J. R. P. (1948). Overcoming resistance to change. *Human Relations, 1*, 512–532.

Dachler, H. P., & Mobley, W. H. (1973). Construct validation of an instrumentality-expectancy-task-goal model of work motivation: Some theoretical boundary conditions. *Journal of Applied Psychology, 58*, 397–418.

Dachler, H. P., & Wilpert, B. (1978). Conceptual dimensions and boundaries of participation in organizations: A critical evaluation. *Administrative Science Quarterly, 23*, 1–39.

DeCharms, R. (1968). *Personal causation: The internal affective determinants of behavior.* New York: Academic Press.

Deci, E. L. (1972). The effects of contingent and noncontingent rewards and controls on intrinsic motivation. *Organizational Behavior and Human Performance, 8*, 217–229.

Deci, E. L. (1975). *Intrinsic motivation.* New York: Plenum Press.

Ekehammer, B. (1974). Interactionism in personality from a historical perspective. *Psychological Bulletin, 81*, 1020–1048.

Festinger, L. A. (1957). *A theory of cognitive dissonance.* Evanston, Ill.: Row, Peterson.

Fisher, C. D. (1978). The effects of personal control, competence, and extrinsic reward systems on intrinsic motivation. *Organizational Behavior and Human Performance, 21*, 273–288.

Ford, R. N. (1969). *Motivation through work itself.* New York: American Management Association.

Goodman, P. S. (1977). Social comparison processes in organizations. In B. M. Staw & G. R. Salancik (Eds.), *New directions in organizational behavior.* Chicago: St. Clair Press.

Goodman, P. S., & Friedman, A. (1971). Adams' theory of inequity. *Administrative Science Quarterly, 16*, 271–288.

Greenberg, J. (1977). The protestant work ethic and reactions to negative performance evaluations on a laboratory task. *Journal of Applied Psychology, 62*, 682–690.

Greenberg, J., & Ornstein, S. (1983). High status job title as compensation for underpayment: A test of equity theory. *Journal of Applied Psychology, 68*, 285–297.

Hall, D. T., & Nougaim, K. E. (1968). An examination of Maslow's need hierarchy in an organizational setting. *Organizational Behavior and Human Performance, 3*, 12–35.

Hall, J. (Summer, 1976). To achieve or not: The manager's choice. *California Management Review, 15*(3), 5–18.

Herzberg, F. (1966). *Work and the nature of man.* Cleveland: World Publishing.

Herzberg, F., Mausner, B., & Snyderman, B. B. (1959). *The motivation to work.* New York: Wiley.

Hulin, C. L. (1971). Individual differences and job enrichment—The case against general treatments. In J. R. Maher (Ed.), *New perspectives in job enrichment.* New York: Van Nostrand.

Ilgen, D. R., Fisher, C. D., & Taylor, M. S. (1979). Motivational consequences of individual feedback on behavior in organizations. *Journal of Applied Psychology, 64*, 349–371.

Ilgen, D. R., Nebeker, D. M., & Pritchard, R. D. (1981). Expectancy theory measures: An empirical comparison in an experimental simulation. *Organizational Behavior and Human Performance, 28*, 189–223.

Jablonsky, S. F., & DeVries, D. L. (1972). Operant conditioning principles extrapolated to the theory of management. *Organizational Behavior and Human Performance, 17*, 340–358.

Jackson, S. E. (1983). Participation in decision making as a strategy for reducing job-related strain. *Journal of Applied Psychology, 68*, 3–19.

Johnston, W. A. (1967). Individual performance and self-evaluation in a simulated team. *Organizational Behavior and Human Performance, 2*, 309–328.

Jurgensen, C. E. (1978). Job preferences (what makes a job good or bad?). *Journal of Applied Psychology, 63*, 267–276.

King, N. (1970). Clarification and evaluation of the

two-factor theory of job satisfaction. *Psychological Bulletin, 74,* 18–31.

Klinger, E., & McNelly, F. W., Jr. (1969). Fantasy need achievement and performance: A role analysis. *Psychological Review, 76,* 574–591.

Koch, S. W. (1965). *Management and motivation.* Summary of doctoral dissertation presented at the Swedish School of Economics, Helsigfors, Finland.

Komaki, J., Heinzmann, A. T., & Lawson, L. (1980). Effect of training and feedback: Component analysis of a behavioral safety program. *Journal of Applied Psychology, 65,* 261–270.

Komaki, J., Waddell, W. M., & Pearce, M. G. (1977). The applied behavior analysis approach and individual employees: Improving performance in two small businesses. *Organizational Behavior and Human Performance, 19*(2), 337–352.

Komaki, S. L., Collins, R. L., & Penn, P. (1982). The role of performance antecedents and consequences in work motivation. *Journal of Applied Psychology, 67,* 334–340.

Korman, A. K. (1976). Hypothesis of work behavior revisited and an extension. *Academy of Management Review, 1,* 50–63.

Korman, A. K. (1977). *Organizational behavior.* Englewood Cliffs, N. J.: Prentice-Hall.

Korman, A. K., & Glick, A. S. (1981). More is not better: Two failures of incentive theory. *Journal of Applied Psychology, 66,* 225–229.

Landy, F. J., & Trumbo, D. A. (1980). *The psychology of work behavior.* 2nd ed., Homewood, IL: Dorsey.

Latham, G. P., & Baldes, J. J. (1975). The practical significance of Locke's theory of goal setting. *Journal of Applied Psychology, 60,* 122–124.

Latham, G. P., & Yukl, G. A. (1975). A review of research on the application of goal setting in organizations. *Academy of Management Journal, 18,* 824–845.

Lawler, E. E., III (1971). *Pay and organizational effectiveness: A psychological view.* New York: McGraw-Hill.

Lawler, E. E., III, & Hackman, J. R. (1969). Impact of employee participation in the development of pay incentive plans: A field experiment. *Journal of Applied Psychology, 53,* 467–471.

Lawler, E. E., III, & Suttle, J. L. (1972). A causal correlational test of the need hierarchy concept. *Organizational Behavior and Human Performance, 7,* 265–287.

Lawler, E. E., III, & Suttle, J. L. (1973). Expectancy theory and job performance. *Organizational Behavior and Human Performance, 9,* 482–503.

Lewin, L. (1938). *The conceptual representation and the measurement of psychological forces.* Durham, N. C.: Duke University Press.

Locke, E. A. (1968). Toward a theory of task motivation and incentives. *Organizational Behavior and Human Performance, 3,* 157–189.

Locke, E. A. (1976). The nature and causes of job satisfaction. In M. D. Dunnette (Ed.), *Handbook of industrial and organizational psychology.* Chicago: Rand McNally.

Locke, E. A. (1977). The myths of behavior mod in organizations. *The Academy of Management Review 2*(4), 543–553.

Locke, E. A., & Schweiger, D. M. (1979). Participation in decision-making: One more look. In B. M. Staw (Ed.), *Research in organizational behavior* (Vol. 1). Greenwich, Conn.: JAI Press.

Locke, E. A., Shaw, K. N., Saari, L. M., & Latham, G. P. (1981). Goal setting and task performance: 1969–1980. *Psychological Bulletin, 90,* 125–153.

Lowin, A. (1968). Participative decision making: a model, literature critique, and prescriptions for research. *Organizational Behavior and Human Performance, 3,* 68–106.

Maslow, A. H. (1954). *Motivation and personality.* New York: Harper & Row.

Maslow, A. H. (1970). *Motivation and personality* (2nd ed.). New York: Harper & Row.

McClelland, D. C. (1961). *The achieving society.* Princeton, N.J.: Van Nostrand.

McClelland, D. C., & Winter, D. C. (1969). *Motivating economic achievement.* New York: Free Press.

McGregor, D. (1960). *The human side of enterprise.* New York: McGraw-Hill.

McGregor, D. M. (1957). The human side of enterprise. *Management Review,* 1957, 22–29, 88–92.

Mawhinney, T. C. (1975). Operant terms and concepts in the description of individual work behavior: Some problems of interpretation, application and evaluation. *Journal of Applied Psychology, 60,* 704–712.

Mawhinney, T. C. (1979). Intrinsic v extrinsic work motivation: Perspectives from behaviorism. *Organizational Behavior and Human Performance, 24,* 411–440.

Miner, J. B., & Dachler, H. P. (1973). Personnel attitudes and motivation. *Annual Review of Psychology, 24,* 379–422.

Miner, J. B., & Smith, N. R. (1982). Decline and

stabilization of managerial motivation over a 20 year period. *Journal of Applied Psychology, 67,* 297–306.

Mischel, W. (1973). Toward a cognitive social learning reconceptualization of personality. *Psychological Review, 80,* 252–283.

Mitchell, T. R. (1974). Expectancy models of job satisfaction, occupational preference, and effort: A theoretical, methodological, and empirical appraisal. *Psychological Bulletin, 82,* 1053–1077.

Mitchell, T. R. (1979). Organizational behavior. *Annual Review of Psychology.* Palo Alto, Calif: Annual Reviews, 30, 243–282.

Myers, M. S. (January–February 1964). Who are your motivated workers? *Harvard Business Review, 42,* 73–88.

Naylor, J. C., Pritchard, R. D., & Ilgen, D. R. (1980). *A theory of behavior in organizations.* New York: Academic Press.

Nealey, S. M. (1964). Determining worker preferences among employee benefit programs. *Journal of Applied Psychology, 48,* 7–12.

New Tool: "Reinforcement" for good work. *Business Week,* December 18, 1971. 76–77.

Parker, D. F., & Dyer, L. (1976). Expectancy theory as a within-person behavioral choice model: An empirical test of some conceptual and methodological refinements. *Organizational Behavior and Human Performance, 17*(1), 97–117.

Peak, H. (1955). Attitude and motivation. In M. R. Jones (Ed.), *Nebraska Symposium on Motivation.* Lincoln: University of Nebraska Press.

Porter, L. W. (1962). Job attitudes in management: I. Perceived deficiencies in need fulfillment as a function of job level. *Journal of Applied Psychology, 46,* 375–384.

Porter, L. W., & Lawler, E. E., III (1968). *Managerial attitudes and performances.* Homewood, Ill.: Dorsey Press.

Pritchard, R. D. (1969). Equity theory: A review and critique. *Organizational Behavior and Human Performance, 4,* 176–211.

Pritchard, R. D., Campbell, K. M., & Campbell, D. J. (1977). The effects of extrinsic financial rewards on intrinsic motivation. *Journal of Applied Psychology, 62,* 9–15.

Pritchard, R. D., Dunnette, M. D., & Jorgenson, D. O. (1972). Effects of perceptions of equity and inequity on worker performance and satisfaction. *Journal of Applied Psychology, 56,* 75–94.

Pritchard, R. D., Leonard, D. W., Von Bergen, C. W., Jr., Kirk, R. J. (1976). The effects of varying schedules of reinforcement on human task performance. *Organizational Behavior and Human Performance, 16,* 205–230.

Rhode, J. G., Sorensen, J. E., & Lawler, E. E., III (1976). An analysis of personal characteristics related to professional staff turnover in public accounting firms. *Decision Sciences, 7,* 771–800.

Ronan, W. W., Latham, G. P., & Kinne, S. B. (1973). Effects of goal setting and supervision on worker behavior in an industrial situation. *Journal of Applied Psychology, 58,* 302–307.

Scheflen, K. C., Lawler, E. E., III, & Hackman, J. R. (1971). Long-term impact of employee participation in the development of pay incentive plans: A field experiment revisited. *Journal of Applied Psychology, 55,* 182–186.

Schlenker, B. R., Soraci, S., & McCarthy, M. (1976). Self-esteem and group performance as determinants of egocentric perceptions in cooperative groups. *Human Relations, 29,* 1163–1187.

Schneider, B. (1983). Interactional psychology and organizational behavior. In L. L. Cummings & B. M. Staw (Eds.), *Research in organizational behavior* (Vol. 5). Greenwich, Conn.: JAI Press.

Staw, B. M. (1977). Motivation in organizations: Toward synthesis and redirection. In B. M. Staw & G. R. Salancik (Eds.). *New directions in organizational behavior.* Chicago: St. Clair Press.

Stedry, A. C., & Kay, E. (1966). The effects of goal difficulty on performance. *Behavioral Science, 11,* 459–470.

Steers, R. M., & Porter, L. W. (1974). The role of task-goal attributes in employee performance. *Psychological Bulletin, 81,* 434–452.

Steers, R. M., & Porter, L. W. (Eds.) (1983). *Motivation and work behavior* (2nd ed.). New York: McGraw-Hill.

Terborg, J. R. (1977). Validation and extension of an individual differences model of work performance. *Organizational Behavior and Human Performance, 18,* 188–216.

Terkel, S. (1972). *Working: People talk about what they do all day and how they feel about what they do.* New York: Pantheon.

Tolman, E. C. (1932). *Purposive behavior in animals and men.* New York: Century.

Vecchio, R. P. (1981). An individual-differences interpretation of the conflicting predictions generated by equity theory and expectancy theory. *Journal of Applied Psychology, 66,* 470–481.

Vroom, V. J. (1964). *Work and motivation.* New York: Wiley.

Vroom, V. H., & Yetton, P. W. (1973). *Leadership and decision-making.* Pittsburgh: University of Pittsburgh Press.

Weiss, H. M., & Adler, S. (1984). Personality and organizational behavior. In B. M. Staw & L. L. Cummings (Eds.), *Research in organizational behavior* (Vol. 6). Greenwich, Conn.: JAI Press.

Where Skinner's theories work. *Business Week,* December 2, 1972, 64–65.

White, R. W. (1959). Motivation reconsidered: The concept of competence. *Psychological Review, 66,* 297–333.

15

Job Satisfaction, Attitudes, and Opinions

As human beings, members of work-oriented organizations have thoughts and feelings which strongly influence their behavior on the job. These thoughts and feelings are part of their conscious states and provide the inputs used by them to make decisions about their actions and reactions to their jobs. Therefore, we must understand more about these conscious states. Those who study human behavior, label the conscious states of interest to us here *attitudes* and *beliefs*.

First we define beliefs or opinions and attitudes and then we discuss, in detail, job satisfaction as a particular subset of attitudes. We explore both the nature of job satisfaction and its relationship to several aspects of work-related behavior. Following this we turn our attention to individual reactions and organizational programs designed to affect job satisfaction and employee well-being.

BELIEFS OR OPINIONS[1]

Beliefs are thoughts (cognitions) held about some objects, concepts, or events, or the relationship between these things. "My cash register is jamming," "The pressure in the tank is up to 150 pounds per square inch," "You are working harder than she is" all are beliefs. Note that all are subjective belief states of the individual. Most are very concrete and, more than likely, represent true states of affairs, but they may not be. For example, the pressure in the tank might not be 150 pounds per square inch; the individual may have misread the dial or the pressure

---

[1]The terms *beliefs* and *opinions* tend to be used interchangeably. We do the same. For example, psychologists who study attitudes tend to talk about beliefs. However, sample surveys constructed to ask people about what they believe tend to be labeled opinion surveys.

gauge may be incorrect. Regardless of the accuracy of the belief, to the individual it represents the basis on which he or she responds.

One final point should be made about beliefs: They do not necessarily convey any information about goodness or badness, liking or disliking by the belief holder. Consider the belief that my cash register is jammed. In and of itself, this does not say anything about whether the person who holds this belief sees it as good or bad. If he or she is the store manager and customers are backed up waiting to check out, this is probably bad. However, if the person is a cashier who has not had a break in 6 hours, he or she may be delighted to have the cash register break down.

ATTITUDES

Definition

Attitudes, like beliefs, are conscious states. Unlike beliefs, they do represent the degree of affect felt by the individual who holds them. They are the feelings the individual has toward some object, and these feelings are manifested in some judgment about the goodness or badness of the attitude object from the individual's point of view.

We define an attitude as *the affective orientation toward a particular attitude object*. This definition is consistent with much of the major research on attitudes at the present time (Fishbein & Ajzen, 1975). Note two things about this definition. First, attitudes are toward some attitude object. They do not exist in a vacuum. The object may be very specific, such as an attitude toward the letterhead on a piece of stationery, or it may be very general, such as an attitude toward big business. In all cases there is some object toward which the affective response is directed. Second, the term attitude as used in the statement, "She has a good attitude" has no meaning in this chapter. In this statement,

the term attitude really has no specific attitude object. It is a very general description incorporating much more than is usually included in precise treatments of attitudes.

Importance

The attitudes of employees are important to the employees themselves and to those who manage organizations. Employees' attitudes serve several functions. They provide information about employees' reactions to other individuals, events, or objects. For example, an individual who does not like being in or around water knows better than to try a career as a skin diver.

Attitudes may also guide behavior. If we assume that, other things being equal, employees will seek to approach or obtain attitude objects toward which they hold positive attitudes and avoid those for which they hold negative ones, then they should intend to behave in order to attain positive and to avoid negative attitude objects. Whether the behavior actually occurs depends, of course, on many factors which aid or inhibit the behavior. Nevertheless, the attitude does reflect an *intended* behavior if the behavior is feasible.

Attitudes are even related to the physical health of employees. Sales (1969) found a significant negative correlation between employees' serum cholesterol levels while working on 1-hour laboratory tasks and their degrees of enjoyment of the tasks. Sales and House (1971) found that job satisfaction was negatively correlated with the rate of deaths from arteriosclerotic heart disease across groups of employees. Although the Sales and House data are correlational, they certainly deserve further attention.

Employees' attitudes are important to employers for at least two reasons. As mentioned earlier, attitudes indicate intended responses. Therefore, knowledge of those attitude objects on the job to which employees respond favorably and to which they respond unfavorably can provide a basis for job design, policy, and practice decisions. When possible, positive features should be strengthened and negative ones altered or removed. At a more general level, employees' attitudes are important to employers for philosophical reasons. Today it is not sufficient to be content simply with providing work for employees. It is well accepted that employers should provide meaningful and satisfying work, to the extent that it is possible to do so. Although it is often argued that it is not technically possible to provide satisfying jobs, the technical limits are not quite as restrictive as many employers had once believed. It is perfectly reasonable for employers to be concerned with positive employee attitudes as an end in itself rather than simply as a means to some end such as lower turnover. More is said about ways to improve working conditions later.

JOB SATISFACTION

Job satisfaction is a specific subset of attitudes held by organization members. It is the attitude they have toward their jobs. Stated another way, it is their affective responses to their jobs.

Job satisfaction has been the primary attitude of interest to both practitioners and researchers over the years. In 1976, Locke reported that there had been well over 3000 published studies on job satisfaction between the early work of Hoppock in 1935 and Locke's review and critique in 1976. Because of the interest in, and importance of the topic, we devote most of the remainder of the chapter to discussing it.

Dimensions of Job Satisfaction

Specific Job Dimensions. The concept of a job is very complex. It has many facets, such as the nature of the work, the supervisor, the company, pay, or promotional opportunities.

The job itself seldom serves as a unitary attitude object. Rather, the attitude, in this case the satisfaction that the individual associates with his or her job, is really the degree of satisfaction with a number of different dimensions of the job.

Over the years considerable time and effort have been devoted to discovering the dimensions of job satisfaction. The best conclusion to draw from this work is that, although there are many very specific and diverse job dimensions which are related to job satisfaction, there is a set of dimensions common to most jobs that is sufficient to describe most of the predictable variance in job satisfaction. The size of the set varies roughly from five to twenty job dimensions, but seldom is it necessary to assess the degree of satisfaction using more than ten. The number in this set may vary somewhat depending on the nature of the job and the purpose for which job satisfaction is being investigated. As we shall see, a common core of job dimensions is a good index of job satisfaction over a wide variety of jobs.

Locke (1976) presented a summary of job dimensions that had consistently been found to contribute significantly to employees' job satisfaction. Figure 15.1 illustrates Locke's discussion by organizing specific job dimensions according to the classification scheme he introduced in 1973. The specific dimensions listed in Figure 15.1 represent those job characteristics typically used to assess job satisfaction. They are relatively specific attitude objects for which the organizational members have some position on a like-dislike continuum. They are also work characteristics salient to most people. For example, consider work itself and pay. Job incumbents quickly form very definite attitudes about the work they do. After very little experience on the job, they have definite feelings about how interesting the work is, how routine, how well they are doing, and, in general, how much they enjoy doing whatever it is they do.

GENERAL CATEGORIES	SPECIFIC DIMENSION	DIMENSION DESCRIPTIONS
I. Events or Conditions		
1. Work	Work Itself	Includes intrinsic interest, variety, opportunity for learning, difficulty, amount, chances for success, control over work flow, etc.
2. Rewards	Pay	Amount, fairness or equity, basis for pay, etc.
	Promotions	Opportunities for, basis of, fairness of, etc.
	Recognition	Praise, criticism, credit for work done, etc.
3. Context of Work	Working Conditions	Hours, rest pauses, equipment, quality of the workspace, temperature, ventilation, location of plant, etc.
	Benefits	Pensions, medical and life insurance plans, annual leaves, vacations, etc.
II. Agents		
1. Self	Self	Values, skills, and abilities, etc.
2. Others (In-Company)	Supervision	Supervisory style and influence, technical adequacy, administrative skills, etc.
	Co-workers	Competence, friendliness, helpfulness, technical competence, etc.
3. Others (Outside Company)	Customers	Technical competence, friendliness, etc.
	Family Members*	Supportiveness, knowledge of job, demands for time, etc.
	Others	Depending upon position—e.g., students, parents, voters.

* Not included in Locke's discussion.

Likewise, feelings about pay are quite clear. The same amount of pay may lead to quite different feelings about how good it is, but, nevertheless, almost all will have formed for themselves some feeling about that amount.

The general categories of job dimensions depicted on the left-hand side of Figure 15.1 are not addressed by most researchers who attempt to identify the job dimensions important to job satisfaction. Locke (1973, 1976) introduced the general categories in order to cluster common dimensions into more theoretically meaningful groups. We feel his system is useful, for it provides some basis for considering the adequacy of the set of dimensions as well as a basis for better understanding how and why some dimensions are liked or disliked. For example, according to Locke (1976), "every Event or Condition ultimately is caused by someone or something, and . . . every Agent is liked or disliked because he is perceived as having done (or failed to do) something . . ." (p. 1302). To the extent that this is so, it is clear that in some settings in which supervisors have considerable control over the work done by their subordinates and over their pay, we should expect to find satisfaction with supervision closely related to satisfaction with the work itself and the pay. In other settings, in which supervisors influence very little the work done by subordinates, and subordinates' pay is based upon some companywide scale, we should expect less covariation among satisfaction with work itself, pay, and supervision.

Single or multiple dimensions. Should job satisfaction be considered a single entity or should satisfaction with each of the dimensions of interest be considered separately? The answer depends on one's reason or reasons for being concerned about job satisfaction. If job-satisfaction measures are used to diagnose potential problem areas in the job setting, then separate dimensions are more valuable than an overall measure. The individual job facets can be considered in order to learn which ones seem to be producing positive and which ones negative feelings on the part of employees. If, on the other hand, the interest is in the relationship between a general response to the job, such as quitting, a measure of overall job satisfaction may be more appropriate.

Combining dimensions of job satisfaction. It seems intuitively obvious that all of a job's dimensions are not equally important to all people in determining overall satisfaction with their jobs. Some people may consider their pay very important and working conditions less so; others may consider the reverse. Therefore, when combining measures of satisfaction with several dimensions of a job, it is tempting to weight the dimensions by their relative importance to the particular individual. With few exceptions (e.g., Butler, 1983), the data are very clear for this issue: It does *not* work (Ewen, 1967). It is much better to select a set of job dimensions that have been found to apply to most jobs and then simply weight each dimension score equally to calculate overall satisfaction.

Several reasons have been suggested for why importance ratings do not work. The most compelling is that when individuals rate their satisfaction with any single dimension of a job, they also indirectly indicate the dimension's importance (Dachler & Hulin, 1969; Locke, 1976). That an individual has either strong positive or strong negative feelings about a dimension indicates that the dimension is important enough for that person to feel strongly about it. On the other hand, an individual's having neutral feelings of satisfaction usually means that the factor really does not matter much. Therefore, weighting satisfaction ratings by importance is redundant and adds nothing.

Theoretical Views of Job Satisfaction

Job satisfaction is often treated as if it were the same as or very similar to work motivation. For example, it is not uncommon to treat both topics in a single chapter. It should be clear from our discussion so far that we consider the two topics quite distinct. Job satisfaction is concerned with the *feelings* one has toward a job, and work motivation is concerned with the *behaviors* that occur on the job. Nevertheless, it is not surprising that the two topics are not clearly differentiated. This occurs for two reasons. First, satisfaction is a hedonic response of liking or disliking the attitude object. It is often assumed that individuals will approach those things with which they are satisfied and avoid those things with which they are dissatisfied. As a result, job satisfaction is frequently associated with job behaviors just as motivation is. Second, most theories of motivation have an underlying hedonic assumption that individuals are motivated to seek that which is pleasant to them. Therefore, many theories of work motivation are also considered, at least in part, theories of job satisfaction.

In the discussion that follows we have not addressed all of the individual theories of job satisfaction. We suggest five general orientations toward job satisfaction, all of which describe the processes by which job satisfaction is determined for individuals.

Comparison processes. The most widely accepted view of job satisfaction assumes that the degree of affect experienced results from some comparison between the individual's standard and that individual's perception of the extent to which the standard is met. The amount of satisfaction that results is a function of the size of the discrepancy between the standard and what the individual believes he or she is receiving from the job. Vroom (1964) labeled this view a *subtractive* theory of job satisfaction.

There is one issue with regard to the comparison-process view of job satisfaction: the specification of what is used as the standard to which the job is compared. Some have argued that the individual's needs serve as a standard (Morse, 1953; Porter, 1962, 1963). Locke (1976) believes that the individual's values, rather than his or her needs, serve as a standard. Smith, Kendall, and Hulin (1969) developed a popular job-satisfaction measure, the Job Descriptive Index (JDI), which considered the cognitive state of an individual's frame of reference as the standard to which the job is compared. The evidence seems to show that both values and frames of reference serve as standards more than needs.

Instrumentality theory. A second view of job satisfaction is that individuals calculate the degree to which their jobs are satisfying by considering the extent to which the jobs lead to valued outcomes. It is assumed that each individual has a set of judgments about how much he or she values certain outcomes such as pay, a promotion, or good working conditions. The individual then estimates the extent to which holding the job leads to each of these outcomes. Finally, by weighting the perceived value or attractiveness of each outcome and by considering all outcomes in the set, the individual arrives at an estimate of the satisfaction he or she feels will come from the job. This process, labeled instrumentality theory for its emphasis on the extent to which

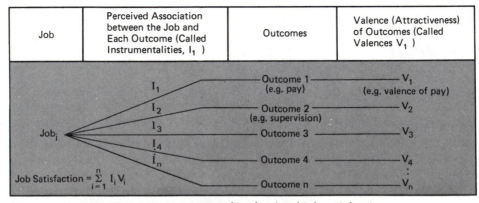

FIGURE 15.2 Instrumentality theory of job satisfaction.

a job is instrumental in producing satisfaction, is illustrated in Figure 15.2.

Pulakos and Schmitt (1983) used an instrumentality view of job satisfaction to predict the degree of satisfaction students entering the job market would have on their new jobs. Measures were obtained of the types of outcomes each student felt were important (valences) as well as the extent to which they believed their first jobs would provide such outcomes for them (instrumentalities). Outcomes were such factors as good pay, challenging work, and friendly co-workers. Nine months and 20 months later Pulakos and Schmitt found that job satisfaction was significantly related to the product of the instrumentalities and valences obtained prior to reporting to the new jobs. When the measures were explored individually, it was found that the instrumentalities were more predictive of satisfaction than were valences. This is probably because all the students in the sample agreed pretty closely on the level of importance of any given outcome such as pay. As a result there was little variance in the outcomes, and the lack of variance reduces the size of the correlation that can be expected. On the other hand, there was considerable variance in the beliefs about the extent to which their new jobs would provide any particular outcome.

Social influence. Salancik and Pfeffer (1977) questioned comparison theories of job satisfaction and suggested that perhaps people decide how satisfied they are with their jobs not by processing all kinds of information about them but by observing others on similar jobs and making inferences about others' satisfaction. In a similar vein Weiss and Shaw (1979) suggested that an individual simply infers a level of his or her own satisfaction from observing others. In a sense they were saying that individuals may come into new jobs not knowing how satisfied they will be with them. They look around, see others like themselves who are satisfied (or dissatisfied) with them, and are then influenced by these observations about how satisfied (or dissatisfied) they are with their jobs.

Research by White and Mitchell (1979) and Weiss and Shaw (1979) showed that people are indeed influenced by their perceptions of others' satisfaction. Weiss and Shaw had people first view a training film showing others working on an electrical assembly task. While working on the tasks, those in the film either made incidental comments which indicated that they liked the tasks (for example, "This task is OK" or "I don't mind doing this at all") or they exhibited neutral positions toward the task. Following the film, the participants in the study worked on the same task they saw demonstrated in the film and rated their degrees of satisfaction. The results clearly showed that the feelings about the tasks were influenced by others' reactions as well as by properties of the task themselves.

The social-influence theory of job satisfaction is interesting because it recognizes the social nature of work and suggests a way of determining job satisfaction that has been ignored for a long time. It seems obvious that social factors do influence satisfaction and that they deserve more attention than they have received in the past.

Two interpretations of the social-influence theory have sprung up: the strong and the weak. The strong interpretation argues that social cues provide the *only* basis for satisfaction with work. The weak suggests that satisfaction is affected by social forces but does not deny that some or perhaps a major portion of satisfaction may be derived in other ways. Part of the confusion has arisen because of the way Salancik and Pfeffer (1977) discussed their social-influence view. From that discussion some have inferred that the strong interpretation most closely reflects their position. In our opinion, it is not necessary to interpret Salancik and Pfeffer in the strong sense; indeed, only the weak interpretation seems supportable. Clearly people are influenced by what others say about their jobs but this is not the only factor that affects their satisfaction.

Equity theory. Equity theory also contains a social element in which the individual compares his or her inputs and outcomes to those of others. The theory was discussed in detail in Chapter 14. For job satisfaction the same process is hypothesized as for work motivation. It differs from that presented thus far in that it predicts that too much of a good thing is dissatisfying—that is, that receiving more than is equitable will produce less satisfaction.

The evidence seems to indicate that equity norms do operate and that overpayment inequity can exist (for example, Pritchard, Dunnette, & Jorgenson, 1972). Because the conditions occur relatively infrequently and because it is uncertain how long individuals will continue to experience overpayment inequity before adjusting their points of view to allow them to receive the same returns without feeling overcompensated, it does not appear to us that an equity framework controls a major portion of the job-satisfaction variance.

Two-factor theory. Herzberg (Herzberg, 1966; Herzberg, Mausner, & Snyderman, 1959) proposed that job satisfaction stemmed from an entirely different set of causes than job dissatisfaction. He argued that "satisfiers," which were such work-related dimensions as recognition, autonomy, and responsibility, and the work itself could affect only satisfaction and not dissatisfaction, whereas the opposite effect occurred for "dissatisfiers," such as pay, working conditions, and human-relations behaviors of supervisors or co-workers. This position generated considerable research and debate during the 1960s. By now it is clear that the position has no support (see King, 1970; Locke, 1976; Miner & Dachler, 1973, for reviews). Both facets contribute to both satisfaction and dissatisfaction, although satisfiers seem, in general, to contribute more to both than dissatisfiers do. The two-factor theory no longer deserves consideration.

Conclusions about theories. Of the five theories presented, comparison-process views seem to be the most important. That is, they appear to explain more variance in job satisfaction than other points of view. Neither the social-influence nor equity views should be overlooked, however. These seem to influence job satisfaction over and above the comparison process. Also, in settings in which social comparisons are quite prominent, these processes may in fact dominate. Comparative research on different theories is sorely lacking and is needed for firm conclusions.

Job Satisfaction and Behavior

Turnover. One of the most consistent findings about job satisfaction is that it correlates negatively with turnover (Mowday, Porter, & Steers, 1982). Some of the best research in this area was done by Hulin (1966, 1968). In his 1966 study, Hulin compared clerical workers who subsequently quit to a matched sample of those who did not quit. Job-satisfaction measures were obtained from both groups prior to the resignation of those who quit. Turnover was clearly related (negatively) to job satisfaction. In a follow-up study (1968), Hulin made changes in the jobs to correct some of the dissatisfying factors mentioned by those who quit. These changes led to significant decreases in turnover.

The consistency of the negative relationship between job satisfaction and turnover has led investigators to look more closely at other factors that might be related to issues of turnover and job satisfaction. Jackofsky and Peters (1983) argued that dissatisfaction with the job should only lead to turnover when the employees believed that alternative employment is available to them. This position followed directly from the classic work of March and Simons (1958), which posited that dissatisfaction leads to a search for alternative jobs and that search increases the likelihood that alternatives will be found. Jackofsky and Peters (1983) simply argued that, if this were true, only those who believe alternative jobs exist which they are likely to obtain will quit when they are dissatisfied. Data from a sample of retail employees in several southwestern cities confirmed this prediction; the relationship between job satisfaction and turnover was stronger among those employees who believed that they could find alternative employment.

Spencer and Steers (1981) found a strong negative relationship between job satisfaction and turnover only for hospital employees who were relatively low performers. These authors felt that high-performing employees who became dissatisfied were encouraged to stay by receiving whatever inducements could be provided to change their feelings. Low performers, on the other hand, received no such encouragement; therefore, job satisfaction was more likely to be related to quitting for them than for the high performers.

Finally, there has been some tendency to question the point of view that turnover is always a condition to avoid. Typically, turnover is considered to be very costly to an organization, and attempts are made to reduce it. Dalton, Krackhardt, and Porter (1981) proposed, however, that turnover is a good way to allow the people who do not fit well into an organization to leave and thus to open up positions for others who might fit better. They gathered data from 1389 employees primarily from California banks. Supervisors were asked to rate the performance of these employees and to judge the extent to which they thought each employee would be easy to replace. The researchers classified those who were good performers and also difficult to replace as dysfunctional turnovers and those who were poor performers and easy to replace as functional turnovers. Of the 32% who quit voluntarily, 18% were classified as

dysfunctional and 13% as functional. Although no one would argue that 18% turnover is a good thing, that percentage is far below the 32% that would typically be considered problematic if the distinction between functional and dysfunctional turnover had not been made.

Absenteeism. Absenteeism also tends to show a negative correlation with job satisfaction, but the strength of the correlation tends not to be very high. In fact, in many cases, the relationship is zero.

One of the reasons offered for the poor relationship between absenteeism and job satisfaction is that conditions other than those that influence satisfaction influence absenteeism (Ilgen & Hollenback, 1977). Smith (1977) demonstrated this quite clearly. He surveyed many managers in the Chicago headquarters of a large organization shortly before a crippling snowstorm. Smith argued that on the day after the snowstorm, the managers had a built-in excuse not to come to work. This should have removed any constraints on attendance behavior so that attendance should have been more a function of attitudes (job satisfaction) than other conditions. His data clearly show job satisfaction negatively correlated with absenteeism under this condition. A control group in New York, where there was no snow, showed no correlation between job satisfaction and attendance on the same day.

Terborg, Lee, Smith, Davis, and Turbin (1982) argued from a statistical point of view that the correlation between job satisfaction and absenteeism in any one study is likely to be an underestimate of the true relationship between these two variables. Using a statistical procedure for aggregating data across samples, Terborg et al. combined six separate studies of absenteeism in retail stores. In none of the six studies did the correlations between measures of job satisfaction and absenteeism exceed −.124. However, when certain assumptions were made about the measures, the estimated true correlations between absenteeism and dimensions of job satisfaction were much higher ($-.21$ for satisfaction with work; $-.37$ for satisfaction with pay; and $-.16$ for satisfaction with communication).

Performance. Although it is intuitively appealing to conclude that satisfied employees are better performers, the data simply do not support such a position. Major reviews by Brayfield and Crockett (1955), Herzberg, Mausner, Peterson, and Capwell (1957), and Vroom (1964) refuted this view. Clearly, it is no longer acceptable to hold such a position.

What is less clear is why the two are unrelated (Fisher, 1980). At one extreme it could be argued that job attitudes are unrelated to performance behavior. A more moderate and more appealing position to us is that the two may be related, but only under certain conditions—when performance behavior is not constrained or controlled. For example, performance on a machine-paced job is influenced much more by the speed of the machine than by job satisfaction. Similarly, a sales representative's dollar volume in sales may be more a function of the quality of the district than of his or her satisfaction. Therefore, Herman (1973) argued, job satisfaction should relate to performance (and to any other behavior) only when other influences on behavior have been removed. Complex behaviors, such as those represented by work performance, are frequently influenced by other factors; we would suggest that often they are not strongly related to job satisfaction. This is much different from saying that, across the board, job satisfaction is unimportant to performance.

Behaviors in general. Two final comments about job satisfaction and behaviors need to be made before we leave the topic. First, as we have already mentioned, one must ask if the behavior in question could possibly be related to job satisfaction. Frequently behavior is constrained by outside factors not related to job satisfaction. In addition, the dimen-

sions on which satisfaction is measured may be only weakly related to the behavior in question. Ilgen and Hollenback (1977) raised this issue with regard to absenteeism. If employees do not believe that company policies give much weight to absences in making pay and promotional decisions and if supervisors and co-workers accept absenteeism as a way of life, then satisfaction with company policies, supervision, and co-workers should not be expected to be negatively correlated with absenteeism.

A second comment questions the adequacy of the set of behaviors most frequently related to job satisfaction. The focus has been on a narrow set closely associated with productivity goals of the organization—for example, absenteeism, turnover, and individual performance. Nord (1977) castigated researchers for their myopic focus and challenged them not to abandon the old as wrong but to expand the domain of concern. He stressed that research on job satisfaction must consider existing social, political, and economic variables which will allow us to place job satisfaction in a more realistic perspective, given today's organizational climates and attitudes toward work. His position is well taken and deserves attention.

Finally, Naylor, Pritchard, and Ilgen (1980) question the extent to which job satisfaction should be strongly related to any behavior. In a general theory of behavior in organizations, these authors suggest that many other factors are much more closely related to the employee's decisions about which behaviors to display than is job satisfaction. As a result, even though in some cases job satisfaction will correlate with behavior, if one is really interested in understanding why a behavior occurs, there are many more important variables to consider than job satisfaction. Job satisfaction simply is not the most prevailing force behind job behaviors in most settings.

Regardless of the mean level of job satisfaction, there have been major changes in the value and meaning of work in a large enough segment of the working population to make these issues relevant to many organizations. The desire to share one job between two individuals and the emergence of a large number of dual-career families among managerial and professional staff are just a few of these changes. Such changes simply emphasize the need to become more aware of the attitudes and opinions of the work force in order to maintain effective human-resource systems within organizations. These issues demand attention that focuses on job satisfaction and opinions from a broader perspective than simply trying to correlate attitudes and opinions with performance or attendance. Exploring the impact of families, group norms, and other factors of attitudes or opinions as suggested by Nord (1977) appears to be a good start for a more in-depth analysis of these issues.

The Measurement of Job Satisfaction

Job-satisfaction instruments. Hundreds of studies—and many different scales—have been used to measure job satisfaction over the last 40 to 50 years. The scales fall into two general categories. One consists of *tailor-made* scales, which are constructed for a particular setting or project. The second set is comprised of *standardized* scales, which were developed to establish general group norms and to insure reliability and validity. With the present level of knowledge about job satisfaction and the availability of good measures of it, there is almost no reason to use tailor-made scales. Unfortunately, tailor-made scales are still being used quite frequently.

We devote all our attention here to two standardized scales. The first, the Job Description Index (JDI), has been well developed and is used widely. The second, the Kunin faces scale, is presented for its uniqueness. Several other good scales are available;

we leave it to those who are interested to check the literature on them.

Job description index (JDI). The Job Description Index (JDI),[2] developed by Smith and some of her associates over the years, was reported by Smith et al. (1969). In earlier versions of the scale, individuals were asked to describe the jobs they would most like to have (their "best" jobs) and the ones they would least like to have (their "worst" jobs). Responses thus elicited were used in an item analysis to identify those items which tended to be most discriminating; such items were then included in the final scale. In its final form the scale measures attitudes in five areas: work, supervision, pay, promotions, and co-workers. The scale consists of a series of adjectives or statements for each of these categories, and the individual is asked to mark each one as yes (Y), no (N), or cannot decide (?) as it relates to his or her job. A few examples are given:

Work

_____Fascinating
_____Routine
_____Frustrating

Supervision

_____Hard to please
_____Praises good work
_____Stubborn

Pay

_____Adequate for normal expenses
_____Less than I deserve

Promotions

_____Promotion on ability
_____Dead-end job

[2]The Job Description Index is copyrighted by Dr. Patricia C. Smith, Bowling Green State University. Inquiries about it should be addressed to her at Bowling Green State University, Bowling Green, Ohio 43403.

Co-workers

    _____Stimulating
    _____Talk too much

Although the scale actually "describes" one's job, the "description" implies the individual's evaluation of it. Scores based on this scale have been found to be related to other measures of job satisfaction.

The internal-consistency reliability of the JDI, derived by correlating scores of random split-halves of the items for eighty men, ranged from .80 to .88 for the five separate scales. The intercorrelations of the five scales for a sample of 980 men ranged from .28 to .42. These intercorrelations reflect only moderate relationships, thus implying that the five scales were tapping somewhat separate facets of job satisfaction. Schneider and Dachler (1978) replicated the low intercorrelations among dimensions in a large utility company and also showed that the test-retest reliabilities of the subscales were good ($r = .57$) when compared over a 16-month period.

"Faces" job-satisfaction scale. A rather different scheme for measuring job satisfaction was developed by Kunin (1955). This consists of a series of drawings of people's faces with varying mouth expressions, ranging from a broad smile to a deep frown, as illustrated in Figure 15.3. the respondent simply marks that face which best expresses how

Put a check under the face that expresses how you feel about your job in general, including the work, the pay, the supervision, the opportunities for promotion and the people you work with.

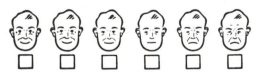

FIGURE 15.3 Illustration of the "Faces" scale for measuring job satisfaction. (From Kunin, 1955.)

he feels about his "job in general." Dunham and Herman (1975) found that such a scale worked just as well for women as a set of new faces drawn to clearly be women's faces.

Employee-attitude surveys. Large corporations are discovering that they can learn much about the state of their human resources if they systematically survey employee opinions, attitudes, and satisfaction. It is recommended that such surveys be conducted on a regular basis, such as every 1 to 3 years. Survey data serve as an audit of the human resources and provide valuable information that can be used for: (1) giving feedback to specific work units for the development of employees in the unit and/or altering policies, practices, and conditions in some way to better meet the needs of the work force in the unit; (2) diagnosing problems that may exist; (3) communicating employees' expectations to management in a way that protects the anonymity of the employees; and (4) establishing training programs (Dunham & Smith, 1979). Dunham and Smith provide an excellent description of the development and use of attitude surveys. They first describe the preliminary steps that are needed to determine if a survey is needed, who should be surveyed, what should be done with the data from the survey, and how to introduce the survey to managers, employees, and unions in such a way that each group realizes the value of the survey to them. This latter phase is particularly important. In many cases, surveys are poorly accepted by employees and particularly unions because they have often been used to gain information managers felt would be useful for preventing unionization. For the most part, these "quick-fix" surveys, initiated when management fears that union organization is imminent, are of little value to management or to employees. This accounts, in a sense, for their earned bad reputations. On the other hand, if surveys are established as an ongoing process in the human-resource management system rather than as one-shot attempts to deal with longstanding problems, they can be quite valuable.

Following a detailed description of the initial phase of the survey process, Dunham and Smith (1979) describe the design of a specific survey, the administration of such a survey, the analysis of survey data, and the use of such data by the organization. Anyone interested in conducting an organizational survey should refer to this book for very helpful information. The detail needed to develop employee surveys goes beyond our purpose here. We conclude simply that such surveys can be very useful and deserve careful consideration.

Trends in Job Satisfaction

Beginning in the late 1960s there was a great deal of concern about major shifts in the values of people about work. With respect to job satisfaction, the popular position was that people were much less satisfied with their work than they used to be. A well-publicized study entitled *Work in America* (U.S. Department of Health, Education, and Welfare, 1973) suggested that people at that time were much less satisfied with work than they had been in the past. Given the data available today, this conclusion appears to be an overreaction.

There is some evidence of a slight decline in job satisfaction—for example, Smith, Scott, and Hulin's (1977) comparison of employee responses to an attitude survey administered at Sears Roebuck over the past 25 years. Organ (1977) showed, however, that when a similar downward trend in job satisfaction was corrected for the employees' ages, job satisfaction stayed relatively constant. Organ argued that the work force was simply getting younger over the time period surveyed, and younger employees, in general, tend to be less satisfied. He hypothesized that when the "baby boom" of the 1940s and early 1950s

moved through the work force, job satisfaction would reflect the age changes of this group. We are just entering this phase in the early 1980s, as the mean age of the work force actually has increased to some extent. However, it is too early to see the effects of this change on job satisfaction. Regardless of its effect, however, the data of many studies indicate that it will not be very large and that the mean level of satisfaction is not so low as to be cause for alarm. For example, Weaver (1980) reported data from a survey of 4,709 full-time employees in the United States conducted on an annual basis from 1972 through 1978. He used a scale with four anchors, two of which reflected satisfaction with the job (*Very Satisfied* and *Somewhat Satisfied*). The range in percent of the sample that reported being satisfied with their jobs varied from a low of 85.8% in 1972 to a high of 89.2% in 1979. These levels of satisfaction do not imply a need to be alarmed about the general degree of satisfaction with work.

QUALITY OF WORKING LIFE

Although, as we have indicated, early fears that the work force in the United States was becoming much less satisfied with work are, for the most part, unfounded, there have been some rather dramatic shifts in the beliefs and values that people hold about work. Public-opinion surveys by Yankelovich and others (Katzell & Yankelovich, with Fein, Ornati, & Nash, assisted by Berman, Deliberto, Morrow, & Weiss, 1975) have documented shifts in work values. In general, people believe that work should not simply be a means of producing income but should also provide a means for enhancing or maintaining their dignity through their own greater involvement in the decisions that involve them in the work place. These values grew out of a combination of many forces, not the least of which were a general increase in the educational level of the work force, a greater international interdependence with an exposure to the diverse work values of cultures other than our own, and legal pressures created by the desire to protect the rights of women and minority-group members.

Some of the most visible reactions on the part of organizations to the current work values are programs that go under the general label of *Quality of Work Life* (QWL). Because QWL is used in different ways by different people, it is frustrating at times to attempt to define what it is and what it is not. At the core of all QWL, however, is an orientation or philosophy with respect to the relationship between the organization and the people who work for that organization. In his book entitled *Quality of Work Life in Action*, Stein (1983) describes five components that underlie QWL:

1. More control and autonomy for employees.
2. Recognition for those who have made contributions to meeting the goals of the organization through work on the job.
3. A sense of belonging to the organization.
4. The opportunity for progress in personal growth and development on the job.
5. Material (extrinsic) rewards for work.

To this list, Stein adds the need on the part of the organization to provide decent working conditions and a sense of dignity for the employees. In many respects these additions are meant to encapsulate the more specific conditions of 1 through 5 and to summarize the philosophical orientation of QWL toward people at work.

There are about as many variations of programs, policies, and practices that are labeled QWL as there are organizations attempting to apply or establish them. This may be because the whole concept is quite new, so there are many aspects of it that need to be tried. Some may argue that this diversity is necessary because, after all, the needs of specific work forces are so diverse that in order

to best meet them, it is necessary to tailor the QWL to the specific situations. This may be true, but it has one undesirable consequence: Organizations can label just about anything a QWL effort and claim that they are dealing with the quality of working life of their employees. In some respects, this condition exists today; it is not a good state.

In spite of the diversity, there are some common themes that run through most QWL programs. The most central of these is the establishment of labor-management committees. These committees are composed of members of both management and worker groups and include union spokespersons, if the workers are represented by a union or unions. These committees are given some general guidelines for issues to address, but they are also given considerable freedom to draw up their own agendas. The overall goal of these committees is to gain inputs from worker and management perspectives in a problem-solving rather than an adversary role.

A second component of almost every QWL effort is the establishment of means for every individual employee to provide inputs into that part of the organization's function related to his or her job. This may be accomplished by Quality Circles, which are small teams that meet on a regular basis to discuss problems related to the way a job is done in a particular area. Quality Circles represent adaptations of the Japanese procedures for soliciting worker involvement. Other means of soliciting worker opinions are suggestion boxes, opinion surveys, representative councils elected by the employees from within their work groups, and the redesign of work into small teams that are responsible for the multiple functions of the team that had previously been allocated to supervisors of the work groups.

In sum, QWL is a growing concern in U.S. industries. It represents the development of a work norm that places a high premium on the job satisfaction of the work force and on the value of the human resources that make up that work force. It is not any particular bag of tricks for dealing with individuals at work, even though at times it appears to be so. Although the focus of QWL is to be applauded and encouraged, caution must be shown in the selection and development of procedures to deal with QWL issues. There are, at the present time, a large number of specific programs being peddled as QWL with exaggerated claims about their abilities to meet organizational and/or individual needs. Considerable effort will be required in the coming years to design and evaluate the effectiveness of QWL.

STRESS

It is well known that our psychological reactions to the world around us can create wear and tear on our bodies that may eventually manifest themselves in physiological conditions such as high blood pressure, ulcers, headaches, and other health problems. The conditions may also create psychological conditions of nervous tension, feelings of depression, and so on—all of which affect our well-being The combination of physiological and psychological reactions that negatively affect an individual as a result of conditions in the environment are often viewed as results of stress on the person; such environmental conditions are labeled *stressors*.

It has been recognized for some time that jobs may create conditions that cause stress for people at work. In 1981, the importance of stress at work was dramatized by the national strike of the Air Traffic Controllers' union, which was justified on the basis that the controllers' jobs were so stressful. The controllers argued that the tension created by the work load and the great responsibility for human life required that they be given shorter work hours with more frequent breaks in order to release some of that tension and

also that they be paid at a higher level to compensate for the threats to their health created by the stressors of the job.

Research does show that some jobs do have a higher number of stress-related illnesses than others, but, as Ivancevich and Matteson (1980) point out, this does not necessarily mean that the illnesses are caused by the jobs. It could just as easily be that people with tendencies for these illnesses tend to select certain kinds of jobs. One study that minimizes the possibility of the selection effect looked at dimensions of jobs rather than at the jobs themselves. Shaw and Riskind (1983) combined data from a large number of studies that had information on the frequency of stress-related illnesses. They analyzed the jobs using the Position Analysis Questionnaire and compared the frequency of illnesses with the dimensions of the jobs in which these illnesses occurred. Five of twenty-seven job dimensions were related to half of the stress-related illnesses investigated. These five dimensions were:

1. Using various sources of information.
2. Making decisions.
3. Performing controlled manual and/or related activities.
4. Communicating judgments and/or related information.
5. Working in businesslike situations.

Although these data are still open to the alternative explanation that people with health weaknesses migrate toward jobs with these characteristics, this possibility seems a little less plausible when the dimensions are represented in a wide variety of jobs with very different job titles. The data are of further interest because they offer some suggestions for the types of things in jobs that may lead to stresslike reactions to work.

Research that has related measures of job stress to job satisfaction consistently finds that high stress is related to low job satisfaction. For example, Kavanagh, Hurst, and Rose

(1981) measured the degree of stress experienced by air traffic controllers by means of a structured interview. They then compared the amount of stress to measures of job satisfaction. Table 15.1 shows that as stress went up, satisfaction with the nature of the work itself, with co-workers, and with the level of group morale went down.

Looking at stress and satisfaction over time among a sample of hospital employees, Bateman and Strasser (1983) found evidence that indicated a reciprocal relationship between job satisfaction and stress. In their case, stress was inferred from a subjective measure of felt tension. Their data indicated that employees' dissatisfaction with the work itself and with their working relationships with physicians at the hospital lead to increased tension. Increased tension, in turn, lead to dissatisfaction with supervision and with pay.

Given the increased concern for the quality of working life, greater attention will inevitably be paid to job stress and to the kinds of variables that cause stress-related responses at work. Hopefully, this work will provide a basis on which to either redesign jobs to reduce stress and/or to make people aware of the possible risks of stress in these settings so that they can make more reasoned job choices. Another approach will be for employees to learn more about how to deal with stressors so that negative physiological and psychological effects do not occur. Such research is also likely to remove some of the myths that surround what we believe may cause stress but really do not know for sure. One such example is the recent work (Brett, 1982) with people who are frequently transferred from one job to another and are required to move their places of residence. Counter to popular opinion, transferred families experienced no more difficulties with acceptance into communities and school-friendship groups than did members of the control group, who were transferred infrequently or not at all.

DISCUSSION

Job satisfaction has been an important topic in industrial-organizational psychology; indeed, several thousand studies of job satisfaction have been conducted over the last 50 years. Its importance continues to remain high, yet the reason for concern has shifted. Initially, job satisfaction was of interest primarily because of the relationship it was believed to have to performance. It made good intuitive sense to expect that satisfied workers were better workers, but the data did not agree. Clearly our understanding of the relationship between satisfaction and performance has advanced a long way from the initial, rather naive assumption just mentioned. Today, we realize that job satisfaction

TABLE 15.1 Mean job satisfaction scores for three levels of stress for a sample of air traffic controllers

| | SUBJECTIVE STRESS AS MEASURED BY INTERVIEWS | | | |
	NO/LOW	MILD	MODERATE	SEVERE
Number of Cases	390	20	5	0
JDI-Work[a]	50.64	40.65	42.40	
JDI-Co-workers	50.36	43.15	43.20	
Group Morale	50.35	43.75	45.20	

[a]JDI is the Job Descriptive Index of Smith, et al., 1969.
Adapted from Kavanagh, et al., 1981.

is important for other reasons. It is useful to know the level of satisfaction of the work force because such knowledge can help us to provide conditions necessary to improve working conditions. It is important because of its possible relationship to physiological reactions to work. Finally, it is important in its own right, as one of the goals of an organization becomes that of improving the quality of working life for all of those who comprise the work force of that organization.

REFERENCES

Bateman, T. S., & Strasser, S. A. (1983). A cross-lagged regression test of the relationships between job tensions and employee satisfaction. *Journal of Applied Psychology, 68,* 439–445.

Brayfield, A. H., & Crockett, W. H. (1955). Employee attitudes and employee performance. *Psychological Bulletin, 52,* 396–424.

Brett, J. B. (1982). Transfer and well-being. *Journal of Applied Psychology, 67,* 450–463.

Butler, J. K. (1983). Value importance as a moderator of the value-fulfillment-job satisfaction relationship: Group differences. *Journal of Applied Psychology, 68,* 420–429.

Dachler, H. P., & Hulin, C. L. (1969). A reconsideration of the relationship between satisfaction and judged importance of environmental and job characteristics. *Organizational Behavior and Human Performance, 4,* 252–266.

Dalton, D. R., Krackhardt, D. M., & Porter, L. W. (1981). Functional turnover: An empirical assessment. *Journal of Applied Psychology, 66,* 716–721.

Dunham, R. B., & Herman, J. B. (1975). Development of a female faces scale for measuring job satisfaction. *Journal of Applied Psychology, 60,* 629–632.

Dunham, R. B., & Smith, F. J. (1979). *Organizational surveys.* Chicago: Scott, Foresman.

Ewen, R. B. (1967). Weighting components of job satisfaction. *Journal of Applied Psychology, 51,* 68–73.

Fishbein, M., & Ajzen, I. (1975). *Belief, attitude, intention, and behavior: An introduction to theory and research.* Reading, Mass.: Addison-Wesley.

Fisher, C. D. (1980). On the dubious wisdom of expecting job satisfaction to correlate with performance. *Academy of Management Review, 5,* 607–12.

Herman, J. B. (1973). Are situational contingencies limiting job attitude–job performance relationships? *Organizational Behavior and Human Performance, 10,* 208–24.

Herzberg, F. (1966). *Work and the nature of man.* New York: Van Nostrand.

Herzberg, F., Mausner, B., Peterson, R. O., & Capwell, D. F. (1957). *Job attitudes: Review of research and opinion.* Pittsburgh: Psychological Service of Pittsburgh.

Herzberg, F., Mausner, B., & Snyderman, B. B. (1959). *The motivation to work.* New York: Wiley.

Hoppock, R. (1935). *Job satisfaction.* New York: Harper and Brothers.

Hulin, C. L. (1966). Job satisfaction and turnover. *Journal of Applied Psychology, 50,* 280–85.

Hulin, C. L. (1968). Effects of changes in job satisfaction levels on employee turnover. *Journal of Applied Psychology, 52,* 122–126.

Ilgen, D. R., & Hollenback, J. H. (1977). The role of job satisfaction in absence behavior. *Organizational Behavior and Human Performance, 19,* 148–61.

Ivancevich, J. M., & Matteson, M. T. (1980). *Stress and work: A managerial perspective.* Glenview, IL: Scott, Foresman.

Jackofsky, E. F., & Peters, L. H. (1983). Job turnover versus company turnover: Reassessment of the March and Simon participation hypothesis. *Journal of Applied Psychology, 68,* 490–495.

Katzell, R. B., & Yankelovich, D., with Fein, M., Ornati, O. A., & Nash, A., assisted by Berman, J. A., Deliberto, R. A., Morrow, I. J., & Weiss, H. M. (1975). *Work productivity and job satisfaction: An evaluation of policy-related research.* New York: Psychological Corporation.

Kavanagh, M. J., Hurst, M. W., & Rose, R. (1981). The relationship between job satisfaction and psychiatric health symptoms for air traffic controllers. *Personnel Psychology, 34,* 691–708.

King, N. (1970). Clarification and evaluation of the two-factor theory of job satisfaction. *Psychology Bulletin, 74,* 18–31.

Kunin, T. (1955). The construction of a new type of attitude measure. *Personnel Psychology, 8,* 65–78.

Locke, E. A. (1973). Satisfiers and dissatisfiers among white and blue collar employees. *Journal of Applied Psychology, 58,* 67–76.

Locke, E. A. (1976). The nature and causes of job satisfaction. In M. D. Dunnette (Ed.), *Hand-*

book of industrial and organizational psychology. Chicago: Rand McNally.

March, J. G., & Simons, H. A. (1958). *Organizations.* New York: Wiley.

Miner, J. B., & Dachler, H. P. (1973). Personnel attitudes and motivation. *Annual Review of Psychology, 24,* 379–422.

Morse, N. C. (1953). *Satisfaction in the white-collar job.* Ann Arbor: University of Michigan Press.

Mowday, R. T., Porter, L. W., & Steers, R. M. (1982). *Employee-organization linkages: The psychology of commitment, absenteeism, and turnover.* New York: Academic Press.

Naylor, J. C., Pritchard, R. D., & Ilgen, D. R. (1980). *A theory of behavior in organizations.* New York: Academic Press.

Nord, W. R. (1977). Job satisfaction reconsidered. *American Psychologist, 32,* 1026–1035.

Organ, D. W. (1977). Inferences about trends in labor force satisfaction: A causal-correlational analysis. *Academy of Management Journal, 20,* 510–519.

Porter, L. W. (1962). Job attitudes in management: I. Perceived deficiencies in need fulfillment as a function of job level. *Journal of Applied Psychology, 46,* 375–384.

Porter, L. W. (1963). Job attitudes in management: II. Perceived importance of needs as a function of job level. *Journal of Applied Psychology, 47,* 141–148.

Pritchard, R. D., Dunnette, M. D., & Jorgenson, D. O. (1972). Effects of perceptions of equity and inequity on worker performance and satisfaction. *Journal of Applied Psychology, 56,* 75–94.

Pulakos, E. D., & Schmitt, N. (1983). A longitudinal study of a valence model approach for the prediction of job satisfaction of new employees. *Journal of Applied Psychology, 68,* 307–312.

Salancik, G. R., Pfeffer, J. (1977). An examination of need satisfaction models of job satisfaction. *Administrative Science Quarterly, 22,* 427–456.

Sales, S. M. (1969). Organizational role as a risk factor in coronary disease. *Administrative Science Quarterly, 14,* 325–336.

Sales, S. M., & House, J. (1971). Job dissatisfaction as a possible risk factor in coronary heart disease. *Journal of Chronic Diseases, 28,* 861–873.

Schneider, B., & Dachler, H. P. (1978). A note on the stability of the Job Descriptive Index. *Journal of Applied Psychology, 63,* 650–653.

Shaw, B. J., & Riskind, J. H. (1983). Predicting job stress using data from the Position Analysis Questionnaire. *Journal of Applied Psychology, 68,* 253–262.

Smith, F. J. (1977). Work attitudes as predictors of attendance on a specific day. *Journal of Applied Psychology, 62,* 16–19.

Smith, F. J., Scott, K. D., & Hulin, C. L. (1977). Trends in job-related attitudes of management and professional employees. *Academy of Management Journal, 20,* 454–460.

Smith, P. C., Kendall, L. M., & Hulin, C. L. (1969). *The measurement of satisfaction in work and retirement.* Chicago: Rand McNally.

Spencer, D. G., & Steers, R. M. (1981). Performance as a moderator of the job-satisfaction-turnover relationship. *Journal of Applied Psychology, 66,* 511–514.

Stein, B. A. (1983). *Quality of work life in action: Managing effectiveness.* New York: American Management Association.

Terborg, J., Lee, T. W., Smith, F. J., Davis, G. A., Turbin, M. S. (1982). Extension of the Schmidt and Hunter validity generalization procedure to the prediction of absenteeism behavior from knowledge of job satisfaction and commitment. *Journal of Applied Psychology, 67,* 440–449.

U.S. Department of Health, Education, and Welfare (1973). *Work in America.* Cambridge, Mass.: MIT Press.

Vroom, V. H. (1964). *Work motivation.* New York: Wiley.

Weaver, C. (1980). Job satisfaction in the United States in the 1970s. *Journal of Applied Psychology, 65,* 364–368.

Weiss, H. M., & Shaw, J. B. (1979). Social influences on judgments about tasks. *Organizational Behavior and Human Performance, 24,* 126–140.

White, S. E., & Mitchell, T. R. (1979). Job enrichment vs social cues: A comparison and competitive test. *Journal of Applied Psychology, 64,* 1–9.

16

Group Processes and Leadership

In this chapter we shift our emphasis from the individual to groups of individuals. Organizations, by definition, are composed of more than one individual. Usually individuals are clustered into groups, either formally or informally, and often they must interact with others to accomplish their tasks. In fact, any particular individual in an organization may be a member of several groups all within the same organization. Whereas traditional bureaucratic organization guidelines minimized multiple group memberships, modern organizational theory encourages them. (See Likert's [1967] notion of linking pins and descriptions of matrix organizations such as that of French [1978].) Whether individuals are members of one or more groups, it is reasonable to conclude that members of organizations are members of groups. Therefore, social factors do influence human behavior at work.

NORMS AND ROLES

In any organization in which people are required to work together with others, there must be ways to insure that each person performs a set of behaviors that makes it possible for the whole system to function. A first step for obtaining reliable sets of behaviors from individual members is to communicate to them what is required of them; the second step is to encourage compliance with the set of required behaviors. In both cases, interpersonal communications with and the reactions of those with whom the persons work play a major role in soliciting and maintaining effective behavior at work. In the first case, others communicate to individuals what is expected of them (*expected behaviors*); in the latter, the person learns—either through talking with others, watching what happens to others when they perform a certain set of behaviors (modeling), or directly by behaving and receiving the consequences of that behavior—the *rewards* and *sanctions* that are associated with particular behaviors.

Norms

Norms are shared expectations about appropriate behaviors. As you observe people at work, you will quickly notice that there are certain sets of behaviors that almost everyone does most of the time. Norms may apply to all kinds of behaviors. Consider, for example, norms related to meeting times. It is not unusual for norms to develop with respect to the meaning of the starting time for a meeting. In some organizations, when a meeting is set for 10:30 A.M., that meeting starts right at that time. If you watch the people who are to attend, they will begin to arrive and have a seat 5 or 10 minutes before the meeting is to begin so that at 10:30 everyone is ready to go. In other organizations, 10:30 means the time that people start arriving. No one expects to begin at 10:30 even though the time is set for that. More than likely, a norm will exist for the amount of time after the starting time that is acceptable to begin, and meetings will begin at that time. Once the norm is learned, both practices can function very effectively even though "a 10:30 A.M. meeting" has a different meaning at each location.

Another example of an interesting norm was observed in a large corporation. Here a norm existed for holding the door when a number of persons were walking together. In this case, the most senior-ranking person in the group held the door open for all the others. The norm was a subtle one that outsiders often did not notice. At first, new members, especially those with quite junior rank, were often confused if they tried to get the door to hold it and found themselves being "challenged" for the right to do so. Nevertheless, after a few awkward experiences, they too fell in line.

Although norms exist for an infinite variety of behaviors—attendance, dress, work speed, and many others—several dimensions are considered with respect to them. First, norms vary in the degree to which they are formalized. Some formal norms are explicitly stated as part of an organization's policy. For example, norms related to dress at fast-food establishments often state explicitly that anyone who interacts directly with customers or who works in the area where customers will be eating must wear a particular uniform. Less formal norms may never be explicitly stated but are, nonetheless, just as important to the individual. In a shop in which there is a long-standing practice of stopping work 20 minutes before closing time to clean up, imagine the problem of a new supervisor who decides that he or she will have people work right up to quitting time and "clean up on their own time."

A second characteristic of a norm is the range in behavior that is considered acceptable for complying with the norm. In general, the more important the norm in the opinion of the group, the less the tolerance for violating it. Consider a quality circle group that meets each Thursday afternoon to discuss ways the group might improve their work procedures; there may be a reasonable degree of tolerance of those who are 5 to 10 minutes late. On the other hand, a weekly panel that assembles to discuss the impact of events in the news to a live television audience cannot accept tardiness from any of its members.

A third dimension important to norms is the severity of the sanctions that are associated with violating them. For the most part, the severity of the sanctions varies as a function of the extent to which the norm holders believe that compliance with a particular norm is central to their well-being. So, for example, if the group believes that working too fast and producing too much is quite likely to lead to a loss of jobs, the group will monitor the performance of all members and deal with anyone who does not restrict production to the level that is believed to be acceptable. On the other hand, if the behavior is felt to be less important, sanctions tend to be less severe.

Another factor that influences the severity of the response to norm violations is some judgment about the person who violated the norm. If the person is a newcomer who could not have been expected to know the norm (for example, that "Higher-ranking persons hold the door for lower-ranking ones around here."), then violations of the norm are more likely to be tolerated. At the other extreme are individuals (discussed by Hollander, 1964) who have earned the respect and acceptance of the group and may be able to violate some norms without reprisal. Hollander suggested that with respect and acceptance come the accumulation of "idiosyncratic credits" that can be cashed in to allow the person to violate a norm and still be accepted. However, when "credits" are spent, the person has to do something to deserve the continued support of the group. Regardless of the labels attached to the process, it is clear that sanctions received for violating group norms are varied, to some extent, as a function of the person who performs the behavior.

Roles

Like norms, roles are also expected patterns of behavior. They differ from norms primarily in terms of their specificity. Norms tend to be patterns of behavior that apply to most, if not all, members of the group. Roles are focused upon specific positions within the group and are directed toward the particular individuals who occupy those positions.

Role episode. The best accepted way of looking at roles and how they operate is a rather simple model called the role episode, introduced by Robert Kahn and his colleagues (Kahn, Wolf, Quinn, Shoek, & Rosenthal, 1964; Katz & Kahn, 1978) and illustrated in Figure 16.1. The figure describes two sets of actors in the role episode: the focal person and role senders. The focal person is the one for whom the role behaviors are prescribed. Role senders are usually persons who have some vested interest in the behavior of the focal person. They may or may not be members of the organization. Supervisors and co-workers would almost always be considered role senders for a focal person in a work organization, but, in addition, so would the person's spouse. A spouse certainly has an interest in work-related behaviors that impact on the person's life—promotions, transfers, or office working hours on weekends and/or in the evenings.

The behaviors that others (role senders) believe should be performed by the focal person are labeled *role expectations* in Figure 16.1. Role expectations are beliefs that the role senders have about what is and what is not appropriate for the focal person in order for him or her to perform the role effectively. Note that the model as it is drawn implies a single role expectation for the whole role set. Obviously, this is not the case. Often members of the role set have very different role expectations for the focal person. Supervisors may believe that the person should produce more units and work faster whereas co-

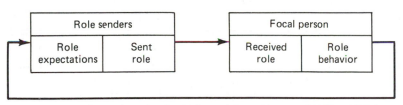

FIGURE 16.1 The role episode. (Adapted from Katz and Kahn, 1978.)

workers may believe that the most appropriate response is to slow down and produce less. For the moment, we describe the sending of one role before we introduce the issues created by multiple role senders.

Assuming the existence of a role expectation, the next phase in the role episode involves communicating the role expectation to the focal person. This is represented in Figure 16.1 as the *sent role*. Once communicated the sent role is received by the focal person (*received role*). The separation of the sent role from the received role emphasizes the fact that what the focal person believes is expected of him or her may be quite different from what the role senders believe they sent to the focal person. Such misunderstandings can occur for any number of reasons. The role senders may not have been clear about what they expected or they may have sent conflicting cues about what was to be done; also, the focal person may simply have misunderstood the role that was sent to him or her.

The first point that any actual behavior enters the role episode is near the end in the *role-behavior* box. This represents the fact that the focal person behaves on the basis of what he or she believes should be done. This behavior is then observed by the role senders and serves as an input to start the sequence over again. Presumably, if the role senders believe that the focal person performed the behavior successfully, their role expectations remain pretty much intact, and they "send" the same role back to the person as the cycle repeats itself. If there is not a match between expected behaviors and what the role senders believe actually occurred, they may either modify the role expectations and send a different role to the person or they may indicate their disapproval of the previous behavior and repeat the same role expectations.

Role compliance. Having received a role from one or more role senders does not imply that the focal person will necessarily comply with that role. In order to comply, the person must both have the necessary skills and abilities to comply with the role demands and also be willing to comply to them (Naylor, Pritchard, & Ilgen, 1980). Since most treatments of roles assume that the focal persons possess the necessary skills and abilities to accomplish the roles, interest in role compliance shifts to the motivational component of willingness to comply. For the most part, this involves the existence of rewards and sanctions administered by the role senders for compliance with their role demands. The mechanisms for this process are the same for roles as they are for norms.

Role making. The role process described thus far assumes a rather passive focal person whose major task is to understand the role demands of others and then to decide the extent to which to conform or not conform to the roles being sent. Graen and his colleagues (Dansereau, Graen, & Haga, 1975; Graen, 1976) argued that people do not simply "take" roles by attempting to ascertain the demands of others and then to conform to them assuming that they are interested in attaining the rewards offered by the group and avoiding the sanctions. Instead, individuals "make" roles. Role making is a combination of accepting the role demands of others and of attempting to influence the nature of the role that is sent in the first place. That is, the focal person tries to create, to some extent, role expectations in role senders that are likely to be favorable to himself or herself. If a person accepts a position in an advertising agency that involves devoting about equal amounts of time to both soliciting new accounts and working closely with long-established accounts, the person who likes to meet new people and is very good at it will attempt to change the role expectations so that he or she is involved more in soliciting new accounts than in maintaining old ones. The process of establishing this new mix geared to the focal person is role making rather than role taking. In practice, a role-making model is probably more accurate than the role-taking one.

Role Conflict. We mentioned earlier that not all role senders expect the same behaviors of the focal person. In fact, at times they may expect very different behaviors, so different that it is not possible for the focal person to meet the role demands of all the persons who are sending him or her roles. This situation is known as *role conflict,* and is a common source of dissatisfaction at work.

Naylor et al. (1980) proposed that the nature of role conflict could be described in terms of two major dimensions: the nature of the conflict among behaviors and the sources of the role conflict. This two-dimensional system is illustrated in Figure 16.2. Behavioral differences are of two types. By far the more common are behaviors that conflict because

of time constraints. All jobs occasionally require more things to be done than there is time to complete them. Time conflict becomes more severe when more than one person or set of persons is sending role expectations to the focal person. Often the different groups or individuals have no idea about what others expect. The second form of conflict among behaviors is less frequent, but more problematic. In this case, the behaviors themselves are mutually exclusive, that is, contradictory. We gave an earlier example of such behavior related to production rates: The supervisor may expect the focal person to produce more and his or her peers may expect conformity to pressures to restrict production. Another example would be role expectations to conform to a sales code of ethics that requires no payments to potential customers and simultaneous strong role de-

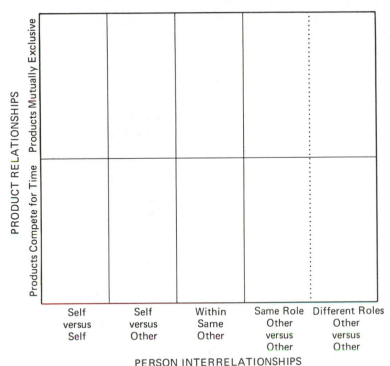

FIGURE 16.2 Conditions of role conflict. (With permission from Naylor, Pritchard, and Ilgen, 1980.)

mands to complete sales in foreign markets whose salespersons do not accept such ethical codes.

The second dimension is that of the persons within the role set who are sending conflicting role demands. Here, we can think of the focal person himself or herself as a role sender. In most cases, that person has certain expectations about what is and is not appropriate behavior to accomplish the job. These expectations can be in conflict with what others expect and can cause considerable dissatisfaction.

The final factor that affects role conflict (but which is not illustrated in Figure 16.2) is the nature of the consequences associated with compliance or noncompliance with conflicting role demands. If two roles are very much in conflict in terms of either time demands or the nature of the behaviors, and the focal person sees no advantage or disadvantage associated with compliance with one of the role senders but at the same time sees major advantages of conforming to the other, then there is not likely to be much experienced conflict. The answer to the problem is clear; the person will go with the role that has the greater payoff for role compliance. Experienced conflict, according to Naylor et al., is greatest when the payoff associated with both of the conflicting roles is about equal and high, such that there is much to gain by conforming to either one and much to lose by not conforming to either one.

Role ambiguity. Role ambiguity occurs when the focal person is uncertain about what behaviors are appropriate for fulfilling the role successfully. The uncertainty leads to two undesirable states. First of all, if the person does not know what to do, it is unlikely that he or she will do the right thing. Thus, role ambiguity often leads to poor role performance. Second, the person often experiences tension or stress when he or she recognizes that he or she is supposed to do something and do it well but what that some-

thing is is unknown. The tension or anxiety is increased when the person knows that important things are riding on doing the job well—a promotion, successful completion of a probationary time period, acceptance by ones' co-workers, and so on. Role ambiguity is very common among new employees.

CONFORMITY

Influences on Individual Behavior

Conformity is yielding to group pressure, either real or imagined. A classic study of conformity done in the laboratory (Asch, 1958) illustrates the group-conformity effect. Seven undergraduates were told that they would be presented with a picture of a line on a screen and that under the line would be three other lines. Their task was simply to look at the other three lines and to tell which one most closely matched the line at the top of the screen in length. In addition, the people who were seated in the room would, in turn, announce which line they thought was the best match. Unknown to the subjects, several of the others in the room actually were not subjects; they were part of the experiment and would choose lines that were not the best match to the standard as their supposed best guess of the correct line. In the strongest conformity experience, the first six people were participating in the experiment and all six identified the same incorrect line as the correct one. When this happened, the seventh person who was the subject in the experiment also said that he or she thought the incorrect one listed by the others was the best match.

This experiment dealt with a rather trivial behavior in a setting that, for the most part, was not very important to the participants. It was a psychology experiment. The subjects did not know the others in the room, and they also knew that they, more than likely, would never see them again. Yet the trivial and contrived nature of the setting stresses the importance of conformity behavior. If people will go along with the group even when the group has no real power over them, conformity should be even more likely if, for example, the group can impact on the future career opportunities of the person or the group can influence the extent to which the teenager will or will not be accepted.

Most of the research on conformity behavior can be described in terms of two dimensions. The first deals with the nature of the conformity behavior. The second addresses the factors that influence conformity. Conformity behavior can be ordered along a continuum of the extent to which the individual accepts the behavior to which he or she conforms. At one extreme, the individual internalizes the behavior by taking it as his or her own standard. Once this occurs, the person will display the behavior even in the absence of external pressure from the group. Organizations often strive for this level of conformity from employees on behaviors that are believed to be central to the effective functioning of the organization. For example, it is hoped that new employees who may initially conform to a norm for high-quality standards will internalize that norm and voluntarily behave in line with it because they believe in maintaining high standards of quality. At the other extreme is conformity only when being observed by others who have the power to administer rewards and sanctions. In such situations, as soon as the person believes he or she is not being observed, the conforming behavior will disappear.

Conformity behavior has also been studied in terms of the types of factors that do or do not affect the degree of conformity. For the most part, conformity behavior is influenced by the same types of variables that influence other behavior. In this sense, the behavior responds the same way as motivation. Conformity behavior is best viewed in terms of

the utilities associated with conforming or not conforming in a manner described by expectancy theory in Chapter 14. The more a person believes that it is beneficial to conform to group pressure, the more likely is conformity behavior. Keep in mind that "beneficial" is not determined simply in terms of some external standard of the extent to which the person can gain something from others. It also involves the extent to which the person sees the behavior as fitting his or her own personal standards.

Conformity behavior has a bad reputation, some of it deserved, but not all. Most people look at conforming to group expectations as a loss of personal freedom and, therefore, as undesirable. In many cases, this may be true. But, in many others, it is not. If it were not for some conformity, no organization could function. Some personal freedom must be sacrificed in exchange for the benefits that are accrued from holding a steady job. To do such means that the freedom to sleep as long as is desired in the morning, and other behaviors, must be regulated to meet the needs of a position. The task is to strike an appropriate balance between individual needs and group demands that does not compromise the needs and values of those who comprise the group.

Group Think

In organizations, important decisions are often made in groups. Committees of high-level executives often decide about entering new markets, building new plants, acquiring new business, and many other matters vital to the success of the organization. Often these groups are composed of people who share a common set of goals and attitudes and have been working together for a long time so that many of them are very close personal friends as well as business colleagues. Such conditions are ripe for a phenomenon known as *group think*.

Group think is a term coined by Irving Janis (1972) in a provocative book that analyzed the foreign-policy decisions of the Kennedy and Johnson administrations. Group think refers to the fact that, through the process of working together in a group, very conscientious and bright decision makers can mislead themselves during the decision-making process. Often they are unaware that they are being misled. The consequence is that some very unwise decisions are reached in groups—decisions that, when analyzed later, seem obviously flawed. Perhaps the best example analyzed by Janis from a group-think perspective was the decision by President Kennedy and his advisors to conduct the Bay of Pigs invasion of Cuba. The defeat and embarrassment that resulted for the United States should have been anticipated, or at least the possibility of it entertained by the group. Yet the group failed to give proper attention to the possible negative consequences of the action.

According to Janis, several factors are likely to produce group think. First, as we have already mentioned, it is likely to occur in groups that tend to share a common perspective and also are composed of members who have a high degree of mutual respect, either because of their expertise or because of friendship ties for each other. Other characteristics are: an illusion of invulnerability, a tendency to moralize by believing that what they are about to do is for the good of a large number of people, a feeling of unanimity among the group members, and pressure toward agreement among all members of the group—either an implicit or explicit call for consensus. The presence of most of these conditions is likely to lead to the group-think phenomenon. Other examples of group think besides the Bay of Pigs were decisions during the Johnson administration regarding commitment of troops to VietNam and the actions of President Nixon and his compatriots regarding Watergate. Group think is likely in any of a number of decisions in organizations—for example, the decision of a power company to build several new nuclear reactors.

STATUS DIFFERENCES

Even the most cursory view of the behavior of people in groups leads to the conclusion that there are differences in power and influence among group members. These differences evolve quite quickly after a group is formed, even without any formalized structural demands. In organizations, the status differences among group participants is apparent because specific policies and practices state the formal power relationships among group members. Because of felt needs for establishing accountability for individuals' actions in the organization, lines of authority are established. At the primary group level, this means that usually one person is held responsible for the group's goal-directed behavior and is designated the supervisor or manager.

Individuals in supervisory or managerial positions are expected to plan, coordinate, direct, and control the task-relevant activities of those individuals for whom they have responsibility, so as to accomplish the goals established for their group. In other words, they are expected to demonstrate "leadership" by influencing group members to contribute to the group's task. Because it is so essential to the organization that work group members direct their activities toward organizational goals and because the extent to which they do this is often credited, rightly or wrongly, to the supervisor's or manager's ability to lead, it is not surprising that leadership has been studied so extensively. In the next few sections we first consider definitions of leadership, and then we discuss the need for leadership in organizations. Next, we consider theoretical approaches to leadership and, when appropriate, applications of these theories to improving leader effectiveness.

LEADERS AND LEADERSHIP: POSITIONS, PERSONS, OR PROCESSES?

Leadership is an illusive concept because it is often used to mean very different things. Three viewpoints are considered here.

Position

To some, leadership resides in a position within an organization. From this point of view, a position is a set of prescribed behaviors for the person assigned to it. Persons in this position acquire a certain set of behaviors expected of them. These behaviors may be those normally considered leadership behaviors. Thus, the individual in this position may be expected to direct the behavior of others and to reward and to reprimand others according to the quality of their performance. In a strict sense, leadership, according to this view, is little more than exercising the role or roles defined as part of the position. Taken to its extreme, little credit for leadership is given to the individual who occupies the position. Most of the behavior is seen as coming from the power, authority, and other aspects delegated to the position. Historians who place most of the causal emphasis on the events and the conditions of the times rather than praise the accomplishments of the leaders exemplify this view. Although the positionist view of leadership recognizes that interaction between leaders and their position requirements influences leadership, the emphasis is on the position itself and the role or roles defined by it.

Person

A second view of leadership focuses on the person. The answer to the historical question in this case is that a person contributed more to events than did the conditions of the times. The search for an understanding of leadership from this point of view has addressed the leader's personal characteristics. Abilities, personality variables, interests, and values have been investigated as possible explanations of differences among effective and ineffective leaders.

Process

A third focus is on the process by which leaders lead. The question is what do they do to lead. At the most general level, leaders influence others; they must achieve group goals by soliciting the aid and commitment of those under them to contribute time and effort toward the accomplishment of group goals. Yet, as Katz and Kahn (1978) explained, this influence must be more than merely routinely exercising the power of the role or position. The prison guard who "influences" the prisoner to move from the exercise yard by pointing his gun could hardly be considered to be demonstrating leadership. Leadership is influence, but it must be some degree of influence that can be attributed to the individual in the leadership position. If everyone in the same position always had the same degree of influence, regardless of what he or she did, then this would not be leadership.

In many ways, the process orientation toward leadership combines the position and the person by recognizing that the major component of what is called leadership is the leader's ability to influence his or her subordinates. The influence process obviously is affected by the situation, which is primarily composed of properties of the leader's position. For example, some leadership positions make available to individuals in them the ability to control valued rewards of the subordinates; other positions offer little in the way of rewards for the position holder to use. Similarly, some individual characteristics affect the person's ability to influence others. For example, a leader's own skill will influence his or her ability as an expert and will guide the behavior of subordinates by the use of expert power. Mainly, process approaches to leadership recognize the separate contributions of situational and individual factors as well as the interaction between the two as they impact on the influence process.

We view leadership in organizations as influence, exerted by individuals in leadership positions, that is not entirely determined by the position itself. Thus, ours is a process orientation. We limit our discussion to those in leadership positions. These positions may be identified from organization charts or they may be positions within other organizations concerned with behavior in that organization. An example of the latter is a union steward. Although we recognize that any number of individuals in a group may emerge and serve leadership functions, we ignore these possibilities in our discussion.

We accept the incremental-influence notion of Katz and Kahn (1978)—that is, that the degree of influence must be more than just applying standard operating procedures. Graen and his colleagues (Dansereau et al., 1975; Graen, 1976) distinguish this quite clearly by differentiating leadership from supervision. Supervision is influencing subordinates to do nothing more than simply fulfill the minimum requirements of their jobs to avoid being fired. Leadership is influencing them to participate actively in the group's activities. Furthermore, leadership is knowing who within the work group needs merely to be supervised and who needs to be stretched beyond the minimum requirements of his or her job.

THEORIES OF LEADERSHIP

Many diverse theories of leadership have been presented over the years. Most of these theories can be grouped into three categories based upon their primary emphases. In this section, we address each of the three major orientations: *trait, behavior,* and *situational-moderator* theories.

Trait Theories

Systematic research on leadership has often focused on the leader's personal traits or characteristics. Explanations of leader effectiveness were thought to be his or her aggressiveness, intelligence, or other personal characteristics such as age or physical attractiveness. The typical research strategy measured personal characteristics, then correlated them with evaluations of leader effectiveness.

Although a large number of studies were conducted to discover the traits that distinguished leaders from nonleaders and good leaders from bad, the results were rather disappointing. No traits clearly identified leaders, especially effective ones. In general, leaders tended to be somewhat stronger than nonleaders in such characteristics as intelligence, social skills, or task skills, but the differences were small and the number of nonleaders who had the same characteristics was large. As a result several reviews of leadership by the mid-1950s (for example, Gibb, 1954) concluded that there was little reason to pursue leader traits.

Opinion has changed somewhat in the past few years. Reviews directed at managerial positions in organizations have offered some hope for trait concerns (Campbell, Dunnette, Lawler, & Weick, 1970; Stogdill, 1974). This change can be credited to at least two factors. First, Ghiselli (1971) demonstrated that through careful consideration of a specific leadership position—that of manager in formal work organizations—a set of relevant traits can be identified and measured which relates to managerial effectiveness. Figure 16.3 describes several of the traits and their relationship to managerial success in a national sample of managers. Some similar traits were also identified as important by Campbell et al., 1970.

A reconsideration of the information gained by understanding leader traits may

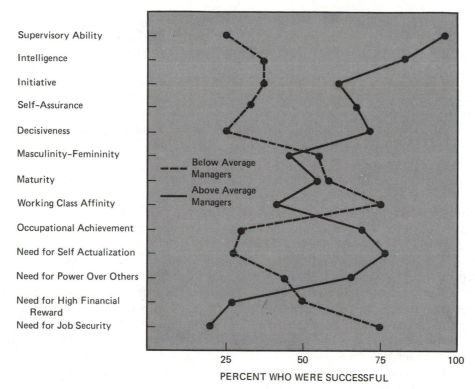

Supervisory Ability
Intelligence
Initiative
Self–Assurance
Decisiveness
Masculinity–Femininity
Maturity
Working Class Affinity
Occupational Achievement
Need for Self Actualization
Need for Power Over Others
Need for High Financial Reward
Need for Job Security

- - - Below Average Managers
——— Above Average Managers

25   50   75   100

PERCENT WHO WERE SUCCESSFUL

FIGURE 16.3 Mean scores for managers high or low on job success across the thirteen traits measured by Ghiselli's self-description inventory. (Adapted from Figures 2, 6, and 10 in Ghiselli, 1971.)

also have influenced the tendency to evaluate trait theories more carefully. Although traits do not show extremely strong associations with managerial effectiveness, given the high degree of importance of many managerial jobs to the effectiveness of the organization, even modest relationships between managerial traits and success can be useful. From this standpoint, smaller degrees of association between the trait or construct under consideration and effectiveness can be tolerated as the importance of being effective increases. Therefore, it is safe to conclude that, although leadership traits are not strongly associated with leader effectiveness, some generalizations can be made about a number of traits and these can be useful for

understanding and identifying leaders, particularly for managerial jobs.

Behavior Theories

Leadership research shifted its focus from leader traits to leader behavior mostly because of dissatisfaction with the lack of progress with traits. This shift was also very reasonable for understanding leadership. After all, if a leader is to influence the group in some fashion, the influence should be most closely related to the way he or she behaves. Therefore, leader behaviors should be the most immediate manifestations of influence.

Behavior dimensions. There were two general approaches to identifying leader behaviors and their effects on such measures of leader effectiveness as group productivity, group member satisfaction, and grievances. At the University of Michigan investigators looked at large numbers of work groups in diverse organizations, from railroad gangs to office workers in insurance companies. Effective and ineffective groups with similar types of tasks were selected, and then leader behaviors were measured and compared. This procedure identified two primary leader behaviors. One was labeled employee-centered, the other, production-centered supervision. The former covered behaviors directed toward the social and emotional needs of group members, whereas the latter were behaviors directed toward task accomplishment. Although the early work tended to see these two as dependent, in the sense that leaders who were strong in one should be weak on the other, later work recognized that the two dimensions were relatively independent.

When the behaviors were related to group performance, there was clear support for the belief that employee-centered behaviors led to improved social and emotional responses. For example, leaders strong in this dimension usually had more satisfied group members than leaders weak in this dimension. Somewhat less clearly, the Michigan research also supported the human-relations position that employee-centered behavior led to higher group productivity than production-centered behavior.

In a field experiment, Morse and Reimer (1956) demonstrated that employee-centered behavior actually created higher morale and higher productivity. Office managers in insurance offices were selected and trained to be employee-centered or production-centered; then performance and attitudinal measures were taken over the next year. The data clearly showed that employee-centered leaders were superior with regard to employee attitudes. Although productivity data

tended to favor production-oriented leaders when the field experiment was terminated, the authors concluded that, had the experiment continued, the employee-centered leadership would have been more successful in the long run. Subsequently, a computer simulation using the parameters of Morse's and Reimer's research substantiated their conclusions about the time effects (Brightman, 1975).

Taking a different tack, researchers at Ohio State University converged on two very similar leader behaviors. Here the focus was on developing an instrument to measure leader behavior with relatively independent dimensions of leader behavior when the scale was subjected to factor analyses. There were two scales. One asked group members to describe leader behaviors (the Leader Behavior Description Questionnaire, LBDQ) and the other had leaders describe their own behavior (the Leader Opinion Questionnaire, LOQ).

Two relatively independent dimensions of leader behavior emerged, labeled Initiation of Structure and Consideration. Table 16.1 lists the items that describe each. It is obvious that these describe behaviors very similar to those found by the University of Michigan group. Subsequent research from a variety of perspectives tends to support the conclusion that leader behaviors can be categorized into two major classes, one for social-emotional behaviors, the other for task-related ones.

Unlike the Michigan research, conclusions about the relationship of leader behavior to leader effectiveness were less clear. Consideration was positively related to social-emotional factors, such as member satisfaction with the leader and the group, but its relationship to productivity was not consistent. Initiation of structure, on the other hand, was not consistently related to either social-emotional behavior or performance. At this time, the best conclusion we can reach about leader behavior is that person-oriented behaviors are

TABLE 16.1 Items from the leader behavior description questionnaire (Form XII) used to define consideration and initiation of structure

CONSIDERATION ITEMS
1. Is friendly and approachable.
2. Does little things to make it pleasant to be a member of the group.
3. Puts suggestions made by the group into operation.
4. Treats all group members as equals.
5. Gives advance notice of changes.
6. Keeps to himself or herself. (Reverse scored)
7. Looks out for the personal welfare of group members.
8. Is willing to make changes.
9. Refuses to explain actions. (Reverse scored)
10. Acts without consulting the group. (Reverse scored)

INITIATION OF STRUCTURE ITEMS
1. Lets group members know what is expected of them.
2. Encourages the use of uniform procedures.
3. Tries out ideas on the group.
4. Makes attitude clear to the group.
5. Decides what will be done and how it shall be done.
6. Assigns group members to particular tasks.
7. Makes sure that role in the group is understood by the group members.
8. Schedules the work to be done.
9. Maintains definite standards of performance.
10. Asks that group members follow standard rules and regulations.

Source: The Leader Behavior Description Questionnaire, copyrighted by Ohio State University.

usually positively correlated with the social-emotional responses of subordinates, but whether person-oriented or production-oriented behaviors are related more closely to other types of criteria of leader effectiveness depends on several other considerations. Some of these are addressed in the following section.

Concerns about leader behaviors. As researchers began to look closely at leader behavior and to conclude that there were two major dimensions of leader behavior, several reservations developed. First, it was obvious that there was no simple relationship between leader behavior and effectiveness other than that of consideration and social-emotional responses. It was apparent that there were no specific behaviors that were going to be best for all situations. Therefore, leadership research shifted from the behaviors to an attempt to discover the conditions under

which certain leader behaviors were or were not effective. We discuss this issue more extensively later in the chapter.

Second, Schreisheim, House, and Kerr (1976) suggested that the inconsistent findings related to initiation of structure behavior may have been because the behavior was described by different items on different questionnaires. Three questionnaires had been used over the years to measure initiation of structure. Although the items on each were similar, there were some notable exceptions. In particular, the earliest measure contained items on punitive behaviors designed to persuade members to exert more effort, whereas later scales did not contain such items. In addition, later scales contained more items on organizing the leader's work and and the work of others than earlier scales did. Schreisheim and others found that in considering these differences, several of the inconsistencies among findings from different research studies could be explained by the measures they used. Nevertheless, there still are many differences in conclusions about which behaviors are more effective.

A third issue is the direction of causality between leader behaviors and effectiveness. Up to now we have been assuming that when leader behaviors were related to group effectiveness, the behaviors caused effectiveness. Morse's and Reimer's (1956) field experiment demonstrated that leader behaviors can cause group responses. However, it is possible that the causal sequence may go the other way in many work settings. For example, assume that consideration behavior correlates positively with group performance in some settings. Perhaps, in these cases, the leader did not show consideration behaviors until the group was performing well. At that time the leader may have decided that he or she could afford to show more considerate behaviors. It is not possible to tell from field research whether a positive correlation between consideration and group performance is because leader behavior causes performance or the other way around.

In a laboratory experiment Lowin and Craig (1968) studied just this issue. They had leaders assigned to groups but manipulated the group's performance independently of what the leader did. They found that through these manipulations the group could cause leader behaviors which paralleled the findings in field settings. Therefore, although Lowin's and Craig's findings did not exclude the possibility that leader behavior affects group effectiveness, they did emphasize that the direction of causation may be reversed and that the interaction patterns between leaders and group members are complex, with the direction of influence going both ways.

Finally, the efficacy of reducing all leader behavior to two dimensions has been questioned. Bowers and Seashore (1962), for example, although recognizing that two factors

can be used, suggested that a four-category system may be more useful. These four were supportive behavior, in which the leader addresses interpersonal, supportive matters in the group; goal emphasis, which stresses goal accomplishment; work facilitation, which is specific behavior designed to help subordinates with their particular tasks; and interaction facilitation, which is directed toward aiding interactions among group members as well as between group members and others in the organization. Hammer and Dachler (1975) went even farther. They suggested that the two major dimensions are so general that they do little to specify guidelines for leaders. For the latter, a much more particularistic behavior taxonomy is needed, which may vary from situation to situation.

The concerns about leader behaviors question the assumption of general behaviors effective in all situations. This we feel is legitimate. The researchers also found that much more particularistic behavior descriptions might be more useful to leaders. Yet, the concerns still lead to the conclusion that what a leader does (that is, how he or she behaves) is important and needs to be understood in order to improve leadership effectiveness and management in organizations. After a brief digression in the next section, we examine some current leadership approaches which maintain behavioral concerns while emphasizing situational influences on leadership.

An application of leader behaviors. Blake and Mouton (1964, 1969) established an elaborate commercial program for training leaders based on the two leader dimensions. In their model, these are labeled *concern for people* and *concern for production*. They treated the two dimensions as independent and concluded that the most effective leaders in organizations are those strong in both dimensions.[1] Their program first assesses the

---

[1]We have already indicated that it is very unlikely that one style fits all situations. This conclusion opposes Blake's and Mouton's assumption.

current style of managers in the two-dimensional leader-behavior space (known as the managerial grid) and then attempts to move them to the desired state of strong in both (cell 9, 9 in their two-dimensional grid with nine points for each dimension).

The procedure for accomplishing the training is an elaborate one that involves the entire managerial staff of the whole organization in a multistep, self-evaluation of their leadership styles. The program attempts to change participants in the direction suggested by the grid. The process is really a complete organizational development package of which the leadership training is a central part but certainly not the only part. Since contribution of the leadership portion is nested within the whole program, it is impossible to evaluate the effectiveness of the leadership training per se.

Situational-Moderator Theories

The evidence seems clear; the same leaders and/or the same leader behaviors are not equally effective in all situations. In some situations some people do better than others; likewise, certain behaviors are effective in some settings but not in others. With this realization, the task seems simple enough; all that is needed is a description of what works best under what conditions.

Unfortunately, the problem is not so simple. It is complex because there are no well-accepted taxonomies of situations. The only real standard for describing situations is that the classification scheme be useful for the purpose at hand. Within the area of leadership are several systems which are quite reasonable in their own right, yet quite different from each other. Furthermore, there has been no attempt to integrate all into a single system. Therefore, we have selected three approaches from among many. They were chosen because they represent a range of possible situational views and, to some extent, because of the current interest in them.

The contingency model. The contingency model of leadership, developed by Fred E. Fiedler (Fiedler, 1964, 1967, 1971), is by far the best-known model to explain situations. The model posits a motivational style for leaders, defines situations, and describes the relationship between different leadership styles and situations as they relate to the effectiveness of the group.

According to Fiedler (1971), leaders can be described as having one of two motivational orientations which create a leadership style for them. Some leaders are *task oriented*. These leaders prefer to accomplish group goals by structuring and working with the task. Other leaders are *person oriented*. For them, group goals are best accomplished by working closely with the interpersonal relations in the group. Although these are very similar to the two behavior dimensions discussed earlier, there are two differences. First, the preferred style does not mean that the leader will use behaviors consistent with the preferred style. For example, a person-oriented leader may want to be considerate but may feel he or she needs to work with the task. Therefore, style and behavior are not the same. The second difference is that Fiedler feels that leader style is relatively permanent and unchanging. He would not advocate trying to change leader style.

Leader style is measured by the Least Preferred Co-worker (LPC) scale. Respondents are asked to think of all the persons with whom they have worked, then to describe the person with whom they have had the most difficulty working. The scale contains bipolar adjectives such as "friendly . . . unfriendly" and "cooperative . . . uncooperative." Those who score high on the scale are said to have a relationship-oriented style (and are termed high LPC leaders), and those with low scores are described as having a task-oriented style (low LPC leaders).

Turning to the situation, the model focuses upon the extent to which it facilitates or inhibits the leader's ability to influence his or her subordinates. A single dimension is created, termed situational favorability, which is said to index the leader's ease of influence in a particular setting. It has three factors: (1) leader-member relations; (2) task structure; and (3) position power. Each of these is then dichotomized and combined so that good leader-member relations, a highly structured task and a position with great power define the most favorable conditions for influence and the opposite on all three, the least favorable. The top two-thirds of Figure 16.4 shows how the dimensions are combined by the model.

Figure 16.4 also illustrates how leader style relates to situational favorability. Based on a review of many studies in a variety of settings, such as high-school basketball teams, voluntary church groups, tank crews, and supermarket employees, Fiedler (1964, 1967) concluded that low LPC leaders outperformed high LPC leaders in either very favorable or very unfavorable settings. High LPC leaders, on the other hand, were better in moderately difficult situations.

Since its introduction, the contingency model has generated considerable research

and controversy. Some have concluded that the model has little or no validity (see, for example, Ashour, 1973; Evans & Dermer, 1974; Graen, Alverez, Orris, and Martella, 1970). Strube and Garcia (1981) did a major review of research on the model prior to 1981. Although they admitted that often studies did not support the model, they concluded that, overall, there was more support than nonsupport. Vecchio (1983) countered Strube's and Garcia's conclusion by arguing that they had failed to include some rather important studies in their review. When these were included, the results were less favorable with respect to the model. The debate goes on.

Perhaps more useful than looking at the model as a whole is to address some of the specific issues raised by the critics. First, there is still considerable doubt as to what is being measured by the LPC scale. Fiedler's (1971) description of it as a motivational orientation is interesting but lacks strong empirical support. In a very complete review of research on LPC, Rice (1978) concluded that there did seem to be support for the general notion that low LPC scores indicated a task orientation and high ones a relationship orientation. Beyond that it is hard to say what is being measured.

Second, the relationship between leader

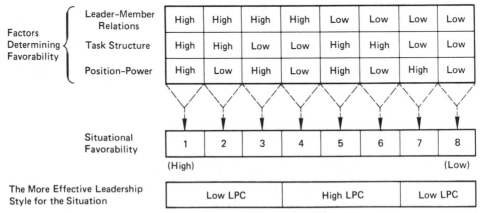

FIGURE 16.4 The relationship between leadership style and situational favorability according to the contingency model. (Adapted from Fiedler, 1967.)

style and situational favorability depicted in Figure 16.4 is often not empirically demonstrated even by Fiedler and his colleagues. Fiedler often attributed the lack of support to some moderating variable such as the intelligence or the experience of the leader. Others, such as Graen et al. (1970), simply have doubted the validity of the model.

At present the issues raised are not resolved. The criticisms of the LPC measure and of the degree to which leaders and situations interact as the model says they do are very well taken. Nevertheless, Fiedler made a significant contribution to the study of leadership by focusing attention on the leader-situation interaction and by attempting to describe that interaction. In addition, research using the LPC scale and the concepts of the model continues to find enough support to warrant further investigation.

An application of the contingency model. Recently Fiedler, Chemmers, and Maher (1976) advocated applying the model through a self-paced training program entitled *Leader Match*. The idea of the program is that, although leader style is relatively unchangeable, leaders can be trained to diagnose the situation and perhaps alter it to better fit their own styles.

The training consists of a self-paced programmed learning text which presents the leader with a series of cases or incidents to which he or she responds by choosing from a set of alternative answers. If the correct answer is chosen, the individual advances to the next problem. Incorrect choices are explained, and the individual chooses again until correct. Before the presentation of incidents, the individual is presented with the notion of leadership styles and situational favorability according to the contingency model. In addition, the participant takes the LPC scale and scores it himself or herself. The purpose of the training is to teach the person how to diagnose situations and to alter them to fit leader styles in general and his

or her own style in particular. This text takes 3 to 4 hours to complete.

In the one published study that used *Leader Match*, Csoka and Bons (1978) found that leaders trained with the manual outperformed those who did not have access to it. The differences in performance between trained and untrained leaders, although not large, was statistically significant and occurred in two independent samples. One was a laboratory sample and the other a field sample of West Point cadets who were assigned leadership positions in Army units for 2 to 4 weeks. Csoka and Bons noted that the group differences may have been due to factors other than the knowledge of the model, such as an increase in self-confidence for those who had completed the training.

Kabanoff (1981) raised an interesting point with respect to the utility of the *Leader Match* training program. To understand his argument recall that the model says that in easy situations low LPC leaders will outperform high LPC leaders and that in moderately difficult situations the reverse is true. Also recall that *Leader Match* would recommend that, if a person were a high LPC leader and he or she were in an easy situation, he or she should attempt to change the situation to a moderately difficult one for which it is predicted that the high LPC style is better than the low. Note that the situations only deal with which of the two styles are better. It does not say that, overall, a high LPC leader in an easy situation will perform less well than the same high LPC leader in the moderately difficult situation. It could easily be the case that all leaders do worse in moderately difficult situations than in easy ones even though in the latter case high LPC leaders do better than low LPC ones. If so, it is poor advice to suggest the shift that *Leader Match* training advocates. Kabanoff calls this the fundamental error of the logic behind *Leader Match*.

Vroom-Yetton model. To Vroom and Yetton (1973), the most important aspect of leadership was the leader's actions related to distributing the decision-making functions within the group. As is illustrated in Figure 16.5, leaders have a number of options for distributing decision making in the group. According to Vroom and Yetton, which options they choose depend on several situational factors. Factors such as the amount of time that can be allowed to make the decision, the subordinates' knowledge of the issues, and the degree to which subordinates must be committed to the final decision all influence leaders' choice of decision-making strategies.

Vroom and Yetton emphasized that the proper choice of a decision-making strategy is critical to two major components of leader effectiveness—the quality of actions reached from the decision and the degree to which subordinates are motivated to work toward the chosen course of action. To aid the leader in choosing decision strategies and thus im-

prove his or her effectiveness, the model describes a series of conditions, then advocates one or several decision-making strategies that fall along the continuum of Figure 16.5. It is a normative model because the strategies prescribed for a given set of conditions are based on a compilation of research and practice prior to 1973. On the basis of the literature, Vroom and Yetton then concluded which decision-making procedure(s) was best for each setting.

The model is used to train leaders by asking them a series of questions about their own situations. The questions can be answered either yes or no, so the series represents a flow chart with branches that eventually lead to a statement of which decision-making style should be best in their settings. In essence, the training's primary goal is to train leaders to diagnose their own leadership situations. If the diagnosis is correct (that is, diagnosed as the model says it should be), then the leader

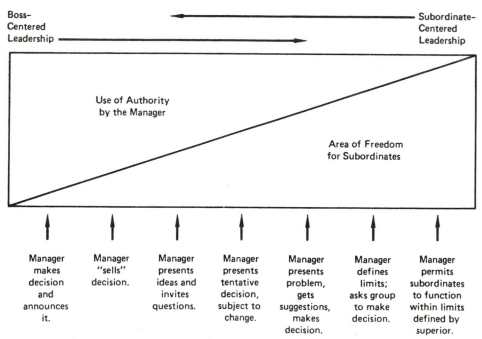

FIGURE 16.5 Possible distributions of decision-making in groups. (Adapted from Sutemeister, 1958.)

should know what decision-making style to use.

The model and its application are relatively new, so there are few data on which to judge either the model's validity or the training's effectiveness. What data do exist are on the model and not on the training. Vroom and Jago (1978) had ninety-six managers who were unaware of the model describe two actual problem-solving situations that they had encountered on their jobs. One problem was to have been handled effectively, the other ineffectively. Once the managers had described the situations, they were trained on the model. They then reanalyzed the problems they had described in the first session, according to the model. The result was a set of problem descriptions in which the managers either did or did not do what the model recommended. In addition, the manager described his or her degree of success in each situation. It was argued that if the model really did describe the proper way to make decisions, then when the managers' actions matched the model's prescribed set of actions, the actions should have been successful. When there was not a match, the actions should not have been successful. Table 16.2 supports this point of view.

The Vroom and Jago (1978) study has two major limitations. First, it would have provided more support for the model if it had been a predictive rather than a concurrent study. That is, a stronger test would have consisted of observations of actual behaviors followed by a waiting period in which actual behaviors would have been observed and evaluated. If the model is correct, the behaviors that fit the model should be the more successful ones. Second, by having managers code their own responses after they had been trained on the model, there may have been a tendency for them to bias their descriptions in favor of matching the model. Nevertheless, the data do offer an initial attempt at validation of the model and suggest that it does have some validity. Field (1982) avoids the latter problem by experimentally manipulating leader behaviors and situations. In general, his data support the model, but the study is a laboratory one not dealing with on-going groups. Therefore, the best conclusion about the theory at this point is that it definitely seems worth further exploration as a guide for training managers. However, more support is needed.

Subordinate-focused situational models. Our final set of approaches to leadership emphasizes the interaction between the leader and the situation by focusing on the subordinate as the key situational component. Two models have taken this perspective. They were labeled the *Path-Goal* model and the *Vertical Dyad Linkage* (VDL) model by their proponents.

The path-goal model of leadership concen-

TABLE 16.2 The frequency with which descriptions of successful and unsuccessful actions by managers agree with the Vroom and Yetton model

MANAGER'S JUDGMENT OF THE QUALITY OF HIS OR HER COURSE OF ACTION	DEGREE OF AGREEMENT BETWEEN THE MANAGER'S COURSE OF ACTION AND THE MODEL'S RECOMMENDED COURSE OF ACTION	
	AGREE	DISAGREE
Successful	80	14
Unsuccessful	37	50
	$x^2 = 34.00$	$p < .01$

Adapted from Vroom and Jago, 1978, Table 3, p. 115.

trates on the leader's role in the motivation of his or her subordinates (Evans, 1974; House, 1971; House & Mitchell, 1974). Leaders have a major impact on their subordinates' work goals and goal-directed performance through their management of positive and negative rewards for goal accomplishment and through their assignment of tasks to subordinates. Within any work group, members have different desires and needs as well as different skills and abilities, so leaders must be attuned to the differences among their group members to be able to influence and guide their behaviors most effectively.

House and Mitchell (1974) reviewed leadership research according to the path-goal model. Their review identified four general leadership styles or patterns of behaviors: (1) directive; (2) supportive; (3) achievement-oriented; and (4) participative. These styles were then seen to interact with those situational characteristics that influence subordinate motivation. The two situational features were: (1) the environment which affected the leader's freedom to assign tasks and give rewards, as well as the quality of the tasks he or she had to assign; and (2) subordinate individual characteristics, such as their needs. Leadership effectiveness, according to the model, is matching the proper style with the task requirements and individual needs of subordinates so that the subordinates will be motivated to facilitate accomplishment of group goals.

Unfortunately, the path-goal model of leadership linked up with the Ohio State leadership dimensions of Initiation of Structure and Consideration. The path-goal theory assumed that leaders influenced subordinates through their display of these two behaviors (Initiation of Structure and Consideration). As a result, most of the research on the model shows that leaders influence subordinates as predicted with respect to the satisfaction of the subordinates, but rarely their performance (Fulk & Wendler, 1982). Yet, had the

model remained broader in its approach by taking into account many different kinds of behaviors that might influence subordinate motivation, it probably would have had more impact (Hammer & Dachler, 1975). Fulk and Wendler (1982) concluded from their review of research on the model that the model itself has a great deal of promise, but that it should not necessarily be limited to the behaviors of Initiation of Structure and Consideration. We, and others (Hammer & Dachler, 1975; Naylor et al., 1980), agree.

The Vertical Dyad Linkage model, developed by Graen and his colleagues (Dansereau et al., 1975; Graen, Dansereau, & Minami, 1972), also emphasized the individual subordinates. The VDL model confutes the commonly held belief that leaders should treat all their subordinates alike. According to VDL, leaders must form dyadic relationships between themselves and each of their subordinates. Leaders also must identify those subordinates who are capable of expanding their roles by sharing the decision-making and other leadership functions technically delegated to the leader. In one sense, these capable subordinates become informal assistants. Other subordinates who cannot or do not want expanded roles must also be identified by effective leaders. These individuals are assigned the more routine tasks of the group. The result is that the leader must tailor his or her responses according to subordinate capabilities and limitations, then must establish effective dyadic relationships with each so that two subgroups are formed. These are labeled "informal assistants" and "hired hands" in the VDL model.

Although the path-goal model emphasizes positive and negative rewards and the VDL model emphasizes task assignment, each model pertains to some extent to both rewards and task assignments, and therefore the two models are complimentary. Unlike individuals in Fiedler's and Vroom's and Yetton's models, individuals associated with situational models with the subordinate focus have not developed programs to train leaders. Nevertheless, the implications of the models are clear. Leaders must evaluate the needs and capabilities of their subordinates and then modify their own behaviors to meet those needs and abilities. This means that leaders will need to treat individuals within their groups differentially both in the subtasks they assign to them and in the positive and negative rewards they administer in response to each subordinate's behavior.

DISCUSSION

Much of what people do in organizations involves interactions with others. In this chapter we have introduced only some of the most basic and most important interpersonal factors influencing people at work. Clearly, if any organization is going to operate effectively, the behaviors of its members must be shaped and guided along certain dimensions in order to accomplish the needed goals. Much of the process of influencing others is done by people with whom they work as they communicate what is and is not expected of them on the job. We have seen that roles and norms provide the standards against which people's behavior is judged. If the behavior is judged acceptable, one type of message is sent to the person behaving; if it is not acceptable, either another message is sent or the nature of the standard is reconsidered. These are just a few of the interpersonal dynamics of the role episode discussed in this chapter.

For the most part, it is unlikely that any roles would be carried out if people were not willing to alter their behavior and give up some of their personal freedom in order to accomplish the goals of the organization as these are manifested in the roles and norms of its members. Leadership, in a sense, is the flip side of the conformity coin. In this case, the focus is on the person who influences others and creates conditions that facilitate conformity to work roles.

Before leaving the subject of groups, it should be mentioned that leadership is one of the few topics in which there has been a systematic flow of research and thought (Calder, 1977). We have seen how an initial concern with leader traits shifted to the study of leader behaviors when there was little progress with traits. When behaviors were reliably identified and measured, but the relationship between the behaviors and leader effectiveness was unclear, the notion of an interaction between leader behaviors and situational conditions began to dominate thinking about leadership. Although there are still many questions about the impact of leaders on groups, much has been learned. Each of the three major emphases listed has contributed some guidelines for management practice. The work with managerial traits by Ghiselli demonstrated that managers have some stable characteristics. These may not account for a large portion of the variance in managerial behavior, but given the great value of identifying managerial talent, knowledge of such personal characteristics can be useful for selecting and managing managerial staff.

The emphasis on leader behaviors and leadership situations has been useful training for leader behaviors and/or for skills in determining the requirements of various situations. Unfortunately, there is still a considerable lack of consensus on which leader behaviors are most important and on how leader situations should be viewed. We presented several points of view. All represent reasonable approaches; yet none has emerged as clearly superior. Nevertheless, with a few exceptions (for example, Calder, 1977; Korman, 1973), most would agree that there have been advances in our knowledge of the leader-situation interaction and that those in leadership positions must learn more about this interaction in order to improve leader effectiveness.

REFERENCES

Asch, S. E. (1958). Studies of independence and conformity I. A minority of one against a unanimous majority. *Psychological Monographs, 70,* 9 (Whole No. 416).

Ashour, A. S. (1973). The contingency model of leadership effectiveness: An evaluation. *Organizational Behavior and Human Performance, 9,* 339–355.

Blake, R. R., & Mouton, J. S. (1964). *The managerial grid.* Houston: Gulf.

Blake, R. R., & Mouton, J. S. (1969). *Building a dynamic corporation through grid organization development.* Reading, Mass.: Addison-Wesley.

Bowers, D. G., & Seashore, S. E. (1962). Predicting organizational effectiveness with a four-factor theory of leadership. *Administrative Science Quarterly, 11,* 238–263.

Brightman, H. J. (1975). Leadership style and worker interpersonal orientation: A computer simulation study. *Organizational Behavior and Human Performance, 14,* 91–122.

Calder, B. J. (1977). An attribution theory of leadership. In B. M. Staw & G. R. Salancik (Eds.), *New directions in organizational behavior.* Chicago: St. Clair Press.

Campbell, J. P., Dunnette, M. D., Lawler, E. E., III, & Weick, K. E. (1970). *Managerial behavior, performance, and effectiveness.* New York: McGraw-Hill.

Csoka, L. S., & Bons, P. M. (1978). Manipulating the situation to fit the leader's style: Two validation studies of *Leader Match. Journal of Applied Psychology, 63,* 295–300.

Dansereau, F., Jr., Graen, G. B., & Haga, W. J. (1975). A vertical dyad linkage approach to leadership within formal organizations: A longitudinal investigation of the role-making process. *Organizational Behavior and Human Performance, 13,* 46–78.

Evans, M. G. (1974). Extensions of a path goal theory of leadership. *Journal of Applied Psychology, 59,* 172–178.

Evans, M. G., & Dermer, J. (1974). What does the least preferred co-worker scale really measure? *Journal of Applied Psychology, 59,* 202–206.

Fiedler, F. E. (1964). A contingency model of leadership effectiveness. In L. Berkowitz (Ed.), *Advances in experimental social psychology* (Vol. 1). New York: Academic Press.

Fiedler, F. E. (1967). *A theory of leader effectiveness.* New York: McGraw-Hill.

Fiedler, F. E. (1971). Validation and extension of the contingency model of leadership effectiveness: A review of empirical findings. *Psychological Bulletin, 76,* 128–148.

Fiedler, F. E., Chemmers, M. M., & Maher, L. L. (1976). *Improving leadership effectiveness: The leader match concept.* New York: Wiley.

Field, R. G. H. (1982). A test of the Vroom-Yetton model of leadership. *Journal of Applied Psychology, 67,* 523–32.

French, W. L. (1978). *The personnel management process* (4th ed.). Boston: Houghton Mifflin.

Ghiselli, E. E. (1971). *Explorations in managerial talent.* Pacific Palisades, Calif: Goodyear.

Gibb, C. A. (1954). Leadership. In G. Lindzey (Ed.), *Handbook of social psychology* (Vol. 2). Reading, Mass.: Addison-Wesley.

Graen, G. B. (1976). Role-making processes within complex organizations. In M. D. Dunnette (Ed.), *Handbook of industrial and organizational psychology.* Chicago: Rand McNally.

Graen, G. B., Alvarez, K., Orris, J. B., & Martella, J. A. (1970). Contingency model of leadership effectiveness: Antecedent and evidential results. *Psychological Bulletin, 74,* 285–296.

Graen, G. B., Dansereau, F., & Minami, R. (1972). Dysfunctional leadership styles. *Organizational Behavior and Human Performance, 7,* 216–236.

Hammer, T. H., & Dachler, H. P. (1975). A test of some assumptions underlying the path goal model of supervision: Some suggested conceptual modifications. *Organizational Behavior and Human Performance, 14,* 60–75.

Hollander, E. P. (1964). *Leaders, groups, and influence.* New York: Oxford University Press.

House, R. J. (1971). A path-goal theory of leader effectiveness. *Administrative Science Quarterly, 16,* 321–338.

House, R. J., & Mitchell, T. R. (Autumn 1974). Path-goal theory of leadership. *Journal of Contemporary Business, 3,* 81–97.

Janis, I. L. (1972). *Victims of group think.* Boston: Houghton Mifflin.

Kabanoff, B. (1981). A critique of *Leader Match* and its implications for leadership research. *Personnel Psychology, 34,* 749–764.

Kahn, R. L., Wolf, D. M., Quinn, R. P., Snoek, J. D., & Rosenthal, R. A. (1964). *Organizational stress: Studies in role conflict and ambiguity.* New York: Wiley.

Katz, D., & Kahn, R. L. (1978). *The social psychology of organizations* (2nd ed.). New York: Wiley.

Korman, A. K. (1973). On the development of contingency theories of leadership: Some methodological considerations and a possible alternative. *Journal of Applied Psychology, 58,* 384–387.

Likert, R. (1967). *The human organization.* New York: McGraw-Hill.

Lowin, A., & Craig, J. R. (1968). The influences of level of performance on managerial style: An experimental object-lesson in the ambiguity of correlational data. *Organizational Behavior and Human Performance, 3,* 440–458.

Morse, N. C., & Reimer, E. (1956). The experimental change of a major organizational variable. *Journal of Abnormal and Social Psychology, 52,* 120–129.

Naylor, J. C., Pritchard, R. D., & Ilgen, D. R. (1980). *A theory of behavior in organizations.* New York: Academic Press.

Rice, R. W. (1978). Construct validity of the least preferred co-worker score. *Psychological Bulletin, 85,* 1199–1237.

Schreisheim, C. A., House, R. J., & Kerr, S. (1976). Leader initiating structure: A reconciliation of discrepant research results and some empirical tests. *Organizational Behavior and Human Performance, 15,* 297–321.

Stogdill, R. M. (1974). *Handbook of leadership.* New York: Free Press.

Strube, M. J., & Garcia, J. E. (1981). A meta-analytic investigation of Fiedler's contingency model of leadership effectiveness. *Psychological Bulletin, 90,* 307–321.

Sutemeister, R. A. (1969). *People and Productivity,* New York: McGraw-Hill.

Vroom, V. H., & Jago, A. (1978). On the validity of the Vroom-Yetton model. *Journal of Applied Psychology, 63,* 151–162.

Vroom, V. H., & Yetton, P. W. (1973). *Leadership and decision-making.* Pittsburgh: University of Pittsburgh Press.

17

Human Factors in Job Design

The previous chapters have dealt with some of the factors that can influence job criteria (job performance, job attendance, job satisfaction, etc.): individual differences, training, and the organizational and social context of work. In a sense the discussion of these factors has been based on the assumption that the nature of the jobs people perform is "fixed"—that it is preordained and "given." But this is not necessarily so. The nature of jobs—that is, their "content," methods, procedures, and the equipment and physical work situations that can influence the work activities—can be the consequence of any of several influences, some intentional and some unintentional. Within reasonable limits the nature of jobs can be altered.

Over the centuries people have improved methods of doing work and the tools, machines, and devices used to carry out work. Many such improvements have been of an evolutionary nature, and succeeding generations have benefitted from the experiences

of past generations. In recent decades, however, marked developments in technology, which have resulted in many new types of equipment and systems and vast changes in the methods of carrying out traditional types of work, have had a major impact on the types of jobs many people perform. Through sad experience it has been found that some of the jobs resulting from new technologies introduce problems, such as difficulties in operating and maintaining equipment, high error rates, accidents, physical strain, and job dissatisfaction. Such problems argue for systematic attention to the design of jobs so they are reasonably suitable for the people who perform them.

MAJOR APPROACHES TO JOB DESIGN

In the twentieth century three major types of effort have had some impact on the nature of jobs. These approaches to job design are: methods analysis; human factors; and job enrichment.

Methods Analysis

What has become known as methods analysis emerged from industrial engineering. The developments of industrial engineering during the early part of the century were dominated by Frederick W. Taylor (1903), who introduced time-study methods, and by Frank and Lillian Gilbreth (1921), who introduced motion study. These and related developments ultimately formed what is now commonly called methods analysis, which focuses on the development of efficient work methods, and thus has a significant impact on the nature of jobs.

Human Factors

The second effort that has had a major influence on job design is what is now commonly called human factors and human factors in engineering. (In most other countries this is called ergonomics.) This field is concerned generally with insuring that the design of physical equipment and facilities people use and the environments in which people work and live are suitable for human use. Various disciplines are concerned with human factors, including engineering, architecture, industrial design, physiology, biology, anthropology, sociology, and psychology.

Human factors received its first major impetus during World War II when problems arose in operating and maintaining new types of military equipment. However, the human-factors field is relevant to the design, maintenance, operation, and improvement of all kinds of systems, and to the many circumstances in which humans find themselves. Today the human-factors field has relevance to the design of industrial equipment, transportation systems, communication systems, automobiles, health-care systems, recreation, buildings, consumer products, and the general living environment.

Our particular interests in human factors in this text are its implications for influencing the nature of jobs. Its influence arises from two sources: first, from the design of the machines, tools, equipment, and other devices that are used by people in their jobs; and second, from the manner in which such physical items are integrated into operational systems. The integration aspect (and in some instances the design aspect) are frequently carried out by industrial engineers using methods-analysis techniques. Thus, to a considerable degree, the methods-analysis approach of the industrial engineers and the human-factors fields have merged, and many industrial engineers concentrate on both areas of application in job design.

Job Enrichment

The third major approach to job design is called job enrichment or job enlargement. The interest in job enrichment has developed because of concern about the "quality of work life" and what has been referred to as the "dehumanization" of some types of work. This is discussed in the next chapter.

Discussion

The methods-analysis and human-factors approaches to job design often result in the simplification of work activities. The methods-analysis approach in particular has sometimes resulted in highly specialized jobs, typified by automobile assembly-line jobs. On the other hand, job enrichment has been aimed more at expanding jobs, thereby increasing job complexity, decision making, and responsibility. These apparently opposite objectives create a possible dilemma for those concerned with job design. However, the distinction between these apparently opposite directions is not nearly as clear cut as it might at first appear. There is also a definite trend on the part of methods analysts and human-factors personnel to recognize the importance of creating jobs that offer greater opportunities for job satisfaction to more people.

This chapter is an overview of the human-factors field, especially of the way in which the design of the physical equipment and facilities people use influences the nature of their jobs.

CRITERIA FOR EVALUATING HUMAN FACTORS

In Chapter 5 we discussed some of the criteria that may be pertinent to some aspects of industrial psychology. Of the criteria mentioned, those particularly relevant to evaluating human-factors principles and data are performance criteria, physiological criteria, certain subjective criteria, and accident and injury criteria. (Accidents are discussed in Chapter 21.) These criteria can be useful for comparing the appropriateness of one design of equipment to another, of one job design to another, of one set of working conditions to another, and of other job-related variables. Because of the significance of criteria for such purposes, let us take a minute to discuss them further.

Performance Criteria

Probably the most common type of criterion used to evaluate human factors is some measure of performance, such as work output, time taken to complete some job activity, quality of performance, or performance decrement over time. In some circumstances, however, performance measures of more basic human processes—such as visual, motor, or mental performance—may be important. Such criteria are generally most relevant to research in performance measurement.

Physiological Criteria

Human work is accomplished by certain physiological processes. As a person performs work, especially physical work, various changes occur in his physiological condition. If the work is taxing enough or long enough, an individual's physical ability to perform the task deteriorates. The energy used in any muscular task comes from potential energy stored in chemical form in the muscles. Muscle activity triggers, directly or indirectly, quite an assortment of physiological reactions, each of which can be considered an index of the muscle activity itself. These include changes in heart rate, energy expenditure, blood pressure, oxygen consumption, breathing rate, blood composition, and electrical resistance of the skin.

Energy expenditure of the total organism is frequently measured in terms of kilocalories per minute (kcal/min). Some examples of this measure for various work activities are given here (McCormick & Sanders, 1982, p. 190):

ACTIVITY	KCAL/MIN
Light assembly	1.6
Brick laying	4.0
Sawing	6.8
Lawn mowing	7.7
Chopping down a tree	8.0
Stoking furnace	10.2

Edholm (1967) suggested that work loads should preferably be kept below about 2000 kcal/day (per 8-hour day); this is equivalent to an average of about 4.2 kcal/min.

Electromyographic recordings of the electrical output of the muscles are sometimes used to measure the muscular effort in local muscle groups (as opposed to total body-energy expenditure). Khalil (1973) suggested that this technique lends itself quite well for use with industrial jobs. Figure 17.1 shows ex-

Foot-pounds	Deltoid	Biceps	Triceps	Brachiorodialis	Total
60	4.7	30.1	7.1	19.7	63.6
15	1.9	9.7	1.2	5.1	17.9

FIGURE 17.1 Electromyograms recorded for four muscles of a subject maintaining a constant torque of 60 ft-lb and 15 ft-lb. The sum of the four values is an index of the total amount of energy expended. (Adapted from Khalil, 1973, Figure 3.)

amples of such recordings for four muscles of a subject maintaining a constant torque of 60 foot-pounds and 15 foot-pounds. The difference in the recordings for these two work loads is quite evident.

Subjective Criteria

Work may be accompanied by some subjective (psychological) reactions to it. There are various dimensions of such reactions, such as boredom and job satisfaction. In the framework of human factors, other types of subjective responses are sometimes used as criteria—for example, judgments of design features, (such as seating design) or expressions of comfort (such as temperature conditions).

HUMAN FACTORS: A FRAME OF REFERENCE

A helpful frame of reference[1] for viewing human factors as related to human work is illustrated in the following paradigm:

$$S \rightarrow \qquad O \rightarrow \qquad R$$
(Stimulus)   (Organism)   (Response)

[1]Readers interested in human factors are referred to E. J. McCormick & M. S. Sanders (1982). *Human factors in engineering and design* (5th ed.). New York: McGraw-Hill.

Many human work activities conform to this pattern: An individual (the organism) receives stimuli that in turn serve as the instigation of responses.

Using somewhat more operational terms, we can express this paradigm in terms of *information-input* processes, *mediation* (that is, mental) *processes,* and *action processes.* A generalized schematic diagram of these functions is given in Figure 17.2. Consider, for example, an electric power-station operator who receives information from the instruments of his control panel. On the basis of this information (and of previous experience), the operator decides what to do and takes corresponding action, such as opening one switch and closing another.

Because this basic frame of reference is important to human factors, we examine each of these aspects separately. Since we cannot cover each aspect thoroughly, we use relevant examples of research to illustrate how to develop guidelines that can be applied to the design of the things people use in their jobs.

INFORMATION-INPUT PROCESSES

The sensory organs of the body are the avenues through which individuals receive information about their environments, including information necessary to perform their jobs. We commonly think that we have

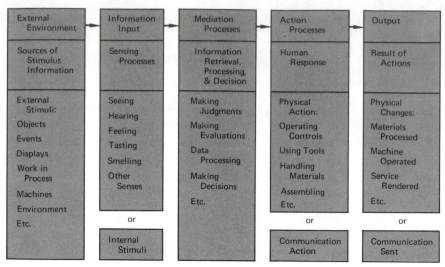

External Environment	Information Input	Mediation Processes	Action Processes	Output
Sources of Stimulus Information	Sensing Processes	Information Retrieval, Processing, & Decision	Human Response	Result of Actions
External Stimuli: Objects Events Displays Work in Process Machines Environment Etc.	Seeing Hearing Feeling Tasting Smelling Other Senses	Making Judgments Making Evaluations Data Processing Making Decisions Etc.	Physical Action: Operating Controls Using Tools Handling Materials Assembling Etc.	Physical Changes: Materials Processed Machine Operated Service Rendered Etc.
	or		or	or
	Internal Stimuli		Communication Action	Communication Sent

FIGURE 17.2 Schematic diagram of the basic functions of human beings in performing work and other activities. A few examples are given for each basic function in the lower part of the figure.

five senses: sight, hearing, touch, taste, and smell. However, we also have other senses: sensations of heat and cold, of body movement, of body posture, of position of body members (such as arms and legs), and probably some others not yet identified. We sense many things in our environments directly, but other information *indirectly*, by the use of manufactured *displays*, such as visual instruments on control panels, machinery, and testing equipment; labels and instructions; blueprints and diagrams; hazard symbols and signs; and various sound signals like those from horns and bells.

Types of Displays

In general, displays can be described as either *static* (signs, printed material, labels, road signs, etc.) or *dynamic* (speedometers, clocks, pressure gauges, radios, etc.). Certain displays have both static and dynamic features—for example, video display terminals (VDTs) that retain certain visual material momentarily and then change.

Selection of Sensory Modality

In designing a display to present information to people, the designer *may* have a choice of the sensory modality to use, although in many circumstances the sensory modality is virtually predetermined by the nature of the case. When there is some option, there are two factors to consider: (1) the relative advantages of one sensory modality over another for the purpose at hand; and (2) the relative demands already made on the different senses.

The visual sense is used most extensively as a display-input channel, followed by audition. The tactual sense is being used by some blind persons (for example, with Braille print) and seems to offer reasonable promise for use in circumstances in which vision and audition are overloaded. When there is some option in choosing one channel over another, consideration of the relative advantages of each can aid in selection. Following is a comparison of the visual and auditory channels:

- Nature of message: Vision better for long, complex, messages. Hearing most suitable for short, simple messages.
- Attention location demands: Vision requires attention to specific location. Hearing does not.
- For demanding attention (as for emergencies): Hearing is best.
- For presenting sequential information to be retained: Vision is best.
- For presenting various types of information (by use of various types of "codes"): Vision is better.
- Rate of presentation of information: Vision usually is better.
- Need for "referral" to information source: Static visual displays can be referred to again. Auditory display information is "lost" unless it is repeated.

Use of Coding in Displays

Displays present stimuli that in turn convey information to people indirectly. (For example, we can read an outdoor thermometer through the window without having to stick our heads outside to find that the temperature is around zero.) The stimuli presented by displays are usually in the form of codes that *represent* the basic information in question. In designing displays (that is, the stimuli), there are certain guidelines that must be followed and others that may be useful in some circumstances. These guidelines are given here (adapted from McCormick & Sanders, 1982):

- *Detectability*. Any stimulus used in coding information *must* be detectable by the relevant sensory mechanism, like those in seeing, hearing, feeling, and the like.
- *Discriminability*. In addition, every code symbol, even though detectable, needs to be discriminable from other symbols of the same class, such as different letters or numerals or tones.
- *Compatibility*. The notion of compatibility is discussed in a later section of this chapter, but generally refers to one's expectations, such as the numbers on a clock face's increasing in a clockwise direction. When relevant, stimuli used in displays should be compatible.

- *Meaningfulness*. This special case of compatibility refers to the desirability (when relevant) of using stimuli that are symbolic representations of the basic information in question and that are most meaningful to the receiver.
- *Standardization*. When coding systems are to be used by different people in different situations, it is desirable to use the same codes.
- *Use of multidimensional codes*. In some circumstances two or more coding dimensions can be used, such as color and shape of signs.

Visual display coding dimensions. Several types of visual coding dimensions can be used in displays. The most common are: letters, digits, geometric shapes, symbols, and colors. Such codes can be used for various tasks or purposes, such as: to identify specific items; to search and locate certain items; to count specific items; and to compare specific items. Research has shown that the effectiveness of different codes varies somewhat with the task. For example, color codes are generally superior for searching and counting tasks, and are better than most other codes for identification tasks. But letter and digit (alphanumeric) codes are better than color codes for identification tasks (McCormick & Sanders, 1982). Furthermore, combinations of codes (such as color and shape) sometimes enhance the reception of information.

However, Christ and Corso (1983) report that, with extensive practice, people learn to use different codes reasonably well; when there are differences in performance with different code sets, the differences are not of major consequence. Although practice does indeed minimize differences with various visual codes, however, if codes are to be used with inexperienced people, the codes that are used should be the ones that are most appropriate for the particular task in question.

Design Features of Visual Displays

A few examples can illustrate the extensive research with visual displays.

Numerical visual displays. Many displays present numerical information, either for "quantitative" reading (to determine an actual numerical value) or "qualitative" reading (to determine an approximate value, or the direction of change of values). Examples shown in Figure 17.3 include displays with moving pointers and fixed scales, those with fixed pointers and moving scales, and counters. Research has found the features shown to be the most suitable.

Such research also reflects that these displays should be designed or selected for specific purposes. For example, if the only purpose of a display is to obtain a quantitative value (*and* if the values do not fluctuate very much), a counter (that is, a digital display) is usually preferable. This was demonstrated, for example, by van Nes (1972) in an experiment with a conventional clock such as (a) in Figure 17.3 and a counter such as (i); the subjects were to rate time differences between pairs of displays of one type or the other. The following are the average times taken by ten subjects to perform the task, along with their errors, when using circular and counter displays:

	AVERAGE TIME	AVERAGE ERRORS
Circular (clock) display	118 sec.	15%
Counter (digital) display	51 sec.	5%

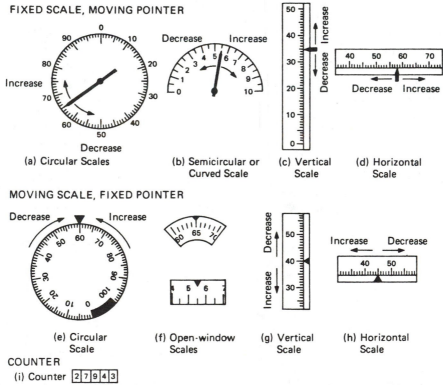

FIGURE 17.3 Some examples of visual displays that present numerical values. Such displays are typically used for quantitative reading tasks but in certain situations may also be used for qualitative reading tasks. (Adapted from McCormick & Sanders, 1982. Copyright © 1982 by McGraw-Hill. Used with the permission of the McGraw-Hill Book Company.)

The relative differences clearly show the superiority of the counter display for this general type of task.

Symbolic designs. For some purposes symbols are used as codes to represent various concepts. When they are used they should represent the concepts as accurately as possible. Various experimental procedures can be used to identify the symbols that best represent any given concept. One procedure is to present various symbols and to ask subjects to identify the meaning of each. This procedure was used by Mackett-Stout and Dewar (1981) with four versions of each of eight different types of symbols of public signs (bus, elevator, men's washroom, etc.). The four elevator symbols are shown in Figure 17.4. The percent of subjects who gave the correct identification is shown below each symbol. In this instance symbol 3 had the highest identification index.

In a broader frame of reference Easterby (1967, 1970) developed a set of principles based on perceptual research that would generally enhance the use of such displays. Some of these principles are summarized there. Examples of their application to machine displays are shown in Figure 17.5.

- Figure/ground. The important features of a display should be clearly discriminable from the "ground" (the background), as shown in (a) of Figure 17.5.
- Figure boundary. A contrast boundary (essentially a solid shape) is preferable to a line boundary, as illustrated in (b) of Figure 17.5.
- Closure. An enclosed figure, such as shown in (c), is usually preferable to one not so enclosed, unless there is some particular reason for doing otherwise.
- Simplicity. Symbols should be as simple as possible, as long as they include all essential features, as shown in (d).
- Unity. Symbols should be as unified as possible. For example, when solid and outline figures are used together, the solid figure should be within the line outline figure, as shown in (e) of Figure 17.5.

Discussion

We have given only a few examples of design features of visual displays that could improve the reception of relevant information by workers. As a generalization, it can be said that whenever job-related information is to be transmitted indirectly to workers, the likelihood of the information's being received can be increased by appropriately designing whatever displays are to be used.

MEDIATION PROCESSES

As indicated earlier, nearly every human activity requires some mediation processes. The grist for these operations consists of input information and information retrieved from storage—that is, from memory. The nature of

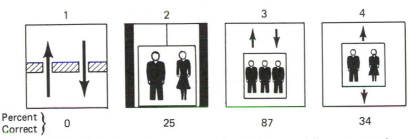

FIGURE 17.4 Symbols used to represent an elevator, and the percent of subjects who identified each correctly. (From Mackett-Stout & Dewar, 1981, Figure 1.)

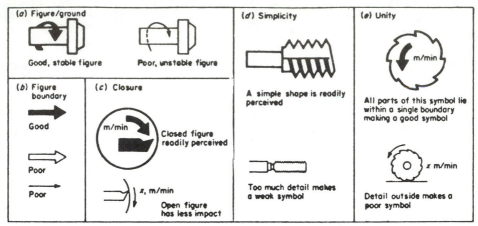

FIGURE 17.5 Examples of certain perceptual principles relevant to the design of visual code symbols. These particular examples relate to codes used with machines. (Adapted from Easterby, 1970, by McCormick & Sanders, 1982.)

these mediation functions naturally varies with the situation but can include judgments and evaluations, reasoning, computations, and other mental operations. Whatever their nature, however, the end result is usually some decision or choice of action. Note, however, that these mediation operations cannot be neatly differentiated from the preceding information-input and the succeeding output (that is, response) functions. For example, the process of perception is inextricably intertwined with both sensation functions and mediation processes, because perception, as a psychological process, includes the attachment of meaning to that which is sensed.

The Nature of Decisions to be Made

Operationally, the nature or "quality" of the mediation processes required in at least some types of human work is influenced by the type or format of the input information presented, by the nature of the responses to be made, and by the interrelationship among them.

Given certain informational input (stimuli), the mediation processes should lead to a decision which, when implemented by a hu-

man response, should produce the most appropriate end result (output). In repetitive operations the decision as to what to do is virtually predetermined, and the human response to a given stimulus is essentially a conditioned response. Such operations, of course, are best mechanized or automated; however, economic factors, the state of the art, or other considerations may argue for retaining human beings in some such operations. In less structured, less predictable circumstances, people's mental capacities are more effectively utilized. In fact, a major reason for incorporating human operators into certain systems is that certain required functions cannot be defined or predicted accurately. In a sense, the human being is needed most when there is an inherent uncertainty in or vagueness about the problem at hand which requires indeterminate responses at indeterminate times. Although human beings certainly have their shortcomings (some more than others), they generally are more adaptable than machines, primarily because of their repertoire of mental abilities.

When, for one reason or another, a human being is used to perform a given function in a system, it may be desirable (and in some circumstances critical) to try to facilitate the mediation and decision processes by appropriate design of the system, including especially the information-input and output (response) features of the system. In doing so, one should focus particularly on the decisions to be made and then work backward to figure out what information should be presented to the individual to help him make such decisions. The displayed information should then be presented so as to facilitate the mediation and decision processes.

Facilitating Mediation Processes

We cannot explore here all the various ways of facilitating the mediation functions in systems. Instead, we briefly discuss one aspect—decision time—as an example.

In fairly well-structured job situations in which specific responses are to be made to specific stimuli, the decision time (or response time) is clearly a function of the number of possible alternatives. This was illustrated by Hilgendorf (1966) with a key-punching task. Hilgendorf's experiment examined the relationship between information input (as measured by the number of equally probable alternative stimuli which could occur) and response time (RT). There were six sets of stimuli and corresponding keys consisting of two, four, ten, twenty-six, 100, and 1000 symbols.

The results, summarized in Figure 17.6, indicate that response time varied directly with the logarithm of the number of alternatives for values up to 1000. Note that the total response time was made up of two values: *recognition time* (the time the subject took to identify the stimulus and raise his hand from a resting position) and *movement time* (the actual time taken to make the response).

The implications of such findings are probably particularly pertinent to circumstances in which a premium is placed on the time to choose, from among various possible reactions, the one that is specifically indicated. In such circumstances, a reduction of the number of possible actions (if feasible)

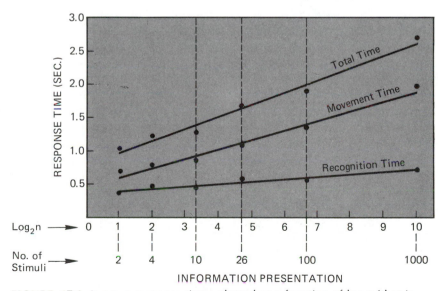

FIGURE 17.6 Average response times plotted as a function of $\log_2 n$ (that is, the number of "bits" of information) and as the number of possible stimuli. (Adapted from Hilgendorf, 1966, Figure 1.)

would tend to bring about a more rapid response.

Compatibility

The concept of compatibility in the human-factors field refers to the spatial, movement, or conceptual features of stimuli and
responses, individually or in combination,
which are most consistent with human expectations. It has been repeatedly demonstrated that compatible relationships definitely improve human performance in terms
of time, accuracy, and other criteria. Some
examples illustrate this concept.

Compatibility relationships (sometimes
called stereotypes) generally arise from one of
two basic sources. Certain relationships are
intrinsic to a situation (such as turning the
steering wheel to the right to turn right). Others are culturally acquired (such as learning
that red means to stop and green means to
go). However, as S. L. Smith (1981) points out,
some relationships are much stronger than
others in that they are recognized by more
people than others. Following are some examples of different types of compatibility.

Spatial compatibility. Spatial compatibility is the compatibility of the physical features, or the arrangement, of items or
modules such as displays or controls. An example of a serious lack of compatibility is
shown in Figure 17.7, an illogical arrangement of certain modules on the display panel
of a nuclear power plant. In this instance the
operators added the arrow cues to alert themselves to the pairs of displays that were operationally related to each other.

Figure 17.8, another example relating to
spatial compatibility, shows two arrangements of a set of eight displays and their corresponding controls. Of these, the arrangement on the right is the more compatible because of the closer, one-to-one relationship of each control to its corresponding

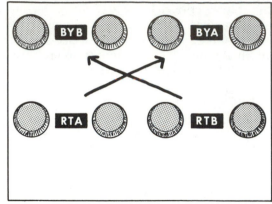

FIGURE 17.7 Illogical and incompatible
arrangement of pairs of certain display modules
on the control panel of a nuclear power plant.
The operators improvised the arrow cue to aid
them in recalling the pairs that were
operationally related to each other. (Adapted
with permission from the Electric Power
Research Institute, EPRI NP–1118, November
1979, Figure 5–2.)

display, although the one on the left is also
acceptable.

Movement compatibility. There are several variants of movement compatibility, but
they all pertain to the relationship between
the direction of some physical movement
(usually of a control device) and the direction
of response of the system. Frequently the response of the system is shown by a display.
Note, however, that there is some parallel to
the chicken-and-egg conundrum here; in
some circumstances the control action is to
correspond with some indication such as a
display—whereas in others the indication reflects the consequence of the control action.
In general, those linkages most consistent
with human expectations result in superior
human performance.

Certain principles have been postulated to
account for those expectations. In connection with the relationships between rotary
controls (such as knobs) and their associated

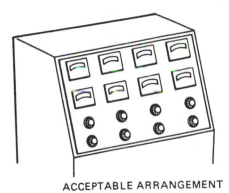 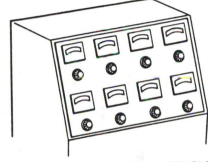

ACCEPTABLE ARRANGEMENT   PREFERRED ARRANGEMENT

FIGURE 17.8 Illustration of spatial compatibility of a set of displays and their corresponding controls. The arrangement on the right is the more compatible because of the closer, one-to-one relationship of each pair of displays and controls, although the one on the left also represents a reasonably compatible pattern.

linear quantitative displays, for example, four different principles have been proposed:

1. Warrick's principle: The pointer of the display should move in the same direction as the nearest point on the control knob.
2. Clockwise for increase: A clockwise turn of the knob is associated with an increase.
3. Up for increase (on a vertical scale).
4. Scale side: The pointer moves in the same direction as that part of the control knob which is on the same side of the knob as the scale markings, the directional part of the pointer, or both.

As Brebner and Sandow (1976) point out, however, there are circumstances in which there may be conflicts between certain of these principles. These conflicts can account for individual differences in the perceived compatible relationships. Figure 17.9 shows some examples of compatible relationships of rotary controls and quantitative displays in which the majority of subjects demonstrated the relationships depicted.

Conceptual compatibility. This applies to circumstances in which some concept is best represented by a feature of a display. Red for stop and green for go are examples. These as-

sociations, of course, are ones we have learned; others are symbolic codes that represent certain concepts—for example, informational road signs with such symbols as telephones, deer, pedestrians, and so on. Still other examples, shown later in Figure 17.12, illustrate how the shapes of control knobs represent their functions.

Discussion

Not all mediation and decision processes are contingent on the design features of the physical objects people use in their jobs. But there are indeed some job situations in which design features of the physical equipment used can facilitate the mediation and decision processes. When this is the case efforts should be made to incorporate design features that do facilitate such processes.

ACTION PROCESSES

Quite a variety of physical actions can be involved in different jobs: walking a tightrope, controlling the movement of a crane, assem-

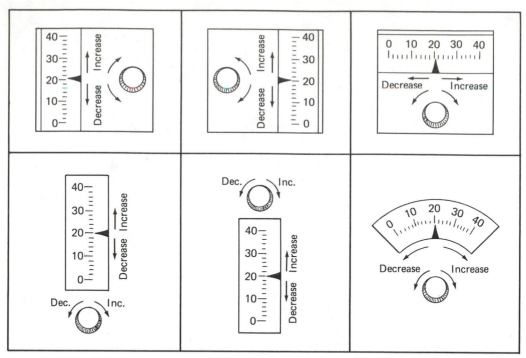

FIGURE 17.9 Some examples of compatible relationships between rotary controls (such as knobs) and displays. (Adapted in part from Brebner & Sandow, 1976; Petropoulos & Brebner, 1981; and Warrick, 1947.)

bling watches, and handling boxes in a warehouse. For illustrative purposes we discuss some aspects of physical handling, control devices, and hand tools.

Physical Handling

Although the human effort involved in jobs has been markedly reduced over the years by the development of mechanical devices, there are still many jobs that involve physical effort, such as moving and handling parts, boxes, bags, and so on. At present there are no regulations by the Occupational Safety and Health Agency (OSHA) regarding maximum permissible weights considered safe to avoid injury (especially of the lower back), fatigue, and so on, when lifting items. The establishment of such standards would have to

take into account individual differences sex; task variables such as frequency, height of lift, and so on; and the criteria to be used in establishing safe limits. As an example of research relating to lifting, we summarize part of the research by Garg and Saxena (1980) involving the lifting of tote boxes. The subjects (male college students) lifted boxes of different sizes, with and without handles, all filled with lead weights to their maximum acceptable levels. The results, summarized in Figure 17.10, show clearly that the maximum acceptable weight was greater for boxes that had handles, and that the dimensions of the boxes also affected the maximum acceptable weight. (The acceptable weight was also greater for boxes with shorter width and length and more depth than for boxes with greater width and length and less depth.) Al-

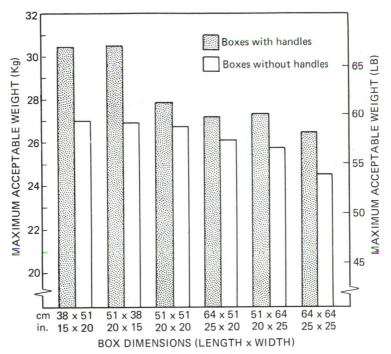

FIGURE 17.10 Effects of handles and box dimensions on maximum acceptable weight for boxes lifted from the floor to bench height. (From Garg & Saxena, 1980, Figure 1.)

though these specific results are not earth-shaking, they clearly demonstrate the effects of design features on human performance.

Because several variables can affect lifting activities, it is not yet feasible to set forth comprehensive specifications of "safe" lifting limits. However, Ayoub, Mital, Bakken, Asfour, and Bethea (1980) have developed a set of maximum recommended liftable weights for males and females—in terms of box dimension and frequency of lift—for six "heights" of lifts. For example, for one size box (30.5 cm or 12 inches) the mean weights for females for lifting from the floor to knuckle height ranged from 19.8 kg (44 lb.) for one lift per minute to 11.4 kg (25 lb.) for twelve lifts per minute. For males the corresponding mean weights ranged from 30.3 kg (67 lb.) to 17.8 kg (39 lb.).

Control Devices

Three points should be discussed with respect to the many types of control devices that we use, each of which can affect their use. These are: (1) correct identification, essentially a coding problem; (2) specific design features; and (3) location.

Coding of control devices. When a number of control devices of the same general class are to be used, mistakes may occur because of failure to distinguish one from another. Under such circumstances, some form of coding can usually reduce errors. Different methods of coding can be used, such as shape, size, location, texture, and color. In coding control devices the same guidelines as for coding displays are applicable. For control devices, however, the tactile and kinesthetic

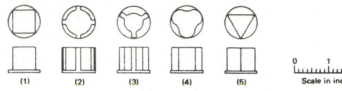

FIGURE 17.11 Design of fractional rotation knobs seldom confused by touch. (Adapted from Hunt, 1953.)

						Scale in inches
(1)	(2)	(3)	(4)	(5)		0 1 2

senses are frequently the most important. The tactile sense is relevant when discriminating individual controls from each other, if they are to be used without visual control, and the kinesthetic sense is relevant if people are to reach for controls in various locations without visual control.

Hunt (1953) experimented with various designs of three classes of knobs in order to identify those that could be identified accurately by touch alone. The subjects who tried to identify the various designs did so under conditions in which they could not see them. A few of the designs that could be accurately identified are shown in Figure 17.11, particularly so-called fractional rotation knobs (those that are not rotated beyond one full turn). Sometimes knobs with symbolic associations can be used, such as those shown in Figure 17.12.

Design features of control devices. There are many types of control devices, including cranks, handwheels, knobs, levers, pedals, push buttons, and selector switches. Recommendations of the suitability of various controls for different situations are given in other sources, such as the *Applied Ergonomics Handbook* (1974), and are not repeated here. It should be noted, though, that variations in the design of any given type of control device can influence its effectiveness in actual use. For example, Kohl (1983) investigated the hand-turning forces that could be exerted by females turning knobs of five different shapes: triangular, square, pentagonal, hexagonal, and circular. As expected, greater forces could be applied with larger knobs (as 5.5 and 4.5 inches) than with smaller knobs (as 3.5 and 2.5 inches). But more particularly, under adverse conditions, with "greased" hands, the forces that could be applied were greatest with the triangle, and were progressively less with squares, pentagons, hexagons, and circles.

Location of control devices. The results of a study by Snyder (1976) on relative locations of the brake and accelerator in motor vehicles illustrates the effects of the location of control devices on their use. In a mockup of a vehicle cab, three combinations of relative locations of the brake and accelerator were used, each characterized by the lateral and vertical separation between the two, as shown here. The mean movement times from the accelerator to the brake are also given.

LANDING FLAP | LANDING GEAR | FIRE EXTINGUISHER

FIGURE 17.12 Some shape-coded control knobs. Although these can be differentiated by touch, they also have symbolic association with their uses.

CONDI-TION	LATERAL SEPARATION (IN)	VERTICAL SEPARATION (IN)	MEAN MOVEMENT TIME (MSEC)
1	2.5	2	202
2	4	0	152
3	8	0	168

The mean movement times were least for conditions 2 and 3, in which the brake and accelerator were even with each other (zero vertical separation). Under emergency conditions the saving of even a few milliseconds in applying the brake could be important.

Hand Tools

An example of the application of human factors considerations in the design of hand tools is illustrated by the redesign of cutting pliers as reported by Yoder, Lucas, and Botzum (1973). These pliers are used to cut injection-molded parts for boxes in a pharmaceutical plant. With the conventional pliers the operators complained of muscle fatigue and a condition called wrist tenosynovitis, presumably caused by the angle at which the wrist was bent, as illustrated in Figure 17.13. The use of these pliers depended most on the third and fourth fingers of the hand. A redesigned pair of pliers is also shown in Figure 17.13, along with the cutting position when using them. An electromyographic

analysis found that the redesigned pliers utilized a greater portion of the muscles of all of the fingers, and thus reduced the fatigue and tenosynovitis. Many other types of hand tools could likewise be redesigned in order to minimize physiological stress or to make them more efficient for human use.

WORKSPACE DESIGN

Fixed work stations should be so designed that the individuals can perform their tasks effectively, comfortably, and safely. Two major aspects of this design problem concern the total workspace and the arrangement of the facilities and features of that workspace.

Workspace Envelope

The workspace envelope can be viewed as a three-dimensional space around an individual which can be used for the physical activities he will be expected to perform. For a seated individual this typically consists of

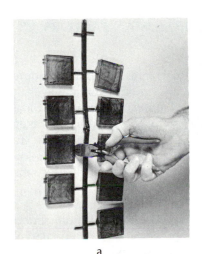 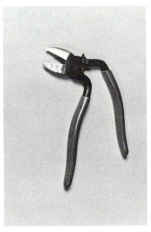 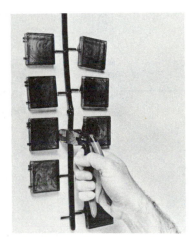

a   b   c

FIGURE 17.13 Cutting pliers used to cut parts for injection-molded plastic boxes. The original design (shown in *a*) caused fatigue and wrist tenosynovitis. The redesigned pliers (*b* and c) improved wrist posture and better distributed the work load across all the fingers, thus basically correcting the problem with the original design. (From Yoder et al., 1973, Figures 7 and 8.)

whatever space he or she can reach conveniently by hand. Of course, this leads to the problem of individual differences, and the types of actions people are to take with their hands. Kennedy (1964) conducted research relating to the workspace envelope. The subjects were presented with a vertical rack of measuring staves, each pointing toward the right shoulder and each with a knob on the end. Each subject grasped each rod between the thumb and forefinger and moved it out until the arm was fully extended without pulling the shoulder away from the back. This was done with the racks at 15° intervals around an imaginary vertical line, beginning at a seat reference point behind the subject. Figure 17.14 shows the distances for the fifth-percentile subjects for three vertical levels—namely, for the seat reference level (SAL) and for 10 inches, 25 inches, and 40 inches above the seat reference level.

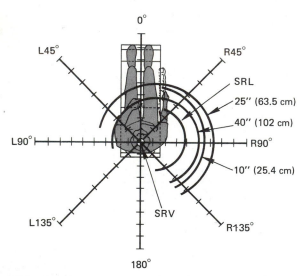

FIGURE 17.14 Distances of reach of the fifth percentile of a sample of Air Force personnel in grasping a knob at various angles at the seat reference level (SRL) and at 10″, 25″, and 40″ above the SRL. Such data can define the workspace envelope within which most people can conveniently work. (Adapted from Kennedy, 1964.)

Data like these can, of course, be used to create the immediate workspace for seated personnel. The fifth-percentile values are frequently used for setting the outer limits that individuals would be expected to reach, since those beyond the fifth percentile (95% of the population) would also be able to reach the locations that those of the fifth percentile can reach.

Arrangement of Facilities

When people use various displays, controls, tools, materials, parts, and so forth, in their jobs these should be arranged within the workspace according to some guiding principle or principles, such as *importance* (putting the most important things where they are most easily used), *frequency of use, functional relationships,* or *sequence of use.* An example of the functional-relationship principle is illustrated later in Figure 17.16 (see page 366).

EXAMPLES OF HUMAN-FACTORS PROBLEMS

Human-factors problems abound all around us—in our jobs and in our everyday lives. In the *Wall Street Journal,* for example, Sloan (1983) bewailed some of the problems he encountered in using hotel showers with "futuristic banks of levers, knobs and dials—no two of which are ever alike or do the same thing twice" (p. 34). Although many human-factors design features in our lives have only a nuisance value, others are of more serious proportions. Here, we discuss briefly certain such problems in two types of systems—namely, control rooms of nuclear power plants and video display terminal (VDT) workstations, used with computers and word processors.

Control Rooms
of Nuclear Power Plants

Occasional events at nuclear power plants (such as the one at Three Mile Island) have focused attention on some of the human-factors problems in the control rooms of such plants. In 1977 the Electric Power Research Institute (EPRI) sponsored an extensive research program, carried out by Lockheed Missiles and Space Company, Inc., to analyze the human-factors features of five nuclear power plants. The research turned up a wide range of human-factors problems; a couple of examples are shown in Figure 17.15. Other human-factors problems included: situations in which an operator could not see the displays while communicating with others; lack of clear identification of displays and controls; numerous problems associated with maintenance; information overload of operators; and lack of compatibility of system modules (EPRI report, 1979; Seminara & Parsons, 1982). Figure 17.7 (earlier in this chapter) shows two pairs of displays whose arrangements were incompatible with their functional relationships.

As one phase of the EPRI study, recommendations were made to modify existing consoles to minimize the human-factors faults (EPRI report, 1979). One such recommendation consisted simply of adding outlines to functionally related modules, as illustrated in Figure 17.16.

The Nuclear Regulatory Commission (NRC) commissioned a Human Factors Society (HFS) study group to analyze human-factors safety issues in the nuclear industry. That group made fifty-one recommendations for a long-range plan for nuclear-reactor regulation, most of which have been or will be implemented by the NRC. The human-factors problems associated with existing nuclear power plants will not go away overnight, although certain modifications can at least minimize the possibility of future accidents.

The design of future installations is, of course, a major challenge to those involved in human factors.

Video Display Terminal
(VDT) Workstations

There is no escape from the inexorable tide of technology. We are now told that no household should be without a personal computer or a word processor. Although there will indeed be holdouts against this trend, computers and word processors are becoming part and parcel of the facilities used by large numbers of workers. Here, we discuss some of the human-factors aspects of video display terminals (VDTs) and the workstations associated with them.

A VDT typically consists of a keyboard and a cathode ray tube display (basically the same as a TV) for presenting alphanumeric data. (The word processor shown in Figure 17.17 is an example of a VDT.) There is considerable diversity in the predominant mode of interaction with VDTs in various jobs, including: data entry (using the keyboard to enter data): data acquisition (calling up information from a computer component and reading it from the screen); interactive communication (such as that of airline-reservation personnel); word processing (essentially a replacement for the conventional typewriter, except that the "typed" material is presented on the VDT instead of on a sheet of paper); programming (of computers); and computer-assisted instruction.

Human-factors problems with VDTs. There have been numerous reports of complaints by VDT operators. In one, M. J. Smith, Cohen, and Stammerjohn (1981) used a questionnaire to solicit the reactions of 250 VDT operators and 150 nonoperator control subjects about various aspects of their work, including job stress and health complaints. Some of the work-attitude items (called stressors) that characterized the VDT operators

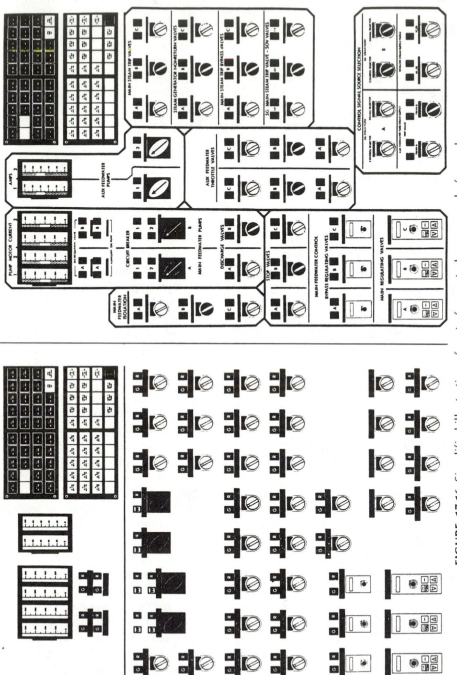

FIGURE 17.16 Simplified illustration of part of a control-room panel of a nuclear power plant, showing the original design (on the left), and an enhancement of that same arrangement made by drawing lines around related groups of modules (on the right). Since the nature of the functional groups is not relevant for illustrative purposes (and because of the reduced size), the labels of the groups are not given. (Reproduced with permission from the Electric Power Research Institute report, 1979.)

FIGURE 17.15 A couple of human-factors problems in a nuclear power plant. In the photo on the left, the control console is so arranged that certain controls could be accidentally activated by the knee or the hand used to brace the operator when reaching for the farthest controls. In the photo on the right, certain of the displays are at a height that makes reading or lamp replacement a problem. Special stepladders are required. (Photographs courtesy of the Electric Power Research Institute [EPRI], based on research they sponsored.)

FIGURE 17.17 An example of a video display terminal (VDT)—in particular, a word processor. This shows the display itself (which is a cathode ray tube) and the keyboard. With this particular model the keyboard is movable, and can be positioned at the convenience of the operator. (Courtesy of CPT Corporation, Minneapolis, Minnesota.)

were: boredom; necessity for increased concentration; having to work too hard; having to work too fast; and having heavy work loads. Some of the many health complaints were: fatigue; pain down arm; irritated eyes; burning eyes; eye strain; back pain; sore shoulder; neck pain into shoulder; and hand cramps. The most common human-factors problems are those dealing with visual complaints and muscular discomfort. In addition, however, there is considerable concern about other aspects, such as radiation emissions and psychosocial stress (associated with performance of highly repetitive tasks and lack of "control" over one's job activities).

National Research Council Evaluation of VDTs. Because of the widespread use of VDTs, the National Research Council (NRC) established a panel to assess the impact of video viewing on workers' vision (this review, however, also covered other aspects of VDTs). In general the panel concluded, on the basis of available evidence, that most of the complaints and reported symptoms cannot be attributed directly to the use of VDTs as such; for example, the panel reported that there was no evidence that the occupational use of VDTs as such was *directly* associated with increased risk of ocular (visual) diseases, cataracts, physiological damage to the visual system, or hazardous levels of emitted radiation, or to the reported physical complaints. However, the panel did acknowledge that some of the reported problems with VDTs may be attributable to features of the work situation—that is, the way VDTs are used and the specific design features of the VDTs and their associated workstations. It is this point that we would like to emphasize.

Design features of VDTs. A number of human-factors aspects are relevant for the design of VDTs and their workstations; presumably, the appropriate design of these features would help minimize the complaints that have been reported. A few such features are discussed next, with particular reference to their human-factors aspects.

Aside from the numerous human-factors aspects of the design features of VDTs as such, variations in the extent to which individuals use VDTs in their typical work routines also can influence the complaints of operators. Most of the surveys of VDT users have covered individuals who spend most or all of their time using VDTs. However, millions of people use VDTs incidentally, as only part of their work routines. It is probable that deficiencies in the design of VDT systems can be tolerated much more by these occasional users than by regular users. If further research indicated that full-time use of VDTs imposes excessive stress on operators, in some circumstances, work schedules might be able to be adjusted so that VDT operators could be rotated occasionally to other duties during the work day.

Contrast and color. In general terms, visual task performance is enhanced by increases in the contrast of the characters (as letters and numerals) against their backgrounds. However, this contrast can be either of light characters on a dark background, or vice versa. The U.S. convention is to call light characters on a dark background *positive* contrast and dark on light, *negative* contrast; European convention reverses these terms. There are some inklings that negative-contrast displays (dark on light) yield greater legibility than positive-contrast displays (Bauer & Cavonius, 1980; Radl, 1980); however, further research is probably in order to confirm (or reverse) these findings. The colors of VDT displays are influenced by the colors of the phosphors that are used. Most displays use either white or green phosphors. However, some displays using white phosphers have a color filter to change the observed color, such as to orange, yellow, and amber. *The Seybold Report on Office Systems* (October 1982) reports that based on their research the trend in European countries seems to be toward the use of amber, yellow, and green. In fact, Sweden has mandated that all terminal screens be yellow or amber.

However, although there is a trend toward amber, yellow, and green screens, the National Research Council report (1983) concludes that there are no known performance differences associated with differences in the colors of the phosphors used, as long as the blue and red extreme ends of the spectrum are avoided. The report also concludes that differences between white and green phosphors are totally subjective; preferences for either are reported approximately equally often.

Although there is no overwhelming research evidence to support the advantage of using positive contrast (black on white) versus negative contrast (light on dark), on the basis of the research of Bauer and Cavonius (1980) and Radl (1980), we are inclined to recommend the use of positive contrast.

Glare. What is called reflected glare is the result of reflections from polished or glassy surfaces. In the case of a VDT display, such glare is caused by improper positioning of the VDT screen relative to the light source, such as a window or luminaire. Such glare can be reduced by positioning the VDT screen perpendicularly to the place of the light source; shielding or screening the light source; using VDTs whose angular positions can be adjusted; and placing a hood around the screen. Reflective glare is thus not an intrinsic feature of VDTs, but rather the consequence of the visual environment, and can be minimized or eliminated by appropriate action as just discussed.

Keyboards. The increased use of keyboards with computers and word processors has raised a long-dormant issue regarding the arrangement of the keys. The conventional typewriter keyboard (called the QWERTY keyboard because these are the first letters on

the top line) was designed by the Sholes brothers in 1873 to minimize the jamming of type bars in the early design of the typewriter. Although various other designs have been proposed over the years, the design that has been given most attention is that developed by Dvorak and copyrighted in 1932. Some of the back-up research was later reported by Dvorak (1943). Both the QWERTY and the Dvorak designs are shown in Figure 17.18.

The Dvorak keyboard (called the Dvorak Simplified Keyboard or DSK) was designed to minimize the amount of travel time by placing the most used keys on the "home-base" row (the second from the bottom) and to better balance the fingers on the two hands. Lamb (1983) reports that Virginia Russell, head of the Dvorak International Federation, claims that more than 4000 words can be typed using only the home-base row of the DSK, while only 100 words are thus possible with the QWERTY. Further, Russell claims that with the QWERTY arrangement the fingers of an average (full-time) typist travel 16 miles a day, as contrasted with 1 mile with the Simplified Keyboard. Lamb (1983) states that in a comparison of the two arrangements, estimates of productivity gains with the Simplified Keyboard range as high as 60%, although he reports that Dick Land (head of Instructional Laboratories at Harvard University) believes that a 10% to 20% gain is a more accurate estimate. In turn, Norman (1983) estimates the advantage to be only 5% to 10%. Norman acknowledges the advantage of the Simplified Keyboard, but believes the advantage (even if it is as high as 10% to 20%) is not big enough to matter. This evaluation is based on the assumption that many persons who use keyboards perform a variety of other activities, so the increased typing efficiency with the Simplified Keyboard would therefore be relatively nominal. However, in the case of persons using a

QWERTY KEYBOARD

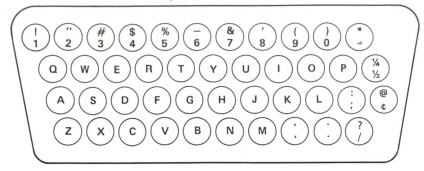

DVORAK SIMPLIFIED KEYBOARD

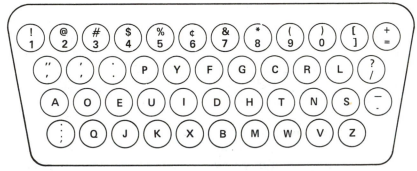

FIGURE 17.18 The conventional QWERTY keyboard and the Dvorak Simplified Keyboard (DSK). The DSK conforms to the American National Standard (ANSI) X4–22–1983 as an optional alternative to the conventional QWERTY keyboard.

keyboard a substantial portion of the work day, it would seem that efficiency could be expected to increase by 5% or 10% (or perhaps more) with the Simplified Keyboard.

A major factor in considering the possible use of the Simplified Keyboard is that there are millions of QWERTY keyboards in existence, and millions of people trained in their use. In view of this a complete conversion to the Simplified Keyboard would be entirely impractical. The most feasible approach to the possible use of the simplified model is as an alternative, especially for persons who are not completely committed to the QWERTY by training or experience. In fact, Smith-

Corona has offered a simplified model for some years. With the increased use of keyboards with computers and word processors, certain computer manufacturers are also poised to offer the simplified model as soon as consumer demand warrants it. As an aside, it is technically feasible to program certain computers so they can be converted to the Simplified Keyboard. The flurry of interest in the simplified model for use with computers and word processors has been such that the American National Standards Institute (ANSI, 1983) has accepted the Simplified Keyboard as an official alternative to the QWERTY version.

VDT workstations. Some of the postural complaints about VDTs arise from the design of the workstation, including the table or desk on which the VDT is placed, the position of the keyboard, and the design of the chair. Because of individual differences in physical dimensions it is desirable to provide for adjustments for certain features of workstations, including dimensions of some and angles of others. Figure 17.19 illustrates the means of the preferred angle values for the three angular features that are most relevant to the posture of the trunk and arms. A set of design recommendations for various features of the workstation, shown in Figure 17–20 (Kroemer & Price, 1982), is based on data from various studies. Note that the recommendations of Grandjean, Hunting, and Pidermann (1983) on keyboard table height and seat height are somewhat higher than those of Kroemer and Price. (See page 372.)

A few suggestions of the National Research Council panel regarding VDT workstations are as follows: The screen should be in front of the operator and preferably near the keyboard; the screen and source document should preferably be a few degrees below the straight-ahead line of sight (this can minimize neck and shoulder discomfort); the keyboard should be detachable (so it can be placed in the most comfortable position for the operator); a convenient writing surface should be provided; leg room should provide for space to accommodate variations in posture; hand, wrist, and arm should be supported for long-term periods of VDT operation (but there are little data on the presumed advantages); the backrest should have adjustable depth, height, and angle with respect to the seat pan; the seat pan itself should have a slight cavity in its center and it should be well rounded along its front edge.

Discussion of VDTs. Our discussion of the human-factors aspects of VDTs has been more extended than would normally be appropriate for a survey text such as this. This has been done intentionally, however, to illustrate the variety of human-factors aspects that can be involved with any given system. Even so, we have still not mentioned other human-factors aspects of VDTs that are also generalizable to other systems: the luminance of the display; the "flicker" rate of the displayed material; the illumination on the workstation; the possibility of an adjustable-angled keyboard, especially for short operators (as suggested by Miller & Suther, 1983); certain psychosocial problems (such as a possible lack of a sense of "control" by operators), and the need to cope with technological change.

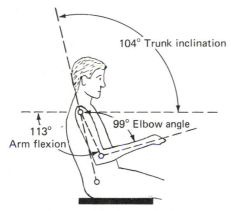

FIGURE 17.19 The "mean body posture" preferred by sixty-eight VDT operators. This shows the means of the preferred angle values for the three angular features that are most relevant for the posture of the trunk and arms. (From Grandjean et al., 1983, p. 15.)

DISCUSSION

Although this text is not intended to make readers "human-factors experts," it should at least contribute to an awareness of the importance of design for people's jobs.

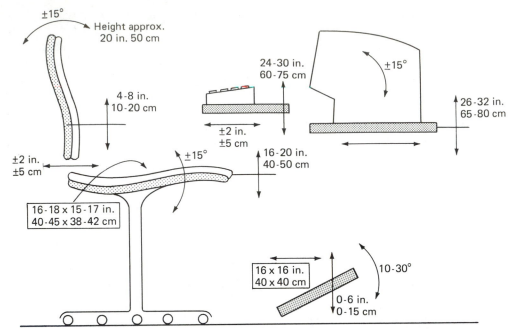

FIGURE 17.20 Design recommendations for certain VDT workstation features. (Adapted from Kroemer & Price, 1982, and reproduced with permission of Industrial Engineering. Copyright © Institute of Industrial Engineers, Inc., Norcross, Georgia 30092.) Note: On the basis of subsequent research, Grandjean et al. (1983) make the following recommendations which are a bit higher than shown in the figure):

Keyboard table height: range from 65 to 82 cm (26 to 33 in.) to allow for keyboard heights from table of 3 to 8 cm (1.2 to 3.2 in.).

Seat height: range from 42 to 55 cm (17 to 22 in.).

REFERENCES

American National Standards Institute (ANSI) (1983). *ANSI Standard X4.22.*

Ayoub, M. A., Mital, A, Bakken, G. M., Asfour, S. S., & Bethea, N. J. (1980). Development of strength and capacity norms for manual materials handling activities: The state of the art. *Human Factors, 22*(3), 271–282.

Bauer, D., & Cavonius, C. R. (1980). Improving the legibility of visual display units through contrast reversal. In E. Grandjean & E. Vigliani (Eds.), *Ergonomic aspects of visual display terminals.* London: Taylor & Francis.

Brebner, J., & Sandow, B. (1976). The effect of scale side on population stereotypes. *Ergonomics, 19*(5), 571–580.

Christ, R. E., & Corso, G. M. (1983). The effects of extended practice on the evaluation of visual display codes. *Human Factors, 25*(1), 71–84.

Dvorak, A. (1943). There is a better typewriter keyboard. *National Business Education Quarterly, 11,* 58–66.

Easterby, R. S. (1967). Perceptual organization in static displays for man/machine systems. *Ergonomics, 10,* 195–205.

Easterby, R. S. (1970). The perception of symbols for machine displays. *Ergonomics, 13,* 149–158.

Edholm, O. G. (1967). *The biology of work.* New York: World University Library, McGraw-Hill.

Electric Power Research Institute (November 1979). *Human factors methods for nuclear control room design, Volume 1: Human factors enhancement of existing nuclear control rooms.* Palo Alto, Calif.: EPRI NP–1118. (Prepared by Lockheed Missiles & Space Co., Inc.)

Garg, A., & Saxena, U. (1980). Container characteristics and maximum acceptable weight of lift. *Human Factors, 22*(4), 487–495.

Gilbreth, F. B., & Gilbreth, L. M. (December 5–

9, 1921). *First steps in finding the one best way to do work.* Paper presented at the annual meeting of the American Society of Mechanical Engineers, New York, New York.

Grandjean, E., Hunting, W., & Pidermann, M. (1983). VDT workstation design: Preferred settings and their effects. *Human Factors, 25*(2), 161–175.

Hilgendorf, L. (1966). Information input and response time. *Ergonomics, 9*(1), 31–37.

Hunt, D. P. (August 1953). *The coding of aircraft controls.* U.S. Air Force, Wright Air Development Center (Tech. Rep. 53–221).

Kennedy, R. W. (1964). *Reach capability of the USAF population: Phase 1. The outer boundaries of grasping-reach envelopes for the shirt-sleeved seated operator.* U.S. Air Force, Aerospace Medical Research Laboratory, TDR 65–59.

Khalil, T. M. (1973). An electromyographic methodology for the evaluation of industrial design. *Human Factors, 15*(3), 257–264.

Kohl, G. A. (July–August 1983). Effects of shape and size of knobs on maximal hand-turning forces applied by females. *The Bell System Technical Journal, 62*(6), 1705–1712.

Kroemer, K. H. E., & Price, D. L. (1982). Ergonomics in the office: Comfortable work stations allow maximum productivity. *Industrial Engineering, 14*(7), 24–32.

Lamb, G. M. (May 25, 1983). Goodbye to QWERTY—new typing keyboard is faster. *Christian Science Monitor.*

Mackett-Stout, J., & Dewar, R. (1981). Evaluation of public information signs. *Human Factors, 23*(2), 139–151.

McCormick, E. J., & Sanders, M. S. (1982). *Human factors in engineering and design.* New York: McGraw-Hill.

Miller, W., & Suther, T. W., III (1983). Display station anthropometrics: Preferred height and angle settings of CRT and keyboard. *Human Factors, 25*(4), 401–408.

National Research Council, Panel on Impact of Video Viewing on Vision of Workers (1983). *Video displays, work, and vision.* Washington, D.C.: National Academy Press.

Norman, D. A. (September 1983). The DVORAK revival: Is it really worth the cost? *CP News* (Consumer Products Technical Group, The Human Factors Society, Santa Monica, Calif.) 8(3).

Petropoulos, H., & Brebner, J. (1981). Stereotypes for direction-of-movement of rotary controls associated with linear displays. *Ergonomics, 24*(2), 143–151.

Radl, G. W. (1980). Experimental investigations for optimal presentation mode and colors of symbols on the CRT screen. In E. Grandjean & E. Vigliani (Eds.), *Ergonomic aspects of visual display terminals.* London: Taylor & Francis.

Seminara, J. L., & Parsons, S. O. (1982). Nuclear power plant maintainability. Applied Ergonomics, 13.3, 177–189.

Shackel, B. (Ed) (1974). *Applied Ergonomics Handbook.* Surry, England: IPC Science and Technology Press. *13*(3), 177–189.

The Seybold Report on Office Systems (October 1982). *5*(10), 5–8. Seybold Publications, Inc. P.O. Box 644, Media, PA.

Sloan, B. (August 30, 1983). Designers of hotel showers are all wet. *Wall Street Journal,* p. 34.

Smith, M. J., Cohen, B. G. F., & Stammerjohn, L. W., Jr. (1981). An investigation of health complaints and job stress in video display operations. *Human Factors, 23*(4), 387–400.

Smith, S. L. (1981). Exploring compatibility with words and pictures. *Human Factors, 23*(3), 305–315.

Snyder, H. L. (1976). Braking movement time and accelerator-brake separation. *Human Factors, 18*(2), 201–204.

Taylor, F. W. (1903). Shop management. *Transactions of the American Society of Mechanical Engineers, 24,* 1337–1481.

van Nes, F. L. (1972). Determining temporal differences with analogue and digital time displays. *Ergonomics, 15*(1), 73–79.

Warrick, M. J. (1947). Direction of movement in the use of control knobs to position visual indicators. In P. M. Fitts (Ed.), *Psychological research on equipment design* (Research Rep. No. 19). Army Air Force, Aviation Psychology Program.

Yoder, T. A., Lucas, R. L., & Botzum, G. D. (1973). The marriage of human factors and safety in industry. *Human Factors, 15*(3), 197–205.

18

Job Enrichment

The application of methods-analysis and human-factors principles discussed in the preceding chapter often created jobs that were more simple than were the ones to which the techniques were applied. That is, the new jobs required fewer of the job holders' skills and abilities to perform the jobs successfully than did the jobs as originally designed. Technological advances also contributed to a general trend toward simpler jobs. More automated production processes often demanded little from those whose jobs were automated.

As the number of oversimplified jobs expanded, so did the resistance to them. On the one hand, job simplification was criticized for failing to meet the same criterion (efficiency) that had led to limiting the scope of many jobs in the first place. Frequently, as the jobs were simplified to the point at which almost anyone could perform them with little or no training, lack of involvement, boredom, and frustration lowered performance.

Job simplification was also criticized from a philosophical standpoint. It was argued that since work occupied a major part of most people's lives, the dissatisfaction with work assumed to accompany simple jobs adversely affected the quality of life available to those with simple jobs.

Both criticisms attributed reactions to simple jobs to similar factors, and both recommended similar changes. In particular, both assumed a humanistic orientation. Humans were seen as needing to grow and develop throughout life. To do this, it was necessary to provide opportunities for growth and development at work. Therefore, regardless of the initial reasons for questioning the design of jobs with limited scope, the suggested solutions were the same: Increase the complexity of jobs.

Increasing job scope—that is, *job enrichment*—is a motivational concern. This is in contrast to methods analyses and human-factors analyses discussed in the previous chapter. The latter do not ignore motivation, but their emphasis is more on an individual's requisite knowledge, skills, abilities, and capabilities. Job-enrichment concentrates on motivational issues. In this chapter we describe and evaluate job-enrichment principles and practices.

JOB ENRICHMENT: A DEFINITION

The term job enrichment has been used to describe the expansion of the number of duties and responsibilities associated with a particular job. This expansion can occur along two dimensions. One, frequently called *horizontal loading*, increases the number of subtasks required on a job without increasing the amount of responsibility or complexity. For example, the job of cashier at a supermarket could be expanded horizontally by requiring the cashier to also bag groceries and perhaps to stock shelves when there are no customers ready to check out. Similarly, job rotation often represents horizontal loading. In this case, the cashier could operate the cash register for a while, then move to bagging groceries for a time, and finally spend a period of time stocking shelves. In all these cases, the employee does more activities in the course of the day, but the skill level of any job that is being done at one time is about the same and is also not very high.

Jobs can also be expanded vertically (*vertical loading*) by expanding the ability and skill requirements as well as the amount of responsibility and autonomy required from the job holders. Changes which require job holders to complete more complex tasks, make decisions about various aspects of the work, and so forth, are changes representing vertical loading. The salesperson whose job is changed from simply selling items to customers to selling, keeping a running inventory, going along on seasonal buying trips to buy for the department, and hiring additional staff for the department is changed vertically. The sum total of the changes requires the use of considerably more skills and abilities and the exercise of more responsibility than did simply selling goods to customers.

The literature has tended to use the term job enlargement to refer to horizontal loading and job enrichment to refer to vertical loading, although the earlier literature on the subject often used job enlargement to refer to both types of job change. In this chapter we use job enrichment to refer primarily to vertical loading, when the enriched job requires the use of more complex skills and abilities, responsibility, and/or autonomy.

TWO EXAMPLES

Enriching a Job at TI: An Example (From Weed, 1971)

Before 1967, cleaning and janitorial services at a Texas Instruments plant were performed by four contract cleaning companies. Three hundred forty people were employed for this, and a company-developed rating scheme rated cleanliness at 65%, with 100% being theoretically perfect. Turnover ranged from 100% to 400%, and the average education of the employees was lower than the third-grade level.

A decision was made to drop the contract services and to develop an in-house staff to handle cleaning services. In setting up the new staff, the goal was to change several factors associated with the job. Specifically, it was decided to improve the cleaning technology and equipment, to improve selection and training of employees, to increase pay over 40%, and to increase the scope of the jobs to allow all individuals more control over planning their own activities and over their own behavior on the job. The focus of the project was on job scope.

Weed (1971) reported that the program was

very successful. Teams of cleaning-services staff were given areas of responsibility and the freedom to design their own ways of doing the tasks. These teams took the responsibility given to them and developed more efficient ways of doing their jobs. Following the introduction of the program, the cleanliness rating of the facilities improved from 65% to around 80%, turnover dropped to below 20%, and the total number of cleaning personnel needed to get the job done dropped over 30%. These effects were attributed primarily to the benefits of job enrichment.

An Experimental Field Study in a Government Agency

Locke, Sirota, and Wolfson (1976) applied job enrichment in the headquarters of a large federal agency to a number of groups of employees in relatively low-level jobs. After extensive pretesting to diagnose how the jobs might be changed, agency supervisory personnel were instructed in the nature of the changes to be introduced. Then, specific changes were made in some units, but not in others. The latter served as control groups. Nearly 11 months were required to prepare to implement change.

Following the change, the enriched job groups and controls were observed and compared for 7 months. The results are summarized in Table 18.1. On the surface there seemed to be strong support for job enrichment with the exception of attitude changes. Yet, Locke's and others' elaboration of these findings were instructive. First, they showed that much of the performance change was probably due to more efficient work procedures. The same changes that led to more responsibility also led to better methods for doing the job. Therefore, a by-product of the job enrichment was a positive effect that could not be credited to increases in responsibility per se.

Second, the lack of any attitude differ-

TABLE 18.1 Summary of results of job-enrichment experiment

	GROUP	
MEASURE	EXPERIMENTAL UNITS	CONTROL UNITS
Productivity	+23%[a]	+2%
Absenteeism	−5%	+7%
Turnover	−6%	+20%
Complaints and disciplinary actions	0	4
Attitudes	no change	no change

[a]Percent change over time.
Source: Locke et al., 1976. Copyright 1976 by the American Psychological Association, copied by permission.

ences was attributed to the fact that employees initially responded quite positively. But, they also felt that if they were to do more work, they should be paid more and should be promoted to higher civil-service ratings. Not receiving the extrinsic rewards led to disappointment and even lower attitudes than before the change. This effect has been observed by others. It has also been avoided by still others—for example, by increasing extrinsic rewards when the jobs are enriched, as Texas Instruments did by increasing the pay level 40%. These studies and others lead to the general conclusion that enriching a job is usually not sufficient for improved responses to the job. The study in the federal agency also emphasizes the complex interrelationships among many facets of jobs and that there is no simple fix that can be accomplished by changing one or two of their dimensions.

REACTIONS TO RESEARCH

The TI study is typical of many of the earlier job-enrichment studies. Certainly impressive changes accompanied the change in job scope. There was reason to believe that enriching jobs might be very beneficial, but the support was not nearly as strong as the proponents advocated. This was because the job-enrichment changes were always accompanied by many other changes. The TI study is a good example. As we have already mentioned, pay was also increased significantly. In addition, an orientation program was added, the educational level of applicants was higher, and a better benefit package was provided, all of which allowed TI to attract and hold higher-quality employees. Any of these factors either alone or in combination with other conditions could have caused the observed changes in cleanliness, turnover, and amount of work accomplished by each individual. This study and many others done at the Ford Motor Company, General Foods, Polaroid Corporation, and other major United States corporations were interesting, but the extent to which the observed improvements were due to the effects of job enrichment were still suspect (Fein, 1974).

Besides the difficulty of isolating the job-enrichment effect, there was also the problem of attempting to state specifically what type of change represented a job-enrichment change. Most of the early investigators used Herzberg's two-factor theory (Herzberg, Mausner, & Snyderman, 1959) as the theoretical underpinning for selection of job-enrichment dimensions. Remember from our earlier discussions in Chapters 14 and 15 that this theory considered motivators to be those features of the job that were intrinsic to the work: recognition, achievement, responsibility, and the work itself. From this point of view, increases in job enrichment attempted to enhance one or more of these characteristics of the job.

Recall also that the two-factor theory itself was under considerable attack at about the same time as the job-enrichment work began and that, by now, the theory is pretty much discredited. As a result, job enrichment was on the horns of a dilemma: Desirable effects were believed to be due to it, but the theoretical foundation leading to the research in the first place was crumbling. In the mid 1970s, another perspective developed not so much to prop up the failing base represented by the two-factor theory as to replace it entirely. This position is discussed in the following section.

JOB-CHARACTERISTICS MODEL

For their view of the nature of jobs, Hackman and his colleagues (Hackman & Lawler, 1971; Hackman & Oldham, 1976, 1980) leaned heavily upon the work of Turner and Lawrence (1965), who identified seven core dimensions of jobs. Of particular interest for job enrichment were *variety, feedback, autonomy,* and *identity.* The first three of these are self-explanatory; the last is the extent to which the individual is allowed to complete some identifiable part of the task and therefore take some responsibility for it. Tasks high in identity allow the worker to see the completed unit and often to test whether what was done was done correctly—for example, does the light light, the radio play, or the shirt have two arms and all its buttons on correctly? Low task identity occurs when the person works on some small piece of a larger unit that is not really a distinguishable part of it. Assembly-line work, as it is often constructed, is the epitome of low task identity.

Studying 208 employees who held thirteen jobs in the Bell System, Hackman and Lawler (1971) obtained ratings of the critical job dimensions for job enrichment from both employees on the job and outside raters. With some possible exceptions (feedback in particular), these dimensions correlated significantly with job satisfaction, performance, and withdrawal. Furthermore, higher-order needs for achievement and growth moderated the observed correlations so that job-scope correlations with satisfaction and performance

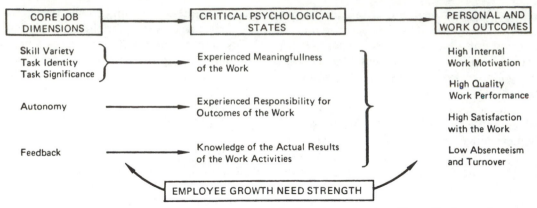

CORE JOB DIMENSIONS → CRITICAL PSYCHOLOGICAL STATES → PERSONAL AND WORK OUTCOMES

Skill Variety
Task Identity
Task Significance
→ Experienced Meaningfullness of the Work

Autonomy → Experienced Responsibility for Outcomes of the Work

Feedback → Knowledge of the Actual Results of the Work Activities

High Internal Work Motivation

High Quality Work Performance

High Satisfaction with the Work

Low Absenteeism and Turnover

EMPLOYEE GROWTH NEED STRENGTH

FIGURE 18.1 The job-characteristics model of work motivation. (From Hackman & Oldham, 1976.)

were stronger for those with greater higher-order needs.

Hackman and Oldham (1976, 1980) refined and supplemented the concepts explored by Hackman and Lawler (1971). The result was the model presented in Figure 18.1. The model identifies five basic job dimensions which affect psychological states, and then act as the bases of various responses to the jobs. Finally, employee differences in "Growth Need Strength" moderate the links between the jobs and the psychological states, as well as the psychological states and reactions to the job.

The five core dimensions are described as follows:

1. *Skill Variety* is the degree to which the job requires a variety of different activities to carry out the work. These activities vary in the number of *different* skills and talents needed by the individual on the job. Simply increasing the number of activities without increasing skill demands is not sufficient to affect skill variety.
2. *Task Identity* is the degree to which the job requires the completion of a whole unit of work. This unit of work should be obvious to the job holder so that he or she is aware of the unit and accepts credit or blame for its quality.
3. *Task Significance* is the extent to which the job has a substantial impact on the lives and work of other people.

4. *Autonomy* is the freedom the job holder has to schedule his or her activities on the job and to determine the procedures to use to carry them out.
5. *Feedback* is the degree to which the individual obtains direct and clear information about the effectiveness of his or her performance.

Besides describing the job dimensions and the psychological processes involved in them, Hackman and Oldham specified how the dimensions should be combined to establish a unidimensional measure of job scope. This dimension was termed the *Motivation Potential Score (MPS)* of a job and was defined as:

$$MPS = (\frac{SV + TI + TS}{3}) \times A \times F$$

in which

MPS	=	Motivational Potential Score
SV	=	Skill Variety
TI	=	Task Identity
TS	=	Task Significance
A	=	Autonomy
F	=	Feedback

In order to test the theory, an instrument was developed to study jobs—the Job Diagnostic Survey (JDS) (Hackman & Oldham, 1975). This instrument, or a short form of it, was administered both to the job incumbents and to supervisors of the job incumbents.

Overall, the theory looked quite promising and was received with considerable ethusiasm. It offered a framework for future job-design research, recognized that individuals may react to jobs differently, and posited an individual-difference characteristic—Growth Need Strength (GNS)—which provided cues about how people should respond to their jobs. Needless to say, it generated considerable research. Much of the early research was relatively primitive and, in general, tended to support the model. The primary criticism was leveled at the Job Diagnostic Survey as a measuring instrument (Dunham, 1976) rather than at the relationships between job dimensions and employees' responses that were outlined in Figure 18.1. Later on, however, as more data accumulated, there were some major reservations and modifications suggested.

CRITIQUE OF THE JOB-CHARACTERISTICS MODEL

Roberts and Glick (1981) provide a major review of research on the job-characteristic model through 1981. Griffin, Welsh, and Moorhead (1981) also reviewed similar literature but focused entirely upon the use of job enrichment for improving performance. Both groups of reviewers recognized the strengths of the model, but they also raised some serious questions.

The major reservations with respect to the job-characteristics model and the research related to it centered on either the model itself, or the measures used to access it. Two concerns stand out in each of these two areas. Recall that Hackman and Oldham (1976, 1980) developed an instrument, the Job Diagnostic Survey (JDS), to measure the variables in the model. Dunham (1976) reported factor-analytic work that showed a general

lack of independence among the dimensions of the JDS. That is, whereas Hackman and Oldham had argued that the job dimensions of feedback, task identity, task significance, autonomy, and so on, were separate characteristics of jobs, Dunham countered that the high degree of correlation among the measures of these dimensions indicated that there was not sufficient justification to consider them separate characteristics. Roberts and Glick (1981) raise the same objection. We certainly agree from the standpoint of parsimony: A large number of overlapping measures is to be avoided and also, from a theoretical point of view, if several supposedly separate dimensions overlap significantly it makes little sense to speak of the dimensions as separate characteristics. On the other hand, simply observing an empirical correlation between dimensions is not sufficient either to conclude that there is no justification for separate dimensions or that it is not useful to consider the dimensions separately. There are reasons why dimensions may covary that are not related to their usefulness. Therefore, we are less concerned about this particular problem with the JDS than are many of its critics.

A second more critical problem deals with the distinction between the actual situation and perceptions of that situation. Clearly, the dimensions of jobs described by the model deal with actual characteristics of those jobs. For example, the degree to which a job provides job incumbents with feedback about their performance is a property of the job itself, not of the people who hold the job. Hackman and Oldham would have no trouble agreeing with this position. Unfortunately, when it comes to measuring job characteristics, the JDS is administered to the people who hold the jobs, and they describe their jobs using the instrument. The critics argue, justifiably, that the description obtained may reflect the nature of the job itself, but that it is no more than the incumbent's *perceptions* of that job. For example, the job itself may have many opportunities to receive feedback about performance, but the person in the job either does not know what to look for or ignores the feedback that is coming to him or her, and, as a result, reports that the job is low on feedback. To the extent that the actual job situation does not mirror perceptions of it by those who are on the job, the model is severely limited. After all, any changes that are made to alter the job in order to build in more enriching characteristics must be made to the job itself with the assumption that such changes will change perceptions and reactions to the changes by the job holders. Thus, the heavy reliance upon job perceptions is potentially limiting to the model, although this limitation can be overcome by using independent observers to measure job characteristics rather than the people who are in those jobs.

The two just-described criticisms are not inherent to the model but deal with the way it has been applied or the way research on it has been conducted. Two other criticisms deal with the process outlined by the model. The first concerns the individual characteristic of Growth Need Strength (GNS). Recall that the job-characteristics model hypothesized that job enrichment features increased job holders' psychological reactions to their jobs with respect to the meaningfulness of the work, feelings of autonomy, and knowledge of results about their work which, in turn, could lead to feelings of accomplishment. These psychological states were the immediate precursors of responses to the job: satisfaction, commitment, performance, and so on. However, these reactions were only to occur for those who were high on GNS; nothing was said about the reactions of those low on GNS. The absence of any statement implied that job enrichment would not affect these people. Research since then does tend to show that job enrichment effects are lower for those low in GNS, but that there is some

effect on these people as well (Stone, 1976). Roberts and Glick (1981) criticize Hackman and Oldham (1976) for ignoring the low GNS group.

A more critical concern with GNS is a methodological dilemma created by measures of it. This problem is that the items on the scale are very similar to the items that are used to measure job satisfaction and other beliefs and attitudes about a job. Therefore, the empirical relationship observed between the construct GNS and belief and attitude responses to a job is inflated by the common methods used to measure each. Given the nature of the need construct and those of attitudes and beliefs, this problem cannot be overcome in any simple manner.

A final valid criticism made by Roberts and Glick (1981) was that the Motivational Potential Score (MPS; see page 378 cannot be justified. There is no basis for the empirical weighting system suggested by Hackman and Oldham (1976). Furthermore, when the variables in the equation tend to be positively correlated, which they do in this case, almost any linear combination of the variables will lead to an index that correlates highly with any other combination. Given this, the criticism is a valid one, but the practical impact is minor; as long as the same variables are used to assess MPS, the nature of the way they are combined is not that important.

The best conclusion about the job-characteristics model of job enrichment is that some of the luster has worn off. The large amount of initial research on it using the JDS in a rather uncritical manner is no longer justified. On the other hand, it is still premature to abandon the model. It has offered a reasonable structure that can be explored more fully. This exploration needs to be guided by the notions that Growth Need Strength is probably not going to add much to the development of job enrichment, that job incumbents' perceptions of their jobs cannot be taken as necessarily valid descriptions of the actual jobs, and that other variables in the job context and the individual are likely to impact on the effects of enriching jobs. In the section that follows, we explore some of these possible other variables.

OTHER FACTORS AND JOB ENRICHMENT

Goal Setting

Umstot, Bell, and Mitchell (1976) hired individuals to work for 4 days on a job identifying and coding parcels of land with appropriate zoning codes. The job had been subcontracted to the researchers by a county government in the Seattle area. The actual jobs for particular employees were constructed so as to be either high or low on MPS as defined previously. In addition, employees were assigned either high or low performance goals.

The results showed that enriched jobs led to higher job satisfaction but not to higher performance. Performance was measured in terms of quantity of items completed. The authors pointed out that if performance had allowed for quality differences, the results might have been different. Interestingly, performance was most strongly affected by goals such that more difficult goals led to higher performance. In addition, high goals *and* high MPS created the most favorable condition. Jobs low on MPS and on goals created conditions which led to the lowest level of performance. In sum, under well-controlled conditions, job enrichment only affected satisfaction, and goal setting affected performance. There was, however, some evidence that the two common motivational procedures complimented each other such that the most favorable condition tended to be the one in which the job was high on enrichment characteristics and the goals were difficult,

and the opposite condition was the least favorable.

Nonparticipating Groups

In some instances, job redesign may inadvertently have negative effects upon other employees who observe and/or interact with those on the enriched jobs (Katzell & Yankelovich with Flein, Ornati, & Nash, assisted by Berman, Deliberto, Morrow, & Weiss, 1975). The most common difficulty is with supervisors on redesigned jobs as compared to those on new jobs. In the former case, the jobs are often expanded by relegating some of the responsibility and decision-making power formerly held by the supervisor to the employees in the redesigned jobs. The result is a supervisor in a position described as responsible for behavior of the employees under him or her but without the authority to influence these same employees. Such circumstances can be avoided when the enriched job is a completely new one where one level of supervision often can be eliminated.

Employees less directly involved with those on the enriched jobs, other than their supervisors, may also be dissatisfied with the changes. Feelings of jealousy and of being left out of the action have been observed in some settings among those whose jobs were not involved. Locke and his colleagues (Locke et al., 1976) reported these types of effects among the civil-service employees who observed the enrichment changes but were not actually involved in the changes themselves.

Other Individual Differences

We have already mentioned that Growth Need Strength (or some similar personality variable) was the focal individual difference variable in most job enrichment research and that differences in reactions to jobs between those that were high on GNS as compared to those that were low were not nearly as pronounced as had been expected. Some researchers have suggested that other individual differences are important.

Cherrington and England (1980) argued that GNS and other related variables had been selected as important for affecting the nature of the relationship between job enrichment and job satisfaction because people high on these variables were assumed to have a stronger desire for enriched jobs. That is, the personality variables (GNS, and so on) were indirect measures of the more direct notion of desire for enriched jobs. Cherrington and England reasoned that the relatively weak showing of all of these types of measures may have been because investigators failed to go after the variable that has the most direct effect: desire for an enriched job. When they measured desire for enriched jobs directly, they found that this variable acted as a moderator of the relationship between job characteristics and job satisfaction more strongly and more consistently than did indirect measures such as work values. Nevertheless, as has been the case with most of the individual-difference research, the effects were not particularly strong.

Perhaps the most reasonable conclusion about individual differences in desire for enriched jobs was reached by Ganster (1980) who explored the extent to which four individual variables affected the relationship between job enrichment and reactions to the job. The four variables were: Protestant Ethic, GNS, Need for Achievement, and Arousal-Seeking Tendency. Of the four only Need for Achievement acted as a moderator variable, and the effect was *opposite* that expected: Higher levels of job enrichment led to lower task satisfaction for those high on the need for achievement than for those low on the need. Considering these results and the results of others at that time Ganster (1980) wrote that, "there is no justification for choosing employees to be recipients of job enrichment on the basis of some individual difference measure" (p. 145). The conclusion still holds today. Differences between individuals are found, such as those described by Cherrington & England (1980), but they do not appear to be so strong as to advocate withholding enrichment from particular individuals on the basis of the beliefs and values of the individuals alone.

DISCUSSION

The general conclusion that changing the structure and nature of the job can affect behaviors that are important in the workplace is as relevant today as it was 10 years ago. Furthermore, the notion of changing jobs in the direction that has come to be labeled job enrichment can also impact on behavior. However, it is naive to believe that such changes will always be for the better. It is clear that sweeping changes in large numbers of jobs in order to meet social values related to the quality of working life and/or in order to increase productivity are not possible and, furthermore, probably are not desirable given the diversity of organizations, work groups, and individuals involved in such jobs. Nevertheless, it is equally clear that there exists a sizable number of jobs that could be improved through some form of job enrichment and that such changes would positively affect the individuals in those jobs. Our task is to identify these jobs and to consider such changes. Already there are some bases for these changes; for example, the job-characteristics model offers some cues about what could be changed. Yet more work is needed to develop ways to diagnose jobs which do not rely so heavily upon the job incumbents' perceptions if we are to be able to better evaluate the nature of the effects of such changes on the job incumbents.

REFERENCES

Cherrington, D. J., & England, J. L. (1980). The desire for an enriched job as a moderator of the enrichment-satisfaction relationship. *Organizational Behavior and Human Performance, 25,* 139–159.

Dunham, R. P. (1976). The measurement and dimensionality of job characteristics. *Journal of Applied Psychology, 61,* 404–409.

Fein, M. (1974). Job enrichment: A re-evaluation. *Sloan Management Review,* 69–88.

Ganster, D. C. (1980). Individual differences and task design: A laboratory experiment. *Organizational Behavior and Human Performance, 26,* 131–148.

Griffin, R. W., Welsh, A., & Moorhead, G. (1981). Perceived task characteristics and employee performance: A literature review. *Academy of Management Review,* 655–664.

Hackman, J. R., & Lawler, E. E., III (1971). Employee reactions to job characteristics. *Journal of Applied Psychology, 55,* 259–286. (Monograph)

Hackman, J. R., & Oldham, G. R. (1975). Development of the Job Diagnostic Survey. *Journal of Applied Psychology, 60,* 159–170.

Hackman, J. R., & Oldham G. R. (1976). Motivation through the design of work: Test of a theory. *Organizational Behavior and Human Performance, 16,* 250–279.

Hackman, J. R., & Oldham, G. R. (1980). *Work redesign.* Reading, Mass. Addison-Wesley.

Herzberg, F., Mausner, B., & Snyderman, B. (1959). *The motivation to work.* New York: Wiley.

Katzell, R. A., & Yankelovich, D., with Fein, M., Ornati, O. A., & Nash, A., assisted by Berman, J. A., Deliberto, R. A., Morrow, I. J., & Weiss, H. M. (1975). *Work productivity and job satisfaction: An evaluation of policy-related research.* New York: Psychological Corporation.

Locke, E. A., Sirota, D., & Wolfson, A. D. (1976). An experimental case study of the successes and failures of job enrichment in a government agency. *Journal of Applied Psychology, 61,* 701–711.

Roberts, K. H., & Glick, W. (1981). The job characteristics approach to task design: A critical review. *Journal of Applied Psychology, 66,* 193–217.

Stone, E. F. (1976). The moderating effect of work-related values on the job scope-job satisfaction relationship. *Organizational Behavior and Human Performance, 15,* 147–167.

Turner, A. H., & Lawrence, P. R. (1965). *Industrial jobs and the worker: An investigation of responses to task attributes.* Boston: Graduate School of Business Administration, Harvard University.

Umstot, D. D., Bell, C. H., Jr., & Mitchell, T. R. (1976). Effects of job enrichment and task goals on satisfaction and productivity: Implications for job design. *Journal of Applied Psychology, 61,* 379–394.

Weed, E. D. (1971). Job enrichment "cleans up" at Texas Instruments. In J. R. Maher (Ed.), *New perspectives in job enrichment.* New York: Van Nostrand Reinhold.

19

Job Evaluation

In the labor market, individuals have certain potentialities, skills, or other qualities that they seek to "sell" to prospective employers. In turn, the intent of employing organizations is to offer wages that will attract personnel who can perform the available jobs. Thus, the proffered wages are intended to serve as an incentive to accept employment. But there is more to it than that. Lawler (1971), for example, stated that pay is typically thought of as performing a number of functions that contribute to organizational effectiveness; in particular, it serves as a reward to make employees satisfied with their jobs, to motivate them, to gain their commitment to the organization, and to keep them in the organization.

To meet these ends, pay, of course, must serve as an incentive that is perceived as fulfilling certain needs of individuals. In this regard it is obvious that for most people money does provide the wherewithall to keep body and soul together—in effect, to fulfill what

Maslow described as the individual's physiological needs. Its instrumentality for the satisfaction of other needs depends on the need in question. For example, Lawler indicated that generally money is perceived primarily as satisfying the need for esteem, secondarily as being instrumental in satisfying the autonomy and security needs, and finally as being only marginal for satisfying the social and self-actualizing needs. In effect, Lawler suggested that the importance of pay to any given individual is the combined effect of the importance of the various needs to the individual and the extent to which the individual perceives pay as being "instrumental" in satisfying those needs.

Some of the motivational aspects of pay, including equity theory, were discussed in Chapter 14 and are not repeated here. The primary purpose of this chapter is to discuss the process of job evaluation, which is the dominant procedure for establishing rates of pay for various jobs. Before getting into the different methods of job evaluation, however, we touch briefly on various forms of compensation, the labor market, legal factors that influence wage rates for jobs, and alternative procedures for setting wage rates (job evaluation is one such procedure).

FORMS OF COMPENSATION

There are different forms of compensation for work performed, some of which are associated with specific types of jobs. Some of the forms of compensation are: salary (per week, month, or year); hourly wage rate; incentive pay (some form of piece rate); commission (especially for sales jobs); tips; bonus; and profit sharing. The total compensation for an individual on a given job can include combinations of some of these forms.

FACTORS THAT INFLUENCE WAGE RATES

Wage levels in general and wage rates for individual jobs are influenced by various factors that operate in the labor market and by certain legal requirements. (We use the terms *wage rates* and *wage level* in a general sense, to cover hourly, salary, and other forms of compensation.)

Wages and the Labor Market

An organization obtains its employees from one or more labor markets. A labor market comprises that general pool of people who are prospective candidates for employment in some type of occupation. For example, the labor market for hourly paid and office jobs is usually the local community, whereas that for certain types of professional and managerial jobs may be regional or national in scope, comprising those who have the particular qualifications required, wherever they

may be. Whatever the labor market in question, an organization that expects to obtain its employees from that market must be able to compete with other organizations in the market, and wage rates are one of the important bargaining ingredients.

The general wage level in any given labor market depends on a number of different factors: supply and demand, general economic conditions, regional and industrial factors (wages are higher in certain regions and industries than in others), union-contract provisions, productivity, and so on. Such factors tend to result in the establishment of "going rates" for various jobs and occupations in the labor market. It is our conviction that there is a hierarchical value system that underlies the wages paid to all jobs throughout the entire occupational structure of the economy. This value system is based on two postulates: (1) pay for work is influenced by such job-related factors as skill, effort, responsibility, type of work, and working conditions; and (2) pay for work is largely a function of the supply of, and demand for, individuals who are capable of performing, and willing to perform, various jobs at certain wage rates.

The labor market is not a vague, ethereal concept. Rather, it is comprised of live people with motivations and sets of values which are reflected—in the labor market—by their behavior in offering their services and accepting or rejecting employment under specified conditions.

This inescapable fact reminds us of our earlier discussion of equity theory in Chapter 14. Granting some question about certain aspects of this theory, we can nonetheless see how individual members of the labor market might, in a general way, apply an outcome/input ratio to themselves, based on their perceptions of the combination of the various types of outcomes and what they would put into the work situations. Further, we can see that individuals might apply this "ratio" to themselves in relationship to their perceptions of how the corresponding factors relate to *others* in the labor market. Thus, individuals would be most likely to consider employment as "equitable" if the perceived outcomes and inputs are reasonably in line with those of *others* in a similar line of work. (Of course, people probably tend to be more perceptive of inequity of the "underreward" variety than of the "overreward" variety.)

Thus, we can say that the "going rate" for a particular type of work is a very rough-and-ready reflection of the notion of "equity," in that it reflects the approximate level of (at least) the financial "outcomes" for the typical "inputs" in the type of work in question. It thus provides individuals with a basis for their perceptions of the outcome/input ratios of *other* people whose inputs into a job (that is, their job-related skills and other factors) might be comparable to their own. If an organization offers rates of pay that are appreciably below the going rates for similar work, it will have difficulty in attracting and keeping qualified workers. If it pays substantially above the going rates, it might have to price itself out of the market for its goods and services.

Legal Requirements

Certain laws in the United States deal with rates of pay for employed workers. The Fair Labor Standards Act, for example, sets minimum hourly wages for those covered by the Act. Beginning in January, 1979, the minimum wage was $2.65 with provision for subsequent increments at specified dates. As of 1984, the rate was $3.35. Further, the Equal Pay Act of 1963 requires that there be "equal pay for equal work," meaning that men and women are to be paid the same if they are doing "equal work." In particular, the act specifies that if work requires equal *skill, effort,* and *responsibility,* and if it is performed under similar *working conditions,* employees of both sexes must be paid the same. In turn, the Civil Rights Act of 1964 specifies in Title VII that it is unlawful for an employer to discriminate against individuals with regard to compensation (as well as with regard to hiring) because of race, sex, color, religion, or national origin. These acts establish the primary legal boundaries for compensation practice in the United States.

The comparable-worth issue. In recent years there has been considerable interest in the concept of comparable worth, with proposals that the prevailing legal concept of "equal pay for equal work" be replaced by the concept of "equal pay for jobs of comparable worth." Generally, this means that wage rates for jobs that are of "comparable worth" should be the same, even though the jobs are different in content and therefore do not involve "equal work." The issue applies primarily to the wage rates for jobs held primarily by women, which generally are less than the wage rates for jobs held primarily by men. However, the issue also applies to jobs held by minority groups, although the primary concern relates to female-dominated jobs versus male-dominated jobs because of the large number of people on such jobs.

A major thesis of the proponents of the comparable-worth doctrine is that the wage rates for female-dominated jobs are less than they "should be" because the jobs are held largely by women, and that this represents a form of discrimination (sometimes called institutional discrimination). The National Academy of Sciences appointed a Committee on Occupational Classification and Analysis to examine the issues involved in the comparable-worth concept. The report of that committee (Treiman & Hartmann, 1981) presents considerable data on comparative earnings for men and women, and includes the following statement in the conclusion: "On the basis of a review of the evidence, our judgment is that there is substantial discrimination in pay" (p. 91).

In reflecting about possible discrimination, however, we need to differentiate between that implied by the concepts of equal work versus comparable worth. In the equal-work frame of reference, comparative data on the earnings of men and women are very treacherous to interpret, in part because of the broadness of the job or occupation categories usually used. (For rigorous comparative purposes one needs to be sure that the jobs covered are the same; such assurances are usually not available.) Further, as Roberts (1980) points out, there are serious statistical problems involved in attributing differences in earnings between men and women (on the same job) to discrimination. Some portion of the differences may be attributable to such factors as experience, tenure, length of service, qualifications, and so on (Mecham, 1982; Roberts, 1980). Even allowing for such limitations, however, the weight of evidence seems to suggest that the legal and conceptual aspects of "equal pay for equal work" are not always fulfilled, thus implying that some such discrimination still exists in this respect.

The evidence is much more ambiguous regarding discrimination in the frame of reference of comparable worth, which concerns the "comparability" of jobs of different types. Although it is alleged that the pay for female jobs is less than it "should be," there is no generally accepted concensus as to the definition of comparable worth, let alone as to the methods for measuring it. The often-repeated statement that women are paid on the average 60% (or 59% or 58%) the average of men is simply not relevant because it does not take into account the fact that many of the jobs men hold are different from those held by women. Although this statistic has frequently been cited as evidence of discrimination, William H. Knapp (1981) states that "this point simply is that the comparison of median earnings by sex without more refinement is by no means an indicator of sex discrimination" (p. 21).

A number of court cases in the United States have dealt with alleged discrimination in pay for women versus men on jobs that are different in content but that are alleged to be "comparable." The decisions in a number of these cases have hewn to the "equal pay for equal work" provisions of federal laws. However, certain subsequent court decisions, the passage of certain municipal ordinances and state laws, and the appointment of some state commissions to consider the issue, suggest that the comparable worth concept will be an important legal issue in the coming years.

Discussion

The current comparable-worth issue raises the question about the basis on which to establish wage rates for specific jobs. In our opinion there is no conceptually appropriate, economically viable, or practical basis for determining the comparability of jobs other than that reflected by the going rates of pay in the labor market (McCormick, 1981). In other words, it is argued that the wage policy of an organization should be aimed at the establishment of wage rates for jobs that are within striking range of the going rates in the labor market for similar work. To do otherwise would court one of two consequences: Marked underpayment would make it difficult to attract and keep qualified workers, and marked overpayment would risk problems in competing in the sale of goods or services offered by the organization.

PROCEDURES FOR SETTING WAGE RATES

Starting with the assumption that an organization wants to establish wage rates for jobs that are reasonably in line with those in the labor market (i.e., that approximate the "going rates"), the organization can follow one of two basic procedures. In the first place, if the jobs in question have direct counterparts in the labor market, the prevailing wage rates can be used directly, specifically by setting the rates within the organization at the prevailing rate or slightly above or below. Obviously, such a procedure is most feasible if there are similar organizations with similar jobs in the labor market.

In the second place, an organization can use some type of job-evaluation system. Such systems generally provide some systematic procedure for deriving indexes of job values or for creating classes of jobs that, in turn, provide for setting wage rates for the jobs in question. Job-evaluation systems are used by most large organizations. This chapter deals primarily with such systems.

Installing a Job-Evaluation Program

Although it is not appropriate here to detail the development, installation, and operation of a job-evaluation program, let us at least get an overview of these processes, which typically include the following steps.[1]

1. Establishing responsibility. Usually a job-evaluation committee is set up to be responsible for a job-evaluation program, although in some circumstances this responsibility is assigned to one individual.
2. Developing or selecting the job-evaluation system to be used.
3. Preparing job descriptions.
4. Evaluating jobs.
5. Converting evaluations to money values. This process frequently includes carrying out a wage or salary survey of going rates in the labor market.
6. Providing for evaluation of new jobs.

---

[1]The reader interested in further discussion of compensation administration is referred to such texts as: D. W. Belcher (1974). *Compensation administration*, Englewood Cliffs, N.J.: Prentice-Hall; J. G. Berg (1976). *Managing compensation*, New York: AMACOM, American Management Association; R. Henderson (1976). *Compensation management*, Reston, Va.: Reston Publishing Company; B. Livy (1975). *Job evaluation: A critical review*, New York: Wiley; H. G. Zollitsch & A. Langsner (1970). *Wage and salary administration*, Cincinnati: South-Western Publishing; and *Selected sample of job evaluation systems* (1978), New York: Organization Resources Counselors.

METHODS OF JOB EVALUATION

Four rather traditional job-evaluation methods are based on individuals' judgments of job characteristics. In addition, a more statistical approach to job evaluation, based on structured job-analysis data, seems to offer considerable promise for establishing rates of pay. These are:

1. Ranking method;
2. Classification method;
3. Point method;
4. Factor-comparison method;
5. Job-component method.

Ranking Method

In the *ranking method*, jobs are compared with each other, usually on the basis of judged overall worth. Most typically, these judgments are obtained by a simple ranking of jobs. Because jobs can be judged relative to others by other procedures, such as the paired-comparison procedure, this method could more appropriately be called the *job-comparison* method. The reliability of the evaluations is usually increased by having several individuals—preferably people already familiar with the jobs—serve as evaluators. When there are many jobs to be evaluated, however, it is usually impossible to find individuals familiar with all of them. Although there are ways of combining evaluations when each rater evaluates only some of the jobs, this method is usually most suitable to small organizations with limited numbers of jobs.

Classification Method

The *classification method* consists of several categories of jobs along a hypothetical scale. Each such classification is usually defined and is sometimes illustrated. Each job is assigned to a specific classification on the basis of its judged overall worth and its relation to the descriptions of the several classifications.

The classification method is rather simple to develop and use. Unless special care is taken, however, it tends to perpetuate possible inequalities in existing rates of pay if it is used to evaluate existing jobs with already designated rates.

Point Method

The *point method* of job evaluation is without question the most common. It is characterized by the following: (1) the use of several job-evaluation factors; (2) the assignment of "points" to varying "degrees" or levels of each factor; (3) the evaluation of individual jobs in terms of their "degree" or

level on each factor, and the assignment to each job of the number of points designated for the degree or level on the factor; and (4) the addition of the point values for the individual factors to derive the total point value for each job. This total point value is then converted to corresponding wage or salary rates.

One of the most common point systems is that of the National Metal Trades Association (NMTA) Associates. Their system for manufacturing, maintenance, warehousing, distribution, and service positions is shown in Table 19.1 (They also have systems for three other classes of positions.) The eleven factors and the point values assigned to the five degrees of the factors are illustrated. With this particular system the point values for the "1st

TABLE 19.1 Points assigned to factor degrees of job-evaluation system for manufacturing, maintenance, warehousing, distribution, and service jobs of the NMTA associates

FACTOR	1ST DEGREE	2ND DEGREE	3RD DEGREE	4TH DEGREE	5TH DEGREE
SKILL					
1. Knowledge	14	28	42	56	70
2. Experience	22	44	66	88	110
3. Initiative and Ingenuity	14	28	42	56	70
EFFORT					
4. Physical Demand	10	20	30	40	50
5. Mental or Visual Demand	5	10	15	20	25
RESPONSIBILITY					
6. Equipment or Process	5	10	15	20	25
7. Material or Product	5	10	15	20	25
8. Safety of Others	5	10	15	20	25
9. Work of Others	5	10	15	20	25
JOB CONDITIONS					
10. Working Conditions	10	20	30	40	50
11. Hazards	5	10	15	20	25

Source: The National Position Evaluation Plan, Unit 1, NMTA Associates, c/o MIMA The Management Association, Westchester, Illinois.

degree" of all factors add up to 100; thus these "1st degree" points imply the intended weights of the eleven factors. The points for each higher degree increase by equal intervals, so the sum of the "5th degree" values adds up to 500.

Although most point systems share basic similarities, there is some variability in the factors that are used and in the weights assigned to varying degrees of the factors. Most systems provide definitions of the factors and guidelines for evaluating individual jobs in terms of the various factors. In the NMTA system, for example, the following guidelines are given for designating various degrees (and point values) for the amount of experience:

DEGREE	AMOUNT OF EXPERIENCE	POINTS
1st	Up to and including 3 months	22
2nd	Over 3 months up to and including 12 months	44
3rd	Over 1 year up to and including 3 years	66
4th	Over 3 years up to and including 5 years	88
5th	Over 5 years	110

Factor-Comparison Method

The *factor-comparison method* was initially developed and described by Benge, Burk, and Hay (1941). The system must be tailor made for the organization for which it is to be used. The development is time-consuming and complex, which probably accounts in part for its somewhat limited use. Once the system is developed, however, its implementation is relatively straightforward. Our discussion of the system focuses on the procedures used in its development.

In this method, fifteen or twenty tentative "key jobs" are selected. These are jobs that have current rates not subject to controversy and that are considered by the job-evaluation committee to be neither underpaid nor overpaid. These jobs are then compared to others in terms of factors common to all jobs. The factors used in the Benge, Burk, and Hay system are:

- Mental requirements;
- Skill requirements;
- Physical requirements;
- Responsibility;
- Working conditions.

The key jobs are then *ranked* and *rated* by several "judges," usually members of a committee. The ranking consists of ranking the key jobs on each of the factors. In the rating process the judges "allocate" the going rate (hourly or salary) to the individual factors in terms of how much they consider the going rate is being "paid" for each factor; jobs are subsequently rank ordered on each factor on the basis of these "allocated" rates. (In both the ranking and rating processes the judgments of the several judges are pooled to produce a single set of values.) Table 19.2 is an illustration of the hypothetical results of these processes for six jobs. This table shows, for each factor and for each job, the "allocated" money values (in dollars), the rank order of the judgmental ranking process (identified by $ under the "Rank Order" heading), and the rank order of the money values based on the "direct" ranking of those values (designated as "D"). The objective of such a presentation is to identify any inconsistencies in the two sets of rank orders. Table 19.2 illustrates such inconsistencies for physical requirements. Jobs for which such inconsistencies are found (and for which the inconsistencies cannot reasonably be adjusted) are eliminated. In this illustration jobs K and B would be eliminated. The money values for the remaining jobs on each factor then represent benchmarks to use in the subsequent evaluation of nonkey jobs. In the actual application of the system, other jobs are evaluated on each factor by being

TABLE 19.2 Data for a hypothetical sample of key jobs as used in the factor-comparison method of job evaluation

JOB	GOING RATE OF PAY[a]	MENTAL REQUIREMENTS $	RANK ORDER $	RANK ORDER D	SKILL REQUIREMENTS $	RANK ORDER $	RANK ORDER D	PHYSICAL REQUIREMENTS $	RANK ORDER $	RANK ORDER D	RESPONSIBILITY $	RANK ORDER $	RANK ORDER D	WORKING CONDITIONS $	RANK ORDER $	RANK ORDER D
L	$6.30	1.85	1	1	2.30	1	1	.70	5	5	1.05	2	2	.40	5	5
G	5.35	1.15	3	3	1.70	2	2	.95	4	4	1.00	3	3	.55	4	4
K	5.20	.55	4	4	.90	4	4	1.85	②	①	.70	4	4	1.20	2	2
R	4.50	1.35	2	2	1.60	3	3	.15	6	6	1.25	1	1	.15	6	6
B	4.20	.25	6	6	.40	5	5	1.90	①	②	.40	5	5	1.25	1	1
P	3.50	.30	5	5	.25	6	6	1.60	3	3	.30	6	6	1.05	3	3

[a]Note: Rates are illustrative and for comparison purposes only.
Legend:
 Going rate of pay: Prevailing hourly rate for the job.
 $_: Amount of pay judged to be paid for the factor in question as based on rating process.
 Rank order-$: Rank order of these amounts for the jobs.
 Rank order-D: Rank order of jobs based on the "direct" ranking process.
Source: Adpated from Zollitsch and Langsner, 1970, Table 7.5, p. 183.

compared with the jobs that represent the scale for the factor; each job is assigned a value for each factor. Following are the hypothetical key jobs in Table 19.2 (except for K and B) with their scale values for mental requirements (in actual practice the scales have several or many jobs):

JOB	$ VALUE ON MENTAL REQUIREMENTS
L	1.85
R	1.35
G	1.15
P	.30

Each job being evaluated would then be compared with these key jobs and would be assigned values accordingly. The sum of the values for the five factors would be the total value for the jobs. Although the original values are actually money values, inflation would cause such values to become obsolete; thus these are usually considered as point values.

The factor-comparison system is admittedly time-consuming and complex to develop, and is therefore not in common use in its pure form. However, certain modifications have been developed that are in use.

Job-Component Method

Behind what we call the *job-component method* of job evaluation is the implicit assumption that similarities in job content impose similar job demands on the incumbents and should therefore warrant corresponding rates of pay. One could then argue that any given job component carries its own "value," regardless of the combination of other job components with which it might occur in any given job. The application of this rationale in job evaluation leads to structured job-analysis procedures that make it possible to identify and measure the level of each of many job components as they occur in jobs.

One illustration of this approach is the Clerical Task Inventory[2] (originally called the

[2]The Clerical Task Inventory (CTI) is copyrighted by C. H. Lawshe, Jr., and is available through the Village Book Cellar, 308 West State Street, West Lafayette, Indiana, 47906.

Job Analysis Check List of Office Operations) as reported by Miles (1952). In this task inventory, the analyst rates the importance to the job of each of many office operations. This study found that a weighted combination of the five most important office operations resulted in total values that were highly correlated with going rates for the jobs.

A more generalized example of the job-component approach is represented by the Position Analysis Questionnaire (PAQ)[3], which was described in Chapter 4. Because the PAQ is a structured job-analysis questionnaire that provides for the analysis of jobs in "worker-oriented" terms, it can be used with most types of jobs. In its use in a job-evaluation context an equation has been derived that consists of statistically weighted job-dimension scores that produce total job-evaluation points. In various studies such point values for samples of jobs have resulted in respectable correlations with going wage rates, ranging from the mid 80s to the mid 90s (McCormick, Jeanneret, & Mecham, 1972; Robinson, Wahlstrom, & Mecham, 1974; Taylor, 1971). In one study job-evaluation points based on the PAQ were correlated with those resulting from four other methods (Robinson et al., 1974). The correlations ranged from .82 to .95, indicating that the PAQ produced evaluations that were essentially the same as those resulting from other job-evaluation systems.

A possible advantage of the job-component method over other methods is that the job values are derived statistically, which eliminates the typical subjective "evaluation" phase of other job-evaluation methods. The equation that is used is an example of what

[3]The Position Analysis Questionnaire (PAQ) is copyrighted by the Purdue Research Foundation. The PAQ and related materials are available through the University Book Store, 360 West State Street, West Lafayette, Indiana, 47906. Further information about the PAQ is available through PAQ Services, Inc., 1625 North, 1000 East, Logan, Utah, 84321.

has been named a policy-capturing approach because it "captures," statistically, the prevailing pay policy reflected in the pay rates of the jobs in the sample. In effect, the statistical underpinnings of the equation result in deriving estimates of the money values in the labor market of individual job dimensions as based on the analysis of jobs with the PAQ.

The job-component method of job evaluation based on the PAQ has practical applications in numerous organizations in both the private and public sectors. For example, it was used by a large banking organization to evaluate jobs held by over 13,000 individuals.

The job-component method and wage discrimination. The job-component method of job evaluation offers substantial promise in efforts to minimize possible wage discrimination between men and women, from the standpoints of both equal pay for equal work and comparable worth. A job-oriented type of structured job-analysis procedure would be relevant in equal pay for equal work analyses since such questionnaires provide for analyzing jobs in terms of specific tasks within some occupational area (automobile mechanics, clerical workers, etc.). With the results of such job analyses for specific jobs it is possible to measure statistically the degree of similarity between jobs—in other words to determine the extent to which jobs comprise "equal work."

The relevance of the job-component method in the frame of reference of comparable worth is predicated on the acceptance of two assumptions:

1. That basic "human behaviors" involved in jobs (as measured by "worker-oriented" job-analysis questionnaries such as the PAQ) serve as the appropriate " job components" or common denominators for determining the comparability of different types of jobs.
2. That the going rates of pay for such job components serve as the basis for determining the money values of such components and for total job values.

Such an approach seems to be especially relevant in the comparable worth frame of reference because there is evidence that the analysis of jobs with the PAQ is not influenced by the sex of the job incumbent (Arvey, Passino, & Lounsbury, 1977).

Discussion

There are differences both in the *techniques* of evaluation and in the *bases* of evaluation among the four traditional job-evaluation methods (ranking, classification, point, and factor comparison). These differences are illustrated here:

	TECHNIQUE OF EVALUATION	
BASIS OF EVALUATION	BY COMPARISON WITH OTHER JOBS	BY EVALUATION AGAINST A "STANDARD"
Whole job	Ranking method	Classification method
Job factors	Factor-comparison method	Point method

The job-component method does not involve the subjective evaluation of jobs, as required by the conventional methods, but rather it provides for the derivation of relative job values by the use of a statistical equation.

CONVERTING JOB-EVALUATION RESULTS TO PAY SCALES

Job-evaluation systems typically result in jobs being placed at varying positions along a scale of relative job values as reflected by point values, rank orders, or job classifications. The most common indexes of relative job values, point values, are used in the following discussion.

The conversion of point values to money values usually involves the development of a "going-rate" curve and an "organization-rate" curve.

Developing a Going-Rate Curve

At some stage of developing a wage- or salary-administration program, it is necessary to determine the relationship between evaluations, usually of a sample of key jobs, and rates of pay for corresponding jobs in the labor market. If data on the going rates of such jobs are not available, a wage or salary survey is made. For illustrative purposes, the median monthly salaries of twenty-two hypothetical jobs and their hypothetical job-evaluation point values are presented graphically in Figure 19.1. The line drawn through the dots on the graph represents the going-wage curve. Although this particular relationship is linear,

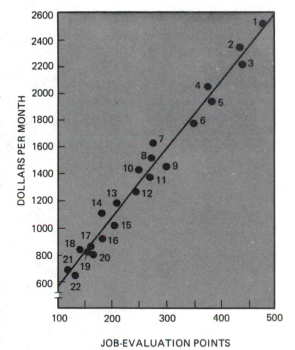

JOB-EVALUATION POINTS

FIGURE 19.1 Relationship between job-evaluation points and median monthly pay rates for twenty-two hypothetical jobs. (The "going rate" for each job in such an analysis is usually the median of the rates for several similar jobs in the labor market.) The line of best fit (in this case a straight line) reflects the relationship of the job-evaluation points to going rates.

it is curvilinear for some job-evaluation systems.

Setting an Organization-Rate Curve

The next stage is to establish a wage or salary curve for the specific organization. (In private companies this is called the company wage or salary curve.) This curve is set so it has some predetermined relationship to the going-rate curve—the same as the going-rate curve or a bit above or below it. This curve is then used by the organization to establish rates of pay for all of the jobs covered. This assures that all the jobs covered have their rates of pay established on the same basis.

Figure 19.2 shows an organization wage curve for the same jobs illustrated in Figure 19.1. In this case it is shown as slightly below the going-rate curve of the labor market. Where this curve is actually set with respect to the going-wage curve in any give case, however, is a function of various considerations, including economic conditions, contract negotiations, and fringe benefits. Thus, it can be at the level of the going-wage curve or at various levels above or below.

Different practices may be followed to convert job-evaluation points to actual rates of pay. It would be possible to take the evaluated points for a given job and to derive the corresponding exact rate that would be applicable. Thus, every slight difference in points would result in some difference in

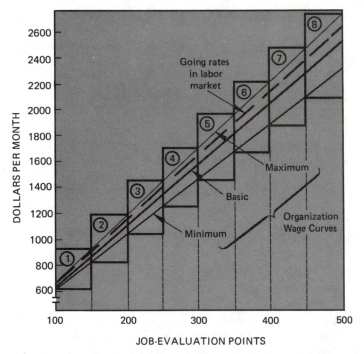

FIGURE 19.2 Illustration of an "organization" wage curve and of one pattern of conversion of job-evaluation points into rates of pay. In this particular example, the point values are converted into nine pay grades, each of which has a range of rates.

hourly rate. In practice most organizations (and unions) feel that the inherent lack of perfect accuracy in the judgments that underlie a set of job evaluations makes it desirable to bracket together jobs of approximately the same point value and to consider these jobs as equal in setting up the wage structure. This bracketing results in so-called *labor grades*. The number of labor grades found in specific wage structures varies from around eight or ten to twenty or twenty-five. The tendency of most current union demands in wage contract negotiations is to favor a relatively small number of labor grades.

When the jobs have been bracketed in labor grades, provision is usually made for wage increases within each labor grade, as illustrated in Figure 19.2. Various procedures have been used in granting wage increases within labor grades, as well as in upgrading employees to higher categories. Some organizations use an automatic acceleration schedule under which specified increases automatically become effective after a specified period of time on the job. This principle is used most frequently in the lower labor grades and with new employees, but it is sometimes used in higher levels in the wage structure as well. Regular personnel evaluations are also used by some organizations as a means of identifying employees who are eligible for a pay increase under the prevailing pay structure.

As already mentioned, there are various policies for converting points to rates of pay, but we only discuss two or three variations here. Figure 19.2 shows an increasing range of rates with higher pay grades; in actual practice the range may be constant, or it may be greater or less than that illustrated. In some systems the width of the pay grades (in terms of job-evaluation points) increases with higher rates; these increases may be systematic or adapted in some way to the concentration of jobs along the evaluation scale.

FACTORS IN JOB-EVALUATION SYSTEMS

The most common type of job-evaluation system is the point system, which provides for the evaluation of jobs on various factors. Although individual job-evaluation systems vary in the factors that are included, there is a fairly substantial degree of similarity between and among systems. The weights assigned to the different factors in a system are usually determined by a committee. (Recall that examples of weights for the system used by the NMTA Associates are given in Table 19.1.) In discussing such weights, however, let us hark back to the discussion in Chapter 6 of the weighting of factors in performance-evaluation systems. The point was made there that the *actual* or *effective* weights of factors (as opposed to the *intended* weights) are in part influenced by the variability (specifically the standard deviations) of the values assigned on the various factors to different cases in the sample. Thus, if the values on a given job-evaluation factor which are assigned to different jobs show little variation, then that factor would have relatively nominal effective weight—*unless* appropriate statistical steps are taken to give it its intended weight.

Optimum Combinations of Factors and Weights

As just stated, the usual practice in developing a job-evaluation system is for a committee to select the factors and to designate the intended weights. The optimum combination of factors and weights, however, can be determined by statistical procedures. Such procedures involve the following steps: (1) developing an "experimental" job-evaluation system with several factors; (2) evaluating the sample of jobs using this system; (3) determining the going rates for the jobs in the labor market (by a wage or salary survey); and

(4) applying appropriate statistical procedures (specifically some form of regression analysis). The factors and their statistically determined weights could then be used in the organization with reasonable assurance that the rates of pay based on the system would have a reasonable relationship with rates in the labor market.

DISCUSSION

Wage and salary administrators must feel that they are continuously walking a tightrope because of the conflicting pressures on them. A wage and salary program must provide positive work incentives for the employees, must be generally acceptable to employees, must be reasonably competitive with conditions in the labor market, and must keep the organization solvent. Obviously, there are no pat and simplistic resolutions to meet these various objectives. The note on which we would like to close this discussion is that insight into and knowledge relevant to the problem, derived through research, can aid in developing a satisfactory program.

REFERENCES

Arvey R. D., Passino, E. M., & Lounsbury, J. W. (1977). Job analysis results as influenced by sex of incumbent and sex of analyst. *Journal of Applied Psychology, 62*(4), 411–416.

Benge, E. J., Burk, S. L. H., & Hay, E. N. (1941). *Manual of job evaluation* (4th ed.). New York: Harper & Row.

Knapp, W. H. (1981). *The comparable worth issue: A BNA special report.* Washington, D.C.: The Bureau of National Affairs.

Lawler, E. E. (1971). *Pay and organizational effectiveness: A psychological view.* New York: McGraw-Hill.

McCormick, E. J. (1981). Minority report. In D. J. Treiman & H. I. Hartmann (Eds.), *Women, work, and wages: Equal pay for jobs of equal value.* Washington, D.C.: National Academy Press.

McCormick, E. J., Jeanneret, P. R., & Mecham, R. C. (1972). A study of job characteristics and job dimensions as based on the Position Analysis Questionnaire (PAQ). *Journal of Applied Psychology, 56*(4), 347–368.

Mecham, R. C. (1982). Personal communication, 1982.

Miles, M. C. (1952). Studies in job evaluation: A. Validity of a check list for evaluating office jobs. *Journal of Applied Psychology, 36,* 97–101.

Roberts, H. V. (1980). Statistical biases in the measurement of employment discrimination. In E. R. Livernash (Ed.), *Comparable worth issues and alternatives.* Washington, D.C.: Equal Employment Advisory Council.

Robinson, D. D., Wahlstrom, O. W., & Mecham, R. C. (1974). Comparison of job evaluation methods: A "policy-capturing" approach using the Position Analysis Questionnaire (PAQ). *Journal of Applied Psychology, 59*(5), 633–637.

Taylor, L. R. (1971). Personal communication.

Treiman, D. J., & Hartmann, H. I. (Eds.) (1981). *Women, work, and wages: Equal pay for jobs of equal worth* (Report of the Committee on Occupational Classification and Analysis). Washington, D.C.: National Academy Press.

Zollitsch, H. G., & Langsner, A. (1970). *Wage and salary administration* (2nd ed.). Cincinnati: South-Western Publishing.

20

Working Conditions

Working conditions in the United States and in many other industrial countries have improved markedly over the last century or so, probably because of such things as increased social concern by management, pressures from employees and unions, improved technology, and tighter legal and regulatory requirements. In the United States, the Occupational Safety and Health Administration (OSHA) of the Department of Labor is charged with administering the Occupational Safety and Health (OSH) Act, which sets certain standards for working conditions. Granting significant improvements over the years, further improvements can still be made in working conditions for some types of jobs.

Our discussion of working conditions covers two general categories. The first is the physical environment, particularly illumination, thermal conditions, and noise. The second is various aspects of time, such as work schedules (hours of work), and rest pauses.

ILLUMINATION

Although visual skills differ among individuals, our interest here is in terms of the features of the illumination environment that are appropriate for performing the visual tasks involved in various types of work. The "appropriateness" of the illumination environment for a given visual task depends on two classes of criteria; visual performance and visual comfort.

The Measurement of Light

Before we discuss "how much" light should be provided for any given task, however, we need to define certain terms used in the measurement of light. [Incidentally, such terminology gets rather complicated due to the fact that U.S. terminology (US) is somewhat different from that of the International System of Units (SI). With the SI system distance is measured by meters (m) rather than feet (ft)].

Light at the source: luminous intensity or candlepower. Unit of measure: *candela (cd)* or *luminous flux* measured in *lumens (lm)*.

$$1 \ cd = 1257 \ lm$$

Light on a surface: illuminance or illumination. Depends on candlepower at source and distance, following the inverse square law:

$$\text{Illuminance} = \frac{\text{candlepower } (cd)}{\text{D (distance)}^2}$$

Units of measure:

US: *footcandles (fc)*
SI: *lumens/D² or lux (lx)*
   (1 *lm/m² = 1 lux = 0.0926 fc*)

Following are some examples of the relationships between *candlepower (cd)*, distance (*D*), and illuminance:

DISTANCE	1 cd	2 cd	3 cd
1 ft	1 fc	2 fc	3 fc
2 ft	1/4 fc	2/4 fc	3/4 fc
3 ft	1/9 fc	2/9 fc	3/9 fc
1 m	1 lx	2 lx	3 lx
2 m	1/4 lx	2/4 lx	3/4 lx
3 m	1/9 lx	2/9 lx	3/9 lx

Light reflected from a surface: illuminance.

Units of measure:

US: *footlambert (fL)*
SI: *candela per square meter (cd/m²)*

The luminance (in *fL* or *cd/m²*) depends on the reflectance of the surface (ranging from 100% to 0%). If a surface reflects 100% (which seldom is the case) the luminance (in *fL* or *cd/m²*) would be the same as the illuminance falling on the surface (in *fc* or *lx*).

Factors that Influence Visual Performance

Visual performance can be thought of as the extent to which people make the visual discriminations that are required by a task. Such performance is influenced by the intrinsic characteristics of the visual task itself and by the characteristics of the luminous environment. The intrinsic characteristics of the task that affect the ability to make visual discriminations include the brightness contrast of the "details" to be discriminated against their backgrounds, the size of the details to be discriminated, and the time available for seeing.

A couple of sets of data relating to task variables illustrate the effect of such variables on visual performance. The first set of data, shown in Figure 20.1, shows the relationship between brightness contrast and visual per-

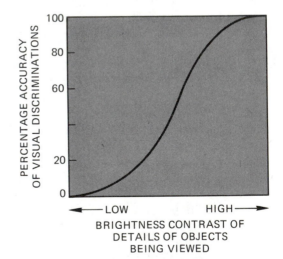

FIGURE 20.1 Generalized relationship between brightness contrast of visual detail and accuracy of visual discrimination. (Adapted from *IES Lighting Handbook, Reference Volume*, 1981, Figure 3–29.)

formance. An example of low brightness contrast is gray printing on a slightly lighter gray paper; an example of high contrast is black printing on very white paper.

The second set of data, shown in Figure 20.2, shows the relationship between viewing time and brightness contrast, as related to background luminance. The curves of Figure 20.2 show the combinations of luminance, time, and contrast that produce the same level of visual discriminability for any given level of luminance; for example, if viewing time is decreased the contrast must be increased to maintain the same level of visual discriminability. Likewise, for any given viewing time, a tradeoff exists between luminance and contrast; higher levels of luminance are required as contrast decreases.

Prescribing Illumination Standards

The specifications of illumination standards for kumquat inspectors, doughnut hole punchers, pinball machine assemblers—or any other job—is based on extensive research that we need not cover in detail here. Much of this research was carried out by Blackwell (1959, 1972). The illumination specifications for various types of situations formerly established by the Illuminating Engineering Society (IES) were based rather directly on Blackwell's work, especially on the Visibility Reference Function (VRF) shown in Figure 20.3. This represents the task contrast required at different levels of task background luminance to achieve equal visual discrimination for a standard visual task viewed for

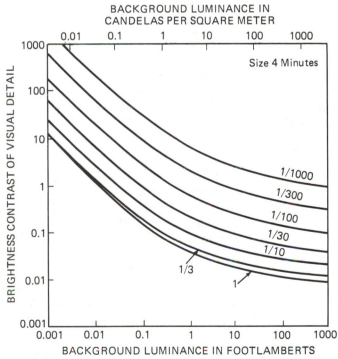

FIGURE 20.2 The relationship between brightness contrast of visual detail, luminance, and viewing time required for equal visual discriminability for a specified size of visual target (4 minutes of visual angle). (From *IES Lighting Handbook, Reference Volume*, 1981, Figure 3–31.)

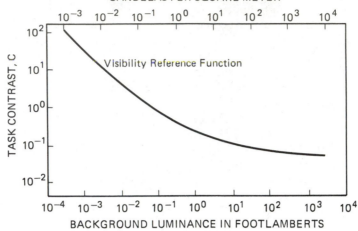

FIGURE 20.3 Visibility Reference Function (VRF) representing visual task brightness contrast required at different levels of task background luminance to achieve equal (threshhold) visual discriminability for a specified size of visual target (4 minutes of visual angle) exposed for 1/5 second. (From *IES Lighting Handbook, Reference Volume,* 1981, Figure 3–30.)

1/5 second. Illumination standards based on the VRF involved various procedures and adjustments we need not describe, but the end result consisted of standards for specific work situations.

More currently the IES has adopted a somewhat simplified procedure for establishing illumination specifications, although these still have their roots in Blackwell's earlier work. The new procedure uses ranges of illumination, accompanied by weighting factors, to select the specific recommended illumination level (*IES Lighting Handbook, Application Volume,* 1981). In this procedure the visual task in question is first classified in one of the types of activity categories given in Table 20.1. This classification, in turn, specifies the general illuminance category and the ranges of illuminance. Each range has three values: low, middle, and high. A correction factor, based on the weighting of three task and worker characteristics, determining which of these three values to use follows:

	WEIGHT		
CHARACTERISTIC	−1	0	+1
Age	Under 40	40–55	Over 55
Speed or accuracy	Not important	Important	Critical
Reflectance of task background	Over 70%	30–70%	Less than 70%

The weights for the three characteristics are added algebraicly (i.e., +1, 0, −1) to derive the total weighting factor (TWF). (Since categories A, B, and C of Table 20.1 do not involve active visual tasks, the speed or accuracy characteristic is not used for these categories; the average reflectance of the room, walls, and floor is used instead of task background reflectance.) The following guidelines

TABLE 20.1 Illuminance categories and illuminance values for generic types of activities in interiors

TYPE OF ACTIVITY	ILLUMINANCE CATEGORY	RANGES OF ILLUMINANCES		REFERENCE WORK-PLACE
		LUX	FOOTCANDLES	
Public spaces with dark surroundings	A	20–30–50	2–3–5	General lighting throughout spaces
Simple orientation for short temporary visits	B	50–75–100	5–7.5–10	
Working spaces where visual tasks are only occasionally performed	C	100–150–200	10–15–20	
Performance of visual tasks of high contrast or large size	D	200–300–500	20–30–50	Illuminance on task
Performance of visual tasks of medium contrast or small size	E	500–750–1000	50–75–100	
Performance of visual tasks of low contrast or very small size	F	1000–1500–2000	100–150–200	
Performance of visual tasks of low contrast and very small size over a prolonged period	G	2000–3000–5000	200–300–500	
Performance of very prolonged and exacting visual tasks	H	5000–7500–10000	500–750–1000	Illuminance on task, obtained by a combination of general and local (supplementary lighting)
Performance of very special visual tasks of extremely low contrast and small size	I	10000–15000–20000	1000–1500–2000	

Source: *IES Lighting Handbook, Application Volume,* 1981, p. 2–5, Table I.

are then used to select the low, middle, or high value of the category for the task:

FOR CATEGORIES A,B,C	FOR CATEGORIES D THROUGH I
TWF = −1 or −2: use low value	TWF = −2 or −3: use low value
TWF = O: use middle value	TWF = −1, 0, or +1; use middle value
TWF = +1 or +2: use high value	TWF = +2 or +3: use high value

Following are the illuminance categories for a few types of activities or situations (*IES Lighting Handbook, Application Volume,* 1981, Table II):

B: Stairways and corridors
C: Handling rough, bulky items (warehouse)
D: Wrapping, packing, labeling
D: Reading typed originals
E: Mail sorting
E: Repair work (garage)
F: Fine bench and machine work (woodworking)
G: Very difficult inspection
G: Extra fine hand painting and finishing (paint shop)
H: Surgical task lighting

For any given activity or situation, the level of illumination to be provided within its designated category (low, middle, or high) would be based on the weighting previously mentioned; this takes into account age, speed or accuracy, and background reflectance.

Glare

There are two sources of glare: (1) *direct glare,* caused by light sources in the field of view; and (2) *reflected* or *specular* glare, caused by high brightness from polished or glossy surfaces that are reflected toward the individual. Three variations in the *level* of glare have also been categorized (IES Nomenclature Committee, 1979): (1) *discomfort* glare, which produces discomfort, but does not necessarily interfere with visual performance or visibility; (2) *disability* glare, which reduces visual performance and visibility, and is often accompanied by discomfort; and (3) *blinding* glare, which is so intense that for an appreciable length of time after it has been removed no object can be seen.

Reduction of glare. There are various ways to reduce glare. A few samples follow:

- To reduce direct glare from luminaires: Position luminaires away from the line of sight; use several low-intensity luminaires instead of a few very bright ones; use light shields, hoods, and visors when glare source cannot be reduced.
- To reduce direct glare from windows: Use windows that are set some distance above the floor; use shades, blinds, or louvers.
- To reduce reflected glare: Keep luminance of luminaires as low as feasible; use surfaces that diffuse light, such as flat paint, nonglossy paper, and so on; avoid bright metal and glass where feasible; position luminaires or work area so reflected light will not be directed toward the eyes.

Discussion

Improper illumination can affect people's work performance and can cause various forms of visual discomfort. Correcting some illumination problems involves the services of illuminating engineers. However, some improvements can be made by using common sense and by applying some of the information and guidelines just discussed.

THERMAL CONDITIONS

We usually only become aware of the temperature of our environment when we have distinct sensations of heat or cold. Such awareness occurs when there is an imbalance of the thermal interchange between ourselves and our environment. Such an imbalance can affect our health and performance as well as our comfort.

The Heat-Exchange Process

The food we eat and the air we breathe are the "inputs" to the chemical process called metabolism. The metabolic process produces the energy we require in our every-day activities and heat. The body continually attempts to maintain thermal equilibrium with its environment. Under most conditions we have surplus heat to transmit to the environment, but in cold conditions the body tries to preserve its heat. There are four ways in which the heat-exchange process can take place:

- Convection: The transmission via the air (which technically is a fluid).
- Evaporation: Of perspiration, and to some degree of the vapor exhaled from the lungs.
- Radiation: The transmission of thermal energy between objects, as between the sun and the earth, or between ourselves and the walls, ceilings, and other surfaces—such as cold windows or hot metal furnaces—in our environment.
- Conduction: The transmission of thermal energy by direct contact, as walking barefoot on a cold floor or putting one's hand on a hot stove. Our clothing usually insulates us so well that this method is of negligible importance and is not considered in most methods of measuring heat exchange.

Heat-balance equation. The fundamental heat-exchange process is set forth by the general heat-exchange equation (*ASHRAE Handbook*, 1981, p. 8–1):

$$S = M + [\pm W] \pm E \pm R \pm C$$

which means:

Storage = Metabolism + (± Work) ± Evaporation ± Radiation ± Convection.

If the body is in a state of equilibrium the S (Storage) is zero. In conditions of imbalance the body temperature can increase (if high enough it can cause heat stroke or death), or decrease (which can also cause death in extreme conditions).

Environmental Factors that Influence Heat Exchange

The heat-exchange process is, of course, very much affected by certain environmental conditions—in particular, air temperature, humidity, air flow, and the temperature of objects in the environment (such as the walls, ceilings, windows, furnaces, or the sun). The interaction of these conditions is quite complex and cannot be covered in detail here. But we can point out that under high air-temperature and high wall-temperature conditions, heat loss by convection and radiation is minimized, so that heat *gain* to the body may result. Under such circumstances the only remaining means of heat loss is by evaporation. But if the humidity is also high, evaporative heat loss will be minimized, with the result that body temperature rises. In winter high humidity and wind have an unhappy cooling effect. The wind-chill index, frequently given in weather reports, is based on the cooling effects of the combinations of low temperatures and wind.

Indexes of environmental effects. Two of the various indexes of the effects of combinations of environmental factors are described here. One of these is the Wet Bulb Globe Temperature (WBGT). This index, used in enclosed environments, is a weighted average of dry bulb temperature, t_{db} (the usual measure of air temperature), and what is called the "naturally" convected wet bulb temperature, t_{nwb}. (Wet bulb temperature takes into account the effects of humidity in combination with air temperature and air movement, and is especially useful when the human body is near its upper limits of temperature regulation by sweating.) The WBGT is derived with the following equation (*ASHRAE Handbook*, 1981, p. 8.17):

$$WBGT = 0.3\, t_{db} + 0.7\, t_{nwb}.$$

The other index we mention is Effective Temperature. Actually there are two versions of this index. The original version (ET) was intended to equate varying combinations of temperature, humidity, and air movements in terms of equal sensations of warmth or cold. For example, an ET of 70° characterized the thermal sensation of a 70° temperature in combination with 100% humidity, but that value also characterized other (higher) temperatures and other (lower) humidities that gave the same thermal sensations (such as 81° temperature and 10% humidity). Although ET has been widely used, and has been a useful index, it overemphasizes the effects of humidity in cool and neutral conditions and underemphasizes the effects in warm conditions; also, it does not fully account for air velocity in hot-humid conditions.

Because of these limitations of the original ET, a newer index, identified as ET^x, was developed. It is derived by a complicated formulation based on the effects of environmental variables on the physiological regulation of the body.

Although these (and other) indexes of thermal conditions are expressed in terms of temperature (either degrees Fahrenheit, °F, or Celsius, °C), their values cannot be interpreted in terms of conventional "dry bulb" temperature values since they also take into account other variables (such as humidity, air flow, etc.).

Effects of Heat on Performance

The effects of heat on the performance of people engaged in heavy physical activities have been well documented. But there are indications that heat can also affect performance on tasks that do not involve much physical activity. Beshir, El-Sabagh, and El-Nawawi (1981), for example, report distinct effects of heat on performances on a tracking task. Figure 20.4 shows the mean error scores of subjects during three work cycles when engaged in the tracking task under three temperature conditions as measured by WBGT.

Errors were clearly greater under the "high" temperature conditions than under the more normal WBGT temperature of 65°F (20°C).

Fine and Kobrich (1978) compared the mean errors of subjects on four cognitive tasks when working under conditions of 95°F (35°C) heat with those of subjects in two control groups working at more normal temperatures. The error rate for subjects in the hot conditions increased during 7 hours to about twice that of subjects in the control conditions. Thus, very high levels of heat can cause degradation in performance on various kinds of work.

Heat-Exposure Limits

The level of heat that can be tolerated depends on several variables such as: work load; rest periods; humidity; and air velocity. Various individuals and organizations have set forth recommended limits of exposure for certain specified work loads. Ramsey (1978) proposed the following set of "abbreviated guidelines" for four levels of work load:

WORKLOAD (KCAL/HOUR)		RECOMMENDED LIMITS (WBGT)[a]	
		°F	°C
Light	<200	86	30
Moderate	201–300	82	28
Heavy	301–400	79	26
Very heavy	>401	77	25

[a]To account for differences in air velocity and clothing Ramsey proposes the following adjustments: Add 2°C (3.6°F) if air velocity is greater than 1.67 meters/sec or if worker is wearing shorts, and subtract 2°C (3.6°F) if worker is wearing standard clothing plus a jacket.

In discussing recommended tolerance limits Ramsey and Chai (1983) point out that there can be considerable variability in the derivation of allowable WBGT values under certain circumstances, as when the metabolic work load on air velocity must be estimated. In view of this they express the opinion that

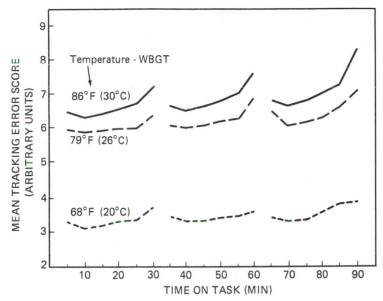

FIGURE 20.4 Mean errors of subjects on a tracking task performed during three cycles under three temperature conditions (as measured by WBGT). Errors are clearly greater under the two "high" temperature conditions than under the more normal temperature of 68°F. (Adapted from Beshir et al., 1981.)

a simplified set of decision rules can serve the same purpose as seemingly more precise approaches.

High temperature conditions can be tolerated if a person is provided with adequate rest. Figure 20.5 gives one set of permissible heat-exposure limits for various WBGT values for continuous work (over an 8-hour day) and for various combinations of work and rest. This shows, for example, that for heavy work of 500 kcal/hr, if the WBGT is as high as 86°F, people should work only 25% of the time (and rest 75%), whereas if the WBGT is as low as 77 the same work can be carried on continuously.

Wing (1965) summarized the results of fifteen different studies of tolerance limits for carrying out mental activities. The generalized results are shown in the lower line of Figure 20.6. The environmental conditions of the various studies were characterized in terms of ET. The lower line shows the tolerance limits (in terms of time) for carrying out mental activities without impairment of the work activity under different ET conditions. Work beyond the indicated time limits typically suffered some degradation. The upper line, in turn, shows the recommended upper limit of exposure in terms of heat tolerance as based on other data.

Effects of Cold

Exposure to cold is accompanied by a number of physiological changes, including the vasoconstriction of the peripheral blood vessels, which reduces the flow of blood to the surface of the skin and results in reduced skin temperature. This is a protective response of the body to minimize heat loss (although it numbs the fingers and toes). In fact, our subjective sensations of cold are very closely related to mean skin temperatures (the mean temperature of the total body surface).

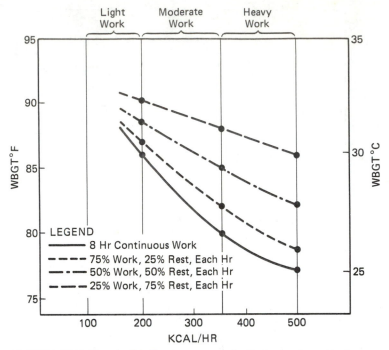

FIGURE 20.5 Permissible heat-exposure limits for various work loads and combinations of work and rest. (From Dukes-Dobos & Henschel, 1971, as presented in *ASHRAE Handbook,* 1981, Figure 13, p. 8.17.)

The critical subjective tolerance limit, without any numbing sensation, appears to be about 77°F (25°C) (*AHSRAE Handbook,* 1981, p. 8.14); however, during moderate to heavy activity, such skin temperatures may still be comfortable.

Although mean skin temperature is a significant factor in sensations of comfort, the temperature of the extremities is more frequently the critical comfort factor since one of the first responses to cold exposure is vasoconstriction and reduced circulation of heat to the hands and feet. In this regard various levels of subjective sensations are associated with the hand-skin temperatures (HST):

Uncomfortably cold	68°F (20°C)
Extremely cold	59°F (15°C)
Painful	41°F (5°C)

As would be expected, reduced performance on manual tasks stems from the physical lowering of HST. Clark (1961) found the critical skin temperature to be in the 55°F to 60°F range (12.8°C to 15.6°C), and indicated that manual performance is not affected by temperatures above 60°F (15.6°C), but that decrements may be expected below 55°F (12.8°C).

Some evidence of the effects of cold on manual performance is provided by Tanaka, Tochihara, Yamazaki, Ohnaka, and Yoshida (1983), who had subjects perform a psychomotor key-pressing task at 15-minute intervals over an hour under three air-temperature conditions. Figure 20.7 shows the "counting" performance (i.e., the number of times the subjects pressed the key in a 15-second period) for the three conditions. Performance

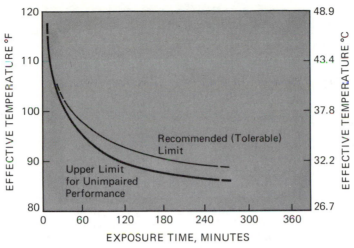

FIGURE 20.6 Upper limit for unimpaired mental performances based on fifteen studies. For any given effective temperature, the point on the curve horizontally to its right represents the time limit (read along the base) within which mental activity is typically not impaired; a longer period of work would usually result in work decrement. The upper curve, in turn, gives the recommended upper limit of exposure in terms of human tolerance to heat, as based on other research findings. (Adapted from Wing, 1965, Figure 9.)

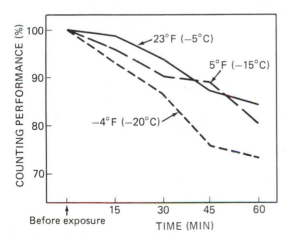

FIGURE 20.7 Performance on a key-pressing "counting" task during cold exposure at three conditions of air temperature. Performance is given as a percentage of the preexposure control value. (Adapted from Tanaka et al., 1983, Figure 2.)

deteriorated more under the coldest condition (−4°F, −20°C) than under the other conditions. Incidentally, performance was significantly correlated with hand-skin temperature.

Although most people work indoors in temperature-controlled climates, there are still some jobs that involve exposure to the elements and the danger of hypothermia (reduction of body temperature): construction work, fishing, the operation of oil rigs, and road maintenance, for example. In such instances the primary method of protection is appropriate apparel, although in some cases providing rotating shifts may also help.

NOISE

We have human technology to blame for the noise people encounter in everyday life and in some jobs, since the primary sources of noise are man-made: automobiles, machines, aircraft, and sound amplifiers. Before discussing some of the effects of sound we mention certain aspects of the measurement of sound and of the subjective sensations it produces.

Measurement of Sound

Sound, of course, is a form of energy. Its two primary characteristics are frequency and intensity. Vibrating objects (such as tuning forks and machines) cause fluctuating changes in air pressure to spread out away from them. This is something like the waves in a pond that are generated by a pebble thrown into it, except that sound waves travel in all directions. For an object that has a *single* frequency, these waves, if shown graphically, form a sine (sinusiodal) wave; the number of repetitions per second is the frequency. Frequency really refers to the number of vibrations or cycles per second (cps); however, it is now common practice to use the term hertz (Hz) rather than cycles per second (cps). Actually, most vibrating sources generate complex waves rather than pure waves; thus, although middle C on the piano and on a trumpet have the same dominant frequency (256 Hz), their "qualities" are different because of the differences in the *other* frequencies also generated. Incidentally, a given octave has twice the frequency of the one below it.

The intensity of sound is usually measured by decibels (dB). The decibel scale is actually a logarithmic scale, which accounts for the fact that a ten-decibel difference actually reflects a tenfold difference in sound level. With a logarithmic scale the zero value is not an absolute zero; "0 dB" is about the level of the weakest sound that can be heard by a person with very good hearing in an extremely quiet location. Figure 20.8 shows examples of the dB levels of some typical sounds.

The measurement of sound level is really

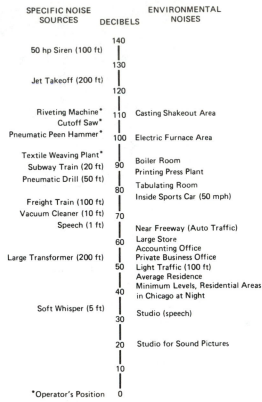

FIGURE 20.8 Decibel (dB) levels for various sounds. These are A-weighted sound levels measured with a sound-level meter. (From Peterson, 1980, Figure 2–1.)

quite complicated. The dB levels of sounds, for example, usually involve one of several "weighting" systems that take into account variations in the sensitivity of the ear to different frequencies. These are designated as A, B, and C. The most common is the A weighting system, which is the one used in Figure 20.8. But the measurement complications do not stop here, because of problems involved in measurement of power and power level (which we do not get into).

Measurement of Subjective Aspects of Sound

There have been numerous efforts to develop scales for measuring various subjective reactions to sound, such as loudness, loudness level, "noisiness," "annoyingness," "objection ability," or how "disturbing" sounds are. We burden the reader with only one example—namely, the *sone*, a measure of loudness. The judged loudness of a 1000 Hz tone of 40 dB is taken to be 1 sone. A sound that sounds twice as loud has a loudness of 2 sones, and so on. Following are a few examples:

NOISE SOURCE	dB	LOUDNESS, SONES
Residence inside, quiet	42	1
Household ventilating fan	56	2
Automobile, 50 ft.	68	14
"Quiet" factory area	76	54
18-in automatic lathe	89	127
Nail making machine, 8 ft	111	800

Clearly, loudness is sones increases markedly with increases in dB.

Stevens (1972) developed a revision of his earlier procedure for deriving an estimate of the sones for any given sound. The procedure (labeled Mark VII) is the one in most current use.

Effects of Noise on Hearing

There are two types of hearing loss: (1) *nerve* deafness, which results from damage or degeneration of the hair cells in the inner ear; and (2) *conduction* deafness, which is caused by some condition of the outer or middle ear that affects the transmission of sound waves to the inner ear. Through age most people experience some hearing loss (nerve deafness).

In addition to hearing loss through age, however, people can experience hearing loss through noise exposure. Exposure to high levels of noise is usually accompanied by some temporary hearing loss compared with preexposure levels. This is called the temporary threshold shift (TTS). With exposure over an extended period of time the "temporary" hearing loss can become more "permanent." Following are some generalizations about noise-induced permanent hearing loss (Peterson, 1980):

- Hearing damage from exposure to excessive noise is cumulative; both level and exposure time are important factors.
- At any given level, low-frequency noise tends to be less damaging than noise in the midfrequency range.
- Individuals are not all equally susceptible to noise-induced hearing loss.
- The hearing loss from noise tends to be most pronounced around 4000 Hz, but it spreads over the frequency range with increased exposure time and level. (The loss is not typically at the frequency of greatest exposure.) (p. 18)

Figure 20.9 is an example of a survey of hearing loss. This figure shows the hearing loss of sixty-six earth-moving machine operators with different durations of exposure to the noise from their equipment, which ranged from 90 to 120 dB. Hearing tests were given to the men before their work shift, and the results were compared with the hearing losses that typically occur through age for individuals of comparable age.

Effects of Noise on Performance

Evidence about the effects of noise on work performance represents a mixed bag. If you scrounge through the literature you can find examples that would show that noise produces a decrement, no effect, or an improvement in performance (Broadbent, 1979; Gawron, 1982; Hockey, 1978). Recognizing this ambiguous state of affairs, it probably is possible to tease out a few generalized inklings about the effects of noise on perfor-

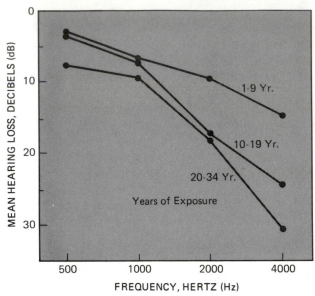

FIGURE 20.9 Hearing loss of three groups of earth-moving equipment operators varying in length of exposure. These data are corrected for age—that is, the hearing loss shown is that over and above the normal hearing loss for men of corresponding age. (Adapted from LaBenz, Cohen, & Pearson, 1967, Table 6.)

mance. To begin with, such possible effects are probably related to the types of tasks being performed, although even on this score there is probably no clear-cut distinction between the types of tasks on which performance is, or is not, affected. To add further qualms, most of the relevant research has been carried out in laboratories, and may not be applicable to actual work situations over extended periods of time.

Given these caveats, then, the inklings that are available suggest that noise may cause degradation in such tasks as: monitoring activities; complex mental tasks; tracking tasks; tasks that call for skill and speed; tasks that demand a high level of perceptual capacity; and tasks that require considerable short-term memory. When noise does affect performance it usually has to be fairly high. Hockey expresses the opinion that—for most types of tasks—the level required to expect reliable

performance effects is 95 dBA. On the other hand, it seems that simple, repetitive, routine tasks are relatively insensitive to the effects of noise.

It should be added that, even if high noise levels do not affect performance on tasks, there can be subtle effects, such as annoyance, irritability, interference with communications, and long-term health effects. With regard to health effects, Cohen (1972) reported that a 5-year, follow-up study of 500 workers subjected to noise levels of 95 dB or above revealed a higher incidence of somatic complaints of illness and diagnosed disorders than another group of workers not subject to such noise levels. Cohen also reported a higher absence rate for those working in high noise levels, which may indicate greater psychological stress.

The most definitive conclusion about the effects of noise on performance seems to be that, in general, if noise levels are kept within reasonable bounds in terms of *other* criteria (especially in terms of avoiding hearing loss), such levels typically would not have any serious effects on performance of most tasks.

Regulations Regarding Workplace Noise

In the United States the Occupational Safety and Health Administration (OSHA) has established a set of legal, permissible noise exposures for persons working in industry (*Federal Register*, 1971). These regulations are based primarily on considerations of hearing loss. In general terms the regulations limit an employee's noise exposure to 90 dBA, as an 8-hour time-weighted average. (Reducing the level to 85 dBA on the grounds that this would further reduce hearing-loss risks is being considered; however, this possibility will depend on further consideration of such factors as health risks, feasibility, and economic impact.)

The present 90 dBA standard is based on the concept of "daily noise dose" (D), which takes into account the estimated effects of noise level and duration on hearing loss. Although certain procedures and equations can be used to estimate the daily noise dose, the following data reflect the nature of the trade-offs of intensity and duration to keep the daily exposure to one daily noise-dose level:

DURATION PER DAY (HOURS)	SOUND LEVEL dBA
8	90
6	92
4	95
3	97
2	100
$1\frac{1}{2}$	102
1	105
$\frac{1}{2}$	110
$\frac{1}{4}$ or less	115

The regulations also limit the noise level of any sound to 115 dBA.

The sound-level limits just given (and the 115 dBA maximum) are based on the measurement of the "effective noise level." This applies to limits for workers who do not wear ear protectors, or, in the case of those who do, the level that takes into account the protection they get.

Noise Control

The control of noise is very much an engineering problem. Generally, it can include the following approaches: reducing the noise at the source (such as by proper machine design, lubrication, or mounting); enclosing the noise; and using baffles and soundproofing materials. If these steps still do not bring the noise level within acceptable limits, using ear-protection devices is in order.

WORK SCHEDULE

Work schedules have various aspects, including the total number of hours worked per week, the four-day work week, flexible work hours, shift work, and provision for rest periods.

Hours of Work

In many countries, including the United States, work schedules for many people have settled down at somewhere around the conventional 40-hour week. For whatever historical interest it might be, a survey was carried out, by Kossoris, Kohler, and others (1947), of the experiences of thirty-four plants with varying work schedules during and after World War II. In general the results indicated that the (then) fairly common 44-hour week was best in terms of efficiency, absenteeism, and injuries. Although the 40-hour week has substantially replaced the post-War 44-hour week in the United States, the results of that study probably still have implications for overtime work and the rather common practice of moonlighting (people's holding two jobs).

Four-Day Work Week

Given the fairly standard 40-hour work week, the next matter is the distribution of these hours over the week. The most common arrangement is the 5-day, 8-hour-per-day schedule (5/40). Several years ago there was quite a flurry of interest in other work schedules, especially the 4-day, 10-hour-per-day schedule (4/40) (Poor, 1973). The fact that such schedules have not become epidemic in proportion probably implies that they have not been broadly perceived as being preferable to the 5/40 schedule. Even though the 4/40 (or other similar schedules) have not become common practice, however, it is relevant to wonder about the results of such schedules where they have been used.

From a questionnaire survey of 434 clerical and forty supervisory employees who had been on a 4/40 schedule for a year, Goodale and Aagaard (1975) reported "mixed and somewhat inconsistent reaction" to the schedule. In reply to a general question, 80% reported that they did not want to revert to a traditional 5-day work week. Replies to more specific questions, however, were more mixed. For example, 62% felt they were making better use of their leisure time, and 53% had not adopted an earlier bedtime to compensate for an earlier starting time. In another survey of workers in a 4/40 schedule, Fottler (1977) interviewed employees of the food and nutrition department of a large hospital and found that about 56% were in favor of continuing the schedule. This percentage is at the low end of the range of responses reported from other studies.

In synthesizing the results of various opinion studies, Dunham and Hawk (1977) indicated that the 4/40 schedules are viewed most favorably by younger workers with low job levels, low income levels, and low satisfaction with job-related components.

In summary, it appears that data on employees' attitudes toward the 4/40 schedule represent something of a mixed bag and do not support some of the early enthusiastic claims that the 4/40 schedule is the wave of the future. This is not to say that such a schedule should not be considered, but rather suggests that it should not be viewed as a panacea for employee discontent and urges that consideration of such a program take into account the attitudes of the employees toward it, along with the practical feasibility of scheduling work.

Flexible Work Hours

Another innovation in work scheduling is the adoption of flexible work hours (sometimes referred to as flexitime). Such programs have been adopted by a number of companies in the United States, Europe, and Canada. There are many variations of the flexible work-hours scheme, but in general they provide that employees work for a specified number of hours (such as 35 or 40 hours per week) but permit flexibility in terms of individuals' reporting for work each day.

Curiosity about the results of the flexible work week includes interest in the attitudes of employers toward it and whether it has had any effect on work-related behavior. Golembiewski and Proehl (1978) summarized the results of sixteen studies from which we can draw some conclusions about both types of criteria.

We cannot present all of the results of the attitude data from these studies. In the nine studies in which people were asked if they wanted the program continued, however, we can report that the percentages who urged continuation were as follows: 80, 83, 85, 96, 98, 98, 99, 100, and 100. Although data on other attitude factors reflected some variability, the pattern of attitudes is very definitely on the plus side. As expressed by the authors, "... the attitudinal data summarized ... provide major motivation for (flexible workweek) applications" (Golembiewski & Proehl, 1978, p. 849).

On the behavioral side, the "hard" data available from the studies were skimpy but included, in some instances, data on sick leave and absenteeism, tardiness, turnover, overtime, and trends in costs. Although such data were limited, Golembiewski and Proehl concluded that, by and large, the benefits of flexible work schedules far outweigh their costs and indicated that such schedules do not seem to induce negative or managerially undersirable behaviors at work. In addition, a side effect of the use of flexitime by a large number of organizations in a limited geographical area is that it helps minimize rush-hour traffic, since local people have different work schedules. A possible constraint on the use of flexible hours could exist in organizations in which the operations require full staffs during scheduled hours of work.

Shift Work

Since human beings evolved in a world with a 24-hour day-night schedule, they have developed a temporal "program" called the circadian rhythm. This rhythm is accompanied by certain physiological changes during the 24-hour period. For example, oral temperature is typically lower early in the morning (around 4:00 A.M.) than during the day or early evening. In addition, there are indications that performance in certain types of activities tends to vary over the 24-hour period. Folkard and Monk (1979), for example, summarized data from six studies that show job performance vary over the 24 hours, with

the low point being very late at night or very early in the morning.

Adjustment of circadian rhythm. The degree to which night workers' circadian rhythms adjust themselves may influence their performance. Folkard and Monk (1979) state that it is now recognized that experienced shift workers may show some form of long-term adjustment as a result of prolonged experience with a particular shift system. They emphasize, however, that the degree of adjustment is greater with permanent night-shift workers ("full timers") than with those on rotating shifts ("part timers").

Individual differences in adjustment. However, Folkard and Monk also indicate that individuals do indeed differ in the degree to which their circadian rhythms adjust to night work. Such differences seem to be somewhat related to the differences between "morning" and "evening" types of individuals. Breithaupt, Hildebrandt, Döhre, Josch, Sieber, and Werner (1978) reported that predominantly morning types react to late shift work with sleep deficiency and its accompanying pathological symptoms. In turn, they add that evening types are inherently less vulnerable to delayed sleep simply because their delayed circadian rhythms are more in phase with night work.

Effects on health and safety. Fairly consistent evidence indicates that the quantity and quality of sleep is associated with shift work (Smith, Colligan, & Tasto, 1982; Tilley, Wilkinson, Warren, Watson, & Drud, 1982). The results of one survey by Smith et al. are shown in Table 20.2. The effects of shift work on sleep (especially the quality of sleep) were most accentuated for the night and rotating shift workers. The afternoon workers fared a bit better than the day workers in this survey, presumably because of the early-rising hours of the day workers.

The much higher frequency of injuries and sick absences shown in Table 20.2 for the ro-

TABLE 20.2 Health and safety effects of shift work: 883 food-processing workers

	SHIFT			
EFFECT	DAY	AFTERNOON	NIGHT	ROTATION
Sleep: average hours	7.0	7.4	6.4	6.8
Sleep: fair or poor (%)	23	27	52	53
Injuries: % with 1 or more (6 mo)	19	22	16	39
Injuries: av. no. per worker	0.28	0.34	0.25	0.69
Sickness: % with 1 or more (6 mo)	51	66	60	72

Source: Smith et al., 1982, Tables 2, 3, 6, and 7.

tating shift implicates rotating shift work as the most detrimental to work safety and health for the workers in the survey. Although the specific results from other surveys vary somewhat, the general pattern tends to be the same: For at least some people shift work tends to induce sleep problems, and perhaps in part because of such problems tends to increase health and safety risks. The effects seem to be especially associated with the rotating shift.

Effects on leisure activities. People who work at fixed hours usually adapt their lifestyles and patterns of leisure activities to their regular work schedules. For those on rotating shifts some leisure activities can be affected adversely, but some can actually be facilitated or unaffected. An indication of these differential effects comes from a survey done in Sweden by Herbert (1983), who obtained data from sixty-one workers over a period of $2\frac{1}{2}$ years. All the workers were first employed at the same time when a factory began its operations. Some of Herbert's results are shown in Figure 20.10. The activities that were hindered most were: watching TV; seeing others; and sleep. Those that were facilitated most were: house work; shopping; maintenance of house, garden, car, etc.; travelling; and errands to post office, bank, etc. Of course, the usual individual differences must be recognized, but at least some people per-

ceive rotating shift work to have some positive, facilitative effect on some of their nonwork activities.

Effects on performance. Although it is commonly accepted that work performance is at a low ebb during night shifts, hard data on this matter are rather sparse. Folkgard and Monk (1979) present data from six studies that show variations in job performance over a 24-hour period; their results are shown in Figure 20.11. These results do tend to show declines during the late night and early morning (and thus tend to conform to the implications of the circadian rhythm). However, one needs to be wary about accepting generalizations. As Folkard and Monk point out, performance on night shifts can be affected (for better or worse) by such factors as the choice of the shift system, the nature of the task, the performance demands of the task (such as for air controllers), adjustment of individuals to the task and shift, and the ubiquitous fact of individual differences.

Attitudes toward shift work. Most people take a dim view of shift work. But this is not a universal attitude. For example, on the basis of survey of 315 rotating shift workers in the British steel industry, Wedderburn (1978) reported the following responses to the question:

"On the whole how do you feel about working shifts?"

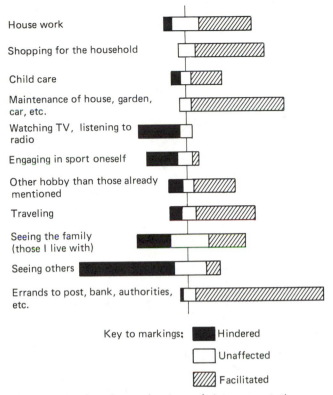

House work

Shopping for the household

Child care

Maintenance of house, garden, car, etc.

Watching TV, listening to radio

Engaging in sport oneself

Other hobby than those already mentioned

Traveling

Seeing the family (those I live with)

Seeing others

Errands to post, bank, authorities, etc.

Key to markings: ■ Hindered

☐ Unaffected

▨ Facilitated

FIGURE 20.10 Indexes of ratings of sixty-one rotating shift workers who rated their shift work as being hindered, unaffected, or facilitated by their work-shift schedules. (The nature of the rating index is not described, so the results should be viewed as reflecting relative patterns of responses.) (From Herbert, 1983, Figure 1, p. 570.)

Response	Percent
I like it very much.	18
I like it more than I dislike it.	29
I neither like it nor dislike it.	22
I dislike it more than I like it.	23
I dislike it very much.	8

Although these results indicated more favorable than unfavorable attitudes toward the "general" question asked, this does not mean that those who do like shift work are completely enthralled by it, for responses of the same individuals indicated considerable dislike of it for certain reasons: effects on social life, 61%; irregular sleeping times, 47%; working at night, 44%; irregular meal times, 38%; and early rising, 35%.

The descriptive items of the survey questionnaire that tended to be dominant in the responses of workers to the three shifts were the following:

• Day shift: Gives me more spare time. Good for family life. Does not restrict my social life.
• Afternoon shift: Restricts my social life. Wastes the day. Is least tiring.
• Night Shift: Tiring. Restricts my social life. Is not good for family life. Disturbs my sleep. Gives me more spare time.

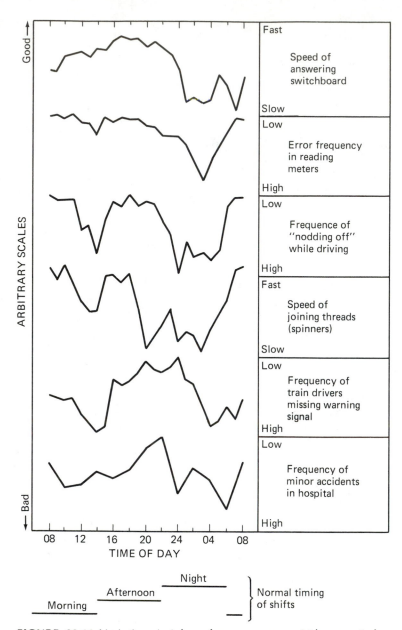

FIGURE 20.11 Variations in job performance over a 24-hour period for six types of activities. (From Folkard & Monk, 1979, Figure 1, p. 284. The original sources are given in Folkard and Monk.)

Although rotating shift work frequently involves three shifts of 8 hours each, an interesting variation was used with police officers in the city of Dartmouth (as reported by Peacock, Glube, Miller, Cline, 1983). The original and new schedules are:

Original 8-hour, 12-day schedule; rotating 8-hour shifts (day, evening, and night) with about 4 days off.

New 12-hour, 8-day schedule; rotating 12-hour shifts (day and night) with about 4 days off.

The most striking result was the overwhelming support for the 12-hour, 8-day schedule on the part of the officers, especially because they felt their sleep patterns were not disturbed as much as with the 8-hour, 12-day schedule. As an aside, no evidence indicated any deleterious effect in terms of physiological measures. Although this study was based on small numbers, it argues for further experimentation with innovative work schedules, such as the 12-hour, 8-day schedule, when services must be provided on an around-the-clock basis.

Discussion of shift work. There is obviously no way to eliminate evening and night work, since some of the work of the world needs to be carried on during all hours of the day and night. Realizing that there are no absolute, across-the-board pronouncements that can be made about work schedules and shift work, a few general (but qualified) comments can be made on the basis of available research regarding shift work and work during the witching night hours:

- Work activity during the evening and night tends to be at odds with the circadian rhythm.
- People can adjust somewhat to a schedule that involves evening or night work, but some people can adjust better than others.
- A permanent night schedule permits more adjustment than a rotating shift. One implication of this is that in situations in which the cost of an error may be extremely high (e.g., in a large chemical plant), a permanent shift system

should be used if at all possible (Folkard & Monk, 1979).
- Rotating shift work and regular evening and night shifts tend to hinder the nonwork activities of many people, although such schedules can also facilitate some such activities for some individuals.
- Because of individual differences in opinions about shift work, it seems desirable that individuals be given their preference for shift work when this is feasible.

Rest Periods

In considering rest periods we need to differentiate different types of work, because of the differences in their relevant criteria. Here, we discuss rest periods for the following: general physical work; psychomotor work; monitoring tasks; and light and sedentary work.

Rest for general physical work. Some types of light physical work activities can be carried out over the usual 8-hour work period without physical impairment to the individual or reduction in work output. However, the energy requirements of heavier work can result in physical impairment or reduction in work output. The typical estimates of the acceptable limits of energy expenditures for a work day range from 2000 to 2500 kcal/day (averaging about 4.0 to 5.0 kcal/min) (McCormick & Sanders, 1982). If the work requirements are well below, say, the 4.0 kcal/min limit a person in good physical condition could continue the work over a work day without rest. But if the energy requirements are higher, rest periods should be provided. In general, the rest periods should be scheduled to minimize the accumulation of physiological stress. Perhaps the most objective way of doing this is to use physiological measures as guidelines, as proposed by Davis, Faulkner, and Miller (1969). They compared the effects on heart rate of two different rest breaks (one for 2 minutes, the other for 7 minutes) interspersed between 10-minute work periods of a lifting task. The heart-rate

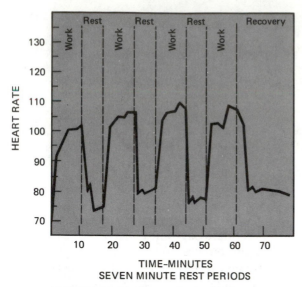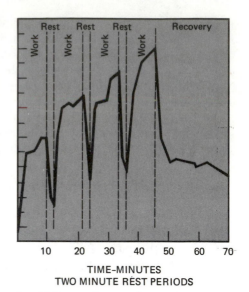

FIGURE 20.12 Comparison of heart-rate patterns for a lifting task carried out under 2-minute and 7-minute rest-break schedules. The 2-minute break is clearly inadequate in that it permits continued increase in the heart rate during successive work periods. (From Davis, Faulkner, & Miller, 1969, Figures 2 and 3.)

patterns for these two rest-break schedules are shown in Figure 20.12. Note that the 7-minute rest breaks kept the heart rate fairly steady, as contrasted with the 2-minute schedule. If it is not feasible to measure physiological conditions, such as heart rate, to use as the basis for scheduling rest breaks—for example, in the case of heavy physical work—it may well be that the workers should be encouraged to take rest breaks when they feel they need them.

Rest periods for psychomotor work. Most types of psychomotor work (as repetitive assembly work) involves the use of certain muscle groups. If the rate of contraction is slow enough, the work can be continued without complications. But at higher rates a muscle group can become physiologically fatigued, even to the point that it can no longer function. One procedure for measuring the activity of local muscle groups (and of their muscular fatigue) is by the use of electromyographic recordings (EMG) (which were il-

lustrated in Figure 17.1 in Chapter 17). If there are indications of cumulative fatigue, rest periods should be provided to minimize it.

Rest periods for monitoring tasks. Some types of jobs require monitoring one or more displays, usually to identify a change in the displayed information. (The stereotypical monitoring task is watching a radar scope for possible targets such as invading aircraft.) In a sense, the most demanding monitoring tasks involve a single display, in which the changes (the "signals") to be observed seldom occur. In such tasks attention tends to wane after 20 to 30 minutes, which sometimes results in failure to identify signals that do occur. People simply are not very good at performing such tasks. If the detection of the signals is critical in such circumstances, operators should be given rest periods or changes of duty after 20 to 30 minutes. If the signals to be detected occur rather frequently, or if the operator is kept more active by monitoring a variety of displays or with other related duties, monitoring sessions can probably be more extended. In other words, more frequent signals to respond to, or more activity of other types, helps to prevent lag of attention.

Rest periods for light and sedentary tasks. There is no clearly evident physiological basis for change in work performance over the work period for these types of tasks. Scheduling rest periods for such work is usually based on "boredom," "fatigue," and other "affective" reactions. Hard data about such reactions are sparse, but some are reported by Nelson and Bartley (1968) on the basis of a survey of seventy-five female office workers. These women were asked to report, for the hours of each half day of each work day, the hour when they felt "most tired," "most bored," and "most rested." Figure 20.13 summarizes the results. Note that the first hour is a period in which work demands are easily

met by most workers (as shown by the high percentage who reported feeling most "rested"), but that some workers actually reported this as the period in which they were most "tired." At the tag end of the morning there was an upswing in the percentages who reported "most tired" and "most bored." The early afternoon had the highest percentage responding "most rested," and end-of-the-day increases occurred in the "most-tired" and "most-bored" categories.

Data from other studies indicate that the greatest feelings of "fatigue" tend to occur during the fourth and eighth hours of the 8-hour work shift, which tends to jibe with the results shown in Figure 20.13 for the "most-tired" and "most-bored" responses.

Although there is limited evidence available about the effects of rest periods on light and sedentary work, the bits and pieces of evidence that are available suggest that rest

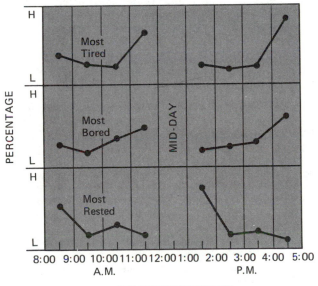

FIGURE 20.13 Percentage of female office workers reporting hours during each half day when they felt most tired, bored, or rested. Data points are plotted at midpoints of the hours. (Adapted from Nelson & Bartley, 1968, Figure 1.)

periods typically do not reduce output (even though there is less total time worked), and in fact in some instances tend to increase total work output. It is probable, though unconfirmed, that for light and sedentary jobs, the possible benefits from rest periods are more from "psychological" factors, such as alleviation from boredom or some vague desire for a change, than from any significant change in physical or physiological conditions.

DISCUSSION OF WORKING CONDITIONS

Although working conditions in many countries have improved over recent decades, the conditions for some workers are still not what they should be—either in terms of the effectiveness of the work itself or the health and welfare of the workers. Thus, working conditions should be a continuing concern for management. A special aspect of such concern should be those work situations in which various combinations of adverse conditions exist, such as heat, long hours of work, and noise.

REFERENCES

ASHRAE handbook, 1981 fundamentals (1981). Atlanta, Ga.: American Society of Heating, Refrigerating and Air-Conditioning Engineers.

Beshir, M. Y., El-Sabagh, A. S., & El-Nawawi, M. A. (1981). Time on task effect on tracking performance under heat stress. *Ergonomics,* 24(2), 95–102.

Blackwell, H. R. (June 1959). Development and use of a quantitative method for specification of interior illumination levels. *Illumination Engineering,* 54(6), 317–353.

Blackwell, H. R. (October 1972). *A human factors approach to lighting recommendations and standards.* Proceedings of the Sixteenth Annual Meeting of the Human Factors Society. Santa Monica, Calif.: The Human Factors Society.

Breithaupt, H., Hildebrandt, G., Döhre, D.,

Josch, R., Sieber, U., & Werner, M. (1978). Tolerance to shift of sleep, as related to the individual's circadian phase position. *Ergonomics,* 21(10), 767–774.

Broadbent, D. (1979). Human performance and noise. In C. Harris (Ed.), *Handbook of noise control.* New York: McGraw-Hill.

Clark, R. E. (February 1961). *The limiting hand skin temperature for unaffected manual performance in the cold.* Natick, Mass.: Quartermaster Research and Engineering Command (Tech. Rep. EP–147).

Cohen, A. (September 1972). *The role of psychology in improving worker safety and health under the Occupational Safety and Health Act.* Paper given at the meetings of the American Psychological Association, Honolulu, Hawaii.

Davis, H. L., Faulkner, T. A., & Miller, C. I. (1969). Work physiology. *Human Factors,* 11(2), 157–166.

Dukes-Dobos, F., & Henschel, A. (1971). *The modification of the WBGT index for establishing permissible heat exposure limits in occupational work.* Washington, D. C.: U. S. Public Health Service, ROSH, TR–69.

Dunham, R. B., & Hawk, D. A. (1977). The four-day/forty-hour week: Who wants it? *Academy of Management Journal,* 20(4), 656–668.

Federal Register, May 29, 1971, Vol. 36, No. 105.

Fine, B. J., & Kobrick, J. L. (1978). Effects of altitude and heat on complex cognitive tasks. *Human Factors,* 20(1), 115–122.

Folkard, S., & Monk, T. H. (1979). Shiftwork and performance. *Human Factors,* 21(4), 483–492.

Fottler, M. D. (1977). Employee acceptance of a four-day work week. *Academy of Management Journal,* 20(4), 656–668.

Gawron, V. J. (1982). Performance effects of noise intensity, psychological set, and task type and complexity. *Human Factors,* 24(2), 225–243.

Golembiewski, R. T., & Proehl, C. W., Jr. (October 1978). A survey of the empirical literature on flexible workhours: Character and consequences of a major innovation. *The Academy of Management Review,* 3(4), 837–853.

Goodale, J. L., & Aagaard, A. K. (1975). Factors relating to varying reactions to the 4-day work week. *Journal of Applied Psychology,* 60(1), 33–38.

Herbert, A. (1983). The influence of shift work on leisure activities: A study with repeated measurement. *Ergonomics,* 26(6), 565–574.

Hockey, G. (1978). Effects of noise on human work efficiency. In D. May (Ed.), *Handbook of noise assessment*. New York: Van Nostrand Reinhold.

IES lighting handbook, application volume (1981). New York. Illuminating Engineering Society of North America, 1981.

IES lighting handbook, reference volume (1981). New York: Illuminating Engineering Society of North America.

IES Nomenclature Committee (1979). *Proposed American national standard nomenclature and definitions for illuminating engineering* (prosposed revision of 27.1R 1973). *Journal of the Illuminating Engineering Society, 9*(1), 2–46.

Kossoris, M. D., Kohler, R. F., and others (1947). *Hours of work and output*. Washington, D.C.: U.S. Department of Labor, Bureau of Labor Statistics, Bulletin No. 917.

LaBenz, P., Cohen, A., & Pearson, B. (March–April 1967). A noise and hearing survey of earthmoving equipment operators. *American Industrial Hygiene Association Journal, 28*, 117–128.

McCormick, E. J., & Sanders, M. S. (1982). *Human factors in engineering and design*. New York: McGraw-Hill.

Nelson, T. M., & Bartley, S. H. (1968). The pattern of personal response arising during the office work day. *Occupational Psychology, 42*(1), 77–83.

Peacock, B., Glube, R., Miller, M., & Cline, P. (1983). Police officers' responses to 8 and 12 hour shift schedules. *Ergonomics, 26*(5), 479–493.

Peterson, A. P. G. (1980). *Handbook of noise measurement* (9th ed.). Concord, Mass.: GenRad, Inc.

Poor, R. (Ed.) (1973). *Four days forty hours*. New York: Mentor.

Ramsey, J. D. (1978). Abbreviated guidelines for heat stress exposure. *American Industrial Hygiene Association Journal, 39*, 491–495.

Ramsey, J. D., & Chai, C. P. (1983). Inherent variability in heat-stress decision rules. *Ergonomics, 26*(5), 495–504.

Smith, M. J., Colligan, M. J., & Tasto, D. (1982). Health and safety consequences of shift work in the food processing industry. *Ergonomics, 25*(2), 133–144.

Stevens, S. S. (February 1972). Perceived level of noise by Mark VII and decibels (E). *Journal of the Acoustical Society of America, 51*(2, Part 2), 575–601.

Tanaka, M., Tochihara, Y., Yamazaki, S., Ohnaka, T., & Yoshida, K. (1983). Thermal reaction and manual performance during cold exposure while wearing cold-protective clothing. *Ergonomics, 26*(2), 141–149.

Tilley, A. J., Wilkinson, R. J., Warren, P. S. G., Watson, W. B., & Drud, M. (1982). The sleep and performance of shift workers. *Human Factors, 24*(6), 629–641.

Wedderburn, A. A. I. (1978). Some suggestions for increasing the usefulness of psychological and sociological studies of shiftwork. *Ergonomics, 21*(10), 827–833.

Wing, J. F. (September 1965). *A review of the effects of high ambient temperature on mental performance* (Tech. Rep. AMRL–TR–65–102). USAF, Aerospace Medical Research Laboratories, Wright-Patterson Air Force Base.

21

Accidents and Safety

Dramatic improvement of safety in industry has occurred in the United States and in many other countries over the past half-century or century. Such evidence is in the reduction of death rates, injury-frequency rates, and injury-severity rates (National Safety Council, 1980). But such improvements should not bring a sigh of relief, because the human and economic costs of accidents and injuries are still of major proportions. Accidents and safety represent a logical concern of the various branches of psychology that deal with human beings in industry: industrial-organizational psychology, human-factors psychology, and clinical psychology.

DEFINITIONS

The term *accident* has been used with various shades of meanings. For certain purposes the

National Safety Council considers an accident to be "any unexpected event that interrupts or interferes with the orderly progress of the production activity or process." In this frame of reference, an accident may cause damage to equipment or materials or it may delay production, without resulting in an injury or fatality. For our purposes, however, we generally consider accidents to be events in which injuries or fatalities do occur.

Most countries have procedures for recording and reporting accidents. In the United States, the Occupational Safety and Health Act of 1970 provides for reporting injuries and illnesses that are:

- Fatalities;
- Lost work day cases (these are sometimes called disabling injuries);
- Nonfatal cases that do not involve lost work days (these cases result in transfers to other jobs or termination of employment, or they require medical treatment other than first aid).

THE "CAUSES" OF ACCIDENTS

The objective of accident research is to ferret out data that can be used as the basis for taking action which will reduce the possibilities of subsequent accidents. Thus, determining the "causes" of accidents is very important. The "causes" of accidents are sometimes attributed to some device or material that is involved (such as a punch press or an electric wire) or to some event (such as falling). Such information, however, contributes little to "explaining" the circumstances and behaviors that contribute to accident occurrences. Unfortunately, the basic causes of accidents are very elusive, so we usually have to deal largely with empirical relationships between possible relevant variables and accidents.

In this regard one can hypothesize (with substantial confidence) that accidents are the consequence of two classes of variables: *situational* and/or *individual*. Before discussing these further, however, we present a model of the accident phenomenon.

A MODEL OF THE ACCIDENT PHENOMENON

Various models have been set forth as frameworks for viewing the behavioral events that lead up to accidents. One such model, based in part on the one presented by Ramsey (1978), is shown in Figure 21.1. This shows the hypothesized stages in the occurrence or avoidance of accidents on the part of individuals in a potentially hazardous situation. The first stages deal with the *perception* and *cognition* of the hazard. Failure to perceive and recognize the hazard typically leads to unsafe behavior, although in some instances a person might happen to make a decision that leads to safe behavior. At the *decision-making stage* (following perception and cognition), the individual can make a decision to try to avoid an accident, or, conversely, to take whatever risk is implied.

If the individual decides to take action to minimize the risks of an accident—and decides to take an action that would reduce such risks—the next stage depends on the person's *ability* to take action. The fulfillment of this sequence typically would result in the execution of some form of "safe" behavior. Failure to fulfill these stages typically would result in some form of "unsafe" behavior. But then the factor of "chance" enters the picture. In one sense there is no such thing as chance, because each event has some precipitating circumstances. The term *chance* can then be thought of as applying to events we cannot predict. Such unpredictable circumstances (i.e., "chance") certainly play their part in causing or avoiding accidents. Thus, even "safe" behavior might still not prevent an accident, and "unsafe" behavior might still avoid an accident.

The distinction between situational and individual variables as these can influence accident occurrences is evident in Ramsey's model. The type of work situation to which individuals are "exposed" obviously influences the probability of accidents because of variations in the risks associated with different situations. In turn, the following stages in the model are, of course, associated with individuals. (The list of attributes and characteristics on the right-hand side of the model is discussed later.)

SITUATIONAL FACTORS IN ACCIDENT OCCURRENCE

The accident liability rates of different work situations can be influenced by such factors as: the nature of the job activities; the presence or use of potentially accident-producing agents (such as machinery, tools, moving objects, chemicals, etc.); the work methods; en-

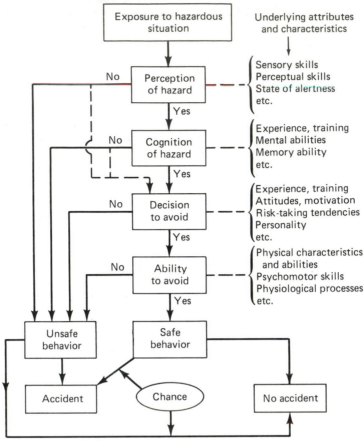

FIGURE 21.1 Sequential model representing various stages in the occurrence or avoidance of accidents in a potentially hazardous situation. At the right are examples of the human attributes and characteristics that underlie the perception, cognition, decision, and ability stages. (Adapted in part from Ramsey, 1978.)

vironmental circumstances (such as slippery floors, high temperature, etc.); the presence and use of protective clothing and gear; and work schedules. A few of these aspects are discussed briefly here.

Job Factors

One of the important situational variables is the job itself. Following are some indications of differences in accident rates for certain jobs in construction work in England (Pimble & O'Toole, 1982). These are ex-

pressed as the rate per 1000 persons at risk per year:

JOB	ACCIDENT RATE
Carpenters, joiners	39
Roofing slaters	44
Painters	19
Plumbers	83
Scaffolders	170
Gangers, foremen	12
Other light occupations	114

Such differences can arise from the variations in the nature of the work involved, the tools and equipment used, the features of the work situation involved, and so on.

Work Schedule

On the basis of a review of accident research, Surry (1968) found the following tendencies in accident rates in some situations during the day and night schedules:

Day workers: Increase from beginning of morning work period with peak during latter part of the morning, with a drop before lunch; low rate immediately after lunch with peak in midafternoon, with subsequent decline or maintenance of midafternoon level.

Night workers: High at beginning of shift, followed by drop; slight increase after work break and then decline.

Although various "explanations" have been offered for such patterns, as yet no clear-cut reasons have been discovered. Incidentally, these particular patterns are by no means universal; other patterns occur in other situations. But whatever pattern exists in any given situation, it does characterize the accident liabilities during the work period.

Atmospheric Conditions

In certain studies of atmospheric conditions, a ∪ shaped form of curve has been found to characterize the relationship between temperature and accidents; the accident rate is lowest near an "optimum" temperature and higher in lower and higher temperatures (Surry, 1968). The optimum temperature in any given circumstance depends on the nature of the task work, the clothing worn, the degree of acclimatization of the workers, and even the age of the individuals. In one study of British industrial workers to which Surry refers, the optimum temperature was in the upper 60s.

INDIVIDUAL DIFFERENCES IN ACCIDENT OCCURRENCE

The extent to which individuals contribute to the occurrence—or avoidance—of accidents is influenced by the extent to which their work activities tend to be "safe" behaviors or "unsafe" behaviors. Referring back to the model in Figure 21.1 we can hypothesize that the nature of work behaviors (whether safe or unsafe) would depend on the underlying human attributes or characteristics associated with each of the four "stages" of the model that lead up to the work behavior (perception, cognition, decision, and ability). Figure 21.1 lists examples of some attributes or characteristics associated with each of these stages.

Unsafe Behaviors and Accident Liability

It seems reasonable to believe that errors in the perception, cognition, and decision stages, or lack of relevant ability, would contribute to unsafe behaviors, and conversely that the fulfillment of these stages would contribute to safe behaviors. However, we would feel more comfortable if we had evidence to support this assumption. Some such evidence comes from the results of a study of industrial workers by Whitlock, Clouse, and Spencer (1963). Using the critical incident technique, the supervisors of 350 employees recorded the "unsafe behaviors" of the employees for 8 months. The number of unsafe behaviors served as an "accident-behavior" score for each individual. These scores, in turn, were correlated with injuries recorded during the 8-month period and for as long as 5 years after the study. The correlations, for 284 employees for whom injury records were available for various periods of time, were as follows:

Time period: (years)	1	2	3	4	5
Correlation:	.35	.49	.29	.51	.56

Additional evidence comes from a survey conducted in nineteen production plants (Edwards & Hahn, 1980). By a procedure we need not describe, these researchers obtained reports from 3330 workers of the "unsafe acts and conditions" they had observed. They then developed a summated index of these for each of the nineteen plants. In turn, these indexes were correlated with records of actual accidents in the plants. The correlation for a few of the unsafe acts and conditions were as follows:

UNSAFE ACT OR CONDITION	CORRELATION WITH ACCIDENTS
Handling unsafe material unsafely	.69
Workers did not understand how to do job	.62
Horseplay during work	.51
Climbing on or over moving equipment	.56
Loading or feeding material too fast	.46
Waste or scrap left in work area	.77
Using equipment without permission	.90

On the basis of studies such as these we must thus accept the assumption that unsafe behaviors are in fact related to accident occurrence. As we contemplate the unsafe behaviors of individuals, however, we run up against these three questions:

1. Are there *significant differences* among people in their frequency of unsafe behaviors and of accidents *within* specific work situations?
2. Is there such a thing as generalized accident proneness?
3. What specific personal factors (if any) are related to accident occurrence (or avoidance)?

Unsafe Behavior and Accidents within Specific Situations

The first of the preceding three questions deals with the frequency of unsafe behavior and accidents involving individuals within specific work situations in which the liability is the same for all individuals. There are indeed differences in the frequency of accidents among individuals within such situations. The critical question, however, is whether there are some individuals who have significantly *more* accidents than can be attributed to chance. The accident literature is strewn with instances in which individuals with above-average accident records have been erroneously labeled as "accident prone" when, in fact, their accident rates might be within chance expectations. In connection with chance distributions (versus statistically significant differences) we can draw an analogy with the tossing of coins. If 1000 individuals were each to toss ten coins, the average number of heads per person would be very close to five. But the individuals would vary in the number of heads from very few (perhaps none) to many (perhaps ten). If we simply identify those who tossed heads eight or more times, and call these "heads-prone," we would be making the same error that is made when individuals who have more than the average number of accidents for one period of time are called "accident-prone."

Given any specified number of individuals (with equal liability) and a specified number of accidents, it is possible to determine, statistically, the "expected" distribution of accidents *if* they were distributed by chance. Such an expected distribution is illustrated in Figure 21.2, which shows the expected distribution of 1470 minor injuries suffered by 1060 individuals over a specified period of time. From this we can see (in the center panel) that fifty-one individuals (42 + 6 + 3) would be *expected* (by chance) to have four or more accidents, even though the average

NUMBER OF ACCIDENTS (N)	NUMBER OF MEN SUFFERING N ACCIDENTS	TOTAL NUMBER OF ACCIDENTS
0	266	0
1	368	368
2	256	512
3	119	357
4	42	168
5	6	30
6 or more	3	35

(Bracket annotations: men suffering 3 or more accidents = 170 (16%); 4 or more = 51; men with 1 or more accidents = 75%; total accidents 600 (40%); 100%.)

FIGURE 21.2 Estimated "chance" distribution of 1470 accidents among 1060 individuals, all equally liable (From Froggatt & Smiley, 1964, as adapted by Surry, 1968, Table B.4, p. 189.)

would be only 1.4. We can see that 170 individuals (16%) would be expected (by chance) to have 600 (40%) of the accidents (center and right-hand panels).

Granting that chance factors can (and typically do) result in some people having more accidents than others, there are indeed specific situations in which some individuals have more accidents that can reasonably be attributed to chance. To determine if some individuals do have more accidents than can be attributed to chance, however, one needs to carry out some type of statistical analysis. One procedure is to compare the *actual* distribution of accidents (for people with similar liability) with the (chance) *expected* distribution (such as the expected distribution shown in Figure 21.2). If the actual distribution differs significantly from the expected distribution, it can then be inferred that some individuals do in fact have more accidents than can be accounted for by chance. This is illustrated by a hypothetical example in Figure 21.3. The expected distribution in that figure is the one represented in Figure 21.2, but the "actual" distribution is hypothetical and is exaggerated in order to illustrate the

point. The shaded area between the two curves represents the extent to which the actual distribution stretches beyond the expected distribution and thus indicates the probable influence of individual factors on accident occurrence.

Another statistical procedure that can be used is to compare the number of accidents of individuals over time, such as for two periods of time. Such correlations, of course, would have to be statistically significant to demonstrate the comparison.

Statistical evidence developed by either of these (or other) methods can support the hypothesis of what we call *accident repetitiveness* in the situation—that is, the systematic tendency for some individuals to have more accidents than can be attributed to chance. (Note that we are avoiding the term *accident proneness*.)

Evidence of accident repetitiveness. Such statistically confirmed evidence has been presented for many different jobs and other situations, indicating that—in such circumstances—there is a tendency for individuals to maintain their accident rates over time. In a study by one of the present authors, an in-

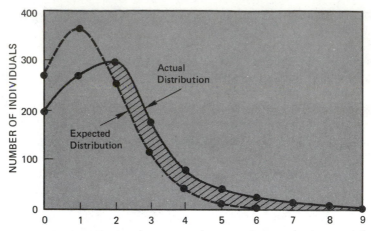

FIGURE 21.3 Comparison of an expected (chance) distribution of 1470 accidents (based on data in Figure 21.2) and a hypothetical actual distribution to illustrate tendency toward accident repetitiveness on the part of some individuals (illustrated by the lined area).

jury index was derived for employees on three jobs. This index, based on the frequency of accidents per 1000 hours worked, was derived separately from two 6-month periods, and these were then correlated. The correlations were as follows:

JOB	CORRELATION
Drill press	.86
Assembler	.88
Machine operator	.74

Further examples come from the study by Whitlock et al. (1963) mentioned before. The correlation between the numbers of unsafe behaviors between the odd-numbered weeks and the even-numbered weeks for the 8-month period was .74. (The corresponding correlation for a sample of workers in a chemical plant was .93.) In turn, correlations of numbers of injuries for odd-numbered months and even-numbered months were also derived; these were computed separately for personnel for whom data were available for the different periods of time. The result-

ing correlations were .63 for 1 year of data; .58 for 2 years; .75 for 3 years; .66 for 4 years; and .67 for 5 years.

Thus, there is substantial evidence for at least certain work situations that people tend to maintain their own rates of unsafe behavior and accidents over time, regardless of whether these rates are high, average, or low. Keep in mind that this pattern is for individuals *within* individual work situations, in which the accident liability is the same for all workers.

Accident Proneness

As we shift to the discussion of unsafe behaviors and accidents *across* situations, we can no longer stave off a discussion of the notion of generalized accident proneness. There are two disparate interpretations of the term *accident proneness*. One interpretation implies the existence of particular personal qualities which predispose the individual—"a personality type"—toward having repeated accidents, in whatever circumstance that person finds himself. The evidence in support of this concept of accident proneness is not conclusive. Thus, the use of the term in this sense should probably be avoided.

The second interpretation of accident proneness is essentially a statistical concept, characterized by the tendency for some people to be accident repeaters in virtually any situation—that is, to have more accidents in general than can be attributed to chance. This interpretation is then essentially "descriptive." It does not "explain" the tendency. At present there is no unequivocal evidence to confirm the notion that there are people who are "accident repeaters" in the sense that they tend to have high accident rates in all kinds of situations. (Although such evidence is not now available, future evidence may support this contention.) There is evidence, however, that there are accident repeaters *within* specific types of work situations.

Thus, if the term accident proneness is used, it should be considered as being situational—that is, as being applicable to those specific types of work situations in which there is statistical evidence of accident repetitiveness.

Specific Personal Factors Related to Accidents

In the types of situations in which accident repetitiveness does exist, the most logical explanation for it is based on the following premises:

- That "safe" (versus "unsafe") work behaviors in different types of work situations depend on various combinations of the four sequential stages that precede the behavior (perception, cognition, decision, ability).
- That there are variations across work situations in the specific aspects of perception, cognition, decision, and ability that are relevant to safe (or unsafe) behavior.
- That specific types of behavior based on these variations, in turn, depend on certain underlying human attributes or characteristics. (For example, visual skills may be more important to the perceptual function of some jobs than other jobs; the execution of physical activities of some jobs may depend very much on physical strength, and for other jobs more on reaction time.)

A few examples can illustrate the range of personal variables that have been found to be related to the accident rates of individuals in certain types of work situations.

Vision. Jobs vary, of course, in their dependence on various types and degrees of visual skills in connection with the "perceptual" stage shown in the model in Figure 21.1. The most extensive research relating to the vision of workers is that carried out some years ago by Dr. Joseph Tiffin of Purdue University. That research resulted in the establishment of visual standards for various jobs and job families, as discussed in Chapter 9. Substantial evidence from that program indicated that on many jobs those persons who did not meet the visual standards had significantly higher accident rates than those who did meet such standards. One example of these results is shown in Figure 21.4.

Perceptual style. Although for some jobs the performance at the perceptual stage may depend very much on vision, for other jobs there may be greater dependence on perceptual skills of some type. For example, some interesting research has been carried out with what is referred to as perceptual style, especially as related to the concept of field dependence versus field independence. This construct is viewed as a continuum along which individuals may be differentiated with respect to their perceptual abilities to discriminate figures in a complex background (or to "pull" a figure from an embedded context). Those who do not do this well are referred to as field dependent (that is, the visual "field" somehow inhibits their perception of the "embedded figure" in the field); those who are better at "seeing" a figure in an

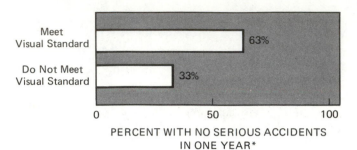

FIGURE 21.4 Vision in relation to serious accidents among 104 paper-machine operators. *A "serious" accident is one requiring the attention of the plant physician.

embedded background are referred to as field-*in*dependent.

This construct has been used especially in vehicle-driving situations. In a laboratory experiment with subjects using a driving simulator, for example, Barrett and Thornton (1968) found that persons who were field independent were able to decelerate more rapidly in an "emergency" situation that those who were field dependent. In addition, in an analysis of the accident records of vehicle drivers over a period of 3 years, Harano (1969) found that field-independent drivers had better accident records than field-dependent individuals.

From a review of relevant studies of perceptual style Goodenough (1976) stated that evidence suggested that field-dependent drivers do not quickly recognize developing hazards, are slower in responding to embedded road signs, have difficulty in learning to control skidding vehicles, and fail to drive defensively in high-speed traffic. More data are necessary to nail down the relevance of perceptual style to vehicular driving, but the current cues suggest that this may be important to minimizing vehicular accidents.

Perceptual-motor relationships. On the basis of an early study of accidents Drake (1940) postulated that the relationship between perceptual speed and motor speed may be a factor in the accident liabilities of individuals. Drake describes the relationship as follows: "In other words, the person who reacts quicker than he can perceive is more likely to have accidents than is the person who can perceive quicker than he can react."

Subsequently, Babarik (1968) tested this hypothesis with taxi drivers, specifically with regard to emergency stops made when cars ahead came to abrupt stops. Babarik argued that drivers who make up for long "initiation" time with fast movements (that is, have short movement times and thus stop their vehicles more abruptly after applying the brake) would be expected to have more rear-end accidents than drivers who—in the same time—initiate movements more rapidly but make less abrupt stopping movements. A ratio of these was found to be significantly related to rear-end accidents with a sample of 104 taxi drivers. Those with the most markedly different such ratios were referred to as having "desynchronizing" reaction patterns, whereas the others were referred to as "normal." The results are summarized briefly here, in particular showing the percentage of drivers in these two groups who had two or more rear-end accidents.

REACTION-PATTERN GROUP	DRIVERS WITH TWO OR MORE REAR-END ACCIDENTS
Normal	10 percent
Desynchronizing	38 percent

Although certain other findings from this study left the water a bit murky, these results do tend to confirm Drake's perceptual-motor hypothesis. But here, again, let us emphasize that certain personal variables may be related to accident occurrence in some work situations but not in others—depending on the relevance of the variable to the specfic work-related behaviors involved.

Personal factors. Although there is no strong evidence to support the hypothesis that people of a particular "personality type" are "accident prone," personal factors have been related to accident frequency in some specific work situations. For example, Kunce (1967) derived a certain combination of scores based on the Strong Vocational Interest Blank (SVIB) that he referred to as an "accident-prone" index. Scores based on this index were related to accident rates of employees in a food-processing plant, as shown in Figure 21.5.

Adjustive behavior. As indicated in the accident-sequence model (Figure 21.1), decisions in hazardous situations are in part influenced by people's attitudes. In this regard McGlade (1970) proposed the construct of *adjustive behavior* as being conducive to safe work behavior. He defined this construct

as follows: *Consistent* successful performance of an activity, in the face of possible unplanned interruptions, is *adjustive* behavior leading to safe performance. Expressed another way, such behavior, according to McGlade (1970), is the capacity to "mesh" a person's "abilities, skills, and tasks into a meaningful whole which brings about successful performance of an activity in virtually all situations and under almost all conditions."

In a sense, adjustive behavior can be viewed as a consistent predisposition toward safe behavior—essentially an attitude. Persons with such a predisposition presumably would make decisions that would generally result in safe behaviors.

Although McGlade's construct of adjustive behavior still needs to be considered as a hypothetical formulation, it offers a potentially intriguing frame of reference for viewing the decision aspects of behavior in hazardous situations. Perhaps the attitude implied by the construct (a predisposition toward safe behavior) might ultimately be nailed down as a common denominator related to safe behavior on an across-the-board basis in various types of work (perhaps even the basis for a generalized form of accident proneness).

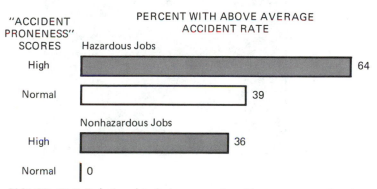

FIGURE 21.5 Relationship between an "accident-proneness" index (based on the Strong Vocational Interest Blank) and accident rates of sixty-two male employees on jobs rated hazardous and nonhazardous in a food-processing plant. (Adapted from Kunce, 1967.)

Experience. As one might expect, work experience tends to minimize the likelihood of accidents. Experience can have its impact primarily on the behaviors involved in the cognitive, decision, and ability stages of the basic model shown in Figure 21.1. Some data to illustrate the relevance of experience come from an analysis of accident records of 776 enlisted personnel in the U.S. Navy on fifteen destroyer-type ships (Butler & Jones, 1979). The jobs involved were in the deck and engineering divisions of the ships. Following is a list of months of service of those having no accidents, or one, or more than one:

	AVERAGE MONTHS OF SERVICE OF THOSE HAVING		
DIVISION	NO ACCIDENTS	ONE	TWO OR MORE
Deck	43	27	21
Engineering	60	47	35

Although experienced personnel generally tend to have lower accident rates than those with limited experience, this is not a universal pattern.

Age. Advanced age can bring about deterioration in several human attributes, such as vision and certain physical abilities. On the other hand, the experience that accompanies age can contribute to decisions that result in safer work behavior. (For some individuals, advanced age can, of course, affect the decision processes.) In general, age could be expected to have different kinds of effects on accident rates, depending on the situation.

The consolidated results of three age-injury surveys carried out by the California Division of Labor Statistics and Research (1961, 1966, 1969) covering over 450,000 males in the labor force are shown in Figure 21.6. Notice the sharp rise in accidents, which peaks around age 20, then subsequently declines and then dips sharply in the 60- to 70-year range. These data include workers on different types of jobs, so, in part, they may reflect differences in accident liability. Perhaps very young and older workers might have been placed in jobs not as hazardous as

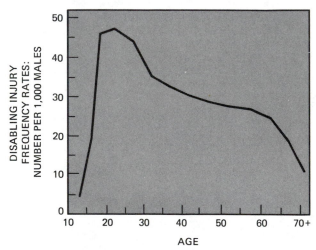

FIGURE 21.6 Age profile of disabling-injury frequency rates per 1000 males in the civilian labor force, as based on surveys of the California labor force. (From Gordon, Akman, & Brooks, 1971, p. 211, based on California work-injury surveys.)

those on which men in their 20s were placed. Despite this possible source of distortion, however, the impression remains that accident rates tend to be associated with age across a variety of jobs in the labor market, and that the most suspectible ages are the early 20s.

But we need to be cautious in assuming that this is a broad, universal pattern. A different pattern, for example, is shown in Figure 21.7. This is a statistically generalized curve of the relationship between age and "days out" for workers in Maine sawmills (Cooke & Blumenstock, 1979). ("Days out" is, in effect, an index of severity, not frequency, of accidents.) This curve shows high rates for young and old workers, with the dip being in the late 40s. The postulated explanation is: The younger workers are presumably more ignorant of work hazards (because of limited experience) and are less attentive; and mature, married men with families tend to be more cautious and responsible in their work behavior and therefore are more likely to avoid accidents.

The form of the relationship for Maine sawmill workers (Figure 21.7) is obviously very

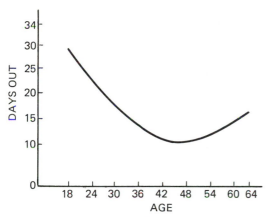

FIGURE 21.7 A statistically generalized curve of the relationship between age and "days out" of workers in Maine sawmills; "days out" is an index of accident severity. (From Cooke & Blumenstock, 1979, p. 119.)

different from that of the varied sample surveyed in California (Figure 21.6). Such a difference indicates that, at least for some jobs, the age-accident relationship may be situational—that it may depend on the nature of the work activities.

THE REDUCTION OF ACCIDENTS

From our previous discussion, it follows that efforts to reduce accidents must be in the direction of (1) reducing the liability of the situation or (2) minimizing the possible influence of any relevant personal factors. The wares of the safety engineers cover a spectrum of techniques, procedures, and guidelines directed toward reducing situational liability. In our discussion we touch on at least a few of the possible approaches to reducing accidents from the human-liability side of the coin, rather than from the situational side.

Personnel Selection and Placement

When it has been demonstrated that some personal factor is *significantly related* to accident frequency on a given job or in some other circumstance, it is then possible to select those individuals with characteristics associated with good accident records. Such an objective would be based on the personnel-selection procedures discussed in Chapters 7 through 11.

Safety Training

Safety-training programs are fairly common, especially with new employees and in some instances with current employees. In such training programs it is important to apply sound principles of learning, as discussed in Chapter 12. Following are some critical aspects of such training (adapted from Cohen, Smith, & Anger, 1979):

1. Stress the learning of safe behaviors as opposed to the unlearning of unsafe acts.
2. Provide for practice that insures the transfer of learned behavior to the real situation.
3. Provide frequent feedback during training.
4. Establish meaningful rewards for safe behaviors.

In connection with safety-training programs the National Safety Council (1980) ranks the communication media on a scale from concrete to abstract—the more concrete the method, the more effective it is. The ranking of the methods is as follows:

DO—Actual experience (most effective)
DO—Acting role
TELL AND SHOW—Demonstration
SHOW—Live on spot
SHOW—Display or exhibit
TELL AND SHOW—Sound film, TV
TELL—Lecture
SHOW—Charts
TELL—Recordings

One needs to accept such a ranking with a few grains of salt since the effectiveness of communications depends very much on the type of material to be communicated. Some safety-training material might best be transmitted by methods not near the top of such a list, but such a list can provide some general guidance in selecting training methods.

Training and feedback. The importance of feedback in training has been demonstrated time and again. In the specific context of safety training, Komaki and her associates (Komaki, Collins, & Penn, 1982; Komaki, Heinzmann, & Lawson, 1980) have investigated the effects of feedback in relation to the safety practices in several situations. In the investigations trained personnel observed specified types of worker behaviors and rated the behaviors as "safe" or "unsafe." On the basis of such observations a mean safety-level index was derived—specifically, the percentage of incidents performed safely divided by the total number of incidents observed.

In one study (Komaki et al., 1980) such observations were made in four sections of the vehicle-maintenance division of a large Western city during the five following periods (covering 45 weeks):

1. baseline (before training);
2. training only;
3. training and feedback;
4. training only; and
5. training and feedback.

The safety training consisted of 30- to 45-minute sessions during the regular work day. The feedback need not be described in detail, but included the posting of graphs showing the safety level before any training and during the preceding training session(s). Following are the safety-level indexes for the maintenance section for these periods:

PERIOD	SAFETY LEVEL
Baseline (no training)	49
Training only	61
Training and feedback	76
Training only	64
Training and feedback	75

The safety levels were higher for the training periods with feedback than for the training periods without feedback.

Somewhat similar results, reported from another study in a poultry-processing plant, are summarized here (Komaki et al., 1982):

PERIOD	SAFETY LEVEL			
	DEPT. 1	DEPT. 2	DEPT. 3	DEPT. 4
Baseline	78	63	79	72
Training only	83	66	84	90
Training plus feedback	95	85	92	96

Reinforcement

Reinforcement consists of some form of reward for particular types of behavior. In work situations rewards can be in the form of bonuses, promotions, feedback (as discussed before), praise (a form of social reinforcement), and special privileges (time off, preferred parking locations, etc.). An example of the use of praise in the safety context dealt with potential eye injuries in a shipyard with over 20,000 employees (Smith, Anger, & Uslan, 1978). The supervisors of five work groups were given special training in certain fundamentals of behavior modification. An important aspect of this training was focused on praising subordinates for wearing safety equipment such as safety goggles. Following are the eye-accident rates for the workers in these five groups as compared with thirty-nine other groups:

WORK GROUPS	EYE ACCIDENT RATES		
	BEFORE	AFTER	CHANGE
Experimental (5)	11.8	4.3	−7.5%
Control (39)	5.8	4.7	−1.2%

It seems that some form of reinforcement for safe-behavior practices can have a beneficial effect on such behavior. However, such reinforcement cannot be a one-time proposition. It needs to be continued, as implied by the results of the feedback studies just discussed.

Propaganda

Various forms of propaganda are used in many safety programs: posters, placards, handouts, and so on. Propaganda is an attempt to change the attitudes of people so they are more inclined to engage in safe behavior. Some approaches to propaganda, however, have not been effective in achieving such an objective. Although it is not appropriate here to discuss the specifics of research dealing with propaganda, we summarize the conclusions of an extensive review of such research by Sell (1977). Sell concludes that, to be effective, safety posters and other propaganda should:

1. Be specific to a particular task and situation.
2. Back up a training program.
3. Give a positive instruction.
4. Be placed close to where the desired action is to take place.
5. Build on existing attitudes and knowledge.
6. Emphasize nonsafety aspects.

In turn, they should *not:*

1. Involve horror (because this can bring in defense mechanisms in the people at whom the propaganda is aimed).
2. Be negative (because this can show the wrong way of acting).
3. Be general.

DISCUSSION

Accidents are such a pervasive aspect of life that it is unreasonable to expect that they can be eliminated from work situations, but it is reasonable to believe that they can be minimized. In general, the reduction of accident rates needs to be approached from two points of view. In the first place, efforts can be made to reduce the liability of work situations, as by improved design of work situations in terms of human-factors considerations and improved working conditions. In the second place, efforts can be directed toward minimizing the unsafe behaviors of individuals. Such an effort needs to be fortified with an understanding of the human processes that contribute to unsafe behaviors (and conversely to safe behaviors), and of human attributes and characteristics that underlie these processes. In addition, such efforts need to be fortified with relevant research regarding the approaches and programs that would be effective in reducing the unsafe behaviors of people.

REFERENCES

Babarik, P. 1968. Automobile accidents and driver reaction pattern. *Journal of Applied Psychology, 52*(1), 49–54.

Barrett, G. V., & Thornton, C. L. (1968). Relationship between perceptual style and driver reaction to an emergency situation. *Journal of Applied Psychology, 52*(2), 169–176.

Butler, M. C., & Jones, A. P. (1979). Perceived leader behavior, individual characteristics, and injury occurrence in hazardous work environments. *Journal of Applied Psychology, 64*(3), 299–304.

California work injuries, 1960, 1965, and 1968 (November 1961, December 1966, and September 1969). San Francisco: State of California, Department of Human Relations, Division of Labor Statistics and Research, Tables 16.

Cohen, A., Smith, M. J., & Anger, W. K. (1979). Self-protective measures against workplace hazards. *Journal of Safety Research, 11*(3), 121–131.

Cooke, W. N., & Blumenstock, M. W. (1979). The determinants of occupational injury severity: The case of Maine sawmills. *Journal of Safety Research, 11*(3), 115–119.

Drake, C. A. (1940). Accident proneness: A hypothesis. *Character and Personality, 8,* 335–341.

Edwards, D. S., & Hahn, C. P. (1980). A chance to happen. *Journal of Safety Research, 12*(2), 59–67.

Froggatt, P., & Smiley, J. A. (January 1964). The concept of accident proneness. *British Journal of Industrial Medicine, 21,* 1–12.

Goodenough, D. R. (1976). A review of individual differences in field dependence as a factor in auto safety. *Human Factors, 18*(1), 53–62.

Gordon, J. B., Akman, A., & Brooks, M. L. (1971). *Industrial accident statistics: A re-examination.* New York: Praeger.

Harano, R. M. (October 1969). *The relationship between field dependence and motor vehicle accident involvement.* Washington, D.C.: American Psychological Association, Experimental Publication System, Issue No. 2, Ms. No. 065B.

Komaki, J. L., Collins, R. L., & Penn, P. (1982). The role of performance antecedents and consequences in work motivation. *Journal of Applied Psychology, 67*(3) 334–340.

Komaki, J., Heinzmann, A. T., & Lawson, L. (1980). Effect of training and feedback: Component analysis of a behavioral safety program. *Journal of Applied Psychology, 65*(2), 261–270.

Kunce, J. T. (1967). Vocational interest and accident proneness. *Journal of Applied Psychology, 51*(3), 223–225.

McGlade, F. S. (1970). *Adjustive behavior and safe performance.* Springfield, Ill.: Charles C Thomas.

National Safety Council (1980). *Accident prevention manual for industrial operations: Administration and programs* (8th ed.). Chicago: National Safety Council.

Pimble, J., & O'Toole, S. (1982). Analysis of accident reports. *Ergonomics, 25*(11), 967–974.

Ramsey, J. D. (May 1978). *Ergonomic support of consumer product safety.* Paper presented at the American Industrial Hygiene Association Conference.

Sell, R. G. (1977). What does safety propaganda do for safety? A review. *Applied Ergonomics, 84,* 203–214.

Smith, M. J., Anger, W. K., & Uslan, S. S. (1978). Behavioral modification applied to occupational safety. *Journal of Safety Research, 10*(2), 87, 88.

Surry, J. (June 1968). *Industrial accident research: A human engineering approach.* Toronto: University of Toronto, Department of Industrial Engineering.

Whitlock, G. H., Clouse, R. J., & Spencer, W. F. (1963). Predicting accident proneness. *Personnel Psychology, 16*(1), 35–44.

APPENDIX A

Elementary Descriptive Statistics

DESCRIPTIVE VERSUS SAMPLING STATISTICS

Statistical methods have two purposes. One is to describe a body of data. This is done using *descriptive statistics*, which reduces a body of data by graphic methods, computational methods yielding numerical measures, and tabular methods. The sole aim of *descriptive statistics* is to reduce the original data to charts, graphs, averages, and the like, so that the facts concerning the data will be more apparent.

The second purpose of statistical methods is to enable experimenters to learn how safely they can generalize from *descriptive statistics* obtained from a sample. This approach is known as *sampling statistics*. It applies the mathematics of probability and is very important to industrial-organizational psychology.

This Appendix deals with only certain concepts of *descriptive statistics*, but the impor-

tance of *sampling statistics* should not be underestimated, and every serious student of industrial-organizational psychology should become familiar with these methods.

Descriptive statistics in industrial-organizational psychology are used to summarize various types of raw data, such as test scores, attitude measures, and criterion values.

GRAPHIC REPRESENTATION OF DATA

In discussing various types of descriptive statistics, let us us use as an example a set of data like that shown in Table A.1. These data represent the number of defects identified by each of sixty inspectors during a week.

Frequency Distribution

A frequency distribution shows the number of cases in each of various *class intervals*

TABLE A.1 Number of defects detected by each of sixty inspectors during 1 week of work

15	36	40	37	32	13	35	20	33	36	33	16	38	19	33	34	24
36	25	29	27	39	42	31	21	26	28	53	23	51	21	26	39	28
30	31	32	30	29	49	39	30	44	34	37	35	38	35	41	37	43
42	38	45	22	46	41	47	48	34								

of the value in question; in this case it would be the number of inspectors for each of the various class intervals of numbers of defects detected. The steps in constructing a frequency distribution are as follows:

1. Determine the range of the values in the raw data. Quickly glance through the data to determine the *highest* and the *lowest* values. The range is the difference between these values. For the sixty inspector records, the highest figure is 53 and the lowest is 13. The range is therefore 53 – 13 = 40.
2. If we find that the range of the data is large (that they are widely spread), it usually will be more convenient to group them by class intervals (abbreviated c.i.) with a range in each c.i. of more than 1 unit. A simple rule to help decide on the correct size of the c.i. is to divide

the range by 15 (because, on the average, this is the most desirable number of c.i.'s), and to take as the c.i. the whole number nearest to the quotient. In our problem, the range divided by 15 would be 40 ÷ 15 = 2.66. As 3 is the whole number nearest to 2.66, 3 would be the size of the c.i. to use.
3. Arrange the adjacent c.i.'s in a column, leaving a blank space immediately to the right of this column. The arrangements of the c.i.'s preparatory to constructing a frequency distribution are illustrated in the first column of Table A.2.
4. Place a tally mark for each value in the original list of raw data opposite the appropriate class interval. As the first value among the sixty listed in Table A.1 is 15, the first tally mark should be in the 15–17 c.i. The second value, 36, is represented by a tally mark in the 36–38 c.i. It is usually advisable to tally the fifth entry in each c.i. with a line across the preceding four tally

TABLE A.2 Illustration of data relating to a frequency distribution and of data used for computing the arithmetic mean and median

1	2	3	4	5	6	7	8
CLASS INTERVAL (c.i.)	TALLY MARKS	FREQUENCY (f)	CALCULATION OF PERCENTAGE	PERCENTAGE	d	fd	CUMULATIVE f
51–53	//	2	2/60 = .033	3	6	12	60
48–50	//	2	2/60 = .033	3	5	10	58
45–47	///	3	3/60 = .050	5	4	12	56
42–44	////	4	4/60 = .066	7	3	12	53
39–41	ЖHT /	6	6/60 = .100	10	2	12	49
36–38	ЖHT ////	9	9/60 = .150	15	1	9	43
33–35	ЖHT ////	9	9/60 = .150	15	0	0	34
30–32	ЖHT //	7	7/60 = .117	12	−1	−7	25
27–29	ЖHT	5	5/60 = .083	8	−2	−10	18
24–26	////	4	4/60 = .066	7	−3	−12	13
21–23	////	4	4/60 = .066	7	−4	−16	9
18–20	//	2	2/60 = .033	3	−5	−10	5
15–17	//	2	2/60 = .033	3	−6	−12	3
12–14	/	1	1/60 = .017	2	−7	−7	1
	Total =	60		100	$\Sigma fd =$	−7	

marks. When all the tallies have been made, they will appear as in column 2 of Table A.2. Column 3 simply reflects the count of the tally marks for each.

In some circustances it may be desirable to show the percentage of cases in each class interval instead of (or in addition to) the frequency. This may be done by dividing each *f* value (in the third column) by the total number of cases in the distribution. Each quotient thus obtained indicates the percentage of the total number of cases that fall in the respective c.i.'s These computations are shown in column 4 of Table A.2; the computed percentages are shown in column 5.

Frequency Polygon

A frequency polygon is a graphic representation of the frequency data—in this case, the data in column 3 of Table A.2. In making a frequency polygon, first lay off appropriate units on cross section or graph paper in such a manner that the midpoints of the c.i.'s can be plotted on the base line, as shown in Figure A.1, and the frequencies can be plotted on the vertical axis, as shown by the left-hand vertical scale of that figure. Then place a dot

representing each frequency and connect these dots as shown in the figure. When it is desirable to compare a frequency polygon with other polygons, plot the *percentages* (as given in column 5 of Table A.2) rather than the actual *frequencies* (as shown in column 3). Such a polygon would have the same form as that based on frequencies, but the vertical scale would be shown as percentages, as illustrated by the right-hand vertical scale of Figure A.1. In either form (whether based on frequencies or percentages), a frequency polygon gives a graphic impression of the data represented.

The Normal Distribution

The shape of the frequency polygon shown in Figure A.1 is typical of the kind of distribution usually found when data obtained from a group of people are plotted. Note that the curve is approximately "bell-shaped"—that is, it is high in the center and tapers off toward the base line at both ends. If we were to divide the area under this curve by drawing a perpendicular line from the central high point to the base line, the two parts would be approximately equal in area and

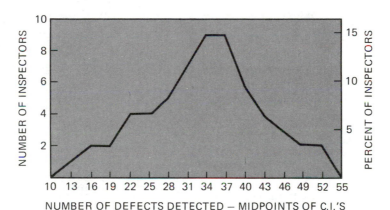

FIGURE A.1 Frequency polygon of data given in Table 21.2. The figure as characterized by the left-hand scale illustrates a polygon based on *frequencies,* and that characterized by the right-hand scale illustrates one based on *percentages.*

would be bilaterally symmetrical in shape. It is generally recognized that all, or nearly all, measurements of human traits and abilities result in distributions of approximately this form. These distributions are caled *normal distributions*. A strictly normal distribution conforms to a symmetrical bell-shaped curve defined by a mathematical equation, the basis of which is beyond the scope of this discussion. It suffices for the beginning student to know that:

1. A normal distribution is bell-shaped—that is, it is high in the center and low at both ends. Its two halves are symmetrical.
2. Measurements obtained from a group of persons usually approximate this type of distribution.

MEASURES OF CENTRAL TENDENCY

For some purposes it is desirable to have a single numerical value, called a measure of central tendency, that "represents" a set of data. A measure of central tendency may be defined as a single figure or value representative of the entire set of data. Three such measures in common use are the *arithmetic mean*, the *median*, and the *mode*.

The Arithmetic Mean

The arithmetic mean, sometimes simply called the mean, may be defined as the sum of the measures divided by the number of measures. For the sixty values previously discussed from which a frequency polygon was constructed, the mean is obtained by finding the total of the sixty measures and dividing this total by 60, thus:

$$\text{Arithmetic Mean} \atop (\text{A.M.}) = \frac{\text{Sum of measures}}{N}$$

$$= \frac{2016}{60} = 33.6$$

This is the procedure for computing the exact value of the arithmetic mean of any set of values. In practice, a shorter method of computation utilizing data as tabulated in a frequency distribution and yielding an approximation (rather than the exact value) of the mean is often used. This shorter method assumes that each score as tabulated in a frequency distribution has the same value as the midpoint of the c.i. in which it falls. For further convenience in calculation, the mean is first computed in c.i. units from an arbitrary base selected near the center of the distribution at the midpoint of one of the c.i.'s. The base selected is entirely arbitrary—it may be taken as any point in the distribution. We have chosen one near the center of the distribution to simplify computation.

If this method is used, columns such as 6 and 7 in Table A.2 should be prepared. Column 6 (d) represents the number of c.i. units of each c.i. above or below the c.i. that has been arbitrarily chosen as the base for the calculations. (For example, the c.i. 51–53, which has two scores, is 6 c.i. units above the arbitrary base.) The values in column 7 (fd) are derived by multiplying for each class interval the f value by the d value. (For the 51–53 c.i. this value is 12, which is the product of the f of 2 multiplied by the d of 6.) The scores tabulated in c.i.'s below the arbitrary base are represented by negative values in the fd column. The arithmetic mean (A.M.) is computed with the following formula:

Formula for Computing A.M.
$\text{A.M.} = M° + c.i.(c)$
$M° = \text{assumed mean}$
$c.i. = \text{size of } c.i.$

$$c = \frac{\Sigma fd}{N} = \text{summation of deviations}$$
$$\qquad\qquad \text{from assumed mean divided by } N$$

$$\text{A.M.} = 34 + 3\left(\frac{-7}{60}\right) = 34 - .35 = 33.65$$

In this formula the fd value is the algebraic sum of the values in the fd column (column 6). This sum divided by the number of cases indicates how far the computed mean will deviate from the assumed mean (base) in terms of c.i. units. From the tabulation, this deviation in c.i. units from the arbitrarily base (assumed mean) is defined as:

$$\text{Deviation in c.i. units from base} = \frac{\Sigma fd}{N}$$

This computation for the data under consideration shows that:

$$\text{Deviation in c.i. units from base} = \frac{\Sigma fd}{N}$$
$$= \frac{-7}{60} = -.117$$

This is interpreted to mean that the A.M. is .117 of a class interval below the midpoint of the arbitrary base (see formula in illustrative problem). In order to transmute this deviation $(-.117)$ into raw-score units, we would multiply it by 3 (the size of the class interval). Thus, in raw-score units, the deviation is $-.35$. The mean, as computed by this method, is therefore .35 raw-score units below the midpoint of the 33–35 c.i. As the midpoint of this is 34, the mean is $34 - .35 = 33.65$. This approximation does not agree exactly with the exact method in which all raw data are added and the sum is divided by the number of cases, but the approximation is sufficiently close to justify its use in many cases.

The Median

The median is a measure of central tendency defined as that score (or value) that exceeds, and is exceeded by, half the measures— that is, it is that point in the distribution above and below which 50% of the values lie. A logical (though laborious) method to determine the median consists of arranging all the raw data in rank order from lowest to highest and counting off the bottom half of the measures. The value at this point is the median. If this method is followed for the data in Table A.1, the following arrangement of the scores is obtained:

53	45	41	38	36	34	32	29	26	21
51	44	40	38	36	34	31	29	25	20
49	43	39	37	35	33	31	28	24	19
48	42	39	37	35	33	30	28	23	16
47	42	39	37	35	33	30	27	22	15
46	41	38	36	34	32	30	26	21	13

Counting from the lowest score up, we find that the thirtieth from the low end is 34, and the thirty-first from the low end is also 34. The median score would therefore be 34. If there had been a difference between the thirtieth and the thirty-first scores, the median would be the value half-way between these scores. If an odd number of cases were included in the original set of scores (sixty-one instead of sixty), the median would be the value of the middle score.

In practice, the median as well as the mean may be conveniently approximated from a tabulated frequency distribution. This requires the preparation of a *cumulative f* column, shown in column 8 of Table A.2. This column shows the cumulative frequencies by c.i., starting with the lowest c.i. The median value in this distribution is that value which separates the lower thirty from the upper thirty, which is within the c.i. of 33–35. There is a procedure for determining the specific value within this c.i. that characterizes the median, but that procedure is not discussed here.

The Mode

A third measure of central tendency is the mode, defined as the measure appearing most frequently. This value, as well as the mean and the median, may be determined directly from the raw data (if one value appears more often than any other) or it may be approximated from a frequency distribution of the data. In computing the mode directly from the raw data, the values are inspected to determine which one appears most frequently.

Sometimes, as in the values shown in Table A.1, several of the measures appear an equal number of times. In this case, each of the values 30, 33, 34, 35, 36, 37, 38, 39 appears three times. In such an instance, an approximation of the mode may be obtained from a frequency distribution using the following empirical formula:

$$Mode = 3(Median) - 2(Mean).$$

For the data we have been discussing, this formula gives the following value for the mode:

$$Mode = 3(34.2) - 2(33.65) = 35.30.$$

When to Use the Mean, Median, and Mode

Why is it necessary to have three different measures to indicate the central tendency of a set of data? The answer is that each is best adapted to certain uses—that is, in some cases one may be most representative of a set of data, but in other cases another measure may be most suitable. The mean is ordinarily used if the distribution is approximately normal. (If the distribution is perfectly normal, the three measures of central tendency have the same value.) If, on the other hand, there is a preponderance of extreme cases at either end of the distribution, the mean may give an incorrect impression of the central tendency of the data. Under these circumstances, the median or mode is more suitable. Consider, for example, the following monthly incomes of five persons:

$800 $900 $850 $750 $5000.

The mean for these five incomes is

$$\frac{\$800 + \$900 + \$850 + \$750 + \$5,000}{5} =$$

$1,660

This figure, though an accurate statement of the mean, is not typical of the group as a whole because it is so markedly affected by the one income of $5000. The median income is $850, and this value is more typical for the group as a whole than is the mean income of $1660. We may generalize this illustration by saying that if a distribution is very much *skewed* (that is, if it contains more cases at one extreme than at the other), the median or mode is more likely to be representative of the typical score than is the mean.

MEASURES OF VARIABILITY

Besides a need for measure or value to represent the central tendency of a set of data, there is also quite frequently a need for some measure of the spread, or variability, of the data. The need for a measurement of this type may be seen by comparing the data shown in Table A.1 (the mean of which, computed from the frequency distribution, was found to be 33.65) with another set of data that, as an example, we might assume to consist of twenty-one scores of 33 and thirty-nine scores of 34, making sixty scores in all. The mean of these sixty scores is 33.65.

$$\frac{(21)(33) + (39)(44)}{60} = 33.65$$

Although both distributions have the same mean, they differ markedly in variability or spread. The former is made up of scores varying from 13 to 53, and the latter consists entirely of scores of 33 and 34. A quantitative measure of variability is therefore valuable. There are statistical procedures that yield a single value describing this variability; as in means and medians, these measures tell us something about the group as a whole.

The Standard Deviation

The standard deviation is the most widely used measures of variability. It is defined as the square root of the mean square deviation. Defined by formula:

$$\text{Standard Deviation} = S.D. = \sigma = \frac{\sqrt{\Sigma D^2}}{N}$$

in which ΣD^2 is read "the sum of the squared deviation of the scores from their mean," and N is the number of cases. S.D. and σ are abbreviations for the standard deviation and are used interchangeably.

Although the standard deviation may be computed directly from a set of raw data by means of the formula

$$S.D. = \sqrt{\frac{\Sigma D^2}{N}}$$

this process is laborious. For example, for the set of data we have been using as an example (tabulated in Table A.1), we would proceed by determining the difference between each raw score and the mean of the sixty scores, squaring these differences, summing the sixty squared differences, dividing by 60, and extracting the square root of the quotient. The first score tabulated is 15. The difference between this value and the mean of the sixty scores (as computed directly from the raw data is $D = 33.6 - 15.0 = 18.6$. D^2 would therefore be $(18.6)^2 = 345.96$. This process must be repeated for every one of the sixty scores before the sum of the squared deviations can be obtained.

Because it is tedious to compute the S.D. directly from the raw data, a simple process that approximates the true value of the S.D. has been developed. This is used in the computations shown in Table A.3, in which the standard deviation of the data shown previously in Table A.2 is computed.

The standard deviation is the most commonly used measure of variability. Usually when the mean value of a set of data is given, the S.D. is also given to indicate the variability of the data.

COMPARABLE SCORES

The S.D. can also be used to compare individual scores from different distributions. For example, suppose that two inspectors from departments A and B, who are working at different inspection jobs, detect respectively 45 and 89 defects during a week of work. How can we compare the effciency of these two employees? Obviously, a direct comparison of the figures 45 and 89 is not valid because the two inspection jobs may be very different. Also little can be said about the position of these inspectors in their respective groups without knowing their relation to the mean of their group in inspection work. To make a comparison, then, we must first compute the mean number of defects spotted by all inspectors in department A, and the mean number spotted by all inspectors in department B. Suppose that those means are respectively 38 and 95. We thus see that the inspector from department A is $45 - 38 = 7$ pieces *above* the mean for that department and that the inspector from department B is $89 - 95 = -6$, or 6 pieces *below* the mean of inspectors from that department. We can say, at this point, that the inspector from department A is above average in ability on the job and that the inspector from department B is below average. But how about their relative distances from the average? To answer this we must compute the S.D.s of the two

TABLE A.3 Computation of the standard deviation from a frequency distribution*

c.i.	f	d	fd	fd²
51–53	2	6	12	72
48–50	2	5	10	50
45–47	3	4	12	48
42–44	4	3	12	36
39–41	6	2	12	24
36–38	9	1	9	9
33–35	9	0	0	0
30–32	7	−1	−7	7
27–29	5	−2	−10	20
24–26	4	−3	−12	36
21–23	4	−4	−16	64
18–20	2	−5	−10	50
15–17	2	−6	−12	72
12–14	1	−7	−7	49
Total = 60			Σfd = −7	Σfd² = 537

$$\text{Mean} = M° + c.i. \left(\frac{\Sigma fd}{N}\right)$$

$$\text{Mean} = 34 + 3\left(\frac{-7}{60}\right) = 33.65$$

$$\text{S.D.} = \sqrt{\frac{\Sigma D^2}{N}} = c.i. \sqrt{\frac{\Sigma fd^2}{N} - \frac{\Sigma fd^2}{N}}$$

$$= 3 \sqrt{537/60 - (.117)^2}$$

$$= 3 \sqrt{8.950 - .014}$$

$$= 3 \sqrt{8.936}$$

$$= 3(2.99)$$

$$\text{S.D.} = 8.97$$

*The data used in this table are from Table A.2

distributions and determine how many S.D.s each inspector is above or below average.

Suppose we find the S.D. of the operators in department A to be 5.5 pieces. Our first inspector is, therefore,

$$\frac{45 - 38}{5.5} = 1.27 \text{ S.D.s}$$

above average. If the S.D. of the inspectors in department B is 9.5, the inspector from the group who detected 89 pieces is

$$\frac{89 - 95}{9.5} = -.63 \text{ or } .63 \text{ S.D.s}$$

below average. *The deviation of a score from the means of the distribution expressed in S.D. units results in a measurement comparable with similarly determined measurements from other distributions.* Thus, we may say that our first inspector is about *twice* as far above average, in terms of comparable scale units, as

the second operator is below average. Scores computed in this manner are known as z-scores. The formula for a z-score is as follows:

$$z\text{-score} = \frac{\text{Raw Score} - \text{Mean of Raw Scores}}{\text{S.D. of Raw Scores}}$$

The z-score is helpful not only when comparing scores from one distribution to another, but also when, for any reason, it is desirable to combine scores with the same or differential weighting. An example of an industrial situation that requires this technique is combining factors in a personnel-evaluation system, such as those illustrated in Chapter 6. Let us suppose, as an example, that we want to combine the evaluations of each person on these two factors into an overall rating. (If more than two factors are included in the system, as is usually the case, the procedure is identical). Suppose that an employee, A, has received 40 points on industriousness and 30 points on knowledge of job, making a total of 70 points, if the ratings are added directly. Suppose that another employee, B, has received 30 points on industriousness and 40 points on knowledge of job, which also results in a total of 70 points, if the ratings are added directly. Such a direct and immediate combination of ratings would result in identical overall ratings for these two employees. The question we may raise is whether such a statement of equal ratings is justified. The answer is that it is not. If the mean rating of all employees on industriousness was 33 with a S.D. of 3, then A's rating would be

$$\frac{40 - 33}{3} = 2.33, \text{ or } 2.33 \text{ S.D.s}$$

above the mean, and B's would be

$$\frac{30 - 33}{3} = -1.00, \text{ or } 1.00 \text{ S.D.}$$

below the mean on this trait. If the mean rating for all employees on knowledge of job were 25, with a S.D. of 6, A would be

$$\frac{30 - 25}{6} = +.83, \text{ or } .83 \text{ S.D.s}$$

above average in knowledge of job and B would be

$$\frac{40 - 25}{6} = 2.50 \text{ or } 2.50 \text{ S.D.s}$$

above average in this respect. Now, the proper combination of the two factors, if we wish to weight them equally, are shown in Table A.4.

Changing ratings into z-scores and adding the z-scores show that the two employees A and B are not equal in rating (as we would infer if the raw ratings were added), but rather that A is definitely higher than B. The procedure described is based on the assumption that the two factors should receive equal weights and shows how they can combined with equal weight into a composite score. One might think that conversion of raw scores to z-scores is not necessary if the raw scores are to be given equal weight in the combination score. Actually, if we do not give the raw scores equal weight by converting them into z-scores, the scores will weight themselves according to the size of their respective standard deviations. In other words, if combined directly, the raw scores will be weighted too much or too little, depending on their position relative to the means of their respective distributions and on the variability of the distribution of which they are a part. When scores are combined, they are *always* weighted in some manner, whether deliberately or not. It is important, therefore, to weight them deliberately (either with equal weight or otherwise) by converting them into z-scores and then combining them.

It does not follow from this discussion that combined scores should always be weighted equally. Indeed, it is often desirable to weight various scores according to some plan that has been decided before the scores are combined. When this is desired, such weighting can be done easily by multiplying each z-score by the appropriate weight before they are combined. In our example, suppose that we have de-

TABLE A.4 Illustration of use of z-scores for giving equal weight to ratings on two factors for two employees.

EMPLOYEE	RATING IN INDUSTRI-OUSNESS	RATING IN KNOWLEDGE OF JOB	Z-SCORE IN IN-DUSTRIOUSNESS	Z-SCORE IN KNOWLEDGE OF JOB	SUM OF SCORES FOR BOTH UNITS
A	40	30	+2.33	+83	+3.16
B	30	40	−1.00	+2.50	+1.50

TABLE A.5 Effects on combined ratings for two employees of weighting two factors 2 and 1.

EMPLOYEE	Z-SCORE IN INDUSTRI-OUSNESS	Z-SCORE IN KNOWLEDGE OF JOB	WEIGHTED Z-SCORE IN INDUS-TRIOUSNESS (WEIGHT-2)	WEIGHTED Z-SCORE IN KNOWLEDGE OF JOB (WEIGHT-1)	COMBINED WEIGHTED Z-SCORES
A	+2.33	+.83	+4.66	+.83	+5.49
B	−1.00	+2.50	−2.00	+2.50	+.50

cided that *industriousness* should be given twice as much weight as *knowledge of job* in determining the total rating. This is shown in Table A.5.

The combined ratings so obtained show a still greater difference between employees A and B than was obtained when the scores were equally weighted. If, on the other hand, we decide to give the rating on *knowledge of job* twice as much weight as the rating on *industriousness*, the computations would be made as shown in Table A.6.

Essentially the same procedures can be followed when combining other set of data with specified weights—for example, subcriteria, job-evaluation factors, or test scores. As an example, in selecting candidates for electrical-apprentice training, one company assigned differential weights to four factors according to the judged importance of these factors to apprentice training. These weights were as follows:

General intelligence	40%
Knowledge of electricity	30%
Merit rating	20%
Seniority of service with the company	10%

To score the candidates according to this plan, each was given a general intelligence test and a test covering technical phases of electricity. Merit ratings and seniority were obtained from the company records. Each of the four scores for each candidate was converted into a z-score, and the four resulting z-scores were respectively multiplied by 40, 30, 20, and 10. For each candidate the sum of the weighted z-scores was used to indicate whether or not he was selected for apprenticeship training.

PERCENTILES

The discussion of comparable scores should have made clear that a raw score on any test is relatively meaningless unless it is interpreted in relation to its location in a distribution of other scores made by other people. If a test has seventy-five very easy questions, a score of 65 might be near the bottom of the distribution and hence should be interpreted as a very low score. On the other hand, if a test has seventy-five very difficult questions, a score of 65 might be at or near the top of the distribution and should therefore be considered a very high score. In other words, a raw score of 65 might be a low score or a high score, depending on the distribution of scores from which it is drawn.

TABLE A.6 Effects on combined ratings for two employees of weighting two factors 1 and 2.

EMPLOYEE	Z-SCORE IN INDUSTRI-OUSNESS	Z-SCORE IN KNOWLEDGE OF JOB	WEIGHTED Z-SCORE IN INDUS-TRIOUSNESS (WEIGHT-1)	WEIGHTED Z-SCORE IN KNOWLEDGE OF JOB (WEIGHT-2)	COMBINED WEIGHTED Z-SCORES
A	+2.333	+.833	+2.333	+1.666	+4.0
B	−1.000	+2.500	−1.000	+5.000	+4.0

One convenient and widely used method of interpreting a raw score is by using *percentile ranks*. A percentile rank may be defined as the number showing the percentage of the total group equal to or below the score in question. Thus, on a certain test, if 65 percent of the total group scored 129 or below, the score of 129 would be at the sixty-fifth percentile or would have a percentile rank of 65. Note that the fiftieth percentile is the same as the median as previously defined.

A convenient, practical method of determining by close approximation the percentile equivalents of a set of raw scores uses a cumulative frequency distribution like that tabulated in Table A.7. This tabulation is based on the same distribution previously used in Table A.2.

The percent values in column 4 of Table A.7 are obtained by dividing each of the values in the cumulative *f* column (column 3) by the total of column 2, in this instance 60. The percent values in column 4 are then plotted against the upper limits of the class intervals, as shown in Figure A.2. The percentile ranks of the raw scores may be read directly from

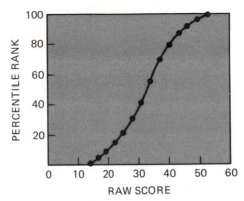

FIGURE A.2 Chart for converting raw scores into percentile ranks for illustrative data in Table 21.4.

Figure A.2, with sufficient accuracy for most purposes.

The manual published with standardized tests usually includes percentile tables enabling the conversion of raw scores into percentile ranks. Because the percentile rank of a given raw score is dependent on the nature of the group used in constructing the conversion table, several raw-score-to-percentile-rank conversion tables, based on different groups, are often published with standardized tests.

TABLE A.7 Cumulative frequency distribution used in determining percentile ranks of raw scores

(1) CLASS INTERVALS	(2) *f*	(3) CUMULATIVE *f*	(4) PERCENT
51–53	2	60	100
48–50	2	58	96
45–47	3	56	93
42–44	4	53	88
39–41	6	49	81
36–38	9	43	71
33–35	9	34	56
30–32	7	25	42
27–29	5	18	30
24–26	4	13	22
21–23	4	9	15
18–20	2	5	8
15–17	2	3	5
12–14	1	1	2
Total = 60			

CORRELATION

For quantitative data on a sample from a population (such as a sample of people), there may be two items of data for each of the cases so related that they vary, or tend to vary, with each other. An obvious example would be people's height and weight—two variables that are somewhat related. A correlation is a statistical index of the degree of relationship between two such variables. A correlation can range from +1.00 (a perfect positive relationship) through to −1.00 (a perfect negative relationship).

A graphic example of a correlation is

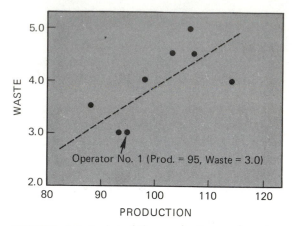

FIGURE A.3 A plot of the production and waste records for the eight punch-press operators shown in Table A.6.

shown in Figure A.3; this is based on data for eight punch-press operators for whom we have two items of data: (1) production for a given period of time; and (2) pounds of waste (material wasted by mispunching or otherwise). Following are these data for the eight operators:

OPERATOR	PRODUCTION	WASTE
1	95	3.0
2	103	4.5
3	88	3.5
4	98	4.0
5	93	3.0
6	107	4.5
7	114	4.0
8	106	5.0

The graphic representation of these data in Figure A.3 was made by plotting the values on coordinate axes, with one variable (production) being represented on the X or horizontal axis and the other (waste) on the Y or vertical axis. Such a representation gives a better indication of the relationship between the two variables than the data in the preceding columns do. It is even possible to draw in, by inspection, a line or curve that repre-

sents this relationship in an approximate form.

Although this simple method of studying the relationship between two variables is sometimes adequate for very simple problems or for those using only a small amount of data, it is not adequate for an exact study because it does not give a quantitative statement of the degree of relationship. The slope of the dotted line cannot be considered a quantitative statement because: (1) this line is drawn in by inspection; and (2) its slope depends on the units of measurement on both the X and Y axes. Two quantitative methods commonly used to measure the degree of relationship between two paired sets of data are rank-order correlation and product-moment correlation.

Rank-Order Correlation

This method may be described by applying it to the data for the eight punch-press operators.

In Table A.8 two two columns headed *Rank* give, respectively, the rank of the operators on the two measures (production and waste). The highest-producing operator (in this case the seventh in the list) is given a rank of 1, the second highest a rank of 2, and so on. In like manner, the rank of each operator in wastage is placed in the waste-rank column. If two or more operators are tied for a given rank (as are the second and sixth operators, who are tied at 4.5 pounds of waste each), the tied scores are all given the same rank, the average of the ranks that would have been assigned to the tied scores if they had not been tied. The values in the D^2 column are obtained by squaring each D value. The sum of the D^2 column is determined and the correlation is computed using the formula:

$$Rho = 1 - \frac{6\Sigma D^2}{N(N^2 - 1)}$$

TABLE A.8 Computation of rank-order correlation

OPERATOR	PRODUCTION	WASTE	RANK IN PRODUCTION	RANK IN WASTE	DIFFERENCE IN RANK (D)	(D)²
1	95	3.0	6	7.5	1.5	2.25
2	103	4.5	4	2.5	1.5	2.25
3	88	3.5	8	6.0	2.0	4.00
4	98	4.0	5	4.5	.5	.25
5	93	3.0	7	7.5	.5	.25
6	107	4.5	2	2.5	.5	.25
7	114	4.0	1	2.5	3.5	12.25
8	106	5.0	3	1.0	2.0	4.00
						25.50

$$\text{Rho} = 1 - \frac{6\Sigma D^2}{N(N^2 - 1)} = 1 - \frac{153}{504} = .70$$

in which N is the number of cases entering into the computation.

This formula for the rank-order correlation is empirical. It yields a value of $+1.00$ if the data are in exactly the same rank order. (The reason for this is that if all ranks are the same, all D's are zero, all D^2 values are zero, ΣD^2 is zero, and the formula becomes $1 - 0 = 1$.) If the data are in exactly reverse order (that is, if the individual who ranks highest on one series is lowest on the other, and so on), the formula will yield a value of -1.00, but if there is no relationship between the two sets of data, a correlation of zero will be found.

If there are an appreciable number of cases, however, the rank-order method of computing the degree of relationship is extremely laborious. For this reason—and for other reasons of a mathematical nature—it is ordinarily used only when the data are limited to a very few cases (less than thirty).

The Product-Moment Correlation

This is the most widely used measure of relationship. Like the rank-order correlation, it may vary from $+1.00$ (indicating perfect positive relationship) through zero (indicating no relationship) to -1.00 (indicating per-

fect negative relationship). The product-moment correlation, represented by the symbol r, may be defined in several ways. One of the simplest definitions is that r is *the slope of the straight line that best fits the data after the data have been plotted as z-scores on coordinate axes*—that is, it is the tangent of the angle made by this line with the base line.

Several terms in this definition require further definition. *Slope* means the steepness with which the line rises. The slope of a straight line drawn in any manner across coordinate paper is defined as the distance, y, from any given point on the line to the x intercept, minus the distance, a, from the origin to the y intercept, divided by the distance, x, from the point on the line to y intercept. Thus the slope, which we call b, is defined in Figure A.4 as follows:

$$b = \frac{y - a}{x}$$

Remember that, on coordinate axes, distances above and to the right of the origin are positive, but distances measured below and/or to the left of the origin are negative. The slope of any line that *rises* as it goes from left to right will therefore be positive (the

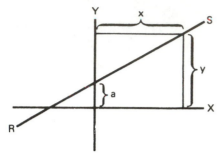

FIGURE A.4 The slope of the line RS is defined as $b = \dfrac{y-a}{x}$.

greater the rise in a given distance to the right, the larger the positive value of the slope), and the slope of any line that *falls* as it goes from left to right will be negative (the greater the fall in a given distance to the right, the great the negative value of the slope).

The line of *best fit* in the definition is a line so drawn that the sum of the squared deviations in a vertical direction from the original points to the line is less than the sum would be for any other straight line that might be drawn.

A rough approximation of the value of r may be obtained by plotting the z-scores of the two variables, fitting a straight line to these points by inspection and graphically measuring the slope of this straight line. Although this method is never used in practical

computation (because it is both inaccurate and laborious), the application of it to a set of representative data may clarify the meaning of the correlation coefficient, r. Returning to the data for which we have previously computed the rank-order correlation (see Table A.8), we first compute the z-scores for each measure as shown in Table A.9.

These pairs of z-scores are used as the x and y values for eight points plotted on co-ordinate axes, as in Figure A.5. The straight line that seems to best fit these points is then determined (as with a stretched string that is moved about until the desired location is obtained) and drawn on the graph. The correlation, r, as determined by this crude method, is obtained by measuring the slope of this line. The procedure applied to Figure A.5 gives a value of $r = .61$, but note that this value is affected by:

1. The accuracy with which the straight line has been located, and
2. The accuracy with which the slope of the line has been measured after it has been drawn.

Points 1 and 2 both eliminate the possibility of complete accuracy in this method of determining a correlation coefficient. Therefore, a mathematical method has been devised to make the computation, so that no plotting of points or graphic measurements

TABLE A.9 Production and waste for eight punch-press operators with corresponding z-scores of the production and waste figures

OPERATOR	PRODUCTION	WASTE	Z-SCORE IN PRODUCTION	Z-SCORE IN WASTE
1	95	3.0	−.69	−1.38
2	103	4.5	+.31	+.82
3	88	3.5	−1.56	−.65
4	98	4.0	−.31	+.09
5	93	3.0	−.94	−1.38
6	107	4.5	+.81	+.82
7	114	4.0	+1.69	+.09
8	106	5.0	+.69	+1.56
Mean	100.5	3.94		
S.D.	8.0	.68		

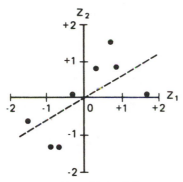

FIGURE A.5 A plot of the z-scores for production and waste records of the eight punch-press operators shown in Table A.6.

are required. This method requires deriving the equation of the straight line that, if plotted, would best fit the points and computing the slope of this straight line of best fit from the equation.

It may be proved mathematically that the slope of the straight line of best fit is given by the following equation:

$$\text{Slope} = r = \frac{\Sigma Z_x Z_y}{N}$$

in which $\Sigma z_x z_y$ is read "the sum of the products of the z-scores for the pairs of points or values."

Applying the formula to the data in Table A.9, we may compute the correlation, as in Table A.10. The value of r thus obtained by computation, .67, differs from the value of .61 obtained by plotting and inspection. The plotting and inspection method yielded a value that was somewhat incorrect for the data in question.

Although the z-score method of computing a correlation coefficient as illustrated in Table A.10 may be used with any number of cases and will yield the correct mathematical value of r, when many pairs of data are to be correlated this method is very laborious. It is therefore recommended, under such circumstances, that a modification of the fundamental formula

$$r = \frac{\Sigma Z_x Z_y}{N}$$

which makes it possible to compute r from raw-score values rather than z-scores values, be used. One convenient formula for determining the coefficient of correlation directly from the raw data is:

$$r = \frac{N\Sigma XY - \Sigma X \Sigma Y}{\sqrt{N\Sigma X^2 - (\Sigma X)^2} \sqrt{N\Sigma Y^2 - (\Sigma Y^2)}}$$

TABLE A.10 Computation of r by z-score method between production and waste figures

OPERATOR	PRODUCTION	WASTE	z-SCORE IN PRODUCTION	z-SCORE IN WASTE	$(z_1 z_2)$
1	95	3.0	−.69	−1.38	+.95
2	103	4.5	+.31	+.82	+.25
3	88	3.5	−1.56	−.65	+1.01
4	98	4.0	−.31	+.09	−.03
5	93	3.0	−.94	−1.38	+1.30
6	107	4.5	+.81	+.82	+.66
7	114	4.0	+1.69	+.09	+.15
8	106	5.0	+.69	+1.56	+1.08
					+5.38

$$r = \frac{\Sigma z_x z_y}{N} = \frac{+5.38}{8} = .67$$

When we apply this formula to the data tabulated in Table A.10, the computations shown in Table A.11 result.

When many pairs of data are to be correlated, the use of a chart further simplifies the computations. Several forms of such a chart have been prepared. One convenient form is shown in Figure A.6. This chart shows the computation of the correlation between time used in inspecting 300 pieces of material and the number of defective pieces detected. In using this chart, the following steps should be followed:

1. Decide upon appropriate class intervals for one of the variables (using the rules given before), and write these in on either the X or the Y axis.
2. Decide upon appropriate class intervals for the other variable, and write these in on the axis not used in step 1.

3. Place one tally mark on the scattergram for each pair of values being correlated. For example, if an inspector spotted thirty-three defects in 16.5 minutes, the tally mark would go in the cell that is found at the intersection of the *row* containing thirty-three defects and the *column* containing 16.5 minutes.
4. After all tally marks have been placed on the chart, the rows should be added horizontally and the sum of the tally marks in each row should be written opposite this row in the f_y column (column *l*).
5. The tally marks in each column should be added and the sum written at the bottom of each column in the row (A), the f_x row.
6. The f_y column should be added and the sum written opposite N at the bottom of this column. *The value of N thus obtained may be checked by adding the values in the f_x row. The sum of these values should also give the value of N.*
7. Each value of f_y in the column so headed should be multiplied by the value of d_y opposite it and the resultant product written in

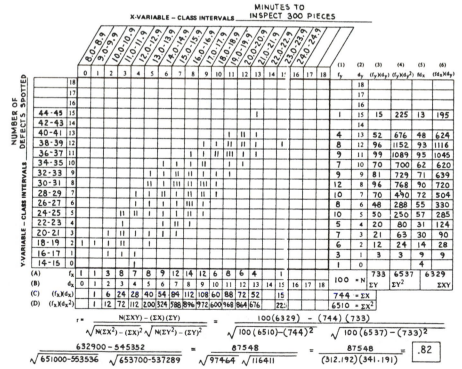

FIGURE A.6 A chart used to compute a product movement coefficient of correlation.

452

TABLE A.11 Computations of r directly from raw data

OPERATOR	PRODUCTION (X)	WASTE (Y)	X^2	Y^2	XY
1	95	3.0	9,025	9.00	285.0
2	103	4.5	10,609	20.25	463.5
3	88	3.5	7,744	12.25	308.0
4	98	4.0	9,604	16.00	392.0
5	93	3.0	8,649	9.00	279.0
6	107	4.5	11,449	20.25	481.5
7	114	4.0	12,996	16.00	456.0
8	106	5.0	11,236	25.00	530.0
	$\Sigma X = 804$	$\Sigma Y = 31.5$	$\Sigma X^2 = 81,312$	$\Sigma Y^2 = 127.75$	$\Sigma XY = 3,195.0$

$$r = \frac{N\Sigma XY - \Sigma X \Sigma Y}{\sqrt{N\Sigma X^2 - (\Sigma X)^2}\ \sqrt{N\Sigma Y^2 - (\Sigma Y)^2}}$$

$$r = \frac{8(3,195) - (804)(31.5)}{\sqrt{8(81,312) - (804)^2}\ \sqrt{8(127.75) - (31.5)^2}}$$

$$r = .67$$

column 3, headed $f_y d_y$. *The sum of column 3 is the value of* ΣY *used in the formula.*

8. Each value in column 3, the $f_y d_y$ column, should be multiplied by the corresponding value in column 2, the d_y column, resulting in the values for column 4, or the $f_y d_y^2$ column. *The sum of column 4 is the value of* ΣY^2 *which is used in the formula.*

9. The values going into column 5, the fd_x column, are determined by finding, for each row, the sum of the products of the number of cases in each cell times the x value of that cell. For example, in the first row in which a tally mark appears, there is only a single case, which appears in the cell under an x value of 13. The value to go into the blank in column 5 is therefore $(1)(13) = 13$. In the next row no tally marks appear; therefore, this row is blank. In the next row, one tally mark appears in the cell under an x value of 11, two in the cell with an x value of 12, and one in the cell with an x value of 13. The value to go into the blank cell in column 5 is therefore $(1)(11) + (2)(12) + (1)(13) = 48$. The remaining cells in column 5 are filled in a similar manner.

10. The cells in column 6, the $fd_x d_y$ column, are filled with values obtained by multiplying each value in column 2, the d_y column, by the value in that same row appearing in column 5, the fd_x column. The value in the first cell in column 6 is therefore $(15)(13) = 195$. *The sum of*

column 6 is the value of ΣXY used in the formula.

11. The values in row C are obtained by multiplying each value in row A, the f_x row, by the value directly below it in row B, the d_x row. The values appearing in row A have already been obtained (see step 5). The resultant values are entered in row C, the $f_x d_x$ row. *The sum of the values appearing in row C is the value of* ΣX *used in the formula.*

12. Each value in row B, the d_x row, should be multiplied by the value directly below in row C, the $f_x d_x$ row. The resultant values should be entered in row D, the $f_x d_x^2$ row. *The sum of the values in row D is the value of* ΣX^2 *used in the formula.*

13. The value for N (see step 6), ΣY (see step 7), ΣY^2 (see step 8), ΣXY (see step 10), ΣX (see step 11), and ΣX^2 (see step 12) are now entered in the formula. The indicated arithmetic computations are then performed, yielding the value of r.

This method assumes that each measure has the value of the midpoint of the class interval in which it falls. The computations indicated on the chart produce not only the value for r but also the mean and the standard deviations of both the X and Y arrays.

Taylor-Russell Tables (Institutional Prediction)

Tables of the proportion who will be satisfactory among those selected for given values of the proportion of present employees considered satisfactory, the selection ratio, and r.

EMPLOYEES CONSIDERED SATISFACTORY	r	SELECTION RATIO										
		.05	.10	.20	.30	.40	.50	.60	.70	.80	.90	.95
10 percent	.00	.10	.10	.10	.10	.10	.10	.10	.10	.10	.10	.10
	.10	.14	.13	.13	.12	.12	.11	.11	.11	.11	.10	.10
	.20	.19	.17	.15	.14	.14	.13	.12	.12	.11	.11	.10
	.30	.25	.22	.19	.17	.15	.14	.13	.12	.12	.11	.10
	.40	.31	.27	.22	.19	.17	.16	.14	.13	.12	.11	.10
	.50	.39	.32	.26	.22	.19	.17	.15	.13	.12	.11	.11
	.60	.48	.39	.30	.25	.21	.18	.16	.14	.12	.11	.11
	.70	.58	.47	.35	.27	.22	.19	.16	.14	.12	.11	.11
	.80	.71	.56	.40	.30	.24	.20	.17	.14	.12	.11	.11
	.90	.86	.69	.46	.33	.25	.20	.17	.14	.12	.11	.11
	r	.05	.10	.20	.30	.40	.50	.60	.70	.80	.90	.95

EMPLOYEES CONSIDERED SATISFACTORY	r	SELECTION RATIO										
		.05	.10	.20	.30	.40	.50	.60	.70	.80	.90	.95
20 percent	.00	.20	.20	.20	.20	.20	.20	.20	.20	.20	.20	.20
	.10	.26	.25	.24	.23	.23	.22	.22	.21	.21	.21	.20
	.20	.33	.31	.28	.27	.26	.25	.24	.23	.22	.21	.21
	.30	.41	.37	.33	.30	.28	.27	.25	.24	.23	.21	.21
	.40	.49	.44	.38	.34	.31	.29	.27	.25	.23	.22	.21
	.50	.59	.52	.44	.38	.35	.31	.29	.26	.24	.22	.21
	.60	.68	.60	.50	.43	.38	.34	.30	.27	.24	.22	.21
	.70	.79	.69	.56	.48	.41	.36	.31	.28	.25	.22	.21
	.80	.89	.79	.64	.53	.45	.38	.33	.28	.25	.22	.21
	.90	.98	.91	.75	.60	.48	.40	.33	.29	.25	.22	.21
30 percent	.00	.30	.30	.30	.30	.30	.30	.30	.30	.30	.30	.30
	.10	.38	.36	.35	.34	.33	.33	.32	.32	.31	.31	.30
	.20	.46	.43	.40	.38	.37	.36	.34	.33	.32	.31	.31
	.30	.54	.50	.46	.43	.40	.38	.37	.35	.33	.32	.31
	.40	.63	.58	.51	.47	.44	.41	.39	.37	.34	.32	.31
	.50	.72	.65	.58	.52	.48	.44	.41	.38	.35	.33	.31
	.60	.81	.74	.64	.58	.52	.47	.43	.40	.36	.33	.31
	.70	.89	.82	.72	.63	.57	.51	.46	.41	.37	.33	.32
	.80	.96	.90	.80	.70	.62	.54	.48	.42	.37	.33	.32
	.90	1.00	.98	.90	.79	.68	.58	.49	.43	.37	.33	.32
40 percent	.00	.40	.40	.40	.40	.40	.40	.40	.40	.40	.40	.40
	.10	.48	.47	.46	.45	.44	.43	.42	.42	.41	.41	.40
	.20	.57	.54	.51	.49	.48	.46	.45	.44	.43	.41	.41
	.30	.65	.61	.57	.54	.51	.49	.47	.46	.44	.42	.41
	.40	.73	.69	.63	.59	.56	.53	.50	.48	.45	.43	.41
	.50	.81	.76	.69	.64	.60	.56	.53	.49	.46	.43	.42
	.60	.89	.83	.75	.69	.64	.60	.55	.51	.48	.44	.42
	.70	.95	.90	.82	.76	.69	.64	.58	.53	.49	.44	.42
	.80	.99	.96	.89	.82	.75	.68	.61	.55	.49	.44	.42
	.90	1.00	1.00	.97	.91	.82	.74	.65	.57	.50	.44	.42
50 percent	.00	.50	.50	.50	.50	.50	.50	.50	.50	.50	.50	.50
	.10	.58	.57	.56	.55	.54	.53	.53	.52	.51	.51	.50
	.20	.67	.64	.61	.59	.58	.56	.55	.54	.53	.52	.51
	.30	.74	.71	.67	.64	.62	.60	.58	.56	.54	.52	.51
	.40	.82	.78	.73	.69	.66	.63	.61	.58	.56	.53	.52
	.50	.88	.84	.78	.74	.70	.67	.63	.60	.57	.54	.52
	.60	.94	.90	.84	.79	.75	.70	.66	.62	.59	.54	.52
	.70	.98	.95	.90	.85	.80	.75	.70	.65	.60	.55	.53
	.80	1.00	.99	.95	.90	.85	.80	.73	.67	.61	.55	.53
	.90	1.00	1.00	.99	.97	.92	.86	.78	.70	.62	.56	.53
	r	.05	.10	.20	.30	.40	.50	.60	.70	.80	.90	.95

EMPLOYEES CONSIDERED SATISFACTORY	r	SELECTION RATIO										
		.05	.10	.20	.30	.40	.50	.60	.70	.80	.90	.95
60 percent	.00	.60	.60	.60	.60	.60	.60	.60	.60	.60	.60	.60
	.10	.68	.67	.65	.64	.64	.63	.63	.62	.61	.61	.60
	.20	.75	.73	.71	.69	.67	.66	.65	.64	.63	.62	.61
	.30	.82	.79	.76	.73	.71	.69	.68	.66	.64	.62	.61
	.40	.88	.85	.81	.78	.75	.73	.70	.68	.66	.63	.62
	.50	.93	.90	.86	.82	.79	.76	.73	.70	.67	.64	.62
	.60	.96	.94	.90	.87	.83	.80	.76	.73	.69	.65	.63
	.70	.99	.97	.94	.91	.87	.84	.80	.75	.71	.66	.63
	.80	1.00	.99	.98	.95	.92	.88	.83	.78	.72	.66	.63
	.90	1.00	1.00	1.00	.99	.97	.94	.88	.82	.74	.67	.63
70 percent	.00	.70	.70	.70	.70	.70	.70	.70	.70	.70	.70	.70
	.10	.77	.76	.75	.74	.73	.73	.72	.72	.71	.71	.70
	.20	.83	.81	.79	.78	.77	.76	.75	.74	.73	.71	.71
	.30	.88	.86	.84	.82	.80	.78	.77	.75	.74	.72	.71
	.40	.93	.91	.88	.85	.83	.81	.79	.77	.75	.73	.72
	.50	.96	.94	.91	.89	.87	.84	.82	.80	.77	.74	.72
	.60	.98	.97	.95	.92	.90	.87	.85	.82	.79	.75	.73
	.70	1.00	.99	.97	.96	.93	.91	.88	.84	.80	.76	.73
	.80	1.00	1.00	.99	.98	.97	.94	.91	.87	.82	.77	.73
	.90	1.00	1.00	1.00	1.00	.99	.98	.95	.91	.85	.78	.74
80 percent	.00	.80	.80	.80	.80	.80	.80	.80	.80	.80	.80	.80
	.10	.85	.85	.84	.83	.83	.82	.82	.81	.81	.81	.80
	.20	.90	.89	.87	.86	.85	.84	.84	.83	.82	.81	.81
	.30	.94	.92	.90	.89	.88	.87	.86	.84	.83	.82	.81
	.40	.96	.95	.93	.92	.90	.89	.88	.86	.85	.83	.82
	.50	.98	.97	.96	.94	.93	.91	.90	.88	.86	.84	.82
	.60	.99	.99	.98	.96	.95	.94	.92	.90	.87	.84	.83
	.70	1.00	1.00	.99	.98	.97	.96	.94	.92	.89	.85	.83
	.80	1.00	1.00	1.00	1.00	.99	.98	.96	.94	.91	.87	.84
	.90	1.00	1.00	1.00	1.00	1.00	1.00	.99	.97	.94	.88	.84
90 percent	.00	.90	.90	.90	.90	.90	.90	.90	.90	.90	.90	.90
	.10	.93	.93	.92	.92	.92	.91	.91	.91	.91	.90	.90
	.20	.96	.95	.94	.94	.93	.93	.92	.92	.91	.91	.90
	.30	.98	.97	.96	.95	.95	.94	.94	.93	.92	.91	.91
	.40	.99	.98	.98	.97	.96	.95	.95	.94	.93	.92	.91
	.50	1.00	.99	.99	.98	.97	.97	.96	.95	.94	.92	.92
	.60	1.00	1.00	.99	.99	.99	.98	.97	.96	.95	.93	.92
	.70	1.00	1.00	1.00	1.00	.99	.99	.98	.97	.96	.94	.93
	.80	1.00	1.00	1.00	1.00	1.00	1.00	.99	.99	.97	.95	.93
	.90	1.00	1.00	1.00	1.00	1.00	1.00	1.00	1.00	.99	.97	.94
	r	.05	.10	.20	.30	.40	.50	.60	.70	.80	.90	.95

Source: H. C. Taylor, & J. T. Russell (1939). The relationship of validity coefficients to the practical effectiveness of tests in selection: Discussion and tables *Journal. of Applied Psychology, 23*, 565–578. Note: The Tables as given here omit r values of .05, .15, .25, and so on. The complete tables are given in the seventh and earlier editions of this text.

APPENDIX C

Lawshe Expectancy Tables (Individual Prediction)

EMPLOYEES CONSIDERED SATISFACTORY		INDIVIDUAL PREDICTOR CATEGORIES				
	r	HI 1/5	NEXT 1/5	MIDDLE 1/5	NEXT 1/5	LO 1/5
30 percent	.15	38	32	30	28	22
	.20	40	34	29	26	21
	.30	46	35	29	24	16
	.40	51	37	28	21	12
	.50	58	38	27	18	09
	.60	64	40	26	15	05
	.70	72	42	23	11	03
	.80	80	44	20	06	01
	.90	90	46	12	02	00
40 percent	.15	48	44	40	36	32
	.20	51	45	40	35	30
	.30	57	46	40	33	24
	.40	63	48	39	31	19
	.50	69	50	39	28	14
	.60	75	53	38	24	10
	.70	82	58	36	19	06
	.80	89	61	34	14	02
	.90	97	69	29	06	00

EMPLOYEES CONSIDERED SATISFACTORY		INDIVIDUAL PREDICTOR CATEGORIES				
	r	HI 1/5	NEXT 1/5	MIDDLE 1/5	NEXT 1/5	LO 1/5
50 percent	.15	58	54	50	46	42
	.20	61	55	50	45	39
	.30	67	57	50	43	33
	.40	73	59	50	41	28
	.50	78	62	50	38	22
	.60	84	65	50	35	16
	.70	90	70	50	30	10
	.80	95	75	50	25	05
	.90	99	85	50	15	01
60 percent	.15	68	64	60	57	52
	.20	71	63	60	56	48
	.30	76	66	61	54	44
	.40	81	69	61	52	37
	.50	86	72	62	50	31
	.60	90	76	62	47	25
	.70	94	80	64	43	18
	.80	98	86	66	39	11
	.90	100	94	71	31	03
70 percent	.15	77	73	69	69	62
	.20	79	75	70	67	59
	.30	84	76	71	65	54
	.40	88	79	72	63	49
	.50	91	82	73	62	42
	.60	95	85	74	60	36
	.70	97	89	77	58	29
	.80	99	94	80	56	20
	.90	100	98	88	54	10

Source: C. H. Lawshe, R. L. Bolda, & G. Auclair, (1958). Expectancy charts, III: Their theoretical development. *Personnel Psychology, 11,* 545–599. Note: The Tables as given here omit *r* values of .25, .35, .45, and so on. The complete Tables are given in the original source and in the sixth and seventh editions of this text.

APPENDIX D

Representative Personnel Tests

This appendix lists some of the personnel tests that are used in business, industry, and other organizations and addresses of their publishers or distributors. The list includes most of the tests mentioned in this text, along with some that are not mentioned. The tests are divided into various classes. The numbers following the tests are the identification numbers of the publishers or distributors, whose addresses are given later in this appendix.

Two comprehensive sources of information about tests of various kinds (including personnel tests) are as follows:

- *Tests: A Comprehensive Reference for Assessments in Psychology, Education and Business*, R. C. Sweetland and D. J. Keyser (eds.). Kansas City, Missouri: Test Corporation of America, 1983.
- *The Eighth Mental Measurements Yearbook*, O. K. Buros (Ed.). Highland Park, New Jersey: Gryphon, 1978.

TESTS

Mental Ability Tests

Adaptability Test	14
D.A.T. Abstract Reasoning	11
D.A.T. Numerical Ability	11
D.A.T. Verbal Reasoning	11
Purdue Non-Language Personnel Test	19
SRA Nonverbal Form	14
SRA Verbal Form	14
Thurstone Test of Mental Alertness (TMA)	14
Wonderlic Personnel Test	20

Clerical, Stenographic, and Typing Tests

D.A.T. Clerical Speed and Accuracy	11
General Clerical Test	11
Minnesota Clerical Test	11
PRI Clerical Battery	10
Purdue Clerical Adaptability Test	19
Seashore-Bennett Stenographic Proficiency Test	11
SRA Clerical Aptitudes	14
SRA Typing Skills Test	14
Typing Test for Business	11

459

TEST PUBLISHERS

1. American Guidance Service
   Publishers' Building
   Circle Pines, MN 55014
2. American Optical Corporation
   14 Mechanic Street
   Southbridge, MA 01550
3. Bausch and Lomb, Inc.
   1 Lincoln First Square
   Rochester, NY 14600
4. Consulting Psychologists Press, Inc.
   577 College Avenue
   Palo Alto, CA 94306
5. Industrial Psychology, Inc.
   515 Madison Avenue
   New York, NY 10022

6. Keystone View Company 2212
2212 East 12th Street
Davenport, IA 52803
7. Lafayette Instrument Co.
Sagamore Parkway
P.O. Box 5729
Lafayette, IN 17903
8. NSC Interpretive Scoring Systems
P.O. Box 1416
Minneapolis, MN 55440
9. PAQ Services, Inc.
1625 North, 1000 East
Logan, UT 84321
10. Personnel Research Institute (PRI)
Psychological Research Services
Case Western Reserve University
11220 Bellflower Road
Cleveland, OH 44106
11. Psychological Corporation
757 Third Avenue
New York, NY 10017
12. Psychological Services, Inc.
Suite 1200
3450 Wilshire Boulevard
Los Angeles, CA 90010

13. Saville and Holdsworth Ltd.
18 Malbrook Road
London SW15 6UF
England
14. Science Research Associates
155 North Wacker Drive
Chicago, IL 60606
15. Sheridan Psychological Services, Inc.
P.O. Box 6101
Orange, CA 92667
16. Stanford University Press
Stanford, CA 94305
17. Stoelting Company
1350 Koster Avenue
Chicago, IL 60623
18. Titmus Optical Company
Petersburg, VA 23803
19. University Book Store
360 State Street
West Lafayette, IN 47906
20. E. F. Wonderlic and Associates
P.O. Box 7
Northfield, IL 60093

Index

SUBJECTS